James & V
Intellectual Property
Law in New Zealand

JAMES & WELLS INTELLECTUAL PROPERTY LAW IN NEW ZEALAND

IAN FINCH

GENERAL EDITOR

PUBLISHED BY:
Brookers Ltd
Level 1, Guardian Trust House
15 Willeston St
Wellington

The law is stated as at 14 September 2007.

ISBN 978-0-86472-611-7

Typeset by Thomson Brookers XBook Processor

Production Editor: Matthew Heaphy

Printed by Printlink, Wellington, New Zealand

FOREWORD

When I first entered the legal profession more than 40 years ago, the law on intellectual property was something of a Cinderella. One superficial lecture in an omnibus course, entitled "Personal Property", was all that was thought necessary for the education of LLB students on this topic. The 1953 trio of Acts concerning patents, designs and trademarks had been enacted for just a few years. These Acts were then regarded as arcane by most practitioners. Their operation was confined to an enlightened few — mainly patent and trademark attorneys. The average lawyer did not wish to be involved in a recondite specialty, seen to have its own corps of professionals. In that era, there was little New Zealand case law on intellectual property. British textbooks were used. Concepts such as plant variety rights and layout designs were unknown.

Over the last two decades, the position has changed dramatically. New Zealand Courts have been making many significant decisions in intellectual property law. New legislation to deal with situations, never conceived ten years previously, is passed frequently. The breathtaking growth of information technology and the advent of the internet (now a normal accompaniment of daily life) has meant that case and statute law has burgeoned to keep pace with these phenomena.

It is therefore extremely timely that a work has been produced which deals with the numerous facets of intellectual property law in New Zealand. A glance at the Table of Contents shows just how diverse the field has become. For example, there is a whole section devoted to domain names and to other issues in electronic commerce. That often-pleaded supplement to the venerable tort of passing off, the Fair Trading Act 1986, deservedly receives a chapter of its own. These are but examples of the variety of concepts which any comprehensive work has to cover. Subscribers will be obliged to keep up to date because of the constant changes. Fortunately for them, there will be an ongoing service.

James & Wells, specialists in intellectual property law, has accepted with distinction the daunting task of producing this work, which, in the standard cliché of a legal foreword, "fills a need for the busy practitioner". The work will provide a starting-point for anybody seeking guidance when exploring the thickets of existing law and the new ground of developing law. I have no doubt that opinions expressed in this work will be cited frequently before Courts and Tribunals.

The authors are to be commended for producing such a comprehensive work. It will become essential equipment for all players in a fast-growing field, notably, patent and trademark attorneys, lawyers, information technology consultants, computer buffs and many more. The world of intellectual property now reaches into many areas of life, not previously known to excite the law's interest. That is why the potential outreach for this excellent work is substantial.

I wrote the above four years ago when the on-line version of this work was launched. That is now to become a hard-copy version which will extend the outreach considerably.

Developments in intellectual property law over the last four years have been quite notable. Particularly, the introduction of the .nz domain name dispute resolution system. This and other recent developments are covered in the work.

The Hon Sir Ian Barker QC

Bankside Chambers

September 2007

PREFACE

In 2001 I took a sabbatical from my litigation practice at James & Wells and lived out of a backpack for 8 months in various parts of Europe and Asia. When I returned I was told that we were writing a book on intellectual property and I was to be project leader. I should have caught the next flight out of the country. But due to my relaxed frame of mind at the time, I innocently accepted the daunting task of assigning the authorship of various chapters to members of the firm (myself included), directing the writing and research, filling in gaps, and compiling and editing the many contributions into a cohesive whole.

The text was initially meant to be 200 pages and written in plain English for the benefit of (primarily) business people. After 8 months of work it became apparent that our enthusiasm for the task was going to lead to something far more comprehensive. While the style remained (hopefully) accessible to the layman, the content became more detailed as an obsessive drive emerged to create a reference work which was more complete than any of its predecessors. And so *James & Wells Intellectual Property Law in New Zealand* was born.

I don't envy anyone the task of writing a legal text, especially one in the constantly changing legislative arena that intellectual property seems to be of late. So it's appropriate to thank those who have contributed so much time, labour, skill and judgment in its development.

Firstly thank you to the authors who wrote or co-wrote the original chapters. In no particular order: Tim Walden, David Marriott, Amanda Holling, Matt O'Neill, Mary Lane, Kate Wilson, Simon Pope, Frith Tweedie, Carrick Robinson, Simon Rowell, John Allen, Simon Murphy, Mardi Lewis, Robert Snoep and Ceri Wells.

Thank you to those who have contributed to researching and updating material as the legislation has changed and case law has developed, to those who contributed to the re-writes in 2003 and 2005: Simon Rowell, Carrick Robinson, David Marriott, Amanda Holling, Tim Mahood, Matt O'Neill, Mardi Lewis, Mary Lane, Meg Scally, Tim Walden and Tracey Lucas.

Thanks to my partners Ceri Wells, Kate Wilson, Jason Rogers, Simon Rowell and David Marriott, and to Claire Tompkins and Tim Walden for reviewing and amending the content in anticipation of this hard copy print.

Thanks to the team at Thomson Brookers, for making the product happen, and especially to Matthew Heaphy for his ongoing support in keeping the product online and topical, and Sarah Hunt for making out a business case for its publication (call me old fashioned but it's great to see the words on the page as well as a screen).

Finally thanks to our all knowing and long suffering support staff. You know who you are. Without your input in turning musings into text the entire product would have remained mere intellectual property.

Ian Finch

14 September 2007

About James & Wells

This text has been written by the professional staff of James & Wells.

James & Wells is a national firm with offices in Auckland, Hamilton, Tauranga and Christchurch, specialising in intellectual property law and intellectual property protection in New Zealand and worldwide.

James & Wells comprises a patent attorney practice and an affiliated law firm.

The patent attorney practice provides clients with advice from experts with industrial and technical experience, who work in specialised teams of patent and trade mark attorneys, barristers and solicitors, engineers, physicists, chemists, biologists and commerce graduates. They assist clients to obtain the intellectual property rights discussed in this text, and to exploit those rights with effective contract negotiation and technology transfer arrangements (such as licences, assignments, franchises etc).

The affiliated law firm, James & Wells Lawyers, employs a dedicated team of New Zealand's leading intellectual property lawyers. Their sole focus is on the enforcement of registered and unregistered intellectual property rights, defending against actions initiated by others, general civil litigation as it relates to intellectual property issues and alternative methods of conflict resolution such as mediation and arbitration.

James & Wells recognises that the true value of intellectual property lies in its effective exploitation. Hence it is also heavily involved in the development and implementation of intellectual property strategies for its clients. This includes providing training on intellectual property matters for the staff of clients and helping clients set up in-house procedures for protecting IP, safeguarding confidential information and establishing ownership of inventions and other IP. It is this in-depth involvement with the commercial side of its clients' businesses that is the characterising feature of James & Wells's unique approach to intellectual property law services.

More information on James & Wells can be found on their website (www.jaws.co.nz).

James & Wells thanks everyone who was involved in the researching, writing, typing, and editing of this text.

Please forward any feedback to the project coordinator, Ian Finch (ianf@jaws.co.nz).

CONTENTS

Chapter 1

Introduction to Intellectual Property Law in New Zealand

1.1 What is intellectual property?

Intellectual property is a term that refers to the ownership of an intangible thing — be it the innovative technology behind a new product, the brand name affixed to it, the goodwill the company making the product enjoys, or the manner in which the product and associated material are presented. Intellectual property is now often recognised as the most valuable asset in a business.

Although intangible, the law recognises that the rights arising out of intellectual property are property rights. As such they can be sold, licensed, damaged and, in a recent development, converted or unlawfully detained.

The intangible nature of intellectual property, and the ease with which software and other information stored in digital media can be copied and disseminated, makes it especially

1

vulnerable to infringement. Consequently, clearly defining the ownership and scope of the rights to intellectual property, and effective enforcement of those rights, assumes increased importance.

Intellectual property rights have developed through case law and statute. These laws both define, and clarify the process of enforcing, intellectual property rights and include:

* Patent rights (see chapter 2);

* Plant variety rights (see chapter 3);

* Copyright rights (see chapter 4);

* Layout design rights (see chapter 5);

* Design registrations (see chapter 6);

* Trade and service marks (see chapter 7);

* Domain names and other issues in electronic commerce (see chapter 8);

* Passing off (see chapter 9);

* The Fair Trading Act 1986 (see chapter 10); and

* Border control (see chapter 11).

Each of these areas of law is discussed in this text.

1.2 The value of protecting intellectual property

To be successful in business you need to have a competitive advantage. This advantage may be cost-driven or may arise through differentiation. Intellectual property protection seeks to ensure that differences between products and processes are defined and thereby maintained.

However, intellectual property is often the most valuable but least understood asset of any successful business. The importance of protecting and exploiting that asset is often not recognised by many businesses, particularly during their start-up stages. The following are some real world examples of the value of protecting and exploiting intellectual property.

* IBM added US$900 m per annum to its bottom line by conducting a simple intellectual property mining exercise. IBM examined its old patents and licensed out a number of these to its competitors. Thus, it was able to tap into an income stream without having to re-invest in product development or marketing.

* Dell estimates the value of a single business plan patent it holds to be in the order of US$500 m. This patent has been challenged and found to be both valid and infringed.

* Smirnoff sold its "Smirnoff" trade mark for US$1 b.

The full value of each of these companies' intellectual property could not have been realised unless that intellectual property had been protected in some form, usually at an early stage.

Intellectual property law is a commercial tool that must be considered when developing business strategy. Ideally an intellectual property strategy should be fully integrated with a business strategy.

The penalties for breach of intellectual property rights can be substantial. Civil remedies can include temporary or permanent injunctions, payment of damages or an accounting of profits, corrective advertising and delivery up or destruction of infringing goods. Many breaches also carry criminal sanctions. These can act as a significant deterrent to potential competitors, or a trap for unwary businesses.

1.3 Rationalisation for grant of exclusive intellectual property rights

The grant of exclusive intellectual property rights is rationalised on the basis that it provides an incentive for authors, inventors, creators, artists, innovators and entrepreneurs to create new works. In addition, the limited duration of the exclusive rights ensures that ultimately, the knowledge inherent in the intellectual property falls into the public domain for use by all, spurring further creativity and innovation.

Generally speaking, intellectual property rights in New Zealand fall into two basic categories:

- Those that can be registered; and

- Those that subsist solely as a creature of statute or at common law.

1.3.1 Registered intellectual property rights

Registered intellectual property rights are obtained by means of an application process, and include:

- **Patents**: a patent provides protection for the ideas embodied in novel technologies, products and processes. Patents cover a principle or idea and not just a single physical form of an invention. Therefore, the monopoly granted can be wide in scope and cover many variations.

- **Design registrations**: a design registration provides protection for aspects of the appearance of an article, such as its shape, configuration, pattern or ornamentation. Unlike patents, a design registration does not protect functional aspects of an article unless they also contribute to its appearance. As most manufactured articles involve an element of designer choice, design protection is generally available.

- **Trade marks**: a trade mark may comprise any marking such as a word, phrase, symbol, picture or any combination of these. A trade mark may also be a colour, label or even a smell or sound if these are capable of being represented graphically.

  The purpose of a trade mark is to indicate a connection between certain goods or services and the trade mark owner. More recently it has been recognised that the connection may comprise a licence permitting other parties to use the mark with the owner's consent, and that trade marks may have a secondary purpose, which is to indicate the quality of goods or services rather than simply their origin.

- **Plant variety rights**: plant variety rights give the breeder of a new variety the exclusive right to produce and sell the variety for a finite period of time. Protected varieties must be new, distinct, homogenous, and stable.

1.3.2 Unregistered intellectual property rights

Unregistered intellectual property rights subsist either as a creature of statute or at common law. They typically operate to prevent unscrupulous people from capitalising on the creative or intellectual effort of the intellectual property rights-holder in order to save time or money. Unregistered intellectual property rights include:

- **Copyright**: copyright is a property right that exists automatically in certain categories of original works, such as literary, dramatic, musical or artistic works, irrespective of their quality. There is no requirement to register copyright in New Zealand. Copyright rewards the time, labour, skill and judgment expended in creating a work. Copyright rights can be exercised to prevent others from piggy-backing on that effort by copying the work or a substantial part of it.

- **Layout design rights**: layout design rights are akin to copyright rights and subsist specifically in the layout of integrated circuits.

- **Goodwill and reputation**: goodwill is the "attractive force which brings in custom". Goodwill and reputation can subsist in anything from the name of a business, to the shape and appearance of a product, or the look and feel of a web site. Goodwill and reputation can be protected via an action under the tort of passing off (where one person disguises his goods or services as those of another so as to pass off those goods and services as the original) and/or an action under the Fair Trading Act 1986 (to restrain misleading or deceptive conduct and/or false or misleading representations).

- **Confidential information and trade secrets**: where information is communicated in circumstances importing an obligation of confidence it may be possible to restrain unauthorised use of that information until it lawfully enters the public domain.

1.4 When should rights be registered?

The decision whether to apply for registration of an intellectual property right depends on a number of factors. Perhaps the most important of these is the market value of the product or service and the leverage that protection can provide the owner.

In some cases registration may not be appropriate and the intellectual property owner may rely on unregistered rights such as copyright, or goodwill and reputation (via the tort of passing off, or consumer protection legislation such as the Fair Trading Act 1986).

The two key indicators of whether it is worth applying for registration are:

- The amount of money, time, and effort spent in researching and developing a particular product or market; and

- How long that product or market will present a return on that investment.

When a product or process has a high degree of research and development ("R & D") associated with it, then a correspondingly high R & D cost component must be added to the price of the product. Without intellectual property protection, a competitor can often enter the market simply by copying the original product or process. In so doing, the competitor avoids the associated R & D costs and can therefore undercut the innovator.

Intellectual property protection gives rights holders a monopoly in the product. Premium prices can be fixed to a product in order to recoup R & D costs and secure a profit without instigating an unfair price war.

1.5 New Zealand and international intellectual property law

1.5.1 New Zealand

New Zealand has a well developed system of intellectual property protection, which is derived from statute, case law and international agreements. Like most Commonwealth countries, New Zealand's intellectual property-related legislation was originally inherited from the UK, and has been developing for over 150 years. Consequently, case law from the UK, and other Commonwealth countries such as Australia and Canada, may influence the application of New Zealand intellectual property legislation where New Zealand case law does not assist.

1.5.2 Paris Convention

Since 20 June 1984, New Zealand has been a member of the Paris Convention (along with the majority of countries worldwide).

The Paris Convention provides reciprocal rights to citizens and residents of member nations regarding the acquisition and enforcement of intellectual property rights. In the interests of consistency it also provides a system under which a person can obtain the same filing date for an application made in multiple jurisdictions within a certain time frame. This time frame is known as the "convention period".

The convention period for patents is 12 months from the filing date of the first (or "originating") application to protect the same intellectual property in any country which is a member of the Paris Convention.

The convention period for registered trade marks and registered designs is 6 months.

(1) *Advantages of claiming convention priority*

The advantages of the Paris Convention are readily apparent:

- It provides a grace period in which to file additional applications overseas;

- The convention period allows for patentable inventions to be disclosed and for the commercial viability of inventions, designs, and trade marks to be assessed before incurring the expense of filing corresponding applications overseas; and

- It deters overseas competitors from claiming intellectual property acquired from New Zealand as their own during the convention period.

1.5.3 Other international developments

The development of New Zealand intellectual property law is heavily guided by international agreements such as TRIPS (Trade-Related aspects of Intellectual Property Rights) and GATT (General Agreement on Trade and Tariffs).

The New Zealand-Australia Closer Economic Relations Trade Agreement ("CER") has also resulted in significant harmonisation between trans-Tasman economic policies and legislation in recent years (notably the Trade Practices Act 1974 (Aust) and the Fair Trading Act 1986 (NZ)).

In addition, the recent trend toward including intellectual property related provisions in bi-lateral and multi-lateral free trade agreements may influence New Zealand's intellectual property regime in future years.

1.5.4 Novelty

(1) *Absolute novelty*

To patent an invention or register a design it must be novel. Most countries have an "absolute" novelty requirement. This means that the invention or design must not have been made available or used anywhere in the world before the date on which protection is sought (or the convention date, if applicable).

(2) *Local novelty*

In contrast, New Zealand currently has a "local" novelty requirement for patents and designs. This means that the invention or design must not have been known or used in New Zealand before the date on which protection is sought (or the convention date if the application is filed in New Zealand under the Paris Convention). Publication outside New Zealand does not generally affect rights here.

Applications to register patents and designs that originate from overseas can be filed in New Zealand outside the convention period if there has been no disclosure of the invention or design in New Zealand (even if it has been disclosed elsewhere in the world).

A draft Patents Bill was released in 2004, which introduces an absolute novelty requirement in relation to patents in New Zealand. The absolute novelty requirement would be consistent with our major trading partners and reflects the reality that publication of material on the Internet has global not local effect. The draft Bill is expected to be introduced into the House in late 2007 and is discussed in more detail in the patents chapter at 2.22.1 ("Draft Patents Bill 2004").

(3) *No novelty requirements for trade marks*

There are no novelty requirements for applications to register trade marks in New Zealand. Generally speaking the owner of a trade mark in New Zealand is the first to use, or to apply to register, the mark in relation to the specified goods or services here. This means that in certain circumstances it is legitimate to register a trade mark in New Zealand that has been acquired from overseas.

(4) *Different novelty requirements for plant varieties*

The novelty requirements for plant varieties differ according to the type of plant protected. They are discussed in more detail in the plant variety rights chapter of this text (chapter 3).

1.6   The Intellectual Property Office of New Zealand

The Intellectual Property Office of New Zealand ("IPONZ") is the trading name of New Zealand's Patent and Trade Marks Office. This is the Government body through which registrable intellectual property rights such as patents, design registrations and trade mark registrations are obtained.

In recognition of its role in commerce, IPONZ is run under the auspices of the Ministry of Economic Development.

IPONZ has a website (www.iponz.govt.nz), which:

- Provides an overview of the services that IPONZ offers;

- Contains useful information and a number of Practice Notes or "how to" guides for applicants; and

- Hosts electronic searchable Registers of registrable intellectual property rights.

Each application for patent, trade mark or design rights must be examined by IPONZ examiners. These examiners generally have tertiary qualifications which are matched to the subject matter they are examining.

Decisions of examiners may be appealed to the Commissioner of Patents, Trade Marks or Designs. Likewise the Commissioner's decisions may be appealed to the High Court.

Further information regarding the patent, trade mark and design examination procedure can be found in the patents, design registrations, and trade marks chapters of this text (chapters 2, 6, and 7 respectively).

1.7   The Plant Varieties Office

The Plant Varieties Office ("PVR Office") is now part of IPONZ and oversees the examination and grant of plant variety rights.

The PVR Office has a website (www.pvr.govt.nz), which:

- Gives an overview of the services it provides;

- Contains useful information and a guide for applicants; and

- Hosts an electronic searchable database ("register") of plant variety rights.

Further information regarding plant variety rights can be found in the plant variety rights chapter of this text (chapter 3).

1.8   Patent attorneys

Patent attorneys specialise in the protection of intellectual property, especially registrable intellectual property rights. Most patent attorneys will have a background in science, engineering and/or law.

A survey conducted some years ago of the New Zealand profession showed that the average patent attorney has at least two tertiary qualifications. It is currently common for attorneys working in the trade mark and litigation side of practice to have both law and commerce degrees. In the patent side of the practice it is common for attorneys to have doctorates in science.

In addition to being specialists in New Zealand intellectual property law, most patent attorneys have a good working knowledge of international intellectual property legislation and practice. They generally have a large network of associates overseas whose expertise they can readily call upon when required.

1.8.1 Only a patent attorney may act as patent agent

Patent attorneys are the only people (under s 101 Patents Act 1953) legally entitled to prepare documents, draft patent specifications and conduct business concerning patent rights on behalf of others. Section 103(5) allows law practitioners, who are not registered patent attorneys, to provide similar services to patent attorneys, although they cannot describe themselves as patent attorneys. In practice few do, mainly because very few law practitioners have the technical knowledge required to deal with patent specifications. Provisions comparable to ss 101 and 103(5) Patents Act 1953 appear in the draft Patents Bill 2004 (cls 181 and 187-188).

1.8.2 Patent attorney training

To qualify as a registered patent attorney a trainee must have had at least 3 years' experience working for a registered patent attorney (or IPONZ) and have passed a series of examinations (prescribed in the Patents Act 1953, Designs Act 1953 and Trade Marks Act 1953) on the law and practice relating to intellectual property.

1.8.3 New Zealand Institute of Patent Attorneys

Most patent attorneys are members of the New Zealand Institute of Patent Attorneys ("NZIPA"), which is a self-regulating body.

Chapter 2

PATENTS

12

2.1 Introduction

A patent provides protection for ideas and principles embodied in novel technologies, products, and processes, and is not limited to the physical form of the product itself.

Patent legislation is designed to provide an incentive for innovation and the introduction of new technology into New Zealand.

The legislation gives the registered proprietor the exclusive right to make, use, or sell the invention in New Zealand and to authorise others to do the same.

Because a patent confers a monopoly on the patentee which is potentially broad in scope, it is granted for a limited duration only. In addition, the patentee must fully disclose the best method of making or carrying out the invention as a condition of grant.

Full disclosure of the invention enables others to make and use the invention once the patent expires, which benefits New Zealand society at large.

New Zealand patent law follows international trends, and the Patents Act 1953 complies with obligations under the General Agreement on Trade and Tariffs ("GATT") to which New Zealand is a signatory.

2.2 Legislation, treaties, and conventions

2.2.1 Governing law

Patent law and practice in New Zealand is currently governed by:

- Patents Act 1953 ("the Act");

- Patents Regulations 1954;

- Case law as developed by the Courts;

- Intellectual Property Office of New Zealand ("IPONZ") practice notes; and

- Decisions of the Commissioner of Patents.

The Act has been amended in recent times by:

- Patents Amendment Act 1992 (repealed s 51 of the Principal Act, which dealt with inventions relating to food or medicine and gave effect to New Zealand becoming a member of the Patent Cooperation Treaty);

- Patents Amendment Act 1994 (extended the term of a patent from 16 years to 20 years);

- Patents Amendment Act 1999 (redrafted s 77, which provided for the recognition of convention countries); and

- Patents Amendment Act 2002 (inserted a new s 68B permitting use of a patented invention for regulatory purposes).

The Act is substantially the same as the Patents Act 1949 (UK) (and amendments), which was repealed by the Patents Act 1977 (UK).

Accordingly, the application of the Act is interpreted by reference to case law originating from:

- New Zealand;

- The United Kingdom (before 1977); and

- Commonwealth countries with similarly worded legislation, such as Australia.

2.2.2 International conventions

New Zealand is a contracting State to the following conventions and treaties:

- Paris Convention (International Union) 1883-1934 ("the Paris Convention"). New Zealand has complied with the Paris Convention's substantive provisions since becoming a member on 20 June 1984;

- The Stockholm text of 1967 amending the Paris Convention, but only as to its administrative provisions, such as arts 13-30;

- The Convention establishing the World Intellectual Property Organisation 1967 ("WIPO Convention"), which took effect in New Zealand on 20 June 1984;

- Reciprocal arrangements with India, Sri Lanka, and Taiwan;

- Trade Related aspects of Intellectual Property Rights ("TRIPS") negotiated as part of the General Agreement on Trade and Tariffs; and

- Patent Cooperation Treaty ("PCT"), which took effect in New Zealand from 1 December 1992. This is discussed at 2.2.3 ("The Patent Cooperation Treaty") later in this chapter.

2.2.3 The Patent Cooperation Treaty

Since December 1992 New Zealand has been a contracting state to the Patent Cooperation Treaty ("PCT"). The PCT simplifies the procedure, and reduces the cost, of filing patent applications internationally.

The PCT system allows an applicant to make an international (PCT) application from New Zealand, and to nominate any of the countries that are a party to the PCT (around 125 countries). This one application reserves the applicant's right to file for separate patent protection in each of the nominated PCT countries, and retain the filing date of the original New Zealand application.

The PCT offers reciprocal rights to citizens and residents of other nations which are members of the PCT when filing in New Zealand.

A full list of the contracting states can be found at the World Intellectual Property Organisation ("WIPO") website (www.wipo.org).

The advantages of a PCT application include:

- **Prior searching and examination** — a comprehensive international patent search is conducted and the application can be examined before the substantive costs associated with filing patent applications in individual overseas countries are incurred;

- **Costs are delayed** — the cost of filing patent applications in overseas countries can be deferred by up to 31 months from the date of filing the New Zealand patent application, while maintaining the option to obtain patents in around 125 different countries; and

- **Decisions on where to patent are deferred** — the PCT applicant can nominate all countries to which the PCT applies in an application. However, the final decision on where to apply for patent rights can be deferred by up to 31 months from the date of filing the New Zealand patent application. Before making this decision, the applicant is able to assess:

- The strength of the patent application;

- The commercial potential of the invention; and

- The countries in which it has become apparent that there is a need for protection of the invention.

2.2.4 Proposed legislation

The Ministry of Economic Development released a discussion paper in March 2002 entitled *Review of the Patents Act 1953: Boundaries to Patentability* ("the Report"), reviewing the standard of patentability applied under our current Act. The Ministry received submissions on the Report which formed the basis for proposed amendments to the Act. In December 2004, the Ministry released an exposure draft of the Patents Bill 2004 ("the draft Bill"). The deadline for submissions on the draft Bill was 11 March 2005. The draft Bill is expected to be introduced into the House in late 2007 and is discussed in more detail at 2.22.1 ("Draft Patents Bill 2004") and in other sections of this chapter as appropriate.

2.3 Types of patents

When making an application for a patent, the patent can be in either of the following two forms:

- A patent of invention; or

- A patent of addition.

A patent of invention may also include:

- A divisional patent application; and

- A cognated patent application.

The ability to choose between one or other of these patents offers the patent applicant some flexibility when securing patent protection.

2.3.1 Patents of invention

The overwhelming majority of patents filed fall within the standard classification of patent of invention. They are simply known as "patents".

(1) Meaning of "invention"

For an invention to be patentable, it must fall within the definition of "invention" in s 2(1) Patents Act 1953, which provides:

> "'Invention' means any manner of new manufacture the subject of letters patent and grant of privilege within s 6 of the Statute of Monopolies and any new method or process of testing applicable to the improvement or control of manufacture; and includes an alleged invention."

Section 6 Statute of Monopolies 1623 states:

"Provided also (and it be declared and enacted) that any declaration beforementioned shall not extend to any letters patents and grants of privilege for the term of fourteen years [now twenty years] or under, hereinafter to be made, of the sole working or making of any manner of new manufactures within this realm, to the true and first inventor and inventors of such manufactures, which others at the time of making such letters patents and grants shall not use, so as also they be not contrary to the law, or mischievous to the state, by raising prices of commodities at home, or hurt of trade, or generally inconvenient."

Therefore, under the Act, an invention must:

- Be a manner of manufacture;

- Be new; and

- Involve an inventive step

These concepts are discussed at 2.4 ("Patentable subject matter") and 2.7.2 ("Novelty requirements") later in this chapter.

Under cl 13 of the draft Patents Bill 2004, an invention must also be "useful" in order to be patentable. Under cl 10 of the draft Bill, an invention will be useful if it has a specific, credible and substantial utility.

(2)   *Unity of invention*

Patents provide rights in relation to a specific invention. Sections 10(4) and 29(4) Patents Act 1953 state that a patent must relate to a single general inventive concept. Compare cls 35(2)(a) and 96(1) of the draft Patents Bill 2004. This is known as "unity of invention".

Unity of invention was discussed in *Celanese Corp of America's Application* (1952) 69 RPC 227. The case involved inventions that included processes with intermediate steps. It held that if an investigation into the novelty of the intermediate step renders an investigation into the novelty of the final product unnecessary, the claims regarding the intermediate steps and the final product may be regarded as relating to a single invention.

In 1997, the Intellectual Property Office of New Zealand ("IPONZ") issued a Practice Note to ensure a consistent practice was followed when examining patent applications for unity of invention. It directed that there will be unity of invention if there is a technical relationship between inventions involving one or more corresponding special technical features.

"Special technical features" are those features which define the contribution the claimed invention as a whole makes over the "prior art".

"Prior art" in this context relates to all of the technology and disclosures known before the priority date of the claimed invention. Prior art is discussed in more detail at 2.7 ("Obtaining grant of rights" below).

The issue of unity of invention only arises during the examination of a patent application by IPONZ. It is therefore not possible to object to the grant of a patent on this ground. Compare cl 96(2) of the draft Bill.

Other grounds of objection are discussed at 2.9 ("Opposition to the grant of a patent application") later in this chapter.

2.3.2 Patents of addition

Section 34(1) Patents Act 1953 provides for the grant of patents of addition. Compare cl 98 of the draft Patents Bill 2004. Patents of addition are granted for improvements or modifications to an invention for which the applicant already has a granted patent or a patent application. The first patent is known as the "parent" patent.

A patent of addition cannot be filed before the date of filing of the parent patent: s 34(3). Compare cl 100(1) of the draft Bill. A patent of addition cannot be sealed before the parent patent is sealed: s 34(4). Compare cl 100(2) of the draft Bill.

Under s 34(2), after a patent of addition has been filed, there are two options available to the patentee. They are to:

- Maintain both the parent and the patent of addition; or

- Ask the Commissioner to revoke the parent in favour of the patent of addition.

If the parent patent is revoked, the patent of addition can be converted into an independent patent. Compare cl 99(2) of the draft Bill.

A patent of addition cannot be revoked or invalidated for the following reasons:

- That it lacks an inventive step over the invention the subject of the parent patent,

- That the invention should have been the subject of an independent patent.

This was confirmed in *Canadian Industries Ltd's Application* (Commissioner's Decision No P06/1984, 3/5/84, Asst Commr Burton).

The term of a patent of addition is the unexpired term of the parent patent. Compare cl 101(1) of the draft Bill. Section 34(6) states that no renewal fees are payable in respect of a patent of addition unless it becomes an independent patent. If the patent of addition is converted into an independent patent, the same fees will be payable as if the patent had been originally granted as an independent patent. Compare cl 102 of the draft Bill. Renewal fees are discussed further at 2.10 ("Duration, renewal, and restoration") later in this chapter.

2.3.3 Divisional patent applications

A New Zealand patent application must refer to a single invention. This is known as "unity of invention". Independent claims for apparatus, and methods of using that apparatus, are permissible. However, it is not possible to include independent claims for apparatus and methods which do not share a common inventive feature. Unity of invention is discussed in more detail at 2.3.1(2) ("Unity of invention") earlier in this chapter.

The Commissioner can raise unity of invention objections during examination of a patent application. It is often possible for the applicant to overcome this objection by dividing the part objected to out of original patent application (the "parent application") and filing a separate application covering that subject matter. This separate application is known as a "divisional patent application".

Divisional patent applications are governed by s 12(5) Patents Act 1953. Compare cl 31 of the draft Patents Bill 2004.

Divisional applications can only be filed subject to the following restrictions:

- The divisional application must be filed before the parent application has been accepted for grant by the Commissioner;

- To retain the priority date of the parent application, the subject matter of the divisional application must be fairly based on the subject matter disclosed in the parent application. Priority dates and fair basis are discussed in more detail at 2.7.2 ("Novelty requirements") and 2.7.3(3) ("Fair basis") later in this chapter;

- While the claims of a divisional application can be broader than the claims of the parent application, the priority date of the parent application can only be retained if the broadened claims are fairly based on the subject matter disclosed in the parent application. Fair basis is discussed at 2.7.3(3) ("Fair basis") later in this chapter; and

- If the subject matter and/or broadened claims of the divisional application are not fairly based on the subject matter disclosed in the parent application, the divisional application takes the date the new matter was introduced as its priority date.

In practice, if more time is required to overcome the examiner's objections to a parent application, a divisional application containing identical subject matter and claims to the parent application may be filed before the expiration of the period for placing the parent application in order for acceptance. Note however that such "whole content" divisionals may be excluded by cl 31(1) of the draft Bill, which seems to permit only applications covering "any part" of the patent application.

2.3.4 Cognate patent applications

If an applicant files more than one patent application for the same invention, s 9(3) Patents Act 1953 allows the applications to be cognated (combined) into a single application, provided there is unity of invention. Compare cls 33(4) and (5) of the draft Patents Bill 2004. Unity of invention is discussed at 2.3.1(2) ("Unity of invention") earlier in this chapter.

Cognated applications are commonly used to derive the benefits of multiple priority dates from the additional applications which include further subject matter to that in the earlier filed applications.

A single complete specification can also be filed where two or more applications (accompanied by a provisional specification) are cognated. The difference between a provisional and complete specification is discussed at 2.7 ("Obtaining grant of rights") later in this chapter.

2.4 Patentable subject matter

For an invention to be patentable it must fall within the definition of "invention" in s 2 Patents Act 1953. The definition is an exclusive one. It means:

> "any manner of new manufacture the subject of letters patent and grant of privilege within s 6 of the Statute of Monopolies and any new method or process of testing

applicable to the improvement or control of manufacture and includes any alleged invention."

At present, there is only one statutory bar to patentability. Under s 17, the Commissioner may refuse to grant an application for patent protection if he or she deems that use of the invention claimed in the specification would be contrary to morality. This is discussed later in this chapter.

The following subject matter is also barred from patentability at common law:

- Naturally occurring products;

- Pure discoveries;

- Mere information (for example, a mathematical formula); and

- Methods of medical treatment (discussed later in this section).

Under cl 13 of the draft Patents Bill 2004, an invention will be patentable if:

- It is a manner of manufacture within the meaning of s 6 Statute of Monopolies 1623;

- When compared to the prior art base as it existed before the priority date of the claim, the invention:

  - Is novel; and

  - Involves an inventive step;

- It is useful; and

- It is not excluded from patentability under cls 14 or 15 of the draft Bill.

An invention will be excluded if:

- Commercial exploitation of the invention is contrary to public policy or morality;

- It is a human being or a biological process for the generation of human beings;

- It is a diagnostic, therapeutic, or surgical method for the treatment of human beings; or

- It is a plant variety.

The draft Bill also establishes a Maori advisory committee to advise the Commissioner (upon request) whether an invention claimed in a patent specification is derived from Maori traditional knowledge or indigenous plants or animals and, if so, whether the commercial exploitation of the invention is likely to be contrary to Maori values. This is discussed further at 2.22 ("Future developments") later in this chapter.

2.4.1 Manner of manufacture

The key consideration for determining the patentability of an invention is whether the invention is a "manner of new manufacture" within the meaning of s 6 of the Statute of Monopolies, which states:

"Provided also (and be it declared and enacted) that any declaration beforementioned shall not extend to any letters patents and grants of privilege for the term of fourteen years [now twenty years] or under, hereinafter to be made, of the sole working or making of any manner of new manufactures within this realm, to the true and first inventor and inventors of such manufactures, which others at the time of making such letters patents and grants shall not use, so as also they be not contrary to the law, or mischievous to the state, by raising prices of commodities at home, or hurt of trade, or generally inconvenient."

GEC's Application (1943) 60 RPC 1, at p 4, formulated the rule that has most often been applied to determine if an invention is a manner of manufacture. In accordance with that rule a method or process is a manner of manufacture if it:

- Results in the production of some vendible product;

- Improves or restores to its former condition a vendible product; or

- Has the effect of preserving from deterioration some vendible product to which it is applied.

These are known as "Morton's Rules".

The meaning of the words "any manner of new manufacture" was further discussed by the High Court of Australia in *National Research Development Corp v Commissioner of Patents* (1959) 102 CLR 252; (1961) 78 RPC 134; 1A IPR 63, at p 75. The case is significant for a number of reasons:

- It confirmed Morton J's proposition in *GEC's Application* that "manufacture" may encompass both a process and a product;

- It qualified Morton's Rules by holding that a "product" in relation to a process is simply "something in which the new and useful effect may be observed"; and

- It found that a new use of a known product was patentable.

Both *GEC's Application* and *NRDC* have been affirmed in New Zealand in *Swift & Co v Commissioner of Patents* [1960] NZLR 775. In that case, the invention was a new method of tenderising meat products. Enzymes were injected into an animal before it was killed and distributed in the animal's circulatory system. The Court of Appeal held that, as the animal fell within the scope of a "vendible product", the process was patentable.

Currently, a broad range of subject matter is considered to fall within the "manner of manufacture" definition and is therefore patentable in New Zealand. Examples of patentable subject matter are discussed later in this section.

2.4.2 Applicant entitled to benefit of doubt

In disputes concerning the patentability of an invention , the patent applicant will be given the benefit of the doubt: *Swift & Co v Commissioner of Patents* [1960] NZLR 775.

Similarly, in *Commissioner of Patents v Microcell Ltd* (1959) 1A IPR 52, at p 58, the High Court of Australia held:

"it is well settled that the Commissioner ought not to refuse acceptance of an application and specification unless it appears practically certain that letters patent granted on the specification would be held invalid."

This was affirmed in *Hughes Aircraft Co's Application* (Commissioner's Decision No P03/1995, 3/5/95, Commr Popplewell).

Under the draft Patents Bill 2004, the standard of proof in disputes concerning the patentability of an invention will change to the balance of probabilities.

2.4.3 Collocation of integers

Where there are two integers (for example, for an axle and a wheel) and each performs its own proper function independently of the other, that is not a patentable combination. However, if the axle and wheel work together to produce a new or improved result then the combination is patentable.

In *Williams v Nye* (1890) 7 RPC 62 (CA), a machine used to make sausages, which combined two machines that had previously been used separately, was not considered patentable. The ultimate result was novel and useful but there was no difficulty to overcome and no inventive power or genius in developing the machine. Accordingly, the Court held there was no invention.

The argument that an invention is a collocation of known integers is often used by patent examiners to overcome a shortfall in the legislation which precludes examiners from examining patent applications for an inventive step. Under the draft Patents Bill 2004, examiners will be required to examine a patent application for an inventive step.

The concept of collocation is discussed in more detail at 2.9 ("Opposition to the grant of a patent application") below.

2.4.4 New use of a known product

A new use of a known product or process is patentable provided the use satisfies the statutory requirements of patentability.

The patentability of new uses was considered as early as the nineteenth century. See, for example, *Lane Fox v Kensington & Knightsbridge Electric Lighting Co* [1892] 3 Ch 424.

However *National Research Development Corp v Commissioner of Patents* (1959) 102 CLR 252; (1961) 78 RPC 134; 1A IPR 63 is viewed as the first authority to unequivocally hold that a new use of a known product is potentially patentable.

In *Wellcome Foundation Ltd v Commissioner of Patents* [1983] NZLR 385 (CA), at p 388, the New Zealand Court of Appeal approved *NRDC* stating:

> "The suggestion ... that a discovery of a new use for a known product cannot provide the basis for a grant [of Letters Patent] must, in a bald form, be rejected as outmoded."

2.4.5 Selection inventions

A selection invention is one in which the invention is based on the discovery that one or more members of a class of product have some special advantage over other products which do not form part of that class, when used for some particular purpose. Selection inventions are often used in relation to chemical compounds.

I G Farbenindustrie AG's Patents (1930) 47 RPC 289, at p 323, laid out the following conditions governing the patentability of selection inventions:

- The selection must be based on securing a substantial advantage (or substantially avoiding some disadvantage) by the use of the selected members;

- Substantially all the selected members must possess the advantage in question; and

- The selection must be in respect of a "quality of a special character", which can fairly be said to be peculiar to the selected group.

The "quality of special character" must not be one that would be obvious to someone skilled in the art.

If a substantial number of the selected members do not possess the advantage (or avoid the disadvantage) then the selection will be defective and the patent invalid.

In New Zealand, selection inventions have been approved in *Wellcome Foundation Ltd v Commissioner of Patents* [1983] NZLR 385 (CA).

2.4.6 Invention by importation

The Patents Act 1953 retains a legislative throwback from the Patents Act 1949 (UK) regarding invention by importation.

A person (but not a company) who brings an invention into New Zealand from abroad may be regarded as the "true and first inventor" for the purposes of making a patent application.

The Act provides New Zealand with local novelty. Therefore, an importer can only obtain a New Zealand patent if the invention was not known in New Zealand at the time the application for patent protection was filed.

Under the draft Patents Bill 2004, the novelty of an invention would be determined by reference to the prior art base, which will include any matter made available to the public (whether in New Zealand or elsewhere) by written or oral description, use, or in any other way, before the priority date of the claim.

This new absolute novelty requirement will eliminate the grant of patents in respect of imported inventions that have been made available to the public in foreign jurisdictions. This is discussed in more detail at 2.7.2 ("Novelty requirements") later in this chapter.

2.4.7 Morality

Under s 17 Patents Act 1953, the Commissioner may refuse a patent application if the use of the invention would be contrary to morality.

This is the only statutory exception to patentability.

The Court of Appeal in *Wellcome Foundation Ltd v Commissioner of Patents* [1983] NZLR 385 (CA) refused a patent for a method of treating disease or illness in humans on the basis that use of the invention was contrary to morality under s 17 of the Act. This case is discussed in detail later in this section.

The general exclusion against patents that are contrary to morality survives in the draft Patents Bill 2004 independent of a specific exclusion against patents for the treatment of human beings. Under cl 14(1), an invention would not patentable if its commercial exploitation would be contrary to public policy or morality, whereas, certain methods of treating humans would be excluded from patentability under cl 15(2).

2.4.8 Methods of medical treatment

Article 27 of TRIPS specifically excludes patents for diagnostic, therapeutic, and surgical methods of treatment of humans.

Presently, the Commissioner does not allow claims for methods of treatment of humans on the basis that they are contrary to morality under s 17 Patents Act 1953, which states that the Commissioner may refuse an application to register a patent if the use of the invention would be contrary to morality. In *Wellcome Foundation Ltd v Commissioner of Patents* [1983] NZLR 385 (CA), this prohibition was affirmed on policy grounds, at p 391:

> "If the practice of not granting patents for methods of treating human illness or disease is to be altered or modified, it is best left to Parliament."

IPONZ issued a practice note in March 1996 confirming that the decision in *Wellcome* is determinative of the law in New Zealand and setting out several types of methods considered patentable.

That practice note was based heavily on Assistant Commissioner Popplewell's decision in *Joseph H Handleman's Application* (Commissioner's Decision No P02/1993, 23/2/93, Asst Commr Popplewell), which held that claims relating to a method of treating humans might be considered patentable in the following situations:

- Where the human is not ill;

- Where the treatment is cosmetic;

- Where the treatment is of contributive effects (symptoms) of a continuing condition such as baldness, obesity, aging, and acne;

- Where the treatment is an elective treatment of a condition which is not itself an illness. For example, contraceptive treatment (*Schering AG's Application* (1971) 88 RPC 337) and smoking;

- For methods of diagnosis, where there are no surgical steps included (*Bio-Digital Sciences Inc's Application* (1973) 90 RPC 668);

- Where the treatment relates to health and hygiene, in particular herbal remedies and vitamins; and

- Where the treatment is of a condition not requiring treatment of the human itself, such as lice on the body.

In accordance with that decision (and practice note), where a human is treated for something other than an illness or a medical condition, a method of treatment claim may be valid.

If an objection is made to a patent claim on the basis that it describes a method of medical treatment, a strategy which is often used is to convert the claims to "Swiss-type" claims (discussed later in this section).

The *Wellcome* decision was unsuccessfully challenged in *Pfizer Inc v Commissioner of Patents* [2005] 1 NZLR 362; (2004) 60 IPR 624 (CA). The case involved a patent for a method of medical treatment, the use of a new compound to treat psychotic disorders. The High Court (*Re Pfizer Inc* 30/8/02, Ellis J, HC Wellington AP257/00) rejected an attempt by Pfizer to overturn the Commissioner's ruling that the application was contrary to morality. On appeal, the full bench of the Court of Appeal unanimously confirmed the High Court's decision, ruling that methods of medical treatment of humans are not patentable in New Zealand. However, the ruling was based upon the definition of "invention" in s 2 of the Act, rather than upon s 17 (which permits the Commissioner to refuse an application for a patent where the use of the invention would be contrary to morality).

The Court of Appeal held that the definition of invention in s 2 incorporated s 6 Statute of Monopolies 1623, which defined the patentability of an invention, but also limited it with the requirement that it "be not contrary to law, nor mischievous to the State, by raising prices of commodities at home, or hurt of trade, or generally inconvenient". On policy grounds Pfizer's invention was found to be generally inconvenient to protect, and the appeal rejected.

The Court of Appeal also considered the *Wellcome* decision in *Pharmaceutical Management Agency Ltd v Commissioner of Patents* [2000] 2 NZLR 529; (1999) 9 TCLR 429; [2000] RPC 857 (CA) concerning Swiss claims, noting that it did not overrule its decision in the *Wellcome* case. The Court re-stated their view, at para 83, that:

> "reform of this area of the law is better undertaken through the Parliamentary process"

and later, at para 128, that:

> "Parliament would have to legislate in the clearest and most unequivocal terms before New Zealand law could be taken as having gone any further in the direction of unlimited protection of pharmaceutical patents, than the allowance of Swiss-type claims"

Thus, the *Pfizer* decision on appeal affirms the approach in *Wellcome* that, if methods of medical treatment are to be patentable, it must be through an Act of Parliament in clear and unequivocal terms. This decision is discussed in IPONZ, "Information for Clients", Issue 32, 23 July 2004.

In accordance with art 27 of TRIPS, cl 15(2) of the draft Patents Bill 2004 excludes from patentability an invention that is a diagnostic, therapeutic and surgical method for the treatment of human beings. It states that such methods "are not patentable inventions". Presumably, inventions that fall within the exceptions to the rule described by Assistant Commissioner Popplewell in *Handleman's Application* would still be patentable. The general exclusion of inventions that are contrary to public policy or morality when exploited commercially would continue under cl 14 of the draft Bill.

2.4.9 New medical use of a known substance: Swiss-type claims

Swiss-type claims provide for a second and subsequent medical use of a known substance or composition.

An example of a second and subsequent medical use of a known pharmaceutical compound is Asprin™ (acetylsalicylic acid). Asprin™ has been used for over 100 years to alleviate headaches. However, its anticoagulant (to prevent heart attacks and strokes) and anti-inflammatory (to alleviate arthritic symptoms) properties were only recently discovered. Accordingly, Asprin™ became the subject of a patent having Swiss-type claims.

In the landmark decision *Pharmaceutical (Pharmac) Management Agency Ltd v Commissioner of Patents* (1999) 46 IPR 655, the Court of Appeal upheld the legitimacy of Swiss-type claims. The Court found that such claims are patentable, provided all the prerequisite requirements for acceptance (such as novelty) are met, and the claim is made in an accepted format, for example:

> "The use, in the manufacture of a medicament, of [the active compound] as an active ingredient in a [the newly invented activity] composition in admixture with an inert carrier."

This is only one example of a Swiss-type claim accepted by IPONZ as patentable.

The decision in *Pharmac* is in accord with the Commissioner's practice note, 7 January 1997 that, in light of the trend to liberalise the definition of invention, Swiss-type claims should not be refused.

The allowability of Swiss-type claims was also implicitly affirmed by the High Court in *Merck & Co Inc v Arrow Pharmaceuticals (NZ) Ltd* 29/9/06, Harrison J, HC Wellington CIV-2006-485-817. The invention the subject of that decision related to a novel dosing regime for a known medical composition for treating afflictions such as osteoporosis. The High Court decision was an appeal of an earlier decision of Assistant Commissioner Hazlewood (*Merck & Co Inc v Arrow Pharmaceuticals (NZ) Ltd* (Commissioner's Decision No P03/2006, 31/1/06, Asst Commr Hazlewood)) in which the Assistant Commissioner held that Swiss-type claims directed to a new dosage regime were patentable. Surprisingly, shortly after the decision issued IPONZ published an examination guideline stating that it regarded a dosage regime to be a method of medical treatment, and therefore unpatentable. In a subsequent decision (*Genentech Inc & Washington University's Application* (Commissioner's Decision No P01/2007, 23/1/07, Asst Commr Popplewell)) Assistant Commissioner Popplewell confirmed that such claims are allowable after reviewing United Kingdom, European, and New Zealand law on the issue. This decision, and the High Court's decision in *Merck & Co*, are binding on IPONZ and accordingly any inconsistency between the examination guidelines and those authorities should be resolved in a manner consistent with the underlying rationale of those decisions, which is to permit Swiss-type and dosage regime claims in New Zealand.

2.4.10 Computer software

Computer software is currently patentable in New Zealand provided it meets the test formulated by Burchett J in *International Business Machines Corp v Commissioner of Patents* (1992) 22 IPR 417. For computer software to be patentable it must:

- Embody a novel concept; and

- Have a commercially useful affect.

The invention at issue in the *IBM* case was an improved method and apparatus for representing curve images in computer graphic displays. The Court held, at p 425:

> "the formula is applied to achieve an end, the production of the improved curve image. A method of producing that by computer, which is novel and inventive, is entitled to the protection of the patent laws."

Computer software was first held to be patentable in New Zealand in *Clark's Application* (Commissioner's Decision No P12/1993, 30/6/93, Commr Burton). The patent application related to the use of a computer to produce patterns for shoe manufacture. Although Commissioner Burton expressed reservations regarding the patentability of the subject matter, he granted the patent.

The issue was laid to rest in *Hughes Aircraft Co's Application* (Commissioner's Decision No P03/1995, 3/5/95, Commr Popplewell), which involved computer programs for calculating conflict alert status in aircraft. Applying the *IBM* case, the Commissioner found the computer program was patentable as it resulted in improved air traffic control, which was deemed to be a commercially useful effect.

In a more recent development, the data structures that enable computer systems to process information have also been deemed patentable in New Zealand on the basis that the data structure may enable data to co-operate with a computer programme in a more efficient way — which can be a commercially useful effect: *Microsoft Corp's Application* (Commissioner's Decision No P04/2007, 5/3/07, Asst Commr Popplewell).

Clause 13(c) of the draft Patents Bill 2004 requires that an invention must be useful in order to be patentable. Under cl 10, an invention is useful if it has specific, credible, and substantial utility.

2.4.11 Business methods

Business methods are currently patentable within New Zealand.

To be patented, a business method must:

- Produce a commercially useful effect; and

- Produce an artificially created state of affairs.

Ordinarily the business method will interact with some tangible apparatus, or other material, to fulfil the "artificially created state of affairs" requirement. For example, customer loyalty programmes that interact with smart cards as part of a business method will be considered patentable, whereas pure methods (ie, new schemes or plans) that are not associated with apparatus will not.

For a more detailed discussion of the current New Zealand position, and the decisions giving rise to that position, see Matt Adams, "The Business of Patenting Business" (2007) 4(12) NZIPJ 312.

Clause 13(c) of the draft Patents Bill 2004 expressly requires an invention to be useful in order to be patentable.

2.4.12   Microbiological processes

Microbiological processes and the products of such processes (such as micro-organisms) are patentable. To be valid, the claims must be fairly based on both the micro-organism and the specification, and the patent must relate to a new strain of micro-organism.

The decision of Assistant Commissioner Burton in *Imperial Chemical Industries Ltd's Application* (Commissioner's Decision No P05/1981, 8/6/81, Asst Commr Burton) also suggests, at p 14, that for inventions using micro-organisms as starting materials, both a description of the morphological characteristics of the micro-organism and a deposit of the micro-organism in a recognised public depository will be necessary for the specification to contain a sufficient description of the subject micro-organism. The same decision confirms that a request to add morphological information to a specification which already identifies the micro-organism by deposit number will not require post-dating of the complete specification as it is an amendment by way of explanation.

However, Assistant Commissioner Burton's decision may be open to challenge as it relies upon the judgment of Lord Diplock in *American Cyanamid Co (Dann's) Patent* (1971) 54 RPC 425 (HL), a dissenting judgment which differs in material respects from the majority judgment of the remaining four Law Lords. The majority held that a patentee need not make a claimed micro-organism available to members of the public in order to meet the sufficiency requirements under the United Kingdom Act. Lord Diplock disagreed, holding that to be valid the specification must not only contain sufficient information to enable a reader to identify the micro-organism, it must also tell the reader where he or she can obtain a culture sample.

In 2004, IPONZ proposed to introduce the following practice note concerning applications relating to micro-organisms:

> "Before an application relating to micro-organisms can proceed to acceptance, it is necessary for the applicant to disclose both a morphological description of the micro-organism, and a deposit number from a recognised culture collection depository. At least one of these requirements must be met at the time of filing the application."

The practice note specifically referenced the decision of Assistant Commissioner Burton. However, the practice note was withdrawn in late 2004 following discussion with members of the patent attorney profession. IPONZ deferred on the basis that the main issues surrounding patent applications relating to micro-organisms could be resolved through the current review of the Patents Act 1953. In that regard, cls 37-40 of the draft Patents Bill 2004 do require deposit of a micro-organism if a person skilled in the relevant art in New Zealand could not reasonably be expected to perform the invention without having a sample of the micro-organism and it is not reasonably available to that person. The Bill is likely to be enacted in late 2007.

2.4.13   Genetic material

Novel genetic material, such as gene or DNA sequences, are patentable in New Zealand.

For genetic material to be patentable an applicant must supply the following information:

- The genetic sequence to be protected (for example, AAT CAG CGC … TGA); and

- The function(s) of the genetic sequence.

Therefore a pure genetic sequence cannot be patented without the applicant disclosing its function(s) (and by implication the effects).

While genetic material is patentable, patents relating to methods of medical treatment of humans are not. This distinction is discussed in more detail earlier in this section.

2.4.14   Board games

Board games (such as MONOPOLY™) are capable of copyright protection.

Patent protection for board games is also relatively easy to obtain in New Zealand (compared to other countries such as Australia).

The patentability of board games is governed by the British Patent Office ruling (43 RPC 137), which states that the claim must include the following:

- An apparatus;

- Playing pieces;

- A board with novelty in the character of its markings (as shown in drawings accompanying the specification); and

- Playing pieces being moved in accordance with rules (as disclosed in the specification).

2.4.15   Foodstuffs

Foodstuffs for humans and animals, and the associated methods of manufacture, are patentable subject matter.

In *Swift & Co's Application* (1962) 79 RPC 37, a method of tenderising meat by injecting enzymes into the animal before slaughter was found to be patentable. This case is often cited as the landmark case for the patentability of methods of producing foodstuffs.

2.4.16   Animals and plants

Genetically engineered or altered animals (excluding humans) and plants are patentable subject matter, except where they occur naturally. For example, the transgenic mouse ("oncomouse") has been patented (New Zealand Patent No 243908). Typically, characterisation by genetic sequence is required.

It must be noted that dual protection is currently available for new strains of plants under both the Patents Act 1953 and the Plant Variety Rights Act 1987. However, under cl 15(3) of the draft Patents Bill 2004, plant varieties would be excluded from patentability.

There is a detailed discussion of the protection of plant varieties in the plant variety rights chapter of this text (chapter 3).

2.4.17   Morality

In accordance with s 17 of the Act the Commissioner may refuse a patent application on the basis that the use of the invention would be contrary to morality.

This is the only statutory exception to patentability.

It was on this basis that the Court of Appeal in *Wellcome Foundation Ltd v Commissioner of Patents* [1983] NZLR 385 (CA) refused a patent for a method of treating disease or illness in humans. This case is discussed in detail in the 2.4.8 ("Methods of medical treatment") earlier in this chapter.

2.5 Rights granted by registration

2.5.1 Exclusive rights

A granted patent gives the registered proprietor the exclusive right to do certain things in relation to the patented invention. These rights are not governed by the Act but rather by the Deed of Letters Patent, which reads:

> "THEREFORE, We by these letters patent give and grant to the patentee our special licence, full power, sole privilege, and authority, that the patentee by himself, his agents, or licensees and no others, may subject to the provisions of any statute or regulation for the time being in force make, use, exercise and vend the said invention within New Zealand and its dependencies during a term of twenty years from [the date of filing the complete specification] and that patentee shall have and enjoy the whole profit and advantage from time to time accruing by reason of the said invention during the term:

> "AND WE strictly command all our subjects whomsoever within New Zealand and its dependencies that they do not at any time during the said term either directly or indirectly make use of or put into practice the said invention, nor in any way imitate the said invention without the consent, licence, or agreement of the patentee in writing under his hand, on pain of incurring such penalties as are prescribed by law and of being answerable to the patentee according to law for his damages thereby occasioned:"

By virtue of the Deed of Letters Patent, the registered proprietor of a granted patent has the exclusive right to:

• Manufacture the patented invention;

• Use the patented invention;

• Exercise the patented invention;

• Vend (ie, sell or license) the patented invention; and

• Import the patented invention.

It is intended to codify the exclusive rights of the patentee under cl 17 of the draft Patents Bill 2004, rather than under the Deed of Letters Patent. That section would give patentees the exclusive right to exploit the invention or to authorise others to do the same.

2.5.2 Territory

Registration of a patent under the Patents Act 1953 has effect throughout New Zealand and its dependencies, specifically Tokelau, Niue and the Cook Islands.

Patents are territorial. Therefore a New Zealand patent will have no effect in other countries. However, it may be possible to enforce acts committed overseas in breach of a foreign patent in New Zealand under the "double actionability" rule. This is discussed in more detail at 2.14 ("Infringement and enforcement of rights") later in this chapter.

2.6   Ownership

Section 7 Patents Act 1953 lists those who can make an application for a patent. They are:

- Any person claiming to be the true and first inventor;

- The assignee of the inventor (whether that be an individual, company or other incorporated body); or

- The legal representative of a deceased person who, immediately before their death, was entitled to make an application: s 7(3).

An application can be made by any person listed above, either alone or jointly with another or others.

Under common law, applicants may also include:

- Anyone to whom the invention was communicated from abroad: *Wegmann v Corcoran* (1879-1880) 13 Ch D 65 (CA); *The NZ Development Authority v Griffith Thomas* (Commissioner's Decision No P04/1982, 20/4/82, Asst Commr Burton); and

- The true and first importer: *Bernard Charles Sherman's Application* (Commissioner's Decision No P13/2000, 1/8/00, Asst Commr Hazlewood); *Edgeberry v Stephens* 1 WPC 35. This is discussed further at 2.4 ("Patentable subject matter") earlier in this chapter.

Under cl 28 of the draft Patents Bill 2004, any person may apply for a patent, either alone or jointly with another person. However, under cl 21 of the draft Bill, a patent may only be granted to the true and first inventor of the invention, any person deriving title from the true and first inventor, or the personal representative of either of those parties if they are deceased.

2.6.1   "True and first inventor"

The "true and first inventor" is the deviser of the actual invention or the person who made the inventive step to arrive at the invention. There can be more than one "true and first inventor". For example, a research team working cooperatively on a project could collectively be the true and first inventor of any new invention that results from their research.

2.6.2   Commissioned inventions

Under s 7 Patents Act 1953, an application for a patent may be made by any person claiming to be the true and first inventor of the invention, their assignee or a personal representative, either alone or jointly with another person. Compare cl 21 draft Patents Bill 2004.

Where an invention is commissioned, the developer ("commissioned party") may apply for ownership of the invention unless the commissioning agreement provides otherwise and directs the commissioned party to execute an assignment of the invention to the commissioning party.

If the commissioning party files an application without an assignment from the commissioned party and/or without naming the commissioned party as an inventor the application may be void, even if the commissioned party has been paid for his or her work.

This is in contrast to s 6(1) Designs Act 1953 and s 21(3) Copyright Act 1994, where the person who commissions the design or copyright work respectively is automatically the owner, in the absence of an agreement to the contrary.

However, it is important to distinguish between a commissioned party who is a true inventor, and one who is merely employed as a technician to put the commissioning party's invention into practice.

2.6.3 Employee inventions

An invention created by an employee during the course of employment may belong to the employer. Ownership will depend on the answer to the following two questions:

- Was the invention made in the course of employment?; and

- Was it part of the employee's duty to make the invention?

If these questions are answered affirmatively then the rights to the invention will belong to the employer.

Each case must be decided on its own facts. The Court will give weight to such matters as:

- The job description of the employee;

- The provisions of any employment contract;

- The nature of duties ordinarily performed by the employee;

- Whether the invention was made in the employee's own time or at work using work facilities and resources; and

- Who paid for any materials used.

See *Staeng Ltd's Patents* [1996] RPC 183 and *Greater Glasgow Health Board's Application* [1996] RPC 207.

The Court's consideration of the above factors was highlighted in the New Zealand Employment Court case of *Empress Abalone Ltd v Langdon* [2000] 1 ERNZ 147. Langdon was employed solely for research on spherical pearls in abalone. Langdon developed an invention related to the production (cultivation) of mabé pearls. The question to be determined was whether the invention was made by Langdon in the course of his employment.

The Employment Court held that Empress had no ownership rights in the invention for the following reasons:

- The invention did not concern the work which Langdon was contracted to perform;

- Langdon had used his own facilities away from the workplace; and

- The invention was worked on in Langdon's own time.

On appeal (*Empress Abalone Ltd v Langdon* [2000] 2 ERNZ 53 (CA)) Empress argued that it was a breach of the duty of fidelity between the employer and employee for the employee to compete with an employer while still employed. The Court of Appeal disagreed, holding, at para 8:

> "The suggested principle of law is, we think, stated too widely. It is not supported either by the cases or by principle. It would mean, for instance, to recall the famous lines of Ralph Waldo Emerson, that had Empress Abalone manufactured mousetraps as well as pearls, Mr Langdon, although employed only in respect of pearl production, would not have been allowed to turn his inventive mind for the benefit of himself and humanity to the manufacture of a better mousetrap. As Mr Couch said for Mr Langdon, any such invention should belong to the inventor, in the absence of a contractual or other legal obligation to the contrary. The English cases to which we were referred support that limit. In those in which the employer succeeded the inventions were discovered by the employees in the course of the duties of their employment. The cases include *British Syphon Co Ltd v Homewood* [1956] RPC 225, 230-231; *Worthington Pumping Engineering Co v Moore* (1902) 20 RPC 41, 46; and *Sterling Engineering Co Ltd v Patchett* [1955] AC 534."

However, the appeal was successful on a criticism that the Judge's approach to the construction of the terms of employment was too narrow, and the case was referred back to the Employment Court for reconsideration.

Having reconsidered the issues, the Employment Court reached the same concluded views as those in its original judgment. It found that Mr Langdon had developed the invention in his own time and without utilising any materials or facilities of Empress and concluded that Empress had not established any legal right to any interest in the subject patent.

The case illustrates the need for clear contractual arrangements in relation to employee inventions.

Only the true and first inventor, a person deriving title from the true and first inventor, or the personal representative of either party (if they are deceased) may be granted a patent under cl 21 of the draft Patents Bill 2004. There are no provisions in the draft Bill regarding employers' rights in inventions created by employees during the course of their employment, or the need for employers to obtain an assignment of the rights in the invention from the employee. Therefore it is anticipated that the present position at common law (described above) will continue.

(1)   *Commissioner may decide disputes*

Where a dispute arises between an employer and an employee regarding their relative rights to an invention (made at least in part by the employee), either party can request the Commissioner to determine the dispute under s 65 Patents Act 1953. The Commissioner may decline to act if he thinks the Court is the proper venue for determination of that particular dispute.

2.6.4 Co-applicants/co-owners

(1)   *Rights and duties of co-owners*

There may be more than one applicant or owner of a patent.

Subject to any agreement to the contrary:

- Where a patent is granted to two or more owners, each owner is entitled to an equal undivided share: s 63(1). Compare cl 23(1) of the draft Patents Bill 2004.

- Each owner is entitled to exploit the invention by making, using, exercising and vending the patented invention for his/her own benefit without accounting to the other owner (s): s 63(2). Compare cl 23(2) of the draft Bill.

- All co-owners must consent to the grant of a licence under the patent, or to the assignment of a share in the patent: s 63(3). Compare cl 23(3) of the draft Bill.

(2)   *Commissioner may decide disputes*

Section 64 Patents Act 1953 empowers the Commissioner to resolve disputes between co-owners of a patent (such as disputes relating to the sale or lease of the patent, or the granting of an interest in the patent). A request must be made to the Commissioner by any one of the co-owners of the patent. Compare cl 25 of the draft Bill.

There is a right of appeal to the High Court from any decision of the Commissioner made under s 64 of the Act.

2.7   Obtaining grant of rights

2.7.1 Search

The first step in obtaining a patent in New Zealand is to conduct a search of the Register at IPONZ. There are two reasons for conducting a search:

- To reveal any patents which may be infringed by the proposed invention; and

- To determine whether there are any patents (whether currently in force or not) which would indicate that the invention lacks the necessary novelty.

2.7.2 Novelty requirements

For an invention to be patentable it must be novel (ie, new or not previously known).

New Zealand currently has a "local novelty" requirement for patentability. This means that a patent will not be novel (and therefore not patentable) if it is either known or used in New Zealand before the priority date. This is known as "anticipation". It is irrelevant whether the invention was known or used overseas.

In contrast, under cls 6, 8, and 13(b)(i) of the draft Patents Bill 2004, an invention must be novel having regard to the prior art base, which includes all matter that as been made available to the public (whether in New Zealand or elsewhere) in any way, before the priority date of the claim.

To that end, the draft Bill creates a new duty upon patentees to inform the Commissioner of the results of any documentary searches conducted in foreign jurisdictions relating to the patentability of the invention the subject of the patent application.

These provisions would effectively repeal New Zealand's local novelty requirement, creating an absolute novelty requirement, and bringing our patent legislation into line with most of our foreign trading partners.

Anticipation under the current Act can occur by either:

- Prior publication; or

- Prior use.

Anticipatory material forms part of the "prior art" for an application. The term "prior art" refers to all relevant publications, technology and methods available or known in New Zealand as at the filing date of a patent application.

Anticipation (in relation to both prior publication and prior use) is discussed at 2.9 ("Opposition to the grant of a patent application") later in this chapter.

(1) *Prior publication*

The term "published" is defined in s 2(1) Patents Act 1953 as follows:

> "'Published' … means made available to the public; and without prejudice to the generality of the foregoing provision a document shall be deemed for the purposes of this Act to be published—
>
> "(a)   If it can be inspected as of right at any place in New Zealand by members of the public whether upon payment of a fee or otherwise; or
>
> "(b)   If it can be inspected in a library of a Government Department or of any institution or public authority and the library is one which is open generally to members of the public who are interested in matters to which the document relates and is a library in which members of the public in search of information related to the subject of the document would ordinarily seek and do in fact seek the information:"

The key consideration is whether a document has been "made available to the public".

In *Molecular Plant Breeding Nominees Ltd's Application* (Commissioner's Decision No P25/2005, 12/9/05, Asst Commr Popplewell), the Assistant Commissioner accepted a submission on behalf of the opponent that a document available electronically via the internet before the priority date of the opposed application met the s 2 definition of "published". The Assistant Commissioner stated, at p 27:

> "it is no longer necessary for a hard copy of a document to be available to comply with the requirements of s 2. The internet, by 1999, was widely available to New Zealanders and, in fact, a search of the 'web', by that date, would have been considered virtually essential for any scientist engaged in a survey of literature relevant to his field. There is no doubt in my mind that in the present case the document concerned has been 'made available to the public'. It could be inspected 'as of right' by the public at any place where a computer with access to the internet was available".

The Assistant Commissioner rejected a submission by the applicant that the definition requires the actual documents to be made available to the public in New Zealand, noting, at pp 27-28:

> "Any person who accesses a document on the Internet is free to download or print it; thus it seems to me that this would be analogous to a facsimile of a document

being sent from overseas to a New Zealand resident — such a document would surely fall within the definition of s 2. I also note, as pointed out by Mr Arthur, that a journal or book unopened on a New Zealand library shelf is still 'published'. Similarly, it seems to me that a document stored electronically on a computer and freely accessible on a computer terminal in New Zealand is 'published' whether or not anyone actually downloads or prints it."

The same test has subsequently been applied by Assistant Commissioner Popplewell in *Agriculture Victoria Services Pty Ltd's Application* (Commissioner's Decision No P26/2005, 12/9/05, Asst Commr Popplewell).

Under cls 6, 8, and 13 of the draft Bill, a patentable invention must be novel having regard to the prior art base, which includes all matter that has been "made available to the public (whether in New Zealand or elsewhere) by written or oral description, use, or in any other way". These provisions would make material made available on the Internet "published" for the purposes of anticipation.

Prior publication is discussed further at 2.9 ("Opposition to the grant of a patent application") later in this chapter.

(a)   *Exceptions to prior publication*

Under s 59(1) Patents Act 1953, certain categories of documents will not be deemed to prior publish an invention. They include:

- Patent specifications filed in New Zealand more than 50 years before the date of filing of the subject patent application that describe the invention;

- Patent specifications that were filed outside New Zealand more than 50 years before the date of filing of the subject patent application that describe the invention; and

- Abstracts or official abridgments of any of the aforementioned patent specifications.

There do not appear to be any corresponding exceptions in the draft Patents Bill 2004.

Further, certain circumstances constitute an exception to prior publication under ss 59 and 60 of the Act. They are:

- Material obtained from the applicant or patentee, which was published without the applicant or patentee's consent. It is immaterial whether the publication occurred in New Zealand or abroad. However, the applicant or patentee must have shown due diligence in making the patent application and must not have compromised their position: *Ethyl Corp's Patent* (1966) 83 RPC 205.

- Disclosures in the form of a patent application (and use or publication as a result of that application) for the same invention which has been made in contravention of the inventor's rights (ie, the invention has been "obtained"). Obtaining is discussed in more detail at 2.9 ("Opposition to the grant of a patent application") later in this chapter.

- Publication as a consequence of use of the invention at a "Gazetted exhibition". An example of "Gazetted exhibition" is the National Agricultural Fieldays at Mystery Creek near Hamilton. This exception can only be relied on if the patent application is filed within 6 months of publication.

There is also some overlap between the exceptions to prior use discussed in the paragraph which follows.

Under the draft Bill, an invention will not be novel if it forms part of the prior art base, being any matter "made available to the public (in New Zealand or elsewhere) by written or oral description, use or in any other way" before the priority date of the claim. Under cl 9, matter disclosed in certain circumstances will not form part of the prior art base, for instance if it was obtained in breach of confidence or unlawfully from the inventor (or a person to whom the inventor made it available in confidence) and disclosed within one year prior to the filing date of the patent application.

(2)   *Prior use*

A single instance of prior use is sufficient to render an invention as lacking the necessary novelty. That use must be prior use in a public manner, rather than necessarily use by the public: *Ralta Ltd's Application* (Commissioner's Decision No P05/1985, 16/4/85, Asst Commr Burton).

For a further discussion on prior use, see 2.9 ("Opposition to the grant of a patent application") later in this chapter.

(a)   *Exceptions to prior use*

Section 60 Patents Act 1953 provides the following exceptions to prior use:

- Communication of an invention to a Government department (or any person authorised by a Government department) for the purposes of investigating the invention or its merits, and/or anything done (in consequence of that communication) to investigate that invention (for example, the provision of details regarding animal remedies for statutory approval under the Agricultural Compounds and Veterinary Medicines Act 1997).

- Displaying the invention (with the inventor's consent) at an international or industrial exhibition (declared a "gazetted exhibition" by the Commissioner) or use of the invention at that exhibition provided the application is filed within 6 months of the exhibition.

- Use of the invention as a result of its display at the gazetted exhibition without the inventor's consent will also not anticipate the invention, provided the application is filed within 6 months of the exhibition.

- Disclosure of the invention in a paper read by the inventor before a learned society, or published (with the inventor's consent) as a result of that reading, will not anticipate the invention, if the patent application is filed within 6 months of the reading/publication.

Compare cl 9(1)(c) and (d) of the draft Patents Bill 2004.

Section 60 also provides that an invention will not be deemed to have been used (ie, worked) if the following criteria are met:

- The invention was used or worked within one year before the priority date of the patent application, for the purposes of reasonable trial only; and

• It was reasonably necessary that the working of the invention was effected in public.

Whether use is "reasonable" is determined having regard to the nature of the invention. Compare cl 9(1)(e) of the draft Bill.

Prior use is discussed further at 2.9 ("Opposition to the grant of a patent application") later in this chapter.

2.7.3 Filing an application

If the invention appears to be novel, the next step is to file an application at IPONZ. The date a patent application is filed becomes its "priority date".

There are three types of application that may be filed:

• **A non-convention application**: a patent application originating in New Zealand, or one filed in New Zealand from overseas, which does not claim priority from any foreign patent application. A non-convention application may be accompanied by either a provisional specification or a complete specification;

• **A convention application**: which is a patent application originating in a foreign country and claiming priority from that foreign application. A convention application must be accompanied by a complete specification; and

• **A national phase application**: in which the application claims priority from an International PCT application. This must be accompanied by a complete specification.

The differences between a complete and provisional specification are discussed in more detail later in this section.

The timeframe for filing a convention application or for filing a complete specification can be extended by the Commissioner under s 93A Patents Act 1953. Extensions of time are discussed in more detail later in this section.

(1) *Requirements of provisional and complete specifications*

Section 10 Patents Act 1953 sets out the minimum requirements of, and contents to be contained within, a patent specification (ie, both a provisional and complete specification). Compare cls 34-36 of the draft Patents Bill 2004 generally.

Every specification must:

• Describe the invention;

• Include a title indicative of the invention; and

• Include a description of the invention.

Drawings depicting the invention are not essential. If drawings are included in a specification they must:

• Be sharply defined;

• Not include any descriptive matter; and

• Be readily identifiable.

A provisional specification generally describes the invention in broad terms. Under New Zealand practice, where a provisional specification is filed the applicant has 12 months (extendable by a further 3 months: s 9(2)) to file a complete specification. The complete specification generally contains a more complete description of the invention, and one or more claims defining the scope of the invention the applicant seeks to protect.

Under the Act, a complete specification must:

- Particularly describe the invention and the method by which it is performed;

- Disclose the best method of performing the invention known to the applicant at the time; and

- Include one or more claims defining the scope of the monopoly.

The claims of a complete specification must:

- Relate to a single invention (see 2.3.1(2) ("Unity of invention");

- Be clear and succinct; and

- Be fairly based on the disclosure contained within the specification (discussed in detail later in this section).

There is no reason in principle why a complete specification cannot be filed in the first instance. However, in practice most applicants file a provisional specification first because they are cheaper to prepare and allow the applicant additional time to develop the invention and to assess its commercial worth. Provided the complete specification is fairly based on the provisional (ie, doesn't introduce entirely new subject matter) it will take the priority date of the provisional specification. "Fair basis" is discussed later in this section.

(2) *Timeframe for filing a complete specification where provisional specification filed*

Once a patent application has been filed, IPONZ will advise the official number and filing date allocated to the application. This normally occurs within a few days of filing the application.

Where an application is accompanied by a provisional specification (rather than a complete specification), a complete specification must be filed within 12 months of filing the provisional. Compare cl 33(1) of the draft Patents Bill 2004. As previously mentioned, s 9(2) Patents Act 1953 allows this period to be extended by 3 months on application. Compare cl 33(2) of the draft Bill.

The advantage in filing a provisional (rather than a complete) specification initially, is that it gives the applicant a 12-month window within which to consider whether to continue with the patent application without losing the advantage of an early priority date.

(3) *Fair basis*

For the claims of patent to have a valid priority date they need to be fairly based on disclosures made within the document from which they claim priority (generally a provisional or complete specification).

In *Mond Nickel Co Ltd's Application* (1956) 73 RPC 189, at p 194, Lloyd-Jacob J formulated a three-stage test to determine whether subject matter is fairly based:

* Is the alleged invention as claimed broadly described in the provisional specification?

* Is there anything in the provisional specification that is inconsistent with the alleged invention as claimed?

* Does the claim include, as a characteristic of the invention, a feature on which the provisional specification is wholly silent?

In this case the test was used to determine whether the claims in a complete specification were fairly based on the provisional specification (external fair basis). However, subsequent cases have held that Lloyd-Jacob J's test applies equally to determining whether the claims of a complete specification are fairly based on the matters disclosed in the body of the complete specification (internal fair basis)

In *Imperial Chemical Industries Ltd's Patent Application* (1960) 77 RPC 223, at p 228, the Court clarified that the term "broadly described" in the first limb of the test meant "in a general sense".

In *Cool 123's Application* (Commissioner's Decision No P11/2006, 13/3/06, Asst Commr Popplewell), the applicant's submission that the rules can be given a broad interpretation, which was based on the following passage from the Superintending Examiner in the *Mond Nickel* case, at p 191 (cited, and not adversely commented on, by Lloyd-Jacob J), appears to have found favour:

> "It may I think be concluded, from the wording of [s 10] that a mere broadening of the protection claimed in a complete specification, while not departing from an invention described in clear terms in the corresponding provisional specification, should not result in a finding that the claim is not 'fairly based' on the provisional specification."

The decision was unsuccessfully appealed to the High Court and the Commissioner's findings in respect of fair basis upheld (*Cool 123 Ltd v Vodafone NZ Ltd* 29/8/07, Simon France J, HC Wellington CIV-2006-485-698).

2.7.4 Examination

Once a complete specification has been filed in respect of an application for a patent, the Commissioner will automatically refer the application (and accompanying specification(s)) to an examiner for examination: s 12(1) Patents Act 1953. Thus, at present no request for examination is required to be filed by an applicant.

Under cl 58 of the draft Patents Bill 2004, the Commissioner is under a duty to ensure the patent application and complete specification are examined, and provide a report as to whether or not the specification complies with the requirements under the Act and whether or not the invention is patentable. Again no request for examination seems necessary.

(1) Advancing examination

The examination process can be accelerated if it can be shown that there is likely to be an infringement of the rights being sought, or if there are other commercial interests that require advanced examination: reg 38.

(2) Investigations undertaken by the Examiner

It is the examiner's role to report whether an application and specification complies with the statutory requirements. Compare cl 58 of the draft Patents Bill 2004.

The examiner may conduct searches for anticipation by prior publication or prior claiming: ss 13 and 14. These concepts are discussed at 2.9 ("Opposition to the grant of a patent application") later in this chapter. There is currently no statutory basis enabling examiners to examine for obviousness.

An examiner may request an amendment if, for example, there has been publication of the invention before its priority date.

The examiner may also inquire whether there are any corresponding overseas applications and request information regarding prior art cited against those applications, and the form of the claims granted overseas: s 15.

Under cl 58 of the draft Bill, the Commissioner must examine the patent application and complete specification, and report on the patentability of the invention. This will involve an enquiry into novelty, usefulness, whether it contains an inventive step, and whether or not it is excluded under cls 14 and 15 of the draft Bill.

In addition, under cl 63 of the draft Bill, applicants have a duty to inform the Commissioner of the results of any documentary searches carried out by foreign patent offices for the purpose of assessing the patentability of the same invention in a corresponding application filed outside New Zealand. Failure to do so may mean that the New Zealand patent cannot be amended at a later date.

(3) Time for placing application in order for acceptance

An application will be in order for acceptance when all requirements imposed by the Patents Act 1953 are met.

Under s 19 Patents Act 1953, an applicant must place the patent application in order for acceptance within 15 months of the date of filing a complete specification. This period may be extended by up to 3 months: s 19(2). In addition, if there is a delay in IPONZ processing or examining the application, further extensions of time may be granted at the Commissioner's discretion. Where an application is not examined immediately, the time under s 19 is customarily extended by IPONZ under s 93.

Under cl 66 of the draft Patents Bill 2004, an applicant must place the patent application in order for acceptance within 18 months of the date that the Examiner's first report is issued under cl 58 of the draft Bill (relating to the patentability of the invention and the compliance of the specification with the Act). This period may be extended under cl 67 of the draft Bill.

During this period, the application must file a Notice of Entitlement (under cl 68) stating that the invention is patentable and the specification complies with the statutory requirements. This procedure appears to be intended to replace the present requirement to obtain a seal of the Patents Office prior to acceptance under the Act.

2.7.5 Acceptance and advertisement

Once an application has been placed in order for acceptance it can be accepted for grant. The Commissioner will give notice to the applicant of that acceptance, and an abstract of the specification and the fact of acceptance will be published in the Intellectual Property Office Journal: s 20. Compare cl 69 of the draft Patents Bill 2004. The nature and content of the Journal is discussed at 2.20 ("Intellectual Property Office of New Zealand") later in this chapter.

Until publication of acceptance, the contents of a patent specification remain confidential. The only details publicly available are:

- The subject matter classification;

- Applicant and inventor details;

- The title of the patent application;

- The application number;

- The filing date; and

- Basic convention details.

As such, a patentee may abandon a patent application before acceptance without compromising the novelty of the invention. The effects of publication of acceptance of a patent application for grant include:

- The contents of the provisional and complete specifications will be made available to the public;

- Damages in infringement proceedings will ordinarily accrue from the publication date; and

- The accepted application enters a three month opposition period. During this period any person interested may lodge a Notice of Opposition opposing the grant of the patent. This is discussed in more detail at 2.9 ("Opposition to the grant of a patent application") later in this chapter.

Under cls 71 and 73 of the draft Patents Bill 2004, the Commissioner must open a complete specification to public inspection (and publish a notice in the Journal advertising the same) 18 months after the earliest priority date claimed in the patent application, unless the patent application is void or has been abandoned. Similar provisions will apply in relation to divisional applications under cl 72 of the draft Bill.

Clause 74 provides that a Treaty application (ie, national phase application) must be taken to be published on the date that it was published under art 21 of the Patent Cooperation Treaty.

Under cl 77 of the draft Bill, the applicant has the same rights after the patent application is published under cls 71-74 as they would have had the application been granted on the date of publication. However, the applicant may not enforce those rights unless a patent is actually granted and the alleged infringing act would, if performed after the actual grant of the patent, have infringed a claim of the specification. Proceedings must be brought within 6 years of the date of the alleged infringement, or 3 years from the date of the grant of the patent, whichever is later. The defendant will not be liable if he or she can prove that the patent could not have been validly granted for the claims (as framed when the allegedly infringing act took place).

2.7.6 Grant and sealing of patent

Before the Deed of Letters Patent will issue, an applicant must request the sealing of the patent application. There are no sealing fees payable.

Request for sealing must occur within 4 months of the date of publication of the complete specification in the Journal. This is in accordance with s 27(2) Patents Act 1953.

Assuming the formalities are met, the Deed of Letters Patent usually issues approximately 6 months after the patent application has been accepted.

Under cl 69 of the draft Patents Bill 2004, the Commissioner must accept the complete specification of the patent application if he or she is satisfied that the specification complies with the statutory requirements.

Under cl 94 of the draft Bill, the Commissioner must grant the patent as soon as is reasonably practicable after three months from the date of publication of the accepted complete specification, provided the Commissioner has decided not to re-examine the patent, no request for re-examination has been made or the Commissioner has decided to grant the patent after re-examination.

Accordingly, it appears as though the requirement that a patent must be sealed prior to grant has been removed from the draft Bill. However, the patentee must file a Notice of Entitlement within 18 months of the first examiner's report stating that the invention is patentable and the specification complies with statutory requirements.

2.7.7 Extending time limits

Under s 93A Patents Act 1953, the Commissioner may extend the time for filing a convention application, or the time for filing a complete specification, on such terms (if any) as he thinks fit, where he is satisfied that the circumstances warrant the extension.

However, the Commissioner is obliged to refuse to grant an extension of time, if, in his opinion:

- The applicant or his agent has not allowed a reasonable margin of time for the delivery to the Patent Office of any documents relating to the matter in respect of which the extension is sought;

- The applicant or his agent has failed to act with due diligence and prudence in respect of such matter; or

- There has been undue delay in bringing the application for the extension of time or in prosecuting it.

As to the application of s 93A Patents Act 1953 generally, see *Shiseido Company Ltd's Application* (Commissioner's Decision No P01/1992, 8/1/92, Asst Commr Popplewell), at p 10:

> "As I see it, [Section 93A] was intended as a remedial provision which empowers the Commissioner to extend the specified times under circumstances effectively outside the control of the applicant or his or her agent.

> "… section 93A was, in my opinion, enacted solely to enable the Commissioner to extend these times under exceptional circumstances, such as instances of force majeure or postal delay which are outside the control of the applicant or his or her agent."

There is no specific form of application under s 93A.

The Commissioner also has a general discretion to grant extensions of time under reg 168 Patents Regulations 1954 (except in certain defined cases mainly dealing with the time limit for sealing a patent and the time limits for opposing certain procedural applications under the Act). Regulation 168 is often utilised to apply for extensions of time for paying fees and other similar administrative oversights which are not of vital importance to the application. For a case on point see *Nederlandse Organisatie Voor Toegepast-Natuurwetenschappelijk Onderzoek Tno* (Commissioner's Decision No P20/2006, 1/5/06, Asst Commr Frankel).

Under cl 288 of the draft Patents Bill 2004, the Commissioner may grant an extension of time for filing an application or complete specification on any terms he or she sees fit, even if the filing date has passed, but must refuse to grant the extension if, in his or her opinion, the applicant or agent failed to act with due diligence and prudence, or there has been an undue delay in applying for the extension of time.

(1)   *Circumstances must warrant the extension*

The requirements of s 93A Patents Act 1953 will usually be met if it is clear, from the circumstances, that the failure to file was unintended by the applicant and/or its agent.

See, for example, *Shiseido Company Ltd's Application* (Commissioner's Decision No P01/1992, 8/1/92, Asst Commr Popplewell), at p 7:

> "To the extent that the failure to file in time was clearly unintended by both the applicant and the New Zealand patent attorney, I am satisfied that an extension is warranted."

(2)   *Circumstances beyond control of applicant or agent*

The "circumstances beyond control" test, which arose out of *Shiseido Company Ltd's Application*, was also applied in *Precision Electronics Ltd's Application* (Commissioner's Decision No P09/1990, 20/7/90, Asst Commr Popplewell), at p 10:

> "In my opinion the 'due diligence and prudence' test of section 93A(3)(b) is essentially the same as asking 'was the failure due to circumstances beyond the control of the applicant or his agent?'"

In that same decision, the Assistant Commissioner accepted the ruling of the House of Lords in *Textron Inc's Patent* (1989) 106 RPC 441 that the failure of an agent or servant to obey instructions may be a supervening and unexpected circumstance beyond the control of the proprietor.

In that case, the proprietor (Textron) received a reminder notice under s 25(5) Patents Act 1977 (UK) to pay a patent renewal fee, but failed to do so. A legal assistant had been instructed to deal with the reminder notices and to refer them to the chief legal counsel if not satisfied that they had been paid. The chief legal counsel deposed that the notice had not been referred to him, and it was apparent that the legal assistant, although qualified and experienced, had, for some unexplained reason, failed to carry out her instructions. In order to restore the patent, Textron needed to show both that it had taken reasonable care and that the fees were not paid because of circumstances beyond its control. The application for restoration was refused by the UK Patent Office, the Patent Court and the UK Court of Appeal (reported at (1988) 105 RPC 177). However, the House of Lords overturned the refusal, on the grounds that it was due to a circumstance beyond the proprietor corporation's control. Lord Templeman, at p 450, lines 38-48, stated:

> "The fees were not paid because of circumstances beyond the control of Textron, namely, the failure of the legal assistant to carry out the instructions of Textron. Textron could and did tell the legal assistant to investigate the report. Textron was entitled to assume, in the absence of any indication to the contrary, that the legal assistant would investigate and report. Textron could not ensure that the legal assistant would investigate and report. Textron could not and did not discover that the legal assistant had not investigated and reported until the renewal six month period had expired. The fees were not paid because of the unexplained and inexplicable failure of a competent employee, appropriately selected, qualified and experienced, to comply with clear and unambiguous instructions which she could be expected to carry out."

and again, at p 451, lines 11-14:

> "The failure of an agent or a servant to obey instructions may be and, in the present case appears to me to be, a supervening and unexpected circumstance beyond the control of the proprietor. It is within the control of the proprietor to ensure that an agent or servant is competent and is given clear and unambiguous instructions but it is not within the control of the proprietor to ensure that an agent or servant invariably obeys instructions."

In a supporting judgment, Lord Oliver of Aylmerton stated, at p 453, lines 49-52:

> "In the instant case, the failure of Mrs Galerstein's legal assistant to carry out her instructions was, in my judgment, a circumstance which was beyond Mrs Galerstein's control and, in so far as Mrs Galerstein was the directing mind of Textron, beyond Textron's control."

(3)   *Due diligence and prudence*

"Diligence" and "prudence" were considered in some detail in *Owens-Illinois Plastic Products Inc's Application* (Commissioner's Decision No P15/1991, 21/10/91, Asst Commr Popplewell). In that case, the Assistant Commissioner accepted the submission of the applicant that "diligence" was a positive requirement that one make the effort to do the necessary job, but rejected the submission that "prudence" was a negative requirement that one does not do something negligent, preferring instead to define prudence as implying a "forethought and deliberation and the ability to foresee the possible consequences of one's action".

In *Adir et Compagnie's Application* (Commissioner's Decision No P05/1990, 8/3/90, Asst Commr Popplewell), the Assistant Commissioner acknowledged, at p 7, that it is essential that the question of due diligence and prudence be measured at the time that the action took place, not with the benefit of hindsight.

In *Mag Instrument Inc's Application* (Commissioner's Decision No P06/1990, 10/4/90, Asst Commr Popplewell), the Assistant Commissioner acknowledged, at p 7, that an isolated aberration on the part of an employee need not necessarily render the entire acts of the agent imprudent or lacking in due diligence, but that evidence of an otherwise high standard of diligence and prudence would be required:

> "Mr Moon further submitted that an isolated aberration on the part of an employee, as in the present case, need not necessarily render the entire acts of the agent imprudent or lacking in due diligence, provided a sufficient and adequate record-keeping system to keep track of foreign filings is in place. While I agree with Mr Moon in principal, I think there needs to be evidence of a high standard of diligence and prudence by the applicant and its agents before an extension of the convention period is granted. When the provisions of section 93A were enacted in 1972 the primary objective was to provide relief from delays caused by circumstances beyond the control of the applicant or its agent, such as failure of or delay in the delivery of mail, in the case of subsection 2, or other factors, in the case of subsection 1. It follows, in my opinion, that extensions of the time laid down in the proviso to section 7(2), necessitated by an error or omission on the part of the applicant or his agent, should only be granted in exceptional circumstances."

2.8 Amendment

It is possible to amend a patent specification both before and after a patent application has been accepted.

2.8.1 Correction of Register by Commissioner

Where a mistake in relation to a patent, or any other document issued under the Patents Act 1953, exists in the Register it can be corrected:

- By the Commissioner, where there has been an error or omission on the part of IPONZ: s 88(1). Compare cl 255 of the draft Patents Bill 2004; and

- On request from an "interested person", where there has been an obvious error or omission on the part of a patentee, applicant or other concerned person (such as a clerical error). However, the section cannot be relied on to correct an error of judgment.

(1) *Obvious mistake*

In *Watership Pty Ltd's Application* (Commissioner's Decision, 19/2/90), Assistant Commissioner Popplewell found for there to be an obvious mistake three factors must be clear from the wording of the specification. They are:

- That a mistake has been made;

- What the mistake is; and

- What amendment is needed to correct the mistake.

In that case, the applicant had mistakenly omitted to include a particular claim in the complete specification. The Commissioner declined to correct the error under s 88 as it was not obvious from the specification that a claim had been omitted.

2.8.2 Amendments to patent specification before acceptance

Before a patent specification proceeds to acceptance, it may be amended in two circumstances:

- **Voluntarily by the applicant**: the request for voluntary amendment must be made in the prescribed form together with payment of the prescribed fee (reg 101); or

- **By the Commissioner**: the Commissioner can request an amendment in an examination report issued under s 12(2)(b) Patents Act 1953 to overcome any objection raised. Compare cl 59 of the Patents Bill 2004.

Generally, any amendment to a patent specification that does not add new subject matter to the specification (ie, matter not in substance disclosed in the pre-amended specification) is allowable before acceptance.

Amendments that introduce new subject matter not fairly based on the initial disclosure (discussed at 2.7 ("Obtaining grant of rights") earlier in this chapter) may result in either:

- A split priority of the application, where the priority date for the new material is the date the amendments were filed and the priority date for the original material remains the same; or

- The need to post-date the entire patent application to the date when the new matter was first disclosed to IPONZ (usually the date of amendment).

Where a patent application is post-dated as a result of amendment, there is a risk that it may be anticipated by the applicant's own disclosures. For example, if a patent application was filed in January then post-dated to June by way of amendment, the invention may be anticipated if the applicant marketed or disclosed the invention between January and June.

There is no provision for amendment of a provisional specification. Thus, a patentee is not able to retrospectively amend a provisional specification to provide fair basis for the claim set of a complete specification.

In *Neose Technologies Inc's Application* (Commissioner's Decision P35/2006, 15/8/06, Asst Commr Popplewell), the Assistant Commissioner confirmed that a request for voluntary amendment under reg 101 can be made at any time before the issue of the Notice of Acceptance of the application, even if the deadline for placing the application in order for acceptance prescribed under s 19 of the Act has already expired.

2.8.3 Amendments to patent specification after acceptance

Section 40(1) Patents Act 1953 permits a patent specification to be amended after the patent application has been accepted. However, amendments after acceptance are limited to three types: disclaimer, explanation, or correction.

In addition, unless the amendment is for the purpose of correcting an obvious mistake, it must not:

• Introduce new material or subject matter to the patent specification; or

• Broaden the scope of the patent so as to claim or describe matter which is not already disclosed:

See *Coory v Amcor Packaging (NZ) Ltd* 14/7/04, Venning J, HC Auckland M1125-SW02, at para 13, and *Polytherm Industries Ltd v Dux Engineers Ltd* 31/10/97, Paterson J, HC Auckland CL32/96, at pp 5-6.

It can be useful for a patentee to amend a patent so as to distinguish between it and any prior art that may have subsequently come to the attention of the patentee, or to include additional claims which specifically cover an allegedly infringing article.

The approach to be taken when assessing whether matter has been added was explained by Aldous J (as he then was) in *Bonzel v Intervention Ltd (No 3)* [1991] RPC 553, at p 554:

> "The decision as to whether there was an extension of disclosure must be made on a comparison of the two documents [the amended and unamended patent] read through the eyes of a skilled addressee. The task of the Court is three-fold:
>
> "(a) To ascertain through the eyes of the skilled addressee what is disclosed, both explicitly and implicitly in the application.
>
> "(b) To do the same in respect of the patent as granted.
>
> "(c) To compare the two disclosures and decide whether any subject matter relevant to the invention has been added whether by deletion or addition.
>
> "The comparison is strict in the sense that subject matter will be added unless such matter is clearly and unambiguously disclosed in the application either explicitly or implicitly."

It should be noted that the test is not akin to that of obviousness. The matter will be additional unless it is clearly and unambiguously disclosed in the application as filed — although that disclosure may be implicit: *IVAX Pharmaceuticals (UK) Ltd v Chugai Seiyaku Kabushiki Kaisha* [2006] EWHC 756, at para 101.

Amendments made after acceptance can be made either with the leave of the Commissioner (under s 38), or the leave of the Court (under s 39).

Where amendments are sought with leave of the Commissioner, the onus is on the applicant to satisfy the Commissioner that the requirements of s 40(1) have been met: *Bernard Charles Sherman's Application* (Commissioner's Decision No P46/2006, 9/11/06, Asst Commr Hazlewood), applying, at p 4, paragraph 3.18 of the *British Manual of Office Practice (Patents)* (2nd ed). Amendments under s 38 cannot be requested while an action for infringement or revocation of the patent is before the Court. This is discussed further at 2.14 ("Infringement and enforcement of rights") later in this chapter.

In *De Laval Ltd v JE Valentine Ltd* 10/11/03, Durie J, HC Palmerston North CIV-2003-454-241, the Court held that a party applying to amend a granted patent need not be restricted solely to the original grounds contained within the application to amend. Accordingly, Durie J allowed an amendment to be made, by way of explanation, despite the fact that explanation had not featured as one of the reasons for such an amendment in the original application.

Under cl 79 of the draft Patents Bill 2004, a patent specification may not be amended after acceptance except for the purpose of correcting an obvious mistake. Even in that limited circumstance, the amendment must not introduce new matter into the specification or broaden the scope of the claims. If such an amendment is permitted, the patentee's right to make the amendment may not be questioned except on the grounds of fraud.

(1) *Disclaimer*

Generally an amendment by way of disclaimer is used to exclude material claimed in a patent in order to overcome relevant prior art.

There are three forms of disclaimer, as follows:

- Limitation of a claim so as to reduce the scope of the monopoly: *AMP Inc v Hellerman Ltd* (1962) 79 RPC 55 (HL);

- Deletion of passages in the complete specification abandoning part of the original disclosure; and

- Specific disclaimer, ie where the patentee disclaims what is specifically disclosed in a prior publication.

There is a detailed discussion of amendments to claims by way of disclaimer in *Bernard Charles Sherman's Application* (Commissioner's Decision No P46/2006, 9/11/06, Asst Commr Hazlewood). The decision confirms that:

- An amendment to add additional features to a main claim will be an amendment by disclaimer, and allowable under the Act, if those additional features are fairly based on the specification;

- The addition of a dependant claim containing further details of an original feature covered by the pre-amended claims fairly based on the specification will also be an amendment by way of disclaimer; and

- The addition of a dependant claim directed to a feature not covered by any of the pre-amended claims will not be permitted: *Quin's Application* (Commissioner's Decision No P13/2006, 27/3/06, Asst Commr Popplewell). Thus, in *Bernard Charles Sherman's Application*, the applicant was permitted to amend independent claim 1 to describe "an essentially complete reaction" but the addition of certain dependant claims was rejected on the basis that the feature of those claims did not relate to the proposed limitation of claim 1 that an essentially complete reaction results.

(2) *Explanation*

Amendment by way of explanation, by definition, describes the invention more clearly so that the specification more accurately reflects the intention of the applicant.

In *Johnson's Application* (1909) 26 RPC 780, the Court stated, at p 783, that:

> "If a man uses a word in an ordinary sense — using it fairly — and if he finds that by some people … that word is taken to mean something that he did not intend it to mean, I think … that it is one of the cases intended to be covered by … explanation."

However, the explanation must not have the effect of broadening the scope of the claim. In *Sealed Air NZ Ltd v Machinery Developments Ltd* 25/8/04, MacKenzie J, HC Wellington CIV-2003-485-2274, Sealed Air NZ Ltd ("Sealed Air") appealed against the Assistant Commissioner's decision, inter alia to allow Machinery Developments to amend its claims by way of explanation in order to remedy an insufficiency in the wording of the specification. Two of the claims originally stated "the apparatus *comprising* tube feed means and tube cut-off means …" (emphasis added). Machinery Developments replaced the word "comprising" with the word "including".

Sealed Air argued that the word "comprising" had the sense of "consisting of", "made up of", "being composed of" or "being constituted of" and, as such, was exclusive of matters other than those specifically stated, citing Lindgren J in *General Clutch Corporation v Sbriggs Pty Ltd* (1997) 38 IPR 359. Machinery Developments on the other hand claimed that the word "comprising" was understood by the patent profession in New Zealand as being intended to signify the non-exclusive "including" and, as such, the amendment did not alter the scope of the claim. MacKenzie J refused the amendment on the basis that, if Machinery Developments was correct the amendment was unnecessary, whereas if Sealed Air was correct it would broaden the scope of the claim. It was therefore unnecessary to consider whether the word "comprising" was best understood in the narrower sense applied by Lindgren J in *General Clutch* or the broader sense understood by the patent profession in New Zealand.

Acknowledgement of prior art to clarify the scope of an invention will be treated as an explanation. The *British Manual of Office Practice (Patents)* also provides the following examples of amendments which have been allowed by way of explanation:

- To show that a mechanism claimed operates only under certain conditions, it being clear from the description that operation under other conditions was not intended;

- To make it clear that a word used in the claim has the same meaning as that given in the description; and

- To include what is clearly implicit in the claims in addition to that which is explicit therein.

These examples were cited with approval by IPONZ in *Lafarge Platres' Application* (Commissioner's Decision No P47/2006, 18/12/06, Asst Commr Hazlewood), at p 7.

Explanation does not include an explanation of the principle upon which the invention is based, as this need not be included in the specification for fair basis.

(3) Correction

For an amendment by correction to be allowed, two requirements must be met:

- A mistake must be shown to have been made; and

- The proposed amendment must provide a proper substitute for the mistake so as to ensure the specification is correct: *Distillers Co Ltd's Application* (1953) 70 RPC 221, at p 223; *Polytherm Industries Ltd v Dux Engineers Ltd* 31/10/97, Paterson J, HC Auckland CL32/96, at p 6.

The general rule is that amendments which result in the introduction of new subject matter (so as to broaden the scope of the invention claimed) are forbidden. However, such amendments are allowed for the purposes of correcting an obvious mistake: *General Tire & Rubber (Frost's) Patent* (1974) 91 RPC 207.

A correction cannot be made for an error of judgment: *Distillers Co Ltd's Application* (1953) 70 RPC 221 and *General Tire & Rubber (Frost's) Patent* (1974) 91 RPC 207.

(4) Discretion of the Court or Commissioner

Whether the Court or Commissioner allows an amendment is discretionary.

The principles to be taken into account when determining whether the discretion should be exercised were set out in *Smith Kline & French Laboratories v Evans Medical Ltd* [1989] 15 FSR 561, at p 569, as follows:

- The onus to establish that an amendment should be allowed is on the patentee, and full disclosure must be made of all relevant matters;

- The proposed amendment must be permitted under the Patents Act 1953;

- The amendment must be sought without delay;

- A patentee cannot obtain an unfair advantage from an amendment to a patent; and

- The enquiry should be as to the conduct of the patentee and not the merit of the invention.

These principles have been confirmed in *PDL Industries Ltd v Jackson Electrical Industries Ltd* 14/8/98, Morris J, HC Auckland CP202/97; *Ancare NZ Ltd v Cyanamid of NZ Ltd* [2000] 3 NZLR 299 (CA), and *Coory v Amcor Packaging (NZ) Ltd* 14/7/04, Venning J, HC Auckland M1125-SW02.

In *Coory*, the High Court observed, at paras 21-23, that these factors are not to be applied mechanically, nor is the discretion to be fettered by Judge-made rules. Rather, a liberal approach is to be adopted toward the exercise of the Court's discretion.

Under the draft Patents Bill 2004, a patentee must be given a reasonable opportunity to amend a specification in revocation proceedings before the Commissioner if, upon re-examination, the Commissioner finds that the invention lacks novelty or an inventive step.

(a)   *Amendment must solve problem*

In *Polytherm Industries Ltd v Dux Engineers Ltd* 31/10/97, Paterson J, HC Auckland CL32/96, the High Court refused to allow an amendment which failed to cure the invalidity it sought to overcome.

Similarly, in *Coory v Amcor Packaging (NZ) Ltd* 14/7/04, Venning J, HC Auckland M1125-SW02, the Court held, at paras 28 and 35, that if the proposed amendment fails to solve the problem giving rise to revocation proceedings, that is one factor which may weigh against the exercise of the Court's discretion to amend the specification.

In *Coory*, the plaintiff held a granted patent in a three positional bottle cap ("the tabnology patent"). The patentee subsequently invented a two positional bottle cap and sought to licence its use to the defendant. The licence negotiations broke down and the plaintiff successfully applied for, and obtained, a patent in respect of the latter invention. The application contained diagrams and figures taken from the tabnology patent, altered slightly to reflect the differences in design between the two inventions. The plaintiff subsequently observed the defendant marketing products featuring a bottle cap with similar properties to his latter invention, and brought a claim against it, and the manufacturer of the cap, for infringement of his granted patent.

The defendants applied to revoke the patent on the basis that it was invalid because, inter alia, it failed to disclose the tabnology patent as relevant prior art. In response, the plaintiff sought leave to amend the patent specification to overcome any invalidity in the original specification. The defendants opposed the application to amend, claiming that the patent would be invalid even if the amendments were allowed.

In considering the application to amend, the Court found that the proposed amendments failed to solve the alleged problems with the patent specification. In particular, it found that they failed to distinguish the latter invention from the subject of the tabnology patent, and that further amendments would be required to do so. Thus the amendment was refused.

Similarly, in *Ancare NZ Ltd v Cyanamid of NZ Ltd* [2000] 3 NZLR 299 (CA), the Court of Appeal observed that only in special circumstances is it appropriate that an existing patent be amended once a defendant makes out a ground on which the patent can be invalidated. The underlying reason for this is a fundamental requirement that a patentee must clearly define the invention and the scope of the monopoly that he or she seeks.

Although the amendment must be sufficient to cure the invalidity it seeks to overcome, note the following comment of the Assistant Commissioner Hazlewood in *Lafarge Platres' Application* (Commissioner's Decision No P47/2006, 18/12/06, Asst Commr Hazlewood), at p 9:

> "The applicant has, I believe, described an invention in the claims that would be clear to the skilled addressee, even though the wording used in the claim might have left a little to be desired. However, a patentee (or applicant for a patent) cannot be denied a patent that is clear from the wording of the claim merely because he could have described the invention in some better manner."

(b)   *Conduct of patentee*

The conduct of the patentee was also said to be a relevant factor in *Coory v Amcor Packaging (NZ) Ltd* 14/7/04, Venning J, HC Auckland M1125-SW02.

The Court reviewed the plaintiff's conduct, noting that the plaintiff owned the tabnology patent, and that the application for the latter patent included diagrams and figures taken directly from that patent specification, indicating the plaintiff's knowledge of the relevant prior art.

Counsel for the plaintiff submitted that the plaintiff and his attorney had not knowingly failed to disclose the prior art. The Court reviewed the authorities concerning the degree of knowledge required in relation to a charge of covetousness, noting that the cases typically related to circumstances in which the patentee had attempted to maintain claims of unjustified width.

Thus, in *Imperial Chemical Industries (Whyte's) Patent* (1978) 95 RPC 11, it was held that a charge of covetousness may only be proved by showing the patentee acted knowingly and deliberately. Similarly, in *Kimberly-Clark Worldwide Inc v Proctor & Gamble Ltd (No 2)* [2001] FSR 339, Humphrey J stated, at para 58, that it would not be a correct exercise of the discretion to refuse amendment in the absence of conduct which can fairly be described as blameworthy. In *Coory*, relying on those decisions, Venning J stated, at para 59:

> "In my judgment the appropriate test is whether the conduct of the applicant, or his agent, the patent attorney in failing to disclose the prior art can be described as blameworthy."

His Honour reviewed the circumstances under which the patent application was made, having regard to the ownership of the tabnology patent, the use of figures and drawings from the tabnology patent in the latter patent application, and the unsatisfactory explanation of contradicting evidence given by the plaintiff's patent attorney. He concluded that the conduct of the plaintiff and his attorney, in failing to disclose the tabnology patent as relevant prior art, was, when assessed objectively, blameworthy.

Venning J also observed that the plaintiff had deliberately maintained a claim of unjustified width in the face of revocation proceedings, having regard to the failure of the proposed amendments to solve the problem in the patent specification. As a result, Venning J declined to exercise his discretion to amend the patent specification in favour of the plaintiff.

(c)   *Duty to disclose relevant facts and matters*

The Court in *Coory v Amcor Packaging (NZ) Ltd* 14/7/04, Venning J, HC Auckland M1125-SW02 also considered whether the plaintiff had an obligation to disclose all privileged correspondence between himself and his patent attorney in order to discharge the onus in the case. Venning J noted, at para 38, that the practice of full disclosure is premised upon the rationale that the plaintiff seeks the indulgence of the Court and is required to set out the full story. Failing to do so will prohibit the Court from making any assumptions in the plaintiff's favour.

However, his Honour also observed that the practice had been criticised in *Oxford Gene Technology Ltd v Affymetrix Inc (No 2)* [2001] RPC 310, where Aldous LJ stated, at pp 317-318, that there is no obligation upon a plaintiff in amendment proceedings to waive privilege in respect of any document, and the obligation to disclose material facts does not warrant the plaintiff throwing all their documents at the Court as a policy of caution. While the plaintiff's case may be best advanced by waiver of the privilege, the obligation to disclose all relevant facts and matters cannot act as a hidden obligation to waive privilege.

Venning J concluded, at para 40, that:

> "there can be no requirement for a patentee to waive privilege. However, the onus is on the patentee to satisfy the Court the amendment sought ought to be granted. In order to satisfy the onus it may, in certain circumstances, be in the applicant's best interest to waive privilege and produce otherwise privileged documentation to the Court. That will only be necessary if the documents are of particular relevance to the issue before the Court. Each case must turn on its own facts."

His Honour held, at para 42, that in the present case the plaintiff had failed to discharge the onus to fully disclose to the Court all relevant facts and matters, including the relevant prior art, and therefore the application was refused.

Similarly, in *PDL Industries Ltd v Jackson Electrical Industries Ltd* 14/8/98, Morris J, HC Auckland CP202/97, the plaintiff was refused leave to amend claims of a specification during an infringement action. The defendant was able to show that the plaintiff was previously aware that its claims should be narrowed based on relevant prior art yet had made a conscious decision not to amend. The Court held that the plaintiff was cognisant of the risk it took in not amending its patent as soon as it became aware of the prior art, and should not be able to do so in infringement proceedings in order to maintain a valid patent.

(d)   *Delay*

Finally, in *Coory v Amcor Packaging (NZ) Ltd* 14/7/04, Venning J, HC Auckland M1125-SW02, Venning J considered several other cases in which the patentee's delay in seeking an amendment ranged from 4 months to 8 years. His Honour concluded that, absent any particular detriment to the opponent or the general public, the delay of $3\frac{1}{2}$ months in the present case would not prevent the exercise of the Court's discretion to amend the patent in favour of the plaintiff. His Honour declined to exercise his discretion in favour of the plaintiff in that case, although on different grounds (discussed above).

2.9   Opposition to the grant of a patent application

On application to the Commissioner the grant of a patent application can be opposed under s 21 Patents Act 1953. The application must be made by:

- An "interested person"; and

- Within 3 months of publication of acceptance of the patent application in the Journal.

Once an opposition is launched, there are no provisions in the Act for withdrawal of the opposition. In practice, however, an opponent can withdraw from the opposition at any point, indicating that he or she does not want to take an active role from that point on. However, there may be cost implications if the opponent withdraws without first reaching an agreement with the applicant.

If an opponent withdraws after the opposition has been launched the Commissioner is bound, in the public interest, to consider any grounds brought to his or her attention and to issue a decision: *Hughes and Kennaugh's Application* (1910) 27 RPC 281 and *Osterstrom and Wagner's Application* (1932) 49 RPC 565.

Oppositions are to be replaced with re-examinations after acceptance (see cls 88-93 of the draft Patents Bill 2004). However, it should be noted that unlike oppositions the party requesting re-examination will have no involvement in the re-examination process and re-examination is only available on the grounds of novelty and inventive step (see cl 90(1)). One advantage over the current patent opposition procedure is that re-examination can be requested at any stage after acceptance, including post-grant.

2.9.1 Burden and onus of proof

The onus of proof lies with the opponent to prove that the application is not suitable for grant.

The burden of proof to be applied is the ordinary civil standard, namely that any matters to be proved must be established on the balance of probabilities. However, the threshold which the opponent must reach on the balance of probabilities is a high one.

In *Sealed Air NZ Ltd v Machinery Developments Ltd* 25/8/04, MacKenzie J, HC Wellington CIV-2003-485-2274, MacKenzie J noted that the question in opposition proceedings is whether the application is "manifestly untenable", following Barker J in *Beecham Group Ltd v Bristol-Myers Co (No 2)* [1980] 1 NZLR 192 and Ongley J in *Saxpack Foods Ltd v J Wattie Canneries Ltd* 11/7/88, Ongley J, HC Wellington M454/85. His Honour noted that opposition proceedings are a means of dealing with patent applications which clearly should not proceed, and that revocation proceedings are the appropriate means of disposing of truly contentious cases.

This view was supported by Harrison J in *Merck & Co Inc v Arrow Pharmaceuticals (NZ) Ltd* 29/9/06, Harrison J, HC Wellington CIV-2006-485-817, at para 22. His Honour also considered the possible prejudice to the applicant in being deprived of the right to defend its invention in properly constituted revocation proceedings to be relevant, citing, at paras 24 and 25, the following passages:

* *Beecham Group Ltd v Bristol-Myers Co (No 2)* [1980] 1 NZLR 192, at p 213, per Barker J:

  "I shall ask myself the questions in respect of each ground of opposition; is the claim to the patent in suit 'manifestly untenable'? Is there a prima facie case for the grant of the patent? Does the justice of the case require the applicant to be permitted to resist the claim for invalidity in properly constituted revocation proceedings? All these tests, although differently stated, really amount to the same thing."

* *Dunlop Holdings Ltd* [1979] RPC 523, at p 544, per Buckley LJ:

  "Whether there would be a real risk that an injustice might be done by depriving the applicant of an opportunity to protect his right to the patent in a full-scale revocation action in the High Court … [That is a factor for] consideration by the Tribunal hearing the opposition proceedings and considering what degree of certainty it should have in relation to the alleged grounds of opposition …"

2.9.2 Standing

To oppose the grant of a patent you must be a "person interested". This is to ensure that only parties directly affected by the grant of a patent are heard.

Standing (or locus standi) must be established as at the time of filing the Notice of Opposition. The burden of proving it rests on the opponent: *Bamford's Application* [1959] RPC 66. The opponent must ensure that it provides sufficient particulars of its relevant activities and supports those statements in evidence. Otherwise, it will be at risk of being found not to have standing to oppose: *Forlong & Maisey's Application* (Commissioner's Decision No P01/2004, 5/1/04, Asst Commr Hazelwood).

There are three traditional grounds on which standing may be based (*Merron's Application* (1944) 61 RPC 91):

- Possession of a patent or pending patent application relating to the same subject matter as the opposed application;

- A manufacturing interest relating to the same subject matter as the opposed application; or

- A trading interest relating to the same subject matter as the opposed application.

However, these grounds are not exhaustive and other grounds have been found to support a claim of standing, for example, a substantial financial interest relating to the same subject matter as the opposed application: *Badische Anilin & Sodafabrik AG's Application* (1963) 80 RPC 19.

In *Propeller Jet Ltd's Application* (Commissioner's Decision No P27/2005, 26/9/05, Asst Commr Popplewell), the Assistant Commissioner was asked to determine, as a preliminary question, whether the opponent had standing in the proceedings. The Assistant Commissioner assessed this by reference to the four grounds for standing set out in the *British Patent Office Practice Manual*, namely:

(1) Whether the opponent has a relevant manufacturing interest in New Zealand;

(2) Whether the opponent has a relevant trading interest in New Zealand;

(3) Whether the opponent possesses patents or patent applications relating to the same subject matter as the opposed application; and

(4) Whether the opponent has a clear financial interest in the subject matter of the patent application.

The decision is notable for its review of other recent IPONZ decisions relating to the issue of standing and also for the Assistant Commissioner's findings that:

- Although the opponent had held earlier patents/patent applications these had all been assigned or voided pre-acceptance and therefore the third ground was not available to the opponent;

- However, a 21 percent shareholding, which was one of the largest parcels of shares, in a company which did have an interest in the subject matter of the patent was sufficient to give the opponent a clear financial interest in terms of the fourth ground.

The grounds of standing were simplified in *Wade's Application* (Commissioner's Decision No P01/1981, 9/1/81, Asst Commr Burton). In that case, it was held that the Court or Commissioner must be satisfied that an opponent has a genuine commercial interest and that there is likelihood that the opponent will suffer real prejudice by the existence of the opposed application.

A future intention to become involved with the subject matter of a patent application has been ruled as insufficient to support a claim to standing: *New Things Ltd's Application* (1914) 31 RPC 45.

The grounds of standing to oppose a patent application are essentially the same as those to revoke a patent application. In *Warren Gregory Tobin's Application* (Commissioner's Decision No P07/2006, 20/2/06, Asst Commr Hazlewood), the patentee questioned the standing of the applicant for revocation to bring the proceeding, and in so doing highlighted an anomaly in the requirement to prove standing brought about by the Office's practice of considering evidence in the public interest. Although the patentee recognised the public interest in the Office doing so, it submitted that this made it possible for an applicant for revocation to provide evidence that might successfully make out a case for revocation notwithstanding that the applicant never had standing to bring the proceeding. In addressing that submission, the Assistant Commissioner noted that, although it is normal for standing to be decided at, and as part of, the substantive hearing, it is open to the patentee to pursue the matter of standing in interlocutory proceedings. This would tend to suggest that there may be some merit in an early application to challenge the standing of an opponent/applicant for revocation where it appears, on the face of preliminary documents filed, that standing will not be able to be established.

In *Warren Gregory Tobin's Application*, the question was whether the applicant for revocation, which operated a call centre, needed to state that it had an imminent desire to use the invention (the preferred embodiment of which involved a call centre that received and processed mobile phone text messages). It was held that the provision of call centre services clearly made the applicant for revocation a person interested in developments in the provision of phone communications including those involving call centres notwithstanding that there was no direct evidence as to nature of the call centre services operated by it. In reaching this conclusion, the Assistant Commissioner cited with approval the following principles for deciding standing laid down in *Mediline AG's Patent* [1973] RPC 91, at p 97:

"(1)   The circumstances of each case must be considered and it is wrong to lay down any hard and fast rule as to the precise nature or extent of the 'interest' which justifies locus.

"(2)   The onus of establishing locus lies on the opponent or applicant for revocation.

"(3)   If the opponent or applicant for revocation can show that he has some genuine interest which will be prejudiced and if the opposition or application to revoke is not frivolous, vexatious or blackmailing, then locus should be granted even if the patentee can throw some doubt on the exact extent of the opponent's interest.

"(4)   It is in the public interest that genuine opposition to a revocation proceeding should be permitted, as normally an opponent or applicant for revocation assists the court or the Comptroller in ensuring that the scope of the patent attacked is properly examined and limited during the application and early stages of its life. The duty of the Comptroller, as a public officer in this connection, is well set out in *Terrell*, 12th edition, paragraph 439."

Under cls 86, 88, and 89 of the draft Patents Bill 2004, any person may request the Commissioner re-examines the complete specification of a patent application for lack of novelty or inventive step. Unlike a request for revocation, the Commissioner has no power to refuse a request for re-examination even if it seems vexatious. (Compare cls 88(1) and 89(1) with cl 104(3) of the draft Bill).

2.9.3 Statutory grounds of opposition

There are eight statutory grounds for opposing the grant of a patent application. They are:

(1)   Obtaining;

(2)   Prior publication;

(3)   Prior claiming;

(4)   Prior use;

(5)   Obviousness;

(6)   Not an invention;

(7)   Insufficiency of description; and

(8)   Convention application not made within 12 months of first foreign application.

Under the draft Patents Bill, it appears that in place of general opposition proceedings, third parties may ask the Commissioner to re-examine a patent application on only two grounds; that the invention lacks novelty or does not involve an inventive step.

(1)   *Obtaining*

Under Section 21(1)(a) Patents Act 1953, the grant of a patent can be opposed if the applicant has obtained the invention from another. The nature of obtaining is described in *Wade's Application* (Commissioner's Decision No P01/1981, 9/1/81, Asst Commr Burton), at p 8, as follows:

"Obtaining ... necessarily involves something more than 'finding out' ... mere 'knowledge' of the invention by a particular party cannot be the basis of an allegation of obtaining. Obtaining must surely involve the *misuse* of such knowledge by some party, ie an application for protection of an invention by a person not entitled to apply in contravention of the rights of a person truly entitled to apply."

Ordinarily, allegations of obtaining can only be made by the person from whom the invention was obtained or his/her personal representative. However, in *A2 Corp Ltd's Application* (Commissioner's Decision No P15/2005, 4/7/05, Asst Commr Popplewell), the Assistant Commissioner cited with approval *International Carbon Corp's Application* [1975] RPC 365 which held that an invention can be obtained through an agent and therefore the person alleging obtaining need not be limited to the person from whom the invention was obtained or that person's personal representative. However, the claim of obtaining was ultimately unsuccessful in that case, the Assistant Commissioner relying on uncontested evidence that the invention as described in an amended claim set submitted during the course of the opposition had been invented by the original patent applicant (who subsequently assigned it to A2 Corp).

A high burden of proof is required to prove obtaining (ie, not simply on the balance of probabilities). A patent application will only be refused on the ground of obtaining if the Court or Commissioner cannot reasonably come to a decision in favour of the applicant: *Stuart's Application* (1892) 9 RPC 452.

However, if the opponent meets this burden the onus shifts to the applicant to prove that the invention was not obtained: *C G Jowsey and J L Doutre's Application* (Commissioner's Decision No P06/1975, 15/5/75, Asst Commr Burton).

An investigation into the ground of obtaining should commence with establishing who owned the invention when the alleged obtaining took place, rather than who the true and first inventor was: *International Carbon Corp's Application* [1975] RPC 365, at p 370, per Whitford J:

> "For my part, I think the question of obtaining involves deciding first whose invention it was at the time when it is alleged the obtaining took place; [and] next whether the invention, assuming it was the opponent's invention, came from the opponents to the applicants."

This approach was endorsed by Assistant Commissioner Poppelwell in *Cool 123's Application* (Commissioner's Decision No P11/2006, 13/3/06, Asst Commr Popplewell). The decision of the Assistant Commissioner was upheld on appeal to the High Court (*Cool 123 Ltd v Vodafone NZ Ltd* 29/8/07, Simon France J, HC Wellington CIV-2006-485-698) although the High Court was not asked to revisit the findings in respect of obtaining.

If obtaining is proved during opposition, and the opponent has filed, or files, an application for the same invention, s 62 enables the Commissioner to direct that the claims of the opponent's application take the same priority date as the opposed application.

(2) *Prior publication*

If an invention which is the subject of a patent application has been published in New Zealand before the priority date of the patent application, then that invention lacks novelty and the patent application may be successfully opposed on the ground of prior publication.

Under s 21(1)(b) Patents Act 1953, an invention will be deemed prior published if, in so far as it is claimed in the complete specification of the patent application, it has been published in New Zealand:

- In any patent specification dated less than 50 years before the filing date of the applicant's complete specification; or

- In any other document provided that document was published before the priority date of the patent application.

Certain exceptions to prior publication are discussed at 2.7.2 ("Novelty requirements") earlier in this chapter.

To successfully oppose a patent application on the ground of prior publication, an applicant must establish that the document relied upon anticipates the invention as claimed and was "published" for the purposes of the Act.

(a)   *Test for prior publication*

The landmark case of *General Tire & Rubber Co v Firestone Tyre & Rubber Co* (1972) 89 RPC 457 (CA) established, at pp 485-486, a "reverse infringement" test for determining whether a document anticipates the invention claimed.

> "If the prior inventor's publication contains a clear description of, or clear instructions to do or make, something that would infringe the patentee's claim if carried out after the grant of the patentee's patent, the patentee's claim will have been shown to lack the necessary novelty, that is to say, it will have been anticipated … if carrying out the directions contained in the prior inventor's publication will inevitably result in something being made or done which, if the patentee's patent were valid, would constitute an infringement of the patentee's claim, this circumstance demonstrates that the patentee's claim has in fact been anticipated.

> "If, on the other hand, the prior publication contains a direction which is capable of being carried out in a manner which would infringe the patentee's claim, but would be at least as likely to be carried out in a way which would not do so, the patentee's claim will not have been anticipated … To anticipate the patentee's claim the prior publication must contain clear and unmistakable directions to do what the patentee claims to have invented … A signpost, however clear, upon the road to the patentee's invention will not suffice. The prior inventor must be clearly shown to have planted his flag at the precise destination before the patentee."

The applicability of the *General Tyre* test was affirmed by the Supreme Court of New Zealand in *Peterson Portable Sawing Systems Ltd (in liq) v Lucas* [2006] 3 NZLR 721 (SC), at para 3.

In *Sealed Air NZ Ltd v Machinery Developments Ltd* 25/8/04, MacKenzie J, HC Wellington CIV-2003-485-2274, MacKenzie J summarised the reverse infringement test as requiring the party opposing the patent application to show the document relied upon clearly:

(a)   Describes something that would infringe the claim;

(b)   Instructs something to be done or made which would infringe the claim; or

(c)   Gives directions, the carrying out of which would inevitably result in infringement of the patent applied for.

The test for prior publication (or "anticipation") and the authorities from which the test arose, were both comprehensively reviewed by the House of Lords in *Synthon BV v Smithkline Beecham Plc* [2005] UKHL 59. In 1997, Synthon and Smithkline simultaneously discovered that a particular salt of paroxetine, a compound used to treat depression, had properties which made it more suitable for pharmaceutical use. Synthon was the first to file a patent application covering this new salt, known as "PMS". Example 1 of the specification described how to make PMS in crystalline form and described the characteristics of the PMS crystals by a number of different readings including infra-red ("IR") spectrum. After Synthon filed its application, but before it was published, Smithkline filed its own application relating to PMS. This patent also claimed PMS in a particular crystalline form by reference to its IR profile. Importantly, this IR profile was different to the profile appearing in the Synthon application. Hence, a person skilled in the art, reading both documents, would think that they identified different crystalline forms of PMS.

Synthon applied to revoke the Smithkline patent on the basis that its own application prior published (or anticipated) any claim to PMS in the Smithkline patent. In response, Smithkline argued that Synthon application was not relevant prior art because of the differences in the IR spectrum readings in each application (which suggested that a different crystalline form of PMS was claimed in each application), and because Synthon's own experiments carried out in the course of preparing for the trial showed that the method in its application failed to produce any crystals at all without further experimentation.

At first instance, Jacob J. held that Synthon's application anticipated the Smithkline patent. His Honour found that PMS was monomorphic (ie, had only one crystalline form) and hence, despite the differences in IR spectra, Synthon and Smithkline were claiming the same compound. He also found that a person skilled in the art, reading Synthon's application, would be able to overcome the mistakes within a reasonable time. The decision of Jacob J was overturned by the Court of Appeal and Synthon appealed to the House of Lords. Delivering the judgment of the House, Lord Hoffmann agreed with Jacob J, that Synthon's application anticipated Smithkline's patent. His Lordship observed that there are two distinct requirements for anticipation: prior disclosure and enablement.

(i) **Disclosure**: To satisfy this first requirement, the matter relied upon as prior art must disclose subject-matter which, if performed, would result in an infringement of the patent. However, the infringement must not be a mere possibility, or even a likely consequence, of performing the invention disclosed by the prior disclosure. It must be the only consequence. Hence, if performance of an invention disclosed by the prior art would not infringe the patent but the prior art would make it obvious to a skilled person how he might make adaptations which resulted in an infringing invention, the patent might be invalid for lack of an inventive step/obviousness but would not be anticipated by the prior publication. For the disclosure requirement, no degree of experimentation on the part of the skilled person is to be assumed.

(ii) **Enablement**: Enablement means that the ordinary skilled person would have been able to perform the invention which satisfies the requirement of disclosure. When determining this, the Court must apply the concept of enablement as it is used throughout the remainder of the body of patent law. Some degree of experimentation by the person skilled in the art is therefore permissible.

As to the interplay between these two requirements, Lord Hoffman was at pains to point out, at paras 30 and 32, that confusion will result if they are not kept distinct:

"I have explained that for the purpose of disclosure, the prior art must disclose an invention which, if performed, would necessarily infringe the patent. It is not enough to say that, given the prior art, the person skilled in the art would without undue burden be able to come up with an invention which infringed the patent. But once the very subject-matter of the invention has been disclosed by the prior art and the question is whether it was enabled, the person skilled in the art is assumed to be willing to make trial and error experiments to get it to work. If, therefore, one asks whether some degree

61

of experimentation is to be assumed, it is very important to know whether one is talking about disclosure or about enablement …

"Likewise, the role of the person skilled in the art is different in relation to disclosure and enablement. In the case of disclosure, when the matter relied upon as prior art consists (as in this case) of a written description, the skilled person is taken to be trying to understand what the author of the description meant. His common general knowledge forms the background to an exercise in construction of the kind recently discussed by this House in [*Kirin-Amgen Inc v Hoechst Marion Roussel Ltd* [2005] RPC 9 (HL)]. And of course the patent itself must be construed on similar principles. But once the meanings of the prior disclosure and the patent have been determined, the disclosure is either of an invention which, if performed, would infringe the patent, or it is not. The person skilled in the art has no further part to play. For the purpose of enablement, however, the question is no longer what the skilled person would think the disclosure meant but whether he would be able to work the invention which the Court has held it to disclose."

(b) *Meaning of "publish"*

If a document can freely be examined by members of the public, as of right, within New Zealand it will be considered "published" for the purposes of the Patents Act 1953.

In *Bristol-Myers Co's Application* (1969) 86 RPC 146, the Court held that a communication to a single member of the public without inhibiting fetter (for example, confidentiality) constituted publication.

In *Monsanto Co (Brignac's) Application* (1971) 88 RPC 153, the Court held that an information disclosure bulletin issued internally to company salespeople for distribution (with no restrictions on subsequent use) constituted publication, despite the fact that the bulletin was not actually distributed externally. The salespeople were deemed to be members of the public.

In *JR Dalrymple's Application* (1957) 74 RPC 449, the Court held that a document that was widely distributed was deemed to be published despite being marked confidential. Although this decision probably turned on the extent to which the document had been disclosed notwithstanding its confidential marking.

In contrast, in *Forlong & Maisey's Application* (Commissioner's Decision No P01/2004, 5/1/04, Asst Commr Hazelwood), Assistant Commissioner Hazelwood confirmed that the test set out in *Humpherson v Syer* (1887) 4 RPC 407 applied in New Zealand, namely that the Hearing Officer should consider whether "the information [had] been communicated to any member of the public who was free in law or equity to use it as he pleased". On the basis of that test, mere public disclosure may not be enough to comprise "publication" if an obligation of confidentiality can be inferred from the circumstances of the disclosure.

Forlong & Maisey concerned an ex-employee of the patent applicant, who claimed to have disclosed an invention the subject of a patent application to a number of third party manufacturers during the course of his role as the patent applicant's research and development manager. The purpose of disclosure was to assess the likely costs of manufacturing the invention. Assistant Commissioner Hazlewood held, at p 15, that in those circumstances "[the ex-employee] must have been aware of the need to keep confidential any research and development that his company was conducting and that came to his attention … He was not free in law or equity to divulge any research and development work of his employer, the applicant."

In *Molecular Plant Breeding Nominees Ltd's Application* (Commissioner's Decision No P25/2005, 12/9/05, Asst Commr Popplewell), the Assistant Commissioner accepted a submission on behalf of the opponent that a document available electronically via the internet before the priority date of the opposed application met the s 2 definition of "published". The Assistant Commissioner stated, at p 27:

> "it is no longer necessary for a hard copy of a document to be available to comply with the requirements of s 2. The internet, by 1999, was widely available to New Zealanders and, in fact, a search of the 'web', by that date, would have been considered virtually essential for any scientist engaged in a survey of literature relevant to his field. There is no doubt in my mind that in the present case the document concerned has been 'made available to the public'. It could be inspected 'as of right' by the public at any place where a computer with access to the internet was available".

The Assistant Commissioner rejected a submission by the applicant that the definition requires the actual documents to be made available to the public in New Zealand, noting, at pp 27-28:

> "Any person who accesses a document on the Internet is free to download or print it; thus it seems to me that this would be analogous to a facsimile of a document being sent from overseas to a New Zealand resident — such a document would surely fall within the definition of s 2. I also note, as pointed out by Mr Arthur, that a journal or book unopened on a New Zealand library shelf is still 'published'. Similarly, it seems to me that a document stored electronically on a computer and freely accessible on a computer terminal in New Zealand is 'published' whether or not anyone actually downloads or prints it."

The same test has subsequently been applied by Assistant Commissioner Popplewell in *Agriculture Victoria Services Pty Ltd's Application* (Commissioner's Decision No P26/2005, 12/9/05, Asst Commr Popplewell).

(3)   *Prior claiming*

Under s 21(1)(c) Patents Act 1953, the grant of a patent application can be opposed on the basis that another patent application (for the same invention) was filed before, but published after, the priority date of the opposed patent application.

In *Traver Corp's Application* (1964) 81 RPC 26, it was held that a challenge on the basis of prior claiming will fail if the prior claim is silent on any essential feature of the claim at issue, even if the later claim falls completely within the scope of the prior claim.

However, in *Commercial Solvents Corp's Application* (1954) 71 RPC 143, it was held that when comparing claims, mere differences in the language (of the claims) that do not substantially differentiate the subject matter of each claim may be disregarded.

An opposition on the ground of prior claiming is technically difficult to prove as the claims have to be virtually identical. Consequently, this ground is rarely invoked.

(4)   *Prior use*

Section 21(1)(d) Patents Act 1953 provides that, where an invention has been publicly used within New Zealand before the priority date of the patent application, and where that use does not fall within one of the statutory exceptions (discussed at 2.7 ("Obtaining grant of rights") earlier in this chapter), the invention can be successfully opposed on the basis that it has been anticipated.

In July 1986, IPONZ issued a practice note based on the decision of *Bristol-Myers Co (Johnson's) Application* (1975) 92 RPC 127. The practice note confirmed that for an opponent to establish prior use he or she must show:

- That the instance of prior use was not a secret use of the invention;

- What was used and by whom it was used;

- Where and when that use occurred; and

- Where any apparatus still in existence can be inspected.

It is clear from the practice note that secret use will not constitute prior use. In *Bristol-Myers Co (Johnson's) Application* (1975) 92 RPC 127, the House of Lords held that the test for secrecy is a subjective one. For use to be secret, the user must have intentionally concealed it. The case also held that the use does not need to be for the purposes of trade. Rather it is sufficient that the user derives a practical benefit.

In *Craig & Connelly's Application* (Commissioner's Decision No P03/1982, 17/3/82, Asst Commr Burton), it was held that a single instance of prior use is sufficient to spoil the novelty residing in a patented invention.

In *Wheatley's Application* (1985) 102 RPC 91, an invention was disclosed to potential purchasers on a confidential basis before the priority date of the application. The patentee received an order but delivery was delayed to allow a patent application to be lodged. The UK Court of Appeal held that there had been use of the invention before the priority date of the application. By agreeing to sell the invention, the applicant had used his invention to achieve his commercial object. It did not matter that the commercial use was undertaken in confidence.

Prior use must be in a public manner, rather than necessarily use by the public. Thus, in *Ralta Ltd's Application* (Commissioner's Decision No P05/1985, 16/4/85, Asst Commr Burton), the private use of a single electric blanket purchased overseas was insufficient to support a claim of prior use.

As to the standard of evidence to establish prior use, Graham J had the following to say in *Seiller's Application* [1970] RPC 103, at p 106:

> "In my judgment it is necessary that proof of prior user in opposition cases should be very clear. Normally, in the absence of cross-examination, this will involve corroboration of a mere statement as to recollection in a declaration, particularly where the time interval involved is considerable. Such corroboration is often best found in documents contemporary with the fact to be proved. Each case, however,

must be considered on its own facts and I say expressly that I am not attempting to lay down any rule as to what is or is not sufficient in any given case."

There are a number of statutory exceptions to prior use, which are discussed in more detail at 2.7.2 ("Novelty requirements") earlier in this chapter. Broadly speaking, however, the exceptions can be summarised as follows:

- Disclosure of the invention at a "gazetted exhibition". This exception is on the proviso that the patent application is filed within 6 months of the exhibition;

- Use for the purposes of reasonable trial and experiment; and

- Disclosure of the invention to a Government department.

In *AHI Whimpway's Application* (Commissioner's Decision No P12/1982, 6/12/82, Asst Commr Burton), the use of a gang-mower on a public golf course was deemed to be reasonably necessary for trial and experimentation having regard to the nature of the invention.

(5) *Obviousness*

Under s 21(1)(e) Patents Act 1953 a patent application may be successfully opposed on the ground of obviousness if the invention is obvious and clearly does not involve an inventive step having regard to one of two things:

- What has already been published in New Zealand; or

- What has already been used in New Zealand.

The opponent must show that the invention is clearly obvious. The benefit of the doubt lies with the patentee. For this reason, oppositions on the ground of obviousness infrequently succeed.

Obviousness is judged as at the priority date of the patent. An opponent cannot rely on ex post facto reasoning to prove obviousness (ie, the assessment must be undertaken without the benefit of hindsight).

The rationale for testing whether an invention is obvious was summarised by Slade LJ in *Hallen Co v Brabantia (UK) Ltd* [1991] RPC 195, at p 209, as follows:

"The word 'obvious' in section 3 [s 21 Patents Act 1953 (NZ)] is I believe directed to whether or not an advance is technically or practically obvious and not to whether it is commercially obvious. Although the law is encapsulated in section 3 of the Patents Act 1977, the law on obviousness goes back many hundreds of years. The basis of the law is that the public are entitled to manufacture that which has been published, in the sense of made available to the public, with obvious modifications. By 'obvious modifications' are meant that which technically or practically would be obvious to the unimaginative skilled addressee in the art. Such a skilled man should be assured that his actions will not be covered by any monopoly granted to another if he does that which is part of the state of the art with modifications which are workshop alterations or otherwise technically or practically obvious alterations. He does not and should not have to look further and consider whether the step he is taking is obvious or not for commercial reasons. The prize for a good commercial decision or idea is a head start on the competition and not a monopoly for twenty years."

In *Beecham Group Ltd v Bristol-Myers Co (No 2)* [1980] 1 NZLR 192, at p 232, the Court held that obviousness is to be judged from the viewpoint of a "notional" person who is:

- Skilled in the "art"; and

- Knowledgeable in all relevant literature; but

- Incapable of a "scintilla of invention".

The test for obviousness most often applied is that set out in *Windsurfing International Inc v Tabur Marine (GB) Ltd* (1985) 102 RPC 59 (CA) where Oliver LJ described, at pp 73-74, the process as follows:

"The first [step] is to identify the inventive concept embodied in the patent in suit. Thereafter the court has to assume the mantle of the normally skilled but unimaginative addressee in the art at the priority date and to impute to him what was, at that date, the common general knowledge in the art in question. The third step is to identify what, if any, differences, exist between the matter cited as being 'known or used' and the alleged invention. Finally the court has to ask itself whether viewed without any knowledge of the alleged invention those differences constitute steps which would have been obvious to the skilled man or whether they require any degree of invention."

Therefore, under the *Windsurfing* test, if the difference between the prior art and the invention claimed would be obvious to the "notional addressee", the ground of obviousness is made out. Note that for the purposes of determining obviousness at the opposition stage the inventive concept is defined by the claims, and advantages which have been described in the specification, but not claimed, should be disregarded: *Lafarge Platres' Application* (Commissioner's Decision No P47/2006, 18/12/06, Asst Commr Hazlewood), at pp 21 and 22.

In *Lucas v Peterson Portable Sawing Systems Ltd* [2003] 3 NZLR 361; (2003) 57 IPR 305, Fisher J confirmed that the starting point for determining obviousness is the four-stage analysis set out in the *Windsurfing* case. His Honour then outlined, at para 69, a series of supplementary principles which might assist in determining the question of obviousness, as follows:

"(a)   Where the invention is the combination of features all of which were individually known, the Court must avoid the danger of concentrating on the integers rather than the whole concept: *Wood v Gowshall Ltd* (1937) 54 RPC 37; *Smale*, supra, at p 43; [*Sabaf SpA v MFI Furniture Centres* [2003] RPC 264 (CA)], 278 at para 40.

"(b)   The Court must also avoid the danger of falling into ex post facto analysis. It must put out of its mind developments since the invention and view the question of obviousness from the perspective of persons skilled in the art immediately before the priority date: *Non-drip Measure Co Ltd v Strangers Ltd* (1943) 60 RPC 135, 142; *Technograph Printed Circuits Ltd v Mills and Rockley (Electronics) Ltd* (1972) 89 RPC 346, 362. The warning against being wise after the event is of special importance in a field, such as the present one, where it is easy to imagine that one is skilled in the art after a relatively brief period looking at a few drawings: *Fichera & Anor v Flogates Ltd & Anor* [1983] FSR 198.

"(c)   There is no inventive step if a known article is applied to a new and analogous purpose: *Morgan & Co v Windover & Co* (1890) 7 RPC 131, 134 (HL); *Smale v North Sails*, supra, at 43.

"(d)   Similarly, there is no inventive step if known features are brought together into a single whole in which the component parts continue to 'do their own thing': *International Paint Co Ltd's Application* (1982) 99 RPC 247 at 275. Thus there is no invention if 'however juxtaposed to the other ingredients of the mixture or parts of the article, each part performs its own function and would do so even in the absence of the other parts.' (ibid). The converse is true if the collocation of features produces a new or improved function by virtue of the novel relationship established between the known features.

"(e)   Obviousness relates to the technical subject matter claimed to be inventive, and not to its commercial worth: *Windsurfing*, supra, at 72.

"(f)   There mere fact that the claim is merely to an improvement to a product already on the market does not preclude an inventive step: *Hickman v Andrews* (1983) 100 RPC 147 at 189.

"(g)   In the end, it is impossible to avoid the conclusion that the distinction between novelty and obviousness is a question rather than classification, at least in a case of the present kind."

Although the decision of Fisher J was ultimately successfully appealed to the Supreme Court (*Peterson Portable Sawing Systems Ltd (in liq) v Lucas* [2006] 3 NZLR 721 (SC)), the Supreme Court confirmed, at para 54, that the test for obviousness advocated in *Windsurfing* remains applicable:

"The law in New Zealand on obviousness was reviewed by the Court of Appeal in *Ancare New Zealand Ltd v Cyanamid of NZ Ltd*. It was determined that the principles are the same as those adopted in England and applicable still under the Patents Act 1977 (UK) (which gave effect to the Convention on the Grant of European Patent (s)). We heard no argument that we should depart from those principles. They are clearly set out in the judgments in [*Windsurfing International Inc v Tabur Marine (GB) Ltd* (1985) 102 RPC 59 (CA)] and [*Mölnlycke AB v Procter & Gamble Ltd (No 5)* [1994] RPC 49."

Documents cited in support of obviousness will often lack features of the invention. Therefore to arrive at the claimed invention the opponent may need to rely on several documents considered simultaneously. This is known as "mosaicing". Mosaicing is only permitted if the documents are of a type that the "notional addressee" would, if researching the subject, normally find together.

In *Ancare NZ Ltd v Cyanamid of NZ Ltd* [2000] 3 NZLR 299 (CA), Gault J stated, at para 43, that:

"the test [for obviousness] is well established. It postulates a person (or, where appropriate, a team) skilled in the field but not inventive, invested with the common general knowledge or prior use relied upon. *Prior documents may be looked at together if that is what the skilled person or team would do.* It asks whether to that person or team the alleged inventive step would be obvious and would be recognised, without bringing to bear any inventiveness, as something that could be done *or is at least worth trying*. That is a question of fact. If any embodiment within the scope of the claim is obvious the claim is invalid." (emphasis added)

As to the "worth a try" test, see the subsequent comments of the Court of Appeal in *Peterson Portable Sawing Systems Ltd v Lucas* 4/3/05, CA64/03; CA97/03, at para 85, in rejecting an argument by counsel for the appellant that Fisher J had erred by failing to mention that test:

"Fisher J identified all the relevant principles, albeit that he did not specifically invoke the 'worth a try' test, the utility of which may well be moot. It seems to add little to the technique of ascertaining obviousness. Anything may be worth a try, depending on acceptable cost for potential benefit, but inventiveness may lie in deciding what to try. The crucial test is the statutory expression examined in terms of the orthodoxy of *Windsurfing*."

It is not permissible for the opponent to mosaic instances of prior use and prior publication to arrive at the invention.

Traditionally, a mere collocation of integers (that is, a combination of separate parts each of which operates independently and does no more than what a person skilled in the art would expect it to do) is not considered to be patentable. Such combinations are usually viewed as being obvious.

In *Sabaf SpA v MFI Furniture Centres* [2003] RPC 264 (CA), the English Court of Appeal held that there is no separate law of collocation, and that "the very act of putting together two or more features may involve an inventive step". The Court cited the following passage from *Wood (Albert) & Amcolite Ltd v Gowshall Ltd* (1937) 54 RPC 37 (CA), at para 40, with approval, where Greene LJ stated, at p 40, that:

"dissection of a combination into its constituent elements and the examination of each element in order to see whether its use was obvious or not is, in our view, a method which ought to be applied with great caution since it tends to obscure the fact that the invention claimed is the combination."

However, the decision of the English Court of Appeal in *Sabaf* was overturned on appeal by the House of Lords (*Sabaf SpA v MFI Furniture Centres Ltd* [2005] RPC 209 (HL)). The House of Lords' decision in *Sabaf* was discussed and adopted by the Supreme Court of New Zealand in *Peterson Portable Sawing Systems Ltd (in liq) v Lucas* [2006] 3 NZLR 721 (SC). In that case, the Supreme Court was asked to consider whether a single claim in a patent relating to a portable sawing mechanism was anticipated or rendered obvious by admitted prior art. The evidence was that the sawmill, as described in the subject claim, was simply a combination of a standard frame in which the sawing rails were not vertically adjustable in unison, and a variation on that standard frame (known as the Lewis Portable Sawmill) which incorporated a winch mechanism by which the rails carrying a saw carriage could be raised and lowered in unison. The sawmill described in the subject claim was said by Lucas to combine these features to produce a non-obvious and inventive "package".

In respect of that claim, the Supreme Court said, at paras 56-62:

> "On this point a recent decision of the House of Lords, *Sabaf SpA v MFI Furniture Centres Ltd*, is helpful. Lord Hoffmann, with whom the other Law Lords agreed, rejected the proposition favoured in the Court of Appeal that where the claimed invention comprises the collocation of two known concepts what must be considered is whether it would be obvious to a person skilled in the art to combine those concepts. Lord Hoffmann, after noting that the principles applied in the European Patent Office are the same as the pre-1977 United Kingdom law (which was based on identical statutory provisions to those in New Zealand), said:

> > 'In my opinion the approach of the Court of Appeal is contrary to well established principles both in England and in the European Patent Office, as stated in the quotation from Lord Tomlin and the EPO Guidelines to which I have referred. I quite agree that there is no law of collocation in the sense of a qualification of, or gloss upon, or exception to, the test for obviousness stated in s 3 of the Act. But before you apply s 3 and ask whether the invention involves an inventive step, you first have to decide what the invention is. In particular, you have to decide whether you are dealing with one invention or two or more inventions. Two inventions do not become one invention because they are included in the same hardware. A compact motor car may contain many inventions, each operating independently of each other but all designed to contribute to the overall goal of having a compact car. That does not make the car a single invention.

> > 'Section 14(5)(d) of the Act provides (following art 82 of the EPC) that a claim shall "relate to one invention or to a group of inventions which are so linked as to form a single inventive concept". Although this is a procedural requirement with which an application must comply, it does suggest that the references in the Act to an "invention" (as in s 3) are to the expression of a single inventive concept and not to a collocation of separate inventions.

> > •   •   •   •   •

> > 'If the two integers interact upon each other, if there is synergy between them, they constitute a single invention having a combined effect and one applies s 3 to the idea of combining them. If each integer "performs its own proper function independently of any of the others", then each is for the purposes of s 3 a separate invention and it has to be applied to each one separately. That in my opinion, is what Laddie J meant by the law of collocation.'

> "In that case [(*Sabaf*)] the invention claimed, in a gas burner, employment of the known concepts of drawing air from above the hob unit and of using a flow path under the flame spreader in which a necessary Venturi effect was present. The advantage was to provide a burner of very low height suitable for modern gas ovens and separate hob units. The two concepts identified had no effect on each other.

Each performed its known function. There was, therefore, no invention in combining them.

"We do not need to decide in this case [(*Peterson*)] whether, and if so in what circumstances, there might be exceptional cases in which there could be an inventive step in identifying and combining known features …

"… It is not claimed in the Lucas patent that there is interaction in the nature of synergy between the concept of separate rails (as used in the Peterson standard frame mill) and the concept of providing moving means by which the rails can be raised or lowered in unison (as in the Lewis mill). Each of the known features performs its known function, just as in the *Sabaf* case. Neither incorporates an inventive concept. Combining them cannot amount to an inventive step.

"Even if it were accepted that, in rare cases, there could be inventiveness in combining known mechanical features without synergistic interaction, this could not be such a case. There cannot be said to be an inventive step in mechanising by standard means, such as a winch, a construction operated manually. Nor could there be an inventive step in taking the Lewis mill, dispensing with the facility to move the rails horizontally, and coupling the rails directly to the vertical sides of the frames.

"Fisher J was impressed with evidence that the Lewis mill required the rails to be raised in unison for a purpose different from that which led Mr Lucas to introduce that feature. But purpose is irrelevant. If it is an obvious step for one purpose it is not inventive to do the same thing for another."

The commercial success of an invention may be used as evidence that the invention as claimed clearly involves an inventive step. However, such evidence is only secondary. Thus, in *Sealed Air NZ Ltd v Machinery Developments Ltd* 25/8/04, MacKenzie J, HC Wellington CIV-2003-485-2274, MacKenzie J confirmed, at para 32, that in determining whether the invention is obvious, the Court is entitled to draw an inference from secondary evidence of the commercial success of the invention, although this is not a substitute for a consideration of the primary evidence as to obviousness. His Honour cited with approval Laddie J's outline of factors relevant to evidence of commercial success in *Haberman v Jackel Intentional Ltd* [1999] FSR 683 including:

(a)   The problem addressed by the invention;

(b)   The duration the problem had existed;

(c)   The significance of the problem;

(d)   The notoriety of the problem and the number likely to be seeking a solution to it;

(e)   The prior art likely to be known to all or most of those expected to be involved in seeking a solution to the problem;

(f)   The extent to which factors existed that would prevent or restrain the exploitation of a solution to the problem even it if was technically obvious;

(g)   The manner in which the invention had been received; and

(h)   The extent to which it can be shown that the commercial success of the invention is due to the technical merits of the invention in so far as they solve the problem.

In *Sealed Air*, MacKenzie J found, at para 34, that the invention addressed a significant problem which had existed for some time. The invention had obtained considerable commercial success and influenced the commercial response of competitors. However, the evidence of commercial success was only secondary, and other factors may have held back the exploitation of the solution even if it was technically obvious. MacKenzie J noted that expertise and knowledge of the prior art in the field could be expected to be more widely held by persons within a different industry to the one in which the invention was applied by the applicant. A solution obvious to a skilled addressee with knowledge of the prior art might not necessarily have been exploited because it would not have served the commercial interests of the parties to whom it would have been technically obvious. Therefore, his Honour placed little reliance on the evidence of commercial success in reaching the conclusion that the invention was not obvious to the skilled addressee with knowledge of the prior art, but without the capacity of inventiveness.

A cautionary approach to evidence of commercial success was also taken by the Supreme Court of New Zealand in *Peterson Portable Sawing Systems Ltd (in liq) v Lucas* [2006] 3 NZLR 721 (SC). In overturning the decision of the trial Judge (Fisher J), who was influenced by evidence that no-one had previously combined the separate features of the invention and as to the effectiveness and commercial success of the product, the Supreme Court emphasised the importance of ensuring that the evidence relates to what is claimed rather than what has been produced. Thus the Supreme Court stated, at paras 63-65:

> "Fisher J was also influenced by evidence that no one had previously combined the separate features. That is a point that tends to elide novelty and obviousness. He also placed weight upon evidence of the effectiveness and commercial success of the 'package' produced by the respondents. Such evidence must be considered with care. Having reviewed what the witnesses said, it appears to us that they did not distinguish between the sawmill construction marketed by the respondents and the combination of features claimed so broadly in claim 7. There were numerous features of the Lucas construction not included in claim 7. Some are described in the patent specification and included in other claims. The 'package' successfully marketed was not the appropriate focus for expert opinion. Even Mr Lucas, as recorded by Fisher J, emphasised the advantage of a 'walk through frame', but claim 7 makes no mention of that. In similar vein, Mr Stevens was impressed with the stability produced by a cantilever effect resulting from the use of an endless chain running round an idler wheel and exerting downward pull on the rails. There is no mention of that in claim 7.

> "When, in the course of cross-examination, Mr Stevens was asked to focus on the claimed inventive concept of providing means for raising and lowering the rails in unison, he came very close to accepting that, if some means were required to facilitate operation of the Peterson standard frame mill, it would be obvious to use winding means which were known. He accepted there would have been the two options of raising and lowering the rails separately or together. The notes of evidence record the following:

>> 'You would have chosen one not the other? I don't know what I would have chosen, it wouldn't have been immediately obvious to come up with simultaneous lifting, I know from experience that simple arrangements such

71

as this are the produce of long thought and it wouldn't have been the first thought to come to mind, it might if I had had direct hands on experience with the standard frame but even then I can't be certain that I would have gone from the first to the second option.'

"The notional person skilled in the art is expected to consider what is known or used in the field and to consider how that might be employed. It cannot be that a step is obvious only if it is first among available options."

See also the Full Federal Court of Australia's decision in *Lockwood Security Products Pty Ltd v Doric Products Pty Ltd* (2005) FCAFC 255. In Lockwood, the question was whether claims relating to a locking mechanism on the inside of a deadlock which could be unlocked from the outside were obvious. The patent was intended to avoid the problem with traditional deadlocks which, when unlocked from the outside, remained locked from the inside. The primary Judge held that the invention was not obvious *(Doric Products Pty Ltd v Lockwood Security Products Pty Ltd* (2001) 192 ALR 306). The Full Federal Court disagreed, interpreting a statement from one of Lockwood's witnesses that it would "never have occurred to him to design such a lock that operated with a safety release mechanism to overcome the problem" as a reference to the preferred embodiment of the lock and not to the lock as broadly claimed. Thus, the statement was related to the "nitty gritty" of effecting a solution to the problem and not the general concept of unlocking the inside lock with the outside key as claimed. In reaching its decision, the Full Federal Court appears to have been influenced by the decision in *Winner v Anmar Holdings Pty Ltd* (1992) 24 IPR 137 which supports the proposition that, if the claimed solution to a problem is the corollary of the problem, and the problem is known, it will be difficult to argue that the solution is inventive. Relating this proposition back to the *Lockwood* case, it was not inventive to say that the solution to the problem of the inside lock not being responsive to the outside key is simply to make it so, especially as the solution was claimed at that level of generality.

Finally, in *Re Ian Conrad Holyoake's Application* (Commissioner's Decision No P09/2005, 15/3/05, Asst Commr Hazlewood), the Assistant Commissioner held that, in determining the issue of obviousness, he was entitled to make use of his own knowledge and experience of the relevant technical background to interpret the invention, particularly in a case where the technology does not appear complex. The Assistant Commissioner relied on the following passage of Diplock LJ in *Johns-Manville Corporation's Patent* [1967] RPC 479, at p 491:

"In determining an issue of obviousness, both the superintending examiner and the Patents Appeal Tribunal are entitled to and do make use of their own knowledge and experience of the relevant scientific and technical background to the subject-matter of the alleged invention."

Finally, in *Cool 123 Ltd v Vodafone NZ Ltd* 29/8/07, Simon France J, HC Wellington CIV-2006-485-698, the question arose as to what documents it is permissible for the Court to assess obviousness against. In an earlier decision the appellant's patent had been found by the Assistant Commissioner to be obvious *(Cool 123's Application* (Commissioner's Decision No P11/2006, 13/3/06, Asst Commr Popplewell)). On appeal, the appellant submitted that obviousness must be assessed only against documents proven to have been located by a diligent searcher who does not have knowledge of the claims or invention, and who has located the documents whilst seeking to obtain information that will be helpful in finding a solution to the particular problem or situation presented. The appellant relied on three New Zealand High Court cases that had followed such an approach — Barker J in *Beecham Group Ltd v Bristol-Myers Co (No 2)* [1980] 1 NZLR 192, Morris J in *Novartis NZ Ltd v Ancare NZ Ltd* 19/6/98, Morris J, HC Auckland CP480/97, and Fisher J in *Gallagher Electronics Ltd v Donaghys Electronics Ltd* (1992) 5 TCLR 31 — and challenged the soundness of the contrary view which finds its primary authority in *Windsurfing International*.

This argument was rejected, albeit in obiter, Simon France J having held that a finding of obviousness was available on the common general knowledge without needing to get into what other documents the unimaginative skilled addressee might consider. In dispensing with the argument, Simon France J made the following observations, at paras 61-70:

- The law is not settled on this aspect. In *Ancare* at the Court of Appeal level, Gault J observed (*Ancare NZ Ltd v Cyanamid of NZ Ltd* [2000] 3 NZLR 299 (CA), para 42):

  "It is to be noted that the same words are used as in s 41(1)(e) in identifying the prior art against which the matter is tested: 'having regard to what was known or used before the priority date of the claim in New Zealand'. That has not always led to acceptance of the same documentary material being taken into consideration under the two subsections [s 41(1)(e) (anticipation) and s 41(1)(f) (obviousness)]. Morris J adopted a narrower approach when considering obviousness, as did Barker J in *Beecham Group Ltd v Bristol-Myers Co (No 2)* [1980] 1 NZLR 192 at p 253 though it was not mentioned in the judgment on appeal: [*Beecham Group Ltd v Bristol-Myers Co* [1981] 1 NZLR 600 (CA)]. Morris J found the ground of invalidity made out even on that [narrower] approach. It is not the approach preferred in the *Windsurfing International* case. Like Morris J, we are able to reach a clear view without reference to documents the availability of which might be contentious and so we do not need to reach a final view on just what documents should be regarded as 'known' for the test of obviousness."

- The statute provides an answer. There are two types of hearing — an opposition to the initial grant and a revocation proceeding where the patent has been issued and there is an application for it to be revoked. The wording of the revocation provision, s 41 Patents Act (as referred to in the passage of Gault J above), is different from the wording of s 21. The plain reading of s 21(1)(b) and (e) together is that obviousness, at the opposition stage, is to be assessed against the same pool of documents that were considered for prior publication under s 21(1)(b). It is difficult to see how else one can read the two provisions.

- The policy reasons advanced by the appellant seem less than compelling. A wider pool of documents will inevitably be identified for a prior publication inquiry. It seems artificial, in the name of avoiding hindsight, to prune that pool and pretend one had not seen half of them. That will surely also lead to unnecessary duplication in evidence and effort if, for example, the primary source of such material for both prior publication and obviousness is the Patent Office library or database. It follows that it was not necessary for the respondents to call further evidence as to the availability of the documents relied upon.

In any event, in cases such as *Ancare* Gault J felt able to look at documents that would plainly come within the diligent searcher test. There is no reference in *Ancare* to the documents having the status of "non-controversial" by virtue of evidence to that effect led at that hearing. By implication there is a pool of documents that are not contentious and they are not contentious because it is plain that they would be located under a diligent searcher approach. Commonsense and experience will make it plain that some documents will inevitably have been found. If that is so, and the documents are already before the trier of fact, it would be odd to describe them as inadmissible on the question of obviousness.

(6) *Not an invention*

A patent application can be opposed under s 21(1)(f) Patents Act 1953 on the grounds that it is not an invention within the meaning of the Act.

"Invention" is defined in s 2 as follows:

> "'Invention' means any manner of new manufacture the subject of letters patent and grant of privilege within section 6 of the Statute of Monopolies and any new method or process of testing applicable to the improvement or control of manufacture; and includes an alleged invention:"

In *L'Oreal's Application* [1970] RPC 265, at pp 269 and 270, the Court said:

> "In cases relating to the objection that the subject of a claim is not 'a manner of new manufacture' the case of *Compagnies Reunies des Glaces et Verres* (1931) 48 RPC 185 shows that 'two basic questions are involved. Is there a manufacture and, if so, is it new? …'

> "This clearly involves inter alia an examination to see whether the specification discloses something which is or can be alleged to be an invention or manner of new manufacture within section 101. Whilst, as stated, if there is doubt it should be resolved in the applicant's favour, the corollary is also necessarily true and, if the Comptroller is satisfied that there is no invention or manner of new manufacture disclosed in the specification, it is his duty to refuse it. The question whether there is a 'manner of new manufacture' the subject of letters patent and grant of privilege disclosed, in our judgment, imposes upon the Comptroller at the application stage the duty of considering whether there is present such consideration as can possibly support a grant. There will be no such possibility if the subject of the claim under review has for example clearly been previously disclosed or is quite plainly obvious in the light of prior available knowledge. There will, in view of the presumption in favour of the applicant at this stage, be very few cases where the Comptroller should take the extreme step of refusal, but in a proper case he is bound to do so. If he is wrong his decision can be reversed on appeal by the Appeal Tribunal, which itself is subject to review by certiorari."

The section is not intended to be a catch-all for grounds not already covered by some other section of the Act: *James Gibbons Ltd's Patent* [1957] RPC 155, at p 157:

> "In my opinion, 'invention' in Ground (f) means an invention as defined in Sec.101 of the Statute of Monopolies. Hence, Ground (f) can only properly be pleaded if it is intended to argue that the invention belongs to one of those types of invention

which are held to be inherently outside the definition, such as systems of business, methods of agriculture, new discoveries, and so on. It cannot be applicable where the invention is a device, apparatus or mechanism which, although it may be shown to be old or obvious, clearly is a 'manufacture'. I am quite satisfied that the Comptroller should not allow Ground (f) to be pleaded merely to form a basis for some unspecified attack upon a patent in the event that the specified grounds of attack provided by Sec. 14 should fail."

Therefore, this ground can be used in relation to an invention that, for example:

- Is not a manner of new manufacture;

- Is a mere discovery;

- Is a collocation of integers;

- Is a method of medical treatment;

- Is a Swiss-type claim which is not correctly formulated; or

- Is a computer program which does not have a commercially useful effect.

A "mere scheme or plan" is not a "manner of manufacture" and thus is not patentable: *D, A, and K's Application* (1926) 43 RPC 155, at p 158, and *Rolls-Royce Ltd's Application* [1963] RPC 251, at p 255.

The mere collation of statistical data is not patentable: *Stahl & Larsson's Application* [1965] RPC 596, at p 600.

Similarly, using a known material for its known properties in a new application for which its properties make it suitable will not amount to an invention: *Commissioner of Patents v Microcell Ltd* (1959) 1A IPR 52, at pp 61-62:

> "it is not an inventive idea for which a monopoly can be claimed to take a substance which is known and used for the making of various articles, and make out of it an article for which its known properties make it suitable, although it has not in fact been used to make that article before ...

> "... We have in truth nothing but a claim for the use of a known material in the manufacture of known articles for the purpose of which its known properties make that material suitable. A claim for nothing more than that cannot be subject matter for a patent, and the position cannot be affected either by the fact that nobody thought of doing the thing before, or by the fact that, when somebody did think of doing it, it was bound to be a good thing to do."

The s 2 definition is discussed in more detail at 2.4 ("Patentable subject matter") earlier in this chapter.

(7)   *Insufficient description*

A patent application with broad, ambiguous and/or speculative claims will be susceptible to an objection of insufficiency: s 21(1)(g).

For the ground of insufficient description to be made out it must be shown that the complete specification does not sufficiently and fairly:

- Describe the invention; or

- Describe the method by which the invention is to be performed.

The Court's approach to a claim of insufficiency under s 21(1)(g) was summarised in *Noton NZ Ltd v Alister Bevin Ltd* (1979) 1 NZIPR 236 as follows:

- The objection is to be considered in two parts — sufficient and fair description of the invention, and sufficient and fair description of the method by which the invention is to be performed;

- If the promised result cannot be achieved because of deficiencies in the information in the specification, there is insufficiency; and

- The Court is to inquire whether the manner in which the invention is to be performed is sufficiently described in the specification to the comprehension of the notional skilled addressee.

The standard by which the sufficiency of the specification should be determined was described by Lindley LJ in *Edison and Swan Electric Co v Holland* (1889) 6 RPC 243, at p 280, as follows:

> "in describing in what manner the invention is to be performed, the patentee does all that is necessary, if he makes it plain to persons having reasonable skill in doing such things as have to be done in order to work the patent, what they are to do in order to perform his invention. If … they are to do something the like of which has never been done before, he must tell them how to do it, if a reasonably competent workman would not himself see how to do it on reading the specification".

While some degree of non-inventive experimentation is acceptable, the description in the specification or claims needs to be sufficient to enable a person skilled in the art to put the invention into practice without an excessive number of such experiments: *Kuo Cheng Shen's Application* (Commissioner's Decision No P12/1994, 11/10/94, Commr Poppelwell).

However the line is not always easy to draw. In *American Home Products Corp v Novartis Pharmaceuticals* [2001] RPC 159, at p 177, Aldous LJ said:

> "There is a difference between on the one hand a specification which requires a skilled person to use his skill and application to perform the invention, and, on the other, a specification which requires a skilled person to go to the expense and labour of trying to ascertain whether some product has the required properties. When carrying out the former the skilled person is trying to perform the invention, whereas the latter requires him to go further and carry out research to ascertain how the invention is to be performed. If the latter is required the specification would appear to be insufficient."

This case also confirms that sufficiency is assessed by reference to the common general knowledge of the skilled addressee. In that regard, the comments of the English Court of Appeal in *Valensi v British Radio Corp* [1973] RPC 337 (CA), at pp 377-378 (cited in *Cryovac Inc's Application* (Commissioner's Decision No P33/2006, 7/8/06, Asst Commr Hazlewood) and *Lafarge Platres' Application* (Commissioner's Decision No P47/2006, 18/12/06, Asst Commr Hazlewood), at p 38) are relevant:

> "the effect of [a number of earlier cases discussed in the judgment] as a whole is to show that the hypothetical addressee is not a person of exceptional skill and knowledge, that he is not to be expected to exercise any invention or any prolonged research, enquiry or experiment. He must, however, be prepared to display a reasonable degree of skill and common knowledge in the art in making trials and to correct obvious errors in the specification if a means of correcting them can readily be found … Further, we are of the opinion that it is not only inventive steps that cannot be required of the addressee. While the addressee must be taken as a person with a will to make the instructions work, he is not to be called upon to make a prolonged study of matters which present some initial difficulty."

Ultimately, the standard of sufficiency is a matter of degree dependant on the facts of each case and the invention at issue. For example, if what is alleged in the specification is the disclosure of an invention to the public that will enable them to achieve a significant improvement on the prior art, and the specification tells them no more than will enable them to get a modest increase over the prior art, the invention the subject of the complete specification has not been sufficiently or fairly described: *Eastman Kodak Co's Application* [1970] RPC 548, at p 564 (cited with approval in *Lafarge Platres' Application* (Commissioner's Decision No P47/2006, 18/12/06, Asst Commr Hazlewood), at p 39).

In *Kubushiki Kaisha Toshiba's Application* (Commissioner's Decision No P08/2005, 11/4/05, Asst Commr Popplewell), the specification contained an error, repeated at least three times in the detailed description, which meant that the invention claimed (a washing machine) would not work. Citing the following passage from *Valensi v British Radio Corp* [1973] RPC 337, at p 377, the Assistant Commissioner found the specification invalid for insufficiency:

> "While the addressee must be taken as a person with a will to make the instructions work, he is not to be called upon to make a prolonged study of matters which present some initial difficulty: and, in particular, if there are actual errors in the specification — if the apparatus really will not work without departing from what is described — then, unless both the existence of the error and the way to correct it can quickly be discovered by an addressee of the degree of skill and knowledge which we envisage, the description is insufficient."

Finally, it should be noted that the enquiry under this ground relates solely to the sufficiency of description in the patent document and not to the practical ability of a reader of the specification to put the invention into practice. The principle is best illustrated by the decision of the House of Lords in *American Cyanamid Co (Dann's) Patent* (1971) 54 RPC 425 (HL).

Dann's Patent concerned an application to revoke a patent for a new antibiotic and a method for its production. The patent was challenged on the basis of insufficiency, lack of fair basis, and false suggestion. It was conceded that the description of the strain in the patent specification was sufficient to enable those skilled in the art to identify the strain in question positively if and when they could acquire it or find it. In addition, the specification used American Type Culture Collection ("ATCC") reference numbers to identify three suitable strains which had been deposited at the ATCC in the United States. There being millions of strains of the bacteria in existence, it was agreed by both parties that, for the purpose of the proceedings, it had to be assumed that in practice the only source open to the interested reader was the ATCC. The original deposits for the ATCC were made with a restriction by the patentee against the acquisition of the strains without the patentee's permission. Those strains were not made available to people in the United Kingdom until some date after the sealing of the patent.

At first instance the trial Judge held that the patentee had to put the addressee of the specification in a position that he knew how to, and was thus able to, obtain any novel material which was essential to performing the invention claimed, and also that the complete specification should be sufficient at its date of filing. As the deposited strain was not publicly available at the date of filing, the trial judge held that the specification did not sufficiently and fairly describe the invention or the manner by which it was to be performed. The patentee appealed directly to the House of Lords.

The House of Lords upheld the appeal. While noting (and indeed having some sympathy for) the applicant for revocation's argument that the failure by the patentee to supply to the public the raw material used in its method or process meant that there was a lack of consideration for the grant of a claim to that method or process, the majority held that, with the codification of the grounds of revocation, there was no longer a statutory basis for refusing the grant of and/or revoking a patent on that ground.

The challenge on the grounds of sufficiency (which was provided for in the statute) was rejected on the basis that the applicant for revocation was unable to point to any aspect of the document itself in which the description of the method and process was deficient. The House of Lords rejected a further submission that the conduct of the patentee (in failing to make the raw material available to the public) would be relevant to the sufficiency of the disclosure in the document holding, per Lord Guest, at p 445:

> "The words of the section are clear. What the section requires is a sufficient *description*. This suggests in the context of a specification a number of words, illustrations, diagrams or symbols. It does not include an obligation to make available with the specification any particular substance. It is illegitimate, in my view, to read into two subsections a requirement that the addressee must be able to perform the invention or that he is able to obtain the starting materials."

and, per Lord Wilberforce, at p 450:

> "My Lords, I fail to see in what sense a failure to give access to strains (admittedly fully described in the specification) can be called a failure of description. It is a failure of action, a failure quite outside the sphere of the specification, a written document whose purpose is to describe, a failure of conduct by the patentee.

> "It cannot be converted into a failure of description by a formula such as 'he failed to perform information enabling the 'addressee to gain access to the culture"."

and, per Lord Guest, at p 443:

> "… [N]owhere in the statutory words can I find or imply an obligation on the part of the patentee himself to supply the starting materials which he amply describes … He must give information so that material can be identified. The emphasis in *Vidal Dyes Syndicate Ltd v Levinstein Ltd* (1912) 29 RPC 245 is on the duty of supplying information. A patentee must not throw upon the public the burden of experimenting in order to ascertain how the invention is to be carried out. It was

pointed out that in preparing his complete specification a patentee has two duties having distinct objects: in the first place he must 'particularly describe and ascertain the nature of the invention' and in the second place he must particularly describe and ascertain 'the manner in which the same is to be performed' (see section 2 of the Patents and Designs Act 1907). Fletcher-Moulton, LJ said (pages 265-6):

> 'The first is to ensure that the monopoly granted by the patentee extends no further than the invention which the applicant for the patent has made. The second is to ensure that the public shall, in return for the grant of the monopoly, be put in full possession of the way to carry out the invention in order that, after the patent has expired, they may enjoy to the full the benefit of that invention.'

"These observations emphasised the need for adequacy of description of method but they were not directed to a situation where there is difficulty in procuring the starting materials unless they are made available by the patentee."

In practice, many practitioners confuse insufficiency with inutility, which is not a ground of opposition but is a ground of revocation. The distinction is succinctly addressed in *Tetra Molectric Ltd's Application* [1977] RPC 290, at p 297 (cited with approval by Davison CJ in *Noton NZ Ltd v Alister Bevin Ltd* (1979) 1 NZIPR 236, at p 238):

> "If you cannot achieve the promised result because of deficiencies in the information given in the specification, there is insufficiency. But, if following that information and having achieved mechanically that which the specification promises you will achieve by so following, the end product will not of itself achieve that promise, then that is inutility."

(8) *Convention application not made within 12 months of first foreign application*

If an application claiming priority from an earlier foreign application (ie, a convention application) is not made within 12 months of the filing of that earlier foreign application, then an objection may be made under this ground: s 21(1)(h) Patents Act 1953.

The rationale for the ground is that, in a situation where the convention application is filed more than 12 months from the earlier foreign application, the relevant invention may have already been disclosed in New Zealand before the date on which the convention application was actually filed in New Zealand, and the Commissioner will have no alternative but to refuse to grant the New Zealand patent application.

However, if there has been no disclosure in New Zealand before the New Zealand filing date the applicant can relinquish the convention priority date and the application may still be granted with no claims to priority.

2.9.4 Documents

To initiate opposition proceedings, an opponent must file both:

* A Notice of Opposition ("the Notice"); and

* A Statement of Case ("the Statement").

The Notice must be filed within 3 months of publication of the accepted application. This can be extended by a further month: s 21(2) Patents Act 1953.

(1)   *Notice of opposition*

The Notice must clearly state the statutory grounds on which the patent is opposed. However, the Notice cannot go beyond the grounds laid out in s 21 Patents Act 1953.

(2)   *Statement of case*

A Statement of Case should accompany a Notice of Opposition to the grant of a patent application. However, as the Statement is often a detailed document, in practice a Notice may be filed along with a request for an extension of time to file the Statement at a later date.

The Statement must set out the opponent's standing, the facts the opponent relies on, and the relief it seeks.

Matters not included in the pleadings cannot be raised at the hearing: *Bradford Dyers Assn Ltd's Application* [1966] FSR 79. However, it is not necessary to elaborate on technical facts in the Statement, unless the patent applicant requires such information.

The Statement is deemed not to have been filed unless copies of the documents referenced in it are also supplied.

Previously, if an opponent withdrew from opposition proceedings before the Statement was filed, or if the Statement was not filed in time, the opposition itself was deemed not to have been launched, and in the latter case the opponent could still avail itself of the belated opposition procedure under s 42. However, that practice has now been overruled by the decision in *LACME v Gallagher Group Ltd* 17/8/05, Fogarty J, HC Wellington CIV-2004-485-2659.

In *LACME*, Gallagher filed a Notice of Opposition and sought a 2-month extension of time to file a Statement of Case under reg 168 Patents Regulations 1954, which was granted by IPONZ. Gallagher subsequently filed and served a Statement of Case, but not until after the deadline had elapsed. The opposition was deemed to have been abandoned.

Once LACME's patent was registered, Gallagher filed an application to revoke the patent under s 42 Patents Act 1953. LACME objected to Gallagher's application on the basis that under s 42 a person may not apply to revoke a patent if they have "opposed" the grant of the patent. Gallagher claimed that, without filing a Statement of Case, the opposition to LACME's patent application had never been formalised. IPONZ agreed in a preliminary opinion. LACME sought a hearing.

At that hearing Assistant Commissioner Hazelwood considered the meaning of "oppose" in s 42 of the Act (*LACME's Application* (Commissioner's Decision No P21/2004, 8/11/04, Asst Commr Hazlewood)) and concluded, at pp 10-11:

> "It seems to me that the time at which the opposition is to be considered launched is when the notice and accompanying statement are forwarded to the applicant. If this is not so then the time of launch would be when the office holds both the notice and statement. I do not think I need to decide quite which of these two points, or any intermediate point, it is that an opposition is to be deemed launched for the

purposes of this decision. Suffice it to say I believe it is at or after the time when both notice and statement are filed with the Office."

Because Gallagher's Statement of Case was filed out of time, Assistant Commissioner Hazelwood deemed the opposition not to have been launched and held that Gallagher was entitled to apply to revoke LACME's patent application.

LACME successfully appealed the Commissioner's decision to the High Court. Fogarty J held that the Assistant Commissioner's requirement that both the Notice of Opposition and Statement of Case be held by IPONZ before an opposition is deemed to have been "launched" introduced a gloss which is not present in the Act itself, and that there was no reason to depart from the plain language of ss 42(1) and 21(3).

(3)   *Amendment of the Notice or the Statement*

The Commissioner has discretionary powers to allow amendment of the Notice and/or the Statement: reg 167 Patents Regulations 1954.

Amendments need to be formulated and submitted as soon as possible before the hearing. In practice, however, IPONZ usually restricts amendments to the period before the applicant files a Counterstatement (ie, within 2 months of the applicant receiving the Statement of Case) unless there is a reasonable explanation as to why the amendments could not have been made earlier.

This practice is consistent with *The Permutit Co Ltd's Application* (1964) 81 RPC 22, in which the following factors were said to influence whether amendments will be permitted:

* The diligence of the opponent in preparing its case;

* The relevance of any new documents;

* The time elapsed since filing the original documents; and

* Whether the delay is unjust to the applicant or against the public interest.

In *Amadeus Global Travel Distribution SA v Sabre Inc* 14/3/03, Ronald Young J, HC Wellington AP126/02, the Court commented that, once the Commissioner has elected to accept an amended Notice of Opposition and Statement of Case, he is obliged to permit the filing of further evidence in support of those amendments, at para 12:

> "The Assistant Commissioner granted the Appellant's application for leave to file the Amended Notice of Opposition and Statement of Case. In that situation as a minimum, he had to allow the Appellant to file further statements of evidence in relation to the amendment. Not to do so would make a mockery of the order to allow the amendments. The Appellant would have had an Amended Statement of Case but without the right to present evidence in support of the amended case ... I accept in saying this that there may be dispute about the extent or indeed the need for evidence at all in support of the amended case. However, that issue could not sensibly be resolved at the interlocutory stage, and as a minimum the Assistant Commissioner had to give limited leave to file further evidence once he allowed the amendments."

2.9.5 Defending opposition proceedings

The applicant must file a Counterstatement within 2 months of receiving the Notice and the Statement.

The Counterstatement needs to set out the responses to the opponent's allegations, and may also contain a brief statement of any other relevant factors in support of the application.

The applicant may unconditionally offer in its Counterstatement to amend the patent application to overcome the objections contained within the opposition. Any amendments will be examined by IPONZ before they can be accepted (see 2.8.3 ("Amendments to patent specification after acceptance") earlier in this chapter).

Failure to file a Counterstatement by the due date is not necessarily fatal to the patent application. It is possible for the Commissioner to exercise his or her discretion to retrospectively grant an extension of time to file the Counterstatement: *Rural Pacific Marketing Pty Ltd v TechniPharm International Ltd* (Commissioner's Decision No P10/1999, 12/8/99, Asst Commr Popplewell).

2.9.6 Evidence

Evidence filed in support of each party's application is given in the form of a statutory declaration or affidavit. Compare cl 262 of the draft Patents Bill 2004.

Any supporting documents, and certified translations of any foreign documents, referred to must be attached as an exhibit to the declaration. If an exhibit (for example, a mechanical model) cannot be copied IPONZ will retain the original and make it freely available for inspection by any party.

Under s 96(1) Patents Act 1953, the Commissioner may receive oral evidence instead of, or as well as, a statutory declaration. In practice this section is rarely (if ever) relied on. The ability of the Commissioner to receive evidence orally is bolstered by cl 264 of the draft Patents Bill 2004, which enables the Commissioner to issue a summons requiring a person to attend a hearing to give oral evidence under oath, and to produce documents relevant to the hearing, under oath if necessary.

In determining the standard of evidence required in opposition proceedings, it is helpful to refer to trade mark opposition and rectification proceedings. In *Royal NZ Yacht Squadron v Daks Simpson Group Plc* [2002] NZAR 187, Young J took a strict approach to the standard of evidence required when proving non-use of a trade mark. It was held that evidence before the Commissioner of Trade Marks must comply with the rules of evidence applicable in the High Court. In *Rainbow Technologies Inc v Logical Networks Ltd* [2003] 3 NZLR 553, it was determined that evidence should be assessed in accordance with the "usual" civil principles.

In *Nufarm Ltd's Application* (Commissioner's Decision No P06/2006, 13/2/06, Asst Commr Popplewell), the Assistant Commissioner confirmed, at p 20, that there was no reason why the approaches in *Rainbow Technologies* and *Royal NZ Yacht Squadron* should not be equally applicable to evidence before the Commissioner of Patents. However, after noting a criticism by Hammond J in *Rainbow Technologies* of the "tribunal's approach" taken by Young J in *Royal NZ Yacht Squadron*, the Assistant Commissioner concluded nonetheless, at p 21, that the admissibility of evidence in patent opposition cases, and the weight to be given to that evidence, is at the discretion of the Commissioner and, while the evidence must be to a high standard (and relevant High Court rules should be kept in mind), the proceedings are before what is effectively a tribunal and some latitude will be allowed where appropriate. A similar approach was taken in *Reel Sa and Asmi's Application* (Commissioner's Decision No P37/2006, 28/8/06, Asst Commr Hazlewood).

Consistent with this approach, in *Warren Gregory Tobin's Application* (Commissioner's Decision No P07/2006, 20/2/06, Asst Commr Hazlewood), the Assistant Commissioner held that evidence that appeared to have been sworn properly, and which had probative value, should not be excluded because of a slight variation from the accepted wording in the swearing portion of the declaration notwithstanding an IPONZ Practice Note published in *Patents Journal* (No 1292) which stated that any such declarations would be inadmissible. The Assistant Commissioner did, however, caution a warning that his finding was not to be taken as a finding that the proper wording is to be trifled with and that any form of wording is permissible.

Any party involved in the opposition proceedings can elect not to file evidence in support of their case, but must notify IPONZ of their intention not to do so.

In *Re Ian Conrad Holyoake's Application* (Commissioner's Decision No P09/2005, 15/3/05, Asst Commr Hazlewood), the Assistant Commissioner held, at p 16, that no adverse inference can be drawn from a failure to file evidence in reply. In that case the applicant for revocation provided evidence of alleged prior use of the invention. The patentee then provided evidence to the effect that the use did not amount to a prior use of the invention as claimed. The applicant for revocation did not provide evidence in reply, and the patentee argued that, as the applicant for revocation had the opportunity to respond to the evidence and failed to do so, it had implicitly accepted the patentee's evidence as to prior use. That argument was rejected by the Assistant Commissioner. The Assistant Commissioner relied on the following passage from D L Mathieson, *Cross on Evidence* (6th ed), Wellington, Butterworths, 1997, at para 2.19:

> **"2.19 Absence of material witness**
>
> "The absence of a material witness cannot be used to make up any deficiency of evidence. If, however, a witness who had knowledge of the circumstances in issue is not called by the defendant, the tribunal of fact may conclude that the evidence given for the plaintiff may more readily be accepted, as well as any inference open from facts directly proved by the plaintiff. The circumstance that the defendant might have proved the contrary is a proper consideration in favour of drawing the inference. But sometimes the only proper inference is that the evidence of the absent witness would not have helped the party not calling that witness.
>
> "The inference which a Court can properly draw in the absence of a witness, *where such absence is not satisfactorily accounted for*, is that nothing which the witness could say would assist the relevant party. But it is incorrect to infer that the absent witness would have given evidence damaging to the case of the accused or other party omitting to call him or her. If the absent witness is independent of both sides, and equally available to them, it has been held that no inference adverse to either party because of that absence should be drawn.

"In *R v Roberts*, the Court of Appeal held that it was not open to a jury to draw an adverse inference from the refusal of a witness to testify. A refusal has no probity or evidential value.

"A Judge in Victoria once stated that 'where uncontradicted evidence, which is inherently reasonable, probable, and conclusive of the matter, has been given, the Court is bound to accept it'. But if this is taken literally, it cannot be reconciled with the general rule that the Courts are free to refuse to accept uncontradicted evidence. Obviously, a Court will rarely reject uncontradicted evidence if it is 'inherently reasonable, probable and conclusive'. If such evidence is rejected, it must be rejected for relevant reasons, which, if the tribunal of fact is a Judge, he or she is obliged to disclose."

In some cases it may be possible to file additional evidence outside of the usual timeframes. The usual rules apply, namely, the evidence must be of a type which could not have been produced within the statutory timeframes, its probative value must outweigh the prejudice to the other party, and the party applying for late filing of the evidence must have acted diligently in the preparation of that evidence and in making that application. There is a detailed examination of the authorities relating to jurisdiction to admit further evidence, and the criteria to be applied when exercising that jurisdiction, in *Synthon BV's Application* (Commissioner's Decision No P25/2006, 19/6/06, Asst Commr Popplewell).

2.9.7 Hearing

On completion of the filing of evidence (if any) the Commissioner will appoint a time for hearing the opposition.

The opposition is heard either before a hearings officer, or on the papers if all parties elect not to be heard in person. The Commissioner will then issue a decision. In practice, the decision is normally reserved.

Decisions of the Commissioner may be appealed to the High Court: s 21(5) Patents Act 1953. Compare cl 268 of the draft Patents Bill 2004.

2.9.8 Relief

Where a patent application has been successfully opposed, the Commissioner may:

- Refuse to grant the patent application; or

- Require that the applicant amend the patent application.

In most cases, the Commissioner will also order the unsuccessful party to contribute to the costs of the successful party.

2.9.9 Section 22 opposition

Anticipatory material can be brought to the Commissioner's attention under s 22 Patents Act 1953 after acceptance of a patent application but before it is sealed.

On the face of s 22, if the Commissioner is satisfied that the invention as claimed has been prior published (see 2.7.2 ("Novelty requirements") and 2.9.3 ("Statutory grants of opposition") earlier in this chapter) the Commissioner may refuse to grant the patent unless it is amended to overcome that anticipatory material. The question arises whether it is possible to raise arguments in respect of the relevance of the cited documents.

Section 22 is infrequently used and there is very little commentary on its application. The section is concerned with documents having the same subject matter as those which may have been cited by the examiner under s 13 of the Act. Section 13 is worded in similar form to s 22 in that s 13(3) seems only to allow for either a challenge to the priority date of the cited document or amendment of the specification. However, in practice, submissions in rebuttal as to the relevance of documents cited under s 13 are routinely filed in response to an examination report. By analogy, the same submissions can be filed under s 22.

Generally the Commissioner will set a deadline for responding to a s 22 objection. Regulation 59 governs the granting of extensions. The total extension period allowed is 6 months and extension applications can be applied for retrospectively. However, the Commissioner also has a general discretion under reg 168 to grant extensions (which arguably could be utilised to obtain extensions beyond the 6 months stipulated in reg 59). As with all extension applications it will be necessary to demonstrate that the applicant has acted diligently in meeting the deadline and that it is in the interests of justice to grant the extension.

In distinction from documents cited under s 13, under s 22 the Commissioner is required to pay regard to priority dates. Thus, he must assess for himself the priority dates of the applicant's claims and only cite a document published on or after the relevant priority date of a claim if he is of the opinion that the claim is not entitled to such priority date (for example, because there is no fair basis). It would be reasonable for a patent applicant to request proof of publication before responding to a s 22 objection.

It is possible for a s 22 opposition to be raised in tandem with a s 21 opposition. The commentary to the equivalent sections of the United Kingdom Act in the *British Patent Office Manual of Office Practice* (Patents) states that if s 21 opposition proceedings have also been instituted, no action in respect of the s 22 opposition is taken, but the matter is brought to the notice of the hearing officer presiding over the s 21 opposition so that, if necessary, the parties can be informed that it appears pertinent to the issues raised in the s 21 opposition. The hearing officer is bound, in the public interest, to consider any alleged prior publication which may be brought to his notice (*Hughes and Kennaugh's Application* (1910) 27 RPC 281) even after the hearing and before the issue of his decision (*Osterstrom and Wagner's Application* (1932) 49 RPC 565). Therefore, a prior publication raised under s 22 can be brought into the s 21 opposition proceedings at any time before grant and the opponent will be given an opportunity to encompass such publication in its Notice and Statement by amendment.

A party bringing material to the Commissioner's attention cannot file submissions in support of those documents.

Under cl 86 of the draft Patents Bill 2004, third parties may notify the Commissioner, at any time after publication of the application but prior to its acceptance, that the invention lacks novelty or does not involve an inventive step. The third party notification must contain reasons for the assertion and supporting documentation must be open to public inspection. Under cl 87 of the draft Bill, the Commissioner must take the third party notification into account in the process of examining the patent application.

2.9.10 Unsuccessful opposition may give rise to cause of action estoppel

Based on recent United Kingdom authority, in certain circumstances an unsuccessful opposition may give rise to an estoppel in subsequent invalidity proceedings launched by the same party and covering the same issues. This is discussed in more detail at 2.15 ("Defences to infringement") later in this chapter.

2.10 Duration, renewal, and restoration

2.10.1 Duration

(1) *Standard patents*

The term and date of a patent is governed by s 30 Patents Act 1953. Compare cl 19(1) of the draft Patents Bill 2004.

The term of a patent is 20 years from:

• The date of filing a convention application in New Zealand;

• The date of filing a PCT application designating New Zealand;

• The date of filing of a complete specification for a non-convention New Zealand application; or

• Some other date as directed by the Commissioner (for example, the date of late addition of new material to the specification).

(2) *Patents of addition*

Under s 34(5) Patents Act 1953, the term of a patent of addition is the unexpired term of the parent patent. Compare cl 101 of the draft Patents Bill 2004. If the parent patent is revoked, the Court or Commissioner may order that the patent of addition become an independent patent for the remainder of the term of the parent patent. Patents of addition are discussed at 2.3 ("Types of patents") earlier in this chapter.

(3) *Divisional patents*

The term of a divisional patent is 20 years from the date of filing the complete specification of the parent patent. This filing date is antedated to the date of the parent application upon request to the Commissioner. Divisional patents are discussed at 2.3 ("Types of patents") earlier in this chapter.

(4) *Extensions of term*

The Patents Amendment Act 1994 repealed ss 31-33 Patents Act 1953 which provided for extensions of the term of a patent. Therefore it is not possible to extend the 20-year period for protection of patented inventions.

In June 2003 the Ministry of Economic Development released a discussion paper entitled "The Pharmaceutical Patent Term in New Zealand", which considered whether extensions of term should be reintroduced for pharmaceutical patents. The paper is discussed in more detail at 2.22 ("Future developments") later in this chapter.

2.10.2 Renewal

Renewal fees for patents are due in the 4th, 7th, 10th, and 13th years of the patent's duration. The renewal dates are generally calculated from the filing date of the complete specification.

(1) *Failure to pay renewal fees in time*

Failure to pay renewal fees within the prescribed period results in a patent ceasing to have effect: s 30(4) Patents Act 1953. Compare cl 19(2) of the draft Patents Bill 2004.

However, the registered proprietor can make an application for an extension of up to 6 months for late payment of the renewal fees. Compare cl 20(2) of the draft Bill.

(2) *Renewal fees on pending applications*

Maintenance fees are not payable on pending applications.

Ordinarily the first renewal fee will fall due 4 years after the filing of the complete specification.

Under s 30(4) Patents Act 1953, where a patent application takes longer than 4 years to proceed to grant, the period for payment is extended to 4 months after the date of sealing if the renewal fees:

- Would normally fall due before the patent is sealed; or

- Fall due within 4 months of the date of sealing of the patent.

Compare cl 20(1) of the draft Patents Bill 2004.

(3) *Renewal fees for patents of addition*

No renewal fees are payable for patents of addition unless the patent becomes an independent patent by virtue of s 34(6). In this case, the same fees must be paid on the same dates as if the patent had originally been granted as an independent patent. Compare cl 102 of the draft Bill. Patents of addition are discussed at 2.3 ("Types of patents") earlier in this chapter.

2.10.3 Restoration

A patentee can apply to the Commissioner to restore a patent and/or patent application in three situations. They are:

- Where a patent has lapsed through failure to pay a renewal fee: s 35 Patents Act 1953. Compare cl 108 of the draft Patents Bill 2004;

- Where a patent has not been sealed by reason only that there was a failure to request sealing: s 36 Patents Act 1953; and

- Where a patent application becomes void due to the applicant's failure to comply with all of the requirements to place the application in order for acceptance within the prescribed time: s 37 Patents Act 1953. Compare cls 66, 68 and 115 of the draft Bill.

The Commissioner may exercise his or her power to restore the patent and/or patent application, provided he or she is satisfied of the following:

- That the failure to pay the renewal fee or request sealing, or the lapsing of the patent application, was unintentional; and

- There was no undue delay in making the application for restoration.

The burden is on the applicant to prove that the failure did not arise intentionally and that there was no undue delay. Such evidence is given by way of statutory declaration, which must accompany the application for restoration. Compare cl 109 of the draft Bill.

Under cl 94 of the draft Patents Bill 2004, the Commissioner must grant a patent as soon as is reasonably practicable after three months from the date of publication of the accepted complete specification, provided the Commissioner has decided not to re-examine the patent, no request for re-examination has been made or the Commissioner has decided to grant the patent after re-examination. The requirement that a patent must be sealed prior to grant has been removed from the draft Bill. Accordingly, there is no provision in the draft Bill for a patentee to restore a patent by reason of a failure to request sealing before grant.

However, under cls 66 and 68 of the draft Bill, an applicant must file a notice of entitlement within 18 months of the first report of the Examiner (or any extension of that period granted under cl 67 of the draft Bill). A patent application will become void if the applicant fails to do so. This procedure appears to replace the requirement to obtain the seal of the Patent Office prior to the grant of a patent.

(1)   *Delay*

The Patents Act 1953 does not specify a time frame in which an application for restoration must be made. Under cls 111 and 116 of the draft Bill, applications for restoration must be made within 12 months of the patent lapsing or the patent application being deemed abandoned or void, although the Commissioner may extend this period provided there was no undue delay in making the application.

Under the current Act, the Commissioner must decide whether there has been undue delay on the facts of each case. The Commissioner will generally assess the period of delay from the date the failure to pay the renewal fee or request sealing, or the lapsing of the patent application, was discovered or ought to have been.

This was highlighted in *W C J Halford's Application* (Commissioner's Decision No P08/1973, 31/7/73, Asst Commr Burton), where it was stated, at pp 2-3, that:

> "The question of undue delay must be assessed from the time when the patentee discovered or might with ordinary and reasonable care have discovered the omission".

In that case, a two year delay between discovery of the lapsed patent application and the application for restoration was held to be excessive.

(2)   *Mistaken belief*

Authorities such as *Atlas Powder Co's Patent* [1995] RPC 357 indicate that, where a patentee consciously elects not to renew a patent (as in that case), the patentee cannot then apply for the patent to be restored, even if that decision had been a mistake. Thus, in the case of a failure to pay the renewal fee, the patent will only be restored if the patentee can show it intended to take steps to pay the fee.

(3) *Reasonable care*

There is an additional requirement that the applicant for restoration show, in the case of a failure to pay the renewal fee, that ordinary and reasonable care was taken in ensuring that patent renewal fees are paid in a timely manner.

In *Ament's Application* [1994] RPC 647, the Court held that a patentee who merely establishes an inability to pay does not establish that he has taken reasonable care to see that the fee was paid.

Two Commissioner's decisions have applied the ordinary and reasonable care requirement in New Zealand.

- In *J W Holmes Application* (Commissioner's Decision No P06/1973, 29/5/73, Asst Commr Burton), the patentee failed to pay two renewal fees despite being sent reminders. The Commissioner observed, at p 4, that:

  > "[the patentee] regarded the patent … as a business asset and yet he does not seem to have taken precautions to ensure the patent was maintained."

  The Commissioner held that the patentee had not exercised reasonable care in maintaining his patent. The Commissioner also held that there had been undue delay in applying to restore the patent, and the application for restoration was decline; and

- In *W C J Halford's Application* a 2-year delay between discovery of the lapsed patent application and application for restoration was held to be excessive, at pp 2-3:

  > "the discovery of the state of the New Zealand patent was by chance and was not the result of a systematic periodic review of the situation by the patentee … consequently the patentee did not exercise ordinary and reasonable care in the maintenance of his New Zealand patent."

2.11   Assignment

Ownership of patent rights can be assigned.

Section 84(4) Patents Act 1953 states that the person (or persons) registered as patentee shall have power to assign, grant licences under, or otherwise deal with the patent, and to give effectual receipts for any consideration for any such assignment, licence, or dealing. Under cl 22 of the draft Bill, the patentee may deal with the patent as the absolute owner thereof subject to any rights vested in other persons entered on the Register.

For further discussion see 2.6 ("Ownership") earlier in this chapter.

2.11.1   Patent applications may be assigned

Section 24 Patents Act 1953 enables the Commissioner (on receipt of a deed of assignment) to direct that a patent application proceed in the assignee's name. The Commissioner will not make such a direction unless one of the following occurs:

- The invention is identified in the assignment document by reference to the patent application number;

- There is an acknowledgment by the assignor that the assignment relates to the invention the subject of the patent application; or

- The Commissioner is otherwise satisfied that the assignee is entitled to the interest of the applicant by virtue of the assignment.

There does not appear to be any equivalent section to cl 24 in the draft Patents Bill 2004. As the sections of the draft Bill which address the right to deal with and/or assign interest in a patent (cls 22 and 154) do not mention "patent applications" it is questionable whether the practice of assigning applications will be permissible under the new Bill.

2.11.2   Form of assignment

The Patents Act 1953 does not specify a particular form that a patent assignment document must take, except that it should be in writing. The assignment of a patent will usually take the form of a deed.

2.11.3   Registration of assignments

An assignment or any other interest must be recorded on the Patent Register: s 84(1) Patents Act 1953. Compare cl 154(1) of the draft Patents Bill 2004.

Despite the existence of s 84(1) there are no sanctions in the Act for failing to record an assignment or other interest. However, if the assignee decides to issue Court proceedings, he or she may be required to provide notice of his or her interest before those proceedings are issued, and may also be required to subsequently record that interest. This is discussed further at 2.14.1 ("Who can initiate infringement proceedings?") later in this chapter.

2.12   Licences

A patentee has the ability to license their patent. This is provided for by the Deed of Letters Patent, the wording of which is discussed in more detail at 2.5 ("Rights granted by registration") earlier in this chapter.

2.12.1   Form of licence

The Patents Act 1953 does not specify a particular form that a patent licence must take. Further, unlike assignments, there is no requirement for the licence to be in writing or to be signed by the patentee. As such oral licences are recognised (even though they cannot be officially entered upon the Register).

The Courts are willing to imply patent licences in situations where a patentee's actions are such that a third party should be entitled to such a licence. For example, if a patentee contracts with a third party to supply a patented product, the Court is likely to imply a licence under the patent to the third party to make the product.

Implied licences are discussed in more detail at 2.15 ("Defences to infringement") later in this chapter.

2.12.2 Co-ownership and licences

Where there is more than one owner of a patent, it is necessary to have the consent of all co-owners of a patent to grant a licence under it. This is subject to any agreement to the contrary. Compare cl 23(3) of the draft Patents Bill 2004.

If the parties are unable to reach an agreement regarding licensing of a patent, s 64(1) Patents Act 1953 enables the Commissioner to settle the dispute. This is discussed in more detail at 2.6 ("Ownership") earlier in this chapter. Compare cl 25 of the draft Bill.

2.12.3 Registration of licences

Section 84(1) Patents Act 1953, requiring registration of assignments, also extends to licences and other interests. Therefore, it is a requirement of the Act that licences are registered. Compare cl 154(1) of the draft Patents Bill 2004.

However, as there are no sanctions for failing to record a licence, very few are recorded on the Patent Register in practice.

2.12.4 Compulsory licences

Compulsory licences are provided for in s 46 Patents Act 1953. Compare cl 159 of the draft Patents Bill 2004.

For a Court to grant a compulsory licence, the party applying for the licence must meet a number of conditions. They must:

- Be a "person interested";

- Apply to the High Court (not the Commissioner);

- Make the application no less than:

  - 3 years after the grant of the patent; or

  - 4 years after the date of the patent (ie, the date of filing a complete specification); and

- Establish that the market in New Zealand for the patented invention is not being supplied, or is not being supplied on reasonable terms.

In practice, compulsory licences are rare.

(1) *"Reasonableness" of supply*

In order to establish a case under s 46 Patents Act 1953, an applicant will need to show that either:

- The patented invention is not being supplied in New Zealand; or

- The patented invention is not being supplied on reasonable terms.

The "reasonableness" of supply is a matter of degree to be decided upon the facts of each case. However, *Kamborian's Patent* (1961) 78 RPC 403 gives some guidance as to the general factors that must be considered when determining whether there has been a "reasonable" supply of the patented invention to the market by the registered proprietor. They are:

- Whether there is a demand for the patented invention;

- If so, what that demand might reasonably be expected to be; and

- The quantum of shortfall in the supply of that expected demand.

In light of such factors, the High Court must be satisfied that the shortfall between supply and demand is sufficient to grant a compulsory licence.

(2)   *Termination of compulsory licence*

A compulsory licence can be terminated by the Court if it is satisfied that the grounds on which the licence was granted no longer exist: s 46(5) Patents Act 1953. Compare cl 160(3) of the draft Patents Bill 2004. Therefore, if the patentee starts to supply the New Zealand market on reasonable terms after the grant of a compulsory licence, the patentee can apply to the High Court to revoke the compulsory licence.

2.12.5   Licences of right

A patentee can apply to the Commissioner at any time after sealing for a patent to be endorsed with the words "license of right": s 44 Patents Act 1953.

If the Commissioner is satisfied that there are no contracts preventing the grant of a license of right, then he or she will endorse the patent accordingly. The Commissioner will then advertise the endorsement in the Journal (discussed at 2.20 ("Intellectual Property Office of New Zealand") later in this chapter).

There does not appear to be a corresponding provision in the draft Patents Bill 2004.

(1)   *Effect of licence of right*

When a patent is endorsed as a "licence of right" any person can, at any time, apply as of right to the patentee for a licence under the patent.

That licence will be on terms negotiated between the patentee and the potential licensee. If an agreement cannot be reached, the parties may apply to the Commissioner for resolution of the dispute: s 44(2)(a) Patents Act 1953.

The renewal fees payable by the patentee of a patent endorsed as a "licence of right" are half the renewal fees for a non-endorsed patent: s 44(2)(d).

A patent endorsed as a "licence of right" is less likely to be infringed, as potential infringers can readily obtain a licence.

(2)   *Current licence holders*

The holder of any licence granted under the patent before the patent was endorsed as "licence of right" may apply to the Commissioner to order that the current licence be exchanged for a licence granted under the endorsement, which may be on more favourable terms than the licensee's current licence.

(3)   *Proceedings for infringement*

Under s 44(3) Patents Act 1953, a licensee of a patent endorsed as a "licence of right" can issue proceedings for patent infringement in his or her own name if the patentee refuses to instigate, or does not instigate, proceedings within 2 months of being asked to do so by the licensee.

Where proceedings are issued in the licensee's own name, the patentee can be joined as a defendant. However, the patentee will not be liable for any costs unless he or she enters an appearance.

In proceedings for infringement of a patent endorsed "licences of right" the defendant may elect to take a licence on terms to be settled by the Commissioner. If a defendant does so, no injunction can be granted, and the potential damages can not exceed double the amount that would have been payable if the defendant was a licensee: s 44(2)(c).

(4)   *Cancellation of "licences of right" endorsement*

Section 45 Patents Act 1953 enables a patentee to apply to the Commissioner for cancellation of the endorsement at any time.

The Commissioner will only revoke the endorsement if there is no existing licence under the patent, or all licensees consent to the cancellation.

The patentee is liable, on cancellation of the endorsement, to pay the balance of renewal fees which would have been payable if the patent had not been endorsed.

2.13   Revocation

Under the Patents Act 1953, a granted patent may be revoked by application to the High Court (s 41) or to the Commissioner (s 42).

For the following reasons, an application for revocation is usually brought under s 41:

- Revocations under s 42 can only be initiated by application to the Commissioner within 12 months of the sealing of the patent. An application under s 41 can be brought at any time during the term of the patent;

- A party who opposed the patent under s 21 cannot bring an application for revocation under s 42. A party who opposed the grant of the patent under s 21 can commence revocation proceedings before the Court under s 41;

- If there are infringement proceedings before the Court in respect of the patent, a s 42 application can only proceed with the leave of the Court; and

- The grounds of revocation under s 42 are limited to the grounds of opposition (under s 21). More extensive grounds for revocation are available under a s 41 application. These additional grounds are discussed later in this section.

As with opposition proceedings, the person applying for revocation must establish standing (locus standi). Standing is discussed in more detail at 2.9.2 ("Standing") earlier in this chapter.

Under cl 104 of the draft Patents Bill 2004, any person may apply to revoke a patent although the Commissioner may refuse an application if it is vexatious (cl 104(3)). Proceedings may be brought before the Commissioner or the Court (no distinction is made between the two forms of proceedings).

The grounds upon which revocation proceedings may be brought before either forum are listed under cl 105 of the draft Bill. Generally they relate either to the patentability of the invention or the non-compliance of the specification with the statutory requirements.

In addition, (under cls 89-93) any person may request the Commissioner to re-examine a patent after acceptance and grant on the limited grounds that the invention lacks novelty or an inventive step. Unfavourable findings may result in revocation of the patent.

Revocation proceedings under cl 104 of the draft Bill appear to be the first opportunity for third parties to object to the grant of a patent for reasons other than that it lacks novelty or an inventive step.

2.13.1 Revocation by the Commissioner

A person interested can, within one year of the sealing of that patent, make an application to the Commissioner under s 42 Patents Act 1953 for the revocation of a patent.

This revocation action is often referred to as a "belated opposition" as the procedure and grounds for revocation before the Commissioner are the same as for s 21 oppositions (discussed in detail at 2.9 ("Opposition to the grant of a patent application") earlier in this chapter).

In *Ancare NZ Ltd v Ciba-Geigy NZ Ltd* 6/6/96, Elias J, HC Wellington AP55/95, an application for revocation was filed exactly 12 months after the patent was sealed but without an accompanying Statement of Case. The question arose as to whether the time limits in s 42 and reg 104 allowed for the Statement of Case to be filed at a later date. It was held that, as the regulation set the time limit for filing a Statement of Case, not s 42, the Commissioner was able to extend the time for filing the Statement of Case under the regulations. By the same reasoning, an extension to file the application for revocation would not be granted.

No action can be taken under s 42 without leave of the Court if there are infringement or revocation proceedings before the Court in respect of the same patent.

Where a s 42 revocation action is filed prior to infringement proceedings, those infringement proceedings are unlikely to be stayed pending the outcome of the s 42 action. Hence, in *Flexiteek International v Tek-Dek NZ Ltd* 12/2/04, Laurenson J, HC Auckland CIV-2003-404-4123, the Court declined an application for stay. See also *Ferro Corp v Escol Products Ltd* [1990] RPC 651, where it was held that an application for stay will only be granted in exceptional circumstances, and the onus is on the party seeking to stay the proceedings.

A s 42 opposition is not available to anyone who has already opposed the same patent under s 21.

2.13.2 Revocation by the Court

Revocation of a patent by the Court is possible at any time during the term of a patent and may be sought by anyone who might be prejudiced by the existence of the patent.

Most commonly an application for revocation by the Court is brought as a defence and counterclaim to a patent infringement suit: *Vigilant Automatic Fire Alarm Co Ltd v Automatic Alarms Ltd* [1963] NZLR 585 (CA).

2.13.3   Grounds for revocation

The grounds for revocation are set out in s 41(1)(a)-(m).

While there is significant overlap between the grounds of opposition and revocation, the grounds of revocation are generally wider. They include:

- Prior grant;

- Obtaining;

- Not an invention;

- Lack of novelty;

- Obviousness;

- Inutility;

- Insufficiency;

- Ambiguity;

- False suggestion/representation;

- Secret use; and

- Contrary to law.

Under cl 105 of the draft Patents Bill 2004, any person may bring proceedings before the Commissioner or Court for revocation of a patent on the following grounds:

- The invention as far as claimed is not patentable:

    - The invention is not a manner of manufacture within the meaning of s 6 of the Statute of Monopolies;

    - The invention is not novel;

    - The invention does not involve an inventive step; or

    - The invention is not useful;

- The invention is excluded from patentability by reason that:

    - Commercial exploitation of the invention is contrary to public policy or morality;

    - The invention is a human being or a biological process for the generation of human beings;

    - The invention is a diagnostic, therapeutic or surgical method for the treatment of human beings; or

    - The invention is a plant variety;

- The patentee is not entitled to the patent;

- The complete specification does not comply with s 35(1) which requires descriptions of the invention, method of performance and claims;

- The scope of a claim is not sufficiently and clearly defined or fairly based on the matter disclosed in the complete specification;

- The patent was obtained by fraud, false suggestion or a misrepresentation;

- The invention was secretly used before the priority date of the claim (other than for the purpose of reasonable trial or experiment by the patentee, the government or any other person to whom the patentee disclosed the invention who used the invention without the consent of the patentee); or

- The patent has been granted contrary to law.

(1)   *Prior grant*

The ground of prior grant can be raised under s 41(1)(a) Patents Act 1953 if the invention was previously claimed in a valid claim in a patent with an earlier priority date in New Zealand.

This ground is similar to s 21(1)(c) (prior claiming) with the exception that the claim alleged to have an earlier priority date must be a "valid" claim. This limitation does not apply in s 21 opposition proceedings.

Prior claiming is discussed in more detail at 2.9 ("Opposition to the grant of a patent application") earlier in this chapter.

(2)   *Obtaining*

Obtaining under s 41 Patents Act 1953 can be alleged in two circumstances:

- Where the patent was granted to a person not entitled to apply for the invention: s 41(1)(b) (compare cl 105(1) of the draft Bill), or

- Where the patent was obtained in contravention of the rights of another person: s 41(1)(c) (compare cl 105(1)(e) of the draft Bill).

Unlike s 21 the party alleging this ground does not have to be the person from whom the invention was obtained or his or her personal representative. However, like obtaining under s 21, a high burden of proof is required to prove obtaining (ie not simply on the balance of probabilities).

Again, mere knowledge does not constitute obtaining. Obtaining must involve misuse of such knowledge: *Wade's Application* (Commissioner's Decision No P01/1981, 9/1/81, Asst Commr Burton).

Obtaining is discussed further at 2.9 ("Opposition to the grant of a patent application") earlier in this chapter.

(3)   *Not an invention*

Under s 41(1)(d) Patents Act 1953, a patent can be revoked on the basis that it is not an invention within the meaning of the Act.

This ground is identical to the equivalent provision in opposition proceedings: s 21(1)(f). For example, inventions claiming methods of medical treatment, or mere collocations of known integers, both fall outside the scope of the s 2 definition of invention and therefore cannot be patented.

This ground is discussed further at 2.9 ("Opposition to the grant of a patent application") earlier in this chapter.

(4)   *Lack of novelty*

For an applicant for revocation to establish lack of novelty under s 41(1)(e) Patents Act 1953, it must be shown that the invention is not new having regard to either:

- What was known before the priority date of the patent in New Zealand; or

- What was used before the priority date of the patent in New Zealand.

This ground is essentially a combination of the opposition grounds of prior publishing and prior use in ss 21(1)(b) and (d) respectively.

However, the ground under s 41(1)(e) is broader as it includes the term "known" rather than simply published. Therefore oral disclosure may be sufficient to anticipate an invention.

Prior publishing and prior use are discussed further at 2.9 ("Opposition to the grant of a patent application") earlier in this chapter.

(5)   *Obviousness*

Under s 41(1)(f) Patents Act 1953, a patent may be revoked if the claimed invention is obvious, and does not involve any inventive step, having regard to:

- What was known before the priority date of the invention in New Zealand; or

- What was used before the priority date of the invention in New Zealand.

Obviousness is easier to establish in revocation proceedings than in opposition proceedings (s 21(1)(e)) for the following reasons:

- The invention does not have to be "clearly" obvious and lacking an inventive step. The higher onus on the opponent to establish obviousness in opposition proceedings was noted by Barker J in *Beecham Group Ltd v Bristol-Myers Co (No 2)* [1980] 1 NZLR 192.

- The ground under revocation incorporates the term "known". Therefore obviousness under s 41 is not limited to published documents — oral disclosures are relevant.

Like the s 21 ground, s 41 obviousness is judged from the view of the "normally skilled but unimaginative addressee": *Windsurfing International Inc v Tabur Marine (GB) Ltd* (1985) 102 RPC 59 (CA).

Obviousness is discussed further at 2.9 ("Opposition to the grant of a patent application") earlier in this chapter.

(6)   *Inutility*

A patent may be revoked under s 41(1)(g) Patents Act 1953 on the basis that the invention is not useful.

The general test for what amounts to a useful invention is found in *Fawcett v Homan* (1896) 13 RPC 398 (CA), at p 405:

> "If an invention does what it is intended by the patentee to do and the end attained is itself useful, the invention is a useful invention."

In *Coopers Animal Health Australia v Western Stock Distributors Ltd* (1986) 6 IPR 545, the Australian Federal Court held that it is the utility of the invention claimed, not the invention described in the body of the specification, that must be examined.

This ground is rarely successful as the invention need only fulfil one of the objectives of the invention (such as provide the public with a useful choice) to avoid a finding of inutility.

(7)   *Insufficiency*

Section 41(1)(h) Patents Act 1953 provides that a patent can be revoked if the complete specification does not:

* Sufficiently and fairly describe the invention and the method by which it is to be performed (compare cl 105(1)(d) of the draft Patents Bill 2004), or

* Disclose the best method of performing the invention known to the applicant (compare cl 105(1)(c) of the draft Bill).

This section, while similar to the ground of opposition in s 21(1)(g), introduces the additional requirement that the patent specification does not disclose the best method of performing the invention known to the applicant at the time of filing. This is in accordance with the requirements set out in s 10(3)(b).

The requirement for the patentee to disclose the best method is also discussed in *E I Du Pont De Nemours & Co v Enka BV* [1988] FSR 69. In that case, the Court established a three-part test for invalidating a patent on this ground:

* There must be a better method of performing the invention than the one disclosed in the patent;

* This method must have been known to the patentee prior to the priority date of the patent; and

* The patentee must have been entitled to claim that better method.

(8)   *Ambiguity*

A challenge to the validity of a patent on the grounds of ambiguity (under s 41(1)(i) Patents Act 1953) can contain two quite distinct arguments:

* That the definition of the invention is not sufficiently and clearly defined; and/or

* That the claims are not fairly based on the disclosures in the complete specification.

This ground is not available in s 21 opposition proceedings.

In relation to the first limb, the case of *Daily v Lightband* (1903) 6 GLR 135, at p 136, has held that, when considering an allegation of ambiguity, the specification needs to be:

> "Assessed by a person of ordinary intelligence, conversant with the subject matter, who will understand it and be able to act upon it."

In relation to the second limb, to determine whether a claim is fairly based on the disclosures in the specification, Lloyd Jacob J's threefold test in *Mond Nickel Co Ltd's Application* (1956)

73 RPC 189, at p 194, is applicable. For further details see 2.7 ("Obtaining grant of rights") earlier in this chapter.

(9)   *False suggestion/representation*

If a patent was obtained on a false suggestion or representation then it may be revoked under s 41(1)(j) (compare cl 105(1)(e) of the draft Patents Bill 2004).

In *Valensi v British Radio Corp* [1973] RPC 337, at p 381, the UK Court of Appeal held that to succeed the applicant for revocation must show that the misrepresentation was of such significance that the governing body (in that case the Crown) was misled into granting the patent.

This ground is not available under s 21 opposition proceedings.

(10)   *Secret use*

If an invention is secretly used in New Zealand before the priority date of the patent, the patent may be revoked under s 41(1)(l) Patents Act 1953. The prohibition on secret use is to prevent someone from extending the period of their monopoly in the invention by using it in secret for a period of time and then subsequently securing a further 20 year monopoly through the patent registration process. Under s 41(2) the following uses will not amount to secret use:

* Reasonable trial or experiment;

* Use by a Government Department; or

* Use by a person without the consent of the patentee.

Compare cl 105(1)(f) and (3) of the draft Patents Bill 2004.

In s 21 opposition proceedings no consideration is given to secret use when considering prior use and obviousness in light of prior use. Compare cl 105(2) of the draft Bill.

(11)   *Contrary to law*

It is possible to revoke a patent under s 41(1)(m) Patents Act 1953 if it has been granted contrary to law. Compare cl 105(1)(g) of the draft Patents Bill 2004.

This ground allows an interested party to apply for the revocation of a patent on any ground on which the patent could have been refused that does not fall within ss 41(1)(a)-(l). For example, on the ground that the application was not filed within 12 months of the first foreign application.

This section was considered (and limited) in *Dow Chemical Co v Ishihara Sangyo Kaisha Ltd* 19/12/85, Eichelbaum J, HC Wellington M653/83. In that case, the Court held that, as the legislature strictly codified the grounds of revocation, this thirteenth "open" ground could not have been intended to open the challenge of a patent to the entire pre-existing common law.

2.13.4 Procedure

Under the Patents Act 1953, the procedure, time limits and the method of giving evidence in s 42 revocation proceedings are the same as for patent opposition proceedings (discussed at 2.9 ("Opposition to the grant of a patent application") earlier in this chapter).

In s 41 revocation proceedings the procedure is governed by the High Court Rules.

Under the draft Patents Bill 2004, revocation proceedings before the Commissioner or Court are both governed by cls 104-106.

A person applying to the Commissioner to revoke a patent under cl 104 of the draft Bill is entitled to a hearing before the Commissioner, as is the patentee. Evidence must be submitted in the form of written affidavits, although the Commissioner has discretion to hear oral evidence and permit cross-examination of witnesses, and the rules of procedure before the Commissioner appear to be subject to the Commissioner's discretion. (see cls 262-274 of the draft Bill). In contrast, revocation proceedings before the Court under cl 104 would be subject to the strict rules of evidence applied by the High Court.

2.14 Infringement and enforcement of rights

Legal action can only be taken against a patent infringer once the Deed of Letters Patent has issued.

Legal proceedings for patent infringement must be commenced in the High Court.

Compare cl 136(1) of the draft Patents Bill 2004. Under that section, after the patent is granted the patentee may sue for infringement between the date the specification became open for public inspection and the date it was accepted. However, it is a defence under cl 78 of the draft Bill to show that the claims as worded when the allegedly infringing act was done could not have been granted. This may cover the situation where the claims are amended after publication but before acceptance.

Also, cl 77(2)(b) prevents proceedings being commenced unless the act would, if done after the grant of the patent, have constituted an infringement of a claim of the granted patent. It is not clear whether "claim" means the claim as it stood at the date when the act was done (ie, before grant), or the claim as it stood after the patent was actually granted. Clause 78(1) suggests that cl 77(2)(b) means the claims as they stood at the date when the act was done, notwithstanding that such claims may not have actually been granted. Clause 136(2) of the draft Bill does not clarify this issue.

Thus, acts that occur after publication but before grant, and which do not infringe the claims as granted, might still be the subject of a successful action if it can be shown that the claims as they stood prior to grant, and at the date of the allegedly infringing act, were valid (indeed the onus is on the alleged infringer to show that the claims as they stood prior to grant were not valid).

Presumably, the intent is to ensure that acts which do not infringe the claims as they stood between publication and grant are not subsequently held to infringe because the claims have been broadened after publication. However, the more likely scenario is that the claims will be narrowed between publication and grant. Arguably the alleged infringer ought not to remain liable for a pre-grant activity which does not fall within the scope of a granted claim, otherwise it would encourage the filing of patents with broad claims as a deterrent, which can subsequently be narrowed to secure acceptance. This might have a chilling effect.

2.14.1 Who can initiate infringement proceedings?

(1) *Registered proprietor*

The registered proprietor of a patent may file proceedings at any time after the patent has been sealed: s 20(4) Patents Act 1953.

Section 20(5) Patents Act 1953 places a limitation on when infringement proceedings can be filed. Proceedings must be initiated by the latter of:

- Six years of the date of the alleged infringement; or

- Three years from the date of sealing of the patent.

There does not appear to be a corresponding clause to s 20(5) in the draft Patents Bill 2004.

(2) *Exclusive licensee*

Section 72 Patents Act 1953 enables an exclusive licensee to take infringement proceedings in respect of any infringement. This right is subject to the provisions of s 85 of the Act, which relate to the recording of an interest in the patent (discussed later in this section).

Under cl 135 of the draft Patents Bill 2004, an exclusive licence is still permitted to bring proceedings but only in respect of infringements that occur after the date of the licence.

If an exclusive licensee takes infringement proceedings in its own name, it must join the patentee as either plaintiff or defendant. However, the patentee will not be liable for any costs unless he or she enters an appearance: s 72(2). Compare cl 137 of the draft Patents Bill 2004.

(3) *Unregistered interests*

Under s 85 Patents Act 1953, where a proprietor/exclusive licensee has an unregistered interest in the patent they must (unless leave of the Court is obtained):

- Give one month's written notice to any potential defendant that he or she intends to commence proceedings, and provide an address for service within New Zealand; or

- Register the interest at least one month before the commencement of proceedings.

In practice a Court is unlikely to refuse leave to commence proceedings on this technicality, as no particular form of expression or notice is required: *Link Technology International Ltd v Port* (1999) 6 NZBLC 102,691.

There does not appear to be an equivalent clause to s 85 in the draft Patents Bill 2004.

2.14.2 No definition of infringement

The Patents Act 1953 does not define "infringement" or acts amounting to "infringement". However, it is generally accepted that a patent will be infringed by any act done in contravention of the exclusive rights conferred by the Deed of Letters Patent. These rights are discussed at 2.5 ("Rights granted by registration") earlier in this chapter.

Generally, infringement will arise through the working of a patented invention (for example, by its manufacture, sale, use or importation) in New Zealand by any person other than the proprietor, without the proprietor's permission.

Infringement can include the sale of a product produced by the defendant using a patented process: s 68A. For such actions to amount to infringement the process must relate to a new product, and the defendant's product must be the same as that of the patentee's. Compare cl 131 of the draft Patents Bill 2004.

"Infringement" is defined in cl 129 of the draft Patents Bill 2004. Under this section, a patent is infringed by a person who does anything that the patentee has the exclusive right to do under the draft Bill. Clause 17 of the draft Bill gives the patentee the exclusive right to exploit the patent or authorise others to do so.

A person also infringes a patent under the draft Bill by supplying another person with the means to put the invention into effect in a manner that would infringe the patent, with knowledge (subjectively or objectively determined) that the person intended to do an act that would infringe the patent (ie, contributory infringement).

2.14.3 Assessing infringement

The approach of the New Zealand Courts in developing patent law has been to adopt the UK position with little qualification. This, in *Smith Kline & French Laboratories Ltd v A-G* [1991] 2 NZLR 560; (1991) 4 TCLR 199 (CA), Cooke P observed, at p 562; p 202:

> "it is as well to add that in relation to patent law one should be wary, in my opinion, of indigenous common law developments unless they are clearly required: see [*Wellcome Foundation Ltd v Commissioner of Patents* [1983] NZLR 385 (CA)]. The New Zealand Courts are operating in an international environment where consistency of approach is important."

As Julian Miles QC notes in his paper "The Pragmatic Approach to Claim Construction in New Zealand", this sentiment has long tempered the approach of the New Zealand Court to claim construction and indeed development of patent law generally.

Thus, traditionally, infringement has been assessed by determining whether the "pith and marrow" of the patent has been taken in accordance with *C Van Der Lely NV v Bamfords Ltd* (1963) 80 RPC 61 (HL), at p 75, per Lord Reid:

> "Copying an invention by picking its 'pith and marrow' without textual [literal] infringement of the patent is an old and familiar abuse which the law has never been powerless to prevent."

The "pith and marrow" doctrine refers to reproduction of the essential novel features of the patented invention.

2.14.4 Claim interpretation

While infringement is generally determined upon the doctrine of "pith and marrow", the New Zealand Courts interpret patent claims in accordance with the "purposive construction" doctrine expounded by Lord Diplock in *Catnic Components Ltd v Hill & Smith Ltd* (1982) 99 RPC 183 (HL).

The "purposive construction" doctrine requires the Court to look at what the patentee intended (ie the purpose of the patent) rather than adopting a strictly literal interpretation of the claims. It was described by Lord Diplock in *Catnic Components*, at p 243, as follows:

> "The question in each case is: whether persons with practical knowledge and experience of the kind of work in which the invention was intended to be used, would understand that strict compliance with a particular descriptive word or phrase appearing in a claim was intended by the patentee to be an essential requirement of the invention so that *any* variant would fall outside the monopoly claimed, even though it could have no material effect upon the way the invention worked."

Thus, under the purposive construction test the scope of a patent is determined by reference to the ordinary meaning capable of being given to the words of each claim by a person skilled in the art. Where there is doubt as to what is meant, or as to the scope of any word or phrase in a claim, reference can be made to the text of the patent specification.

Catnic has been followed in numerous New Zealand cases including *Monsanto Co v Stauffer Chemical Co (No 1)* (1984) 1 NZIPR 518 and *Inglis v Mayson* (1983) 3 IPR 588.

The House of Lords case, *Glaverbel SA v British Coal Corp* (1995) 112 RPC 255, further summarises the principles of purposive construction as follows:

- Interpretation of a patent is a question of law, and therefore the question of construction itself is not a matter for evidence;

- The construction of a patent is an objective test to be assessed by a skilled addressee;

- The Court should have regard to the surrounding circumstances at the date of publication (or perhaps the priority date) but only in so far as those facts would be available to "every skilled addressee";

- The patent specification must be read together with the claims;

- Any claim must be construed in the context of the patent as a whole, but a claim "expressed in clear language … cannot be extended or cut down by reference to the rest of the specification". The purposes of the author of the specification can be used to determine the meaning of the document; and

- The Court must adopt "a purposive construction rather than a purely literal one derived from applying … meticulous verbal analysis", per Lord Diplock in *Catnic*.

Glaverbel has been cited with approval in New Zealand: *Novartis NZ Ltd v Ancare NZ Ltd* 19/6/98, Morris J, HC Auckland CP480/97 and *Peterson Portable Sawing Systems Ltd (in liq) v Lucas* [2006] 3 NZLR 721 (SC).

In the High Court (*Lucas v Peterson Portable Sawing Systems Ltd* [2003] 3 NZLR 361; (2003) 57 IPR 305), Fisher J listed, at para 28, the relevant principles of claim interpretation as follows:

> "(a)   The interpretation of a patent specification is a question of law for the Court to determine but expert evidence can be received as to the meaning of technical terms and concepts found within it.

"(b)   The specification is to be construed objectively through the eyes of a skilled but unimaginative addressee. The test is what an addressee skilled in the particular art in question would understand from the document as a whole.

"(c)   The patent is to be given a purposive construction. Not appropriate is the kind of meticulous verbal analysis to which lawyers can be sometimes attracted.

"(d)   The Court is to have regard to the surrounding circumstances as they existed at the priority date, this including matters of common general knowledge at that time.

"(e)   It is to be assumed that redundancy was not intended. Consequently separate effect should be given to each word and phrase unless no sensible additional meaning can be ascertained from them.

"(f)   The specification is to be interpreted as a whole. Since it is the claims that define the scope of the monopoly, they will normally be the starting point but ambiguity in words or expressions can, in appropriate cases, be resolved by reference to the context of the document as a whole. Importantly, for this purpose the document includes the drawings.

"(g)   The complete specification is broadly divisible into the description or consistory clauses (s 10(1) and (3)(a) of the Patents Act), the best method for performing the invention (s 10(3)(b)), and the claims (s 10(3)(c) and (4)).

"(h)   The description or consistory clauses must identify and describe the essence of the invention in terms which reveal the inventive step or steps. The question is what the skilled addressee would understand as the essential and novel features of the invention.

"(i)   The superlative 'best' when referring to the best method (s 10(3)(b)) implies that more than one embodiment will be possible for any given invention. Passages in the specification introduced by the word 'preferably', or 'in a preferred form', or 'in one embodiment of the invention', or words to similar effect, may tend to indicate what is being described as merely optional and therefore not an essential part of the invention itself.

"(j)   It may be necessary to distinguish between consistory clauses and embodiments for another reason. When referring to the body of the specification for purposes of clarifying ambiguous expressions in a claim, consistory clauses may be exhaustive as to the intended scope of the expression. Embodiments, on the other hand, might help to show the broadness of a claim but presumably never its narrowness.

"(k)   Notwithstanding those technicalities, the overriding requirement will always be to view the specification purposively through the eyes of the technically skilled addressee and not those of a lawyer conducting a line by line analysis of a debenture or will."

Peterson was unsuccessfully appealed to the Court of Appeal (*Peterson Portable Sawing Systems Ltd v Lucas* 4/3/05, CA64/03; CA97/03. However, a subsequent appeal to the Supreme Court of New Zealand (*Peterson Portable Sawing Systems Ltd (in liq) v Lucas* [2006] 3 NZLR 721 (SC)) was successful. Although the Supreme Court took issue with Fisher J's conclusions on anticipation and obviousness, the judgment does not appear to dispute the aforementioned summary of the principles of claim interpretation offered by Fisher J. The Supreme Court did however make the following additional observations, at paras 26-28:

> "A patent specification is to be read as a whole and given a purposive construction. It must be construed as it would be understood by the appropriate addressee — a person skilled in the relevant art.

> "Each part of the specification is to be read objectively in its overall context and in light of the function of that part. The claims are to be interpreted by reference to the object and description in the body of the specification.

> "The claims define the scope of the monopoly conferred by the patent. They limit what others may do. They must clearly define the protected field so others may fairly know where they cannot go. The description in the body of the specification may assist interpretation but it cannot modify the monopoly the inventor has clearly marked out. If his claim is formulated too narrowly so that imitators do not infringe, that cannot be rectified by reference to the description. If it is too wide, consequent invalidity cannot be saved by reading in limitations appearing in the description. The description of a preferred embodiment of the invention is just that and plainly will not confine the scope of an invention claimed more broadly. All of this is well established."

Finally, it is useful to refer to the judgment of the United Kingdom House of Lords in *Kirin-Amgen Inc v Hoechst Marion Roussel Ltd* [2005] RPC 9 (HL) which contains a detailed analysis of the evolution of claim construction in the UK. Amgen was the proprietor of a European patent relating to the production of EPO by recombinant DNA technology. In three consolidated actions, Amgen claimed that Hoechst infringed the patent. Hoechst and another party, TKT, sought a declaration of non-infringement and revocation of the patent. There were two main claims to the patent. The Court of first instance found that one was invalid for insufficiency, but that the other was valid and infringed. On appeal, the UK Court of Appeal found that both claims were valid but that neither was infringed. Both sides appealed, Amgen against the decision that the claims were not infringed, and Hoechst against the rejection of its attack on the validity of the claims. The House of Lords upheld the decision of the Court of Appeal that Amgen's patent was not infringed but reversed the finding that the patent was also valid and in so doing provided the following useful summary as to the English rules of patent construction (which, as aforesaid, will be applicable in New Zealand), at paras 27-34, 41-43, and 50-52:

> "As I indicated a moment ago, it is impossible to understand what the first sentence of the Protocol was intending to prohibit without knowing what used to be the principles applied (at any rate in theory) by an English court construing a legal document. These required the words and grammar of a sentence to be given their 'natural and ordinary meaning', that is to say, the meanings assigned to the words by a dictionary and to the syntax by a grammar. This meaning was to be adopted

regardless of the context or background against which the words were used, unless they were 'ambiguous', that is to say, capable of having more than one meaning. As Lord Porter said in *Electrical & Musical Industries Ltd v Lissen Ltd* (1938) 56 RPC 23, 57:

> 'If the Claims have a plain meaning *in themselves* [emphasis supplied], then advantage cannot be taken of the language used in the body of the Specification to make them mean something different.'

"On the other hand, if the language of the claim 'in itself' was ambiguous, capable of having more than one meaning, the court could have regard to the context provided by the specification and drawings. If that was insufficient to resolve the ambiguity, the court could have regard to the background, or what was called the 'extrinsic evidence' of facts which an intended reader would reasonably have expected to have been within the knowledge of the author when he wrote the document.

"These rules, if remorselessly applied, meant that unless the court could find some ambiguity in the language, it might be obliged to construe the document in a sense which a reasonable reader, aware of its context and background, would not have thought the author intended. Such a rule, adopted in the interests of certainty at an early stage in the development of English law, was capable of causing considerable injustice and occasionally did so. The fact that it did not do so more often was because judges were generally astute to find the necessary 'ambiguity' which enabled them to interpret the document in its proper context. Indeed, the attempt to treat the words of the claim as having meanings 'in themselves' and without regard to the context in which or the purpose for which they were used was always a highly artificial exercise.

"It seems to me clear that the Protocol, with its reference to 'resolving an ambiguity', was intended to reject these artificial English rules for the construction of patent claims. As it happens, though, by the time the Protocol was signed, the English courts had already begun to abandon them, not only for patent claims, but for commercial documents generally. The speeches of Lord Wilberforce in *Prenn v Simmonds* [1971] 1 WLR 1381 and *Reardon Smith Line Ltd. v Yngvar Hansen-Tangen* [1976] 1 WLR 989 are milestones along this road. It came to be recognised that the author of a document such as a contract or patent specification is using language to make a communication for a practical *purpose* and that a rule of construction which gives his language a meaning different from the way it would have been understood by the people to whom it was actually addressed is liable to defeat his intentions. It is against that background that one must read the well known passage in the speech of Lord Diplock in [*Catnic Components Ltd v Hill & Smith Ltd* (1982) 99 RPC 183 (HL)], 243 when he said that the new approach should also be applied to the construction of patent claims:

> 'A patent specification should be given a purposive construction rather than a purely literal one derived from applying to it the kind of meticulous verbal analysis in which lawyers are too often tempted by their training to indulge.'

"This was all of a piece with Lord Diplock's approach a few years later in *The Antaios* [1985] AC 191, 201 to the construction of a charterparty:

> 'I take this opportunity of re-stating that if detailed semantic and syntactical analysis of words in a commercial contract is going to lead to a conclusion that flouts business commonsense, it must be made to yield to business commonsense.'

"Construction, whether of a patent or any other document, is of course not directly concerned with what the author meant to say. There is no window into the mind of the patentee or the author of any other document. Construction is objective in the sense that it is concerned with what a reasonable person to whom the utterance was addressed would have understood the author to be using the words to mean. Notice, however, that it is not, as is sometimes said, 'the meaning of the words the author used', but rather what the notional addressee would have understood the *author* to mean by using those words. The meaning of words is a matter of convention, governed by rules, which can be found in dictionaries and grammars. What the author would have been understood to mean by using those words is not simply a matter of rules. It is highly sensitive to the context of and background to the particular utterance. It depends not only upon the words the author has chosen but also upon the identity of the audience he is taken to have been addressing and the knowledge and assumptions which one attributes to that audience. I have discussed these questions at some length in *Mannai Investment Co Ltd v Eagle Star Life Assurance Co Ltd* [1997] AC 749 and *Investors Compensation Scheme Ltd v West Bromwich Building Society* [1998] 1 WLR 896.

"In the case of a patent specification, the notional addressee is the person skilled in the art. He (or, I say once and for all, she) comes to a reading of the specification with common general knowledge of the art. And he reads the specification on the assumption that its purpose is to both to describe and to demarcate an invention — a practical idea which the patentee has had for a new product or process — and not to be a textbook in mathematics or chemistry or a shopping list of chemicals or hardware. It is this insight which lies at the heart of 'purposive construction'. If Lord Diplock did not invent the expression, he certainly gave it wide currency in the law. But there is, I think, a tendency to regard it as a vague description of some kind of divination which mysteriously penetrates beneath the language of the specification. Lord Diplock was in my opinion being much more specific and his intention was to point out that a person may be taken to mean something different when he uses words for one purpose from what he would be taken to mean if he was using them for another. The example in the *Catnic* case was the difference between what a person would reasonably be taken to mean by using the word 'vertical' in a mathematical theorem and by using it in a claimed definition of a lintel for use in the building trade. The only point on which I would question the otherwise admirable summary of the law on infringement in the judgment of Jacob LJ in [*Rockwater Ltd v Technip France SA* [2004] EWCA Civ 381], at paragraph 41, is when he says in sub-paragraph (e) that to be 'fair to the patentee' one must use 'the widest purpose consistent with his teaching'. This, as it seems to me, is to confuse the *purpose* of the utterance with what it would be understood to *mean*. The purpose of a patent specification, as I have said, is no more nor less than to communicate the idea of an invention. An appreciation of that purpose is part of the material which one uses to ascertain the meaning. But purpose and meaning are different. If, when speaking of the widest purpose, Jacob LJ meant the widest meaning, I would respectfully disagree. There is no presumption about the width of the claims. A patent may, for one reason or another, claim less than it teaches or enables.

"'Purposive construction' does not mean that one is extending or going beyond the definition of the technical matter for which the patentee seeks protection in the claims. The question is always what the person skilled in the art would have understood the patentee to be using the language of the claim to mean. And for this purpose, the language he has chosen is usually of critical importance. The conventions of word meaning and syntax enable us to express our meanings with great accuracy and subtlety and the skilled man will ordinarily assume that the patentee has chosen his language accordingly. As a number of judges have pointed out, the specification is a unilateral document in words of the patentee's own choosing. Furthermore, the words will usually have been chosen upon skilled advice. The specification is not a document *inter rusticos* for which broad allowances must be made. On the other hand, it must be recognised that the patentee is trying to describe something which, at any rate in his opinion, is new; which has not existed before and of which there may be no generally accepted definition. There will be occasions upon which it will be obvious to the skilled man that the patentee must in some respect have departed from conventional use of language or included in his description of the invention some element which he did not mean to be essential. But one would not expect that to happen very often.

•   •   •   •   •

"There is often discussion about whether we have a European doctrine of equivalents and, if not, whether we should. It seems to me that both the doctrine of equivalents in the United States and the pith and marrow doctrine in the United Kingdom were born of despair. The courts felt unable to escape from interpretations which 'unsparing logic' appeared to require and which prevented them from according the patentee the full extent of the monopoly which the person skilled in the art would reasonably have thought he was claiming. The background was the tendency to literalism which then characterised the approach of the courts to the interpretation of documents generally and the fact that patents are likely to attract the skills of lawyers seeking to exploit literalism to find loopholes in the monopoly they create. (Similar skills are devoted to revenue statutes).

"If literalism stands in the way of construing patent claims so as to give fair protection to the patentee, there are two things that you can do. One is to adhere to literalism in construing the claims and evolve a doctrine which supplements the claims by extending protection to equivalents. That is what the Americans have done. The other is to abandon literalism. That is what the House of Lords did in the *Catnic* case, where Lord Diplock said (at [1982] RPC 183, 242:

> 'Both parties to this appeal have tended to treat "textual infringement" and infringement of the "pith and marrow" of an invention as if they were separate causes of action, the existence of the former to be determined as a

matter of construction only and of the latter upon some broader principle of colourable evasion. There is, in my view, no such dichotomy; there is but a single cause of action and to treat it otherwise … is liable to lead to confusion.'

"The solution, said Lord Diplock, was to adopt a principle of construction which actually gave effect to what the person skilled in the art would have understood the patentee to be claiming.

•   •   •   •   •

"In the *Catnic* case [1982] RPC 183, 243 Lord Diplock offered some observations on the relevance of equivalence to the question of construction:

'The question in each case is: whether persons with practical knowledge and experience of the kind of work in which the invention was intended to be used, would understand that strict compliance with a particular descriptive word or phrase appearing in a claim was intended by the patentee to be an essential requirement of the invention so that *any* variant would fall outside the monopoly claimed, even though it could have no material effect upon the way the invention worked.

'The question, of course, does not arise where the variant would in fact have a material effect upon the way the invention worked. Nor does it arise unless at the date of publication of the specification it would be obvious to the informed reader that this was so. Where it is not obvious, in the light of then-existing knowledge, the reader is entitled to assume that the patentee thought at the time of the specification that he had good reason for limiting his monopoly so strictly and had intended to do so, even though subsequent work by him or others in the field of the invention might show the limitation to have been unnecessary. It is to be answered in the negative only when it would be apparent to any reader skilled in the art that a particular descriptive word or phrase used in a claim cannot have been intended by a patentee, who was also skilled in the art, to exclude minor variants which, to the knowledge of both him and the readers to whom the patent was addressed, could have no material effect upon the way in which the invention worked.'

"In *Improver Corp v Remington Consumer Products Ltd* [1990] FSR 181, 189 I tried to summarise this guidance:

'If the issue was whether a feature embodied in an alleged infringement which fell outside the primary, literal or a contextual meaning of a descriptive word or phrase in the claim ("a variant") was nevertheless within its language as properly interpreted, the court should ask itself the following three questions:

'(1)   Does the variant have a material effect upon the way the invention works? If yes, the variant is outside the claim. If no?

'(2)   Would this (ie that the variant had no material effect) have been obvious at the date of publication of the patent to a reader skilled in the art? If no, the variant is outside the claim. If yes?

'(3)   Would the reader skilled in the art nevertheless have understood from the language of the claim that the patentee intended that strict compliance with the primary meaning was an essential requirement of the invention? If yes, the variant is outside the claim.

'On the other hand, a negative answer to the last question would lead to the conclusion that the patentee was intending the word or phrase to have not a literal but a figurative meaning (the figure being a form of synecdoche or metonymy) denoting a class of things which include the variant and the literal meaning, the latter being perhaps the most perfect, best-known or striking example of the class.'

"These questions, which the Court of Appeal in *Wheatly v Drillsafe Ltd* [2001] RPC 133, 142 dubbed 'the Protocol questions' have been used by English courts for the past fifteen years as a framework for deciding whether equivalents fall within the scope of the claims. On the whole, the judges appear to have been comfortable with the results, although some of the cases have exposed the limitations of the method. When speaking of the 'Catnic principle' it is important to distinguish between, on the one hand, the principle of purposive construction which I have said gives effect to the requirements of the Protocol, and on the other hand, the guidelines for applying that principle to equivalents, which are encapsulated in the Protocol questions. The former is the bedrock of patent construction, universally applicable. The latter are only guidelines, more useful in some cases than in others. I am bound to say that the cases show a tendency for counsel to treat the Protocol questions as legal rules rather than guides which will in appropriate cases help to decide what the skilled man would have understood the patentee to mean."

New Zealand counsel would do well to pay attention to Lord Diplock's warning against the application of the *Impacer* questions as legal rules rather than mere guidelines. Judgments in New Zealand since the 1990's have consistently applied the principles set out in *Catnic* without reference to the more structured *Impacer* questions: see, for example, *Smale v North Sails Ltd* [1991] 3 NZLR 19 and *Whangapirita v Allflex NZ Ltd* (1995) 5 NZBLC 103,733.

(1)   *Notional skilled addressee*

As to the meaning of a "notional skilled addressee", see the comments of Jacob LJ in *Rockwater Ltd v Technip France SA* [2004] EWCA Civ 381, at paras 6-11:

"The 'man skilled in the art' is invoked at many critical points of patent law. The claims of a patent must be understood as if read by that notional man — in the hackneyed but convenient phrase the 'court must don the mantle of the skilled man'. Likewise many questions of validity (obviousness, and sufficiency for instance) depend upon trying to view matters as he would see them.

"It is settled that this man, if real, would be very boring — a nerd. Lord Reid put it this way in [*Technograph Printed Circuits Ltd v Mills and Rockley (Electronics) Ltd* (1972) 89 RPC 346] at p.355:

'the hypothetical addressee is a skilled technician who is well acquainted with workshop technique and who has carefully read the relevant literature. He is supposed to have an unlimited capacity to assimilate the contents of, it may be, scores of specifications but to be incapable of scintilla of invention. When dealing with obviousness, unlike novelty, it is permissible to make a "mosaic" out of the relevant documents, but it must be a mosaic which can be put together by an unimaginative man with no inventive capacity.'

"The no-mosaic rule makes him also very forgetful. He reads all the prior art, but unless it forms part of his background technical knowledge, having read (or learnt about) one piece of prior art, he forgets it before reading the next unless it can form an uninventive mosaic or there is a sufficient cross-reference that it is justified to read the documents as one.

"He does, on the other hand, have a very good background technical knowledge — the so-called common general knowledge. Our courts have long set a standard for this which is set out in the oft-quoted passage from [*General Tire & Rubber Co v Firestone Tyre & Rubber Co* (1972) 89 RPC 457 (CA)] at 482 which in turn approves what was said by Luxmoore J in [*British Acoustic Films Ltd v Nettlefold Productions Ltd* (1936) 53 RPC 221] at 250. For brevity I do not quote this in full — Luxmoore J's happy phrase 'common stock of knowledge' conveys the flavour of what this notional man knows ...

"The man can, in appropriate cases, be a team — an assembly of nerds of different basic skills, all unimaginative. But the skilled man is not a complete android, for it is also settled that he will share the common prejudices or conservatism which prevail in the art concerned.

"None of the above is controversial. However, sometimes the requirement that the skilled man be uninventive is used by counsel for a patentee in an attempt to downgrade or dismiss the evidence of an expert called to say that a patent is obvious — 'my witness is more nerdlike than his' is the general theme. I do not find this a helpful approach."

In *Novartis NZ Ltd v Ancare NZ Ltd* 19/6/98, Morris J, HC Auckland CP480/97, it was confirmed, at p 37, that the skilled addressee may compile a team of individuals, each with distinct skills:

"This person is a skilled technician in the art in question, knowledgeable in the relevant literature (including patent specifications and such material as would be discovered on making a diligent search), but unimaginative and with no inventive capacity ... Where the subject matter covers more than one discipline, the notional addressee need not be an individual but may be a research team. In this case such a team would include a toxicologist, chemist and formulator. The Court must consider the whole field of research and the whole field of documents reasonably discoverable or generally known ..."

Moreover, in *Beecham Group Ltd v Bristol-Myers Co (No 2)* [1980] 1 NZLR 192, at pp 232-233, Barker J indicated that the skilled addressee might seek external advice on aspects with which he or she or they are not personally familiar:

"The issue of obviousness is to be judged from the viewpoint of a notional addressee. This, wraith-like legal creature who stalks the Reports of the Patent Cases just as the 'reasonable man' does the treatises on tort, is required to have numerous attributes:

"(i)   He is presumed to be a skilled technician, knowledgeable in the relevant literature, including patent specifications, but incapable of a 'scintilla of invention' (see [*Technograph Printed Circuits Ltd v Mills and Rockley (Electronics) Ltd* (1972) 89 RPC 346], 355 per Lord Reid …

"(ii)   The notional addressee need not be an individual but may be a research team such as the teams employed by both the parties in this case. See [*Olin Matheson Chemical Corp v Biorex Laboratories Ltd* [1970] RPC 157], 184 …

"(iii)   It is to be presumed that the notional addressee would seek advice on aspects with which he is not personally familiar. See *Tetra Molectric Ltd v Japan Imports Ltd* [1976] RPC 547, 583, per Buckley LJ in the Court of Appeal

"(iv)   It is presumed that the notional addressee believes what he finds in the documentation to be true. See *May & Baker Ltd v Boots Pure Drug Co Ltd* (1950) 67 RPC 23, 36 per Lord Normand."

Finally, Tompkins J, in *Smale v North Sails Ltd* [1991] 3 NZLR 19, implied that the skilled addressee is also deemed to be aware of all developments in the relevant art. His Honour said, at p 50:

"I return to what I understand to be the crucial question. The problem, as defined in the specification by the description of the object of the patent, is to minimise stretch or distortion in the luff area. The question, therefore, is whether a skilled addressee, knowledgeable in the art of sail design and construction, aware of all the developments that had previously taken place, considering the problem at the priority date, 16 May 1983, would have found the solution contained in the patent to be obvious."

There is a useful discussion of the notional skilled addressee in A Brown, "The Role of the Skilled Addressee" 59 *Intellectual Property Forum* 42.

As to the distinction between the notional skilled addressee and an expert, see the comments of Assistant Commissioner Hazlewood in *Lafarge Platres' Application* (Commissioner's Decision No P47/2006, 18/12/06, Asst Commr Hazlewood), at pp 13-14. In that case, the evidence of a deponent held out by the opponent as a notional skilled addressee was read down on the basis that he was "qualified well beyond that required of the notional skilled addressee" and more properly categorised as an expert.

(2)   *Common general knowledge*

As will be apparent from the preceding section, the notional skilled addressee by reference to whom the claims of a patent are interpreted (and for that matter the validity of a patent is tested — see the discussion relating to prior publication (at 2.7.2(1)), obviousness (at 2.9.3(5), and insufficiency (at 2.13.3(7)) earlier in this chapter) is deemed to possess the common general knowledge in his or her field at the priority date.

In T A Blanco-White, *Patents for inventions and the protection of industrial designs* (5th ed), London, Stevens, 1983, the author discusses the expression as follows:

"The term 'common general knowledge' is used in patent law to mean that which is 'known to duly qualified persons in that art or science …' …

"The importance of determining the common general knowledge of an art lies in this, that it represents those matters that the skilled man will have in his mind — or at the back of his mind — when he comes to consider the prior art; so that each document has to be regarded as he would regard it in the light of common general knowledge. Thus the mere application of common knowledge to the improvement or elucidation of something read or seen is likely to be obvious in the sense of the patent law; this and some resulting trial and error, are part of the skilled man's 'normal industrial function'."

A useful definition of "common general knowledge" was given by Laddie J in *Raychem Corp's Patent* [1998] RPC 31, at p 40:

"The Court is trying to determine in a common sense way how the average skilled but non-inventive technician would have reacted to the pleaded prior art if it had been put before him in his work place or laboratory. The common general knowledge is the technical background of the notional man in the art against which the prior art must be considered. This is not limited to material he has memorised and has at the front of his mind. It includes all that material in the field he is working in which he knows exist, which he would refer to as a matter of course if he cannot remember it and which he understands is generally regarded as sufficiently reliable to use as a foundation for further work or to help understand the pleaded prior art. This does not mean that everything on the shelf which is capable of being referred to without difficulty is common general knowledge nor does it mean that every word in a common text book is either. In the case of standard textbooks, it is likely that all or most of the main text will be common general knowledge. In many cases common general knowledge will include or be reflected in readily available trade literature which a man in the art would be expected to have at his elbow and regard as basic reliable information."

Sachs LJ, delivering the judgment of the Court in *General Tire & Rubber Co v Firestone Tyre & Rubber Co* (1972) 89 RPC 457 (CA), discussed the distinction between "common general knowledge" and "public knowledge" as follows, at p 482:

"The *common general* knowledge imputed to such an addressee must, of course, be carefully distinguished from what in patent law is regarded as *public* knowledge. This distinction is well explained in *Halsbury's Laws of England*, Vol. 29, para. 63. As regards patent specifications it is the somewhat artificial (see per Lord Reid in the *Technograph* case [1971] F.S.R. 188 at 193) concept of patent law that each and every specification, of the last 50 years, however unlikely to be looked at and in whatever language written, is part of the relevant *public* knowledge if it is resting anywhere in the shelves of the Patent Office. On the other hand, *common general* knowledge is a different concept derived from a commonsense approach to the practical question of what would in fact be known to an appropriately skilled addressee — the sort of man, good at his job, that could be found in real life.

"The two classes of documents which call for consideration in relation to *common general* knowledge in the instant case were individual patent specifications and 'widely read publications'.

"As to the former, it is clear that individual patent specifications and their contents do not normally form part of the relevant *common general* knowledge, though there may be specifications which are so well known amongst those versed in the art that upon evidence of that state of affairs they form part of such knowledge, and also there may occasionally be particular industries (such as that of colour photography) in which the evidence may show that all specifications form part of the relevant knowledge."

In *Merck & Co Inc v Arrow Pharmaceuticals (NZ) Ltd* 29/9/06, Harrison J, HC Wellington CIV-2006-485-817, it was held, at para 33, that scientific publications do not ordinarily form part of the common general knowledge. In reaching that decision, the Court relied upon the legal position as stated by Luxmoore J in *British Acoustic Films Ltd v Nettlefold Productions Ltd* (1936) 53 RPC 221, at p 250:

"It is not sufficient to prove common general knowledge that a particular disclosure is made in an article, or series of articles, in a scientific journal, no matter how wide the circulation of that journal may be, in the absence of any evidence that the disclosure is accepted generally by those who are engaged in the art to which the disclosure relates. A piece of particular knowledge as disclosed in a scientific paper does not become common general knowledge merely because it is widely read, and still less because it is widely circulated. Such a piece of knowledge only becomes general knowledge when it is generally known and accepted without question by the bulk of those who are engaged in the particular art; in other words, when it becomes part of their common stock of knowledge relating to the art."

Note also the comments of Assistant Commissioner Hazlewood in *Lafarge Platres' Application* (Commissioner's Decision No P47/2006, 18/12/06, Asst Commr Hazlewood), at p 14, indicating that care must be taken in opposition cases to judge the evidence against the proven background of common general knowledge in New Zealand, and that it should not be assumed that the common general knowledge will be the same in New Zealand as in other countries: applying *Wellcome Foundation Ltd v VR Laboratories (Aust) Pty Ltd* (1980-81) 148 CLR 262, at p 284.

Finally, in recent years a number of decisions have emerged in Australia which have suggested that information disclosed in the "Background to the invention" section of a patent specification may, without qualification, be taken as an admission of the common general knowledge in the art at the priority date. See, for example, *Bristol-Myers Squibb Co v FH Faulding & Co Ltd* (2000) 170 ALR 439 (FCA), at p 450, and *WM Wrigley JR Co v Cadbury Schweppes Pty Ltd* (2005) 66 IPR 298; [2005] FCA 1035 (FCA), at para 59:

"It follows that what is asserted on the face of the specification, without qualification, to be 'Background of the Invention' can be taken as an admission that what appears therein was part of CGK in Australia at the priority date. This at least is CGK, although evidence may reveal more. The very heading is telling the reader that what appears in that section is known and common place in the art. It is setting the stage, so to speak, for the disclosure of the claimed invention, which, by contrast, will reveal something promised to be new and inventive."

Although the New Zealand Courts have yet to consider the issue, there is no reason why the same reasoning should not apply in principle here. In addition, even though there is currently no equivalent New Zealand authority, the above decisions still have practical implications for those drafting patent specifications in New Zealand (or elsewhere) which are likely to be filed in Australia. For this reason at least one commentator (B Roxborough, "Admissions on the Face of the Specification — Practical Implications for Patent Drafting and Litigation", *Intellectual Property Forum*, Vol 68, March 2007, at p 59) has recommended the use of a suitable disclaimer lest content not commonly known by the skilled addressee in Australia be deemed so merely because it is information on the face of an Australian filed patent specification.

The same author notes that *Gerber Garment Technology Inc v Loctra Systems Ltd* [1995] FSR 492 (CA) may provide relief in those situations where the patent being considered was filed before the above decisions were handed down (and in which a disclaimer will not be present). The UK courts held in *Gerber*, at pp 494-495, that a statement in a specification may constitute an admission "which must necessarily carry great weight, but that it did not estop the patentee or debar him from leading evidence to contradict it."

(3)   *No file wrapper estoppel*

In some jurisdictions, notably the United States, it is permissible to review the prosecution history of a patent in order to determine the scope of the claims and/or the meaning of any integers within a claim. In particular, if the patentee has argued for a narrow interpretation of an integer during prosecution of the patent, they will be estopped from arguing a broader interpretation once the patent is granted. The New Zealand Courts have yet to consider whether file wrapper estoppel applies in New Zealand, although they are likely to follow the Australian Courts which have expressly rejected the doctrine (*Prestige Group (Australia) Pty Ltd v Dart Industries Inc* [1990] 26 FCR 197, and *Baygol Pty Ltd v Foamex Polystyrene Pty Ltd* [2005] FCA 145). The latter decision relied in part on the following comments of Lord Hoffman in *Kirin-Amgen Inc v Hoechst Marion Roussel Ltd* [2005] RPC 9 (HL), at para 35:

> "The Courts of the United Kingdom, the Netherlands and Germany certainly discourage, if they do not actually prohibit, use of the patent office file in aid of construction … It is however frequently impossible to know without access, not merely to the file but to the private thoughts of the patentee and his advisors as well, what the reason was for some apparently inexplicable limitation in the extent of the monopoly claimed … It has been suggested that in the absence of any explanation for a restriction in the extent of protection claimed, it should be presumed that there was some good reason between the patentee and the patent office. I do not think it is sensible to have presumptions about what people must be taken to have meant but a conclusion that they have departed from conventional usage obviously needs some rational basis."

See also *NJ Philips Pty Ltd v Forlong & Maisey Ltd* 3/2/06, Associate Judge Faire, HC Hamilton CIV-2005-419-565, in which the Court struck out a pleading alleging estoppel by misrepresentation arising out of statements made by Counsel for the patentee during the course of an opposition proceeding. The Associate Judge accepted the argument of Counsel for the patentee that submissions of Counsel are simply arguments advanced to persuade a judicial authority that a particular position should be accepted, are addressed to the Hearing Officer not to the other party, are not a statement of fact but are simply Counsel's opinion, can be abandoned, altered or resiled from, and are fundamentally different from formal undertakings which are intended to be relied upon by parties, concluding, at para 51, that submissions are not representations and therefore cannot be found an estoppel by representation. The Associate Judge also seems to have placed some reliance on the fact that New Zealand does not follow the US doctrine of file wrapper estoppel (para 48).

2.14.5 Contributory infringement

For a party to be a contributory infringer, it is necessary to establish procurement or participation. The mere facilitation of an infringement (ie supplying a party with the means to infringe) is not enough.

The supply of apparatus that may be used in an infringing manner does not in itself amount to an infringement: *Sabaf SpA v MFI Furniture Centres* [2003] RPC 264 (CA).

The New Zealand position was first set out in *Whangapirita v Allflex NZ Ltd* (1995) 5 NZBLC 103,733. The action concerned an alleged patent infringement of ear taggers for animals. Allflex produced the ear taggers and subsequently sold them (without instructions for use) to farmers, who then infringed the claims of the patent by using them. Doogue J held that where there is a sale of an object, the use of which might lead to infringement of a patent, this amounts to facilitation but does not of itself constitute an act of procurement of infringement. Accordingly, Allflex was found not to have infringed the patent even though some of its customers had subsequently used the ear tagger in an infringing manner. It is important to note that in this case Allflex did not supply instructions on how to use the ear tagger it supplied.

The position in *Allflex* was confirmed in *Nu-Pulse NZ Ltd v Milka-Ware (ANZ) Ltd* 14/10/99, Master Faire, HC Hamilton CP8/97. In that case, *Milka-Ware* sold a cleaning apparatus for milking machines which did not by itself infringe the claims of the patent. However, when the apparatus was connected to a milking system the patent was infringed. The only possible use for the apparatus was an infringing one. However, the Court struck out the cause of action as untenable on the basis that the selling of non-protected articles to be used for infringement is not of itself an infringement unless there is certainty that they will actually be used in an infringing capacity. In *Milka-Ware*, the Court noted that they could have been exported, thereby avoiding infringement.

The law of contributory infringement was also addressed in *Lucas v Peterson Portable Sawing Systems Ltd* [2003] 3 NZLR 361; (2003) 57 IPR 305. In this case the defendants argued that, as the infringing articles were exported to Australia (or elsewhere) in kitset form, they avoided infringement as they were not assembled until after they left New Zealand. Conversely, the plaintiff argued that a manufacturer infringes even where the kitsets are manufactured and sold in kitset form. The plaintiff relied upon *Windsurfing International Inc v Petit* (1983) 3 IPR 449, at p 459. The plaintiff's argument was not challenged by the defendants, and Fisher J accepted the plaintiff's arguments, finding that the sale of an infringing article in kitset form could constitute infringement. The decision of Fisher J was ultimately overturned on appeal to the Supreme Court of New Zealand (*Peterson Portable Sawing Systems Ltd (in liq) v Lucas* [2006] 3 NZLR 721 (SC)) although for different reasons (the claim which Fisher J deemed infringed was found by the Supreme Court to be both anticipated and rendered obvious by the prior art).

In relation to joint tortfeasors, the leading New Zealand case is *Interpress Assocs Ltd v Fisher & Paykel Production Machinery Ltd* (1996) 34 IPR 390. The Court listed three situations in which joint liability may arise:

(1)   Where A is master and B is servant;

(2)   Where A is principal and B is agent; or

(3)   Where two people are engaged in a joint act in pursuance of a common purpose.

The law regarding joint liability of patent infringement was addressed in *Lucas v Peterson Portable Sawing Systems Ltd* [2003] 3 NZLR 361; (2003) 57 IPR 305. In that case, the first defendant company manufactured, marketed, and sold the infringing product, and as such was the primary infringer. The second defendant was the managing director, employee and sole designer of the first defendant. The Court found that he participated in a common design or concerted action with the primary infringer, and as such he was liable as a joint tortfeasor. The decision of Fisher J was ultimately overturned on appeal to the Supreme Court of New Zealand (*Peterson Portable Sawing Systems Ltd (in liq) v Lucas* [2006] 3 NZLR 721 (SC)) although for different reasons (the claim which Fisher J deemed infringed was found by the Supreme Court to be both anticipated and rendered obvious by the prior art).

Under cl 130 of the draft Patents Bill 2004, it will be an infringement of a patent to supply another with the means to put the invention into effect provided you know that the means are suitable for putting the invention into effect, are intended by the other for putting the invention into effect, and that putting the invention into effect would infringe the patent.

It will not be an infringement to supply a staple commercial product (such as the raw material of a chemical formulation) unless the supply was made for the purpose of inducing another to infringe the patent.

2.14.6   Infringement via the internet

Patents are territorial. Therefore for a defendant's activity to amount to infringement it must occur in New Zealand or a dependency of New Zealand.

However, in *Menashe Business Mercantile Ltd v William Hill Organisation Ltd* (2002) 119 RPC 950, the English Court of Appeal held that it is not a defence to patent infringement to show that a host computer or server, that forms part of a patented invention, is located offshore. In that case the plaintiff had a granted United Kingdom patent for an interactive gaming system in which a host computer was connected with at least one remote terminal, and provided software enabling users to interactively gamble with the host computer. The defendant began supplying United Kingdom customers with software allowing them to access and play similar interactive gambling games over the internet, the only difference being that the defendant's host computer (server) was located offshore. The English Court of Appeal held that the defendant had infringed the patent because:

•   The physical location of the host computer was immaterial;

- It was the input and output of the information that was relevant to infringement; and

- By accessing an infringing system on an offshore server via local terminals, the offshore server was effectively being used in the United Kingdom.

Although this decision relates to a business method using the internet, the same reasoning may apply to the sale of infringing articles through an offshore server.

2.14.7 Pleadings

In *Pfizer Ireland Pharmaceuticals v Eli Lilly & Co* 8/12/05, CA8/05, the Court of Appeal decided that its earlier decision in *Ancare NZ Ltd v Ciba Geigy NZ Ltd* (1997) 11 PRNZ 398 (CA), which held that the usual pleading rules apply in patent revocation cases, did not state the law correctly. The Court of Appeal considered that the structure of the High Court Rules (which require revocation proceedings to be by way of originating application and which make no provision for a patentee to plead to particulars of objection), as well as earlier authorities, meant that Ancare (which held that r 130 (relating to Statements of Defence) applied to revocation proceedings and required the patentee to plead to particulars of objection) should no longer be followed. However, the Court of Appeal observed that rr 425(a) and 429(2) were sufficiently broad to allow a party to seek any directions which might secure the just, speedy, and inexpensive determination of a proceeding. The Court noted, at para 42, that there is "no reason why a party to litigation should not identify the substance of the case to be advanced and this is so irrespective of where the onus of proof lies and whether such identification requires the party to address issues of construction, law or evidence".

2.14.8 Jurisdiction

Although patent rights are territorial, and a New Zealand patent will have no effect in other countries, in certain limited circumstances it may be possible for the owner of the same patent granted in a number of jurisdictions to sue a New Zealand-based defendant for breaches of its foreign patent rights committed in those foreign jurisdictions. The question of whether and in what circumstances such actions are permissible was considered in *Kabushiki Kaisha Sony Computer Entertainment v van Veen* 14/12/06, MacKenzie J, HC Wellington CIV-2004-485-1520. The plaintiffs (collectively "Sony") were the proprietors of the PlayStation 2 computer games system, and owned intellectual property rights in some of the games played on that system. Those games were distributed on CDs and DVDs and, to assist in their protection, Sony embedded codes which prevented copying of the games from the CD or DVD to another medium. The defendants developed and distributed a software programme called HD Loader which enabled a user to circumvent the embedded copy protection code and copy Sony's games. The HD Loader programme was developed by the first defendant who sold or licensed the use of that programme in, amongst other countries, the UK and Hong Kong through the second defendant.

Sony commenced proceedings and obtained a number of interim orders. Following completion of the pleadings the first defendant admitted the material allegations in the Statement of Claim (breach of the New Zealand Copyright and Trade Marks Acts, breach of the United Kingdom Copyright, Designs and Patents Act 1988, breach of the Hong Kong Copyright Ordinance, and wrongful possession and use of confidential information) and Sony applied for judgment against the first defendant.

On each of the causes of action relating to breaches of the New Zealand legislation and wrongful use and possession of confidential information, the admitted facts clearly gave rise to liability which could be enforced in New Zealand. Those causes of action were based on New Zealand law and on actions admitted to have taken place in New Zealand. The more difficult question was whether the Court could determine causes of action relating to alleged breaches of United Kingdom and Hong Kong copyright legislation.

The starting point for the Court was the rule laid down by the House of Lords in *British South Africa Co v Companhia de Mocambique* [1893] AC 602 (HL), which stated that the Court has no jurisdiction to entertain an action for (1) the determination of the title to, or the right to possession of, any immoveable situate out of England (foreign land); or (2) the recovery of damages for trespass to such immoveable. MacKenzie J noted, at paras 9 and 10, that the rule had been applied in Australia and England in several cases involving intellectual property rights, and had been applied by Tipping J in New Zealand in *Atkinson Footwear Ltd v Hodgskin International Services Ltd* (1994) 31 IPR 186 in respect of an application for an interim injunction to restrain the distribution of footwear allegedly infringing the plaintiff's copyright in New Zealand and Australia. Tipping J granted the application with respect to New Zealand but declined to extend it to Australia. However, MacKenzie J noted that since the decision of Tipping J in *Atkinson Footwear* the UK Court of Appeal had carefully reconsidered the position in *Pearce v Ove Arup Partnership Ltd* [1999] 1 All ER 769 (CA), a case involving the construction of a public building in Rotterdam which was a copy of a plan produced by an architectural student in London. The UK Court of Appeal held in *Pearce* that the English Courts did have jurisdiction to entertain a claim in respect of the alleged infringement of Dutch copyright by virtue of actions occurring in Holland on the basis that the *Mocambique* rule involves two limbs, the second of which makes a distinction between proceedings where issue of title, or the extent of rights available under a foreign law arise, on the one hand, and claims where the matter in issue is not the existence or nature of the title or rights, but whether some action has the effect of infringing the unquestioned rights of the plaintiff. MacKenzie J concluded, at para 19:

> "I find the reasoning [in *Pearce*] persuasive in favour of the proposition that, in the case of intellectual property rights governed by the law of a foreign country, the second limb of the *Mocambique* rule should not exclude justiciability in respect of actions for breach of intellectual property rights established under the law of another jurisdiction, when no question of the existence or validity of those rights arises."

adding, at para 22:

> "Nothing which I have said should be taken as questioning the applicability of the first limb of the rule in the *Mocambique* case to questions of title to intellectual property … nor should anything I have said be taken as questioning the applicability of the second limb in the *Mocambique* case to true immoveables such as land … The issue before me is whether the second limb should be extended to items of intellectual property such as those in issue here. The various forms of protection given under intellectual property statutes are territorial in nature, because the statutes conferring them are necessarily territorial in their application. To that extent, they have the characteristics of immoveable property. But the significant difference between such forms of intellectual property and true immoveables such as land is that the same item of intellectual property may be protected by statutory rights in

119

many jurisdictions. A strict application of the second limb of the *Mocambique* case to such rights would mean that, where, as here, a defendant commits infringing acts against a single plaintiff in several jurisdictions, separate proceedings in each jurisdiction will be necessary to deal with those infringements. The inconvenience of such a requirement would outweigh the benefit of certainty that the application of the second limb to such claims would provide. I decline to apply the second limb to this case."

Having concluded that the justiciability of Sony's claim was not excluded by the *Mocambique* rule, MacKenzie J went on to consider whether, on the ordinary principles of the conflict of laws dealing with wrongs committed in another jurisdiction, the New Zealand Court had jurisdiction in the present case. In that regard, the common law double actionability rule applies. The double actionability rule states that, as a general rule, an act done in a foreign country is a tort and actionable as such in New Zealand, only if it is both (a) actionable as a tort according to New Zealand law or, in other words, is an act which, if done in New Zealand, would be a tort; and (b) actionable according to the law of the foreign country where it was done. However, a particular issue between the parties may be governed by the law of the country which, with respect to that issue, has the most significant relationship with the occurrence and the parties.

Having considered the double actionability rule, MacKenzie J went on to address (and resolve) a potential problem in applying that rule to the present case as follows, at paras 24 and 25:

"In applying that Rule, it may be argued that, since the acts complained of must constitute a wrong actionable under New Zealand law, the acts complained of, being infringements in the United Kingdom and Hong Kong, do not constitute a wrong against New Zealand copyright, since New Zealand copyright is territorial in effect. Therefore, a strict application of the first limb of the double actionability rule would lead to the result that the infringement would not be actionable in New Zealand. That Rule was the subject of consideration in *Pearce*. Roch LJ discussed the difficulty which arises in a case such as this, if the first limb of [the Double Actionability] Rule … requires the [New Zealand] court to determine actionability by [New Zealand] domestic law. He dealt with the proposition that, if, despite the rule in the *Mocambique* case, the claim was justiciable, it was bound to fail the requirements in the first limb of the double actionability rule in these terms at page 803:

'If that were a correct analysis, the effect would be that the first limb of r 203(1) imposed a requirement as to jurisdiction; and not simply a rule for the choice of law'

"He went on to note that the view that the first limb of the rule does impose a requirement as to jurisdiction had found expression in the dissenting judgment of Diplock LJ in [*Chaplin v Boys* [1969] 2 All ER 1085 (HL)], but had been plainly rejected by the House of Lords on the appeal. Roch LJ referred to [*Red Sea Insurance Ltd v Bouygues SA* [1994] 3 All ER 749 (PC)], where the Privy Council had accepted that the choice of the lex fori as the applicable law was not an invariable rule; rather that it was 'the general rule' or 'a starting point'. Roch LJ then went on to say, at page 803-804:

'In the present case, the plaintiff's claim would be defeated if the court were to refuse to apply the exception. But the claim (if established on the facts) is one where the English court would have given a remedy, under United Kingdom copyright law, if the facts alleged had occurred in England. This is not a case in which the claim is in respect of some wrong which is conceptually unknown in English law. In our view this is a case where, if the claim is justiciable at all, the exception to the double actionability rule enables English court to apply Dutch law; and the English court ought to do so.'

"I respectfully concur with that reasoning. It seems to me that, in applying the first limb of the double actionability rule, in an intellectual property infringement case, it is necessary to effect a notional transfer to New Zealand, for consideration under New Zealand law, of both the infringing act, and the intellectual property infringed. The infringing act and the intellectual property infringed cannot sensibly be separated in applying the first limb of [the Double Actionability] Rule … The purpose of the rule is to consider how New Zealand law would regard an act, if that act were committed in New Zealand and subject to New Zealand domestic law. Where the act complained of is an infringement of an intellectual property right, a relevant inquiry, in considering the application of New Zealand domestic law, should be whether that particular form of intellectual property is one which is capable of protection under New Zealand law. The focus should be on the nature of the underlying intellectual property, not on the form in which that property is protected by the laws of the foreign jurisdiction. The laws of the foreign jurisdiction are relevant to the second limb, not the first limb, of the double actionability rule."

Accordingly, MacKenzie J entered judgment against the first defendant in respect of all causes of action. Finally, his Honour clarified, at para 27, that in reaching the conclusions which he had as to the applicability of the *Mocambique*, and double actionability, rules his findings should be limited to the case of a defendant who is resident in New Zealand and thereby subject to the jurisdiction of the New Zealand Courts.

Although this judgment relates specifically to allegations of breach of copyright and registered trade mark there is no reason in principal why it should not equally apply to other intellectual property rights, particularly those for which a process of registration is required (therefore providing certainty in terms of the scope of monopoly of the intellectual property right in various jurisdictions) such as patents and registered designs.

2.15 Defences to infringement

There are a number of defences to infringement, including:

- The use of a patented invention for the purpose of bona fide research and experiment (ie to determine if an improvement can be made to the patented invention). This defence excludes experimental use of an invention for commercial advantage: *Monsanto Co v Stauffer Chemical Co (No 1)* (1984) 1 NZIPR 518, at p 531

- The use of a product for the purpose of obtaining regulatory approval: s 68B. For example, the importation of a generic drug to obtain governmental approval will not infringe a current New Zealand patent for that drug. This defence is discussed in more detail below.

- The making and selling of separate components of a combination for which there is a patent. For example, in *Dunlop Pneumatic Tyre Co Ltd v Moseley & Sons Ltd* (1904) 21 RPC 274 (CA), the sale of pneumatic tyre covers without wires did not infringe a patent for pneumatic tyre covers with wires.

- The acts were done with the implied licence or consent of the patentee, for example, the parallel importation of patented product for resale in New Zealand (discussed in more detail below).

- The making and selling of articles that are not of themselves protected by a patent but that can be used for the purposes of infringement: *Beecham Group Ltd v Bristol Laboratories Ltd* (1978) 95 RPC 153 (HL). See 2.14.5 ("Contributory infringement") earlier in the chapter.

- The doing of any of the exclusive acts in relation to a patented invention outside New Zealand. However, a decision of the English Court of Appeal (*Menashe Business Mercantile Ltd v William Hill Organisation Ltd* (2002) 119 RPC 950) has held that this may not be the case if infringement occurs over or via the internet. See 2.14.6 ("Infringement via the internet") earlier in the chapter.

- The patent is invalid on any of the grounds under which it may be revoked under ss 41-42 of the Act. Compare cl 134 of the draft Patents Bill 2004.

2.15.1 Use of a patented invention for research and experimentation

The Patents Act 1953 does not specifically exclude experimental use from patent infringement. However, the New Zealand Courts have adopted this exemption, and subject to such research being of an experimental nature rather than with a commercial advantage in mind. However, in the absence of extensive case law, there is still some uncertainty as to where the line between the two should be drawn.

The best indication of the Court's approach comes from the Court of Appeal's decision in *Smith Kline & French Laboratories Ltd v A-G* [1991] 2 NZLR 560; (1991) 4 TCLR 199 (CA), where Hardie Boys J stated, at p 567; p 205:

> "Doubtless experimentation will usually have an ultimate commercial objective; where it ends and infringement begins must often be a matter of degree. If the person concerned keeps his activities to himself, and does no more than further his own knowledge or skill, even though commercial advantage may be his final goal, he does not infringe. But if he goes beyond that, and uses the invention or makes it available to others, in a way that serves to advance him in the actual marketplace, then he infringes".

On this basis, an academic institution will have no more success in raising the defence than a commercially oriented company.

2.15.2 Regulatory approval

Under s 68B Patents Act 1953, it is not an infringement of a patent for a person to make, use, exercise, or vend the patented invention without the registered proprietor's consent, if these steps are taken for the purposes of obtaining regulatory approval.

This amendment was introduced in 2002, and appears to have been made to facilitate entry into the New Zealand market of generic products, particularly generic pharmaceuticals, and to assist New Zealand manufacturers of generic products to gain access to both New Zealand and export markets.

Essentially the broad wording of the section appears to enable a manufacturer of a generic product to produce any patented product that requires a form of regulatory approval anywhere in the world. As numerous products require regulatory approval, this new exception to infringement has potentially far reaching consequences across many industry sectors.

For example, if a patent existed in New Zealand for an insecticide, and marketing or regulatory approval was required to sell it in Australia, then a manufacturer of insecticides in New Zealand could potentially make, use and sell the insecticide in New Zealand to the extent required to obtain regulatory approval in Australia. If there are no regulatory limits as to the trials required in Australia then, arguably, any amount of use in New Zealand could be deemed use for the purposes of obtaining regulatory approval.

Under cl 133 of the draft Patents Bill 2004, it would not be an infringement of a patent to exploit the invention solely for uses reasonably related to the development and submission of information required under New Zealand law, or the law of another country, regulating the exploitation of the product.

2.15.3   Implied licence to import patented product

The form of patent granted in New Zealand provides the patentee with the exclusive right to make, use, vend and exercise the patented invention. The form of patent expressly prohibits others from directly or indirectly making use of the invention, without the consent, licence or agreement of the patentee in writing.

Notwithstanding this, the Courts have sometimes been prepared to accept that there might be an implied licence to import goods into a particular jurisdiction that goes with the sale of the original patented product overseas. The implied licence finds its origins in *Betts v Willmott* (1871) 6 Ch App 240 in which Betts, the holder of an English and French patent, tried to stop tablets made and sold by him in France from being resold in England. The Court rejected the claim, noting:

> "Where a man carries on the two manufactures himself, and himself disposes of the article abroad … I apprehend that, in as much as he has the right of vending the goods in France, Belgium or England, or in any other quarter of the globe, he transfers with the goods necessarily the licence to use them wherever the purchaser pleases. When a man has purchased an article he expects to have the control of it, and there must be some clear and explicit agreement to the contrary to justify the vendor in saying that he has not given the purchaser his licence to sell the article, or to use it wherever he pleases as against himself."

Subsequent Courts have been prepared to apply *Betts* to insist that, unless the patent owner has expressly disclaimed the purchaser's right to import and resell the goods in a particular jurisdiction, they will be permitted to do so.

Notwithstanding the *Betts* line of authority, Article 28(1)(a) of the WTO's TRIPS Agreement (of which New Zealand is a signatory) purports to limit the ability of signatories to allow parallel importation of patented goods. Where the subject matter of the patent is a product, it requires the patent to confer on its owner the exclusive right to prevent third parties from making, using, offering for sale, selling, or importing that product without the owner's consent.

There is a fundamental inconsistency between the *Betts* line of authority on the one hand, and the Deed of Letters Patent (which requires a patent licence to be in writing) and New Zealand's obligations under TRIPS on the other and therefore the law remains uncertain.

However, the suggestion of an implied license might be defeated by an express provision in the terms of sale of a patented article prohibiting subsequent sale or use. See *B Braun Med Inc v Abbott Labs* 124 F 3d 1419 (CA Fed, 1997), at p 1426:

> "an unconditional sale of a patented device exhausts the patentee's right to control the purchaser's use of the device thereafter. The theory behind this rule is that in such a transaction, the patentee has bargained for, and received, an amount equal to the value of the goods. This exhaustion doctrine, however, does not apply to an expressly conditional sale or license. In such transaction it is more reasonable to infer that the parties negotiated a price that reflects only the value of the 'use' rights conferred by the patentee."

This passage was cited with approval by the US Federal Court of Appeal in *LG Electronics Inc v Bizcom Electronics Inc* 453 F 3d 1364 (CA Fed, 2006). In that case, LG held patents for a number of computer components individually as well as for their combination with other computer components. LG licensed the individual components to Intel on terms which required Intel to notify purchasers of the components that, although it was licensed to sell the components to them, they were not authorised to combine the components with non-Intel components. The Defendants did so and LG successfully brought proceedings asserting that the combination of micro-processors or chip sets with non-Intel components infringed LG's patents covering those combinations.

2.15.4 Innocent infringement

Section 68(1) Patents Act 1953 precludes a plaintiff from recovering damages or an account of profits against an innocent infringer.

An "innocent infringer" is a person who, at the time of infringement, was not aware, and had no reasonable ground for supposing, that the patent existed. In essence, s 68 is a statutory defence to infringement.

A defendant cannot be said to be an innocent infringer if the patented invention is marked with the words "New Zealand" or "NZ", followed by the number of the patent. This is discussed further at 2.15.4(1) ("Marking") below.

The defence of innocent infringement was examined in *Ashmont Holdings Ltd v Jurox Pty Ltd* [2001] 2 NZLR 130. The apparatus in that case carried a patent number but no indication as to the country in which it was registered. The defendants argued that, as the patented invention was not marked correctly, there is a presumption that any infringement is innocent. Fisher J disagreed, stating that there is nothing in s 68(1) of the Act to indicate that when the words "New Zealand" or "NZ" are not used on patented articles the defendant would necessarily lack the requisite knowledge, or reasonable grounds for supposing that a patent was registered in New Zealand. His Honour confirmed that in every case the question whether a defendant is an innocent infringer is one of fact and degree, and that the onus lies with the defendant to establish its innocence.

(1) *Marking*

It is not compulsory to indicate on an article that it is patented. However, a defendant can be found to be an innocent infringer (and therefore not be liable for an account of profits or damages) if the article is not correctly marked. This is discussed further at 2.15.4 ("Innocent infringement") above. Compare cl 139 of the draft Patents Bill 2004.

The recommended marking for a patented invention is: "New Zealand Patent No XXXXXX" or "NZ Pat No XXXXXX"

Inventions the subject of pending applications should be marked: "New Zealand Patent Application No XXXXXX" or "NZ Pat Appln No XXXXXX"

If a party is deemed to be an innocent infringer neither damages nor an account of profits can be awarded by a Court. Nevertheless, a Court may still injunct an innocent infringer to restrain further infringement of the patent.

2.15.5 Cause of action estoppel

A recent decision of the English High Court — Chancery Division, Patents Court, *Coflexip SA v Stolt Offshore MS Ltd* [2003] EWHC 1892 (Patent), has reaffirmed that cause of action estoppel may arise in patent infringement proceedings.

In that case, Stolt was found to have infringed Coflexip's patent, and its counterclaim for revocation was unsuccessful. An inquiry into damages was ordered. The patent was subsequently revoked in an unrelated action by another party and Stolt sought to stay the inquiry into damages. Relying upon *Poulton v Adjustable Cover & Boiler Block Co* (1908) 25 RPC 529 and *Poulton v Adjustable Cover & Boiler Block Co* (1908) 25 RPC 661 (CA), at p 663, Jacob J declined the stay and held:

> "The judgment obtained by the Plaintiff is a judgment which made the matter of infringement and the validity of the Patent *res judicata* between the parties and created a perfect estoppel.

> "An order for the revocation of a patent is conclusive *in rem*, as it extinguishes the patent, but it does not avoid prior estoppels from a prior decision *in personam* that the patent was valid and infringed.

> "There is a difference between a party saying 'there is no patent' and 'there was no patent'. Stolt cannot say there never was a patent, hence orders relating to the inquiry into damages are enforceable, yet an injunction preventing further infringement ceases to have effect, as there is no longer a patent to infringe."

See also *Hormel Foods Corp v Antilles Landscape Investments NV* [2005] RPC 28) in which the High Court of England and Wales barred a second attempt to invalidate a trade mark on the basis of analogous law in the field of patent and registered design which obliges a party attacking the validity to put its full case in support of that attack at trial. Richard Arnold

QC (sitting as a Deputy Judge) noted that, if unsuccessful, the party will be barred by cause of action estoppel from attacking the validity of that right in subsequent proceedings whether the attack is launched on the same or different grounds.

The decision in *Hormel Foods* seems to have been based on the fact that the two actions in the Trade Mark Registry and the High Court were both invalidity actions even though the grounds for the new attack were different.

2.15.6 Groundless threats of infringement

Under s 74 Patents Act 1953, where an aggrieved person is threatened by another person with proceedings for infringement of a patent, and those threats are unjustified, the aggrieved person may be entitled to the following relief:

- A declaration that the threats are unjustifiable;

- An injunction against the continuance of the threats; or

- Damages suffered as a result of the threats.

If the threatening party can prove that the acts in respect of which proceedings were threatened constitute an infringement of the patent then no relief will be available under this section.

In *Tapley (HL) & Co Ltd v White Star Products Ltd* [1957] NZLR 612, North J held that groundless threats can be made orally, and it is immaterial that the threats were made in a bona fide manner if the allegations are not upheld.

Mere notification of the existence of a patent will not constitute a threat of proceedings.

2.16   Remedies for infringement

If infringement of a patent is established, the following principal remedies are available to the patentee:

- An interim and/or permanent injunction restraining the infringing conduct;

- Delivery up or destruction of infringing product(s);

- Delivery up of any machinery adapted to make infringing product(s); and/or

- An account of profits earned by the infringer, or damages suffered by the owner of the patent.

2.16.1 Injunction

Interim and/or permanent injunctions are usually the principal remedy sought. The grant of injunctions (even in the case of innocent infringement) is provided for in s 68(4). An injunction is often sought in conjunction with damages or an account of profits.

The principles for the grant of an interim injunction most often applied by the Courts are set out in *Klissers Farmhouse Bakeries Ltd v Harvest Bakeries Ltd* [1985] 2 NZLR 129, at p 142:

- Whether there is a serious question to be tried?;

- Where the balance of convenience lies?; and

- What is the overall justice of the case?

The Court in *Klissers* emphasised the need for flexibility in all circumstances and the overriding requirement that the matter must be governed by the interests of justice.

Additional factors to be considered by the Court during an application for an interim injunction were set out in *American Cyanamid Co v Ethicon Ltd* [1975] AC 396 (HL). They include:

- The adequacy of other remedies available, in particular damages;

- Where doubt arises as to the adequacy of damages available to either party, the Court must consider where the balance of convenience lies; and

- Wherever possible a Court should attempt to maintain the status quo (that is, the state of affairs existing immediately before the defendant started the acts complained of).

Several recent decisions of the High Court and the Court of Appeal would seem to suggest that the Courts will give increasing primacy to registered intellectual property rights when determining an application for interim relief. In many cases this seems to be at the expense of seemingly conclusive arguments going to the balance of convenience and the overall justice.

In *Aktiebolaget Hassle v Novartis NZ Ltd* 1/5/03, Potter J, HC Auckland CP51-SW/03, the plaintiffs sought an injunction to restrain Novartis from manufacturing an omeprazole product, PROBITOR, which they believed infringed their Patent No 220096 relating to their own similar product sold in New Zealand under the brand name LOSEC. Novartis resisted the application on a number of grounds including:

(1) That it was strongly arguable that the patent was invalid, the equivalent United Kingdom patent having already been overturned on the grounds of obviousness; and

(2) That it had contracted to supply Pharmac with PROBITOR, and was obliged to pay Pharmac $350,000 per calendar month it was unable to supply same (presumably to compensate Pharmac for being obliged to subsidise the more expensive LOSEC during that period).

While recognising the significant losses likely to be suffered by Novartis if injuncted, the Court nonetheless found that the balance of convenience and the overall justice favoured the granting of an injunction, commenting, at para 43:

> "There is a reality to be recognised in the case of the patent, that the patent confers a monopoly during its currency, the benefit of which runs over to the post-patent period because of the strong market position usually developed during the monopoly period. This was expressed by Eichelbaum J in [*Monsanto Chemical Co v Stauffer Chemical Co (No 2)* (1984) 1 TCLR 129; 1 NZIPR 540]."

And later, at para 56:

> "Premature interference with the monopoly position which the patent confers during its currency will also impact on the ability of the proprietor to create or confirm its own market after the expiry of the patent (the 'bridgehead' opportunity)."

The decision of Potter J was upheld by the Court of Appeal in a decision of Blanchard J delivered on 4 July 2003 (*Novartis NZ Ltd v Aktiebolaget Hassle* [2004] 2 NZLR 721 (CA)).

Similar comments have also arisen in the context of applications for interim injunctions to restrain the infringement of registered design rights. See, for example:

- *Handitags Ltd v Warburton* 12/12/01, Glazebrook J, HC Auckland M1586-SW01, at paras 17 and 18:

  > "However, the main reason put forward by Handitags as to inadequacy of damages is the loss of the ability to manage their practical monopoly situation. This is because, at any stage during such a monopoly, an entry of a competitor can cause permanent damage and permanent inability to manage the monopoly and, in particular, the ending of the monopoly which will obviously occur at the end of the design and copyright period. This diminished advantage can mean a permanent effect which Handitags submits is exceedingly hard to quantify. It is noted that there is only some four years left in respect of the design and five years in respect of the copyright so the loss of a portion of the period at the end of the registration for the design and the copyright period is even more significant. These submissions are accepted. It is accepted that damages would not be an adequate remedy for Handitags."

- *BEP Marine Ltd v Aquatech Marine Ltd* 20/12/02, O'Regan J, HC Auckland M1568-SW02 (which applied *Handitags*).

- *Permanent Promotions Pty Ltd v Independent Liquor (NZ) Ltd* 10/6/04, Heath J, HC Auckland CIV-2004-404-2419, at paras 38 and 39:

  > "In my judgment, the scheme of the Act is clear. A Commissioner is appointed to examine designs submitted to him or her. In the course of that examination the Commissioner determines questions of novelty and compliance with statutory definitions. The underlying assumption is that the Commissioner is someone experienced in applying the Act and in making judgments of that sort. The scheme of the Act would be undermined significantly if the Courts failed to recognise the nature of the monopoly that flows from the registration process. In this case the design has been registered. I reject Mr Brown's submission that the Register is prima facie evidence only of what is contained in it rather than the fact that the Commissioner has found the design to comply with the definition contained in s 2(1) of the Act and has found the requisite degree of novelty. No item can be registered unless those conclusions have been drawn. That registration confers a monopoly. On an interim injunction application the Court must be slow to second guess the findings of the Commissioner."

  and, at para 43:

  > "In my view the fact of registration confers a prima facie right sufficient to overcome the hurdle of establishing that a serious question exists to be tried."

If the view expressed by Heath J prevails, then there is considerable advantage to a litigant in having a registered (as opposed to common law) intellectual property right as the basis of the legal proceeding. In particular, it may dispense with the issue as to whether there is a serious question to be tried, and greatly increase the prospects of obtaining interim relief, which in intellectual property cases is more often than not determinative of the proceeding.

However as to balance of convenience and overall justice, some caution needs to be exercised, as the "bridgehead" argument is probably limited to forms of intellectual property in which the rights expire after a finite period. Thus, for example, the bridgehead argument may not be appropriate in a case involving infringement of a registered trade mark. Similarly, if the ownership of the intellectual property is in dispute this may result in refusal of the application: *Golden Homes (1998) Ltd v Blue Chip Construction Ltd* 21/6/05, Allan J, HC Auckland CIV-2003-404-7090. See also *Lesa Systems Ltd v Canzac Ltd* 16/5/06, John Hansen J, HC Christchurch CIV-2006-409-624, at para 34.

It is possible to obtain both Anton Pillar orders and Mareva Injunctions in a patent infringement suit.

An Anton Pillar order is an order made by the Court requiring the defendant to permit the plaintiff to enter and search its premises in order to seize (and therefore preserve) any evidence of infringement.

A Mareva injunction acts to freeze the assets of the defendant until the case has been concluded. This stops the defendant from dispersing its assets during the course of the infringement proceedings in order to defeat any order for damages or an account of profits that might issue at the conclusion of the hearing.

2.16.2 Damages

Section 69 Patents Act 1953 provides the statutory basis for an award of damages. Usually damages are available in all cases unless a defendant can prove he or she was an innocent infringer (discussed at 2.15.4 ("Innocent infringement") earlier in this chapter).

An assessment of damages depends on the facts of each case.

In *Hopkirk v McEwan* (1913) 15 GLR 615 (CA), the defendant was found to have infringed a patent related to a milking machine. Damages were assessed on the loss of sales suffered by the plaintiff with regard to a specific number of machines.

Damages are not available for infringement occurring before publication. However, after publication a patent applicant has the same rights as a patentee: s 20(4). Therefore, although infringement proceedings cannot actually be filed until the Deed of Letters Patent issues, damages run from the date of publication.

Thus, in *Pacific CoilCoaters Ltd v Interpress Assocs Ltd* [1998] 2 NZLR 19 (CA), at p 25, Henry J held:

> "In its terms s 20(4) vests all the privileges and rights in the applicant as if a patent had been sealed. The plain meaning of the words is that the same monopoly rights which are given by a patent are owned by the applicant during the period between publication and sealing."

As only the patentee, or an exclusive licensee, is entitled to bring proceedings for infringement of a patent, it is possible that damages will be limited to those suffered by the patentee/exclusive licensee themselves, rather than other interested parties (such as a non-exclusive licensee or sub-licensee).

See, for example, *Poly-America, LP v GSE Lining Technology Inc* 383 F 3d 1303 (Fed Cir, 2004), in which Poly-America was precluded from recovering lost profits on sales made by a related sister corporation, Poly-Flex, which was a non-exclusive licensee of the patent. There were no sales of the patented products by Poly-America itself. The Court rejected Poly-America's argument that Poly-America and Poly-Flex operated as a single economic unit — primarily on the basis that Poly-America and Poly-Flex could not enjoy the advantages of a separate corporate structure and at the same time avoid the consequential limitation of that structure. Poly-America was also not saved by a clause in its agreement with Poly-Flex which entitled it to collect damages accruing to Poly-Flex, the Court finding that a contract cannot create rights that do not already exist at law. Given that the US and New Zealand concepts of damages are the same, it is arguable that the same result would be reached in New Zealand. Practitioners would be well advised to consider the implications of the *Poly-America* decision upon the relatively common practice of establishing intellectual property holding companies within a corporate group.

Under cl 77 of the draft Patents Bill 2004, a patent applicant has the same rights between publication and acceptance as they would have had if the application had been granted on the date of publication. Proceedings may only be commenced if the patent is actually granted and the allegedly infringing act would, if done after the actual grant of the patent, have infringed the claim of the specification to which the proceedings relate. Proceedings must be commenced within 6 years from the date of the alleged infringement, or 3 years from the date of the actual grant of the patent, whichever is later. It is a defence to these proceedings to show that the claims alleged to have been infringed could not validly have been granted in the form in which they were published (cl 78).

2.16.3 Account of profits

Section 69 Patents Act 1953 specifically provides that a plaintiff is entitled to an account of profits.

The rationale of an award of an account of profits was summarised by the Australian High Court in *Dart Industries Inc v Décor Corp Pty Ltd* (1992) 179 CLR 101; 116 ALR 385 (HCA), at pp 114-115; p 390:

> "The equitable principle of an account of profits is not to compensate the plaintiff, nor to fix a fair price for the infringing product, but to prevent unjust enrichment of the defendant."

Like an award of damages, an account of profits is not available in the following circumstances:

• Where the defendant is an innocent infringer; or

• Where the acts of infringement were carried out before the publication of the acceptance of the patent application.

The remedy of account of profits is not frequently sought because of the difficulty in calculating profits earned by the defendant as a result of the infringement.

2.17 Appeals

Under s 97 appeals against decisions of the Commissioner are to the High Court. Unless leave of the High Court is obtained there are limited rights of appeal to the Court of Appeal (s 98)

Under cl 268 of the draft Patents Bill 2004, a person aggrieved by a decision of the Commissioner may appeal to the High Court, and a decision of the High Court may be appealed to the Court of Appeal (cl 273). There does not appear to be a right of appeal to the Supreme Court in the draft Bill.

In *Sealed Air NZ Ltd v Machinery Developments Ltd* 25/8/04, MacKenzie J, HC Wellington CIV-2003-485-2274, MacKenzie J accepted, at para 7, that the principles to guide the Court on appeals from decisions of specialist bodies are correctly stated in *McGechan on Procedure*, Wellington, Brookers, 1988, at para HR718.03, as follows:

"(a)   The Court is not bound to accept the [Commissioner's] findings of fact;

"(b)   Although the Court must exercise its own judgment, it ought to give proper weight to the expressions of opinion by experienced professionals; and

"(c)   The onus lies on the appellant to satisfy the Court that the decision was wrong."

MacKenzie J adopted, at para 9, the approach taken by Barker J in *Beecham Group Ltd v Bristol-Myers Co (No 2)* [1980] 1 NZLR 192, where his Honour stated, at p 213, specifically in relation to appeals in patent matters, that appeals to the Court from the Commissioner are by way of rehearing and the Court shall have and may exercise the same discretionary powers as are conferred upon the Commissioner. Although Barker J's comments in *Beecham v Bristol-Myers (No 2)* concerned r 26B Patents Rules 1956 (this rule was subsequently repealed and has now been replaced by r 725ZW High Court Rules), the same principles appear to apply. Rule 725ZW states:

"An appeal to the Court shall be by way of rehearing, and the evidence used on appeal shall be the same as that used before the Commissioner, and no further evidence shall be given, except with the leave of the Court."

The applicability of r 725ZW was confirmed in *Merck & Co Inc v Arrow Pharmaceuticals (NZ) Ltd* 29/9/06, Harrison J, HC Wellington CIV-2006-485-817, at para 5. The decision is also notable for the Judge's comment that, as the evidence led before the examiner was uncontested, and the examiner was not called upon to make any findings on disputed facts, but simply applied the law to the relevant evidence, the "whole position is at large": *Beecham Group Ltd v Bristol-Myers Co (No 2)* [1980] 1 NZLR 192, at p 213.

2.18 Offences

The Patents Act 1953 contains a number of criminal offences, which are discussed below. In practice prosecutions under these sections are rare.

If a company offends against the Act, then its officers are deemed to be guilty of the offence unless they can prove that the offence was committed without their consent, and they exercised due diligence in ensuring the offence did not occur: s 108.

2.18.1 Falsification of the Register

Section 105 Patents Act 1953 states that any person who makes, or causes, a false entry in the Register commits an offence under the Act.

The offender is liable upon conviction to imprisonment for a term not exceeding 2 years.

2.18.2 Unauthorised claim of patent rights

Under s 106(1) Patents Act 1953, a person who falsely represents that he or she (or another) is the patentee of an invention, or has applied for patent protection, is liable on summary conviction to a fine not exceeding $200.

Under s 106(2) of the Act, a person who falsely represents that an article sold by them is patented, or the subject of a patent application, in New Zealand is liable on summary conviction to a fine not exceeding $100.

2.18.3 Protection of Royal Arms

Under s 107 Patents Act 1953, the grant of a patent does not authorise the patentee to use a representation as specified in the Flags, Emblems, and Names Protection Act 1981.

2.19 Patent attorneys

Sections 100-104 Patents Act 1953 regulate patent attorneys. Compare cls 179-246 of the draft Patents Bill 2004.

2.19.1 Qualification

In order for a person to qualify to register as a patent attorney he or she must:

• Be of good character;

• Have worked in a patent attorney practice for 3 years, unless he or she is a solicitor; and

• Pass the prescribed exams administered by the New Zealand Institute of Patent Attorneys; or

• Qualify under CER (as a patent attorney in Australia).

Compare cl 190 of the draft Patents Bill 2004.

2.19.2 Patent attorney practice

Section 103(3) Patents Act 1953 provides that patent attorneys have the exclusive right to undertake for gain the:

• Application for, and obtaining of, patents in New Zealand or elsewhere;

• Preparation of specifications or other documents for the purposes of the Act; or

• Giving of advice (other than of a technical or scientific nature) as to the validity of patents or their infringement.

Compare cls 181(3) and 189 of the draft Patents Bill 2004.

Under s 103(5) barristers and solicitors are not excluded from giving professional advice or taking part in proceedings under the Act.

Compare cls 187 and 188 of the draft Patents Bill 2004.

2.19.3 Undertaking practice of patent attorney for gain

Any person who is not a registered patent attorney, or working for a patent attorney practice, and undertakes the practice of a patent attorney is liable on summary conviction to a fine not exceeding $200. Compare cl 181(4) of the draft Patents Bill 2004.

2.19.4 Registration

Upon qualification and payment of the appropriate fee a person may be appointed to the register as a registered patent attorney.

IPONZ publishes a list of registered patent attorneys in the Journal each month

2.19.5 White paper on patent attorney profession

A cabinet white paper was released in July 2003 regarding regulation of the patent attorney profession. For a summary of the white paper recommendations see 2.22.2 ("Regulation of the patent attorney profession") later in this chapter.

2.20 Intellectual Property Office of New Zealand ("IPONZ")

The Patent Office is appointed under s 5 Patents Act 1953 to administer the provisions of the Act. The trading name of the Patent Office is the Intellectual Property Office of New Zealand ("IPONZ").

In accordance with s 3 of the Act, the Commissioner of Patents is appointed under the State Sector Act 1988.

Compare cl 280 of the draft Patents Bill 2004.

2.20.1 The Journal

The "Journal" is defined in s 2 Patents Act 1953 as:

> "the Patent Office Journal published under subsection (1) of section 112 of this Act:"

The Journal is published monthly and contains particulars of all patent applications including:

- The number and date of the application;
- The name of the applicant;
- The name of the inventor; and
- The short title of the invention.

All accepted applications are notified in the Journal. Most details of the application and an abstract of the patented invention are published.

The Journal also contains other information relevant to patent protection in New Zealand, for example, notification of gazetted exhibitions (see 2.7.2(2)(a) ("Exceptions to prior use") earlier in this chapter), or practice notes.

Compare cls 260 and 261 of the draft Patents Bill 2004.

2.21   The Register

Section 83(1) Patents Act 1953 requires IPONZ to keep a Register of Patents ("the Register"). The Commissioner is also required to keep a patents register under cl 247 of the draft Patents Bill 2004.

The Register holds details of:

- Patent applications and granted patents;

- Assignments and transmissions of patents;

- Licences; and

- Any other matter IPONZ is required to keep by the Act.

The Register is open to public inspection. IPONZ currently has an online version of the Register, which is accessible at www.iponz.govt.nz. Through this database the public is able to access the above information found on the Register.

2.22   Future developments

2.22.1 Draft Patents Bill 2004

In March 2002, the Ministry of Economic Development released a discussion paper entitled *Review of the Patents Act 1953: Boundaries to Patentability* ("the Report"). After receiving and reviewing submissions on the Report, in December 2004 the Ministry released an exposure draft of the draft Patents Bill 2004 ("the draft Bill") for consultation. The deadline for submissions on the draft Bill was 11 March 2005. The draft Bill codifies the requirements for patentability of an invention, including certain common law exclusions. In particular, it creates an absolute novelty standard, introduces a usefulness requirement for patentability, and distinguishes the public policy and morality exclusions from the exclusion relating to methods of treatment of human beings. Plant variety rights, human beings, and biological processes for generating human beings would also be excluded from patentability.

The absolute novelty requirement also excludes from patentability an imported invention which has been made available to the public in a foreign jurisdiction, ie invention by importation would no longer be permitted.

Only the true and first inventor of an invention the subject of a patent application, or their personal representative or assignee, may apply for a patent in respect of that invention under the draft Bill.

The draft Bill imposes a new duty upon patentees to provide the Commissioner with the results of any documentary searches in foreign jurisdictions relating to the same invention the subject of a New Zealand patent application.

The patentee must file a Notice of Entitlement of a patent prior to acceptance, and within 18 months from the date of the Examiner's first report as to the patentability of the invention and compliance of the specification with statutory requirements. This procedure appears to replace the current requirement to obtain the seal of the Patents Office on the patent application prior to the grant of a patent.

The draft Bill replaces opposition proceedings with re-examination proceedings before the Commissioner. Under the draft Bill, any person may initiate re-examination proceedings on the limited grounds that an invention lacks novelty or an inventive step, either before acceptance, after acceptance but before grant, or after the grant of a patent.

Any third party that initiates re-examination proceedings must provide reasons for their assertions, and the Commissioner must take notice of the same when re-examining the patent application. However, there is currently no requirement for the Commissioner to take notice of the patentee's submissions as to the patentability of the invention in re-examination proceedings (although it is assumed he will in fact do so).

There do not appear to be any limits to the grounds for which a Commissioner may re-examine a patent of his or her own initiative. Furthermore, he need only report on the patentability of the invention with regard to whether the invention is novel or involves an inventive step. Whether he is required to report on other grounds remains unclear.

Patent applicants must be given a reasonable opportunity by the Commissioner to amend a specification in order to overcome an objection relating to a lack of novelty or inventive step, provided they have not breached the new duty to provide the Commissioner with the results of any documentary searches about the invention in foreign jurisdictions. When making such amendments, the patentee does not appear to be bound by new statutory restrictions regarding the amendment of specifications after acceptance.

There is currently no requirement for the Commissioner to give the patentee a reasonable opportunity to amend the specification to remove any other ground of objection. It appears that the Commissioner may simply revoke the patent if the invention is not patentable on other grounds.

The draft Bill permits any person to apply for revocation proceedings before the Commissioner, or the Courts, on the broad grounds of patentability and compliance of the specification with statutory requirements. This appears to be the first opportunity for third parties to object to the grant of a patent for reasons other than that the invention lacks novelty or an inventive step. The Bill does not distinguish between the grounds for revocation proceedings available before the Commissioner or the Court.

While a person may apply to the Commissioner for re-examination of a patent after acceptance and grant on the grounds only that it lacks novelty or an inventive step (which may result in revocation), that person may also apply to the Commissioner or the Court for revocation of the granted patent on any ground of patentability or by reason of the non-compliance of the specification with statutory requirements. This appears to be an unintended anomaly.

In addition, the Commissioner may refuse an application for revocation that is vexatious, but not a vexatious request for re-examination of a patent.

A person applying to the Commissioner to revoke a patent is entitled, along with the patent applicant, to a hearing before the Commissioner. Evidence must be submitted in the form of written affidavits, although the Commissioner retains his or her discretion to hear oral evidence and permit cross-examination of witnesses. The rules of procedure at such a hearing would be subject to the Commissioner's discretion. In revocation proceedings before the Court, evidence may be submitted orally and would be subject to cross examination, discovery and the strict rules of evidence applied by the High Court.

The Commissioner does not appear to have the power to remit a revocation hearing to the Court, nor the Court to seize it from the Commissioner. However, if a relevant patent proceeding is pending in any Court, an application to the Commissioner to revoke the patent may only be made with leave of the Court.

A person aggrieved by a decision of the Commissioner may appeal to the Court, and a decision of the Court may be appealed to the Court of Appeal in limited circumstances. There does not appear to be any right of appeal to the Supreme Court within the draft Bill.

As the Commissioner has concurrent jurisdiction with the High Court with regard to revocation proceedings, the principle of res judicata may prevent a full appeal hearing in the High Court of a Commissioner's decision in revocation proceedings.

Clause 3(1)(b) of the draft Bill states that one of its purposes is to give greater certainty that the patent is valid. However, by replacing opposition proceedings with limited re-examination proceedings, and expanding the grounds of revocation to reflect new requirements for patentability, the validity of a granted patent is likely to be more vulnerable under the draft Bill than under the Patents Act 1953.

The draft Bill defines infringement of a patent as doing anything the patentee has an exclusive right to do under the draft Bill. Under the draft Bill, patentees have the exclusive right to exploit the invention, or authorise others to do the same,. Under the Patents Act 1953, a patentee's right to exclude others from use of the patented invention originates in the Deed of Letters patent and was subject to statute and regulation. That will no longer be the case.

A person also infringes a patent under the draft Bill by knowingly supplying another person with the means to put the invention into effect in a manner that would infringe the patent.

(1)   *Amending the definition of invention*

Currently the definition of invention is found within s 2(1) Patents Act 1953, and broadly encompasses any new method or process of manufacture.

Under cl 13 of the draft Bill, an invention must be a manner of manufacture within the meaning of s 6 of the Statute of Monopolies.

In order to be patentable, the invention must, when compared to the prior art base as it existed at the priority date of the claim, be novel, and involve an inventive step. In addition, the invention must be useful.

Under cl 3 of the draft Bill, for the purpose of deciding whether or not an invention is novel or involves an inventive step, the "prior art base" means all matter (whether a product, a process, information about a product or process, or anything else) which has at any time before the priority date of that claim been made available to the public (whether in New Zealand or elsewhere) by written or oral description, or in any other way.

The broad definition of "prior art base" excludes from patentability an imported invention which has been made available to the public in a foreign jurisdiction, ie invention by importation would no longer be permitted.

Furthermore, for an invention to be patentable, its commercial exploitation must not be contrary to public policy or morality, it must not be a human being or a biological process for the generation of human beings, and it must not be a diagnostic, therapeutic or surgical method for the treatment of human beings, or a plant variety.

Finally, the draft Bill imposes a new duty upon patentees to provide the Commissioner with the results of any documentary searches in foreign jurisdictions relating to the invention the subject of the patent application.

(2) *Maori and the patenting of bio-technological inventions*

The Report recognised that the granting of intellectual property rights, such as patents, may affect Maori rights and interests in traditional knowledge and native plants and animals.

Accordingly, the draft Bill introduces (in cls 283-286) a Maori advisory committee ("the Committee") to advise the Commissioner about whether an invention claimed in a patent application is derived from Maori traditional knowledge, or from indigenous plants and animals, and, if so, whether the commercial exploitation of that invention is likely to be contrary to Maori values. The Commissioner must consider advice from the Committee but is not bound by it.

(3) *New issues and patentability of bio-technology patents*

Biotechnology is defined as the study or manipulation of one or more of the basic components of living things (including tissues, cells, proteins, genes, or DNA) to create new products or technologies.

At present New Zealand allows patents for animals to be granted. However, IPONZ's current practice is to refuse patent applications that would include human beings within their scope.

A previous review of the Patents Act 1953 recommended that New Zealand repeal s 17, which allows the Commissioner to refuse the grant of a patent if it would be contrary to morality. However, this recommendation was made before increased public interest in genetic engineering and the Royal Commission on Genetic Modification. There is a growing line of argument that genes should not be patentable, as they do not meet the requirements for a patentable invention under s 17.

Under cl 15(1) of the draft Bill, human beings and biological processes for their generation are excluded from patentability. Plant variety rights are excluded under cl 15(3) of the draft Bill.

This is discussed further at 2.4 ("Patentable subject matter") earlier in this chapter.

(4)   *Business methods and software*

Currently, if a method or software achieves an artificially created state of affairs that has utility in the field of economic endeavour, then that method or software is patentable.

Both software and business methods are therefore patentable in New Zealand. However, pure methods (ie mere schemes or plans) do not give rise to an "artificially created state of affairs" and as such are unlikely to be granted patent protection.

There has also been considerable criticism of patent offices worldwide regarding examination of such patents for business methods or software. These criticisms are based on assertions that patent offices lack knowledge of both what is new and what comprises the prior art.

At present, at common law, business methods and computer software must be useful to be patentable. This requirement would be extended to the patentability of all inventions under cl 13(1)(c) of the draft Bill. According to cl 10 of the draft Bill, an invention will be useful if it has specific, credible, and substantial utility.

(5)   *Methods of medical treatment of humans*

IPONZ currently refuses patent applications claiming methods of medical treatment of humans. There are, however, several related methods which are deemed patentable, such as cosmetic treatments, second medical use of a known substance, and Swiss-type claims.

The draft Bill has adopted an exclusion relating to methods of medical treatment corresponding to art 27 of the TRIPS Agreement, to which New Zealand is a signatory. Under the draft Bill, diagnostic, medical or surgical methods for the treatment of human beings are not patentable inventions.

(6)   *Stringency test for patentability*

The Report notes briefly that current practice is to give the patent applicant the benefit of the doubt regarding patentability. Other countries such as Australia and the United Kingdom have adopted a balance of probability approach. The standard is implicitly adopted under the draft Patents Bill 2004.

(7)   *Extension of term for pharmaceutical patents*

The Ministry of Economic Development released a discussion paper in June 2003 entitled "The Pharmaceutical Patent Term in New Zealand" regarding the costs and benefits of patent term extensions.

Until 1994 the Act contained provisions for extending a patent by up to 10 years.

The reasons for allowing extensions of term can be summarised as follows:

* Pharmaceuticals have significant lead times from initial research and development to market. In some cases this process can be longer than the term of any patent protection.

* It would encourage overseas investment and foster relations with companies which may consider research and development operations in New Zealand.

- Some of New Zealand's main trading partners (notably the US, Europe and Australia) have similar term extension provisions. It is thought that enacting similar provisions will enable and enhance commercial relations with these countries.

There is no provision for an extension of term in the draft Patents Bill 2004.

(8) *Genetic material*

In late 2003, Cabinet directed officials from relevant Ministries to prepare a report on the granting of patents for genetic material.

The directive raised concerns that under the present patents regime broad patents for genetic sequences can, and have, been granted. Such patents may have serious implications in terms of:

(1)   Moral, cultural, and economic issues;

(2)   Restrictions upon research and innovation in the genetics field; and

(3)   Implications surrounding the cost of, and access to, health care.

The Ministries were to have reported back in late February 2004.

Notably, genetic material has not been specifically excluded under the draft Patents Bill 2004.

(9) *The progression of the new Patents Bill*

Submissions on the discussion paper closed in July 2002. An exposure draft has been circulated and submissions from interested parties received. A new Patents Bill is currently being prepared by the Ministry of Economic Development for presentation to Parliament. The progression of the Bill will depend on the Government's legislative timetable.

2.22.2   Regulation of the patent attorney profession

In July 2003, a Cabinet white paper proposing to overhaul the patent attorney profession was released from the office of the Associate Minister of Commerce.

The principal recommendation contained within the white paper was that the patent attorney profession should continue to operate under a licensing regime, but with certain modifications to patent attorney practice. The major changes to patent attorney practice that appear likely are:

(1)   Registration as a patent attorney:

- Repeal the current citizenship and age requirements for registration as a patent attorney;

- Allow overseas patent attorney registrations to be recognised in New Zealand; and

- Provide a good character requirement, and prohibit registration of people convicted of dishonesty crimes.

(2)   Regulation of the profession:

- Establish a Patent Attorney's Standards Board to oversee the profession;

- Require a code of conduct be developed and maintained by patent attorneys;

- Implement grounds on which complaints against patent attorneys may be made, specific procedures for making complaints, and establish sanctions which may be ordered following a breach of acceptable standards of service; and

- Establish an independent disciplinary tribunal to determine complaints, and impose sanctions on patent attorneys failing to meet acceptable standards of conduct and/or service.

(3) Patent attorney practice:

- Allow patent attorney practices to trade as limited liability companies, where all directors and shareholders are registered patent attorneys;

- Maintain the current restriction on patent attorney practice whereby parties other than registered patent attorneys are prohibited from preparing or amending patent specifications;

- Increase the maximum fines on summary conviction for people or companies contravening restrictions on trading as a patent attorney;

- Reduce the apprenticeship period from a minimum of 3 years to a minimum of 1 year.

Many of the provisions have been implemented in the draft Patents Bill 2004 (refer cls 179-246).

2.23 References and resources

2.23.1 Websites

Thomson Brookers	www.thomsonbrookers.co.nz
Interim Website of New Zealand Legislation	www.legislation.govt.nz
International Patent Classification	www.wipo.org/classifications/en/index.html
James & Wells	www.jaws.co.nz
Ministry of Economic Development	www.med.govt.nz
Intellectual Property Office of New Zealand	www.iponz.govt.nz
Patents Cooperation Treaty	www.wipo.org/treaties/registration/pct/index.html
TRIPS	www.wto.org/english/tratop_e/trips_e/trips_e.htm
UK Intellectual Property Office	www.ipo.gov.uk
World Intellectual Property Organisation	www.wipo.org

| World Trade Organisation | www.wto.org |

2.23.2 Texts and periodicals

- Blanco White, T A, *Patents for Inventions and the Protection of Industrial Design*, London, Stevens & Sons Ltd, 1983

- Brown, A, and Grant, A, *The Law of Intellectual Property in New Zealand*, Wellington, Butterworths, 1988

- Falconer, D, et al, *Terrell on the Law of Patents* (12th ed), London, Sweet & Maxwell, 1971

- Frankel, S, and McLay, G, *Intellectual Property in New Zealand*, Wellington, Butterworths, 2002

- *Review of the Patents Act 1953: Boundaries to Patentability*, Wellington, Ministry of Economic Development Report, 2002

- *Intellectual Property Forum: The Journal of The Intellectual Property Society of Australia and New Zealand Inc*, Melbourne, Australia

141

Chapter 3

PLANT VARIETY RIGHTS

144

3.1   Introduction

While it is currently possible to obtain protection for new plant varieties under the Patents Act 1953, the primary method of protecting plant varieties is under the Plant Variety Rights Act 1987. The grant of plant variety rights is administered by the Plant Variety Rights Office, now part of IPONZ, Wellington.

Plant variety rights are currently available in New Zealand for varieties of any kind of plant, except algae and bacteria (s 2). A plant variety right will be granted if the variety is new, distinct, homogenous and stable (s 10).

Where the plant variety is:

- A vegetatively propagated fruit or vegetable producing plant, or

- A vegetatively propagated ornamental plant,

the owner of the right may also exclusively propagate the plant variety for the purposes of commercial production of fruit, flowers or other products of the variety (s 17).

3.1.1   Rationale for grant of rights

Plant variety rights provide an incentive to invest in plant breeding in New Zealand. The plant variety rights scheme also allows New Zealanders access to overseas-bred plant varieties, which may not otherwise be released here by their breeders without protection. The result is that farmers, horticultural producers and home gardeners, amongst others, have access to an increasing number and range of plant varieties.

3.1.2   Meaning of "variety"

Following international custom, the word "variety" is used in the sense of a cultivar or cultivated variety, and not in the sense of a botanical variety (as defined in s 2).

3.2   Legislation, treaties and conventions

3.2.1   Governing law

The law relating to plant variety rights is found in the following:

- Plant Variety Rights Act 1987 ("the Act");

- Plant Variety Rights Amendment Act 1990;

- Plant Variety Rights Amendment Act 1994;

- Plant Variety Rights Amendment Act 1996;

- Plant Variety Rights Amendment Act 1999;

- Plant Variety Rights Regulations 1988 and various Plant Variety Rights Orders; and

- Common law expounded by the Courts.

3.2.2 International conventions

New Zealand recognises and conforms to the 1978 Revised International Union of New Varieties of Plants ("UPOV") Convention. It has been a member since 1981.

(1) Convention priority

Section 12 Plant Variety Rights Act 1987 permits a breeder, who has already made an application for plant variety rights in another UPOV country, to claim priority based on that application when filing in New Zealand. If there has been more than one application for the same plant variety overseas, priority can only be claimed in respect of the first application (known as the "originating application"). The originating application should have been filed no more than one year before the date of application in New Zealand.

(2) Advantage of claiming priority

The advantage of claiming priority is that the filing date of the originating application is attributed to the New Zealand application. This is important as both damages and provisional protection run from the filing date. These are discussed in more detail at 3.11 ("Infringement of rights") later in this chapter.

(3) Reciprocal rights available

A New Zealand plant variety rights application can also be used as the basis for a priority claim in another UPOV country, with the same effect.

3.3 Rights granted by registration

Under s 17 Plant Variety Rights Act 1987, a plant variety right gives the holder the exclusive right to produce for sale, and to sell, propagating material of the protected plant variety.

In the case of vegetatively propagated fruit and ornamental varieties, s 17(1) grants the rights-holder the additional exclusive right to propagate the protected plant variety for the commercial production of fruit, flowers, or other products of the plant variety.

3.3.1 Rights-holder may grant licences

Under s 19 Plant Variety Rights Act 1987, the holder of a plant variety right may license others to produce (fruit, flowers and other products) for sale, and to sell propagating material of the protected plant variety. Rights-holders commonly collect royalties from the commercialisation of their protected plant varieties. For more information, see 3.7 ("Licences") later in this chapter.

3.3.2 Rights-holder may bring civil proceedings

As with other types of proprietary rights, the holder of a plant variety right may bring civil action against persons infringing it: s 17(4) Plant Variety Rights Act 1987. For example, the holder of a plant variety right is entitled to seek an injunction and/or can claim damages from another person who, without permission, sells seeds or plants of the protected plant variety. Action can also be taken by the holder of a right against someone who sells propagating material of another variety of the same genus or species using the name approved for the protected plant variety. For more information, see 3.11 ("Infringement of rights") later in this chapter.

3.3.3 Rights may be sold, mortgaged, and assigned

Like other personal property, a plant variety right may be sold, mortgaged or assigned to another person or body: s 17(3) Plant Variety Rights Act 1987. For more information see 3.6 ("Assignment") later in this chapter.

3.3.4 Comparison with patent rights

It is also currently possible for plants to be protected by a patent under the Patents Act 1953. The rights of a patent owner are greater than those of the holder of a plant variety right.

For example, the owner of a plant variety right cannot prevent other breeders exploiting another variety bred from the protected plant variety. A plant variety rights-holder also cannot prevent farmers from saving seed from a previous crop in order to sow a new crop. The grant of a patent, however, prevents the exploitation of essentially derived varieties and also prevents farmers from saving seed for their own use.

The following table outlines the similarities and differences between plant variety rights and patent rights:

	Plant Variety Rights Act 1987	Patents Act 1953
Right to prevent others from producing for sale reproductive material of the protected variety:	Yes	Yes
Right to prevent others from selling reproductive material of the protected variety:	Yes	Yes
Right to prevent others from producing and selling varieties bred from the protected variety:	No	Yes
Right to prevent farmers from sowing saved seed:	No	Yes

(Source: NZ Ministry of Economic Development website)

3.3.5 Territory

Registration of a plant variety under the Plant Variety Rights Act 1987 has effect throughout New Zealand. A grant is also effective in Niue and the Cook Islands under the domestic laws of each country.

3.4 Registrable subject-matter

Plant variety rights are available for cultivated varieties of any kind of plant, except algae and bacteria (s 2). The variety must be:

• New;

- Distinct;

- Uniform;

- Stable; and

- Have an acceptable denomination (ie name) under which it will be registered.

3.4.1 New

To be considered new, propagating material, whole plants or harvested material must not have been sold or offered for sale with the agreement of the owner:

- Within New Zealand; more than 12 months before the date of application for plant variety rights in New Zealand;

- Outside New Zealand; more than 6 years before the date of application for plant variety rights in New Zealand for woody plants; or

- Outside New Zealand; more than 4 years before the date of application for plant variety rights in New Zealand for non-woody plants.

It is usual for the owner to take reasonable precautions to see that no sale occurs that can destroy novelty.

(1) *Exceptions to novelty requirements*

The rules relating to novelty do not apply in certain circumstances. They include:

- Where the sale is part of a contractual arrangement for increasing the applicant's stock under which all of the material produced and any unused propagating material becomes or remains the property of the applicant;

- Where the sale is part of a contractual arrangement for carrying out evaluation trials or tests; or

- Where plant material produced during the breeding, increasing of stock, and trials or tests of the variety, and not required for testing purposes, is disposed of for non-propagating purposes.

3.4.2 Distinct

The plant variety must be distinct from all commonly known plant varieties existing at the date of application, in one or more of the following characteristics:

- Morphological (such as shape, colour);

- Physiological (such as disease resistance); or

- Other (such as commercial application, ie the milling characteristic of a new wheat variety).

3.4.3 Uniform

The plant variety must be sufficiently constant in form or character with regard to the sexual reproduction or vegetative propagation of the plant variety.

3.4.4 Stable

The plant variety will be considered stable if its essential characteristics remain true to its description after repeated reproduction or propagation.

3.4.5 Denomination

Applicants must propose a name for the plant variety on application (s 5(2) Plant Variety Rights Act 1987). This must conform to the internationally accepted UPOV recommendations on variety denominations.

(1) *Correlation with registered trade marks*

The denomination cannot be registered as a trade mark under the Trade Marks Act 2002. This is primarily because people may need to validly use the varietal name in the course of trade and should be able to do so without fear of trade mark infringement.

For similar reasons, no other trade mark must be associated with the denomination unless the denomination is clearly recognisable (s 22 Plant Variety Rights Act 1987).

3.5 Ownership

Under s 2 Plant Variety Rights Act 1987, an applicant for plant variety rights must be the owner of the new plant variety. The applicant will usually be:

- The breeder or discoverer of the plant variety;
- The successor-in-title of the breeder or discoverer of the plant variety;
- The employer of the breeder or discoverer of the plant variety; or
- An assignee of the breeder or discoverer of the plant variety.

3.5.1 Agents may be appointed

An application can be made by an agent (such as a patent attorney or lawyer) on behalf of the owner, provided the Commissioner is satisfied that the agent has the necessary authority to act for the owner.

3.5.2 Proof of assignment required

An assignee can only file in his or her own name if proof of assignment from the breeder is also supplied (in order to establish ownership). For more information, see 3.6 ("Assignment") below.

3.6 Assignment

The right to apply for a plant variety right, the application itself, and the plant variety right once granted, can be assigned like any other item of personal property. An assignment of the plant variety right is made under s 17(3) Plant Variety Rights Act 1987. An applicant claiming to be the successor-in-title of the breeder needs to supply the Commissioner with sufficient written evidence to establish the assignment of rights and ownership.

Likewise, any change of name or address should be recorded with IPONZ as soon as practicable after the change (see 3.10 ("Duration and annuities") later in this chapter).

3.7 Licences

As with other personal property, and under s 19 Plant Variety Rights Act 1987, a plant variety rights-holder can issue a licence to another to grow and / or sell a propagated plant variety. The rights-holder can settle the terms of the licence, and can take action against infringers of the licensed plant variety rights. These plant variety rights are the responsibility of the rights-holder. The Commissioner has no power to intervene in licensing arrangements under normal circumstances. The one exception is in connection with applications for a compulsory licence, or a compulsory sale order, under s 21 Plant Variety Rights Act 1987.

3.7.1 Compulsory licences

On application by an interested person the Commissioner will consider whether a reasonable quantity and/or quality of protected material is available for purchase by members of the public at a reasonable price (s 21(2) Plant Variety Rights Act 1987). If there is not, the Commissioner may make suitable orders, including an order that the plant variety right be licensed to any interested person.

(1) *No application for 3 years from grant*

An application for a compulsory licence cannot be made until 3 years after the granting of a plant variety right.

(2) *Licence may be revoked*

As with compulsory patent licences, under s 21(7) Plant Variety Rights Act 1987, the rights-holder may apply to the Commissioner to revoke or vary the compulsory licence in the event he, she, or it begins selling a reasonable quantity/quality of the plant variety.

3.8 Obtaining grant of rights

3.8.1 Search

The following information/documentation can be obtained from searches of New Zealand's plant variety rights ("PVR") records:

*   Copies of application forms;

*   Technical descriptions (which include descriptions of the variety accompanying any application for PVR);

*   Objective descriptions (which are detailed descriptions of the particular variety by the examiners); and

*   Copies of grant documents.

3.8.2 *New Zealand Plant Variety Rights Journal*

Under s 34 Plant Variety Rights Act 1987, the *New Zealand Plant Variety Rights Journal* is published quarterly by the Plant Variety Rights Office (IPONZ). The journal contains details of applications for, and grants of, plant variety rights, notice of any legislative changes, and general information about plant variety protection in other countries.

(1) *Publication constitutes public notice*

The publication of details of applications and grants in the *New Zealand Plant Variety Rights Journal* constitutes public notification (required under the Act) in order to inform interested persons who may wish to lodge formal objections. It also satisfies the requirements of the UPOV Convention and, in particular, helps to avoid the duplication of approved variety denominations.

3.8.3 Filing requirements

The filing requirements for a plant variety right are covered by s 5 Plant Variety Rights Act 1987.

The filing requirements are described below for:

- All varieties;

- Crop, pasture, amenity grass and vegetable varieties; and

- Fruit, ornamental and tree varieties.

(1) *All varieties*

The following is required under s 5 Plant Variety Rights Act 1987:

- Full name(s) and address(es) of the owner(s);

- Common name and botanical name of the plant variety;

- Proposed denomination (the name under which the grant of plant variety rights is to be registered) and/or breeder's reference and commercial synonyms (if any) (s 5(2));

- Full name and address of original breeder(s) — if other than the owner(s);

- Details of applications for plant variety protection made in other countries (s 12), including:

    - Country;

    - Application date;

    - Application number;

    - Stage of application, and

    - Denomination (or breeder(s) reference).

- Certified correct copy of the overseas application from which priority is claimed (if any) (s 12);

- If an agent is filing on behalf of the applicant, an authorisation of agent form is also required (s 5(1)); and

- A technical questionnaire including information on the technical aspects of the new variety defining the distinctness, uniformity/homogeneity and stability (s 5(1)).

(2) Crop, pasture, amenity grass, and vegetable varieties

(a) Seed sample and germination certificate

For crop, pasture, amenity grasses, and vegetable varieties, in addition to the requirements for all varieties (discussed at 3.8.3(1) ("All varieties") earlier in this chapter), the applicant for plant variety rights must also supply a seed sample and a germination test certificate.

The seed sample must:

- Be fresh and of the highest possible viability. A minimum germination level is required depending on the kind of plant;

- Not have been subject to any chemical treatment;

- Be free of disease and insect contamination;

- Have purity meeting basic seed standards; and

- In the case of cereals, include at least 50 ears of the variety in sound condition.

The germination test certificate must be issued no earlier than 3 months before supplying the seed.

(b) Objective description

Where the new plant variety is protected by plant variety rights outside of New Zealand, and a detailed description prepared by the Overseas Rights Authority is available, then confirmation that the description is the same when plants of the plant variety are grown in New Zealand may be sufficient. Alternatively, recorded values may be altered according to observation of locally grown plants.

(c) Other information

Statements are required as to distinctness, uniformity/homogeneity and stability. Information on the origin and the breeding history of the variety is also required. This is usually incorporated into the technical questionnaire.

(3) Fruit, ornamental, and tree varieties

For fruit, ornamental, and tree varieties, in addition to the requirements for all varieties (discussed at 3.8.3(1) ("All varieties") earlier in this chapter), the applicant must also supply:

- Colour photographs; and

- A statement as to distinctness, uniformity/homogeneity and stability.

(a) Colour photographs of the fruit, ornamental, or tree

Photographs should:

- Characterise, and be capable of identifying, the new variety;

- Preferably include representations of the plant as a whole, as well as flowers, fruit and any distinguishing characteristics of the variety, to illustrate the variety's distinctness;

- Be of the F1 generation, as opposed to the parent plant, to indicate the variety's stability and uniformity; and

152

- Be clear and in focus.

(b)   *Other information*

Statements as to distinctness, uniformity/homogeneity and stability, and information on the origin and the breeding history of the variety, are usually incorporated into the technical questionnaire.

3.8.4 Evaluation of applications

The usual procedure for securing plant variety rights protection in New Zealand is summarised below.

(1)   *Evaluation and detailed description*

Growing plants of the claimed new variety are assessed to verify details provided in the application. A detailed botanical description of the new plant variety is prepared by the plant variety rights examiner.

The procedure for evaluation of a plant variety will depend on the particular plant in question. The evaluation period will vary, depending on the kind of plant and the corresponding growing season.

(2)   *Overseas recommendations accepted*

Recommendations of an overseas plant variety rights authority are accepted without requiring assessment of plants in New Zealand. If further material is required, the Plant Variety Rights Office will issue a request for this information and will set a deadline by which this must be received.

(3)   *Recommendation to Commissioner*

The examiner then recommends to the Commissioner whether a grant of plant variety rights ought to be made on the basis of the results of the variety evaluation.

(4)   *Decision subject to appeal*

An unfavourable determination can be appealed to the District Court. For more information see 3.9.2 ("Objections") and 3.9.3 ("Appeals from decisions of the Commissioner") later in this chapter.

3.9 Grant of rights

Under s 10 Plant Variety Rights Act 1987, when the Commissioner is satisfied that a plant variety meets the criteria for plant variety rights, the applicant is advised and a grant of plant variety rights issues on payment of the grant fee.

3.9.1 Publication

Under s 34 Plant Variety Rights Act 1987, the following details are published in the *New Zealand Plant Variety Rights Journal* upon acceptance of the application:

- Application number;
- Date of application;

- Details of owner or breeder;

- Address for service; and

- Proposed denomination,

The journal is published quarterly. For more information see 3.8.2 ("New Zealand Plant Variety Rights Journal") earlier in this chapter.

Before the granting of the plant variety right, the accepted application and accompanying documents are available at the Plant Variety Rights Office for public inspection. For more information, see 3.8 ("Obtaining grant of rights") earlier in this chapter.

3.9.2 Objections

Under s 6 Plant Variety Rights Act 1987, any person may lodge an objection in writing with the Commissioner:

- Against an application, if the person objecting considers that a proposed denomination should not be accepted (s 6(1)). This must be lodged within 3 months of publication in the *Plant Variety Rights Journal.*

- Against an application or grant of plant variety rights at any time before grant, if the person objecting considers that the applicant is not the rightful owner of the plant variety (s 6(2)). For more information, see 3.5 ("Ownership") earlier in this chapter.

- Against an application or grant of plant variety rights at any time before grant, if the person objecting considers that the variety is not new, not sufficiently distinct, not uniform/homogeneous and/or not stable (s 6(3)). For more information, see 3.4 ("Registrable subject-matter") earlier in this chapter.

In addition, an objection may be made at any time against the making of a grant on the grounds that it contravenes the requirements of the Act.

3.9.3 Appeals from decisions of the Commissioner

Under s 23 Plant Variety Rights Act 1987, within 28 days of receiving any decision of the Commissioner, the applicant (or any other interested party) may appeal on any point relating to:

- An application;

- The declining or cancelling of a grant;

- Imposing a condition on, or declining to modify any aspect of a grant; or

- The issue, variation or revocation of a compulsory licence or sales order.

Under s 24 of the Act, such appeals are made in writing to the District Court.

3.10   Duration and annuities

3.10.1 Duration

Under s 14(2) Plant Variety Rights Act 1987, plant variety rights are granted for a term of either 20 years for non-woody plant varieties, or 23 years for woody plant varieties. The term begins on the date when the plant variety rights are granted: s 14(1).

3.10.2 Annual fees

For plant variety rights to remain in force renewal fees are payable each year on the anniversary date of the grant (s 16(2) Plant Variety Rights Act 1987).

Under s 16(3) of the Act, an extension of time of one month for payment of the annual renewal fee is available, but a surcharge or penalty is currently added. If payment is not made during the one-month extension, the Commissioner will cancel the grant under s 16(2).

The Plant Variety Rights Office generally sends a reminder (by way of an invoice) one month before the due date of the renewal fee (s 16(3)). Hence it is important to ensure that the address for service of notices under the grant is accurate and up-to-date.

3.11   Infringement of rights

Under s 17 Plant Variety Rights Act 1987, the rights-holder has the exclusive right to produce for sale, and to sell, reproductive material of the protected plant variety. The holder also has the exclusive right to propagate the plant variety for the purposes of commercial production of the fruit, flowers, and other products of that plant variety; and the right to import reproductive material into New Zealand.

In *Cropmark Seeds Ltd v Winchester International (NZ) Ltd* 28/9/04, John Hansen J, HC Timaru CIV-2003-476-8, Robert Winchester (the second defendant and director of the first defendant company) organised unauthorised sales of seeds of Cropmark's protected plant variety "Optic". Cropmark brought infringement proceedings against Winchester and his company under s 17 of the Act. Robert Winchester claimed that he was not liable because he merely organised the sales of seeds without directly participating in the sales. John Hansen J considered whether the proprietary rights granted by the Act might be infringed indirectly, by means of organising sales of the protected variety seeds. His Honour noted, at para 32, that, although undefined in the Act, Cropmark's "proprietary rights" consisted of ownership rights in the protected variety seeds. His Honour held that infringement was a violation of those rights and would not be limited to sale. Otherwise, a person "could blatantly organise sales of seed in clear breach of the plaintiff's proprietary rights, but escape all forms of action from the holder of the proprietary right." His Honour commented "I do not consider that was the intention of Parliament, and there are strong policy reasons why it should be so." He concluded, at para 33, that the intention of s 17 captured a person responsible for procuring breaches of the grantee's rights, thus Robert Winchester was found to have infringed Cropmark's proprietary rights in the protected seed.

The decision was upheld on appeal: *Winchester International (NZ) Ltd v Cropmark Seeds Ltd* 5/12/05, CA226/04. In relation to s 17, the Court of Appeal held, at para 40:

"The clear purpose of s 17(1) is to state the nature of the grantee's right and the fact of its exclusivity. Necessarily implicit is that infringement referred to in subsection 4 entails any conduct having the effect of diminishing the grantee's enjoyment of its exclusive right. The section does not attempt any description of what kind of conduct may have that effect: it is left to the courts to make that judgment as a matter of fact."

3.11.1 Licensee may have same rights

Under s 19 Plant Variety Rights Act 1987, a licensee can have the same rights as the holder of a plant variety right. This includes the right to take proceedings in respect of any infringement of the rights committed after the granting of the licence.

3.11.2 Provisional protection

Section 9 Plant Variety Rights Act 1987 grants an applicant interim protection for the candidate plant variety while the application is under consideration. Provisional protection starts once an application has been made and ceases to have effect when the Commissioner either issues the grant of the plant variety rights or refuses the application. While provisional protection is in effect, an applicant who has released the plant variety commercially is entitled to take legal proceedings against anyone whose actions would infringe the plant variety right were it granted.

It is important to note that if the plant variety right is refused, the provisional protection becomes void as of the date of application.

3.11.3 Infringement may involve breach of confidence

In *Franklin v Giddins* [1977] 1B IPR 807 (Qld SC), the Supreme Court of Queensland found that the misappropriation of bud-wood of a unique variety of nectarines amounted to a breach of confidence. The plaintiffs conducted an orchard where they grew "Franklin Early White" nectarines which were highly successful from a commercial point of view primarily because they ripened earlier than conventional fruit. As a matter of genetics it was impossible to repeat the cross-breeding programme followed by the plaintiff in producing the nectarines except by grafting the plaintiff's bud-wood cuttings to root stock. The defendant knew that the plaintiff's bud-wood was not for sale and stole bud-wood cuttings from the plaintiff's orchard. By carrying out the grafting process, the defendant was able to grow Franklin Early White nectarines in competition with the plaintiff. The Court found that the technique of propagating the variety was a trade secret which had been misappropriated by the defendant, and ordered delivery up of the productive bud-wood to the plaintiff for destruction.

3.12 Exceptions to infringement

While the exclusive rights granted include the right to produce for sale and to sell reproductive material (and in some circumstances to propagate fruit, flowers, or other products), s 18 Plant Variety Rights Act 1987 creates a number of exceptions. They are:

- Any person may propagate, grow or use a protected plant variety for non-commercial purposes;

- Using the plant variety for the purposes of hybridisation to produce a new plant variety, and sale of that new plant variety, is not an infringement of a right; and

- The use of reproductive material from a protected plant variety for human consumption, or other non-reproductive purposes, will also not amount to infringement.

3.13   Remedies for infringement

The right to sue is a personal right, and an infringement is actionable as a personal action (s 17 Plant Variety Rights Act 1987). As such, a rights-holder may apply for an interim or permanent injunction, an award of damages (including additional (exemplary) damages), an account of profits or other relief (s 17(4)).

In considering such relief the Court is likely to take into consideration the following:

- Any loss suffered, or likely to be suffered, as a result of the infringement;

- Any profits or other benefits derived by the person infringing; and

- The flagrancy of the infringement.

Where the plant variety right is licensed, the Court may also take into account the position of the licensee when assessing the level of damages to be awarded.

An action for infringement of a plant variety right can be taken in either the District Court or the High Court.

3.13.1   Innocent infringement

Under s 17(8) Plant Variety Rights Act 1987, if, at the time the infringement occurred, the defendant was not aware of the plant variety right, or had no reasonable grounds to suppose it existed, the rights-holder cannot obtain damages against the infringer.

3.14   Offences

The following are offences under s 37 Plant Variety Rights Act 1987:

- To supply false information when making an application;

- To falsely claim someone to be an applicant or holder of plant variety rights;

- To falsely claim that the plant variety is protected by rights or is the subject of an application when selling material; and

- To sell reproductive material of a plant variety without using the approved denomination.

Any person committing one of the above offences is liable on summary conviction to a fine of up to $1,000 (s 37(7)).

3.15   Legislative amendments

3.15.1   MED Cabinet Paper

In March 2002, the Ministry of Economic Development released a discussion document entitled *Review of the Plant Variety Rights Act 1987*. The paper is available through the Ministry's website: www.med.govt.nz. The paper reviews the rights given to plant breeders under the Plant Variety Rights Act 1987 and considers what changes may be required to take into account recent developments in plant breeding techniques and in international standards for plant variety protection. Other issues considered in the paper include biodiversity and food security, and Maori concerns over the granting of plant variety rights in relation to indigenous plant varieties.

A Cabinet Paper, dated 6 August 2003, outlines the changes recommended by Cabinet, summarised below.

(1)   *UPOV*

Although a member of UPOV (International Convention for the Protection of New Varieties of Plants), New Zealand ratified the 1978 version not the 1991 version. The paper questions whether New Zealand should ratify the 1991 version and amend legislation accordingly.

The principal areas where the Plant Variety Rights Act 1987 ("the 1987 Act") does not extend as far as the 1991 UPOV Convention are:

- The right to authorise propagation is only for the purposes of commercial marketing;

- There is no right to authorise exports and only a limited right to authorise importing;

- There is no right to authorise stocking for any of the above purposes;

- There is no right to any plant varieties essentially derived from the protected plant variety;

- There is no right to any downstream bred plant varieties, unless repeated use of the protected plant variety is required; and

- Farm-saved seed usage is allowed although the term in New Zealand is less than required under the 1991 UPOV Convention.

3.15.2   Maori concerns

The Ministry of Economic Development Cabinet Paper raised particular questions as to Maori concerns regarding granted plant variety rights over indigenous plant varieties or new plant varieties derived from indigenous plant varieties. It also questioned whether there should be specific consultation with Maori or a special provision within the Plant Variety Rights Act 1987 for Maori to object to the granting of plant variety rights on cultural grounds. It is not possible, under either the 1978 and 1991 drafts of UPOV, or the 1987 Act, to refuse the granting of plant variety rights on cultural grounds.

3.15.3 Saved seed

A further contentious issue was whether farmers should be permitted to save seed from protected plant varieties. This is the traditional means by which farmers acquire seed for the following year's crops. There are some who support the unrestricted right of farmers to use saved seed, and some (predominantly rights-holders) who consider it a breach of the plant variety rights of the plant breeder. The suggested options for dealing with this issue included:

- Payment of a full royalty on farm-saved seed;

- Payment of a reduced royalty on farm-saved seed;

- Allowing farmers a limited right to use saved seed; or

- Allowing an unrestricted right.

None of these options took into account the general contractual arrangements that commercial seed suppliers often have with farmers to produce seed, nor any possible existing patent rights. It is common to see an exception in such agreements that seed cannot be saved, and many of the above options threatened to undermine such relationships.

3.15.4 Greater PVR rights than patent rights

The paper considered whether the plant variety rights granted under the Plant Variety Rights Act 1987 should also include a right to authorise export. The proposal that there be a right to authorise export would make the rights granted under the Act stronger than those currently granted to a patentee under the Patents Act 1953. If product is purchased from a patentee in New Zealand, unless there is a contractual arrangement as to the purpose for which the product is to be used (or the area in which it is to be used), the buyer is usually free to deal with the goods as he or she sees fit (in accordance with the doctrines of implied right of use and exhaustion of rights).

3.15.5 Greater control on commercial use

A similar question arose with the right to authorise stocking, propagation, conditioning, selling, offering for sale, or authorising export/import. What happens if a party has stocked up for further offers for sale? Where there has been an authorisation of propagation of a protected plant variety, surely it is implicit that this includes an authorisation to stock for this purpose. At present, the Plant Variety Rights Act 1987 does not include such authorisation, but in ratifying the 1991 UPOV Convention New Zealand would have to allow this additional right. This may give the rights-holder considerable power to control the business of a seed propagator or others working commercially downstream of a seed or plant variety rights-holder.

3.15.6 Cabinet recommendations

The following recommendations were made by Cabinet on 28 July 2003:

- That the 1991 UPOV Convention not be ratified, pending the outcome of the WAI262 claim (see below). This was primarily in order to ensure that the Government was not constrained in any future amendments as a result of any decision in that claim;

- Amend the Plant Variety Rights Act 1987 to extend plant breeders' rights in accordance with art 14 of the 1991 UPOV Convention; and

- Amend the Act to incorporate the concept of "essential derivation".

These recommendations, plus a subsequent proposed amendment to s 18, were to allow for the coverage of essentially derived plant varieties under the original plant variety right.

Additional recommendations included:

- Amending the definition of "owner" to remove varieties which are discovered, not bred. This aims to limit the scope of registration of indigenous varieties; and

- Retaining the exemption from infringement for saved seed, but excluding sold varieties from the exemption.

3.15.7 Draft Plant Variety Rights Amendment Bill

Following the aforementioned Cabinet Paper, a draft Bill was prepared for public consultation. An electronic version can be found at www.med.govt.nz/buslt/int_prop/plantvarietyreview/draftbill/index.html.

The aim of the Bill is to amend the existing Act to be compliant with the International Union for the Protection of New Varieties of Plants 1991 Convention (UPOV 91) as well as address issues of indigenous rights arising from the WAI262 Claim. WAI262 is a claim against the New Zealand government to rights in respect of matauranga Maori or Maori knowledge, and indigenous flora and fauna. The claimants say these rights are guaranteed under the Treaty of Waitangi. The claim raises issues in respect of intellectual property rights that have not been addressed before.

The main changes proposed by the Bill are as follows:

- Currently the owner of a variety is defined as a person who bred or discovered the variety. The Bill clarifies that there must be a degree of human input into the development of the variety. Mere discovery is not sufficient;

- The Bill introduces a requirement that the Commissioner, when approving a denomination proposed for a new variety, consider whether the denomination will be offensive to a significant section of the community, including Maori;

- Under the current Act, a grant gives its owner the exclusive right to sell and produce for sale the reproductive material of a protected variety and, if the protected variety falls into specified categories, the exclusive right to propagate that material for commercial production of fruits, flowers and other products. Under the Bill a right holder will have more extensive rights to prevent other people from exploiting the protected variety. These additional rights include the right to prevent other people from producing or reproducing, conditioning for propagation, selling or marketing, or importing or exporting, the reproductive material of a protected variety. They also include the right to prevent other people stocking that material for any of those purposes, or authorising other people to do any of those things;

- Currently the Act prevents the importation of the produce of a protected variety from countries in which it is not possible to obtain the equivalent of a grant under the Plant Variety Rights Act. The Bill gives broader rights in respect of any unauthorised use of such material in New Zealand if the owner has not had a reasonable opportunity to exercise his or her rights in relation to the reproductive material;

- The current Act does not provide any protection for varieties that are predominantly derived from a protected variety (the initial variety) although distinct from it. The Bill introduces the concept of essentially derived varieties ("EDVs") and proposes that the right holder has the same rights in relation to an EDV as in relation to the initial variety. In practice, this will mean that it will be possible for a third party to get a grant in respect of an EDV but they will need the permission of the person who holds the grant of the initial variety in order to exploit the EDV; and

- The proposals to expand the rights of variety right holders in the Bill impact on the ability of farmers to save seed from crops for replanting. The Bill proposes an exception to allow that practice to continue.

The Ministry of Economic Development invited submissions on the draft Bill. The purpose was not to repeat or re-open the policy development process, but rather to determine the practical effects of the proposed changes to help ensure that the legislation gives proper effect to the policy decisions that have already been made, and thus to minimise the risk of unintended consequences of change. Submissions closed on 7 October 2005, although no further action appears to have been taken by the Ministry.

3.16 References and resources

3.16.1 Websites

Thomson Brookers	www.thomsonbrookers.co.nz
Interim Website of New Zealand Legislation	www.legislation.govt.nz
International Patent Classification	www.wipo.org/classifications/en/index.html
International Union (UPOV)	www.upov.org
James & Wells	www.jaws.co.nz
Ministry of Economic Development	www.med.govt.nz
Plant Variety Rights Office	www.pvr.govt.nz
UK Intellectual Property Office	www.ipo.gov.uk
UK Plant Variety Rights Office and Seeds Division of the Department for Environment Food and Rural Affairs	www.defra.gov.uk
World Seed Industry Organisation	www.worldseed.org

3.16.2 Articles and texts

- Plant Variety Rights Office, *Guide to Plant Variety Rights*, Lincoln University Printery, September 1999. Also available at: www.pvr.govt.nz/info.htm.

- *Review of the Plant Variety Rights Act 1987*, Wellington, Ministry of Economic Development, March 2002. Also available at: www.med.govt.nz/buslt/int_prop.html.

- Hallett-Hook, T, "The rivers north of the future: assessing the efficacy of the Draft Plant Variety Rights Amendment Bill's essential derivation provision" (2006) 4(7) NZIPJ 151.

- Hampton, D, and Baker, A, "Protecting Plant Breeders' Investment: Patents and New Plant Cultivars in New Zealand" (2000) 2(9) NZIPJ 269.

Chapter 4

COPYRIGHT

165

4.1 Introduction

Copyright is the term used to describe the rights given to creators of various works. Copyright protects the form of expression in an original work.

Copyright aims to balance the rights of copyright owners with the rights of potential users. It protects original works against unauthorised copying, piracy or plagiarism for a limited duration. This protection provides an incentive for authors to create more original works. It also provides them with recognition for their creative efforts. In return, after copyright in a work expires, it falls into the public domain and may be used freely by members of the public.

The ambit of copyright has expanded greatly in recent times with the development of new technologies (in particular digital technologies). Constant advancements and increased dependence on the transfer of information in electronic form have brought new challenges to copyright laws. Rapid reform of copyright laws is currently being considered so that it remains a vital and effective form of protection for creators of new works.

4.1.1 Scope of this chapter

As this text has been written for legal practitioners (primarily for giving advice to businesses) this chapter will mainly focus on the Copyright Act 1994 as it relates to commercial products.

Aspects of the Act that deal with fair use by educational institutions and the like will not be discussed in detail. More comprehensive information can be obtained from the sources listed at 4.16 ("References and resource sites") later in this chapter.

4.2 Legislation, treaties and conventions

4.2.1 Governing law

The law relating to copyright in New Zealand is found in the:

- Copyright Act 1994 ("the Act");

- Copyright Amendment Act 1997;

- Copyright (Removal of Prohibition on Parallel Importing) Amendment Act 1998;

- Copyright Amendment Act 1999;

- Copyright (Parallel Importation of Films and Onus of Proof) Amendment Act 2003;

- Copyright Amendment Act 2005; and

- Decisions of the Courts.

The Act is divided into 11 parts:

- Part 1 — Description, Ownership, and Duration of Copyright

- Part 2 — Infringement of Copyright

- Part 3 — Acts Permitted in Relation to Copyright Works

- Part 4 — Moral Rights

- Part 5 — Dealing with Rights in Copyright Works

- Part 6 — Remedies for Infringement

- Part 7 — Border Protection Measures

- Part 8 — Copyright Licensing

- Part 9 — Performers' Rights

- Part 10 — Copyright Tribunal

- Part 11 — Miscellaneous Provisions

(1) *Overseas case law relevant*

The Copyright Act 1994 substantially complies with the requirements set out in the Uruguay Round Agreement on Trade Related aspects of Intellectual Property Rights ("TRIPS"). The Act also reflects similar provisions contained in the Copyright, Designs and Patents Act 1988 (UK). Therefore, case law from the UK and other Commonwealth countries (such as Australia) is relevant.

(2) *Many provisions unique to New Zealand*

Although the Copyright Act 1994 draws heavily from international conventions and the legislation of other jurisdictions, it contains some notable features that are unique to New Zealand. These differences highlight how far the Act has moved away from its predecessor, the Copyright Act 1962. Some of these include:

- Introduction of cable programmes as a copyright work;

- Specific recognition of copyright in computer programs and multi-media works;

- Broadening of moral rights;

- An absence of copyright in works such as Bills, Acts and regulations, New Zealand Parliamentary Debates, and judgments of any Court or tribunal;

- Introduction of performers' rights; and

- Removal of the prohibition on parallel importing.

Many of these features are discussed in more detail later in this chapter.

4.2.2 Current developments / legislative amendments

In July 2001, the Ministry of Economic Development released two discussion papers entitled "Digital Technology and the Copyright Act 1994: A Discussion Paper" and "Performers' Rights: A Discussion Paper". These papers examined a possible review of the Copyright Act 1994 in relation to digital technology and performers' rights respectively.

(1) *Digital technology discussion paper*

Following submissions in response to a discussion paper entitled "Digital Technology and the Copyright Act 1994", the Cabinet Economic Development Committee ("CEDC") made a number of policy recommendations to Government, and proposed corresponding amendments to the Copyright Act 1994. The amendments proposed by the CEDC included:

- Redefining the term "copying" to clarify its application to digital works;

- Extending copyright protection to all communication works;

- Limiting the potential liability of internet service providers for both primary and secondary infringement in certain circumstances;

- Expanding technological protection measures to prevent interference with copy protection mechanisms (such as prohibiting the supply or manufacture of devices, means or information that could infringe the exclusive rights of the copyright owner);

- Clarification of the extent of the making of digital copies by libraries and archives as a fair use of copyright works; and

- The introduction of protection for Electronic Rights Management Information ("ERMI"), which identifies content protected by copyright and the terms and conditions of its use; and providing criminal penalties for large scale dealings of copyright material where the ERMI has been knowingly removed.

The amendments proposed by the CEDC were designed to ensure that New Zealand's copyright legislation keeps pace with developments in digital technology and is consistent with new international standards. Many of the CEDC's proposals have been taken up in the Copyright (New Technologies and Performers' Rights) Amendment Bill which was introduced into Parliament on 4 December 2006. The stated intention of the Bill is to "clarify the application of existing rights and exceptions in the digital environment and to take account of international developments". It also seeks to create a more technology neutral framework for the Act. Key aspects of the Bill include:

- A limited exception to the reproduction right for transient copying undertaken by computers or communication networks as a result of an automatic or inevitable technical process;

- Extension of the protection currently afforded to signals that carry program content in broadcasts and cable programs to a more technology neutral category of "communication works";

- Repealing s 88 of the Act, which allows cable program services to re-transmit free-to-air television broadcasts without the permission of the broadcaster;

- Limiting the potential liability of internet service providers ("ISPs") for both primary and secondary infringement in appropriate circumstances. In order to achieve this, the Bill introduces a definition of "ISP" and provides an exception to primary infringement where the ISP is merely providing the physical facilities to enable a communication to take place. The Bill also limits secondary liability in respect of caching and storing of infringing material where the ISP does not know or have reason to believe that the material is infringing, and acts within a reasonable time to delete it or to prevent access to it upon obtaining such knowledge. These limitations on liability are not intended to preclude copyright owners from obtaining injunctive relief against ISPs;

- Amending the provisions relating to technological protection measures ("TPMs") to expand the prohibition against the making, importing, hiring, and selling of devices, services or information designed to circumvent "copy protection" so that it covers devices, services, or information that circumvent all economic rights provided to copyright owners including communication rights. This amendment recognises the increasing importance of communication rights and provides an incentive for the provision of on-line and digital services. The Act will also be amended to make it easier for consumers to exercise permitted acts where TPMs have been applied unnecessarily (for example, the zoning of DVD's to restrict their use to certain jurisdictions). This amendment is consistent with New Zealand's position on parallel importation of legitimate goods;

- The Bill introduces a new provision to protect against the intentional removal and alteration of copyright management information ("CMI") and commercial dealing in copyright material where the dealer knows that the CMI has been removed or altered. CMI refers to the information that identifies content protected by copyright and the terms and conditions of use. This information provides copyright owners with a crucial tool in identifying legitimate copies of works and, in turn, identifying pirated copies and their source. CMI does not include those aspects that track the use of the copyright material as this is outside the scope of copyright protection and also raises privacy issues;

- The Bill introduces two new offence sections (each carrying a penalty of a fine not exceeding $150,000 or a term of imprisonment of up to 5 years, or both) for commercial dealing in devices, services, or information designed to circumvent TPM and for commercial dealing in works where the CMI has been removed or altered;

- The Bill seeks to clarify and amend the exceptions to copyright owners' exclusive rights, particularly those relating to fair dealing, library, archival and educational use; and

- The Bill introduces a limited exception permitting decompilation, copying or adapting a computer programme if that is necessary for its lawful use. Perhaps more controversially it also permits format shifting of legitimately acquired sound recordings for private and domestic use (for example the transfer of sound recordings from a CD to an MP3) provided only one copy is made. This amendment will be reviewed after 2 years to determine its impact.

On 27 July 2007, the Commerce Committee released a report recommending the Copyright (New Technologies & Performers' Rights) Amendment Bill be passed with a number of amendments. The amendments include changing the Bill's name to the less cumbersome but more accurate "Copyright (New Technologies) Amendment Bill", the insertion of a new section to clarify that a lawful user of a computer programme may observe, study or test the functioning of the programme under certain circumstances without infringing copyright, and amendments to the "format shifting" recommendation to clarify that the copy must be solely for the personal use of the person who made it (or a member of his or her household) and that person must retain possession of the original recording. A further recommendation would allow copyright owners to contract out of the format shifting sections. Minor amendments were also recommended for the sections dealing with ISP liability and TPMs. Finally, the paper signals the following issues as requiring further review: off-air recordings of television programmes to educational establishments, directors' rights, orphaned works, and access to works for print-disabled persons.

The Bill is likely to be enacted in late 2007.

Further information relating to the proposed amendments can be viewed on the Ministry of Economic Development website.

(2) *Performers' rights discussion paper*

The impact of digital technology on performers' rights, particularly in the music industry, was explored in the Ministry of Economic Development's discussion paper entitled *Performers' Rights: A Discussion Paper*. The Cabinet Economic Development Committee ("CEDC") received and considered submissions in response to that discussion paper, and released a review paper in December 2003.

The CEDC recommended that no substantive changes should be made to the Copyright Act 1994, at this time, but noted that the extension of performers' rights should be reviewed at a later date. The CEDC recommended that Part 9 of the Act be amended to extend a technology-neutral right of communication from copyright to performers' rights. At present, the protection of performers' rights under the Copyright Act is technology-specific, and relates to sound recordings, films, broadcasts, and cable television. Advances in technology have rendered these provisions less than adequate. The amendment recommended by the CEDC would provide greater protection to performers and would take account of technological advances by applying to any form of communication.

The main amendments proposed by the CEDC appear to have been adopted in the Copyright (New Technologies & Performers' Rights) Amendment Bill which was introduced into Parliament on 4 December 2006. The Bill is discussed in more detail in the preceding section.

(3) *The Commissioning Rule, Contracts and the Copyright Act 1994*

In April 2006, the Ministry of Economic Development released a discussion paper entitled "The Commissioning Rule, Contracts and the Copyright Act 1994". Submissions were invited on two issues. The first concerned the adequacy of the so-called "commissioning rule" under s 21(3) Copyright Act 1994 which deals with the first ownership of certain commissioned copyright works. The second related to the question of works being made available subject to contractual conditions particularly in the digital environment. The discussion paper seems to be a response to concerns raised by members of the photographic industry as to the effect of the commissioning rule on the commercial arrangements between photographers and their clients.

Following the first round of submissions, MED released a further discussion paper proposing to abolish the commissioning rule and seeking further submissions on same. This second round of submissions closed on 28 August 2007. On the issue of copyright and contract, the same paper announced that no further action would be taken.

See www.med.govt.nz.

(4)   *Resale royalty rights for visual artists*

The New Zealand Government has been examining international developments relating to a resale royalty right for visual artists and a possible application of such right in New Zealand. The right allows visual artists to receive a royalty payment each time their original artwork is resold. In April 2007, the Ministry for Culture and Heritage prepared a discussion paper entitled "A resale royalty right for visual artists: options for its possible application to New Zealand". Submissions on the discussion paper closed on 22 June 2007. Of the submissions made, most were either in favour of, or neutral toward, the establishment of the right in New Zealand. The Ministry is currently finalising its analysis of the submissions.

4.2.3 International conventions and treaties

New Zealand is a contracting State to the Berne Copyright Convention 1886, having become a party to the Convention in April 1928. The most recent revision was the Paris Revision 1971 (amended in 1979) concerning the requirement that literary, dramatic and musical works be recorded in some form, but not necessarily in writing.

New Zealand is also a signatory to the Universal Copyright Convention and World Trade Organisation ("WTO") Agreement, parts of which relate to copyright protection.

(1)   *Conventions offer reciprocal rights*

International conventions to which New Zealand is a contracting state or signatory provide equivalent copyright protection in New Zealand for works originating overseas. For example, copyright in a manuscript originating from Australia (also a party to the Berne Convention) will be recognised and is enforceable in New Zealand.

Similarly, works originating from New Zealand will be given the same protection in countries that are parties to the Berne Convention, Universal Copyright Convention and WTO Agreement as are afforded to works created in those countries.

(2)   *Internet treaties*

In 1996, the World Intellectual Property Organisation ("WIPO") adopted two treaties — the WIPO Copyright Treaty ("WCT") and the WIPO Performances and Phonograms Treaty ("WPPT") (often referred to together as the "internet treaties"). The aim of the internet treaties is to provide safeguards and improve existing international protection of rights of copyright owners in response to the risks posed by digital technology. The internet treaties provide that owners' rights continue when, for example, the works are transferred into digital form or disseminated over the internet. Copyright owners are also able to use digital technology to protect their rights and to license their works online.

Both treaties came into force in mid-2002.

Some countries, such as the US and Australia, have already ratified both treaties and have made changes to their respective laws (the Digital Millennium Copyright Act (US) and the Copyright Amendment (Digital Agenda) Act 2000 (Aust)). New Zealand has yet to ratify the treaties.

The Ministry of Economic Development released a discussion paper in 2001 and a position paper in 2003, both addressing the impact of digital technology on New Zealand's copyright legislation. The papers, entitled *Digital Technology and the Copyright Act 1994: A Discussion*

Paper and *Digital Technology and the Copyright Act 1994: A Position Paper* respectively, may be accessed at www.med.govt.nz. These papers are discussed in more detail at 4.2.2(1) ("Digital technology discussion paper") earlier in this chapter.

4.3   Subsistence of copyright

Copyright is a property right that vests automatically in certain categories of original works, irrespective of artistic merit. There is no requirement to register copyright in New Zealand, and therefore no cost associated with doing so.

The Copyright Act 1994 is the foundation of all rights in relation to copyright in New Zealand. Copyright is essentially a creature of statute: *Brooker v John Friend Ltd* [1936] NZLR 743, at pp 746-747.

4.3.1   Qualification for copyright

Section 17 Copyright Act 1994 states that for copyright to exist, at least one of the following three qualifications must be met:

- The author is:

  - A New Zealand citizen, domiciled or resident in New Zealand or a body incorporated under the laws of New Zealand; or

  - A citizen, domiciled or resident in, or an incorporated body of, a prescribed country (s 18(1) and (2)); or

- The work was first published in New Zealand or a prescribed country (s 19(1)); or

- In the case of broadcasts or cable programmes, the work was made or sent from a place in New Zealand or any other prescribed country (s 20(1) and (2)).

Where the work is of joint authorship, and authorship is relied upon for qualification, at least one of the authors must satisfy the authorship requirements for the work to qualify for copyright protection (s 18(3)).

4.3.2   Originality

Under s 14(1) Copyright Act 1994, copyright only subsists in a work if it is original.

Section 14(2) provides that a work is not original if:

- It is a copy of another work; or

- It infringes copyright in another work.

(1)   *Low threshold of originality*

The threshold for originality under s 14(1) is not high. It does not relate to artistic or literary merit, nor does it equate with the novelty requirements in patent law. In *University of Waikato v Benchmarking Services Ltd* (2004) 8 NZBLC 101,561 (CA), the New Zealand Court of Appeal held that the determining factor is whether sufficient time, skill, labour, or judgment have been expended in producing the work. The Court also restated the following passage from its own decision in *Wham-O MFG Co v Lincoln Industries Ltd* [1984] 1 NZLR 641 (CA), at p 664:

"The originality that is required by the Act relates to the manner in which the claimant to the copyright has expressed his thought or ideas. The Act does not require that the work be novel in form but that it should originate from the author and not be copied from another work."

Pursuant to s 14(2), a work is not original to the extent that it is a copy of another work. Perhaps self evidently this means that items which have been produced by a reprographic process, or for which minimal effort has been expended in producing them, will not attract copyright and cannot form the basis of a claim for copyright infringement. For example, the manufacturer of a novel chair should sue on the original design drawings underlying the chair rather than the chair itself. That is because the physical product is a reproduction of those design drawings and therefore unoriginal.

Although not specifically mentioned in any judgment, the series of decisions between Holdfast NZ Ltd and Henkel KgaA illustrate the point.

Henkel manufactured and sold adhesive products under the QuickTite brand in New Zealand and the SuperBonder brand in North America. Henkel's products were packaged in blister wrap on a cardboard card, coloured deep blue with red, yellow, and white bands and bold red and blue lettering. Henkel commissioned graphic artists to create design drawings for the packaging, known as the Blue Image Design.

Holdfast had sold adhesive products in New Zealand under the Fixit Super Glue brand since the 1980s. The Fixit products were also packaged in a cellophane blister on cardboard. Until 2002, the card was predominantly coloured red with lesser amounts of yellow and blue. In 2001, Holdfast learnt of the Blue Image Design. Subsequently, it re-branded the Fixit product under the trade mark SuperBonder. The packaging for the SuperBonder product was admitted to have been copied from the Blue Image Design.

Henkel brought proceedings against Holdfast for, inter alia, copyright infringement. The parties settled the dispute without admission of liability on the basis that Holdfast cease using the SuperBonder packaging which incorporated the Blue Image Design. Subsequently, Holdfast re-branded its SuperBonder product Ultra Bonder and commissioned a graphic designer to create new packaging based upon the old SuperBonder packaging.

Henkel again brought proceedings against Holdfast for, inter alia, copyright infringement, alleging the new Ultra Bonder packaging still substantially incorporated Henkel's Blue Image Design.

In the High Court (*Henkel KgaA v Holdfast Manufacturing Ltd* 5/11/04, Harrison J, HC Auckland CIV-2003-404-2641), Harrison J held, at paras 13-15, that the Blue Image Design embodied in the SuperBonder and QuickTite packaging was a new graphic work in the form of drawings or diagrams and was thus an artistic work, and the packaging for the SuperBonder and QuickTite products was a development or modification of the Blue Image Design in which copyright could subsist.

Holdfast challenged the originality of the Henkel's packaging on the basis that it was a copy of the Blue Image Design drawings, ie, there was insufficient skill, labour and talent expended in the production of the packaging as it was a mere facsimile copy of the underlying Blue Image Design drawings. Harrison J rejected this argument. His Honour held, at paras 25-26, that:

> "While I did not hear direct evidence on the point, I have no difficulty in inferring that both the Super Bonder and Quicktite [packaging] are modifications of [the Blue Image Design drawings]. I do not require a witness to inform me that the Super Bonder or Quicktite packaging differs in certain respects from [the] drawings for [other adhesive products manufactured and sold by Henkel] which I have already found to be original. Obvious differences lie in the substitution of different lettering, the inclusion of a yellow strip, the inclusion of photographs and other miscellaneous changes. Of themselves, these differences are sufficient to satisfy me that the packaging is itself original, and represents more than a minimal input of skill, labour and talent on Henkel's part.

> "… The Super Bonder and Quicktite [packaging] cards are, like [the other adhesive products manufactured and sold by Henkel], produced from the same foundation, namely the [Blue Image Design drawings]. They are simply an extension in the process based upon [the Blue Image Design drawings]. I cannot see any reason why copyright should not subsist in them on that basis, especially when they do not infringe Henkel's existing copyright in the original Blue Image Design."

The decision of Harrison J was successfully appealed by Holdfast to the Court of Appeal (*Holdfast NZ Ltd v Henkel KgaA* [2007] 1 NZLR 336 (CA)). Delivering the principal judgment, Baragwanath J rejected the suggestion that copyright could subsist in the Blue Image Design as a new graphic work in a series of drawings or diagrams commenting, at paras 25-26:

> "Copyright can subsist in a series of drawings … But where it is alleged that copyright has been infringed in relation to one of a series of drawings, each drawing must be considered on its own: *UPL Group Ltd v Dux Engineers Ltd* [1989] 3 NZLR 135, 143.

> "Consequently, where copyright in a particular part of a series of drawings is allegedly infringed, whether there has actually been copying can be established only by comparison between the infringing article and the particular drawing in the series. The immediate question is whether Henkel can establish that the whole of its Blue Image Design has been infringed when any specific drawings of QuickTite and SuperBonder deriving from them have not been produced."

His Honour noted that, although Henkel had failed to produce any drawings underlying its QuickTite and SuperBonder packaging, it had produced a series of original drawings relating to the Blue Image Design and asserted that the QuickTite and SuperBonder packaging had its genesis in those drawings. Thus, it was arguable in law that Henkel also had copyright in the unidentified drawings from which the QuickTite and SuperBonder packaging derived. However, whether that had been established in fact was a matter of inference from the whole of the evidence and, while Baragwanath J was prepared to infer the existence of a work underlying both the QuickTite and SuperBonder packaging, there was no evidence that Henkel was the owner of the copyright which might subsist in that work. Accordingly, the claim in respect of both the SuperBonder and QuickTite packaging failed.

A useful summary of the point can also be found in the judgment of William Young P, at para 127:

> "Henkel's case was not assisted by its failure to address in detail the design path which led to the SuperBonder and QuickTite packaging ... I am certainly prepared to infer that there must have been drawings from which the packaging was immediately derived. It is, however, a striking feature of the case that these drawings were not produced. This renders impossible any comparison between them and the allegedly infringing Holdfast Ultra Bonder packaging ...".

Henkel unsuccessfully appealed the decision of the Court of Appeal to the Supreme Court (*Henkel KgaA v Holdfast NZ Ltd* [2007] 1 NZLR 577 (SC)). Although the Supreme Court found fault with the approach taken by Baragwanath J on the question of infringement, it agreed that the works relied upon by Henkel on appeal were not pleaded and that, on a correct comparison, there would have been no infringement even if they were.

For other analogous cases see:

- *AHI Operations Ltd v New Lynn Metalcraft (No 1)* (1982) 1 NZIPR 381, where the plaintiff claimed infringement of a portfolio of drawings of a vertical filing cabinet, of which 11 were original. Although containing minor differences the remaining 41 drawings were deemed not to be original, Thorp J found, at p 387:

  > "The other drawings relating to the card cabinet for which copyright is claimed, all appear to me to be drawings which differ only in dimension from the 11 drawings listed, and in many cases not even to have involved manual copying but to have been produced, at least in part, by photographic copying. Notwithstanding the citation from *Laddie* (supra) set forth above [as to the degree of originality required], I believe it is both unrealistic and unnecessary to regard those drawings as original artistic works; ... because the extent of skill, labour and talent expended in their production is so slight".

- *J & S Davis (Holdings) Ltd v Wright Health Group Ltd* [1988] RPC 403, where the plaintiff sought to rely on a number of sculptures and drawings relating to its dental impression tray products. The drawings and models upon which the trays were based were no longer in existence — although the plaintiff sought to rely on them, as well as some surviving casts which were made in dental stone from the models. The Court rejected, at p 409, the claim to copyright in the casts on the basis that "they were no more than reproductions of the models and could not, in my view, properly be described as original works". The claim to copyright in the drawings was also rejected as they were brought about by tracing sections cut from casts at 10 mm intervals, Whitford J commenting, at p 412:

  > "I do not think that a tracing of so simple a character could sensibly be described as an original artistic work".

- *Watson v Dolmark Industries Ltd* (1986) 1 TCLR 357; 7 IPR 279, where the defendant successfully applied to rescind an order for interim injunction on the basis that the works alleged to have been infringed were not original. The evidence showed that the plaintiff's product (stackable trays which pivoted around a spigot) was virtually identical to an equivalent product sold in the UK. After looking at the differences Tompkins J held, at p 363; pp 286-287, that minor alterations to what were otherwise direct copies of drawings did not show sufficient independent skill and labour to qualify the later works for copyright protection.

(2) *Effort is the determining factor*

When determining whether a work is original, for the purposes of ascertaining if copyright subsists in the work, the Court will usually ask whether sufficient time, skill, labour and judgment have been expended in producing the work.

However, a recent Australian case suggests that the time, skill and labour must relate to the authorship of the work. In *Desktop Marketing Systems Pty Ltd v Telstra Corp Ltd* (2002) 55 IPR 1; [2002] FCAFC 112 (FCA), in determining whether the white and yellow pages of the appellant had been copied, the Court noted the concept of originality correlates with that of authorship. Thus it was held that in manually inputting all of the data from the appellant's pages the infringer did not generate a new copyright work as none of the skill and labour involved related to the authorship of the work.

See also *CCH Canadian Ltd v Law Society of Upper Canada* (2004) 60 IPR 650 (SCC), in which the Supreme Court of Canada posited the test as sitting somewhere between the "sweat of the brow" doctrine and a higher "creativity" standard, at para 16:

> "For a work to be 'original' within the meaning of the Copyright Act, it must be more than a mere copy of another work. At the same time, it need not be creative, in the sense of being novel or unique. What is required to attract copyright protection in the expression of an idea is an exercise of skill and judgment. By skill, I mean the use of one's knowledge, developed aptitude or practiced ability in producing the work. By judgment, I mean the use of one's capacity for discernment or ability to form an opinion or evaluation by comparing different possible options in producing the work. This exercise of skill and judgment will necessarily involve intellectual effort. The exercise of skill and judgment required to produce the work must not be so trivial that it could be characterised as a purely mechanical exercise. For example, any skill and judgment that might be involved in simply changing the font of a work to produce 'another' work would be too trivial to merit copyright protection as an 'original' work."

(3) *Extent of originality relevant*

Although the standard of originality for a work to qualify for copyright protection is undoubtedly low, the extent of originality may still be relevant to the question of infringement. Thus, in *Land Transport Safety Authority of NZ v Glogau* [1999] 1 NZLR 261, at p 271, McGechan J stated:

> "Where the originality is low, it is to be expected that anything other than almost exact reproduction will not support an inference of copyright amounting to infringement, whereas where there is a higher degree of originality in the work an inference of copying will more readily be drawn even where the degree of similarity is less. In this way, the reward in the scope of protection will tend to be related to the degree of originality. Retaining a low threshold for protection therefore presents no real harm."

In *Holdfast NZ Ltd v Henkel KgaA* [2007] 1 NZLR 336 (CA), the Court of Appeal rejected a claim for breach of copyright in a series of drawings embodying a packaging design in part because each of the elements of that design was "part of the common things of life" and therefore required relatively distinct treatment for that collocation to give rise to copyright. Reaching this conclusion the Court relied upon comments from:

- Lord Hoffmann in *Designers Guild v Russell Williams (Textiles) Ltd* [2001] 1 All ER 700; [2000] 1 WLR 2416; [2001] FSR 113 (HL), at para 25:

    "certain ideas expressed by a copyright work may not be protected because, although they are ideas of a literary, dramatic or artistic nature, they are not original, or so commonplace as not to form a substantial part of the work".

- Lord Pearce in *Ladbroke (Football) Ltd v William Hill (Football) Ltd* [1964] 1 WLR 273 (HL), at p 293:

    "The reproduction of a part which by itself has no originality will not normally be a substantial part of the copyright and therefore will not be protected. For that which would not attract copyright except by reason of its collocation will, when robbed of that collocation, not be a substantial part of the copyright and therefore the Courts will not hold its reproduction to be an infringement. It is this, I think, which is meant by one or two judicial observations that 'there is no copyright' in some unoriginal part of a whole that is copyright."

- Tipping J in *Bonz Group (Pty) Ltd v Cooke* [1994] 3 NZLR 216; (1994) 6 TCLR 23, at p 220; p 27:

    "Where ... the Plaintiff relies for its copyright on a collection of individual features, none of which on their own would attract copyright, this has ramifications when it comes to infringement. To infringe in such circumstances the defendant must have used the same or a substantially similar arrangement or collection of the individual features. If the defendant has copied the individual features but has made its own arrangement of them, this will not represent an infringement. That is because the plaintiff has no monopoly in the individual features as such but only in their arrangement or collocation."

The Court of Appeal in *Holdfast* also adopted the comments of Peter Smith J in *Baigent v The Random House Group Ltd* [2006] EWHC 719 (Ch) as to certainty in the subject matter of the monopoly commenting, at paras 44 and 45:

    "To be substantial:

        'there must be certainty in the subject matter of the monopoly given by copyright in order to avoid [in]justice to the rest of the world': [*Baigent v The Random House Group Ltd* [2006] EWHC 719 (Ch)]

    "In that recent decision concerning the book *The Da Vinci Code* the English High Court dismissed a claim for alleged breach of copyright. The Judge accepted the defence submission that:

        'if what is asserted to be infringed is so general that it cannot be certain that would lead to a conclusion that it is such a level of abstraction that no protection should be afforded to it.' "

The decision of the Court of Appeal was upheld on appeal to the Supreme Court (*Henkel KgaA v Holdfast NZ Ltd* [2007] 1 NZLR 577 (SC)). The Supreme Court held, at paras 38 and 41:

> "The threshold for originality is a low one and it can be material for other purposes how original the work is; that is, how much skill and labour has gone into its creation. In general terms, the greater the originality, the wider will be the scope of protection which copyright affords and vice versa ...

> •   •   •   •   •

> "As we observed earlier, it may be relevant for infringement purposes to determine how much skill and labour went into the making of the copyright work. This point can have particular relevance in arrangement cases. The skill and labour which has given rise to the arrangement is what gives the work its originality and if that skill and labour is not great, another arrangement of the same unoriginal underlying features may not have to depart greatly from the copyright arrangement in order to avoid infringement. If the level of originality in the copyright arrangement is low, the amount of originality required to qualify another arrangement of the same elements as original, is also likely to be low. Substantial reproduction of those aspects of the work in which the originality lies must be shown to establish infringement. This is consistent with the purpose of the law of copyright which is to recognise and protect the skill and labour of the author of the copyright work."

The test for infringement is discussed in more detail at 4.10 ("Infringement and enforcement of rights") later in this chapter.

(4)   *Proving originality*

In an action for breach of copyright, the plaintiff must put sufficient evidence before the Court to establish the nature of the materials in which copyright is claimed. See *Wham-O MFG Co v Lincoln Industries Ltd* [1984] 1 NZLR 641 (CA), at p 651:

> "When materials in which copyright is claimed are not produced at the hearing then their nature must be proved by other evidence."

That is not to say that a plaintiff cannot advance a claim if the original copyright work underlying a product no longer exists, or cannot be located. A similar situation arose in *Wham-O*. However, what is required is evidence to prove the form of the materials in which copyright is claimed to subsist, and to link up those materials in a causative chain to the creation of the product put before the Court as evidence of the existence of that work.

Thus, for example, in *Wham-O*, the Court had detailed evidence before it as to the process of manufacture of the products at issue and, as a consequence, any underlying copyright works.

Wham-O was cited with approval in *Fleming v Fletcher Concrete & Infrastructure Ltd* 1/12/06, Wild J, HC Auckland CIV-2005-404-4598, at paras 83-85. Similarly in *Tiny Intelligence Ltd v Resport Ltd* 21/11/05, John Hansen J, HC Christchurch CIV-2003-409-352, a case involving breach of copyright in a toy plastic trumpet and sword produced for the Canterbury Rugby Union, the Court was prepared to accept that the original computerised drawings of the sword could not be produced because of a computer malfunction. Although the Court first regarded that explanation with some suspicion, it was subsequently satisfied after hearing evidence from the person responsible for producing the drawings, reviewing exchanges in emails between the respective parties, and reviewing evidence from the defendant in cross-examination which seemed to show that he accepted the existence and originality of the drawings.

The evidence relied upon by Hansen J in *Tiny Intelligence* can perhaps be contrasted with the lack of evidence in *Henkel KgaA v Holdfast Manufacturing Ltd* 5/11/04, Harrison J, HC Auckland CIV-2003-404-2641. The decision in *Holdfast* was overturned on appeal (*Holdfast NZ Ltd v Henkel KgaA* [2007] 1 NZLR 336 (CA)), in part because the plaintiff had failed to prove ownership of the pleaded works (it had also failed to put the pleaded copyright works into evidence and had asked the Court to infer their existence). The decision of the Court of Appeal was upheld on appeal to the Supreme Court (*Henkel KgaA v Holdfast NZ Ltd* [2007] 1 NZLR 577 (SC)) although on different grounds. The Supreme Court found that Henkel had failed to plead the works alleged on appeal to have been infringed.

4.4 Categories of subject matter entitled to copyright protection

Under s 14(1)(a)-(f) Copyright Act 1994, copyright subsists in an original work provided it falls within one of the following categories:

- Traditional subject matter such as literary, dramatic, musical and artistic works, including:
  - Product design;
  - Software; and
  - Compilations;
- Sound recordings;
- Films;
- Broadcasts;
- Cable programmes;
- Typographical arrangements;
- Multimedia works and CD ROMs; and
- Digital works.

4.4.1 Literary, dramatic, musical, and artistic works

(1) Literary works

A literary work is any work that is written, spoken or sung, other than a dramatic or musical work. It includes a table or compilation and a computer program.

Under s 2(1) Copyright Act 1994, a literary work need not have any artistic merit. This was confirmed by Peterson J in *University of London Press Ltd v University Tutorial Press Ltd* [1916]

2 Ch 601, at p 608, where, considering whether exam papers constituted a literary work, his Honour stated:

> "In my view the words 'literary work' cover work which is expressed in print or writing, irrespective of the question whether the quality or style is high. The word 'literary' seems to be used in a style somewhat similar to the use of the word 'literature' in political or electioneering literature, and refers to written or printed matter."

The Courts have recognised the following as original literary works in which copyright subsists:

- A list of bingo numbers published in a newspaper: *Mirror Newspapers Ltd v Queensland Newspapers Pty Ltd* [1982] Qd R 305;

- Programme scripts of the news and news reporters: *TVNZ Ltd v Newsmonitor Services Ltd* [1994] 2 NZLR 91;

- A directory of names and addresses of lawyers: *Waterlow Directories Ltd v Reed Information Services Ltd* (1990) 20 IPR 69;

- White and yellow pages directories: *Desktop Marketing Systems Pty Ltd v Telstra Corp Ltd* (2002) 55 IPR 1; [2002] FCAFC 112 (FCA) and (for the purposes of an interim injunction) *YPG IP Ltd v Yellowbook.com.au Pty Ltd* 13/7/07, Allan J, HC Auckland CIV-2007-404-2839; and

- Financial data survey results compiled with certain ratios calculated and tabulated for comparison, published for report and sale: *University of Waikato v Benchmarking Services Ltd* (2004) 8 NZBLC 101,561 (CA).

In some cases the literary content of the work protected may be something as simple as selected data displayed under particular headings. Thus, in *University of Waikato* (above), the Court of Appeal, at paras 39-40, cited with approval the decision of the Federal Court of Australia in *Desktop Marketing Systems Pty Ltd v Telstra Corp Ltd* (2002) 55 IPR 1; [2002] FCAFC 112 (FCA). The latter case concerned the alleged infringement of copyright in telephone directories published by Telstra. Desktop admitted copying the data from the directories, but argued that copyright did not subsist in the data. The Federal Court held, at para 160, that copyright subsisted in the directories, even though the labour and expense incurred by Telstra was substantially in collecting, verifying, recording, and assembling the relevant data. The Federal Court also held, at para 180, that copyright subsisted in the headings adopted by Telstra in its directories.

(a)   *Software*

In *International Business Machines Corp v Computer Imports Ltd* [1989] 2 NZLR 395, the Court held that the source code of a computer program is protected by copyright as a literary work. The Court stated, at p 409, that:

> "source code is protected as a written compilation of instructions, expressed in comprehensible mathematics and English."

In that case, the Court held that separate copyright cannot subsist in object code as an original literary work because it is only a series of electrical impulses and therefore is not in printing or writing. However, copyright subsisted in the object code as a translation (ie, a representation of the source code in a form that is machine readable).

Subsequently, a computer program has been specifically included within the definition of a literary work under s 2(1) Copyright Act 1994.

Copyright might also subsist in programmes which have been derived from existing code if sufficient time, labour, skill, and judgment have been expended in the production of the new programme. Thus in *The Callista Group v Zhang* 11/7/05, Laurenson J, HC Auckland CIV-2003-404-5127, the plaintiff, Callista Group Ltd, sued Zhang, a former employee, for infringement of copyright in computer software developed by Callista. The Court held that copyright subsisted in Callista's programmes, notwithstanding that they had been derived from a combination of original code and code from other sources, because the form produced was original and resulted from the time, skill, labour, and judgment of Callista. Zhang's use of the programmes was as a template, ie, he had merely translated Callista's code into another code for a different end purpose. The Court held that this use of the copyright work was an adaptation within s 2 of the Act and thus an infringement.

(2) Dramatic works

A dramatic work includes (but is not limited to) a work of dance or mime and a scenario or script for a film. The definition does not include films themselves.

The Courts have attempted to expand on this definition, suggesting that while a dramatic work does not have to be in the nature of a play there is a minimum requirement of some type of performance. In *Green v Broadcasting Corp of NZ* [1988] 2 NZLR 490 (CA), an action for copyright infringement in the scripts and dramatic format of a TV programme, *Opportunity Knocks*, failed as the Court found that the format was incapable of performance.

Similarly in *Davies v TV3 Services Ltd (Canwest TV Works Ltd)* 13/6/05, Williams J, HC Auckland CIV-2004-404-1130, TV3 successfully sought further particulars of the "format" of a television programme Ms Davies alleged to hold copyright in. The Court noted that copyright could not subsist in "format" alone without reference to a literary or dramatic work.

However, in *Aristocrat Leisure Industries Pty Ltd v Pacific Gaming Pty Ltd* (2000) 50 IPR 29, Tamberlin J held, at p 43, that a performance need not be by a human being and can include performances by characters (such as in the animated television programme *The Simpsons*).

(3) Musical works

A musical work consists of music, exclusive of any words intended to be sung or spoken with the music (which are literary works) or any actions intended to be performed with the music (which are dramatic works).

(4) Artistic works

The definition of an artistic work is divided into three categories:

- Graphic works (ie a painting, drawing, map, engraving), photographs, sculptures, collages, or models, irrespective of artistic quality;
- Works of architecture, being a building or a model for a building; and

- Works of artistic craftsmanship that do not fall within the two other categories (for example, hand knitted woollen sweaters: *Bonz Group (Pty) Ltd v Cooke* [1994] 3 NZLR 216; (1994) 6 TCLR 23 (CA)).

The definition also specifically excludes layout designs or integrated circuits. The effect of this exclusion is discussed in more detail in the Layout Designs chapter of this text (chapter 5).

(a)   *Product design*

New Zealand copyright law is unusual in that it specifically provides protection for product design by recognising that a product design is derived from an artistic work.

In one of the leading New Zealand cases on design copyright, *Wham-O MFG Co v Lincoln Industries Ltd* [1984] 1 NZLR 641 (CA), copyright was held by the Court of Appeal to subsist in the design of a flying disc as an artistic work. The wooden models were sculptures, and the mould, die and finished plastic products were each considered an engraving.

(b)   *Industrially applied artistic works*

A product design or artistic work intended for industrial application may also be protected by copyright. Under s 75(4) of the Act, a product design or artistic work is considered to have been industrially applied if:

- More than 50 copies in three dimensions are made for sale or hire;

- The work is copied in three dimensions in one or more objects manufactured in lengths, for the purposes of sale or hire; or

- The work is copied as a plate (ie industrial processing) and used to produce works defined in the previous two categories.

The subsistence of copyright in industrial design extends beyond mere drawings. As aforesaid, in *Wham-O MFG Co v Lincoln Industries Ltd* [1984] 1 NZLR 641 (CA), copyright was found to exist in wooden models, moulds or dies, and plastic moulded products of a flying disc.

(c)   *Packaging*

In *Henkel KgaA v Holdfast Manufacturing Ltd* 5/11/04, Harrison J, HC Auckland CIV-2003-404-2641, the High Court found that copyright subsisted in the packaging of a product independently of the copyright in the design drawings on which the packaging was based.

In that case, Henkel manufactured and sold adhesive products under the QuickTite brand in New Zealand and the SuperBonder brand in North America. Henkel's products were packaged in blister wrap on a cardboard card, coloured deep blue with red, yellow, and white bands and bold red and blue lettering. Henkel commissioned graphic artists to create design drawings for the packaging, known as the Blue Image Design.

Holdfast had sold adhesive products in New Zealand under the Fixit Super Glue brand since the 1980s. The Fixit products were also packaged in a cellophane blister on cardboard. Until 2002, the card was predominantly coloured red with lesser amounts of yellow and blue. In 2001, Holdfast learnt of the Blue Image Design. Subsequently, it re-branded the

Fixit product under the trade mark SuperBonder. The packaging for the SuperBonder product was admitted to have been copied from the Blue Image Design.

Henkel brought proceedings against Holdfast for, inter alia, copyright infringement. The parties settled the dispute without admission of liability on the basis that Holdfast cease using the SuperBonder packaging which incorporated the Blue Image Design. Subsequently, Holdfast re-branded its SuperBonder product Ultra Bonder and commissioned a graphic designer to create new packaging based upon the old SuperBonder packaging.

Henkel again brought proceedings against Holdfast for, inter alia, copyright infringement, alleging the new Ultra Bonder packaging still substantially incorporated Henkel's Blue Image Design.

Harrison J held, at paras 13-15, that the Blue Image Design embodied in the SuperBonder and QuickTite packaging was a new graphic work in the form of drawings or diagrams and was thus an artistic work, and the packaging for the SuperBonder and QuickTite products was a development or modification of the Blue Image Design in which copyright could subsist.

His Honour held, at para 19, that collectively the drawings of the packaging based upon the Blue Image Design were also an original work.

Holdfast challenged the originality of the Henkel's packaging on the basis that it was a copy of the Blue Image Design drawings, ie, there was insufficient skill, labour and talent expended in the production of the packaging as it was a mere facsimile copy of the underlying Blue Image Design drawings. Harrison J rejected this argument. His Honour held, at paras 25-26, that:

> "While I did not hear direct evidence on the point, I have no difficulty in inferring that both the Super Bonder and Quicktite [packaging] are modifications of [the Blue Image Design drawings]. I do not require a witness to inform me that the Super Bonder or Quicktite packaging differs in certain respects from [the] drawings for [other adhesive products manufactured and sold by Henkel] which I have already found to be original. Obvious differences lie in the substitution of different lettering, the inclusion of a yellow strip, the inclusion of photographs and other miscellaneous changes. Of themselves, these differences are sufficient to satisfy me that the packaging is itself original, and represents more than a minimal input of skill, labour and talent on Henkel's part.

> •   •   •   •   •

> "The Super Bonder and Quicktite [packaging] cards are, like [the other adhesive products manufactured and sold by Henkel], produced from the same foundation, namely the [Blue Image Design drawings]. They are simply an extension in the process based upon [the Blue Image Design drawings]. I cannot see any reason why copyright should not subsist in them on that basis, especially when they do not infringe Henkel's existing copyright in the original Blue Image Design."

The decision of Harrison J was successfully appealed in *Holdfast NZ Ltd v Henkel KgaA* [2007] 1 NZLR 336 (CA). Delivering the principal judgment, Baragwanath J rejected the suggestion that copyright could subsist in the Blue Image Design as a new graphic work in a series of drawings or diagrams commenting, at paras 25 and 26:

> "Copyright can subsist in a series of drawings … But where it is alleged that copyright has been infringed in relation to one of a series of drawings, each drawing must be considered on its own: *UPL Group Ltd v Dux Engineers Ltd* [1989] 3 NZLR 135, 143.

> "Consequently, where copyright in a particular part of a series of drawings is allegedly infringed, whether there has actually been copying can be established only by comparison between the infringing article and the particular drawing in the series. The immediate question is whether Henkel can establish that the whole of its Blue Image Design has been infringed when any specific drawings of QuickTite and SuperBonder deriving from them have not been produced."

His Honour noted that, although Henkel had failed to produce any drawings underlying its QuickTite and SuperBonder packaging, it had produced a series of original drawings relating to the Blue Image Design and asserted that the QuickTite and SuperBonder packaging had its genesis in those drawings. Thus, it was arguable in law that Henkel also had copyright in the unidentified drawings from which the QuickTite and SuperBonder packaging derived. However, whether that had been established in fact was a matter of inference from the whole of the evidence and, while Baragwanath J was prepared to infer the existence of a work underlying both the QuickTite and SuperBonder packaging, there was no evidence that Henkel was the owner of the copyright which might subsist in that work. Accordingly, the claim in respect of both the SuperBonder and QuickTite packaging failed.

A useful summary of the point can also be found in the judgment of William Young P, at para 127:

> "Henkel's case was not assisted by its failure to address in detail the design path which led to the SuperBonder and QuickTite packaging … I am certainly prepared to infer that there must have been drawings from which the packaging was immediately derived. It is, however, a striking feature of the case that these drawings were not produced. This renders impossible any comparison between them and the allegedly infringing Holdfast Ultra Bonder packaging … But there are other problems for Henkel. We do not know who owns the copyright in these drawings. It is quite likely that copyright was held by the Henkel subsidiary companies which produced the products in question. Further, there is no appropriate evidential basis for finding a causal connection between these drawings and Holdfast's Ultra Bonder packaging."

The claim for infringement of the works which had been produced also failed, although for different reasons (discussed elsewhere in this chapter). Henkel unsuccessfully appealed the decision of the Court of Appeal to the Supreme Court (*Henkel KgaA v Holdfast NZ Ltd* [2007] 1 NZLR 577 (SC)). Although the Supreme Court found fault with the approach taken by Baragwanath J to the question of infringement, it agreed that the works relied upon by Henkel on appeal were not pleaded and that, on a correct comparison, there would have been no infringement even if they were.

4.4.2 Sound recordings

A sound recording is defined by s 2(1) Copyright Act 1994 as:

- A recording of sounds (such as the recording of music or the noise in an office) from which the sounds may be reproduced; or

- A recording of the whole or any part of a literary, dramatic, or musical work from which sounds reproduced in the work may be produced.

4.4.3 Films

A film is defined by s 2(1) Copyright Act 1994 as a recording on any medium from which a moving image may be produced. This includes video cassettes, and discs (for example, DVDs and VCDs) producing moving images as well as aspects of multimedia products.

4.4.4 Broadcasts

A broadcast is defined by s 2(1) Copyright Act 1994 as a transmission, whether or not encrypted, of a programme by wireless communication (s 2(1)). The definition is qualified in that the broadcast must be capable of being lawfully received by members of the public or for presentation to members of the public. Foreign and satellite broadcasts fall within the definition.

4.4.5 Cable programmes

A cable programme is defined by s 4 Copyright Act 1994 as any item included in a cable programme service, that is, a transmission service. A transmission service is the sending of visual images, sounds, or other information by means of a telecommunication system. It does not include wireless communications (ie, broadcasts).

Various exceptions in regards to cable programme services are listed in s 4(2), including:

- A transmission service where the information is received by a person providing the service or another person receiving it using the same system;

- A transmission service run solely for purposes internal to the running of a business; and

- A transmission service run solely for an individual's private and domestic use.

4.4.6 Typographical arrangements of published editions

Separate copyright subsists in typographical arrangements of published editions of literary, dramatic, and musical works as typographical arrangements (s 2(1) Copyright Act 1994). For example, an author of a novel may have copyright rights in relation to the text of the novel (the literary work), while the publisher of the novel may have copyright in the arrangement of the literary work on the page (typographical arrangement).

4.4.7 Other categories of work

There are various works that do not fall within the traditional categories of copyright works but are still capable of copyright protection. The New Zealand Courts have held that copyright subsists in a wide variety of three-dimensional subject matter, including toilet pan connectors, Frisbee™ flying discs, aluminium extrusions, dresses, plastic products, and machinery. Some further examples are discussed below.

(1) *Multimedia / CD ROM*

Certain aspects of multimedia and multimedia CD ROMs are protected. For example, CD ROMs that include moving images are protected as films, and other aspects of the CD ROMs may be protected as software.

Multimedia communicated through television will be capable of copyright protection as a broadcast.

Multimedia works may also be protected as a compilation of individual copyright works (discussed at 4.4.7(3) ("Compilations") later in this chapter).

(2) *Digitally recorded works*

The creation and transmission of a work in digital form does not preclude it from copyright protection even though "digital technologies" and the "internet" are not specifically referred to in the Copyright Act 1994.

Section 15(1) of the Act states that copyright subsists in a literary, dramatic or musical work if recorded "in writing or otherwise". Under s 2(1) of the Act, writing includes any form of notation or code whether by hand or otherwise. A recording of a work in digital form will therefore fall within this broad definition.

(3) *Compilations*

The definition of a literary work in s 2 of the Act includes a compilation. However, s 2(1) also defines "compilation" without reference to the definition of a literary work, suggesting that a compilation may be protected as a separate type of work or a combination of works.

Under s 2(1), a "compilation" includes that which:

- Consists wholly of works or parts of works;

- Consists partly of works or parts of works; and

- Consists of data other than works or parts of works.

Examples of compilations protected by copyright are:

- Football pool coupons: *Ladbroke (Football) Ltd v William Hill (Football) Ltd* [1964] 1 WLR 273 (HL);

- A price list: *Payen Components South Africa Ltd v Bovic Gaskets CC* (1995) 33 IPR 406;

- A manual containing a credit control system: *International Credit Control Ltd v Axelsen* [1974] 1 NZLR 695; and

- A report showing financial survey data, tabulated and converted into certain ratios for comparison: *University of Waikato v Benchmarking Services Ltd* (2004) 8 NZBLC 101,561 (CA).

Databases comprise a compilation of data. Accordingly, on the assumption that a database falls within the definition of "compilation", a database will qualify for copyright protection as an original literary work, provided it is original. While copyright is unlikely to subsist in the individual facts or information contained in a database, copyright will subsist in a database where its creator has applied sufficient effort and expense in the collection and presentation of the data, such that the database constitutes a "literary work" of sufficient "originality" (in terms of s 14(2)).

In *University of Waikato v Benchmarking Services Ltd* (2004) 8 NZBLC 101,561 (CA), the New Zealand Court of Appeal, at paras 39-40, cited with approval the decision of the Federal Court of Australia in *Desktop Marketing Systems Pty Ltd v Telstra Corp Ltd* (2002) 55 IPR 1; [2002] FCAFC 112 (FCA). The latter case concerned the alleged infringement of copyright in telephone directories published by Telstra. Desktop admitted copying the data from the directories, but argued that copyright did not subsist in it. The Federal Court held, at para 160, that copyright subsisted in the directories, even though the labour and expense incurred by Telstra was substantially in collecting, verifying, recording, and assembling the relevant data. The Federal Court also held, at para 180, that copyright subsisted in the headings adopted by Telstra in its directories.

University of Waikato and *Desktop Marketing Systems* were both applied in the High Court in *YPG IP Ltd v Yellowbook.com.au Pty Ltd* 13/7/07, Allan J, HC Auckland CIV-2007-404-2839 in awarding an interim injunction to restrain a breach of copyright in TPG's Yellow Pages directory. The decision is also notable for the observation, at para 58, that, in the case of factual compilations there is no need for visual similarity to exist as a condition of infringement.

However, care also needs to be taken in assessing infringement when the compilation consists of a number of individual features none of which, on their own, would attract copyright. Thus, in *Holdfast NZ Ltd v Henkel KgaA* [2007] 1 NZLR 336 (CA), the Court of Appeal (per Baragwanath J, at para 53) cited with approval the following passage from *Bonz Group (Pty) Ltd v Cooke* [1994] 3 NZLR 216; (1994) 6 TCLR 23, at p 220; p 27:

> "Where … the Plaintiff relies for its copyright on a collection of individual features, none of which on their own would attract copyright, this has ramifications when it comes to infringement. To infringe in such circumstances the defendant must have used the same or a substantially similar arrangement or collection of the individual features. If the defendant has copied the individual features but has made its own arrangement of them, this will not represent an infringement. That is because the plaintiff has no monopoly in the individual features as such but only in their arrangement or collocation."

Baragwanath J continued, at para 54:

> "Consequently, if a defendant were to select a collection of features from the plaintiff's work and used them in a work, so long as the defendant arranges and uses the features differently from the plaintiff, the defendant has not breached the plaintiff's copyright."

Henkel unsuccessfully appealed the decision of the Court of Appeal to the Supreme Court (*Henkel KgaA v Holdfast NZ Ltd* [2007] 1 NZLR 577 (SC)). Delivering the judgment of the Court, Tipping J cited *Bonz* with approval continuing, at para 41:

> "As we observed earlier, it may be relevant for infringement purposes to determine how much skill and labour went into the making of the copyright work. This point

can have particular relevance in arrangement cases. The skill and labour which has given rise to the arrangement is what gives the work its originality and if that skill and labour is not great, another arrangement of the same unoriginal underlying features may not have to depart greatly from the copyright arrangement in order to avoid infringement. If the level of originality in the copyright arrangement is low, the amount of originality required to qualify another arrangement of the same elements as original, is also likely to be low."

There is a further discussion of this concept at 4.3.2 ("Originality") earlier in this chapter.

(4)   *Translations*

Translations are not restricted to the conventional conversion of one language to another. A translation will be protected as an expression of any work in another form or medium requiring a degree of skill and labour.

In *Martin v Polyplas Manufacturers Ltd* [1969] NZLR 1046, the plaintiff made three-dimensional engravings of coins from photographs of the originals. Wild CJ held that the independent labour and skill of the plaintiff in making the engravings afforded him copyright protection as the engravings were an original artistic work.

The object code of a computer program has also been held to be protected, as a translation of the source code: *International Business Machines Corp v Computer Imports Ltd* [1989] 2 NZLR 395.

4.5   Rights conferred by copyright

4.5.1   Idea v expression

In addition to being limited in duration (discussed later in this chapter), the rights conferred upon copyright owners under the Copyright Act 1994 are limited in scope. In particular, copyright protection does not extend to the idea of a work; it merely protects the expression of that idea This was affirmed by Wild CJ in *Martin v Polyplas Manufacturers Ltd* [1969] NZLR 1046, at p 1050, where his Honour stated:

> "Copyright protection is given to literary, dramatic, musical and artistic works and not to ideas, and therefore it is original skill or labour in execution, and not originality of thought, which is required."

The High Court in *Plix Products Ltd v Frank M Winstone (Merchants) Ltd* (1984) 3 IPR 390, at pp 418-419, drew the distinction between two kinds of ideas. Prichard J held that the first kind of idea was the general idea or basic concept of the work. For example, an author has an idea in mind to write a novel about unrequited love. While this idea remains as a thought in the author's mind it is not the subject of copyright. The second kind of idea is where the author of the work transforms the basic concept into concrete form (ie, expresses the idea by furnishing it with details of form and shape). Using the example of the novelist, he or she will think of characters, dialogue, and details of plot. When these ideas are transformed into concrete form, copyright will reside in the form they take.

However, the distinction between idea and expression is not always easy to draw. The submission that a straightforward drawing of a simple utilitarian object could not qualify for copyright protection because the drawing embodied the idea was rejected in *P S Johnson & Assocs Ltd v Bucko Enterprises Ltd* [1975] 1 NZLR 311.

See also *Bleiman v News Media (Auckland) Ltd* [1994] 2 NZLR 673; (1994) 6 TCLR 56; 5 NZBLC 103,446 (CA), at pp 677-678; p 61; p 103,450, where the Court of Appeal commented:

> "In copyright law the conventional distinction between ideas and the expression of ideas is helpful only up to a point. Lord Hailsham in *LB (Plastics) Ltd v Swish Products Ltd* (1979) 96 RPC 551, 621 put it this way:
>
>> 'as the late Professor Joad used to observe it all depends on what you mean by ideas.'
>
> •   •   •   •   •
>
> "It is perhaps more helpful to consider whether the effort, skill and judgment of the copyright owner in the making of his original work has been taken in the making of what appears, on a realistic assessment, to be a reproduction of a substantial part."

4.5.2 Economic rights

The Copyright Act 1994 confers upon the owner(s) of the copyright work the exclusive right to do certain things in relation to that work. These acts fall into nine categories and are listed as "acts restricted by copyright" in s 16 Copyright Act 1994. They include the exclusive right to:

- Copy the work;

- Issue copies of the work to the public, whether by sale or otherwise;

- Perform the work in public;

- Play the work in public;

- Show the work in public;

- Broadcast the work or include the work in a cable programme service;

- Make an adaptation of the work;

- Do any of the exclusive acts in relation to an adaptation of the work; and

- Authorise another person (or company) to do any of the exclusive acts. Therefore, a company director may be personally liable for the actions of his or her company. This is discussed in more detail at 4.10.3(2)(a) ("Liability of company directors") and 4.10.4 ("Secondary infringement") later in this chapter.

(1)   *Economic rights apply to all categories of copyright work*

The exclusive property rights conferred upon a copyright owner under s 16 Copyright Act 1994 are the same for all copyright works, including industrially applied designs. However, they are subject to the provisions in Part 3, which permit certain acts in relation to copyright works, and the provisions in Part 8 regarding copyright licensing schemes.

(2) *Issue copies of the work to the public by sale*

Notably, one of the economic rights granted pursuant to s 16 is the right to issue copies of a work to the public by sale or otherwise. Pursuant to s 29(1) of the Act, this right is infringed by anyone who does so without the license of the owner of this right. However, the right needs to be read subject to s 9 of the Act which defines "issue to the public" as "the act of putting into circulation copies not previously put into circulation" and specifically excludes the subsequent distribution and sale, or subsequent importation into New Zealand, of those copies.

This means that the economic right relating to sale will usually only be breached where the person selling the copied goods in New Zealand is either the manufacturer, or has specifically commissioned the manufacture, of the goods. Where the copied goods have been made by someone else and/or imported, this will amount to a secondary infringement either through importing an infringing copy (s 35) or possessing or dealing with an infringing copy (s 36).

The distinction is important because, for a secondary infringement of copyright, it is necessary to establish that the infringer knows or has reason to believe that the item he or she is dealing with is an infringing copy of the copyright work.

The concepts of primary and secondary infringement are discussed in more detail at 4.10.3 ("Primary infringement") and 4.10.4 ("Secondary infringement") later in this chapter.

4.5.3 Moral rights

In addition to conferring exclusive property rights on the owner of a copyright work, the Copyright Act 1994 also recognises the personal rights of the author/creator of the work. The personal rights of the author/creator of the work are described as moral rights.

Article 6bis of the Berne Convention for the Protection of Literary and Artistic Works, Paris Revision of 1971 provides the legal foundation for the international protection of moral rights as follows:

- Independently of the author's economic rights, and even after the transfer of those rights, the author shall have the right to claim authorship of the work ("attribution") and to object to any distortion, mutilation or other modification of, or other interlocutory action in relation to, the work ("derogatory treatment") which would be prejudicial to his or her honour or reputation;

- The rights granted to the author in accordance with the preceding paragraph shall after his or her death, be maintained, at least until the expiry of the economic rights, and shall be exercisable by the persons or institutions authorised by the legislation of the country where protection is claimed; and

- Each country in which protection is claimed must provide a means of redress for safeguarding the moral rights.

The Act complies with the primary moral rights provided for in the Berne Convention, namely:

- The right of attribution (ss 94-97); and

- The right to object to derogatory treatment of the work (ss 98-101).

The Act also provides for two further rights:

- Against false attribution (ss 102-104); and

- For the privacy of certain photographs and films (s 105).

(1)   *The right of attribution*

Under s 94 Copyright Act 1994, the author of a literary, dramatic, musical or artistic work and the director of a film have the right to be identified as such. The mode of identification varies according to the work (s 95). An author of a commercially published novel has the right to have his/her name marked clearly and reasonably prominently, such as on the cover of each copy of the book, whereas an architect of a building is entitled to have his or her name visible to persons entering or approaching the building (for example, in the form of a plaque).

(a)   *Exceptions to grant of right of attribution*

There are exceptions to the right of attribution under s 97 Copyright Act 1994.

The right does not apply to computer programs, computer generated works or designs of a typeface.

Further, the right is not infringed by an act that would not infringe copyright in the work such as:

- Incidental copying in an artistic work, sound recording, film, broadcast or cable programme;

- Criticism, review and news reporting of the work; or

- Examination of the work, if the work relates to parliamentary and judicial proceedings to Royal Commissions.

Nor does the right extend to works in which Crown copyright exists or works made for the purpose of reporting current events.

(b)   *Right of attribution must be asserted to be enforced*

Before an author's right of attribution can be infringed, the author must assert it. Section 96 Copyright Act 1994 lists the circumstances where a right may be asserted generally. This may include a statement in an assignment of copyright in the work that the author/director asserts his or her right to be identified as the author/director of that work.

(2)   *The right to object to derogatory treatment of a work*

In order to establish the right to object to derogatory treatment of a copyright work, two requirements must be met (s 98 Copyright Act 1994). First, there must be a "treatment" of the work, and secondly the treatment must be derogatory.

(a)   *"Treatment of a work"*

"Treatment of a work" means any addition to, deletion from, alteration to, or adaptation of, the work. It does not include the translation of a literary or dramatic work or an arrangement or transcription of a musical work involving no more than a change of key or register.

(b)   *"Derogatory"*

Treatment of a work will be "derogatory" if, whether by distortion or mutilation (or otherwise), the treatment is prejudicial to the honour or reputation of the author or director.

(c)   *Objective test*

The test as to whether there has been damage to the author/director's honour or reputation is an objective one. In *Pasterfield v Denham* [1999] FSR 168, at p 182, Overend J stated that the plaintiff must establish that the treatment of the work is either a distortion or a mutilation that objectively prejudices the plaintiff's honour or reputation as an artist. It is not sufficient that the author is himself aggrieved by what has occurred.

(d)   *Exceptions to the right to object to derogatory treatment of a work*

Exceptions to the right to object to derogatory treatment of a literary, dramatic, musical or artistic work, or film are listed in ss 100 and 101 Copyright Act 1994 respectively.

In particular the right does not apply to computer programs, computer-generated works and typeface designs (s 100(2)).

(e)   *Infringement of the right to object to derogatory treatment of a work*

Section 99 Copyright Act 1994 states that the right to object to derogatory treatment of a literary, dramatic, or musical work is infringed by a person who:

- Publishes commercially, performs in public, broadcasts or includes in a cable programme a derogatory treatment of the work; or

- Issues to the public copies of a film or sound recording that includes a derogatory treatment of the work. This may include advertisements.

In the case of an artistic work, the right is infringed by a person who:

- Publishes commercially or exhibits in public a derogatory treatment of the work; or

- Broadcasts or includes in a cable programme or shows a film that includes a visual image of a derogatory treatment of the work.

In the case of a sculpture, a work of architecture, or a work of artistic craftsmanship, the issuing to the public of copies of a graphic work representing a derogatory treatment of that work will amount to infringement.

Similarly, infringement will occur where a derogatory treatment of a film has been shown in public, broadcast or included in a cable programme.

(f)   *Right to object to derogatory treatment of a work only available to author*

A claim for infringement of the right not to have a copyright work subjected to a derogatory treatment is open only to the author, not the owner of copyright. In *Benchmark Building Supplies Ltd v Mitre 10 (NZ) Ltd* [2004] 1 NZLR 26; (2003) 10 TCLR 767; 7 NZBLC 104,002 (CA), Gault P stated, at para 45, that:

> "The moral rights of authors are provided to enable authors to protect the integrity of their works even though ownership passes to others. It would be contrary to the very purpose of those rights if the author's right accrued to those employing or commissioning the authors or purchasing the copyright in their works."

and, at para 43:

> "We have no doubt that in the Copyright Act the word 'person' in the definition of author, except where the contrary is expressly stated, does not extend to bodies corporate."

(3) *The right against false attribution*

In contrast to s 94 Copyright Act 1994, s 102 provides that a person has the right not to have a literary, dramatic, musical or artistic work or a film falsely attributed to him or her as an author or director.

Attribution means an express or implied statement as to the identity of the author of the work or the director of the film.

Infringing acts include issuing copies of the work to the public, exhibiting the work in public, performance or broadcast of the work, or the public display of the work.

It is a requirement that the person infringing must know or have reason to believe that the attribution is false.

(4) *The right to privacy of certain photographs and films*

Where a person commissions the taking of a photograph or the making of a film for private and domestic purposes, that person has the right not to have:

- Copies of the work issued to the public;
- The work exhibited or shown in public; and
- The work broadcast or included in a cable programme (s 105).

The right is infringed by the performance of any of these acts.

Section 105(3) lists exceptions to this right. They include:

- Incidental copying of a work in an artistic work, film, broadcast or cable programme;
- Acts done for the purposes of parliamentary or judicial proceedings, or for the purposes of reporting parliamentary or judicial proceedings;
- Acts done for the purposes of the proceedings of a Royal commission, commission of inquiry, ministerial inquiry, or statutory inquiry, or for the purposes of reporting same;
- Where the doing of a particular act is specifically authorised by an enactment; and
- Acts permitted on assumptions as to expiry of copyright or death of the author in relation to anonymous or pseudonymous works.

4.6 Ownership of copyright

4.6.1 Author is generally owner

The general rule under s 21(1) Copyright Act 1994 is that the original owner of copyright is the author of the copyright work, whether a natural person or a company.

(1) Meaning of "author"

"Author" is defined in s 5 Copyright Act 1994 as the person(s) or entity who created the work.

The Act also refers to person(s) responsible for reducing the work to a material form.

People who merely suggest ideas, or directors of a company, are not regarded by the Court as authors: *Kenrick & Co v Lawrence & Co* (1890) 25 QBD 99 and *Hansen v Humes-Maclon Plastics Ltd* (1984) 1 NZIPR 557.

(2) Meaning of "joint authorship"

A "work of joint authorship" is defined in s 6(1) Copyright Act 1994 as "a work produced by the collaboration of 2 or more authors in which the contribution of each author is not distinct from that of the other author or authors". Thus, joint authorship will arise where it is impossible to distinguish each author's individual contribution to the work. This concept is distinct from co-ownership, which arises where each individual author's contribution is distinct and identifiable — such as in the case of an illustrator and writer of a children's book.

4.6.2 Exceptions to author is owner rule

There are two exceptions in the Copyright Act 1994 to the general rule that the author of a copyright work will be the first owner of any copyright that subsists in it. They are:

- **Employers**: where a literary, dramatic, musical, or artistic work (including a product design) is made by an employee in the course of his/her employment, subject to any agreement to the contrary, the employer will be the first owner of any copyright that vests in it (s 21(2)); and

- **Commissioning parties**: subject to any agreement to the contrary, a person or corporate entity who has commissioned certain categories of copyright work will be the first owner of any copyright that vests in it, provided that:

  - The commissioning arose before the work was created; and

  - The work was created in pursuance of the commission (s 21(3)).

The commissioning rule is subject to a discussion paper released by the Ministry of Economic Development in April 2006 entitled "The Commissioning Rule, Contracts and the Copyright Act 1994". This is discussed in more detail at 4.2.2(3) ("The Commissioning Rule, Contracts and the Copyright Act 1994") earlier in this chapter.

(1)   *Exceptions do not apply if contrary agreement*

The exceptions to the general rule of ownership of copyright in s 21 Copyright Act 1994 do not apply if there is an agreement to the contrary. Under s 114, such an agreement normally needs to be in writing, but can be oral.

(2)   *Employee works*

The first exception to the general rule under s 21(2) Copyright Act 1994 is that the employer is the owner of copyright in works created by employees during the course of employment. This raises two questions:

*   When is a person employed for the purposes of the Copyright Act 1994?

*   When is a work deemed to have been produced by an employee "in the course of employment"?

The Australian case of *Redrock Holdings Pty Ltd v Hinkley* (2001) 50 IPR 565 addresses both issues.

The case involved software initially developed by the first defendant before his employment with Redrock. The first defendant continued to develop the software for Redrock after his employment. No discussions were held between Redrock and the first defendant as to the ownership of copyright in the software. The first defendant then left the employment of Redrock taking the source code to the software with him and the Court was asked to determine who owned the software.

One of the questions the Court needed to determine was whether the first defendant was employed under a contract *of* service (in which case his employer, Redrock, would own the software) or a contract *for* services (in which case the first defendant would retain ownership).

In finding that the first defendant was employed under a contract of service, Harper J applied the integration test made famous by Lord Denning in *Stevenson Jordan & Harrison Ltd v MacDonald & Evans* [1952] 1 TLR 101 (CA), at p 111:

> "it is almost impossible to give a precise definition of the distinction [between a contract of service and a contract for services]. It is often quite easy to recognise a contract of service when you see it, but very difficult to say wherein the difference lies. A ship's master, a chauffeur, and a reporter on the staff of a newspaper are all employed under a contract of service; but a ship's pilot, a taxi-man, and a newspaper contributor are employed under a contract for services. One feature which seems to me to run through the instances is that, under a contract of [sic] service, a man is employed as part of the business and his work, although done for the business, is not integrated into it but is only accessory to it."

It was held that the first defendant's work as a software developer integrated into the business of Redrock whose aim was developing intellectual property in its product. Further factors that helped Harper J come to this conclusion were that the first defendant was on a fixed salary with superannuation, was entitled to annual leave, sick leave and long service leave and Redrock provided him with equipment to assist him to write the software.

195

The case highlights that consideration must be given to the employee's duties and obligations to determine whether the first exception to the general rule applies.

The same factors were considered by the High Court of New Zealand in *Fleming v Fletcher Concrete & Infrastructure Ltd* 1/12/06, Wild J, HC Auckland CIV-2005-404-4598. Mr Fleming had accused Fletcher of manufacturing a cattle stop in breach of copyright in certain drawings which the Court found to have been owned by Mr Fletcher. Some of the drawings had been produced through a derivative process involving Mr Fleming as an employee of Fletcher. Those drawings were based on an original drawing produced by Mr Fleming before the period of his employment. Fletcher argued that the derivative drawings were new copyright works and had been produced by a team of Fletcher employees. It further argued that any input by Mr Fleming was as an employee and, accordingly, Fletcher owned the copyright in the works pursuant to s 21(2) Copyright Act 1994. That claim was rejected by the High Court, which held, at paras 97 and 98:

> "the critical words in s 21(2) of the Act are explained by Keith J in [*Empress Abalone Ltd v Langdon* [2000] 2 ERNZ 53 (CA)] at 55. Quoting from Blanco White, *Patents For Inventions and the Protection of Industrial Designs* (5th Ed), London, Stevens, 1983, para 7-004 Keith J said:
>
>> 'Where an employee in the course of his employment made an invention which it was part of his duty to make, the law imported into the contract of employment a term that the invention is the property of the employer.'
>
> "The Judge continued:
>
>> 'The main difficulty in the cases, that text continues, is usually that of determining whether the invention concerned was made in the course of the employment or, in other words, whether it is something that it was the employee's job to invent (para 7-005).'
>
> "Lexis Nexis' *Copyright & Design* in my view accurately summarises the legal position when it states that the effect of s 21(2) is:
>
>> 'The words … clearly mean more than "during the period the employee is employed" … the words mean something more like "as part of the duties the employee is engaged and instructed to undertake".'
>
> "I accept Mr Elliott's [(Counsel for the Plaintiff)] argument that it was no part of Mr Fleming's job to design a cattle stop. Mr Fleming was not employed as a designer or because he had any skills or experience in the design, in particular of cattle stops. He was employed to manage the Onehunga sales centre. The part of his job description relied on by [Fletcher] … did not place on Mr Fleming any design responsibilities. It was limited to Mr Fleming providing product ideas and feedback, of the type generally expected of sales staff."

The relevant part of Mr Fleming's job description referred to above stated:

> "Forecasting:
>
> "To order regularly on a monthly basis form [sic] the various Humes business for: [various product types are then set out].
>
> "…

"This will also include input into new product development."

The High Court also considered it relevant that Mr Fleming did not do any of the design and drawing work in the course of his employment, ie during work hours.

(3) *Commissioned works*

The second exception to the general rule, under s 21(3) Copyright Act 1994, applies where a work has been commissioned.

Commissioning has been likened to "ordering": *Plix Products Ltd v Frank M Winstone (Merchants) Ltd* (1984) 3 IPR 390, at p 412.

In *Hansen v Humes-Maclon Plastics Ltd* (1984) 1 NZIPR 557, at p 570, Hillyer J held that there was no requirement for the commissioning to be expressly stated in a contract. It can be inferred from the facts of the case.

There is a requirement that the commissioning must predate the work (otherwise the work cannot be said to have been created "in pursuance of the commission") and that there is payment or an agreement to pay for the article in which the copyright resides irrespective of whether that article is purchased: *Plix Products Ltd v Frank M Winstone (Merchants) Ltd* (1984) 3 IPR 390.

However, it is important to note that ownership of commissioned works is not contingent on payment. Thus, unless there is an agreement to the contrary, the commissioning party owns the copyright in the commissioned work even if part or all of the consideration is not paid to the person who created the work in pursuance of the commission.

It is always best practice for a written agreement to exist which deals with the issue of who owns copyright in a commissioned work. However, where there is no specific agreement, the law is well settled. *Pacific Software Technology Ltd v Perry Group Ltd* [2004] 1 NZLR 164; (2003) 7 NZBLC 103,950; 57 IPR 145 (CA), contains, at paras 55-60, the following useful summary on the nature of a commission:

- To "commission" simply means to order or request.

- The act of commissioning must pre-date the creation of the work.

- Section 21 Copyright Act 1994 requires a commission and an agreement to pay. An antecedent commissioning usually (but not always) implies an obligation to pay, and the existence of a payment obligation supports the existence of the commission itself. An agreement to pay can be express or implied. For the purposes of a commission, there need not necessarily be agreement as to the precise amount to be paid, but if matters are left too vague, then the supposed commission becomes unenforceable.

- The payment is for the copyright, not the physical embodiment of the copyright work.

- The copyright in the commissioned work belongs to the commissioning party as soon as part of it is done. That is, the commission applies to incomplete, as well as complete, works.

- The notion of a commission is sui generis to copyright law.

(a) *Commissioning exception does not apply to literary works*

The commissioning exception only applies to photographs, computer programs, paintings, drawings, diagrams, maps, charts, plans, engravings, models, sculptures, films, or sound recordings. Works of architecture and literary works are not covered by this exception. See, for example, the comments of the Court in *Pacific Software Technology Ltd v Perry Group Ltd* [2004] 1 NZLR 164; (2003) 7 NZBLC 103,950; 57 IPR 145 (CA).

Therefore, a party who commissions, for example, some computer software and an accompanying manual would (in the absence of an agreement to the contrary) own copyright in the software but not the manual. It is therefore important to fully set out ownership of rights in the contract between the parties before work commences.

4.7 Duration of copyright

The duration of copyright varies according to the type of the work and the circumstances in which it is created and used. Once copyright in a work expires, the work falls into the "public domain" and (in the absence of any other intellectual property rights attaching to the work — such as patent or registered design rights) can be used freely by the public.

4.7.1 Traditional subject matter: literary, dramatic, musical or artistic works

The general rule under s 22(1) Copyright Act 1994 is that the duration of copyright in a literary, dramatic, musical or artistic work expires 50 years from the end of the calendar year in which the author dies. However, this general rule is subject to the exceptions described in paragraphs below.

4.7.2 Computer-generated works

Under s 22(2) Copyright Act 1994, the duration of copyright in a computer generated work is 50 years after the end of the calendar year in which that work was made.

4.7.3 Unknown author(s)

Under s 22(3) Copyright Act 1994, where a work is of unknown authorship, copyright in the work expires 50 years from the end of the calendar year in which it was first made available to the public by an authorised act.

Under s 7 of the Act, an author is "unknown", and thus the copyright work is of unknown authorship, if it is not possible to ascertain the author's identity by reasonable inquiry.

(1) *"Made available to the public"*

The circumstances in which a work is "made available to the public", for the purposes of ascertaining the duration of copyright in a work of unknown authorship, are set out in s 22(4) Copyright Act 1994.

In the case of a literary, dramatic or musical work, the public performance, broadcasting, or the inclusion in a cable programme service, will constitute the work being made available to the public.

In the case of an artistic work, circumstances will include the exhibition of the work in public, the playing or showing in public of a film that includes the work, and the inclusion of the work in a broadcast or in a cable service programme.

(2) *"Authorised act"*

Where a work is of unknown authorship, it may be difficult to determine whether or not the act, by which the work was made available to the public, was "authorised", for the purposes of ascertaining the duration of copyright in the work.

Accordingly, s 65 Copyright Act 1994 provides that copyright in works of unknown authorship will not be infringed where it is not possible to ascertain the identity of the author by reasonable inquiry, and it is reasonable to assume that the copyright has expired, or that 50 years have passed since the author died.

4.7.4 Joint authorship

Under s 22(6) Copyright Act 1994, where a copyright work is of joint authorship, copyright in the work expires 50 years from the end of the calendar year in which the last known author died.

The meaning of "joint authorship" is discussed at 4.6 ("Ownership of copyright") earlier in this chapter.

4.7.5 Industrially applied artistic works

Section 75(1) Copyright Act 1994 provides special exceptions from protection of artistic works that have been applied industrially. A two dimensional (ie, drawing) or three dimensional (ie, product) copy of an industrially applied artistic work will not infringe copyright in that work if the work was first industrially applied by or with the licence of the copyright owner:

- In the case of a work of artistic craftsmanship, more than 25 years before the object or copy is made;

- In the case of a sculpture that is a cast or a pattern for an object that has a primarily utilitarian function, more than 16 years before the object or copy is made; or

- In the case of any other artistic work, more than 16 years before the object or copy is made.

The s 75(1) exception does not apply to:

- A sculpture that is not a cast;

- A pattern for an object that has a primary function other than utilitarian (ie, aesthetic products); or

- A work of architecture, being a building or model for a building.

4.7.6 Sound recordings and films

Under s 23 Copyright Act 1994, copyright in a sound recording or film expires:

- 50 years after the end of the calendar year in which the work was made; or

- 50 years from the end of the calendar year in which the work was first lawfully made available to the public,

whichever occurs later.

As an example, if a sound recording or film made on 1 January 2000 is never made available to the public, it will be protected by copyright until 31 December 2050. If the same work is made available to the public on 13 November 2050, it will be protected until 31 December 2100. Therefore, sound recordings and films could potentially be protected for a period of up to 100 years.

(1) *"Made available to the public"*

Section 23(2) Copyright Act 1994 sets out when a sound recording or film is made available to the public for the purposes of ascertaining the duration of copyright in the sound recording or film. This occurs when the work is first published, broadcast or included in a cable programme service. In addition, in the case of a film or film soundtrack, publication can also occur when the work is first shown or played in public.

The Act does not specify whether these acts must occur in New Zealand or in any other prescribed country.

4.7.7 Broadcasts and cable programmes

Under s 24 Copyright Act 1994, copyright in a broadcast or cable programme expires 50 years after the end of the calendar year in which the broadcast was made, or the cable programme was included in a cable programme service (ie, transmitted). Copyright in a repeated broadcast or cable programme expires at the same time as copyright in the initial broadcast or cable programme.

4.7.8 Typographical arrangements

Under s 25 Copyright Act 1994, copyright in a typographical arrangement of a published edition expires 25 years from the end of the calendar year in which the edition was first published.

4.8 Assignment of rights

Under s 113(1)(a) Copyright Act 1994, ownership of copyright may be assigned. Unlike a licence, an assignment entails a transfer (in full or part) of the ownership of copyright.

4.8.1 Assignment must be in writing

An assignment of copyright is not effective unless it is in writing and signed by or on behalf of the assignor (s 114 Copyright Act 1994). However, there is no preferred form. In *Glogau v Land Transport Safety Authority of NZ and NZ Taxi Proprietors' Federation Inc* [1997] 3 NZLR 353, a letter recording the assignment and a receipt for consideration paid under the assignment was held to be an intention to assign and therefore valid.

4.8.2 Partial assignment of rights

Assignment of copyright may be partial: *J Albert & Sons Pty Ltd v Fletcher Construction Co Ltd* [1974] 2 NZLR 107, at pp 111-112.

A partial assignment of copyright may be limited to:

- One or more, but not all, of the things the copyright owner has the exclusive right to do (discussed in more detail at 4.6 ("Ownership of copyright") earlier in this chapter); and/or

- Part, but not all, of the period for which the copyright subsists (discussed in more detail at 4.7 ("Duration of copyright") earlier in this chapter).

4.8.3 Future copyright may be assigned

Assignment of future copyright, either in its entirety or partially, is provided for by s 116 Copyright Act 1994. An assignment of future copyright is subject to the same requirements as regards an assignment of existing copyright.

4.8.4 Assignment, waiver, and transmission of moral rights

Under s 118 Copyright Act 1994, the author/creator of a copyright work cannot assign their moral rights in the work.

However, under s 107, the author/creator can waive their moral rights in writing. Where a work has multiple authors, a waiver from one does not affect the rights of the other authors (s 108(2)).

Moral rights pass to the estate of the author on his or her death.

4.9 Licences

Copyright may be licensed in New Zealand.

A "copyright licence" is defined in s 2(1) Copyright Act 1994 as a licence to do, or authorise the doing of, any restricted act. Acts (such as copying or selling the work) carried out in pursuance of a licence will not amount to infringement.

4.9.1 Exclusive licences permitted

The Copyright Act 1994 also provides for exclusive licences, which are expressly defined in s 2(1) as follows:

> "'Exclusive Licence' means a licence in writing, signed by or on behalf of a copyright owner, authorising the licensee, to the exclusion of all other persons (including the copyright owner), to exercise a right that would otherwise be exercisable exclusively by the copyright owner:"

In addition to granting the licensee the right to do any of the acts restricted by s 16, an exclusive licence may encompass the right to sue for infringement of the rights granted under the licence: *Biotrading and Financing Oy v Biohit Ltd* [1998] FSR 109, at pp 127-128.

Under s 123 of the Act an exclusive licensee has the same rights and remedies as the copyright owner. However, as these rights are held concurrently, the licence does not preclude the owner from also taking action against third party infringers.

Under s 124, where proceedings are brought by the exclusive licensee or owner in respect of an infringement of the rights licensed, the other party must be joined as either plaintiff or defendant, except with leave of the Court or in the case of an application for interim relief.

An exclusive licensee/owner joined to proceedings under s 124 will not be liable for costs unless he or she takes an active part in the proceedings.

Section 124(4) requires the Court to take into account the terms of the licence and any remedy already granted to the other party in respect of the same infringement when determining what remedies to grant.

4.9.2 Future copyright may be licensed

Under s 116 Copyright Act 1994 it is possible to grant a licence in respect of future copyright. The licence will be binding on the copyright owner when the work comes into existence.

4.9.3 Licences binding on successors in title

In accordance with s 111 Copyright Act 1994, a licence granted by a copyright owner (including a licence of future copyright) is binding on every successor-in-title to that person's interest in the copyright, except a purchaser in good faith for valuable consideration without actual or constructive notice of the licence.

4.9.4 Licences should address electronic right

A number of recent cases have highlighted an emerging problem in relation to pre-internet copyright licences which do not sufficiently provide for use of the work in relation to future technologies.

In *Greenberg v National Geographic Soc* 224 F 3d 1267 (11th Cir, 2001), the plaintiff successfully sued the defendant, National Geographic, for breach of copyright in relation to the use of photographs in a multimedia work. The defendant was licensed to use the photographs but the wording of the licence only covered use in a magazine and did not extend to multimedia works.

Both licensors and licensees would be well advised to bear *Greenberg* and similar cases in mind when drafting copyright licence agreements. One way to avoid problems would be to include a clause that licenses the work for use in "all media now known or to be developed in the future".

4.10 Infringement and enforcement of rights

Copyright is infringed by anyone who, without the authority of the copyright owner or licensee, does any restricted act.

The restricted acts are set out in s 16(1) Copyright Act 1994 and are discussed in more detail at 4.5 ("Rights conferred by copyright") earlier in this chapter.

Legal action may be taken against a person who infringes copyright by:

- The copyright owner; and/or

- An exclusive licensee of the copyright owner (discussed in more detail at 4.9 ("Licenses") earlier in this chapter.

In *World TV Ltd v Best TV Ltd* (2005) 11 TCLR 247, World held an exclusive licence with a third party, CCTV, to broadcast programmes from CCTV1, but not CCTV4. World sought to rely on a letter of authority from CCTV empowering it to enforce CCTV's rights in New Zealand to seek an injunction to prevent Best from broadcasting inter alia programmes from CCTV4. The action was unsuccessful as World was found to be neither an owner nor an exclusive licensee of the copyright works. An action under the Fair Trading Act 1986 also failed as s 124 Copyright Act 1994 was deemed to act as a proviso to the more general provisions of the Fair Trading Act.

Legal action is usually taken in the High Court in the first instance but may be taken in the District Court. The case is heard and decided by a Judge alone. Juries are not used in civil copyright cases.

It is also possible to take legal action to protect an author's moral rights.

4.10.1 Four-part test

For a plaintiff to succeed in an action for infringement of copyright they must satisfy the four-part test established by Chilwell J in *P S Johnson & Assocs Ltd v Bucko Enterprises Ltd* [1975] 1 NZLR 311, at p 315, by proving that:

- There is a work in which the copyright can subsist;

- Copyright does subsist in the work;

- The plaintiff owns the copyright in the work; and

- Copyright in the work has been infringed.

(1)   *There is a work in which copyright can subsist*

In an action for breach of copyright, the plaintiff must put sufficient evidence before the Court to establish the nature of the materials in which copyright is claimed. See *Wham-O MFG Co v Lincoln Industries Ltd* [1984] 1 NZLR 641 (CA), at p 651:

> "When materials in which copyright is claimed are not produced at the hearing then their nature must be proved by other evidence."

That is not to say that a plaintiff cannot advance a claim if the original copyright work underlying a product no longer exists, or cannot be located. A similar situation arose in *Wham-O*. However, what is required is evidence to prove the form of the materials in which copyright is claimed to subsist, and to link up those materials in a causative chain to the creation of the product put before the Court as evidence of the existence of that work.

Thus, for example, in *Wham-O*, the Court had detailed evidence before it as to the process of manufacture of the products at issue and, as a consequence, any underlying copyright works.

Wham-O was cited with approval in *Fleming v Fletcher Concrete & Infrastructure Ltd* 1/12/06, Wild J, HC Auckland CIV-2005-404-4598, at paras 83-85. Similarly in *Tiny Intelligence Ltd v Resport Ltd* 21/11/05, John Hansen J, HC Christchurch CIV-2003-409-352, a case involving breach of copyright in a toy plastic trumpet and sword produced for the Canterbury Rugby Union, the Court was prepared to accept that the original computerised drawings of the sword could not be produced because of a computer malfunction. Although the Court first regarded that explanation with some suspicion, it was subsequently satisfied after hearing evidence from the person responsible for producing the drawings, reviewing exchanges in emails between the respective parties, and hearing evidence from the defendant in cross-examination which seemed to show that he accepted the existence and originality of the drawings.

(2) Copyright does subsist in the work

This requires the plaintiff to establish that the work meets the legislative and statutory requirements for protection. These are discussed in more detail at 4.3 ("Subsistence of copyright") earlier in this chapter.

(3) The plaintiff owns the copyright

Considerations relevant to this enquiry are considered in more detail at 4.6 ("Ownership of copyright") earlier in this chapter.

(4) Copyright in the work has been infringed

This will require the plaintiff to establish a case of primary or secondary infringement, the material considerations of which are discussed below.

4.10.2 Primary and secondary infringement

Infringement of copyright will fall under one of two headings — primary infringement or secondary infringement.

Unlike primary infringement, secondary infringement requires the defendant to have knowledge that his or her act infringes the plaintiff's copyright.

4.10.3 Primary infringement

Sections 29-34 Copyright Act 1994 set out the primary means of infringing copyright.

Sections 30-34 generally correspond to the restricted acts listed under s 16. Accordingly, primary infringement arises by:

- Copying the work (as defined in s 2(1)) (s 30);

- Issuing infringing copies to the public (s 31);

- Performing, playing or showing the work in public (s 32);

- Broadcasting a work, or including it in a cable programme service (s 33); or

- Making an adaptation of a work and/or doing any restricted act in relation to an adaptation (s 34).

The restricted acts are discussed at 4.5 ("Rights conferred by copyright") earlier in this chapter.

(1) Doing restricted act without authority

Under s 29, primary infringement of copyright involves doing any of the restricted acts listed in s 16 without the authorisation of the copyright owner. Under s 16(1)(h), it is a restricted act to do any of the acts restricted by s 16 in relation to an adaptation of a copyright work, and under s 16(1)(i), it is a restricted act to authorise another to do any of the restricted acts.

Under s 29 "restricted acts" include acts carried out in relation to the work as a whole, or in relation to a substantial part of the work, either directly or indirectly. Thus it is an infringement of copyright in an original work (for example, the wooden model of a flying disc) to copy a copy of that work (a plastic flying disc produced from the wooden model for sale). It is also immaterial whether any intervening acts themselves infringe copyright.

Section 29 is subject to the provisions in the Act relating to fair dealing (discussed at 4.11 ("Defences") later in this chapter) and licensing schemes (set out in Part 8 of the Act).

(2)   *Authorising another to do a restricted act*

The meaning of "authorised" was discussed by the English Court of Appeal in *Pensher Security Door Co Ltd v Sunderland CC* [2000] RPC 249 (CA). In that case, the English Court of Appeal held that a defendant, who had commissioned another person to build a door, similar in appearance and materials to a door in which the plaintiff had copyright, had authorised the subsequent infringement. This case was applied in *Spantech Pty Ltd v BPM Contracts Ltd* 16/8/04, Associate Judge Gendall, HC Wellington CIV-2003-454-160.

In *Spantech*, Spantech designed and built a number of storage installations ("the Spantech installations") for the eighth defendant, Heinz Wattie's Ltd. Heinz Wattie's later contracted the first defendant, BPM Contracts, to build another storage installation ("the BPM installation"). Spantech alleged that it owned copyright in the Spantech installations pursuant to s 21(2) Copyright Act 1994. It claimed that Heinz Wattie's had infringed its copyright under s 16(1)(i) of the Act by directing and approving construction of the BPM installation "as per the existing adjacent [Spantech installations]". Heinz Wattie's brought an application for summary judgment against Spantech under r 136(2) High Court Rules, seeking a declaration that it did not authorise BPM Contracts to copy the Spantech installations.

Rejecting the application, Associate Judge Gendall found, at para 39, that by commissioning BPM to build a storage installation "as per the existing adjacent [Spantech installations]", it was clearly arguable that Heinz Wattie's had, impliedly at least, purported to grant BPM the right to manufacture a storage installation of the same design as the Spantech installation, thereby authorising BPM to infringe Spantech's copyright within the meaning of s 16(1)(i) Copyright Act 1994. His Honour noted, at para 42, that the time at which "authorisation" was properly judged was the moment when the contract between Heinz Wattie's and BPM was entered into, and the instructions given.

Two recent decisions (of the US Supreme Court and the Federal Court of Australia) have expanded the concept of "authorisation" as it relates to digital copying technologies.

In *Metro-Goldwyn-Mayer Studios Inc v Grokster Ltd* 545 US 913; 125 S Ct 2764; 75 USPQ 2d 1001 (US, 2005), the US Supreme Court overturned a ruling by the Ninth Circuit that exempted distributors of Peer-to-Peer ("PTP") file sharing software from liability arising from copyright infringement committed by users of the PTP software.

Grokster and StreamCast Networks distributed free PTP software products that allowed computer users to directly share and copy electronic files of music, movies, and other materials. Metro-Goldwyn-Mayer Studios Inc ("MGM") was the owner of copyright in some of the materials shared and copied using that PTP software, and sued Grokster and StreamCast on the basis that they were liable for those infringements.

In their defence, Grokster and StreamCast relied on the Supreme Court's 1984 decision in *Sony Corp of America v Universal City Studios Inc* 464 US 417 (1984), which centred around Sony's Betamax video cassette recorder, a product also capable of being used for copying material subject to copyright protection. In that case, the Supreme Court held that mere distribution of such a product would not make the distributor liable for secondary infringement of copyright if the product was a staple article of commerce "capable of substantial non-infringing uses". The trial and appellate Courts in *Grokster* held that the PTP software products distributed by Grokster and StreamCast satisfied the *Sony* standard of being capable of substantial non-infringing uses.

In concurring opinions, the Supreme Court was split as to the question of whether the evidence satisfied the *Sony* standard. Three Judges held that the PTP software was capable of sufficient substantial non-infringing uses; three that it was not; and three expressed no opinion. However, the *Grokster* decision did not ultimately turn on the characteristics of the PTP software product itself. Instead, the Supreme Court unanimously held that the trial and appellate courts had erred by applying *Sony*'s product-centred standard to the exclusion of evidence that shows "statements or actions directed to promoting infringement".

The Supreme Court highlighted evidence that Grokster and StreamCast each intended the PTP software product to be used for infringing purposes, and took active steps to encourage such infringement by users. Drawing analogy with contributory infringement in patent law, the Supreme Court held that a party can be liable for "inducing" copyright infringement by another. While the Supreme Court was at pains to point out that mere knowledge of infringing potential, or of actual infringing uses, would not be enough to subject a distributor to liability, Grokster and StreamCast's advertising, business planning and internal communications provided substantial evidence of inducement, and the trial and appellate courts' summary judgment rulings in favour of Grokster and StreamCast were overturned.

In *Universal Music Australia Pty Ltd v Cooper* [2005] FCA 972, Tamberlin J found that Cooper, in operating a website MP3S4free.net which contained links to copyright material, authorised copyright infringement by users who downloaded the MP3 files, and by operators of remote websites where the infringing MP3 files were stored, notwithstanding that the MP3 files were never sent to, downloaded onto, or stored on the MP3S4free website itself.

Tamberlin J found that Cooper's actions amounted to more than mere facilitation as the MP3S4free website was operated in a way which was "clearly designed to, and does facilitate and enable [the] infringing downloading", and Cooper had "knowingly permitted and approved the use of his website in this manner and designed and organised it to achieve this result".

Tamberlin J found that Cooper was able to prevent the infringements, either by removing the links to infringing material from his website, or structuring the website so that the operators of the remote sites could not automatically add hyperlinks without some control by Cooper.

Tamberlin J also found that the ISP hosting the MP3S4free website, as well as its director and employees, had authorised infringement, primarily because the director and employees were aware of potential contraventions of copyright which could take place through the use of the website (such awareness being evident from a commercial arrangement between the ISP and Cooper whereby Cooper received free hosting of the website in return for advertising space on it).

The decision is also notable for the finding that disclaimers on the website were insufficient to cure what was otherwise characterised as an authorisation of copyright infringement.

(a) *Liability of company directors*

Generally, a company director who instigates an infringement of copyright by his or her company is liable as a joint tortfeasor: *C Evans & Sons Ltd v Spriteband Ltd* [1985] 2 All ER 415 (CA).

In *Kalamazoo (Aust) Pty Ltd v Compact Business Systems Pty Ltd* (1985) 5 IPR 213, at pp 240-241, it was held that a director of a company will not automatically be liable for any tort that the company commits. However, if a director authorised or directed the particular course that the company followed, the director will be liable for copyright infringement together with the company.

Thus, if a company is formed for the express purpose of doing a wrongful act, the individual officers and company will also be liable for such actions.

Section 133 specifically provides for an officer of a body corporate to be held liable where a body corporate is convicted of an offence under s 131 and the officer knowingly authorises, permits or consents to the offending act or fails to prevent it. This is discussed in more detail at 4.14 ("Offences") later in this chapter.

It is important that a party seeking to lift the corporate veil and join a company director personally to proceedings accurately sets out the basis for doing so, otherwise the Court may strike out the pleading or decline an application for joinder (as was the case in *Bonson Industrial Co Ltd v Plastech Industries Ltd* 20/5/05, Williams J, HC Auckland CIV-2004-404-6386. In that case, the first defendant, Plastech, was accused of infringing copyright in dyes for manufacturing disposable plastic food trays. Plastech claimed to have purchased the alleged infringing dyes from a third party company, CNT Plastics (1998) Ltd and sought joinder of one of the directors of CNT, a Mr Thompson. That application was refused partially on the basis that while Plastech sought to impede Mr Thompson personally, not CNT which was the owner of the dyes, nowhere had it set out in its application why the corporate veil should be pierced or on what basis Mr Thompson was alleged to be personally liable.

(3) *Copying involves reproduction*

Under s 30 Copyright Act 1994, the copying of a work is a restricted act in relation to every type of copyright work and constitutes primary infringement of the work in question. Under s 2(1), "copying" means, in relation to any type of copyright work, reproducing the work in any material form.

The conventional approach to determining whether a copyright work has been reproduced is stated in Laddie, Prescott, and Vittoria, *Modern Law of Copyright* (3rd ed), London, Butterworths, 2001, at para 14.7:

"But there must be some act of reproduction, that is, the making of something that did not exist before. So it is not an infringement of copyright merely to incorporate a work by reference instead of setting it out verbatim (as in 'Subject to the Law Society's Conditions of Sale'). For the same reason, trading in objects already in existence is not reproduction in a material form (eg: cutting pictures out of books and using them to make table mats), although in certain circumstances it might be a breach of the distribution right."

In *Benchmark Building Supplies Ltd v Mitre 10 (NZ) Ltd* [2004] 1 NZLR 26; (2003) 10 TCLR 767; 7 NZBLC 104,002 (CA), Gault P concluded that Benchmark's application of stickers to a Mitre 10 printed brochure did not constitute a reproduction or, indeed, the creation of a new artistic work. Gault P said, at para 32, that:

"By displaying Mitre 10's own brochures Benchmark has done nothing to reproduce the copyright works. Nothing has been copied. Even if a new work is created incorporating the brochures (and we very much doubt that applying stickers has that effect), the representations of the copyright works remained unchanged and no new representations of them were made."

Reproduction requires the creation of something not previously in existence. Only in rare circumstances can a reproduction occur where there is no duplication of the original work. One such example occurred in *Théberge v Galerie d'Art du Petit Champlain Inc* (2002) 210 DLR (4th) 385. In that case, the defendants had purchased lawfully produced posters depicting paintings. Using a chemical process, the ink was lifted from the posters and applied to canvasses that were then offered for sale.

(4) *Three-stage test for primary infringement*

To establish primary infringement of copyright under the Copyright Act 1994, three elements must be proved:

- Reproduction of either the entire copyright work or a substantial part;

- A sufficient objective similarity between the infringing work and the copyright work or a substantial part; and

- A causal connection between the copyright work and the infringing work, in that the copyright work is the source from which the infringing work is derived.

(a) *Substantiality*

One of the indicators of infringement is the degree of similarity between the copyright work and the alleged infringing work. It is not necessary for the work to be copied in its entirety. It is sufficient to establish that such similarity exists between a substantial part of the copyright work and the alleged infringing work.

Whether the part of a copyright work that has been reproduced is a substantial part must be decided by its quality rather than by its quantity. This issue is particularly relevant in claims concerning infringement of copyright in compilations, which are literary works but may be made up of components (for example, data) which are not subject to copyright protection in isolation. This was discussed by Lord Pearce in *Ladbroke (Football) Ltd v William Hill (Football) Ltd* [1964] 1 WLR 273 (HL), at p 293:

"The reproduction of a part which by itself has no originality will not normally be a substantial part of the copyright and therefore will not be protected. For that which would not attract copyright except by reason of its collocation will, when robbed of that collocation, not be a substantial part of the copyright and therefore the courts will not hold its reproduction to be an infringement. It is this, I think, which is meant by one or two judicial observations that 'there is no copyright' in some unoriginal part of a whole that is copyright. They afford no justification, in my view, for holding that one starts the enquiry as to whether copyright exists by dissecting the compilation into component parts instead of starting it by regarding the compilation as a whole and seeing whether the whole has copyright. It is when one is debating whether the part reproduced is substantial that one considers the pirated portion on its own."

The same test was applied in *Wham-O MFG Co v Lincoln Industries Ltd* [1984] 1 NZLR 641 (CA), at p 666; *Land Transport Safety Authority of NZ v Glogau* [1999] 1 NZLR 261 (CA); *University of Waikato v Benchmarking Services Ltd* (2004) 8 NZBLC 101,561 (CA); and *Henkel KgaA v Holdfast NZ Ltd* [2007] 1 NZLR 577 (SC), at para 44.

In *University of Waikato*, the appellants claimed infringement of copyright in a number of compilations, including a questionnaire for an annual survey designed to collect financial data from New Zealand businesses and a report based upon the results of that questionnaire. The report showed data from the questionnaire, tabulated with headings and sub-headings and included additional comparative information. The Court of Appeal confirmed that the starting point for determining whether the respondents had infringed copyright in a substantial part of the appellant's compilations was to consider the particular elements of the works in which copyright subsisted. They stated, at para 42:

"Considered in isolation, some elements of the report are commonplace such as the inclusion of income, the derivation of gross profit, the deduction of overheads, and the calculation of operating profit. But there are a number of unusual or unique features which clearly result from the expenditure of significant creative effort and skill on the appellant's part [including] the headings adopted; the order in which they appear; the selection and calculation of ratios; the presentation and calculation of figures and percentages (designed to show a range of performances of businesses in the category selected); and the overall format and presentation of the report."

The Court of Appeal held, at para 46, that, when compared with the respondents' brochure, there was a striking similarity between it and the appellant's report. The respondents' brochure copied, with only minor changes of detail, the headings and a number of the columns in the report, as well as the format of the report in terms of the placement of dollar figures and percentages (which featured in exactly the same places). Thus, the aspects of the report reproduced in the respondents' brochure were deemed by the Court to form a substantial part of the appellant's compilation.

The decision in *University of Waikato* is also notable because it was a successful appeal from the decision of a Master not to grant summary judgment in proceedings alleging infringement of copyright (see 4.12 ("Remedies") below).

In *TCN Channel Nine Pty Ltd v Network Ten Pty Ltd* (2002) 118 FCR 417; 190 ALR 468; 55 IPR 112 (FCA), the Federal Court of Australia departed from the general rule as to substantiality when considering a copyright infringement action involving broadcasting. The Federal Court held that visual images do not have to comprise a substantial part of a television broadcast, but instead, reproduction of one visual image is sufficient to infringe copyright in the television broadcast. Thus, the Court found that Network Ten had infringed Channel Nine's copyright by broadcasting segments ranging from 8 to 42 seconds duration from Channel Nine's programmes ranging from 30 to 60 minutes. However, the finding was successfully appealed to the High Court of Australia: *Network Ten Pty Ltd v TCN Channel Nine Pty Ltd* (2004) 218 CLR 273; 205 ALR 1, 59 IPR 1 (HCA). On appeal, the majority of the High Court (McHugh ACJ, Gummow, Hayne, and Callinan JJ; Kirby J dissenting) found that, when determining whether or not a substantial part of the television broadcast has been copied, it is necessary to have regard to the whole television broadcast, rather than individual images featured within it. Having defined the correct test, their Honours remitted back to the Federal Court the question whether or not each of the segments of Channel Nine's programmes reproduced by Network Ten constituted a substantial part of Channel Nine's television broadcasts.

In *Designers Guild v Russell Williams (Textiles) Ltd* [2001] 1 All ER 700; [2000] 1 WLR 2416; [2001] FSR 113 (HL), at p 709; p 2426; p 125, per Lord Millet, the House of Lords confirmed that, when the question of substantiality is under consideration, the focus is on the similarities rather than the differences. The pirated part is considered on its own, and its importance to the copyright work is assessed in order to determine whether it forms a substantial part of the copyright work. To do this, there is no need to look at the whole of the infringing work. It is the importance of the pirated part to the original work which matters.

See also the comments of the New Zealand Court of Appeal in *Bleiman v News Media (Auckland) Ltd* [1994] 2 NZLR 673; (1994) 6 TCLR 56; 5 NZBLC 103,446 (CA), at p 679; p 62; p 103,451:

> "However, copyright infringement focuses on what has been taken, the similarities. Differences are of less moment. The fact that separate original work has been added to an infringement does not make it any the less an infringement."

(b) *Objective similarity*

Even if the alleged copy takes a substantial part of the original, it is still necessary that the copy looks objectively similar to the original in order to establish that copyright in the work has been infringed.

Whether there is objective similarity is largely a matter of impression for the Court. As one Judge phrased it "a copy is a copy if it looks like a copy": *Thornton Hall Mfg Ltd v Shanton Apparel Ltd (No 2)* (1988) 13 IPR 463, at pp 470-471.

When determining whether there is sufficient objective similarity the Court's assessment will focus on the similarities between the works.

This assessment was undertaken in *Tidd Ross Todd Ltd v Steelbro NZ Ltd* 1/12/05, Chisholm J, HC Christchurch CIV-2004-409-1386. Steelbro had developed a sideloading container trailer, which Tidd Ross Todd Ltd ("TRT") alleged was based upon their own design known as the "TRT Triple". In making the comparison between the parties' respective trailers, Chisholm J noted the Court of Appeal's comments in *Bleiman v News Media (Auckland)*

Ltd [1994] 2 NZLR 673; (1994) 6 TCLR 56; 5 NZBLC 103,446 (CA), at p 679; p 62; p 103,451, that:

> "copyright infringement focuses on what has been taken, the similarities".

His Honour, however, noted that caution should be taken in the case of commercial designs, stating, at para 42, that "it is necessary to carefully examine the detail and recognise that where there are manufacturing constraints competing products will necessarily be similar and differences may be of particular significance". *UPL Group Ltd v Dux Engineers Ltd* [1989] 3 NZLR 135 was referred to as an example of circumstances where small differences between the parties' respective products were enough to rebut the inference of infringement. In that case, the Court recognised there were limited variations available in the design of common domestic appliances such as lavatory seats and lids and held that Dux's "Twinline" toilet seat was not a reproduction of UPL's "Caroma Uniset".

In *TRT* (above), however, his Honour found, at para 135, that Steelbro had used TRT's design as a spring board, taking "the essence of the TRT design and thereby appropriat[ing] TRT's time, skill and judgment in arriving at [Steelbro's] design" and accordingly that there was infringement of TRT's copyright.

(c)   *Causal connection*

In order to succeed in an action for copyright infringement under the Copyright Act 1994, a plaintiff must also prove that the defendant has directly or indirectly made an unlawful use of the plaintiff's copyright work. In other words, the starting point for the defendant's work must have been that of the plaintiff. This is known as a causal connection.

It is not necessary to show that the defendant has copied directly from the plaintiff's work. It is sufficient for the plaintiff to establish some chain of causation linking the plaintiff's copyright work with the defendant's alleged infringing copy: *Wham-O MFG Co v Lincoln Industries Ltd* [1984] 1 NZLR 641 (CA), at p 668:

> "The copying need not be direct copying. It may be indirect. What must be shown, however, is that either directly or indirectly the alleged defendant copier has in making his copies appropriated the labours of the plaintiff. That copying has taken place is for the plaintiff to establish and prove as a matter of fact. The beginning of the necessary proof normally lies in the establishment of similarity combined with proof of access to the plaintiff's productions: *LB (Plastics) Ltd v Swish Products Ltd* (1979) 96 RPC 551 per Lord Wilberforce at p 619."

In the first copyright case to be referred to the New Zealand Supreme Court (*Henkel KgaA v Holdfast NZ Ltd* [2007] 1 NZLR 577 (SC)) the Court had the following to say regarding causal connection, at para 43:

> "The ultimate issue in a breach of copyright case concerns derivation not similarity, albeit the degree of similarity between the copyright work and the allegedly infringing work has evidentiary significance. Proof of copying will seldom be direct; in most cases the Court will rely on inference. The closer the similarity between the two works the stronger the inference is likely to be that the one was copied from the other. If the alleged infringer has had access to, and therefore an opportunity to copy, the copyright work, and the similarity between the works supports an inference of copying, it may well be appropriate for the Court to conclude, on the balance of

211

probabilities, that there was indeed copying. This of course is subject always to the evaluation of any evidence there may be that no copying actually took place."

(d) *Altered copying*

Bleiman v News Media (Auckland) Ltd [1994] 2 NZLR 673; (1994) 6 TCLR 56; 5 NZBLC 103,446 (CA) is authority for the proposition that, if the starting point of the defendant's design is a copy of the plaintiff's work, the level of effort which the defendant subsequently expends modifying the work may be irrelevant. Again it was emphasised that the correct approach is to establish whether the plaintiff's own skill, effort, and judgment have been taken by the defendant.

The same approach was advocated by the House of Lords in *Designers Guild v Russell Williams (Textiles) Ltd* [2001] 1 All ER 700; [2000] 1 WLR 2416; [2001] FSR 113 (HL), at p 714; p 2431; p 130, per Lord Scott of Foscote:

> "The other type of case in which a question of substantiality may become relevant is where the copying has not been an exact copying of the copyright work but a copying with modifications. This type of copying is referred to in *Laddie* as 'altered copying'. ...

> "The present case is an 'altered copying' case. Helen Burke put together a number of artistic ideas derived from various sources in order to produce her *Ixia* [fabric] design, an original artistic design as it is accepted to be. Ms Ibbotson and Mrs Williams, as the Judge found, copied the *Ixia* design in order to produce their *Marguerite* design. But they did so with modifications. The *Marguerite* design is not an exact copy of *Ixia*, nor is any specific part of the *Marguerite* design an exact copy of any corresponding part of the *Ixia* design. It is an altered copy.

> "The question is, then, where an altered copy has been produced, is what the test should be in order to determine whether the production constitutes a copyright infringement. If the alterations are sufficiently extensive it may be that the copying does not constitute an infringement at all. The test proposed in *Laddie* (pp 92, 93 (para 2-108)) to determine whether an altered copy constitutes an infringement is: 'Has the infringer incorporated a substantial part of the independent skill, labour etc contributed by the original author in creating the copyright work ... ?'

> "My Lords, I think this is a useful test, based as it is on an underlying principle of copyright law, namely, that a copier is not at liberty to appropriate the benefit of another's skill and labour."

The ultimate test is whether the defendant has appropriated the time, labour, skill, and judgment contributed by the original author in creating the copyright work. One test for this may be to enquire whether the defendant has managed to shortcut the design process through use of the copyright work, similar to the springboard enquiry in breach of confidence cases.

4.10.4 Secondary infringement

Secondary (or indirect) infringement of a copyright work is governed by ss 35-39 Copyright Act 1994.

Secondary infringement most commonly arises under s 35 where a person, other than the copyright owner/licensee, imports an infringing copy (of any type of copyright work other than a sound recording, film, or computer program) into New Zealand, other than for that person's private and domestic use and they knew or had reason to believe that the object was an infringing copy. As discussed in more detail below, this test is subjective. In the case of a sound recording, film, or computer program, secondary infringement would arise where a person knew, or ought reasonably to have known, that the imported object was an infringing copy. Thus, the test for sound recordings, films, or computer programmes is objective.

(1) *Meaning of "infringing copy"*

"Infringing copy" is defined in s 12 Copyright Act 1994 as any object the making of which constitutes an infringement of copyright in the work in question.

Where goods are imported, the object is considered to be an "infringing copy" if:

- The making of the object constituted an infringement of copyright in the country in which it was made; or

- The making of the object would have infringed copyright in New Zealand had it been made here by the importer.

Section 12(5A) specifically excludes from the definition of "infringing copy":

- Parallel imported goods (except films, sound recordings and software which are presumed to be infringing copies subject to proof to the contrary);

- Goods in which the owner has failed to secure copyright (where protection was available to them);

- Goods in which copyright protection has expired; and

- Goods industrially applied overseas.

The industrial application of goods is discussed in more detail at 4.7 ("Duration of copyright") earlier in this chapter.

The test for infringement is discussed earlier in this section at 4.10.3(4) ("Three-stage test for primary infringement").

(2) *Knowledge required*

Under s 35(1)(a)(ii) Copyright Act 1994, a person may be liable for secondary infringement of copyright where they import into New Zealand an object (other than a sound recording, film or computer program) that is an infringing copy of a copyright work and they knew, or had reason to believe, that the object was an infringing copy. The person's knowledge must be tested subjectively under this section. In *Crystal Glass Industries Ltd v Alwinco Products Ltd* 15/4/83, Prichard J, HC Hamilton A236/78, Prichard J held, at p 46, that a subjective test for knowledge involved asking the question whether the alleged infringer honestly believed the object was an infringing copy.

Under s 35(1)(a)(i), a person may be liable for secondary infringement of copyright if they import a sound recording, film, or computer program into New Zealand that is an infringing copy of a copyright work and they knew, or ought reasonably to have known, that the sound recording, film, or computer program was an infringing copy. The person's knowledge must be tested objectively under this section.

(3)   *Onus of proof for knowledge requirement*

In most cases, the onus of proving knowledge lies with the plaintiff who must prove subjective knowledge that the object was an infringing copy.

However, in respect of sound recordings, films and computer programs (in some circumstances) the defendant bears the onus of establishing, objectively, that they did not have, and ought not reasonably to have had, knowledge that the object was an infringing copy of the copyright work in question.

(4)   *Ignorance of law no excuse*

A lack of knowledge on the part of the defendant based on an error of law may still amount to infringement.

(5)   *Parallel imports permitted*

Following the enactment of the Copyright (Removal of Prohibition on Parallel Importing) Amendment Act 1998, the parallel importation of genuine products no longer amounts to infringement under the Copyright Act 1994 (s 12(5A)). However, importers must still be aware of other intellectual property rights, particularly trade mark rights.

For example, in *Transport Tyre Sales Pty Ltd v Montana Tyres, Rims & Tubes Pty Ltd* (1999) 43 IPR 481; [1999] FCA 329; (1999) 93 FCR 421, the local distributor of a tyre manufacturer obtained an assignment of the manufacturer's registered trade mark in order to take action against parallel importers. The assignment was on terms that the mark would revert to the tyre manufacturer when the distributorship terminated. The Federal Court of Australia held that the trade mark assignment was lawful even though the assignor retained an option to have the trade mark reassigned to it.

The only New Zealand decision to consider the application of s 12(5A) to date is the decision of Heath J in *Leisureworld Ltd v Elite Fitness Equipment Ltd* 21/7/06, Heath J, HC Auckland CIV-2006-404-3499, an interlocutory decision dealing with Leisureworld's application for an interim injunction. The decision also considers the inter-relationship between the removal of the prohibition on parallel importation under the Copyright Act 1994 and the Trade Marks Act 2002.

Leisureworld and Elite Fitness competed in the New Zealand market for the sale of fitness equipment. In early 2005, Leisureworld acquired the business of a further competitor (Progym NZ) which included a bundle of intellectual property rights for "Infiniti" branded equipment manufactured by an associated Taiwanese company, Progym Taiwan. Among the assets transferred to Leisureworld on settlement were copyright in the products, and two registrations for the "Infiniti" trade mark in New Zealand. Elite subsequently imported "Infiniti" branded fitness equipment made by Progym Taiwan, and Leisureworld sought an interim injunction restraining Elite from continuing to do so on the basis that its actions breached Leisureworld's copyright and registered trade mark rights in New Zealand. Elite's response was that its actions fell within the ambit of the parallel importing exceptions under the Copyright Act 1994 and the Trade Marks Act 2002.

After considering the policy behind the respective amendments to the Copyright Act at length, Heath J reached the following conclusions in respect of the applicability of s 12(5A), at paras 69-72:

"In order to come within the parallel importing exception to infringement of Leisureworld's copyright, the equipment must have been made by or with the consent of the owner of the copyright in the equipment in the country in which the object was made. If no person owns copyright, or other equivalent intellectual property right, in the equipment, then, for the parallel importing provisions to apply, the equipment must have been made in that other country by or with the consent of the owner of the copyright in New Zealand. See s 12(5A)(a) and (b)(iv) of the Copyright Act.

"In my view, Leisureworld faces a potential difficulty in asserting infringement of copyright in New Zealand, at least on an interim injunction application, because of the way in which s 12(5A)(b)(iv) is expressed. There is no doubt that the gymnasium equipment was made in Taiwan pursuant to the arrangements entered into between Leisureworld and Progym NZ when the copyright was transferred to Leisureworld.

"Because Elite bears no onus of proof in relation to the goods in question (see s 35(2) and (6) of the Copyright Act) Leisureworld retains the onus of proving its entitlement to sue for infringement of its copyright.

"On the present evidence, there is a real possibility that s 12(5A)(b)(iv) of the Copyright Act might apply with the consequence that Leisureworld could not sue for infringement. However, in view of the conclusions I have reached on the trade mark point I need not explore this issue further."

Parallel imported sound recordings, films, and software have been specifically addressed by the Government in the Copyright (Parallel Importation of Films and Onus of Proof) Amendment Act 2003, which came into force on 31 October 2003. The 2003 Amendment Act amends s 9(2) and (3) of the principal Act and repeals s 35, replacing it with a new section.

Under the new s 35(1)(a)(i), copyright in a sound recording, film, or computer program is infringed by a person who imports an infringing copy into New Zealand, when that person knows or ought reasonably to know that the object is an infringing copy. A different standard of proof applies in relation to other copyright works, where the importer must actually know or have reason to believe that the object is an infringing copy to be liable (s 35(1)(a)(ii)).

In the case of all copyright works, the importer has a defence if it can be shown that the objects were imported with a copyright licence (s 35(1)(b)) or for the importer's private or domestic use (s 35(1)(c)).

Section 35(2), as amended, creates a presumption that goods are "infringing copies" in civil proceedings brought under s 35, relating to the importation of sound recordings, films, and computer programs. Section 35(2) also protects a defendant against having to disclose information concerning the sources of supply of imported products, if it is unreasonable for him or her to do so. The intention of this provision is to protect the interests of legitimate parallel importers.

The amended s 35(3) introduces a ban on parallel importation of films for commercial purposes for a period of 9 months from a title's first international release. Section 35(3) only remains in effect until 31 October 2008 (see s 35(5)).

The amendments to s 9(2) and (3) of the principal Act clarify the scope of rental rights granted to owners of copyright in films, sound recordings, and computer programs where copies of those works have been parallel imported. This confirms the High Court decision in *Video Ezy International (NZ) Ltd v Roadshow Entertainment (NZ) Ltd* [2002] 1 NZLR 855; (2002) 7 NZBLC 103,524, where it was held that the rental of parallel imported DVDs infringed the rental rights of the owner of copyright in the recently released films.

It is significant that the 2003 Amendment Act only affects s 35 of the principal Act, which relates to importing infringing copies, and not s 36, which relates to possessing or dealing with infringing copies. Importers of infringing goods are often caught by New Zealand Customs. However, the battle against pirated goods usually takes place once they have passed into New Zealand and are in the hands of dealers or purchasers. In these circumstances, the copyright owner must rely on s 36 to bring an action against such infringers. The creation of a presumption that an object is an infringing copy (in the absence of evidence to the contrary) would have been very useful in respect of s 36 infringements.

(6) *Other secondary infringements*

Other acts amounting to secondary infringement include:

- Possessing or dealing with an infringing copy in the course of business in New Zealand where there is reason to believe that it is an infringing copy (s 36);

- Providing a means for making infringing copies (s 37);

- Permitting use of premises for an infringing performance of a literary, dramatic, or musical work (s 38); or

- Providing apparatus for an infringing performance (s 39).

(a) *Providing means for making infringing copies*

The ambit of s 37(1) is quite narrow in the sense that it only applies to an object "specifically" designed or adapted for making copies of a work. An object that was designed for another (lawful or unlawful) purpose but which could be used for making unauthorised copies of a copyright work would not be "specifically designed" and therefore would not meet the requirements of the section.

See for example *CBS Songs Ltd v Amstrad Consumer Electronics Plc* [1987] RPC 429; [1987] 3 All ER 151; [1988] Ch 61 (CA), in which the British phonographic industry unsuccessfully sought to injunct Amstrad selling tape recorders with a high speed copying facility.

However, for the defence (that a means is not specifically used to make infringing copies) to apply the defendants must not have engaged in acts or omissions which encourage users to use the means to make such copies. Two decisions of the US Supreme Court and Federal Court of Australia illustrate this point.

In *Metro-Goldwyn-Mayer Studios Inc v Grokster Ltd* 545 US 913; 125 S Ct 2764; 75 USPQ 2d 1001 (US, 2005), the US Supreme Court overturned a ruling by the Ninth Circuit that exempted distributors of Peer-to-Peer ("PTP") file sharing software from liability arising from copyright infringement committed by users of the PTP software.

Grokster and StreamCast Networks distributed free PTP software products that allowed computer users to directly share and copy electronic files of music, movies, and other materials. Metro-Goldwyn-Mayer Studios Inc ("MGM") was the owner of copyright in some of the materials shared and copied using that PTP software, and sued Grokster and StreamCast on the basis that they were liable for those infringements.

In their defence, Grokster and StreamCast relied on the Supreme Court's 1984 decision in *Sony Corp of America v Universal City Studios Inc* 464 US 417 (1984), which centred around Sony's Betamax video cassette recorder, a product also capable of being used for copying material subject to copyright protection. In that case, the Supreme Court held that mere distribution of such a product would not make the distributor liable for secondary infringement of copyright if the product was a staple article of commerce "capable of substantial non-infringing uses". The trial and appellate Courts in *Grokster* held that the PTP software products distributed by Grokster and StreamCast satisfied the *Sony* standard of being capable of substantial non-infringing uses.

In concurring opinions, the Supreme Court was split as to the question of whether the evidence satisfied the *Sony* standard. Three Judges held that the PTP software was capable of sufficient substantial non-infringing uses; three that it was not; and three expressed no opinion. However, the *Grokster* decision did not ultimately turn on the characteristics of the PTP software product itself. Instead, the Supreme Court unanimously held that the trial and appellate courts had erred by applying *Sony*'s product-centred standard to the exclusion of evidence that shows "statements or actions directed to promoting infringement".

The Supreme Court highlighted evidence that Grokster and StreamCast each intended the PTP software product to be used for infringing purposes, and took active steps to encourage such infringement by users. Drawing analogy with contributory infringement in patent law, the Supreme Court held that a party can be liable for "inducing" copyright infringement by another. While the Supreme Court was at pains to point out that mere knowledge of infringing potential, or of actual infringing uses, would not be enough to subject a distributor to liability, Grokster and StreamCast's advertising, business planning and internal communications provided substantial evidence of inducement, and the trial and appellate courts' summary judgment rulings in favour of Grokster and StreamCast were overturned.

In *Universal Music Australia Pty Ltd v Cooper* (2005) 150 FCR 1; 65 IPR 409 (FCA), Tamberlin J found that Cooper, in operating a website MP3S4free.net, which contained links to copyright material, authorised copyright infringement by users who downloaded the MP3 files and by operators of remote websites where the infringing MP3 files were stored, notwithstanding that the MP3 files were never sent to, downloaded onto, or stored on the MP3S4free website itself.

Tamberlin J found that Cooper's actions amounted to more than mere facilitation as the MP3S4free website was operated in a way which was "clearly designed to, and does facilitate and enable [the] infringing downloading", and Cooper had "knowingly permitted and approved the use of his website in this manner and designed and organised it to achieve this result".

Tamberlin J found that Cooper was able to prevent the infringements, either by removing the links to infringing material from his website, or structuring the website so that the operators of the remote sites could not automatically add hyperlinks without some control by Cooper.

Tamberlin J also found that the ISP hosting the MP3S4free website, as well as its director and employees, had authorised infringement, primarily because the director and employees were aware of potential contraventions of copyright which could take place through the use of the website (such awareness being evident from a commercial arrangement between the ISP and Cooper whereby Cooper received free hosting of the website in return for advertising space on it).

The decision is also notable for the finding that disclaimers on the website were insufficient to cure what was otherwise characterised as an authorisation of copyright infringement.

4.10.5 Jurisdiction

In certain limited circumstances it may be possible for the owner of a copyright work in a number of jurisdictions to sue a New Zealand-based defendant for breaches of its foreign rights committed in those foreign jurisdictions. The question of whether and in what circumstances such actions are permissible was considered in *Kabushiki Kaisha Sony Computer Entertainment v van Veen* 14/12/06, MacKenzie J, HC Wellington CIV-2004-485-1520.

The plaintiffs (collectively "Sony") were the proprietors of the PlayStation 2 computer games system, and owned intellectual property rights in some of the games played on that system. Those games were distributed on CDs and DVDs and, to assist in their protection, Sony embedded codes which prevented copying of the games from the CD or DVD to another medium. The defendants developed and distributed a software programme called HD Loader which enabled a user to circumvent the embedded copy protection code and copy Sony's games. The HD Loader programme was developed by the first defendant who sold or licensed the use of that programme in, amongst other countries, the UK and Hong Kong through the second defendant.

Sony commenced proceedings and obtained a number of interim orders. Following completion of the pleadings the first defendant admitted the material allegations in the Statement of Claim (breach of the New Zealand Copyright and Trade Marks Acts, breach of the UK Copyright, Designs and Patents Act 1988, breach of the Hong Kong Copyright Ordinance, and wrongful possession and use of confidential information) and Sony applied for judgment against the first defendant.

On each of the causes of action relating to breaches of the New Zealand legislation and wrongful use and possession of confidential information, the admitted facts clearly gave rise to liability which could be enforced in New Zealand. Those causes of action were based on New Zealand law and on actions admitted to have taken place in New Zealand. The more difficult question was whether the Court could determine causes of action relating to alleged breaches of UK and Hong Kong copyright legislation.

The starting point for the Court was the rule laid down by the House of Lords in *British South Africa Co v Companhia de Mocambique* [1893] AC 602 (HL), which stated that the Court has no jurisdiction to entertain an action for (1) the determination of the title to, or the right to possession of, any immoveable situate out of England (foreign land); or (2) the recovery of damages for trespass to such immoveable. MacKenzie J noted, at paras 9 and 10, that the rule had been applied in Australia and England in several cases involving intellectual property rights, and had been applied by Tipping J in New Zealand in *Atkinson Footwear Ltd v Hodgskin International Services Ltd* (1994) 31 IPR 186 in respect of an application for an interim injunction to restrain the distribution of footwear allegedly infringing the plaintiff's copyright in New Zealand and Australia. Tipping J granted the application with respect to New Zealand but declined to extend it to Australia. However, MacKenzie J noted that since the decision of Tipping J in *Atkinson Footwear* the UK Court of Appeal had carefully reconsidered the position in *Pearce v Ove Arup Partnership Ltd* [1999] 1 All ER 769 (CA), a case involving the construction of a public building in Rotterdam which was a copy of a plan produced by an architectural student in London. The UK Court of Appeal held in *Pearce* that the English Courts did have jurisdiction to entertain a claim in respect of the alleged infringement of Dutch copyright by virtue of actions occurring in Holland on the basis that the *Mocambique* rule involves two limbs, the second of which makes a distinction between proceedings where issue of title, or the extent of rights available under a foreign law arise, on the one hand, and claims where the matter in issue is not the existence or nature of the title or rights, but whether some action has the effect of infringing the unquestioned rights of the plaintiff. MacKenzie J concluded, at para 19:

> "I find the reasoning [in *Pearce*] persuasive in favour of the proposition that, in the case of intellectual property rights governed by the law of a foreign country, the second limb of the *Mocambique* rule should not exclude justiciability in respect of actions for breach of intellectual property rights established under the law of another jurisdiction, when no question of the existence or validity of those rights arises."

adding, at para 22:

> "Nothing which I have said should be taken as questioning the applicability of the first limb of the rule in the *Mocambique* case to questions of title to intellectual property … nor should anything I have said be taken as questioning the applicability of the second limb in the *Mocambique* case to true immoveables such as land … The issue before me is whether the second limb should be extended to items of intellectual property such as those in issue here. The various forms of protection given under intellectual property statutes are territorial in nature, because the statutes conferring them are necessarily territorial in their application. To that extent, they have the characteristics of immoveable property. But the significant difference between such forms of intellectual property and true immoveables such as land is that the same item of intellectual property may be protected by statutory rights in many jurisdictions. A strict application of the second limb of the *Mocambique* case to such rights would mean that, where, as here, a defendant commits infringing acts against a single plaintiff in several jurisdictions, separate proceedings in each jurisdiction will be necessary to deal with those infringements. The inconvenience of such a requirement would outweigh the benefit of certainty that the application of the second limb to such claims would provide. I decline to apply the second limb to this case."

Having concluded that the justiciability of Sony's claim was not excluded by the *Mocambique* rule, MacKenzie J went on to consider whether, on the ordinary principles of the conflict of laws dealing with wrongs committed in another jurisdiction, the New Zealand

Court had jurisdiction. In that regard, the common law double actionability rule applies. The double actionability rule states that, as a general rule, an act done in a foreign country is a tort and actionable as such in New Zealand, only if it is both (a) actionable as a tort according to New Zealand law or, in other words, is an act which, if done in New Zealand, would be a tort; and (b) actionable according to the law of the foreign country where it was done. However, a particular issue between the parties may be governed by the law of the country which, with respect to that issue, has the most significant relationship with the occurrence and the parties.

Having considered the double actionability rule, MacKenzie J went on to address (and resolve) a potential problem in applying that rule to the present case as follows, at paras 24 and 25:

> "In applying that Rule, it may be argued that, since the acts complained of must constitute a wrong actionable under New Zealand law, the acts complained of, being infringements in the United Kingdom and Hong Kong, do not constitute a wrong against New Zealand copyright, since New Zealand copyright is territorial in effect. Therefore, a strict application of the first limb of the double actionability rule would lead to the result that the infringement would not be actionable in New Zealand. That Rule was the subject of consideration in *Pearce*. Roch LJ discussed the difficulty which arises in a case such as this, if the first limb of [the Double Actionability] Rule … requires the [New Zealand] court to determine actionability by [New Zealand] domestic law. He dealt with the proposition that, if, despite the rule in the *Mocambique* case, the claim was justiciable, it was bound to fail the requirements in the first limb of the double actionability rule in these terms at page 803:
>
>> 'If that were a correct analysis, the effect would be that the first limb of r 203(1) imposed a requirement as to jurisdiction; and not simply a rule for the choice of law'
>
> "He went on to note that the view that the first limb of the rule does impose a requirement as to jurisdiction had found expression in the dissenting judgment of Diplock LJ in [*Chaplin v Boys* [1969] 2 All ER 1085 (HL)], but had been plainly rejected by the House of Lords on the appeal. Roch LJ referred to [*Red Sea Insurance Ltd v Bouygues SA* [1994] 3 All ER 749 (PC)], where the Privy Council had accepted that the choice of the lex fori as the applicable law was not an invariable rule; rather that it was 'the general rule' or 'a starting point'. Roch LJ then went on to say, at page 803-804:
>
>> 'In the present case, the plaintiff's claim would be defeated if the court were to refuse to apply the exception. But the claim (if established on the facts) is one where the English court would have given a remedy, under United Kingdom copyright law, if the facts alleged had occurred in England. This is not a case in which the claim is in respect of some wrong which is conceptually unknown in English law. In our view this is a case where, if the claim is justiciable at all, the exception to the double actionability rule enables the English court to apply Dutch law; and the English court ought to do so.'
>
> "I respectfully concur with that reasoning. It seems to me that, in applying the first limb of the double actionability rule, in an intellectual property infringement case,

it is necessary to effect a notional transfer to New Zealand, for consideration under New Zealand law, of both the infringing act, and the intellectual property infringed. The infringing act and the intellectual property infringed cannot sensibly be separated in applying the first limb of [the Double Actionability] Rule … The purpose of the rule is to consider how New Zealand law would regard an act, if that act were committed in New Zealand and subject to New Zealand domestic law. Where the act complained of is an infringement of an intellectual property right, a relevant inquiry, in considering the application of New Zealand domestic law, should be whether that particular form of intellectual property is one which is capable of protection under New Zealand law. The focus should be on the nature of the underlying intellectual property, not on the form in which that property is protected by the laws of the foreign jurisdiction. The laws of the foreign jurisdiction are relevant to the second limb, not the first limb, of the double actionability rule."

Accordingly, MacKenzie J entered judgment against the first defendant in respect of all causes of action. Finally, his Honour clarified, at para 27, that in reaching the conclusions which he had as to the applicability of the *Mocambique* and double actionability rules his findings should be limited to the case of a defendant who is resident in New Zealand and thereby subject to the jurisdiction of the New Zealand Courts.

4.11 Defences

It is possible to defend a claim of infringement. Some of the more common defences include:

- Copyright is not valid and subsisting in the work and therefore the plaintiff does not meet two of the criteria needed to establish copyright infringement as outlined in *P S Johnson & Assocs Ltd v Bucko Enterprises Ltd* [1975] 1 NZLR 311, at p 315 (discussed at 4.10 ("Infringement and enforcement of rights") above).

- There is no infringement in fact. For example, the copyright work and alleged infringing work are not objectively similar, the defendant has copied the work but has not taken a substantial part or there is no causal connection (each discussed earlier in this chapter).

- Equitable defences such as estoppel, waiver and acquiescence are available to the defendant. The defences of estoppel and acquiescence were (unsuccessfully) argued in *Fleming v Fletcher Concrete & Infrastructure Ltd* 1/12/06, Wild J, HC Auckland CIV-2005-404-4598.

- The act complained of is permitted under the Copyright Act 1994.

4.11.1 Permitted acts

Part 3 of the Copyright Act 1994 lists a number of activities permitted in relation to copyright works. Permissible acts include:

- Incidental copying of an artistic work, a sound recording, a film, a broadcast or a cable programme (s 41). The Act does not define what "incidental" copying is. It is a matter of fact to be determined in each case. An example might be the inclusion in a film of a house (in which copyright subsists) in the background to a scene (which is a reproduction in two dimensions of a three dimensional work);

- Fair dealing (or reasonable use) of the works for the purposes of criticism, review, and news reporting (s 42);

- Fair dealing for the purposes of research or private study (s 43);

- Performing, playing, or showing a literary, dramatic, or musical work in the course of the activities of an educational establishment such as a school (s 47);

- Copying by librarians of a reasonable portion of a published work (s 51);

- Communication of a copyright work to the Crown in the course of public business (s 62);

- Rental of a computer program, sound recording or film by an educational establishment or prescribed library (s 79); and

- Recording a broadcast or cable programme privately, for time shifting of viewing (s 84).

The full list of permissible acts is contained in Part 3 of the Act.

(1) *Fair dealing for purpose of research or private study*

The assessment of whether dealing is fair is a subjective one made by taking all of the facts of the individual case into account. For example, in the case of fair dealing for research or private study the copying must be conducted by the person doing the research. An institute cannot make a master copy for students to further copy: *Copyright Licensing Ltd v University of Auckland* [2002] 3 NZLR 76; (2002) 53 IPR 618; 7 NZBLC 103,585.

"Dealing" and "research" have been widely construed: *TVNZ Ltd v Newsmonitor Services Ltd* [1994] 2 NZLR 91.

The following (non-exhaustive) list of factors may be taken into account when assessing whether the dealing with a work is fair for the purposes of s 43 Copyright Act 1994:

- The purpose of the copying;

- The nature of the work copied;

- Whether the work could be legitimately obtained in a reasonable time at a reasonable price; and

- The substantiality of the part copied.

The application of the equivalent Canadian section was given an extensive review by the Supreme Court of Canada in *CCH Canadian Ltd v Law Society of Upper Canada* (2004) 60 IPR 650 (SCC). The Law Society of Upper Canada maintained and operated a reference and research library in Toronto which also housed one of the largest law collections in Canada. It provided a request-based photocopy service and maintained self-service photocopiers. In 1993, a group of publishers commenced copyright infringement proceedings against the Law Society.

One of the questions for the Court to determine was whether the request-based photocopy service offered by the Law Society fell within the fair dealing defence under s 29 of the Canadian Act which provides that "fair dealing for the purpose of research or private study does not infringe copyright". Delivering the judgment of the Court, McLachlin CJ set out the following six factors which should be considered in assessing whether a dealing was fair:

- **The purpose of the dealing**: Allowable purposes under the Act were said to be research, private study, criticism, review, or news reporting. However, to ensure that users' rights are not unduly constrained, these purposes are not to be given a restrictive interpretation, and research in particular is not limited to commercial or private contexts;

- **The character of the dealing**: The Court must examine how the works were dealt with:

  > "If multiple copies of works are being widely distributed, this will tend to be unfair. If, however, a single copy of a work is used for a specific legitimate purpose, then it may be easier to conclude that it was a fair dealing. If the copy of the work is destroyed after it is used for its specific intended purpose, this may also favour a finding of fairness. It may be relevant to consider the custom or practice in a particular trade or industry to determine whether or not the character of the dealing is fair." (para 55)

- **The amount of the dealing**: The importance of the work should be considered. The quantity of the work taken will not be determinative but may also be relevant:

  > "It may be possible to deal fairly with a whole work ... The amounts taken may also be more or less fair depending on the purpose. For example, for the purpose of research or private study, it may be essential to copy an entire academic article or an entire judicial decision. However, if a work of literature is copied for the purpose of criticism, it will not likely be fair to include a full copy of the work in the critique." (para 56)

- **Alternatives to dealing**: Whether there are any alternatives to dealing with the copyright work;

- **The nature of the work**: For example, if the work is confidential its use and subsequent disclosure might suggest unfairness; and

- **The effect of the dealing on the work**: For example, whether the work which results from the dealing will compete with the original work.

On the facts, McLachlin CJ held that the Law Society did not infringe the plaintiff's copyright.

At least one commentator has advocated the adoption of the Supreme Court of Canada's approach in future fair dealing cases in New Zealand: A Kingsbury, "Finding the Copyright Balance: Originality, Authorisation and Fair Dealing in Canadian and New Zealand Law" (2005) 4(4) NZIPJ 68, at p 73.

(2) *Fair dealing for purpose of criticism, review, and news reporting*

For unauthorised use of a work to constitute fair dealing under s 42 Copyright Act 1994 for the purposes of criticism, review, and news reporting it must be a reasonable use. What is reasonable will depend on the facts of each case.

It is not the quantity of material copied, but the reason that the material has been copied, that determines whether the copying was fair.

In *TCN Channel Nine Pty Ltd v Network Ten Pty Ltd* (2002) 108 FCR 235; 184 ALR 1; 50 IPR 335 (FCA), Conti J in the Federal Court of Australia considered whether, under s 87(c) Copyright Act 1968 (Aust), Network Ten had infringed the copyright in twenty excerpts of Channel Nine's broadcasts by re-broadcasting the same. (See also *TCN Channel Nine Pty Ltd v Network Ten Pty Ltd (No 2)* [2001] FCA 841 (FCA), for Conti J's judgment corresponding to the claim that Network Ten infringed Channel Nine's copyright in the same broadcasts under s 87(a) Copyright Act 1968 (Aust) — the material conclusions of which are the same). Responding to the allegations, Network Ten claimed that the re-broadcast was permitted under the provisions in the Australian Act equivalent to s 42 Copyright Act 1994, for the purpose of criticism and review or news reporting.

To establish infringement, Channel Nine had to establish that Network Ten copied a substantial part of the broadcasts. Conti J held, at para 70, that Network Ten had not copied a substantial part of any of the broadcasts and therefore no infringement had occurred. Accordingly, it was unnecessary to consider whether Network Ten could avail itself of a fair dealing defence. Nevertheless, Conti J reviewed the principles applicable to the criticism or review, or news reporting fair dealing exceptions and made the following conclusions about the fair dealing defence, at para 66:

- Fair dealing involves questions of degree and impression: it is to be judged by the criterion of a fair minded and honest person, and is an abstract concept;

- Fairness (or in the New Zealand context, reasonableness) is to be judged objectively in relation to the relevant purpose (ie, criticism or review, or reporting news);

- Criticism and review are words of wide and indefinite scope which should be interpreted liberally, but nevertheless involve the passing of judgment, which may be strongly expressed;

- Criticism and review must be genuine, not a pretence for some other purpose, but if genuine, need not be balanced;

- An oblique or hidden motive may disqualify reliance upon criticism and review, particularly where the copyright infringer is a trade rival who uses the copyright work for its own benefit, particularly in a dissembling way;

- Criticism and review extends to thoughts underlying the expression of the copyright works;

- News is not restricted to current events; and

- News may involve the use of humour, though the distinction between news and entertainment may be difficult to determine in particular situations.

His Honour examined the application of those principles to the facts of the case, ascertaining the purpose for which each excerpt was used by Network Ten, and concluded, at paras 71-73, that, in relation to a number of the excerpts copied (but not all), the excerpts were used for the purpose of entertainment alone. Accordingly, Network Ten would not have been able to rely upon the fair dealing exception for the purpose of criticism or review, or news reporting, had it been necessary to do so.

On appeal from Conti J (*TCN Channel Nine Pty Ltd v Network Ten Pty Ltd* (2002) 118 FCR 417; 190 ALR 468; 55 IPR 112 (FCA)), Sundberg, Finkelstein, and Hely JJ in the Federal Court of Australia held that Network Ten had infringed copyright in the broadcasts in question and proceeded to consider whether Network Ten would succeed under the fair dealing defence in relation to each excerpt. Sundberg J noted, at para 2, that where Hely J and Finkelstein J differed as to the availability, or otherwise, of the defence in relation to particular excerpts, he upheld the decision of Conti J unless convinced it was wrong. His Honour noted:

> "Fair dealing involves questions of degree and impression, on which different minds can reasonably come to different conclusions."

At para 97, Hely J appeared to accept the principles set out by Conti J in his first judgment (above) as applicable to the fair dealing defence for the purpose of criticism or review, or news reporting. Hely J, at paras 109-131, examined the application of those principles to the facts of the case and determined whether, in relation to each excerpt, the primary Judge, Conti J, had erred in finding that the fair dealing defence was available, or otherwise. In relation to three of the excerpts, Hely J considered that Conti J had erred in finding that the fair dealing defence was available. Conti J's findings as to the availability of the defence were otherwise left unturned.

While Network Ten successfully appealed the decision of the full Federal Court of Australia to the High Court of Australia (*Network Ten Pty Ltd v TCN Channel Nine Pty Ltd* (2004) 218 CLR 273; 205 ALR 1, 59 IPR 1 (HCA), per McHugh ACJ, Gummow, Kirby, and Hayne JJ, and Callinan J (dissenting)), the appeal only concerned the meaning of "television broadcast" under the Copyright Act 1968 (Aust). The Federal Court's findings (of both Conti J and the full Federal Court) regarding the availability, or otherwise, of the fair dealing defence were not at issue in the High Court of Australia and therefore remain applicable.

(3)   *Digital concerns*

The rapid advance of digital technologies, and increased access to works via the internet, has dramatically increased the potential of loss to copyright holders. However, digital technologies also raise issues in respect of the fair use provisions of the Copyright Act 1994.

The fair use provisions are currently drafted with respect to analogue and conventional print technologies. Because of the ease with which works can be copied and stored digitally, some of the fair use provisions may be exercised legitimately in a manner that was not envisaged when the legislation was drafted. For example, educational establishments could, under s 44, make one copy of a work for instructional purposes available online, thereby giving an unlimited number of users access to it.

These and related issues have resulted in a number of proposed amendments to the Act via the Copyright (New Technologies and Performers' Rights) Amendment Bill. The Bill is discussed in more detail at 4.2 ("Legislation, treaties, and conventions") earlier in this chapter.

4.11.2   Innocent infringement

Section 121 Copyright Act 1994 precludes a plaintiff from recovering damages against an innocent infringer.

An "innocent infringer" is a person who did not know and had no reason to believe that copyright subsisted in the work. In essence, s 121 is a statutory defence despite the fact that primary infringement of copyright does not require knowledge.

In *Milwell Proprietary Ltd v Olympic Amusements Proprietary Ltd* (1999) 43 IPR 32, the Federal Court of Australia had to decide whether there was an innocent infringement of prize scales for video gaming machines under the Australian equivalent to s 121. It was held, at p 44, that to obtain the protection of innocent infringement a defendant must establish:

- An active subjective lack of awareness that the act constituting the infringement was an infringement of the copyright; and

- That, objectively considered, he or she had no reasonable grounds for suspecting that the act constituted an infringement.

Ignorance of the law is no excuse: *P S Johnson & Assocs Ltd v Bucko Enterprises Ltd* [1975] 1 NZLR 311, at p 322.

Correct marking of the copyright works and products which reproduce the copyright may help to prevent the defence from being raised. See 4.15 ("Product marking") later in this chapter.

A plaintiff may still obtain an account of profits from an innocent infringer and is still entitled to an injunction to restrain further infringement.

4.11.3   Artistic works on public display

Copyright in a building or a sculpture, model for a building, or work of artistic craftsmanship that is permanently situated in a public place or in premises open to the public, is not infringed by copying the work by making a graphic work representing it, copying the work by making a photograph or film of it, or broadcasting a visual image of the work (s 73). Similarly, copyright is not infringed by the issue to the public of copies, or the broadcasting, of anything whose making was, under s 73, not an infringement of copyright.

The ambit of s 73 was considered by the Courts in *Radford v Hallensteins Bros Ltd* 17/7/06, Judge Hubble, DC Auckland CIV-2005-004-3008). The plaintiff, who was an artist and creator of three sculptures of buildings located in Western Park, Ponsonby, argued, in defence to an application by Hallensteins to strike out causes of action related to its production of tee-shirts featuring images of those sculptures, that s 73 should be construed narrowly and, since there is no specific mention of "commercial copying", the section should only apply to fair and reasonable copying for personal use and not to copying for commercial gain. That argument was rejected by Judge Hubble who concluded, at para 29:

> "Having considered the two points of view, it is clear to me, that the vast weight of academic opinion and practical implementation of s 73 favours the view that the words 'issued to the public' does not prevent commercial exploitation in the form of photography, drawings, post cards and printing onto items of clothing. I can see

no legal basis for the contrary argument and no prospect that it would succeed under the present legislation."

The judgment contains a useful summary of academic commentary on the section.

On appeal (*Radford v Hallenstein Bros Ltd* 22/2/07, Keane J, HC Auckland CIV-2006-404-4881), the appellant argued that, while s 73 permitted sculptures in public places to be replicated, it did not permit replication of the underlying copyright works. After considering in some detail New Zealand's international obligations under the Berne Convention and TRIPS as an aid to statutory interpretation, and examining the context in which the section appears in the Act, and finally considering academic commentary on both s 73 and the UK equivalent, the High Court rejected the argument. Applying the principle of efficacy (which holds that in a confined range of cases the Court may go so far as to add words or omit words or substitute words to correct not just ambiguity, but any obvious drafting error) Keane J held, at paras 34-39:

> "Section 73, as is all too evident from the opposed interpretations on this appeal, does not say enough to make complete sense. On either version words must be implied but with radically different effect and when those interpretations are set against what s 73 does say, I consider, that preferred by the Judge must be correct.

> "To the extent that s 73 does speak, it does so plainly. It sets out to allow members of the public, including players in the market, to copy in two-dimensions sculptures permanently in the public domain and even for profit; and it does so by setting aside any copyright in the work that the author might otherwise enjoy. However s 73 is interpreted, that clear policy is not for compromise.

> "Mr Radford's interpretation does not, I think, allow s 73 that scope and effect. On his argument s 73 does not protect from any possible claim in copyright, as it says it does, anyone who copies sculpture in the public domain. It leaves them vulnerable to a claim in copyright if they indirectly copy any underlying work. It only protects them where there is no such work, or where copyright in it has expired, or where any indirect copy is not a true copy and does not infringe. It erodes the immunity s 73 confers, but without saying so.

> "This interpretation is also impractical. Most sculpture permanently in the public domain will express in fully realised form some underlying work in which copyright could still inhere. Must anyone who copies any such sculpture first discover whether there are underlying works and whether they remain subject to copyright? Must they compare the finished with the underlying work to see whether any indirect copy of the latter would infringe copyright? Any such necessity would erode no less fatally the immunity s 73 apparently confers.

> "The interpretation the Judge under appeal preferred suffers from neither of these deficiencies. His interpretation lies fully with the grain of s 73. It gives the most complete effect to what s 73 expressly permits by completing the logic. To protect from any claim in copyright anyone who copies sculpture permanently in the public domain, his interpretation holds, s 73 must condone indirect copyright of underlying works whether in two or three dimensions and whether or not they too are in the public domain. Only then the Judge says, and I agree, can the immunity s 73 apparently confers have face value.

"On this interpretation, moreover, s 73 remains a true exception. It only exempts copies of three-dimensional works that are permanently in the public domain, not works exhibited temporarily, and only two-dimensional copies. The work itself cannot be replicated in three-dimensions, whether directly or as a copy of one made in two-dimensions. The governing principle of the 1994 Act remains uncompromised."

4.11.4   Saving for expired patents/registered designs

It is not an infringement of copyright if a person produces articles from drawings forming part of a published New Zealand patent specification or registered design that has lapsed (s 74 Copyright Act 1994).

4.12   Remedies

Infringement of copyright is actionable by the copyright owner and/or exclusive licensee. The relief available is the same as for infringement of any other property right.

Section 120 Copyright Act 1994 specifically refers to the principal forms of remedies:

- Damages for any loss suffered by the copyright owner; or

- An account of profits earned by the infringer; and

- Interim or permanent injunctions to restrain the infringing action.

The Act also provides for the availability of:

- Delivery up of infringing articles for destruction (s 122(1)(a));

- Delivery up of any machinery adapted to make the infringing article (s 122(1)(b)); and/ or

- Additional damages (s 121(2)).

4.12.1   Assessment of damages

When assessing damages, the Court will have regard to all the circumstances and in particular to:

- The flagrancy of the infringement;

- Any benefit to the infringer resulting from the infringement; and

- Any other relevant matters: *Raben Footwear Pty Ltd v Polygram Records Inc* (1997) 37 IPR 417.

In *World TV Ltd v Best TV Ltd* 6/9/06, Williams J, HC Auckland CIV-2005-404-1239, the Court was prepared to grant a "modest award of increased damages" (of $15,000) jointly and severally against defendants who had been found to have knowingly breached the plaintiffs' rights to broadcast certain television programmes in New Zealand. In reaching the award, Williams J felt it necessary to balance the flagrancy of the infringement with the fact that significant compensatory damages had already been awarded against the defendants which, once paid to the plaintiffs, would recompense them for what would have been their income had the defendants obtained a license from them to re-broadcast the television programmes and paid the appropriate fee for doing so.

His Honour cited with approval, the judgment of the Court of Appeal in *Wellington Newspapers Ltd v Dealers Guide Ltd* [1984] 2 NZLR 66 (CA). In that case, Wellington Newspapers reprinted in the *New Zealand Truth* large portions of the *Dealers Guide*, a publication listing current prices for second hand vehicles throughout New Zealand. The copying was held by the High Court to be a deliberate plagiarism and an underhand attempt to use information to which Wellington Newspapers was not entitled. Sinclair J held, however, that it was impossible to establish the quantum of compensatory damages, and the taking of an account of profits would be of no benefit to the Dealers Guide. His Honour accordingly fixed additional damages under the then equivalent of s 121(2) at $7,500.

An appeal against that award was dismissed. Dealing first with whether Wellington Newspapers' actions were flagrant, McMullin J in the Court of Appeal observed, at pp 69-70:

> "The ordinary dictionary meaning of flagrant is 'glaring, scandalous, or outrageous'. Flagrancy was described by Brightman J in *Ravenscroft v Herbert* [1980] RPC 193, 208 as:
>
>> 'Flagrancy in my view implies the existence of scandalous conduct, deceit and such like; it includes deliberate and calculated copyright infringements.'
>
> "What is flagrant must of course be a question of fact and degree to be decided against the background of relevant facts. I think that what happened here can certainly be said to be glaring or outrageous. The appellant stole the respondent's property and used it in a publication which it had put together. What it did was to lessen the value of a publication the sale of which was the respondent's sole source of income. It dressed up the material as though it were its own and added it to the range of subjects dealt with in Truth. The inference is that the publication of this material was intended to help maintain, if not increase, the sales of Truth. And, but for the prompt issue of the injunction proceedings, it may well have succeeded at the economic expense of the respondent. Such deliberate deceit fits the description of flagrant."

Then, after paraphrasing the terms of s 24(3) Copyright Act 1962, the then equivalent of s 121(2) Copyright Act 1994, the Court of Appeal continued, at p 70:

> "The additional damages referred to in s 24(3) are to be awarded where the Court is satisfied that the remedies otherwise provided by this section for an action brought under it do not provide effective relief. This would suggest that there may be some damage or loss suffered by a plaintiff which compensatory damages, injunction, the taking of accounts or other remedy would not assuage. It is difficult to see what is contemplated by the additional damages unless it is something in the nature of punishment to the defendant for the hurt done to the plaintiff which the conventional remedies would not provide."

The Court of Appeal concluded, at p 71, in reliance on *Williams v Settle* [1960] 2 All ER 806, at p 812, that the tests are whether the infringement was flagrant, whether there was scandalous conduct and whether the conduct was in total disregard of the plaintiff's legal rights and other circumstances. McMullin J also observed that awards of additional damages must logically and necessarily follow any award for an account of profits (if available) so as to see whether an account provided effective relief.

Thus, compensatory damages already awarded must be weighed before the flagrancy of the defendant's actions can be met by an award of additional damages to punish the defendants for their actions. If, as in the *World TV* case, the size of damages already awarded to the plaintiff is significant, any award of additional damages is likely to be relatively modest.

4.12.2 Conversion and damages

Damages for conversion or detinue subsequent to 1 January 1995 are no longer available under the Copyright Act 1994. However, conversion of copyright (which is a property right) remains available as a common law cause of action.

In *Perry Group Ltd v Pacific Software Technology Ltd* 2/8/02, Williams J, HC Hamilton CP55/01 (affirmed on appeal *Pacific Software Technology Ltd v Perry Group Ltd* [2004] 1 NZLR 164; (2003) 7 NZBLC 103,950; 57 IPR 145 (CA)), the plaintiffs claimed that the first defendant software developer was liable in conversion and/or detinue for wrongfully depriving the plaintiffs of their personal property, namely the copyright in a database that they had commissioned the first defendant to develop on their behalf.

Much of the judgment dealt with questions of fact as to whether a valid commissioning had taken place such that copyright in the commissioned software would vest in the plaintiffs as the commissioning parties. On this point the Court held that, in the absence of a written agreement, a review of the dealings between the parties during the period leading up to and during the development of the software showed that a verbal commission had been undertaken.

The Court of Appeal stated that the notion of a commission is sui generis to copyright law and the existence of the commission may be inferred where there is a requisite arrangement between the parties. The Court of Appeal upheld that a valid commissioning had taken place and stated that, while the better practice is to have a written agreement, inevitably there will be cases where there is no specific agreement. The appeal was dismissed.

On the conversion issue, the defendants sought to make a distinction between the physical medium on which a program was stored, which they conceded could be converted, and intangibles such as the copyright or the information itself, which they argued could not.

The High Court disagreed, preferring instead the plaintiffs' view that:

* Copyright could subsist in software;

* The Act defines copyright as a property right; and

* As "property" copyright is capable of being converted or detained.

Accordingly, the High Court ruled that, by refusing to deliver the software up to the plaintiffs upon demand, the first defendant was liable to the plaintiffs for conversion and detinue.

The Court of Appeal confirmed this point stating, at paras 100-101, that:

> "The relationship of copyright and conversion has attracted a fair measure of juristic debate over the years, for two reasons. The first is because of the abstract debate

over whether the copyright is 'property'. The second is because of the powerful effect of the conversion remedy in damages.

"As to the juristic nature of the copyright, 'great debate', which 'has been conducted, largely over the unconcerned heads of the copyright owners' (Philips and Firfth, *Introduction to Intellectual Property Law* (1st ed, 1986) para 10.3) [sic], is futile. The Act is conclusive. Copyright is a sui generic form of 'personal property'. It is a bundle of rights conferred by law. It is given the status of property, on the terms laid down in statue. Denial of those rights can, on the facts of a given case, amount to conversion."

4.12.3 Account of profits

The remedy of an account of profits is intended to be restorative rather than punitive in nature. Its purpose is to deprive the defendant of any profits it made from its wrong doing rather than to punish the defendant for its wrong doing. The leading authority in respect of an accounting of profits is *Dart Industries Inc v Décor Corp Pty Ltd* (1992) 179 CLR 101; 116 ALR 385 (HCA) in which the rationale for the remedy was summarised by the High Court of Australia as follows, at pp 114-115; p 390:

"The equitable principal of an account of profits is not to compensate the plaintiff nor to fix a fair price for the infringing product, but to prevent unjust enrichment of the defendant."

Dart v Décor also affirmed that in calculating net profits the defendant is entitled to subtract from its gross profits all specific overheads associated with the particular product in issue, as well as a proportion of general overheads attributable to the product. These general overheads are ordinarily calculated by assessing the percentage of the defendant's business associated with the specific product at issue, and then applying the same percentage to the general overheads. Thus, for example, if 10 percent of the defendant's business is associated with making and selling a product which is found to infringe copyright then 10 percent of the general overheads can be subtracted from the gross profit earned from that product.

This methodology is reasonably straightforward where the entire product is deemed to be an infringement of copyright. However, difficulties may arise where a single product comprises both infringing and non-infringing parts. This scenario was addressed by the New Zealand High Court in *ABB Ltd v NZ Insulators Ltd (No 2)* 28/8/07, Courtney J, HC Auckland CIV-2004-404-4829.

The plaintiffs (collectively ABB) had sued NZI for losses sustained as a result of the distribution of NZI's BM miniature circuit breaker. They alleged breaches of the Fair Trading Act, passing off and a breach of copyright. In an earlier judgment (*ABB Ltd v NZ Insulators Ltd* 20/9/06, Courtney J, HC Auckland CIV-2004-404-4829) Courtney J found in favour of the plaintiffs on the Fair Trading Act causes of action and for the third plaintiff on its claim for breach of copyright. The passing off claim failed.

Courtney J's first judgment included a finding that, in copying the S91, NZI had breached copyright in three technical drawings which showed modifications to the S91. The S91 as it existed at the point it was copied was the culmination of many modifications carried out to the original design between 1989 and 1994. Fourteen of those, undertaken in the early to mid 1990's, were detailed in the evidence but copyright was claimed in the drawings relating to only four of those modifications and only three were found to be the subject of infringement by NZI. All of the other parts of the S91 could have been copied lawfully and further aspects of the S91 were designed and made by NZI itself.

The question arose whether there should be an apportionment of the profit to be accounted for given that the BM comprised both infringing and non-infringing parts. Courtney J embarked on a reasonably detailed analysis of the authorities to resolve that noting:

- In cases where the product could not have been manufactured but for the infringing part there will not normally be an apportionment: *Peter Pan Manufacturing Corp v Corsets Silhouette Ltd* [1963] 3 All ER 402 and *Dart Industries Inc v Décor Corp Pty Ltd* (1992) 179 CLR 101; 116 ALR 385 (HCA);

- Conversely, in cases where the product could still have been made without the infringing component an apportionment will be needed to achieve an equitable result: *Robert J Zupanovich Pty Ltd v B & N Beale Nominees Pty Ltd* (1995) 59 FCR 49; 138 ALR 107; 32 IPR 339 (FCA);

- However, none of these cases deals with the difficult issue of a composite article in which both the infringing parts and non-infringing parts are essential to the overall functioning of the whole product; and

- The issue was considered in *Celanese International Corp v BP Chemicals Ltd* [1999] RPC 203 which concerned a chemical manufactured using, in part, a patented process. Laddie J considered that to refuse an apportionment when a significant part of the profits owed nothing to the infringement would be unjust to the defendant, agreeing with the views expressed by the Canadian Federal Court of Appeal in *Imperial Oil v Lubrizole* (1996) 71 CPR (3d) 26 (Can FCA):

  > "The remedy of an account of profits is an equitable one. Its purpose is not to punish the defendant but simply to have him surrender the actual profits he has made at the plaintiff's expense. But if some part of Imperial's profit on the infringing sales can be shown to have been due not to the appropriation of the Lubrizole invention but to some other factor where is the equity? We were told that Lubrizole contends that Imperial's motor oil infringes another of its patents and has sued in respect thereof. May the same profits be claimed a second time? And if not by Lubrizole what of some third party patentee who likewise claims infringement? And even if no other patents were involved, to allow Lubrizole to take profits which Imperial succeeds in showing were solely attributable to some non-infringing feature of its motor oil would be to judicially sanction Lubrizole's unjust enrichment at Imperial's expense."

Courtney J concluded, at para 99:

> "I think it is clear that where both infringing and non-infringing parts play an essential part in the function of the product in question then apportionment is appropriate provided, of course, that there is some evidence on which to make an assessment of the relative contributions of the infringing and non-infringing parts of the product. Not to do so risks the copyright owner being unjustly enriched and the infringer punished which is not the purpose of the remedy."

Her Honour then went on to consider, in the absence of New Zealand authority, the method to be used to determine the extent to which the infringer must account for its profits where the product in question comprises both infringing and non-infringing components. Her Honour cited with approval the approach by Laddie J in *Celanese International* in which he referred to the process of notionally attributing more of the profit to some parts than others as "weighting", using as an example the Canadian case of *Wellcome Foundation Ltd v Apotex Inc* (1998) 82 CPR (3d) 466; 151 FTR 250 (Can FCTD), affirmed on appeal in *Wellcome Foundation Ltd v Apotex Inc* 11 CPR (4th) 218; [2001] 2 FC 618 (Can FCA), in which an apportionment was made based on the relative importance or value of the infringing feature to the product as a whole.

In *Wellcome Foundation* the defendant had manufactured a drug containing two active ingredients, TMP and SMX. Some of the TMP sourced by the defendant had been manufactured through a process that infringed the plaintiff's patent. The defendant's drug contained a TMP/SMX weight ratio of 1:5 but SMX was half the cost of TMP. The defendant argued methods of apportionment that depended either on the profits being split in accordance with the weight ratio of the drugs, or alternatively in accordance with the relative cost of the ingredients. MacKay J rejected these methods saying, at para 58, that they underplayed the significance of TMP as a major potentiating ingredient in the combination drug:

> "In my opinion in this case the proper apportionment is 60% of the profits earned by Apotex from use of infringing TMP with SMX, both active ingredients, in Apo-Sulfatrim. That ratio recognises, albeit in a simplified calculation, that there are two active ingredients, that TMP is the more significant of the two in combination, and that the profit does result at least in part from Apotex's efforts to successfully develop the generic product and its market. I am satisfied that Apotex has shown that a portion of the profits may be attributable to SMX in formulation as an active ingredient and to its successful efforts in developing and marketing Apo-Sulfatrim. Recognition of that warrants apportionment of total profits to be accounted and in my view, fair recognition of that is provided by reserving 40% of Apotex's profits and apportioning 60% to the accounting of profits to be paid to the plaintiffs."

Laddie J, in *Celanese International*, recognised the advantages of the approach in Wellcome Foundation but also warned of its dangers, at para 57:

> "The attractions of following MacKay J's path are obvious. It releases the Judge from mathematical constraints and allows him a wide discretion to pick whatever figure he thinks is fair. Nevertheless Millet J warned against taking relative value into consideration in the absence of compelling evidence. That warning appears to me, with respect, to have much force. Adjusting the apportionment up or down in response to imprecise feelings that one part of a product or process is more or less important or valuable than another will add another layer of unpredictability to an exercise which is already difficult enough. It is also likely to result in the account being burdened with evidence directed to flattering or denigrating the relative merits of different parts when, as a matter of commercial reality, a customer does not really distinguish one part from another. All he wants is the whole product or service. The concept of 'value' is ill-suited to apportionment. It treats each step or part of the process or product as if it had an existence or value of its own. But if the product

or process makes a profit, it does it as a whole. In most cases it is not realistic to say that one part is more important than another. Where the part cannot be severed from the rest and sold or exploited on its own it acquires its value by reason of its co-operation and interaction with the other parts."

Courtney J concluded that an apportionment was appropriate in the present case, commenting, at para 106:

"Attributing revenue and cost to different parts of a building project will usually be a far simpler task than doing so in relation to a small product designed to function as a single unit. In the case of a composite article, however, there is no doubt that the approaches taken in *Wellcome Foundation* and *Celanese International* are preferable. Where, as in this case, the product comprises many components, none of which is especially expensive and all of which operate in unison, the relevant parts are best viewed in the manner described by Laddie J in *Celanese International* ic the value of the infringed parts lies in co-operation and interaction with the other parts."

Finally, her Honour considered who should take the account of profits and, in particular, whether the Court was entitled to do so in light of r 388 High Court Rules which lists only the Registrar, an accountant, or the Registrar and an accountant. Her Honour cited with approval the decision of Williams J in *Aitchison v The Kaitangata Railway & Coal Co Ltd (No 2)* (1900) 21 NZLR 149, in which Williams J pointed out that neither the Registrar nor any other person conducting an inquiry forms a separate tribunal. They are appointed by the Court in order that the Court may exercise its judicial function. If the Court can do that without such assistance, it may proceed to undertake the account itself.

An obvious example of where this might be appropriate, as was the case in *Aitchison*, is where the Judge has already heard the relevant evidence and it would be more convenient and efficient for the Judge to undertake the account rather than have an accountant or the Registrar do so.

The remedy of account of profits is not frequently sought because of the difficulty in calculating profits earned by the defendant as a result of the infringement. An account of profits was sought in the copyright context in *Fleming v Fletcher Concrete & Infrastructure Ltd* 1/12/06, Wild J, HC Auckland CIV-2005-404-4598.

4.12.4 Remedies available to exclusive licensees

Under s 123 Copyright Act 1994, except as against the copyright owner, an exclusive licensee has the same rights and remedies as a copyright owner. Refer to 4.9 ("Licenses") earlier in this chapter.

4.12.5 Remedies available for breach of moral rights

Remedies are also available to owners of moral rights of copyright works under s 125 Copyright Act 1994 by way of damages and injunction. Refer to 4.5.3 ("Moral rights") earlier in this chapter.

4.12.6 Summary judgment proceedings

In *University of Waikato v Benchmarking Services Ltd* (2004) 8 NZBLC 101,561 (CA), the appellant successfully appealed against a decision of Master Christiansen (as he then was) not to grant summary judgment in proceedings for copyright infringement (*University of Waikato v Benchmarking Services Ltd* 11/9/03, Master Christiansen, HC Christchurch CIV-2003-409-1347).

The appellant produced certain compilations including a questionnaire for an annual survey designed to collect financial data from New Zealand businesses, and a report based upon the results of that questionnaire. The report showed the results of the questionnaire, tabulated with headings and sub-headings, and included additional comparative information.

In the High Court, Master Christiansen noted that copyright subsisted in the appellant's compilations, and the appellant owned the copyright in them. The only issue was whether or not the respondents had infringed the appellant's work by copying. After implicitly applying the three-stage test in *Wham-O MFG Co v Lincoln Industries Ltd* [1984] 1 NZLR 641 (CA) to determine whether or not the respondents' work was original, or whether it was a copy of the appellant's work, the Master stated, at para 13, that he could not be satisfied that the appellant's work was truly unique. On that basis, he dismissed the application for summary judgment.

On appeal, the appellant successfully overturned the Master's decision, arguing that the Master had wrongly equated the appellant's requirement to prove that the respondents' work was unoriginal with a defence based upon a lack of novelty or uniqueness in the appellant's compilation.

Delivering the judgment of the Court of Appeal, Randerson J considered at length the suitability of the summary judgment procedure for copyright infringement claims. He noted, at para 61, that under r 136 High Court Rules the appellant must satisfy the Court that the respondents have no defence to the claim, so that the Court is confident, sure, convinced, persuaded to the point of belief, and left without any real doubt or uncertainty. However, his Honour cited with approval the comments of Somers J in *Pemberton v Chappell* (1986) 1 PRNZ 183, at p 185, that, where a defence raises questions of fact upon which the outcome of the case may turn, it will not be right to enter summary judgment, unless the Court is satisfied that the defendant's statements as to matters of fact are baseless. His Honour considered and distinguished *Leco Instruments (UK) Ltd v Land Pyrometers Ltd* (1982) 99 RPC 133 (CA), in which the plaintiff unsuccessfully sought a declaration on summary judgment that certain products it was selling did not infringe copyright in the defendant's drawings. His Honour noted that the issue in *Leco* was whether the plaintiff had copied a substantial part of the defendant's drawings, determined on the basis of a comparison between the product in issue and the drawings relied upon by the defendant. At first instance, the Judge in *Leco* decided that it was appropriate to grant summary judgment in the form of a declaration that the plaintiff did not infringe the defendant's copyright. However, this decision was overturned on appeal. Randerson J noted, at para 64, that *Leco* was an unusual case because the declaration was sought in negative form (ie, a declaration of non-infringement) and the Court in that case was not confident that the defendant had no reasonable prospect of establishing that the copyright in their drawings was infringed.

After reviewing these authorities, Randerson J accepted, at para 64, that while care is necessary before granting summary judgment, in a case of alleged infringement of copyright in literary works it is simply a matter of comparing the relevant aspects of the works in question (in this case, the form and content of the appellant's report with the corresponding material in the respondents' brochures and website). Being satisfied on making this comparison that the appellant had demonstrated the respondents had no defence to the claim of copyright infringement in relation to the report (but not the questionnaire), Randerson J allowed the appeal in part.

While there is no reason in principle why the summary judgment procedure cannot be utilised to obtain a declaration of non-infringement, the party applying will face a difficult task. See, for example, *Spantech Pty Ltd v BPM Contracts Ltd* 16/8/04, Associate Judge Gendall, HC Wellington CIV-2003-454-160. In that case Heinz Wattie's sought an order for summary judgment against Spantech declaring that it did not authorise BPM Contracts to copy a storage installation in which Spantech claimed it owned copyright.

Spantech designed and built a number of storage installations ("the Spantech installations") for the eighth defendant, Heinz Wattie's Ltd. Heinz Wattie's later contracted the first defendant, BPM Contracts, to build another storage installation ("the BPM installation"). Spantech alleged that it owned copyright in the Spantech installations pursuant to s 21(2) Copyright Act 1994. It claimed that Heinz Wattie's had infringed its copyright under s 16(1)(i) of the Act by directing and approving construction of the BPM installation "as per the existing adjacent [Spantech installations]". Heinz Wattie's brought an application for summary judgment against Spantech under r 136(2) High Court Rules.

Associate Judge Gendall reviewed the legal tests to be applied in summary judgment proceedings.

His Honour stated, at para 9, that the starting point is that a plaintiff has the right to have its claim determined following a fair hearing by the Court (citing the Privy Council in *A-G v Jones* [2004] 1 NZLR 433 (PC)). The Privy Council stated, at p 440:

> "Summary judgment should not be given for the defendant unless he shows on the balance of probabilities that none of the plaintiff's claims can succeed. That is an exacting test, and rightly so since it is a serious thing to stop a plaintiff bringing his claim to trial unless it is clearly hopeless."

The Associate Judge noted, at para 10, that in an application for summary judgment for a declaration of non-infringement:

> "[T]he defendant will have the significant burden of establishing that none of the plaintiff's causes of action can succeed. In other words, the defendant must be able to undermine the plaintiff's entire claim. Furthermore, the Court should only give judgment against the plaintiff where the defendant has a clear answer to the plaintiff which cannot be contradicted": *Westpac Banking Corp v MM Kembla NZ Ltd* [2001] 2 NZLR 298 (CA).

Applying the tests, the Associate Judge concluded, at para 43, that Heinz Wattie's had failed to establish that Spantech's claim was clearly hopeless or that it had a clear answer to Spantech's claims which could not be contradicted, and refused the application.

4.12.7 Border protection measures

It is possible to obtain notices empowering the New Zealand Customs Department to seize goods suspected of infringing copyright as the goods enter New Zealand. This is discussed in more detail in the border protection chapter (chapter 11).

4.12.8 Interim injunctions

Several decisions of the High Court and the Court of Appeal would suggest that the Courts will give increased weight to intellectual property rights with a finite duration when determining an application for interim relief. In many cases this seems to be at the expense of conclusive arguments going to the balance of convenience and the overall justice.

In *Aktiebolaget Hassle v Novartis NZ Ltd* 1/5/03, Potter J, HC Auckland CP51-SW/03, the plaintiffs sought an injunction to restrain Novartis from manufacturing an omeprazole product, PROBITOR, which they believed infringed their patent relating to their own similar product sold in New Zealand under the brand name LOSEC (Patent No 220096). Novartis resisted the application on a number of grounds including:

(1) That it was strongly arguable that the patent was invalid, the equivalent UK patent having already been overturned on the grounds of obviousness; and

(2) That it had contracted to supply Pharmac with PROBITOR, and was obliged to pay Pharmac $350,000 per calendar month it was unable to supply PROBITOR (presumably to compensate Pharmac for being obliged to subsidise the more expensive LOSEC during that period).

While recognising the significant losses likely to be suffered by Novartis if injuncted, the Court nonetheless found that the balance of convenience and the overall justice favoured the granting of an injunction, commenting, at para 43, that:

> "There is a reality to be recognised in the case of the patent, that the patent confers a monopoly during its currency, the benefit of which runs over to the post-patent period because of the strong market position usually developed during the monopoly period. This was expressed by Eichelbaum J in [*Monsanto Chemical Co v Stauffer Chemical Co (No 2)* (1984) 1 TCLR 129; 1 NZIPR 540]."

and later, at para 56:

> "Premature interference with the monopoly position which the patent confers during its currency will also impact on the ability of the proprietor to create or confirm its own market after the expiry of the patent (the 'bridgehead' opportunity)."

The decision of Potter J was upheld by the Court of Appeal in a decision of Blanchard J delivered on 4 July 2003 (*Novartis NZ Ltd v Aktiebolaget Hassle* [2004] 2 NZLR 721 (CA)).

Similar comments have also arisen in the context of applications for interim injunctions to restrain the infringement of registered design rights. See, for example:

- *Handitags Ltd v Warburton* 12/12/01, Glazebrook J, HC Auckland M1586-SW01, at paras 17 and 18:

"However, the main reason put forward by Handitags as to inadequacy of damages is the loss of the ability to manage their practical monopoly situation. This is because, at any stage during such a monopoly, an entry of a competitor can cause permanent damage and permanent inability to manage the monopoly and, in particular, the ending of the monopoly which will obviously occur at the end of the design and copyright period. This diminished advantage can mean a permanent effect which Handitags submits is exceedingly hard to quantify. It is noted that there is only some four years left in respect of the design and five years in respect of the copyright so the loss of a portion of the period at the end of the registration for the design and the copyright period is even more significant.

"These submissions are accepted. It is accepted that damages would not be an adequate remedy for Handitags."

- *BEP Marine Ltd v Aquatech Marine Ltd* 20/12/02, O'Regan J, HC Auckland M1568-SW02 (which applied *Handitags*);

- *Permanent Promotions Pty Ltd v Independent Liquor (NZ) Ltd* 10/6/04, Heath J, HC Auckland CIV-2004-404-2419, at paras 38 and 39:

  "In my judgment, the scheme of the Act is clear. A Commissioner is appointed to examine designs submitted to him or her. In the course of that examination the Commissioner determines questions of novelty and compliance with statutory definitions. The underlying assumption is that the Commissioner is someone experienced in applying the Act and in making judgments of that sort. The scheme of the Act would be undermined significantly if the Courts failed to recognise the nature of the monopoly that flows from the registration process.

  "In this case the design has been registered. I reject Mr Brown's submission that the Register is prima facie evidence only of what is contained in it rather than the fact that the Commissioner has found the design to comply with the definition contained in s 2(1) of the Act and has found the requisite degree of novelty. No item can be registered unless those conclusions have been drawn. That registration confers a monopoly. On an interim injunction application the Court must be slow to second guess the findings of the Commissioner."

  and, at para 43:

  "In my view the fact of registration confers a prima facie right sufficient to overcome the hurdle of establishing that a serious question exists to be tried."

- *Viscount Plastics Ltd v Lamnei Plastics Ltd* 13/9/05, Gendall J, HC Auckland CIV-2005-404-3452, in which his Honour, although expressing doubts as to the validity of the plaintiff's registered design, and hence the strength of its case, indicated, at para 16, that a strong case pointing to invalidity would need to be made out before validity could even become relevant in the Court's balancing exercise and that validity alone is unlikely to ever be decisive. His Honour did however note, at para 26, that the size of the market may be relevant to the so called "management of monopoly" argument and stressed, at para 28, that it cannot be elevated to a rigid rule to be applied whenever the plaintiff is the owner of an exclusive patent or license.

Some caution needs to be exercised, as the "bridgehead" argument is probably limited to forms of intellectual property in which the rights expire after a finite period. Thus, for example, the bridgehead argument may not be appropriate in a case involving infringement of a registered trade mark but could well be applicable to copyright works which have been industrially applied.

Similarly, if the ownership of the intellectual property is in dispute this may result in refusal of the application: *Golden Homes (1998) Ltd v Blue Chip Construction Ltd* 21/6/05, Allan J, HC Auckland CIV-2003-404-7090. See also *Lesa Systems Ltd v Canzac Ltd* 16/5/06, John Hansen J, HC Christchurch CIV-2006-409-624, at para 34.

4.12.9 Costs

Costs in legal proceedings are entirely at the Court's discretion. Usually they will be awarded in favour of the successful party.

In *Disney Enterprises Inc v Guan t/a Balmoral Celestial Gifts* 19/6/02, Master Lang, HC Auckland M123-SD02, the plaintiff issued proceedings under s 141(3) Copyright Act. The defendant agreed to have judgment entered by consent once it had made its own determination that the goods the subject of the proceedings had been manufactured and distributed without the plaintiff's authority. The plaintiff sought costs and the defendant opposed.

In ruling that the plaintiff was entitled to its costs, Master Lang acknowledged that enforcement of the plaintiff's copyright interests was of vital importance to it, and that it was entitled to exercise its rights. He went on to say, at paras 45 and 47:

> "I accept also that the proceedings had to be issued as a matter of relative urgency because of the time limits imposed by the Act. The issuing of the proceedings was also a catalyst for the speedy resolution of the dispute, and it is impossible to say that that would necessarily have occurred if the proceedings had not been issued.

> •   •   •   •   •

> "I accept that the Defendant should receive some credit for the fact that it consented to orders being made against it at the earliest opportunity. In my view, however, that credit should be reflected in the fact that costs overall have been minimised through the resolution of the proceedings at an early stage and without resort to further interlocutory processes or unnecessary appearances."

The decision affirms a rights-holder's entitlement to protect its interests by issuing proceedings against an infringer, and further that rights-holders should not be financially impaired as a result.

4.13   Appeals

The decision in *Holdfast NZ Ltd v Henkel KgaA* [2007] 1 NZLR 336 (CA) contains brief but useful comments on the role of the appellate Court in copyright proceedings. After referring to the litigation in *Designers Guild v Russell Williams* at three levels (*Designers Guild v Russell Williams (Textiles) Ltd* [1998] FSR 803; [1998] EWHC Patents 349 (Ch D); *Designers Guild v*

Russell Williams (Textiles) Ltd [2000] FSR 121 (CA); and *Designers Guild v Russell Williams (Textiles) Ltd* [2000] 1 WLR 2416; [2001] FSR 113 (HL)), the Court of Appeal affirmed, at paras 62-65, that it is impermissible for an appellate Court to conduct an examination of its own of facts which are the province of the trial Judge to find. This view was endorsed on appeal to the Supreme Court (*Henkel KgaA v Holdfast NZ Ltd* [2007] 1 NZLR 577 (SC)), at para 44:

> "[T]his [whether a substantial part has been reproduced] is a subject upon which, in borderline cases, minds can reasonably differ and it is appropriate for appellate courts to give to the trial judge's assessment the degree of latitude that conventionally applies to appellate review of a discretion."

In *Holdfast*, the Court of Appeal did carry out its own comparison of the copyright works and the alleged infringing copy but this was permissible because the trial Judge had failed to do so himself.

4.14 Offences

Both civil and criminal remedies may be pursued by a plaintiff under the Copyright Act 1994. A person will be criminally liable for making or dealing with infringing products with the knowledge that the object infringes the copyright work. Section 131 lists various dealings amounting to an offence.

Every person who commits an offence under the Act is liable on summary conviction to:

- A fine up to NZ$10,000 for every infringing copy, with a maximum of NZ$150,000 in respect of infringing copies in the same transaction; or

- A term of imprisonment not exceeding 3 months.

An offender may also be ordered to make reparation to the copyright owner for losses resulting from the criminal infringement and/or deliver up any infringing copies to the copyright owner.

For an example of a criminal sentence under the Copyright Act see *NZ Police v Vile* [2007] DCR 24. Mr Vile was convicted on five charges of breach of s 131(1) Copyright Act 1994 relating to his manufacturing and selling counterfeit CDs from a "relatively sophisticated operation from his home" which he subsequently sold at flea markets and the like. It was clear from the evidence that his CD burning business was significant and involved sophisticated computer equipment, some computers having three CD drives used for burning purposes. The Judge considered it abundantly clear that Vile was well aware that he had no authorisation to make or sell the copies. Noting the absence of any guidance cases about sentencing under s 131 of the Act, the Judge considered the policy behind the legislation, the provisions of the Sentencing Act 2002, and the way in which those provisions should be applied before distilling the following eight principals that could be applied to such sentencing:

- The extent of the commercial infringement, for example, how many copies of each title were being made and how many copies were being sold?

- The manner of the infringement. Is the infringement amateurish or professional? At what level of sophistication is the get-up (ie the printing of CD labels, artwork etc)?

- If the get-up is of a sophisticated nature, is it likely to confuse a consumer? Is there an element of fraud that underlies the defendant's actions?

- How much did the defendant gain from the infringement?

- What was the nature and scale of the distribution system, if any?

- Was the internet, with its apparent anonymity, involved in the course of distribution?

- What was the timeframe over which the activities took place?

- The number of victims (such as authors, producers, those involved in the making or marketing of movies or CDs, distribution networks, all the way down to the store front retailer who are going to be affected, and in that respect the public confidence in purchasing a product must be taken into account. The public is entitled to know into whose pockets the dollars they are spending is going to go).

The Judge observed that the nature of the offending itself is analogous to theft coupled with receiving (in the sense that the infringer is interfering with the copyright owner's rights by making illicit copies but also profiting from the making of those illicit copies by distributing and selling them themselves) before concluding, at paras 34 and 35:

> "It is quite clear that there is a sufficiently large extent of commercial infringement [in the present case]. The manner of the infringement was not amateurish there was getup, and it was at a certain level of sophistication which meant that some of the artwork on the covers was indistinguishable from the originals and in that respect the getup was sophisticated and like to confuse a customer.

> "The gains that could be made from the infringement of course cannot be equated in terms of the figures of reparation but I am satisfied, having regard to the extent of the operation and the account book that was kept by the defendant that this was a fairly sophisticated system and the gains were quite significant."

Rejecting a community based sentence on the basis that it would not send "the correct message about deterrence and denunciation" the Judge sentenced Vile to one year's imprisonment reduced by 3 months for his preparedness to make reparation (in total $8,500). The Judge also ordered destruction of all duplicated and counterfeit CDs and forfeiture of all means of making infringing copies, computer equipment, blank CDs, printers, scanners, and other copiers, concluding, at para 45:

> "It should be made perfectly clear to those who are going to be engaged in commercial copyright infringement that if they are going to embark on this type of activity there will be consequences, that they will be severe, and that if there are going to be downstream consequences for their families then so be it. That this type of activity cannot be allowed to continue and the message must be sent. I trust it has been in this particular case."

A person may also be liable under s 258 Crimes Act 1961 for altering or reproducing a document with intent to defraud. In *Power Beat International Ltd v A-G* [2000] 2 NZLR 288 (CA), the making of copies of a computer program, which had been purchased on CD ROM in the US, was found to constitute an unlawful reproduction in terms of s 266A (the predecessor to the current s 258).

Company directors or persons concerned with the management of a company may also be guilty of an offence where the company has been convicted. Section 133 states that an officer of a company will be guilty where:

- The act that constituted the offence took place with his or her authority, permission, or consent, and

- He or she:

    - Knew, or could reasonably be expected to have known, that the offence was to be or was being committed, and

    - Failed to take all reasonable steps to prevent or stop it.

The liability of directors in a personal capacity was discussed in *P S Johnson & Assocs Ltd v Bucko Enterprises Ltd* [1975] 1 NZLR 311, at p 322. Chilwell J approved the proposition that if a company is formed for the express purpose of doing a wrongful act or it, when formed, those in control expressly direct that a wrongful thing be done, the directors as well as the company are responsible for the consequences.

4.15   Product marking

All copyright works and products derived from copyright works should be marked with the international copyright symbol ©, the author's name and the year of creation. For example, © James & Wells 2007.

This marking acts as a deterrent to would-be copiers, and should, where appropriate, be used on all products, packaging and promotional literature.

The marking may also increase the damages award in a copyright infringement action, as the defendant cannot argue the infringement was innocent if the existence of copyright was known. The defence of innocent infringement is discussed in more detail at 4.11.2 ("Innocent infringement") earlier in this chapter.

Finally, identifying the author in the marking may be important in a claim for infringement as s 126(2) creates a presumption that an author named on a literary, dramatic, musical, or artistic work shall be presumed to be the author, and the first owner, until the contrary is proved. For an example in which the presumption was applied see *YPG IP Ltd v Yellowbook.com.au Pty Ltd* 13/7/07, Allan J, HC Auckland CIV-2007-404-2839, at para 50.

4.16   References and resource sites

4.16.1 Websites

Thomson Brookers	www.thomsonbrookers.co.nz
Copyright Licensing Ltd	www.copyright.co.nz
New Zealand Intellectual Property Office	www.iponz.govt.nz
Interim Website of New Zealand Legislation	www.legislation.govt.nz
James & Wells	www.jaws.co.nz

Ministry of Economic Development	www.med.govt.nz
The Copyright Council of New Zealand	www.copyright.org.nz
World Intellectual Property Organisation	www.wipo.int
World Trade Organisation	www.wto.org

4.16.2   Texts and periodicals

- Brown, A, and Grant, A, *The Law of Intellectual Property in New Zealand*, Wellington, Butterworths, 1988

- Brown, B, et al, *Intellectual Property in New Zealand: Copyright and Design*, Wellington, Butterworths, 2002

- Frankel, S, and McLay, G, *Intellectual Property in New Zealand*, Wellington, LexisNexis Butterworths, 2002

- Garnett, K, et al, *Copinger and Skone James on Copyright*, London, Sweet and Maxwell, 1999

- *New Zealand Intellectual Property Journal*, Wellington, Butterworths

Chapter 5

LAYOUT DESIGNS

5.1 Introduction

In simple terms a layout design (or topography) is the three-dimensional representation of some or all of the elements and interconnections of an integrated circuit. An integrated circuit is one in which the elements of the circuit and some of the interconnections have been formed on a medium and are intended to perform an electronic function.

Integrated circuits are found in numerous electronic items, the most common being the microprocessors found within personal computers.

Layout designs were originally protected via copyright law under the ambit of industrial copyright.

Although copyright for industrial designs is still available within New Zealand, since 1 January 1995 integrated circuits have been protected exclusively by the provisions of the Layout Designs Act 1994.

5.2 Legislation, treaties, and conventions

5.2.1 Governing law

Protection for layout designs (and therefore integrated circuits) in New Zealand is governed exclusively by the:

- Layout Designs Act 1994 ("the Act"); and

- Layout Designs Amendment Act 1999.

The Act is administered by the Ministry of Economic Development.

The Act is divided into five parts:

- Part 1 — Interpretation and Application

- Part 2 — Ownership and Nature of Layout Design Rights

- Part 3 — Exceptions (to infringement)

- Part 4 — Remedies for Infringement

- Part 5 — Miscellaneous.

(1)   *Act applies retrospectively*

Although the Layout Designs Act 1994 did not come into force until 1 January 1995, it retrospectively protects layout designs/integrated circuits created before its enactment (under s 10 of the Act).

(2)   *Circuit Layouts Act 1989 (Aust)*

The New Zealand Act is virtually identical to the Circuit Layouts Act 1989 (Aust).

Therefore decisions based on the Australian Act are likely to be highly persuasive in determining how the New Zealand Act should be applied. There have been few Australian decisions. The majority of provisions contained within both Acts therefore remain untested.

The two leading decisions under the Australian Act are:

- *Avel Pty Ltd v Wells* (1992) 36 FCR 340; 23 IPR 353 (FCA); and

- *Nintendo Co Ltd v Centronics Systems Pty Ltd* (1991) 23 IPR 119 (FCA).

These are discussed in more detail later in this chapter.

5.2.2 International conventions

New Zealand is a member of the WTO and a signatory to GATT and TRIPS.

(1)   *GATT*

Protection of integrated circuits and layout designs is an international requirement under the General Agreement on Tariffs and Trade ("GATT").

(2)   *WTO*

Member countries of the World Trade Organisation ("WTO") are required by the Agreement on Trade-Related aspects of Intellectual Property Rights ("TRIPS"), which forms part of the WTO, to provide protection to layout designs (semi-conductor topographics).

(3)   *TRIPS*

Article 35 of the TRIPS Agreement requires member countries to protect the layout designs of integrated circuits in accordance with the provisions of the IPIC Treaty (the Treaty on Intellectual Property in respect of Integrated Circuits), negotiated as part of WIPO in 1989.

As the protection afforded to layout designs under the Copyright Act 1994 (and its predecessor the Copyright Act 1962) was more than adequate, it appears that the primary reason for enactment of the Layout Designs Act 1994 was to satisfy New Zealand's international obligations under TRIPS.

(a)   *Reciprocal rights*

TRIPS also requires each signatory to provide reciprocal rights to the citizens of other signatory States. Accordingly s 2(2) Layout Designs Act 1994 grants reciprocal rights to a resident or citizen of any country that is either:

- Party to a treaty or convention relating to the protection of layout designs to which New Zealand is a party; or

- A country that the Governor-General of New Zealand is satisfied has adequate provisions for the reciprocal protection of layout designs originating from New Zealand.

The vast majority of New Zealand's trading partners are eligible countries. A full list is found within the Layout Designs (Eligible Countries) Orders (currently the Layout Designs (Eligible Countries) Order 2000).

5.3   Nature of layout design rights

Section 13 Layout Designs Act 1994 confers upon the owner of the layout design rights the exclusive right to do each of the following:

- To copy the layout design, directly or indirectly, in a material form;

- To make an integrated circuit in accordance with the layout design, or a copy of the layout design; and

- To commercially exploit the layout design in New Zealand.

The s 4 definition of exclusive rights also includes the right to authorise any other person to do any of these things:

"For the purposes of this Act, the exclusive right to do an act in relation to an eligible layout design, or an integrated circuit made in accordance with an eligible layout design, includes the exclusive right to authorise a person to do that act in relation to that layout design or integrated circuit."

These exclusive rights are infringed by any person who exercises them in relation to the layout design without the permission of the owner. However, there are a number of exceptions to infringement provided in ss 16-20 of the Act. These are discussed at 5.12 ("Exceptions to infringement / defences") later in this chapter.

5.3.1 Distinction from copyright

Section 2 Copyright Act 1994 specifically excludes protection of layout designs and integrated circuits as "artistic works" under that Act.

Despite the fact that layout designs are now excluded from protection as artistic works under the Copyright Act 1994 the principles of protection under the Copyright Act and the Layout Designs Act 1994 are substantially similar.

The main differences between the protection conferred by the Layout Designs Act 1994 and the protection that might have been available under the Copyright Act 1994 are highlighted in the following table:

	Layout Designs	**Copyright**
Term	From 10 to 15 years.	Maximum protection 16 years for industrially applied articles.
Originality	Must involve intellectual effort and not be commonplace.	Must be original only in the sense that it is the product of the author's own effort and was not copied from another work.
Criminal Offences	No	Yes
Exceptions to Infringement	Broad provisions.	More restrictive.
Innocent Infringement	Innocent commercial exploitation will preclude the granting of an account of profits.	Account of profits available against innocent infringer.
Moral Rights	No moral rights exist.	Moral rights exist in work.

There have been no New Zealand decisions under the Layout Designs Act to date. In the absence of case law dealing specifically with the Layout Designs Act it is likely the Courts will look to analogous case law in the field of copyright when determining how the sections of the Act should be applied.

5.4 Definition of a "layout design"

A layout design is the three dimensional disposition of the elements and interconnections of an integrated circuit.

Section 2 Layout Designs Act 1994 includes the following definition of "layout design":

> "Layout design means the three-dimensional disposition, however expressed, of the elements, at least one of which is an active element, and of some or all of the interconnections, of an integrated circuit; and includes such a three-dimensional disposition prepared for an integrated circuit intended for manufacture:"

5.4.1 No definition of "active elements"

The "active elements" mentioned in the definition of "layout design" in s 2 Layout Designs Act 1994 are not further defined in the Act, but are commonly understood to be elements that determine the path of a current, helping to create the binary code of computer language. They are usually transistors or diodes, which essentially act as a switch (opening or closing the circuit) or one-way valve or gate.

5.4.2 No definition of "interconnections"

Similarly the "interconnections" are not defined, but are commonly understood to be the network of connective pathways connecting the "active elements" of the integrated circuit. This network usually comprises minute aluminium or copper wires.

5.4.3 Meaning of "integrated circuit"

An "integrated circuit" (for the purposes of the Layout Designs Act 1994) is an electronic circuit made from the layout design, where the elements of the circuit are formed in (or on) a material, usually a semiconductor and usually silicon, which performs an electronic function.

"Integrated circuit" is defined in s 2 of the Act as follows:

> "'Integrated circuit' means a circuit, in its final or an intermediate form, in which the elements, at least one of which is an active element, and some or all of the interconnections are integrally formed in or on a piece of material and that is intended to perform an electronic function:"

5.5 Qualification of layout design rights

Layout design rights are proprietary rights that, like copyright, vest automatically in an eligible layout design on its creation.

There is no system of registration for layout designs, and therefore no requirement to register them and no cost.

5.5.1 Eligible layout design

To qualify for layout design rights, the layout design must fall within the definition of "eligible layout design" in s 2 Layout Designs Act 1994:

> "'Eligible layout design' means an original layout design—

"(a)   the maker, or in relation to a jointly made layout design any one or more makers, of which was, at the time the layout design was made, an eligible person; or

"(b)   that was first commercially exploited in New Zealand or in an eligible country;"

An "eligible layout design" is an "original" layout design made by an "eligible person", or first commercially exploited in New Zealand or an "eligible country".

(1)   *Meaning of "eligible person"*

An "eligible person" is defined in s 2 Layout Designs Act 1994 as a:

- New Zealand citizen, resident, or body corporate incorporated in New Zealand; or

- Citizen, resident, or body corporate of an eligible country.

(2)   *Meaning of "eligible country"*

An "eligible country" is one referred to in the Layout Designs (Eligible Countries) Orders (currently the Layout Designs (Eligible Countries) Order 2000). These Orders are discussed in more detail at 5.2 ("Legislation, treaties, and conventions") earlier in this chapter.

(3)   *Meaning of "original"*

For a layout design to be protected under the Layout Designs Act 1994 it must be "original". There is a more stringent test for originality placed on layout designs than is placed on works protected under the Copyright Act 1994.

"Original" is defined in s 6 Layout Designs Act 1994. Without limiting the ordinary meaning of the word, the section states that a layout design will not be deemed to be original if:

- Its making involved no intellectual effort by the maker (for example, it was copied);

- It was commonplace at the time it was made; or

- It comprises elements and interconnections that are commonplace, the combination of which, as a whole, involved no intellectual effort by the maker (ie, creation of the layout design was obvious having regard to the state of the art).

There are to date no New Zealand cases on the application of s 6 (nor on its Australian equivalent s 11 Circuit Layouts Act 1989 (Aust)). Hence, there is no guidance as to the factors the Court is likely to look for in determining whether a layout design is "commonplace", or whether its creation lacked "intellectual effort".

(a)   *Lower threshold of originality than for patentability*

The concept of lack of intellectual effort also arises under patent law in the field of obviousness: *Windsurfing International Inc v Tabur Marine (GB) Ltd* (1985) 102 RPC 59 (CA).

However, it is unlikely that the test for "originality" under the Layout Designs Act 1994 will be analogous to the obviousness test for patentability under the Patents Act 1953.

Layout designs, like copyright, protect the expression of the design, not the idea behind it. This idea/expression dichotomy results in the scope of protection being significantly narrower than patent protection, in the sense that it is permissible to reproduce the idea of a protected layout design (ie, the way in which the integrated circuit works and/or its component parts interact) provided the layout of the integrated circuit is not copied.

This narrower protection will be reflected in the determination of the "level of intellectual effort" required to produce a valid layout design. Further, the Act states in s 6(c) that any combination must involve no intellectual effort by the maker, rather than an inventive step as required in patent law.

In practice, it is likely that very few layout designs will fail to meet the originality threshold established by the Act, as even layout designs that are generated with the assistance of a computer will require some intellectual effort to make (for example, the programming and overseeing of the program that creates the layout design).

5.6 Duration

A layout design is subject to protection for a specified term commencing the day the layout design was made. Provisions are found in s 2 Layout Designs Act 1994 under the definition of "protection period".

The term of protection will depend on whether the layout design has been commercially exploited, and if so, when.

If the eligible layout design is first commercially exploited within 5 calendar years after the calendar year in which the eligible layout design was made, then the protection period is 10 calendar years from the year of first commercial exploitation.

In every other case the protection period is the end of 15 calendar years after the calendar year in which the eligible layout design was made.

5.6.1 Shorter protection for commercially exploited designs

Thus, if a layout design is commercially exploited soon after the layout design is made, the duration of protection will be shorter. In practice, however, this will make little difference, as the commercial lifespan of the vast majority of layout designs will be significantly less than the 15-year protection period provided by the Act.

5.6.2 Meaning of "made"

An eligible layout design is "made" when it is first fixed in a material form (s 5(2) Layout Designs Act 1994).

5.6.3 Meaning of "commercially exploited"

In accordance with s 3 Layout Designs Act 1994, a layout design is "commercially exploited" if it, copies of it, or the resulting integrated circuit, are:

- Sold or hired or otherwise distributed by way of trade;

- Offered or exposed for sale, hire or other distribution by way of trade; or

- Imported for the purpose of sale or hire or other distribution by way of trade.

5.7 Ownership

5.7.1 Maker is first owner

Ownership of eligible layout designs is governed by s 12 Layout Designs Act 1994. The starting presumption is that the person who makes the layout design is the first owner of any rights that vest in it. That is subject to modification in cases where the layout design is made during the course of employment, commissioned or assigned. Each of these is discussed in more detail later in this section.

(1) *Maker must be "eligible person"*

Where the layout design has not been commercially exploited (or was not first commercially exploited in an "eligible country" or New Zealand) at least one of the makers must be an "eligible person" for the layout design to qualify for protection under the Layout Designs Act 1994. The meaning of "eligible person" is discussed in more detail at 5.5 ("Qualification of layout design rights") earlier in this chapter.

5.7.2 Employee designs

Under s 12(2) Layout Designs Act 1994, where a layout design is made during the course of employment under a contract of service or apprenticeship, the employer will be the first owner of the layout design rights.

The operation of s 12(2) can be excluded or modified by agreement between the employer/employee (s 12(4)).

When an employer claims ownership of a layout design, as with copyright, it raises two issues:

- Whether the person was "employed" (rather than being engaged in a contract for services); and

- Whether the layout design was produced by the employee "in the course of employment".

If these two questions are answered affirmatively then the employer is entitled to ownership of the layout design. Whether a layout design was made "during the course of employment" will be a question of fact, and will usually turn on the specific terms of the contract of service or apprenticeship.

The ownership of copyright works created by employees, which requires consideration of similar questions, is discussed in further detail at 4.6.2(2) ("Employee works") in the copyright chapter of this text.

5.7.3 Commissioned designs

Under s 12(3) Layout Designs Act 1994, if the layout design is:

- Commissioned for valuable consideration, and

- Made in pursuance of that commission,

the person who commissioned the layout design will be the first owner of the layout design rights. As with employee designs, the terms of s 12(3) can be excluded or modified by agreement between the parties under s 12(4).

In the copyright context, "commissioning" has been described by the High Court as being analogous to ordering or agreeing to pay for the commissioned work: *Plix Products Ltd v Frank M Winstone (Merchants) Ltd* (1984) 3 IPR 390, at p 412.

While no formal contract of commission is required, the authorities make it clear that the commissioning of the work must predate the making, otherwise the work cannot be said to have been created "in pursuance of the commission": *Hansen v Humes-Maclon Plastics Ltd* (1984) 1 NZIPR 557, at p 570.

Again, whether a layout design has or has not been commissioned is a subjective question to be determined on the individual facts of each case. Further guidance can be found at 4.6.2(3) ("Commissioned works") in the copyright chapter of this text.

5.7.4 Computer-generated works

A significant proportion of layout designs are designed and generated by, or with the help of, machines.

Section 5 Layout Designs Act 1994 governs the situation where a person had some input into the design process but used a computer to make the layout design. This section states that the person who used a computer to make an eligible layout design is deemed to have made the design.

The Act does not include provisions to assign ownership of the rights in layout designs created solely by machines. Where a computer is solely responsible for the design, it is likely that the Courts will look to the Copyright Act 1994 to resolve the question of first ownership.

Section 5(2)(a) Copyright Act 1994 contemplates the creation of a work purely by computer. In such instances, it is the person who undertook the necessary arrangements to create the computer-generated work who is deemed to be the "author" of that work.

Therefore, in the case of a computer-generated layout design, the person who undertook the necessary arrangements to create the design (ie the programmer) is likely to be deemed to have "made" the layout design and therefore to be the first owner of any rights which vest in it.

5.7.5 Joint makers

Section 9 Layout Designs Act 1994 foresees the possibility of joint makers of an eligible layout design.

Under s 12(5) of the Act, where an eligible layout design has been jointly made by people who are not all "eligible persons", s 12 of the Act (defining ownership) applies as if the design had been made solely by those who were eligible persons.

There is no direction in the Act as to how joint rights are held. The relative relationship of rights is likely to be inferred from copyright law, where authors are tenants in common. Thus, a rights-holder is able to instigate infringement proceedings independently of other rights-holders, and rights do not vest in other "tenants" on death or dissolution of a rights-holder.

5.8 Assignment

Layout design rights are personal property. As such they are capable of assignment and may pass by will, or by operation of law (s 39(1)).

Section 39(2) Layout Designs Act 1994 permits a partial assignment of rights. Thus, it is possible to assign any of the rights afforded to the rights-holder, whether separately or in combination, and/or to assign those rights for only part of the protection period.

5.8.1 Prospective owners

Under s 38 Layout Designs Act 1994, a person who will be the owner of rights in future layout designs, when they are made, can assign those layout design rights. An assignment of future rights is binding upon all successors-in-title.

5.8.2 Assignment must be in writing

No assignment of layout design rights will have effect unless it is in writing and signed by, or on behalf of, the assignor (s 39(3) Layout Designs Act 1994).

5.9 Licences

The owner, or prospective owner, of layout design rights can license those rights under the Act (ss 4 and 39).

5.9.1 Licences bind successors-in-title

The grant of a licence of layout design rights binds every successor-in-title to the interest in that right (s 39(4) Layout Designs Act 1994).

However, in the case of a bona fide purchaser for value, if that purchaser had no actual or constructive knowledge of the licence, they will receive clear title to that right.

A person deriving title from that bona fide purchaser for value also receives clear title.

5.9.2 Exclusive licences permitted

The owner of the layout design rights is entitled to grant an exclusive licence of those rights. "Exclusive licence" is defined in s 2 Layout Designs Act 1994:

> "'Exclusive licence' means a licence in writing, signed by or on behalf of the owner or prospective owner of the layout design rights, authorising the licensee, to the exclusion of all other persons, to do an act that, under this Act, the owner would, but for the licence, have the exclusive right to do:"

An exclusive licensee is able to take legal action in his or her own name to enforce the layout design rights licensed. This is discussed further at 5.10 ("Enforcement of rights") later in this chapter.

5.9.3 No compulsory licensing

Unlike under patent and design legislation, there are no provisions in the Act enabling compulsory licensing of layout designs not commercially exploited in New Zealand.

5.9.4 Use of the protected design for defence or national security

Under s 20 Layout Designs Act 1994, use of a layout design (or integrated circuit) by the Crown is not an infringement if it is for the purposes of defence or civil defence.

However, the Crown is only exempt if it has taken all reasonable steps to secure the owner's permission before using the layout design, and has been unable to obtain a licence.

Under s 22 the Crown must also advise the owner of the layout design rights as to its actions as soon as practicable. By s 23 the owner is entitled to remuneration for acts undertaken under s 20. In the event that the parties cannot reach an agreement as to the appropriate level of remuneration, they are able to apply to the Copyright Tribunal for a ruling.

5.10   Enforcement of rights

An action for infringement of the exclusive rights conferred by the Layout Designs Act 1994 can be initiated in either the District Court or the High Court (s 25). As with most civil proceedings, the case will be heard and determined solely by a Judge. A rights-holder (or infringer) cannot elect a jury trial.

5.10.1 Actions by exclusive licensees

Under s 28 Layout Designs Act 1994 an exclusive licensee may commence proceedings for infringement, seeking damages or an injunction, as if they were the owner of the layout design rights. However, as exclusive licensees hold these rights concurrently with the owner they may not take any action for infringement of the layout design rights against the owner itself.

(1)   *Rights of exclusive licensee and owner are concurrent*

The rights that an owner and his or her exclusive licensee have in relation to a layout design are held concurrently. Accordingly, if either the owner or his or her exclusive licensee commences proceedings for infringement seeking damages or a permanent injunction under ss 25 and 26 Layout Designs Act 1994, s 29(1) requires them to join the other as a party to the proceedings.

The requirements of s 29(1) can be waived by the Court, and do not apply in the case of applications for interim injunctions (s 29(2)).

5.10.2 Presumption as to subsistence and ownership of rights

Under s 35 Layout Designs Act 1994, in proceedings for infringement, rights are presumed to subsist in an eligible layout design, and the plaintiff is presumed to be the owner of the layout design rights unless a defendant puts those questions into issue.

5.10.3 Presumption as to knowledge of product marking

If the layout design, integrated circuit, or its packaging was legibly labelled to indicate:

- That layout design rights subsisted in the layout design;

- The identity of the parties with an interest in the layout design rights; and

- The year of first commercial exploitation,

then, under s 36, it is presumed that any person dealing with the layout design had knowledge of those facts.

This presumption may restrict the ambit of the innocent commercial exploitation and innocent infringement defences discussed in more detail at 5.12 ("Exceptions to infringement/defences") and 5.13 ("Remedies") later in this chapter.

5.11 Infringement of rights

Section 13 Layout Designs Act 1994 confers upon the owner of the layout design rights the exclusive right to:

- Copy the layout design, directly or indirectly, in a material form;

- Make an integrated circuit in accordance with the layout design, or a copy of the layout design; and

- Commercially exploit the layout design in New Zealand.

The exclusive property rights also include the right to authorise any other person to do any of these things (s 4).

Under s 14 Layout Designs Act 1994, the exclusive rights are infringed if, during the protection period, a person, without the authority or licence of the owner and/or a licensee, does, or authorises another person to do, anything which it is the exclusive right of the owner to do.

5.11.1 Parallel importation

The parallel importation of integrated circuits and copyright works embodied in integrated circuits is permitted under s 19 Layout Designs Act 1994.

However, this section may need to be read subject to the Copyright Act 1994. While the parallel importation of copyright works is permitted under ss 9(1)(d), 12(3), 12(5A), and 12(6) Copyright Act 1994, the importation of an infringing copy of a computer program stored within an integrated circuit by a person who knows, or ought reasonably to know, that the computer program is an infringing copy is prohibited under s 35(1)(a)(i) Copyright Act 1994.

Although the interplay of these provisions has not yet been considered in New Zealand, a similar issue arose in Australia. In *Avel Pty Ltd v Wells* (1992) 36 FCR 340; 23 IPR 353 (FCA), integrated circuits made by Japanese manufacturers in accordance with protected layout designs were purchased by two of the appellants, Capcom and Tad. Capcom and Tad then programmed the chips with arcade game software of which they were the owners of copyright in Japan. The third appellant, Avel, was the exclusive licensee for the arcade games in Australia.

Wells purchased the chips containing the arcade games in Japan, and imported them for subsequent resale into Australia.

Without s 24(2) Circuit Layouts Act 1989 (Aust) (which is the Australian equivalent to s 19(2) Layout Designs Act 1994) the importation of the chips would have constituted an infringement of the copyright in the software programmed on them under ss 37 and 38 Copyright Act 1968 (Aust). The question arose as to whether the importation was an infringement under the Circuit Layouts Act 1989 (Aust).

Wells argued that s 24(2) was sufficiently broad to permit not only the parallel importation of integrated circuits that had been legitimately commercially exploited overseas, but also any copyright works legitimately embodied in those chips.

In the lower Court, Gummow J held that the importation of the chips did not infringe Capcom or Tad's copyright because of the operation of s 24(2) but on the basis of an erroneous finding that the chips did not constitute an original circuit layout until Capcom and Tad had programmed their arcade game software onto them. On appeal both parties accepted that this finding was wrong.

The sole point on appeal was whether s 24(2) extended to integrated circuits in which a copyright work had been stored subsequent to manufacture. If it did, then Wells' actions in importing the integrated circuits were permissible. If it did not, then the copyright rights subsisting in the computer software embodied in the integrated circuit were infringed by Wells' importation.

After considering the section in some detail, the full Federal Court of Australia held that s 24(2) extended to integrated circuits in which a copyright work was stored, regardless of whether it (the copyright work) was stored there during the manufacture of the integrated circuits or subsequently.

The Court also held that it is not a requirement that an integrated circuit be made by the person who owns the copyright in the work stored on that integrated circuit for s 24(2) of the Act to apply.

Accordingly, Wells' actions were held, at p 348; pp 361-362, not to infringe copyright in the arcade game software:

> "when the subsection speaks of the integrated circuit containing a copy or adaptation of a work, it refers to the storage in the integrated circuit of the work the subject of copyright or a copy or adaptation thereof. The word 'containing' is an apt description of the function of storing data performed by an integrated circuit such as an EPROM or an OTPROM. If a more restricted operation of the subsection had been intended it would not have been difficult to use words appropriate for that task. All that is required to satisfy the words in parenthesis is that the integrated circuit be one that is made in accordance with an eligible layout. When the subsection speaks of the integrated circuit containing a copy or adaptation of a work, it extends to the retention in the integrated circuit of the work the subject of copyright or a copy or adaptation thereof. It is not required that an integrated circuit be made by the person who owns the copyright."

5.12   Exceptions to infringement/defences

The following activities are acknowledged by the Layout Designs Act 1994 as exceptions to infringement and may, in effect, be raised as a defence to infringement proceedings:

- Innocent commercial exploitation (s 15);

- Copying the layout design for private use (s 16);

- Copying the layout design for the purposes of research or teaching (s 17);

- Copying the layout design for the purposes of evaluating or analysing the design (s 18);

- Parallel importation of copies of the layout design (s 19); and

- Use of the layout design by the Crown for the purposes of defence or national security (s 20).

5.12.1   Innocent commercial exploitation

Under s 15 Layout Designs Act 1994, if a person commercially exploits (or authorises the exploitation of) an unauthorised integrated circuit in New Zealand, and at the time they acquired the integrated circuit they did not know, or could not reasonably be expected to have known, that the integrated circuit was unauthorised, that person cannot be liable for infringement of any layout design rights embodied in the circuit.

Under s 3 Layout Designs Act 1994, commercial exploitation includes importing the unauthorised integrated circuit for the purpose of sale or hire, or other distribution by way of trade.

Similarly, under s 35(1)(a)(i) Copyright Act 1994, a person who imports an infringing copy of a copyright work (which arguably includes a computer program stored in an integrated circuit) and knows, or ought reasonably to know, that the computer program is an infringing copy infringes copyright in the computer program.

Thus, a person who imports an unauthorised integrated circuit for the purpose of hire, sale or trade will not infringe either the layout design rights in the integrated circuit or the copyright in any computer program stored in the integrated circuit, provided that they did not know, and should not reasonably have been expected to know, that the integrated circuit was unauthorised at the time they acquired it, and the computer program stored in the integrated circuit was an infringing copy when they imported it (respectively).

(1)   *Actual or constructive knowledge*

In the Australian case *Nintendo Co Ltd v Centronics Systems Pty Ltd* (1991) 23 IPR 119 (FCA), Centronics imported video game machines from Taiwan for resale in Australia. The machines contained a silicon ROM chip incorporating an unauthorised integrated circuit manufactured in breach of Nintendo's layout design rights.

The question arose as to whether Centronics required actual or constructive knowledge of the identity of the owner of the layout design rights (ie Nintendo) or whether it was sufficient for Centronics simply to know that the integrated circuits had been manufactured by a party other than the owner of the rights (and were therefore unlikely to be authorised).

The High Court of Australia held that reference to "the owner" in the Circuit Layouts Act 1989 (Aust) should be regarded as a non-specific reference to a possessor of the attributes that constitute ownership of the relevant right.

The Court also held that actual or constructive knowledge is satisfied if the alleged infringer knew or ought reasonably to have known that intellectual property rights existed in the layout. It does not matter that the alleged infringer neither knew nor could reasonably be expected to know that the integrated circuit (which embodies the layout) was made without the authority of the rights-holder and was therefore "unauthorised".

(2)   *Equitable remuneration*

Under s 15(2) Layout Designs Act 1994 a person who becomes aware that an integrated circuit is unauthorised after innocent commercial exploitation can legitimise subsequent commercial exploitation by paying the owner, or exclusive licensee, of the layout design rights an agreed level of remuneration. In the event that the parties cannot agree to the appropriate level of remuneration they are able to apply to the Copyright Tribunal for a ruling.

(3)   *No innocent commercial exploitation if product marked adequately*

Under s 36 Layout Designs Act 1994, if certain information regarding the layout design rights is marked on the integrated circuit or its packaging, there will be a presumption that any person dealing with that integrated circuit is aware of that information. This may preclude the innocent commercial exploitation defence being available. The nature of marking required is discussed in more detail at 5.10 ("Enforcement of rights") earlier in this chapter.

(4)   *Innocent infringement compared*

The Layout Designs Act 1994 makes reference to both "innocent commercial exploitation" and "innocent infringement". Innocent commercial exploitation appears to be broader than innocent infringement. While both preclude the recovery of damages, an account of profits is still available against an innocent infringer. There does not appear to be any reason for this. Innocent infringement is discussed 5.13.2 later in this chapter.

5.12.2 Private use

A copy made for private use may be commercially exploited without infringement, or may otherwise be distributed by way of trade, to the extent that it does not prejudice the interests of the owner of the rights in the design or circuit.

The private use exception contained in s 16 Layout Designs Act 1994 is similar to that found in the Copyright Act 1994.

It is, however, broader than the copyright exception, as it does not restrict the copier to only one copy of a layout design for the private use of the copier.

5.12.3 Research and teaching

The exceptions to infringement of layout design rights in s 17 Layout Designs Act 1994 are again broader than the corresponding exceptions to infringement of copyright in ss 43 and

44 Copyright Act 1994 as they permit multiple copies of the entire layout design to be made by a reprographic process for the purposes of research or teaching.

In the Australian case *De Garis v Neville Jeffress Pidler Pty Ltd* (1990) 18 IPR 292, at p 298, "research" was defined as:

> "a diligent and systematic enquiry or investigation into a subject in order to discover facts or principles."

In *TVNZ Ltd v Newsmonitor Services Ltd* [1994] 2 NZLR 91, Newsmonitor Services Ltd submitted that s 42 Copyright Act 1994, which provides a "fair dealing" exception to copyright infringement where a copy is made for the purpose of research or private study, covered copies made in the course of providing a commercial news monitoring service. Although Newsmonitor was ultimately unsuccessful, the Court noted, at p 106, that the phrase "research and private study" in s 42 Copyright Act 1994 may cover research undertaken with a commercial end in mind. Thus a research project to develop or improve a specific product will be considered research for the purposes of the Layout Designs Act.

5.12.4 Evaluation and analysis

Section 18 Layout Designs Act 1994 enables parties to copy an existing eligible layout design, or integrated circuit, in order to evaluate and/or create a new, improved or modified layout design based on that existing design, and then to commercially exploit the modified layout design.

The Copyright Act 1994 does not contain similar provisions; however, s 43(2) and (3) could be extended to include such a "fair dealing" exception.

The prospect was considered in the US in *American Geophysical Union v Texaco Inc* (1994) 29 IPR 381, at pp 392-398, where the Court believed such "transformative use" was relevant to fair dealing.

5.12.5 Parallel importation and Crown use

The concepts of parallel importation and Crown use are discussed at 5.11 ("Infringement of rights") and 5.9 ("Licences") earlier in this chapter.

5.13 Remedies

Upon a finding of infringement the Court can award one or more remedies, which may include:

- An interim or permanent injunction restraining the infringing conduct (s 26);

- An account of profits earned by the infringer, or payment of damages incurred by the plaintiff (s 25(1)); and/or

- Additional damages depending on the flagrancy of the infringing act or any benefit accruing to the infringer (s 25(3)).

5.13.1 Interim injunctions

Several recent decisions of the High Court and the Court of Appeal suggest that the Courts will give increasing primacy to intellectual property rights with a finite duration when determining an application for interim relief. In many cases this seems to be at the expense of seemingly conclusive arguments going to the balance of convenience and the overall justice.

In *Aktiebolaget Hassle v Novartis NZ Ltd* 1/5/03, Potter J, HC Auckland CP51-SW/03, the plaintiffs sought an injunction to restrain Novartis from manufacturing an omeprazole product, PROBITOR, which they believed infringed their Patent No 220096 relating to their own similar product sold in New Zealand under the brand name LOSEC. Novartis resisted the application on a number of grounds including:

(1)   That it was strongly arguable that the patent was invalid, the equivalent UK patent having already been overturned on the grounds of obviousness; and

(2)   That it had contracted to supply Pharmac with PROBITOR, and was obliged to pay Pharmac $350,000 per calendar month it was unable to supply same (presumably to compensate Pharmac for being obliged to subsidise the more expensive LOSEC during that period).

While recognising the significant losses likely to be suffered by Novartis if injuncted, the Court nonetheless found that the balance of convenience and the overall justice favoured the granting of an injunction, commenting, at para 43:

> "There is a reality to be recognised in the case of the patent, that the patent confers a monopoly during its currency, the benefit of which runs over to the post-patent period because of the strong market position usually developed during the monopoly period. This was expressed by Eichelbaum J in [*Monsanto Chemical Co v Stauffer Chemical Co (No 2)* (1984) 1 TCLR 129; 1 NZIPR 540]."

and later, at para 56:

> "Premature interference with the monopoly position which the patent confers during its currency will also impact on the ability of the proprietor to create or confirm its own market after the expiry of the patent (the 'bridgehead' opportunity)."

The decision of Potter J was upheld by the Court of Appeal in a decision of Blanchard J delivered on 4 July 2003 (*Novartis NZ Ltd v Aktiebolaget Hassle* [2004] 2 NZLR 721 (CA)).

Similar comments have also arisen in the context of applications for interim injunctions to restrain the infringement of registered design rights. See, for example:

• *Handitags Ltd v Warburton* 12/12/01, Glazebrook J, HC Auckland M1586-SW01, at paras 17 and 18:

> "However, the main reason put forward by Handitags as to inadequacy of damages is the loss of the ability to manage their practical monopoly situation. This is because, at any stage during such a monopoly, an entry of a competitor can cause permanent damage and permanent inability to manage the monopoly and, in particular, the ending of the monopoly which will obviously occur at the end of the design and copyright period. This diminished advantage can mean a permanent effect which Handitags submits is exceedingly hard to quantify. It is noted that there is only some four years left in respect of the design and five years in respect of the copyright so the loss of a portion of the

period at the end of the registration for the design and the copyright period is even more significant. These submissions are accepted. It is accepted that damages would not be an adequate remedy for Handitags."

- *BEP Marine Ltd v Aquatech Marine Ltd* 20/12/02, O'Regan J, HC Auckland M1568-SW02 (which applied *Handitags*).

- *Permanent Promotions Pty Ltd v Independent Liquor (NZ) Ltd* 10/6/04, Heath J, HC Auckland CIV-2004-404-2419, at paras 38 and 39:

> "In my judgment, the scheme of the Act is clear. A Commissioner is appointed to examine designs submitted to him or her. In the course of that examination the Commissioner determines questions of novelty and compliance with statutory definitions. The underlying assumption is that the Commissioner is someone experienced in applying the Act and in making judgments of that sort. The scheme of the Act would be undermined significantly if the Courts failed to recognise the nature of the monopoly that flows from the registration process. In this case the design has been registered. I reject Mr Brown's submission that the Register is prima facie evidence only of what is contained in it rather than the fact that the Commissioner has found the design to comply with the definition contained in s 2(1) of the Act and has found the requisite degree of novelty. No item can be registered unless those conclusions have been drawn. That registration confers a monopoly. On an interim injunction application the Court must be slow to second guess the findings of the Commissioner."

and, at para 43:

> "In my view the fact of registration confers a prima facie right sufficient to overcome the hurdle of establishing that a serious question exists to be tried."

Some caution needs to be exercised, as the "bridgehead" argument is probably limited to forms of intellectual property in which the rights expire after a finite period. Thus, for example, the bridgehead argument may not be appropriate in a case involving infringement of a registered trade mark. Similarly, if the ownership of the intellectual property is in dispute this may result in refusal of the application: *Golden Homes (1998) Ltd v Blue Chip Construction Ltd* 21/6/05, Allan J, HC Auckland CIV-2003-404-7090.

5.13.2 Innocent infringement

If the infringing conduct is deemed by the Court to be innocent, it will not make any order for damages, but can still make an order for an account of profits (under s 25(2) Layout Designs Act 1994). A person will be an innocent infringer if, at the time the infringement was committed, they were not aware, and did not have reasonable grounds for suspecting, that the acts they were doing constituted an infringement.

(1) *Innocent commercial exploitation compared*

If a party is also found to have innocently commercially exploited a layout design, or integrated circuit, the Court cannot award an account of profits. Section 15 Layout Designs Act 1994 expressly states that innocent commercial exploitation is not an infringement of layout design rights.

Innocent commercial exploitation is discussed in more detail at 5.12 ("Exceptions to infringement/defences") earlier in this chapter.

5.13.3 Assessment of damages where exclusive licence granted

In cases where:

- An exclusive licence has been granted in respect of the right which has been infringed; and

- The owner of the layout design rights and exclusive licensee are not both joined as plaintiffs,

the Court is obliged by s 31(1) Layout Designs Act 1994 to take the following into account:

- Any liabilities (such as royalties) to which the licence is subject; and

- Any pecuniary remedy already awarded to the other party under s 25 in respect of the same infringement.

5.13.4 Apportionment of profits between owner and exclusive licensee

Where an owner and exclusive licensee have a concurrent interest in the right that is deemed to have been infringed, and the Court has awarded an account of profits in respect of that infringement, s 32 Layout Designs Act 1994 requires the Court to apportion the profits between those parties.

5.13.5 Limitation for separate proceedings in relation to the same infringement

Section 33 Layout Designs Act 1994 prevents:

- The making of a judgment or granting of an order for the payment of damages in respect of an infringement of rights in favour of the owner or exclusive licensee if a final judgment or order has already been made in favour of the other party directing an account of profits in respect of the same infringement; and

- The making of a judgment or granting of an order for an account of profits in favour of the owner or exclusive licensee in respect of an infringement if a final judgment or order has already been made in favour of the other party awarding damages or directing an account of profits in respect of the same infringement.

5.14 Groundless threats and groundless proceedings

Unlike the Patents Act 1953 and the Designs Act 1953, there are no provisions under the Layout Designs Act 1994 to redress groundless threats of infringement.

Section 40 Layout Designs Act 1994 does provide protection against groundless proceedings. It enables a Court in the case of groundless proceedings to:

- Strike out those proceedings; and

- Order damages to be paid for any loss suffered by the defendant.

5.15   Offences

There are no provisions for criminal offences under the Layout Designs Act 1994.

5.16   References and resource sites

5.16.1   Websites

Thomson Brookers	www.thomsonbrookers.co.nz
Interim Website of New Zealand Legislation	www.legislation.govt.nz
IP Australia	www.ipaustralia.gov.au
	www.ipaustralia.gov.au/ip/circuits.shtml
James & Wells	www.jaws.co.nz
UK Intellectual Property Office	www.ipo.gov.uk
World Trade Organisation — TRIPS material	www.wto.org/english/tratop_e/trips_e/trips_e.htm

Chapter 6

DESIGN REGISTRATIONS

6.1 Introduction

A design registration provides protection for aspects of the appearance of an article, such as its shape, configuration, pattern or ornamentation. Unlike patents, a design registration does not protect purely functional aspects of an article unless they also contribute to its appearance. As most manufactured articles involve an element of designer choice, design protection is generally available.

The procedure for registering a design in New Zealand is relatively uncomplicated. A design that is novel in New Zealand, and that can be applied to an article of manufacture, is capable of registration unless the features of design for which protection is sought are dictated solely by the function of the article.

New Zealand has a local novelty requirement for design registrations. A design will meet this local novelty requirement if it has not been made available to the public in New Zealand before the application date.

Changes to New Zealand's copyright legislation now allow for the parallel importation of copyright works. However, the same does not apply to design registrations. Hence, if the copyright work relates to an article, and a design application covering the article is filed before the article is released in New Zealand, the resulting design registration can be used to block parallel imports of the article.

6.2 Legislation, treaties, and conventions

6.2.1 Governing law

The law relating to design registrations in New Zealand is governed by the:

- Designs Act 1953 ("the Act");

- Designs Amendment Act 1996;

- Designs Amendment Act 1999;

- Designs Regulations 1954 (as amended);

- Decisions of the Commissioner of Designs;

- Intellectual Property Office Practice Notes; and

- Decisions of the Courts.

The Act is derived from the Registered Designs Act 1949 (UK). New Zealand legislation is therefore interpreted with reference to New Zealand case law, case law from the UK, and case law from countries with similar legislation also derived from the UK Act.

6.2.2 International conventions

New Zealand is a contracting State to the following conventions and treaties:

- Paris Convention (International Union) 1883-1934 (substantive provisions; since 20 June 1984);

- The Stockholm text of the Paris Convention of 1967, but only as to its administrative provisions (arts 13–30); and

- The Convention establishing the World Intellectual Property Organisation (WIPO Convention) 1967 (with effect from 20 June 1984).

These agreements allow for the filing date of a foreign design application to be applied to a corresponding application filed in New Zealand within 6 months of the foreign application. Reciprocal rights are also given in foreign countries for applications first filed in New Zealand. Convention applications are discussed further below.

Generally speaking, no international community design application procedure exists. Separate design applications must be filed in each territory in which an applicant wishes to obtain protection.

(1) Convention applications

Ordinarily a design application filed in New Zealand will be given the actual date of filing.

New Zealand has been a member of the Paris Convention since 20 June 1984. The Paris Convention provides reciprocal rights to citizens and residents of member nations regarding the acquisition of intellectual property rights. In the interests of consistency, it also provides a system whereby a person can obtain the same filing date for an application made in multiple jurisdictions within a certain time frame. This time frame is known as the "convention period".

The convention period for registered designs is 6 months from the filing date of the first (or "originating") application to protect the same registered design filed in any country that is a member of the Paris Convention.

Conversely, an application to register a design that is first filed in New Zealand can be used as the basis for a priority claim for corresponding applications filed within 6 months in other countries that are signatories to the Paris Convention treaty.

(2) *Importance of filing date*

The filing date ascribed to an application to register a design is important for two reasons:

- The novelty of the design is assessed as at the filing date. Where the design relates to emerging technologies, the earlier the filing date the less likely it is that there will be prior art that will invalidate the registered design. These concepts are discussed at 6.6.4 ("Novelty requirements") later in this chapter.

- Damages for infringement of a registered design will accrue from the filing date. This is discussed in more detail at 6.15 ("Infringement and enforcement of rights") later in this chapter.

6.3 Rights granted by registration

6.3.1 Exclusive right

A design consists of two-dimensional (pattern and ornamentation) or three-dimensional (shape and configuration) features of an article.

Under s 11(1) Designs Act 1953, the registered proprietor of a design registration has the exclusive right in New Zealand to:

- Manufacture for sale, or for the purpose of any trade or business;

- Import for sale; or for use for the purposes of any trade or business;

- Sell or hire; or

- Offer for sale or hire,

any article in respect of which the design is registered and which embodies the registered design (or a design which is not substantially different), and to make anything for enabling such an article to be made.

(1) *Rights may be licensed*

The registered proprietor may license others to carry out any of these actions.

This is discussed in more detail at 6.9 ("Licences") later in this chapter.

6.3.2 Territory

Registration of a design under the Designs Act 1953 has effect throughout New Zealand, Tokelau (s 50), Niue (by virtue of s 689 Niue Act 1966) and the Cook Islands (by virtue of s 635 Cook Islands Act 1915).

Registered designs are territorial. Therefore, a New Zealand registered design will have no effect in other countries. However it may be possible to enforce acts committed overseas in breach of a foreign design in New Zealand under the "double actionability" rule. This is discussed in more detail at 6.15 ("Infringement and enforcement of rights") later in this chapter.

6.3.3 Comparison with copyright

New Zealand offers concurrent protection of designs through both copyright and design registration.

Copyright is a right that vests automatically in original works. It does not need to be registered to be enforced. Furthermore, copyright protection will extend to articles that do not necessarily qualify as subject matter for a registrable design, or do not meet the novelty requirements of the Designs Act 1953.

Therefore, copyright gives free automatic protection to a wide variety of products without the need to register any details before public disclosure or release of the product in New Zealand. However, the rights afforded by copyright protection are more limited than those offered by design registrations.

In order to establish copyright infringement it is necessary to show that the alleged copy was made with reference to the original. This is known as a "causal connection". If the alleged copy was developed independently there will be no infringement even if it is identical to the original.

Conversely, design registrations offer a monopoly on the design protected, irrespective of how an infringing design was derived or obtained. When assessing whether a registered design has been infringed there is no requirement to prove a causal connection or actual copying of the protected design. For example, a design registration will be infringed by an article to which the same design has been applied even if that article was created independent of any reference to the registered design or a product which embodies the registered design: *UPL Group Ltd v Dux Engineers Ltd* [1989] 3 NZLR 135 (CA), at p 140.

The tests for infringement are also worded differently. Whereas, for copyright infringement it is necessary to show that the alleged infringing article reproduces a substantial part of the copyright work, under the Designs Act 1953 it is necessary to prove that the alleged infringing article is an article "to which the registered design (or a design not substantially different to the registered design) has been applied".

Finally, unlike copyright works, the details of every registered design are recorded in a Register that is open to public inspection. The Register contains representations of every design for which protection has been granted. The particulars of the proprietor and the registration are also available. These details can serve as a tangible record of the proprietor's rights and a strong disincentive to copying or manufacturing similar articles.

6.4 Types of design registration

A design consists of two-dimensional (pattern and ornamentation) or three-dimensional (shape and configuration) features of an article. The features protected are judged solely by the eye of a prospective customer or user of the article to which the design is applied. Hence the design must have at least some element of aesthetic or visual appeal that is not directly dictated by the function to be performed by the article. Ordinarily a design will be applied to a single article of manufacture.

The requirements of a registrable design are discussed in more detail at 6.5 ("Registrable subject matter") later in this chapter.

In addition to standard design registrations applied to a single article, the Designs Act 1953 provides for:

- Registration of minor design variations (known as "Section 8 Registrations"); and

- Registration of a set of articles in a single application.

6.4.1 Section 8 registrations

Under s 8 Designs Act 1953, the proprietor of a registered design can, at a later date, make an application for registration of a design that is not substantially different in character to the earlier registered design (known as the "parent"). Section 8 registrations are used where a design registration has been obtained in respect of one article, and registration is sought for the same design applied to another type of article, or a similar design applied to the same or other articles. For example, if a design registration had already been obtained for a design when applied to a knife and fork, a s 8 registration could be used to gain protection for the same design applied to a spoon.

(1) *No anticipation by parent design*

An application for registration under s 8 Designs Act 1953 is not rendered invalid by prior publication of the parent. That is, in the example above, the examiner at the Intellectual Property Office of New Zealand will not cite the parent registered design (relating to the knife and fork) when examining the novelty of the s 8 application (for the spoon).

(2) *Separate renewal fees payable*

Renewal fees are payable in respect of s 8 registrations.

These are discussed in more detail at 6.5 ("Renewal") later in this chapter.

(3) *Term linked to earlier design*

The term of a registration under s 8 Designs Act 1953 is linked to the parent design registration. A s 8 registration will expire when the parent design registration expires.

6.4.2 Sets of articles

A set of articles is defined in s 2 Designs Act 1953 and can be the subject of a single design registration provided the articles are ordinarily sold, or are intended to be used, together. The articles must share:

- The same design; or

- The same design with modifications or variations not sufficient to alter the character or substantially affect the identity of the design.

For example, it would be appropriate to register a design applied to a set of cutlery, or to a set of salt and pepper shakers, as a design registration for a set of articles.

6.5 Registrable subject matter

Under s 5 Designs Act 1953, a design may be registered in respect of any article or set of articles specified in the application. The word "design" is defined in s 2 to mean:

> "features of shape, configuration, pattern, or ornament applied to an article by any industrial process or means, being features which in the finished article appeal to and are judged solely by the eye; but does not include a method or principle of construction or features of shape or configuration which are dictated solely by the function which the article to be made in that shape or configuration has to perform."

Accordingly, a registered design must:

- Have at least one of the specified features of shape, configuration, pattern, or ornament;

- Be applied to an article by an industrial process or means;

- Have "eye appeal";

- Not be purely functional; and

- Not relate to a method or principle of construction but be "new or original": *Sutton v Bay Masonry Ltd* 28/5/04, Williams J, HC Tauranga CIV-2003-470-260, at para 17.

In *Permanent Promotions Pty Ltd v Independent Liquor (NZ) Ltd* 10/6/04, Heath J, HC Auckland CIV-2004-404-2419, the Court considered an application for interim injunction to prevent the defendant from utilising certain aspects of the plaintiff's registered design. The Court emphasised broadly that there were two aspects to the definition of the term "design" in s 2, namely a positive definition focused on visual appeal and a negative definition excluding features of shape or configuration dictated solely by the function the article performs.

6.5.1 Colour may be an element of design

It is likely that a design applied to an article that comprises an arrangement of certain colours will be capable of registration in New Zealand.

In *Smith Kline & French Laboratories Ltd Design Application* (1974) 91 RPC 253, the Court observed that the effects of colour in designs cannot be ignored, although normally differences in colour are unlikely to be important for the purposes of assessing novelty and/or infringement.

Thus, whether colour makes a material difference will depend on the nature of the design in question. Colours of the pattern of a football jersey were registrable in *Cook & Hurst's Design Application* (1979) 96 RPC 197. However, the registration was as a pattern, not as a three-dimensional shape.

6.5.2 Features of shape, configuration, pattern, or ornamentation

The words "shape" and "configuration" are generally treated as synonymous, and interpreted by the Court as relating to three-dimensional features (ie features of the article itself rather than features applied to an article).

The words "pattern" and "ornament" are also synonymous and are generally considered to relate to two-dimensional features applied to an article (rather than features of the article itself).

See, for example, the comments of Luxmoore J in *Kestos Ltd v Kempat Ltd & Kemp* (1936) 53 RPC 139, at p 152:

> "Shape and configuration are for all practical purposes considered as synonymous … Each signifies something in three dimensions; the form in which the article itself is fashioned. 'Pattern' and 'ornament' can, I think, in the majority of cases be treated as practically synonymous. It is something which is placed on the article for its decoration. It is substantially in two as opposed to three dimensions. An article can exist without pattern or ornament upon it, whereas it can have no existence at all apart from its shape or configuration."

6.5.3 Applied to an article by any industrial process or means

The word "article" is defined in s 2(1) Designs Act 1953 as:

> "any article of manufacture; and includes any part of an article if that part is made and sold separately."

There is some confusion as to the exact extent of items covered by the wording "article of manufacture". However, the words are generally considered to cover any article that is capable of delivery to an end user. For example, in *Collier (RH) & Co's Application* (1937) 54 RPC 253, a prefabricated building was held to be registrable, whereas, in *Concrete Ltd's Application* (1940) 57 RPC 121, a building made in situ was not.

(1)   *"Article" must have secondary purpose*

For the purposes of design protection, an article must have some function other than simply being a vehicle for carrying the registered design: *Littlewoods Pools Ltd's Application* (1949) 66 RPC 309.

For this reason printed matter primarily of a literary or artistic character is specifically excluded from the definition of registrable designs, whereas items such as textiles and wallpaper (which have a secondary purpose) are clearly registrable (reg 33 Design Regulations 1954).

(2)   *Textiles, patterns, wallpaper, and lace registrable*

As previously indicated, textiles, patterns, wallpaper, and lace are all registrable as designs in New Zealand.

6.5.4 Article to appeal to the eye

The features of shape, configuration, pattern, or ornamentation must appeal to and be judged solely by the eye. The eye is to be the eye of an informed ordinary customer of the article in question: *D A Lewis & Co Ltd v Thorn Bros Ltd* (1984) 1 TCLR 236.

In *Sutton v Bay Masonry Ltd* 28/5/04, Williams J, HC Tauranga CIV-2003-470-260, the plaintiffs brought proceedings against the defendants for infringement of their registered design. The design related to a fence post constructed of three members of equal length joined in a squared-off Z shape and attached at right angles. The defendants responded by challenging the validity of the plaintiffs' registered design, seeking rectification of the Register by deletion of the entry on the basis inter alia that the design was not applied to the article for eye appeal, but rather its shape and configuration were dictated solely by function.

In considering whether or not the design appealed to the eye, Williams J adopted, at para 18, the reasoning of the House of Lords in *AMP Inc v Utilux Pty Ltd* (1972) 89 RPC 103 (HL). In *AMP*, Lord Reid held, at pp 108-109, that:

> "the words 'judged solely by the eye' must be intended to exclude cases where a customer might choose an article of that shape not because of its appearance but because he thought that the shape made it more useful to him."

(1) *No requirement design apparent at all times*

In *Ferrero's Design Application* (1978) 95 RPC 473, the Court held that a chocolate egg comprising a layer of dark chocolate outside a layer of white chocolate had eye appeal and that there was no requirement that the article should appeal to the eye at the time of purchase.

In *Sutton v Bay Masonry Ltd* 28/5/04, Williams J, HC Tauranga CIV-2003-470-260 (discussed above), Bay Masonry claimed that the shape and configuration of the Z-shaped fence post were solely dictated by function and had no eye appeal as, once installed, the fence post became invisible to the eye. Williams J rejected the argument, at para 19, noting that:

> "It is no more than the reverse of the argument rejected in *P Ferrero v C.S.p A's Application* [1978] RPC 473, which held that a chocolate egg with differing internal layers invisible at purchase could be a finished article with features judged by the eye as the time of judgment was not limited to the time of purchase."

Accordingly, it appears as though the design need not be apparent at the time of purchase, nor beyond purchase, provided the design was at one point visible and impacted upon the purchaser's decision to purchase the goods in question.

(2) *Design must appeal to the naked eye*

In *AMP Inc v Utilux Pty Ltd* (1970) 53 RPC 397, at p 406, the trial Judge held that in normal circumstances the design must appeal to the eye without magnification. Although the case was taken on appeal to the UK Court of Appeal, and ultimately to the House of Lords, the question of whether magnified vision would suffice was not decided. The decision of the lower Court therefore remains good law.

(3)   *Aesthetic appeal unnecessary*

As with copyright, a design need not be aesthetically pleasing to be registrable. The decisive consideration is simply whether the design has any effect on the eye so as to give the article to which it is applied distinctiveness and individuality of appearance when compared to other articles in which the design is not present: *Harvey & Co (London) Ltd v Secure Fittings Ltd* (1966) 83 RPC 515 (CSess), at p 517.

(4)   *Design may be considered "in use"*

In *Scholle Industries Pty Ltd v AEP Industries (NZ) Ltd* (Commissioner's Decision No D01/2002, 27/11/02, Asst Commr Hazlewood), a design to be applied to a bag was depicted in drawings showing the bag as unfilled. The Assistant Commissioner found that he was entitled to consider what the bag would look like full (i.e. in use), when assessing novelty, at p 7:

> "I accept that all components of shape and configuration have to be taken into account. In addition the bag when filled will have a shape defined by the weld lines of the bag."

6.6 Exceptions to registrability

As previously mentioned, the definition of the word "design" in s 2(1) Designs Act 1953 excludes:

- Methods or principles of construction; and

- Features of shape or configuration that are dictated solely by the function(s) that the article performs.

In addition, the design must be new or original, and not be of a type excluded from registration by the legislation. Each of these concepts is discussed in more detail below.

6.6.1 Not a method or principle of construction

Registrable designs cannot include a method or principle of construction.

Luxmoore J in *Kestos Ltd v Kempat Ltd & Kemp* (1936) 53 RPC 139, at p 151, quoting *Russell-Clarke on Copyright in Industrial Designs*, paraphrased the prohibition as follows:

> "The real meaning is this, that no design shall be construed so widely as to give to its proprietor a monopoly in a mode or principle of construction. What he gets a monopoly for is one particular individual and specific appearance. [If] it is possible to get several different appearances which all embody the general features which he claims, then those features are too general and amount to a method or principle of construction."

6.6.2 Shape or configuration must not be dictated solely by function

Features of shape or configuration that are dictated solely by the function of the article to which the design is to be applied cannot be registered. The rationale behind the prohibition is to prevent design registrations extending to the function of articles (which is the realm

277

of patents) and, by extension, granting an individual (via a design registration) the sole and exclusive right to manufacture articles having the same function.

The test for functionality to be applied is an objective one: *Stratford Auto Components Ltd v Britax (London) Ltd* (1964) 81 RPC 183.

Functionality was considered by the House of Lords in *AMP Inc v Utilux Pty Ltd* (1972) 89 RPC 103 (HL). That case concerned an action for infringement of AMP's registered design for electrical terminals used in Hoover washing machines. The appellants contended that the design contained features that were dictated solely by the function of the terminal.

In the lower Court, AMP's action for infringement was dismissed and an order made to expunge the design from the Register. On appeal, the Court of Appeal held that the design had been validly registered and was infringed by Utilux. Utilux appealed that decision to the House of Lords, which allowed the appeal and restored the lower Court's judgment.

The Court of Appeal's finding, that the design was valid because it was possible to devise terminals in a variety of shapes that performed the same function, was expressly rejected by the House of Lords. In so doing the House of Lords held that, where every feature of shape or configuration was arrived at by considering the function that the article was to perform, then it would be excluded from registration as the shape will have been dictated by its function. The fact that articles of a different shape may perform the same function is irrelevant, as there is no way of ascertaining whether the shape of those articles was not also dictated by the function of the article.

In *Sutton v Bay Masonry Ltd* 28/5/04, Williams J, HC Tauranga CIV-2003-470-260, the plaintiffs brought proceedings against the defendants for infringement of their registered design. The design related to a fence post constructed of three members of equal length joined in a squared-off Z shape and attached at right angles. The defendants responded by challenging the validity of the plaintiffs' registered design, seeking rectification of the Register by deletion of the entry on the basis that its shape and configuration were dictated solely by function.

In considering the issue, Williams J adopted the reasoning of their Lordships in *AMP Inc v Utilux Pty Ltd* (1972) 89 RPC 103 (HL). In *AMP*, Lord Reid, at p 110, confirmed that a registered design must blend industrial efficiency with visual appeal, and a shape that is designed solely to make an article work will be excluded from registration. Lord Morris noted, at p 113, that where a feature of shape or configuration is applied to an article that is designed to perform a particular function, and the feature is not solely dictated or governed by considerations of that function, and results in the article having eye appeal, the design should not be excluded from registration.

Williams J, observed, at para 35, on the evidence presented, that the shape of the Z-post was functionally determined, consisting only of what was necessary to make the article work. Thus his Honour concluded that the Z-post did not have eye appeal and should not have been registered.

In *Permanent Promotions Pty Ltd v Independent Liquor (NZ) Ltd* 10/6/04, Heath J, HC Auckland CIV-2004-404-2419, the plaintiff applied for an injunction to restrain the defendant from inter alia infringing its registered design for the shape of a shot glass. In response, the defendant argued that there was no serious question to be tried as the shape and configuration of the shot glass were dictated solely by function and the registration was therefore invalid. The defendant relied upon certain observations of their Lordships in *Interlego AG v Tyco Industries Inc* [1989] 1 AC 217 (PC), at pp 241, 244, and 245, which clarified the meaning of "design" under the equivalent section of the Registered Designs Act 1949 (UK). The defendant submitted that the second negative aspect of the definition of "design" (ie, not dictated by function and not a method or principle of construction) excluded from protection features of shape or configuration dictated solely by the function that the article to be made in that shape or configuration must perform.

Lord Oliver of Aylmerton delivered the opinion of the Court in *Interlego*. His Lordship noted that three possible constructions of the definition of "design" existed, namely that:

(1)   All that is registrable or able to be considered in connection with an application for registration is that part of the shape or configuration that has eye appeal and purely functional features are excluded from registration;

(2)   Any design that included a feature dictated solely by function is excluded from registration; or

(3)   A design having eye appeal is excluded from registration only if every feature of it is dictated solely by function.

Their Lordships preferred the third construction because it made better sense and was supported by authority. In particular, Lord Oliver, at p 242, relied upon the principle expressed by the House of Lords in *AMP Inc v Utilux Pty Ltd* (1972) 89 RPC 103 (HL), summarised as follows:

> "The negative part of the definition [of 'design'] does not involve, in order to demonstrate that a particular shape is 'dictated solely' by function, showing that the function could have been performed by an article in some other shape. All that has to be shown is that the relevant features of the shape were brought about only by, or are attributable to, the function which the article in that shape is to perform, even if the same function could equally well be performed by an article of a different shape.

> "If every feature of the shape is one which is attributable solely to the function which the finished article is to perform, then the exclusion operates even though the shape may also have eye appeal."

Lord Oliver added in *Interlego*, at p 245, that:

> "There can be no purpose in an exclusion which applies only to a subject matter already excluded. To give the exclusion any operation one has to postulate at least a situation in which the need for the exclusion arises. The necessary condition for the exclusion to operate is the existence of a shape which has eye appeal but which, because of features falling within the latter part of the definition, is nevertheless not to be treated as a design. If the mere coincidence of visual appeal and industrial efficiency were sufficient to entitle the shape to protection as a design, the negative part of the definition would have no scope for operation."

Although ultimately granting the injunction, Heath J regarded the defendant's submissions based upon the observations of their Lordships in *Interlego* as strongly arguable. Heath J indicated that the defendant may well prevail on the question of whether the design was capable of registration by the Commissioner, because it fell within the second exclusionary part of the definition of "design" under s 2 of the Act. However, having regard to his own conclusions about the Register being prima facie evidence of compliance with the requirements for registration (see 6.19 ("The Register") later in this chapter), his Honour was not able to hold that there was no serious question to be tried.

6.6.3 Commercial success

If the features have been chosen because of their appearance and/or are likely to influence consumers in favour of buying the article because of its shape or appearance then their design is more likely to be capable of registration.

In *Blue Point Products Ltd* (Commissioner's Decision No D01/1997, 18/7/97, Asst Commr McCardle), the Assistant Commissioner noted, at p 57, the observation of Lord Avonside in *Harvey & Co (London) Ltd v Secure Fittings Ltd* (1966) 83 RPC 515 (CSess) that:

> "If there is doubt, commercial success may be taken as an indicator that the public has found something eye-appealing about the design."

6.6.4 Novelty requirements

(1) *New or original*

Section 5(2) Designs Act 1953 provides that:

> "Subject to the provisions of this Act, a design shall not be registered thereunder unless it is new or original and in particular shall not be so registered in respect of any article if it is the same as a design which before the date of the application for registration has been registered or published in New Zealand in respect of the same or any other article or differs from such a design only in immaterial details or in features which are variants commonly used in the trade."

There is no definition of "new" or "original" in the Act.

The meaning of the phrase "new or original" was considered by the High Court of New Zealand in *Sutton v Bay Masonry Ltd* 28/5/04, Williams J, HC Tauranga CIV-2003-470-260. In that case, the plaintiffs brought proceedings against the defendants for infringement of a registered design of a fence post constructed of three members of equal length joined in a squared-off Z shape and attached at right angles. The defendants responded by challenging the validity of the registered design, seeking rectification of the Register by deletion of the entry on the basis that, inter alia, the shape depicted in the design was not new or original. The defendants alleged that the shape was the same as a generally available aluminium extrusion made and sold within New Zealand, and a shape published in New Zealand catalogues and on New Zealand websites, prior to the application date.

Williams J, at para 18, cited with approval the meaning of the phrase "new or original" as summarised by the Federal Court of Australia in *Conrol Pty Ltd v Meco McCallum Pty Ltd* (1996) 34 IPR 517 (FCA), at pp 528-529. That case concerned a successful application to revoke a registered design on the basis that the design was not new or original. In *Conrol*, the Court stated that it is necessary to compare the design with prior art in order to determine if it is "new or original". It is not sufficient to point to any difference between the design and previously published designs. Rather, the design must be substantially new or original, having regard to the nature and character of the article to which the design is applied. The design must be assessed as a whole, the test being whether an article made according to the design in suit would be substantially similar in appearance to any article already made.

However, at least one commentator has warned against the wholesale adoption of *Conrol* in New Zealand: C Elliot, "Form Over Function — A Review of Recent Developments in Designs Law" (2005) 62 *Intellectual Property Forum* 10.

(2) *Design must be novel*

The words "new" or "original" simply mean that the design must be novel. A design will not be novel if the features of shape, configuration, pattern, or ornamentation that together comprise the design have been published in respect of the same, or any other, article before the application date. Hence, prior publication will destroy novelty, regardless of whether the article to which the design has previously been applied is different to that in relation to which the design is now sought to be registered.

It is important to note that it is the prior application of those features to an article of manufacture that destroys novelty, not the publication of the features themselves. Hence, there may be novelty in being the first to apply the features of a natural or artistic object to an article of manufacture. For example, in *Saunders v Wiel* (1893) 10 RPC 29, a representation of Westminster Abbey viewed from a particular angle, that had been copied from a photograph and applied to the handle of a spoon, was considered novel. Similarly, there may be novelty in applying a painting to a placemat, even though that painting had been published in a catalogue or publicly exhibited, provided the painting had not previously been applied to an article of manufacture (such as a placemat). Novelty would be destroyed if the same painting had previously been applied as a design on a coffee mug (also an article of manufacture).

In *Sutton v Bay Masonry Ltd* 28/5/04, Williams J, HC Tauranga CIV-2003-470-260, Williams J accepted the reasoning of the Federal Court of Australia in *Conrol Pty Ltd v Meco McCallum Pty Ltd* (1996) 34 IPR 517 (FCA) regarding the requisite degree of novelty for a valid registered design.

In *Conrol*, the Court held, at pp 528-529, that the whole of the design need not be new or original in order to qualify for registration. The design may be novel notwithstanding that all of its parts are old and were common general knowledge at the date of registration. If the combination of two or more old and well known designs, or parts of designs, gives the combination as a whole the appearance of a new design, that design may be novel.

(3) *Higher standard than copyright law*

It is important to understand that the threshold for "originality" in design law is higher than that in copyright law. In copyright law a work will be "original" if it is the product of the author's independent time, labour, skill and judgment and has not been copied from any other work. Under design law, it is not enough to show that the design is the original work of the author: it must also be novel.

(4)   *Local Novelty*

To be eligible for registration, a design must not have been published or publicly used in New Zealand before the priority date of the application.

A consequence of local novelty is that, if there has been no disclosure of the design in New Zealand the owner of the design can register the design in New Zealand outside the convention period and after disclosure of the design elsewhere in the world.

(5)   *Not published in New Zealand*

The article to which the design has been applied must not have been prior published in New Zealand before the priority date of the application.

There is no definition of what constitutes prior publication in the Designs Act 1953. However, the Courts consider prior publication of registered designs in much the same way as prior publication of patentable subject matter. Patentable subject matter is defined in the Patents Act 1953 as being prior published if:

- It can be inspected as of right at any place in New Zealand by members of the public whether upon payment of a fee or otherwise; or

- It can be inspected in a library of a government department or of any institution or public authority, and the library is one that is open generally to members of the public who are interested in matters to which the document relates, and is a library in which members of the public in search of information related to the subject of the document would ordinarily seek, and do in fact seek, the information.

Display for the purposes of sale was held to constitute prior publication in *Smout v Slaymaker & Co* (1890) 7 RPC 90.

(6)   *How close must the prior publication be to the registered design?*

As to the extent to which the prior publication must disclose the design, Lord Eversham MR in *Rosedale Associated Manufacturers Ltd v Airfix Products Ltd* (1957) 74 RPC 239 (CA) stated, at p 244, that:

> "the test of prior publication of an alleged invention should, in my judgment, be no less applicable in the case of a registered design, and as regards to the former, I venture to cite once more the oft-quoted language of Lord Westbury in *Hills v Evans* (1882) 31 LJ (Ch) 457, 463:
>
> > 'The antecedent statement must, in order to invalidate the subsequent patent, be such that a person of ordinary knowledge of the subject would at once perceive and understand and be able practically to apply the discovery without the necessity of making further experiments.'
>
> "By a like reasoning, to my mind, if a document is to constitute prior publication then a reader of it, possessed of ordinary knowledge of the subject, must from his reading of the document be able at least to see the design in his mind's eye and should not have to depend upon his own originality to construct the design from ideas which the document may put into his head."

Lloyd-Jacob J, in *S Travers Ltd's Application* (1951) 68 RPC 255, at p 258, commented:

"It is a fundamental principle of the design law that the privilege of registration should not be given to trifling variations, of the kind which a craftsman might be expected to introduce in carrying out his ordinary day to day trade."

In practice, it is often useful to apply a "reverse infringement test" when considering the relevance of prior publications to a registered design. Thus the prior publication will be relevant if the article depicted in it embodies a design which is "not substantially different" from that depicted in the registration, and would infringe the registered design if made after registration.

(7)   *Immaterial details*

Even when a design is novel it needs to fulfil other requirements in order to be capable of registration. The prohibition on designs that differ only in immaterial details from other known designs introduces an element of "substantiality" to the test for registrability (ie the design must be substantially new or substantially original).

The rationale for this is to prevent the Register from being choked with registered designs, rendering it impossible for honest traders to manufacture an article because all possible permutations of shape and configuration have been monopolised by others. See, for example, the comments of the Court in *Le May v Welch* (1884) 28 Ch D 24 (CA), at p 34, per Bowen LJ:

"It is not every mere difference of cut, every change of outline, every change of length or breadth, or configuration, in a simple and most familiar article of dress like this, which constitutes novelty of design. To hold that would be to paralyse industry and ... make the (Designs Act) a trap to catch honest traders."

However, there always has to be a balance between what appears initially to be a slight or immaterial difference (which does not result in a novel design) and one that does. In cases where the prior art is prolific it may often be that small differences will be regarded as substantial rather than immaterial. Put another way, it may be important not to allow the existence of prolific prior art to rob a design of its value as differences over prior art can often be subtle but important: *Axe Australasia Pty Ltd v Australume Pty Ltd* (2006) 69 IPR 45 (FCA), at para 20.

Thus, in *Samuel Heath & Sons Ltd v Rollason* (1898) AC 499 (HL), at p 503, the Court commented:

"In the present day it is very difficult to register any design that does not contain in it something which has been done before. Very often a very successful design may be one in which the difference from a previous design can on analysis be shown to be very slight, when nevertheless the result is to make the one so much more pleasing than the other that it is a successful design. While on the one hand we certainly ought not to give protection to a design in which the variations are trivial and unimportant so that it is substantially the same design as one already registered or known, on the other hand we ought not to refuse it where the design is practically a different one which may be more attractive."

This passage was cited with approval by the Federal Court of Australia in *Mining Equipment Pty Ltd v Mining Supplies Australia Pty Ltd* (2001) 52 IPR 513 (FCA).

(8)   *Alteration in scale*

In *Blue Point Products Ltd* (Commissioner's Decision No D01/1997, 18/7/97, Asst Commr McCardle), the Assistant Commissioner of Designs noted that a mere alteration in scale is not, in general, sufficient to render a design new or original.

It is possible however that differences in proportion may distinguish one design from another and thus be registrable: *Dalgety Australia Operations Ltd v F F Seeley Nominees Pty Ltd* (1986) 6 IPR 361. The Court in *Dalgety* upheld a design for an evaporative air conditioner with a slim, upright appearance. Traditional conditioners were box-like and chunky, this being the fundamental form of such conditioners.

(9)   *Features commonly used in the relevant trade*

A design that differs only in features that are commonly used in a particular trade will not be novel or original. The rationale for this prohibition is that trade variants are considered to be, and should remain, public domain. As was noted in *Phillips v Harbro Rubber Co* [1920] 37 RPC 233 (HL), at p 240:

> "The introduction of ordinary trade variants into an old design cannot make it new or original. For example, if it is common practice to have, or not to have, spikes in the soles of running shoes, a man does not make a new and original design out of an old type of running shoe by putting spikes into the soles. The working world, as well as the trade world, is entitled at its will to take, in all cases, its choice of ordinary trade variants for use in any particular instance, and no patent and no registration of a design can prevent an ordinary workman from using or not using trade knowledge of this kind."

The knowledge of the trade and features commonly used in the trade must also be the background against which newness or originality is assessed: *Hart v Oz-Post Pty Ltd* (2000) 46 IPR 638, at pp 643-644:

> "A design which differs from an earlier design in small details requires consideration as to whether the differences are immaterial details, since differences in that category will deprive a design of newness or originality. This assessment needs to be made with knowledge of the trade and of prior articles to which the design applies and considered against the fundamental form and development of such articles in the trade up to the time of the application for registration."

In *Sutton v Bay Masonry Ltd* 28/5/04, Williams J, HC Tauranga CIV-2003-470-260, Williams J accepted the reasoning of the Federal Court of Australia in *Conrol Pty Ltd v Meco McCallum Pty Ltd* (1996) 34 IPR 517 (FCA) regarding the requisite degree of novelty for a valid registered design.

In *Conrol*, the Court held, at pp 528-529, that the whole of the design need not be new or original in order to qualify for registration. The design may be novel notwithstanding that all of its parts are old and were common general knowledge at the date of registration. If the combination of two or more old and well known designs, or parts of designs, gives to the combination as a whole the appearance of a new design, that design may be novel.

The Court also discussed the registrability of trade variants, stating, at p 530, that in most cases a design which is a common trade variant will only differ in immaterial details from designs previously published or used, although this is not always so. They stated that to be registrable, a design must be more than a mere trade variant which any skilled workman might make. What constitutes a trade variant is a question of fact. It must be one commonly known and used in connection with a particular article or class of articles. Mere workshop variations which a competent workman might be expected to achieve in the ordinary course of business do not cause a design to be new or original.

In *Sutton*, the proceedings related to a registered design for a fence post constructed of three members of equal length joined in a squared-off Z shape and attached at right angles. The defendants challenged the validity of the registered design, seeking rectification of the Register by deletion of the entry on the basis that, inter alia, the shape of the design was not new or original. The statement of novelty in the plaintiff's registered design omitted any reference to usage, and the design was not described as a fence post. However, the plaintiffs argued the case on the basis that the application of the Z-shape to a fence post lent the design its requisite novelty.

Williams J noted that there was nothing in the evidence presented to suggest the Z-post's utility was confined to fencing, but rather the shape was capable of any number of applications. He held that although the Z-post appeared to be new or original in the sense discussed in the authorities (because producing a fence post of that configuration did not appear to have "occurred to anyone before") the Z-post was in fact not substantially new or substantially original having regard to the evidence of widely available Z-shaped aluminium extrusions, and evidence that the defendant had manufactured and used Z-shaped metal articles in fencing and metalwork previously. Accordingly, the plaintiff's design was found to lack novelty because, prior to registration, a shape similar to the Z-shape had already been applied to articles of manufacture. His Honour held that the Z-shape was no more than a trade variant of those articles, and the Z-post should not have been registered as a design.

(10) *Exceptions to novelty requirements*

In certain circumstances, novelty is not destroyed by confidential disclosure of the design and/or a breach of confidence. The exceptions provided by s 10 Designs Act 1953 include:

- Disclosure made by the proprietor in a situation where use or publication by the recipient would be contrary to good faith;

- Disclosure by a recipient in breach of good faith;

- Disclosure at, or as a result of, an industrial exhibition declared as such by the Governor-General by a Notice in the *Gazette*, provided the application is made within 6 months of the opening of the exhibition (an example of such an exhibition is the Mystery Creek Fieldays at Hamilton); and

- Acceptance of a first and confidential order for textile goods bearing a design intended for registration.

6.6.5 Excluded designs

The following designs are excluded from registration under reg 33 Design Regulations 1954:

- Works of sculpture, other than casts or models for use as models or patterns to be multiplied by any industrial process;

- Wall plaques and medals; and

- Printed matter primarily of a literary or artistic character, including greeting cards, maps, stamps and the like.

The requirement that the design be applied to an "article of manufacture" also excludes naturally occurring items.

6.7 Ownership

Under s 6 Designs Act 1953 the applicant for a registered design may include:

- The designer (or author);

- The assignee of the designer; or

- A person for whom the design was made in return for consideration.

There is no requirement for an applicant to specify in his or her design application whether he or she obtained his or her right to apply from another party.

6.7.1 Joint ownership

It is possible for a design to be jointly authored and/or owned under s 6(2) Designs Act 1953.

Joint owners of a design, may, subject to any agreement between the parties, exploit the design independently of one another.

In *Catley Developments Ltd v Wood* 4/10/71, Wild CJ, SC Auckland, Wild CJ found that a registered design filed in the name of the plaintiff was in fact owned jointly by both the plaintiff and defendant as each party had contributed to the development of the product.

6.7.2 Commissioned designs

Under s 6(1) Designs Act 1953, where the design is created by the author for another person for good consideration, that other person shall be treated as the proprietor. For a discussion on what constitutes "good consideration" with regard to design commissioning, see *Chappell & Co Ltd v Nestle Co Ltd* [1960] AC 87 (HL).

6.7.3 Employee designs

Where a design is created during the course of employment, the employer is the owner of the design and must be named as the applicant. See, for example, *Re Equator Mfg Co; Ex parte Pendlebury* [1926] 1 DLR 1101.

6.7.4 No "right of first importer"

Under the Patents Act 1953, a person can claim to be entitled to file a patent application by virtue of having been the first to import the invention into New Zealand. It is unlikely that the first importing of a design into New Zealand gives the importer the right to apply for registration of that design. This was confirmed by the High Court of New Zealand in *Eveready NZ Ltd v Gillette NZ Ltd* 28/8/98, Elias J, HC Auckland M1130/98.

6.7.5 Agents

An agent can be appointed by an applicant or registered proprietor. The agent must reside, or carry on business, in New Zealand. Under s 40 the duly authorised agent may do any of the acts of the applicant required by the Act (eg prosecute the application to grant, pay fees etc).

6.8 Assignments and other interests

6.8.1 Assignment

Under s 6(2) Designs Act 1953, the proprietorship of a design can be transferred, in whole or in part, to one or more persons by assignment, transmission or operation of law. It is possible to transfer the rights in a registrable design (including the right to file an application) before registration. Such entitlement may be as mortgagee, licensee or beneficial owner. There is a mandatory requirement under s 27 to record those interests on the Register.

6.8.2 Recording an interest on the Register

Under s 27 Designs Act 1953, a person with an interest in a registered design (for example, an assignee or a licensee) may apply to the Commissioner to have notice of that interest entered on the Register of Designs.

There is no sanction for failure to record an assignment, although an assignee cannot commence legal proceedings for infringement unless the assignment is recorded and the assignee noted on the Register as the proprietor of the design.

6.8.3 Trusts

While it is technically possible for an interest in a registered design to be held in an express, implied or constructive trust, s 25(4) Designs Act 1953 prohibits that interest from being recorded on the Register.

6.9 Licences

As with other personal property, the proprietor of a registered design can issue a licence to another to carry out any or all of the acts permitted by registration. The proprietor can settle the terms of the licence and can take action against infringers of the licensed rights.

6.9.1 Recording licences on the Register

Under s 27 Designs Act 1953, licences under a registered design should be recorded on the Register. A copy of the licence is not required to be submitted, but particulars of the licence document (such as its date and the parties to the licence) must be provided.

There is no sanction for failure to record a licence.

6.9.2 Compulsory licences

Under s 14 Designs Act 1953, an interested person may apply to the Commissioner for the grant of a compulsory licence in respect of a design that has not been applied in New Zealand to any articles in respect of which the design is registered to such extent as is reasonable in the circumstances of the case.

In determining what is reasonable the Commissioner will take into account the nature of the item to which the design is to be applied. For example, if the article is a very high cost or specialised item (such as a diamond necklace) less use would be required than, for example, a low cost consumer item (such as a clothes peg).

The proprietor of the design may file evidence against the granting of a compulsory licence. The Commissioner will then hear both sides and make such order as he or she deems fit. Decisions of the Commissioner may be appealed to the High Court.

Any compulsory licence granted shall have effect as a deed executed by the registered proprietor.

Although not specifically provided for, it is presumed that (as with compulsory licences under the Patents Act 1953) the proprietor of the design can apply for cancellation of a compulsory licence if he or she commences supplying a reasonable quantity of articles to which the design has been applied in New Zealand.

6.10 Obtaining grant of rights

6.10.1 Filing a standard application

The following documents and information are required for filing a standard design application:

- The full name, address and nationality of the applicant(s);

- The name of the article, or set of articles, to which the design is applied;

- An application form (which can be signed by the applicant, or his or her agent if the applicant files an Authorisation of Agent form);

- A Statement of Novelty;

- Four representations of the design; and

- In certain circumstances, for example where the design relates to a textile, specimens of the textile design may be supplied. Regulation 28 Design Regulations 1954 requires that any specimens furnished must be mounted in a flat position.

6.10.2 Filing a convention application

For convention applications, in addition to the representations of design, Statement of Novelty and applicant details, an applicant must also provide details of the originating application on which the claim to convention priority is based, including the official filing date, the country of filing and details of the applicant(s).

For more information on convention applications, see 6.2.2 ("International conventions") earlier in this chapter.

6.10.3 Minimum filing requirements

A filing date can be obtained by filing one copy of the representations of the design and a Statement of Novelty. If the applicant does so, the additional documents required and the time limits for filing them are as follows:

- Application form or Authorisation of Agent form signed by the applicant: due within 12 months of filing date;

- Formal representations of the design and specific Statement of Novelty: due within 12 months of filing date;

- Convention priority document: due within 3 months of filing date; and

- Certified translation of Convention priority document (if not in English): due within 3 months of filing date.

6.10.4 Statement of Novelty

The Statement of Novelty sets out those features in which novelty is claimed and for which protection is sought. Where, for example, the features of overall shape or configuration are claimed, a Statement of Novelty should state this. If novelty is claimed in just a part of an article a Statement of Novelty can be limited to this.

Care must be taken when drafting the Statement of Novelty as all features claimed in the statement must be present for there to be infringement. The considerations to be taken into account when drafting Statements of Novelty are explained in *Evered & Co Ltd's Applications* (1961) 78 RPC 105 and *Sommer Allibert (UK) Ltd v Flair Plastics Ltd* (1987) 104 RPC 599 (CA).

A Statement of Novelty is not required for textile articles, wallpaper and lace.

6.10.5 Extensions available

Upon application, under reg 34(2) Designs Regulations 1954 the Commissioner may grant an extension of time of up to 3 months for fulfilling the above requirements.

6.10.6 Examination

The Intellectual Property Office will automatically examine the application within one month of filing and issue an Examination Report. The applicant is allowed 12 months from the date of receiving the examination report to place the application in order. An extension of up to 3 months is available on request.

Examination includes a novelty search and an assessment of registrability.

It is possible to request a hearing before the Commissioner of Designs in respect of any examiner's decision regarding registrability. Unless a hearing is requested, a design application that is not placed in order for acceptance within the time stated in the Examination Report will irrevocably lapse. The effect of lapsing a design registration is discussed at 6.11 ("Duration") and 6.13 ("Restoration") later in this chapter.

One or more designs may be separated or divided out of a parent application in response to an objection raised by an examiner. These divisional applications are discussed in detail at 6.4 ("Types of design registration") earlier in this chapter.

6.10.7 Grant of rights and publication of design registration

Design registrations are commonly granted within 6 months of filing the application. Once the design is registered, basic details of the design (without design representations) are published in the *Intellectual Property Office Journal* and thereafter the design registration is open to public inspection at the Intellectual Property Office.

Details of design representations (except designs applied to textile articles and wallpaper and lace) remain confidential at the Intellectual Property Office until grant of the Design Registration. Under reg 60(2) Designs Regulations 1954, designs applied to textile articles are not open to public inspection until 3 years from the date of registration, and designs applied to wallpaper and lace are not open to public inspection until 2 years from the date of registration

No publication of the representations occurs if an application is abandoned or ultimately rejected. A design application that is abandoned or rejected may be refiled provided the design has not been publicly disclosed in New Zealand.

While an application is pending, the only details available to the public are the application number, applicant details, convention date (where applicable), article, class, and (where applicable) the attorney code.

6.10.8 Certificate of Registration

When a design application is granted the Intellectual Property Office of New Zealand issues a Certificate of Registration. The Certificate of Registration bears the date of registration (the date the application was filed for non-Convention applications or the date of the priority document for Convention applications) and the date the Certificate issued. Convention applications are discussed at 6.2.2 ("International conventions") earlier in this chapter.

6.10.9 No opposition to registration

The Act contains no procedure to oppose the registration of a design. If an "interested party" wants to challenge the registration of a design it must do so once the design registration is granted, using the procedures outlined at 6.14 ("Cancellation") later in this chapter.

6.11 Duration

A standard design registration has a term of up to 15 years from the date of filing the application, or from the priority date of the application, whichever is earlier.

The term of registration under s 8 Designs Act 1953 is the unexpired term of the parent design registration. On expiry, the design is available for exploitation by any other party.

Furthermore, under s 74 Copyright Act 1994, once a registered design has lapsed or expired, the drawings of the registered design can be used to reproduce the three-dimensional product without infringing copyright in those drawings.

6.12 Renewal

Renewal fees are due on the fifth and tenth anniversary of the filing date.

A time extension of 6 months is available in which to pay late renewal fees. If the renewal fees are not paid within (or before) the 6-month extension period, the registration irrevocably lapses.

6.13 Restoration

There is no provision for restoration of a New Zealand design registration once it has lapsed. Thus, in *Rainsford Pty Ltd v Assistant Commissioner of Designs* [2003] 2 NZLR 490; (2003) 10 TCLR 759; 57 IPR 138, Hammond J rejected Rainsford's application to restore a lapsed design to the Register. Due to errors and oversights by Rainsford's agent, the registration had not been renewed. Once the error was discovered, Rainsford tried unsuccessfully to restore the registration by filing a formal request for the correction of an error. That request was rejected *Rainsford Pty Ltd's Application* (Commissioner's Decision No D01/2001, 17/10/01, Asst Commr Popplewell) on the basis that, as the registration had lapsed, there was no error in the Register to correct. Rainsford appealed to the High Court and also brought a fresh application for rectification of the Register. Both the appeal and the application were dismissed. Hammond J held, at para 38, that the lack of legislative provision for the restoration of a lapsed registration was determinative:

> "it seems very difficult, if not impossible, to see how something which has 'lapsed' can be 'corrected' — the registration by definition no longer has any effect. The usual argument, in a variety of legal contexts, which is made against a proposition of the character just stated, is something along the lines of 'if the determining officer had appreciated the proper legal position then the position would have been otherwise'. But that line of argument does not appear to me to be open here — by necessary implication the copyright came to an end at the termination of the original period. As Laddie put it, 'it is lost for good'."

6.14 Cancellation

6.14.1 Cancellation of registration by the Commissioner

Any interested person may apply to the Commissioner for cancellation of a design registration. The grounds provided under s 15 Designs Act 1953 are:

- That the design was not new or original at the date of registration; and

- Any other ground on which the Commissioner could have refused to register the design. More information on these grounds can be found at 6.5 ("Registrable subject matter") earlier in this chapter.

There are no time limits prescribed by the Act or Regulations for the filing of an application for cancellation.

(1) *"Interested person"*

In *Wade's Application* (Commissioner's Decision No P01/1981, 9/1/81, Asst Commr Burton), Assistant Commissioner Burton held that an "interested person" for the purposes of the Patents Act 1953 is one who has a genuine commercial interest in the items the subject of the patent. It is likely that this test would be used for determining whether a person qualifies as "interested" under the Designs Act 1953.

6.14.2   Cancellation of registration by the Court

Under s 28 Designs Act 1953, any person aggrieved by the existence of a registered design can apply to the High Court for an order that the registration be varied or cancelled. For an example of a cancellation by the Court, see *D A Lewis & Co Ltd v Trade Winds Furniture Ltd* (1985) 4 IPR 621.

The High Court, in addition to ordering that a design registration is cancelled, may also instruct a variation to an existing registration.

The grounds for applying to the Court to cancel a design registration are not specified in s 28. In practice they are considered to be the same as those which would entitle the Commissioner to cancel a registration.

6.14.3   Cancellation as defence to infringement proceedings

Cancellation or variation of a registered design by the High Court is possible at any time. Most commonly an application for cancellation or variation of the registered design is brought as a counterclaim to proceedings for infringement of the registered design.

Thus, in *Permanent Promotions Pty Ltd v Independent Liquor (NZ) Ltd* 10/6/04, Heath J, HC Auckland CIV-2004-404-2419 the defendant applied to have the plaintiff's registered design cancelled in response to an application for interim relief by the plaintiff. The Court granted the injunction on the basis that the plaintiff provide a bank guarantee of NZ $100,000 as bond against damages. Although the plaintiff was based in Australia, it had no viable assets within New Zealand, and its financial records failed to provide evidence of its ability to pay damages and costs.

6.15   Infringement and enforcement of rights

A design registration is infringed by the unauthorised manufacture or importation for sale (or for use for the purposes of trade or business) or the unauthorised sale, hire (or offering to sell or hire) of articles incorporating or embodying the registered design in New Zealand.

Legal action can only be taken against an infringer once the Certificate of Registration has issued. Court proceedings are initiated in the High Court. Appeals are possible to the Court of Appeal. The case is heard and decided by a Judge alone, with no jury involvement.

6.15.1   Parallel imports prohibited

As the prohibition applies to importation without the authority of the registered proprietor, a design registration may prove an effective instrument against parallel importation of the articles covered.

6.15.2 Tests for infringement

For an article to infringe a registered design it must be an article to which the registered design, or a design not substantially different from the registered design, has been applied. Putting it another way, it must have substantially the same appearance as the design in question. The question of infringement is a question for which the eye must be the judge. Courts will apply both a side-by-side test and an imperfect recollection test, and will also consider actual usage of the design in question.

The degree of novelty between the prior art and the registered design must also considered. In *UPL Group Ltd v Dux Engineers Ltd* [1989] 3 NZLR 135 (CA), at p 139, the Court commented as follows:

> "There is also a relationship between the degree of novelty or originality of a registered design and the issue of infringement. If there is substantial novelty or originality small variations in the article alleged to infringe will be unlikely to save the defendant. On the other hand if the features of novelty or originality are but little removed from prior art small differences may avoid an infringement."

(1) *Side-by-side test*

The side-by-side test involves comparing the alleged infringing design with the registered design in a side-by-side comparison in order to determine whether one is an obvious imitation of the other.

As with novelty, infringement is to be judged by the eye. The leading New Zealand case in this area is *UPL Group Ltd v Dux Engineers Ltd* [1989] 3 NZLR 135 (CA) where Somers J, delivering the judgment of the Court, stated, at p 139, that:

> "The test is whether the article alleged to be an infringement has substantially the same appearance as the registered design. This involves a comparison between the article complained of and the representations of the article contained in the application for registration. It is not always easy to compare a two-dimensional design with a three-dimensional object. That difficulty and the fact that a design means features of shape etc applied to an article by industrial process makes it evident, and it has been so held (see *Dunlop Rubber Co Ltd v Golf Ball Developments Ltd* (1931) 48 RPC 268, 277, 280 and *Benchairs Ltd v Chair Centre Ltd* (1974) 91 RPC 429, 441, 442) that articles manufactured by the plaintiff which embody the design may be compared with the artefact said to infringe."

(2) *Imperfect recollection test*

Products to which the registered design and the alleged infringing design have been applied will not always be sold or viewed side by side. The Court may therefore also compare designs as if they had been viewed at different times. This is known as the "imperfect recollection" test.

The imperfect recollection test was first described in *Valor Heating Co Ltd v Main Gas Appliances Ltd* (1973) 90 RPC 871, at pp 878, where it was held:

> "This court has taken the view that you must consider infringement not merely upon the basis of a side by side comparison, but also upon the basis of having had a look

293

at the registered design, then having gone away and come back and perhaps been [sic] put in a position of deciding whether some other article is the one you originally saw."

The test was further refined in *Sommer Allibert (UK) Ltd v Flair Plastics Ltd* (1987) 104 RPC 599 (CA), at p 624, where the hypothetical customer through whose eyes the Court was looking was identified as a customer interested in the design of the particular type of article being purchased, instead of one who is content to purchase any such article, without regard to its design.

The imperfect recollection test has been applied in New Zealand in *UPL Group Ltd v Dux Engineers Ltd* [1989] 3 NZLR 135 (CA).

(3) *Actual usage consideration*

Actual usage of the registered design may be considered by the Courts to determine whether the alleged infringing design and the registered design will look similar when the articles carrying the design are in use. For example, if a Court were considering a design to be applied to a clothing item, the Court may take into consideration the eye appeal of the garment while being worn.

6.15.3 Jurisdiction

Although design rights are territorial, and a New Zealand design will have no effect in other countries, in certain limited circumstances it may be possible for the owner of the same design granted in a number of jurisdictions to sue a New Zealand-based defendant for breaches of its foreign design rights committed in those foreign jurisdictions. The question of whether and in what circumstances such actions are permissible was considered in *Kabushiki Kaisha Sony Computer Entertainment v van Veen* 14/12/06, MacKenzie J, HC Wellington CIV-2004-485-1520.

The plaintiffs (collectively "Sony") were the proprietors of the PlayStation 2 computer games system, and owned intellectual property rights in some of the games played on that system. Those games were distributed on CDs and DVDs and, to assist in their protection, Sony embedded codes which prevented copying of the games from the CD or DVD to another medium. The defendants developed and distributed a software programme called HD Loader which enabled a user to circumvent the embedded copy protection code and copy Sony's games. The HD Loader programme was developed by the first defendant who sold or licensed the use of that programme in, amongst other countries, the UK and Hong Kong through the second defendant.

Sony commenced proceedings and obtained a number of interim orders. Following completion of the pleadings the first defendant admitted the material allegations in the Statement of Claim (breach of the New Zealand Copyright and Trade Marks Acts, breach of the UK Copyright, Designs and Patents Act 1988, breach of the Hong Kong Copyright Ordinance, and wrongful possession and use of confidential information) and Sony applied for judgment against the first defendant.

On each of the causes of action relating to breaches of the New Zealand legislation and wrongful use and possession of confidential information, the admitted facts clearly gave rise to liability which could be enforced in New Zealand. Those causes of action were based on New Zealand law and on actions admitted to have taken place in New Zealand. The more difficult question was whether the Court could determine causes of action relating to alleged breaches of UK and Hong Kong copyright legislation.

The starting point for the Court was the rule laid down by the House of Lords in *British South Africa Co v Companhia de Mocambique* [1893] AC 602 (HL), which stated that the Court has no jurisdiction to entertain an action for (1) the determination of the title to, or the right to possession of, any immoveable situate out of England (foreign land); or (2) the recovery of damages for trespass to such immoveable. MacKenzie J noted, at paras 9 and 10, that the rule had been applied in Australia and England in several cases involving intellectual property rights, and had been applied by Tipping J in New Zealand in *Atkinson Footwear Ltd v Hodgskin International Services Ltd* (1994) 31 IPR 186 in respect of an application for an interim injunction to restrain the distribution of footwear allegedly infringing the plaintiff's copyright in New Zealand and Australia. Tipping J granted the application with respect to New Zealand but declined to extend it to Australia. However, MacKenzie J noted that since the decision of Tipping J in *Atkinson Footwear* the UK Court of Appeal had carefully reconsidered the position in *Pearce v Ove Arup Partnership Ltd* [1999] 1 All ER 769 (CA), a case involving the construction of a public building in Rotterdam which was a copy of a plan produced by an architectural student in London. The UK Court of Appeal held in *Pearce* that the English Courts did have jurisdiction to entertain a claim in respect of the alleged infringement of Dutch copyright by virtue of actions occurring in Holland on the basis that the *Mocambique* rule involves two limbs, the second of which makes a distinction between proceedings where issue of title, or the extent of rights available under a foreign law arise, on the one hand, and claims where the matter in issue is not the existence or nature of the title or rights, but whether some action has the effect of infringing the unquestioned rights of the plaintiff. MacKenzie J concluded, at para 19:

> "I find the reasoning [in *Pearce*] persuasive in favour of the proposition that, in the case of intellectual property rights governed by the law of a foreign country, the second limb of the *Mocambique* rule should not exclude justiciability in respect of actions for breach of intellectual property rights established under the law of another jurisdiction, when no question of the existence or validity of those rights arises."

adding, at para 22:

> "Nothing which I have said should be taken as questioning the applicability of the first limb of the rule in the *Mocambique* case to questions of title to intellectual property … nor should anything I have said be taken as questioning the applicability of the second limb in the *Mocambique* case to true immoveables such as land … The issue before me is whether the second limb should be extended to items of intellectual property such as those in issue here. The various forms of protection given under intellectual property statutes are territorial in nature, because the statutes conferring them are necessarily territorial in their application. To that extent, they have the characteristics of immoveable property. But the significant difference between such forms of intellectual property and true immoveables such as land is that the same item of intellectual property may be protected by statutory rights in many jurisdictions. A strict application of the second limb of the *Mocambique* case to such rights would mean that, where, as here, a defendant commits infringing acts against a single plaintiff in several jurisdictions, separate proceedings in each

jurisdiction will be necessary to deal with those infringements. The inconvenience of such a requirement would outweigh the benefit of certainty that the application of the second limb to such claims would provide. I decline to apply the second limb to this case."

Having concluded that the justiciability of Sony's claim was not excluded by the *Mocambique* rule, MacKenzie J went on to consider whether, on the ordinary principles of the conflict of laws dealing with wrongs committed in another jurisdiction, the New Zealand Court had jurisdiction. In that regard, the common law double actionability rule applies. The double actionability rule states that, as a general rule, an act done in a foreign country is a tort and actionable as such in New Zealand, only if it is both (a) actionable as a tort according to New Zealand law or, in other words, is an act which, if done in New Zealand, would be a tort; and (b) actionable according to the law of the foreign country where it was done. However, a particular issue between the parties may be governed by the law of the country which, with respect to that issue, has the most significant relationship with the occurrence and the parties.

Having considered the double actionability rule, MacKenzie J went on to address (and resolve) a potential problem in applying that rule to the present case as follows, at paras 24 and 25:

"In applying that Rule, it may be argued that, since the acts complained of must constitute a wrong actionable under New Zealand law, the acts complained of, being infringements in the United Kingdom and Hong Kong, do not constitute a wrong against New Zealand copyright, since New Zealand copyright is territorial in effect. Therefore, a strict application of the first limb of the double actionability rule would lead to the result that the infringement would not be actionable in New Zealand. That Rule was the subject of consideration in *Pearce*. Roch LJ discussed the difficulty which arises in a case such as this, if the first limb of [the Double Actionability] Rule … requires the [New Zealand] court to determine actionability by [New Zealand] domestic law. He dealt with the proposition that, if, despite the rule in the *Mocambique* case, the claim was justiciable, it was bound to fail the requirements in the first limb of the double actionability rule in these terms at page 803:

'If that were a correct analysis, the effect would be that the first limb of r 203(1) imposed a requirement as to jurisdiction; and not simply a rule for the choice of law.'

"He went on to note that the view that the first limb of the rule does impose a requirement as to jurisdiction had found expression in the dissenting judgment of Diplock LJ in [*Chaplin v Boys* [1969] 2 All ER 1085 (HL)], but had been plainly rejected by the House of Lords on the appeal. Roch LJ referred to [*Red Sea Insurance Ltd v Bouygues SA* [1994] 3 All ER 749 (PC)], where the Privy Council had accepted that the choice of the lex fori as the applicable law was not an invariable rule; rather that it was 'the general rule' or 'a starting point'. Roch LJ then went on to say, at page 803-804:

'In the present case, the plaintiff's claim would be defeated if the court were to refuse to apply the exception. But the claim (if established on the facts) is one where the English court would have given a remedy, under United

Kingdom copyright law, if the facts alleged had occurred in England. This is not a case in which the claim is in respect of some wrong which is conceptually unknown in English law. In our view this is a case where, if the claim is justiciable at all, the exception to the double actionability rule enables the English court to apply Dutch law; and the English court ought to do so.'

"I respectfully concur with that reasoning. It seems to me that, in applying the first limb of the double actionability rule, in an intellectual property infringement case, it is necessary to effect a notional transfer to New Zealand, for consideration under New Zealand law, of both the infringing act, and the intellectual property infringed. The infringing act and the intellectual property infringed cannot sensibly be separated in applying the first limb of [the Double Actionability] Rule … The purpose of the rule is to consider how New Zealand law would regard an act, if that act were committed in New Zealand and subject to New Zealand domestic law. Where the act complained of is an infringement of an intellectual property right, a relevant inquiry, in considering the application of New Zealand domestic law, should be whether that particular form of intellectual property is one which is capable of protection under New Zealand law. The focus should be on the nature of the underlying intellectual property, not on the form in which that property is protected by the laws of the foreign jurisdiction. The laws of the foreign jurisdiction are relevant to the second limb, not the first limb, of the double actionability rule."

Accordingly, MacKenzie J entered judgment against the first defendant in respect of all causes of action. Finally, his Honour clarified, at para 27, that in reaching the conclusions which he had as to the applicability of the *Mocambique*, and double actionability, rules his findings should be limited to the case of a defendant who is resident in New Zealand and thereby subject to the jurisdiction of the New Zealand Courts.

Although this judgment relates specifically to allegations of breach of copyright and registered trade mark there is no reason in principal why it should not equally apply to other intellectual property rights, particularly those for which a process of registration is required (therefore providing certainty in terms of the scope of monopoly of the intellectual property right in various jurisdictions) such as patents and registered designs.

6.16 Defences

The two main defences to infringement proceedings are:

- That the design should not have been registered (the criteria for registration is discussed in more detail at 6.5 ("Registrable subject matter") and 6.6.4 ("Novelty requirements") earlier in this chapter); and

- That there is in fact no infringement (the test for infringement is discussed in more detail at 6.15.2 ("Tests for infringement") earlier in this chapter).

An example of a successful defence is found in *D A Lewis & Co Ltd v Trade Winds Furniture Ltd* (1985) 4 IPR 621. In that case, the Court found that the plaintiff's design did not satisfy the criteria of being new or original.

UPL Group Ltd v Dux Engineers Ltd [1989] 3 NZLR 135 (CA) provides an example where the article manufactured by the defendant was held not to infringe the design registration of the plaintiff.

6.17   Remedies

Remedies for design infringement can include:

- Interim and/or permanent injunctions against the infringing conduct;

- Delivery up of the infringing product;

- Delivery up of machinery adapted to make the infringing product; and

- An account of profits earned by the infringer or damages to compensate loss suffered by the owner of the registered design.

6.17.1   Assessment of damages

The Designs Act 1953 contains no specific provisions in respect of infringements before registration. The Act is also silent as to the date from which damages accrue.

Section 11 gives the registered proprietor exclusive rights in relation to "any article in respect of which the design is registered" (emphasis added).

Section 7(5) states that "a design when registered shall be registered as of the date on which the application for registration was made".

Hence, it is reasonable to conclude that while no action for infringement can be taken before the issuing of the certificate of registration, damages would run from the deemed date of registration, which is the date of filing (or the priority date if the application is a convention application).

In terms of assessing the amount of damages payable, the High Court of Australia had the following to say in *Malec v JC Hutton Pty Ltd* (1990) 169 CLR 638 (HCA), at p 643:

> "If the law is to take account of future or hypothetical events in assessing damages, it can only do so in terms of the degree of probability of those events occurring … But unless the chance is so low as to be regarded as speculative — say less than 1 per cent — or so high as to be practically certain — say over 99 per cent — the court will take that chance into account in assessing the damages. Where proof is necessarily unattainable, it would be unfair to treat as certain a prediction which has a 51 per cent probability of occurring; but to ignore altogether a prediction which has a 49 per cent probability of occurring. Thus, the court assesses the degree of probability that an event would have occurred, or might occur, and adjusts its award of damages to reflect the degree of probability."

See also *Mallet v Monagle* [1970] AC 166, at p 174, and *Davies v Taylor* [1974] AC 207, at pp 212 and 219.

These authorities were cited with approval by the Federal Court of Australia in *Axe Australasia Pty Ltd v Australume Pty Ltd* (2006) 69 IPR 45 (FCA), at para 34. In that case, the plaintiff's registered design for a vandal resistant baton light was found both valid and infringed by the defendant's product. The plaintiff became aware of the defendant's product after it had been unsuccessful in a tender to supply its lights to a prison complex which the defendant won. The plaintiff claimed the gross profit it would have earned had it been awarded the contract to supply the lights. However, the Court found it difficult to assess the probability of the plaintiff's tender being accepted at the tender price, given a lack of evidence as to the tender price paid to the defendant or the prices tendered by third parties. Given that the defendant's product was almost identical to the registered design, the Court was prepared to assume a high probability of the plaintiff's tender being accepted, but not necessarily at the price tendered. The claim was therefore discounted by 35 percent to reflect this.

6.17.2   Interim injunctions

Several decisions of the New Zealand High Court and the Court of Appeal would seem to suggest that the Courts will give increasing primacy to registered intellectual property rights when determining an application for interim relief. In many cases this seems to be at the expense of seemingly conclusive arguments going to the balance of convenience and the overall justice.

In *Aktiebolaget Hassle v Novartis NZ Ltd* 1/5/03, Potter J, HC Auckland CP51-SW/03, the plaintiffs sought an injunction to restrain Novartis from manufacturing an omeprazole product, PROBITOR, which they believed infringed their Patent No 220096 relating to their own similar product sold in New Zealand under the brand name LOSEC. Novartis resisted the application on a number of grounds including:

(1)   That it was strongly arguable that the patent was invalid, the equivalent UK patent having already been overturned on the grounds of obviousness; and

(2)   That it had contracted to supply Pharmac with PROBITOR, and was obliged to pay Pharmac $350,000 per calendar month it was unable to supply same (presumably to compensate Pharmac for being obliged to subsidise the more expensive LOSEC during that period).

While recognising the significant losses likely to be suffered by Novartis if injuncted, the Court nonetheless found that the balance of convenience and the overall justice favoured the granting of an injunction, commenting, at para 43:

> "There is a reality to be recognised in the case of the patent, that the patent confers a monopoly during its currency, the benefit of which runs over to the post-patent period because of the strong market position usually developed during the monopoly period. This was expressed by Eichelbaum J in [*Monsanto Chemical Co v Stauffer Chemical Co (No 2)* (1984) 1 TCLR 129; 1 NZIPR 540]."

and, at para 56:

> "Premature interference with the monopoly position which the patent confers during its currency will also impact on the ability of the proprietor to create or confirm its own market after the expiry of the patent (the 'bridgehead' opportunity)."

The decision of Potter J was upheld by the Court of Appeal in a decision of Blanchard J delivered on 4 July 2003 (*Novartis NZ Ltd v Aktiebolaget Hassle* [2004] 2 NZLR 721 (CA)).

Similar comments have also arisen in the context of applications for interim injunctions to restrain the infringement of registered design rights. See, for example:

- *Handitags Ltd v Warburton* 12/12/01, Glazebrook J, HC Auckland M1586-SW01, at paras 17 and 18:

  > "However, the main reason put forward by Handitags as to inadequacy of damages is the loss of the ability to manage their practical monopoly situation. This is because, at any stage during such a monopoly, an entry of a competitor can cause permanent damage and permanent inability to manage the monopoly and, in particular, the ending of the monopoly which will obviously occur at the end of the design and copyright period. This diminished advantage can mean a permanent effect which Handitags submits is exceedingly hard to quantify. It is noted that there is only some four years left in respect of the design and five years in respect of the copyright so the loss of a portion of the period at the end of the registration for the design and the copyright period is even more significant. These submissions are accepted. It is accepted that damages would not be an adequate remedy for Handitags."

- *BEP Marine Ltd v Aquatech Marine Ltd* 20/12/02, O'Regan J, HC Auckland M1568-SW02 (which applied *Handitags*).

- *Viscount Plastics Ltd v Lamnei Plastics Ltd* 13/9/05, Gendall J, HC Auckland CIV-2005-404-3452, in which his Honour, although expressing doubts as to the validity of the plaintiff's registered design, and hence the strength of its case, indicated, at para 16, that a strong case pointing to invalidity would need to be made out before validity could even become relevant in the Court's balancing exercise and that validity alone is unlikely to ever be decisive. His Honour did however note, at para 26, that the size of the market may be relevant to the so called "management of monopoly" argument and stressed, at para 28, that it cannot be elevated to a rigid rule to be applied whenever the plaintiff is the owner of an exclusive patent or license.

- *Permanent Promotions Pty Ltd v Independent Liquor (NZ) Ltd* 10/6/04, Heath J, HC Auckland CIV-2004-404-2419, at paras 38 and 39:

  > "In my judgment, the scheme of the Act is clear. A Commissioner is appointed to examine designs submitted to him or her. In the course of that examination the Commissioner determines questions of novelty and compliance with statutory definitions. The underlying assumption is that the Commissioner is someone experienced in applying the Act and in making judgments of that sort. The scheme of the Act would be undermined significantly if the Courts failed to recognise the nature of the monopoly that flows from the registration process. In this case the design has been registered. I reject Mr Brown's submission that the Register is prima facie evidence only of what is contained in it rather than the fact that the Commissioner has found the design to comply with the definition contained in s 2(1) of the Act and has found the requisite degree of novelty. No item can be registered unless those conclusions have been drawn. That registration confers a monopoly. On an interim injunction application the Court must be slow to second guess the findings of the Commissioner."

and, at para 43:

> "In my view the fact of registration confers a prima facie right sufficient to overcome the hurdle of establishing that a serious question exists to be tried."

If the view expressed by Heath J prevails, then there is considerable advantage to a litigant in having a registered (as opposed to common law) intellectual property right as the basis of the legal proceeding. In particular, it may dispense with the issue as to whether there is a serious question to be tried, and greatly increase the prospects of obtaining interim relief, which in intellectual property cases is more often than not determinative of the proceeding.

However as to balance of convenience and overall justice, some caution needs to be exercised, as the "bridgehead" argument may be limited to forms of intellectual property in which the rights expire after a finite period. Thus, for example, the bridgehead argument may not be appropriate in a case involving infringement of a registered trade mark. Similarly, if the ownership of the intellectual property is in dispute this may result in refusal of the application: *Golden Homes (1998) Ltd v Blue Chip Construction Ltd* 21/6/05, Allan J, HC Auckland CIV-2003-404-7090. See also *Lesa Systems Ltd v Canzac Ltd* 16/5/06, John Hansen J, HC Christchurch CIV-2006-409-624, at para 34.

6.17.3 Innocent infringement

Under s 13 Designs Act 1953 a defendant who proves that, at the date of infringement, he or she was not aware, and had no reasonable grounds for supposing, there was a relevant registered design may be considered an innocent infringer. Neither damages nor an account of profits can be awarded against an innocent infringer.

An injunction can still be obtained against an innocent infringer preventing further infringement of the design registration.

A defendant cannot be said to be an innocent infringer if the article that is the subject of a registered design is marked with the words "registered design" (or any abbreviation or variant) and "New Zealand" or "NZ" (followed by the number of the registered design). This is discussed in more detail at 6.18 ("Marking") later in this chapter.

6.17.4 Groundless threats of infringement

Section 34 Designs Act 1953 provides remedies for groundless threats of infringement. The remedies available are:

- A declaration that the threats are unjustifiable;

- An injunction against continuing threats; and

- Damages the recipient may have sustained as a result of the threats.

Damages will normally be limited to situations where the recipient of the threat has stopped manufacturing and/or withdrawn the alleged infringing article from sale as a consequence of receiving the threat.

Section 34(3) provides, for the avoidance of any doubt, that notification of the mere existence of a design registration is not considered a threat of infringement proceedings.

6.18   Marking

It is not compulsory to indicate on an article that its design is registered. However, a defendant can be held to be an innocent infringer, and can avoid an account of profits or damages, if the article is not marked properly.

Suitable marking for an article that is the subject of a registered design is:

- "New Zealand Design Registration No XXXXX", or

- "NZ Reg Des No XXXXX".

An article the subject of a pending application should be marked:

- "New Zealand Design Application No XXXXX";

- "NZ Reg Des Appln No XXXXX"; or

- "NZ Reg Des App No XXXXX",

until the Certificate of Registration issues.

6.19   The Register

The Register of Designs is maintained by the Intellectual Property Office of New Zealand. The Register is open to public inspection. It contains the names and addresses of the registered proprietors of registered designs, notices of assignment and transmissions (recorded under s 27 Designs Act 1953), and other particulars, including for example:

- The date on which the application was filed in New Zealand;

- The date of registration; and

- Any priority date to which the application is entitled and details of the convention document.

6.19.1   Register prima facie evidence of contents

Section 25(3) Designs Act 1953 makes the Register prima facie evidence of any matters required by the Designs Act 1953 to be entered into it.

In *Permanent Promotions Pty Ltd v Independent Liquor (NZ) Ltd* 10/6/04, Heath J, HC Auckland CIV-2004-404-2419, the plaintiff sought an interim injunction against the defendant to restrain infringement of its registered design. The defendant opposed the application on the basis that there was no serious question to be tried and, in a counterclaim, sought to revoke the registered design on the basis that it failed to comply with the statutory definition of "design" in s 2(1) of the Act, and did not have the requisite degree of novelty. In so doing, the defendant argued that the Register is prima facie evidence only of what is contained in it, rather than of the registered design's compliance with the statutory definition. That argument was rejected by Heath J, who held that the Register can be taken as prima facie evidence of the registered design's compliance with both the statutory definition and novelty requirements, because every application for registration under the Act is subject to examination and approval by the Commissioner, who is assumed to be experienced in such matters. Heath J stated, at para 38:

"In my judgment, the scheme of the Act is clear. A Commissioner is appointed to examine designs submitted to him or her. In the course of that examination the Commissioner determines questions of novelty and compliance with statutory definitions. The underlying assumption is that the Commissioner is someone experienced in applying the Act and in making judgments of that sort. The scheme of the Act would be undermined significantly if the Courts failed to recognise the nature of the monopoly that flows from the registration process."

Heath J went on to state, at para 39, that, in relation to interim injunction applications, the Court must be slow to second guess the findings of the Commissioner. Where a defendant counterclaims for revocation of a registered design on the basis that it fails to comply with the statutory definitions or lacks novelty, the onus upon them is heavy. His Honour concluded, at para 43, that the fact of registration confers a prima facie right sufficient to overcome the hurdle of establishing that a serious question exists to be tried, and the evidence adduced by a defendant as to the strength of its counterclaim will need to be very persuasive in order to convince the Court that the prima facie rights attaching to registration should be overlooked. See also *Viscount Plastics Ltd v Lamnei Plastics Ltd* 13/9/05, Gendall J, HC Auckland CIV-2005-404-3452.

6.19.2 Search

As the Register of Designs is a matter of public record it can be searched, either physically at the Intellectual Property Office of New Zealand's premises in Wellington, or electronically via its website (www.iponz.govt.nz).

(1) *Reasons for search*

Searching is generally conducted for two reasons:

* To reveal design registrations applying to articles which the proposed manufacture and/or sale of may infringe; and

* Before filing an application, to determine whether any registered designs, whether currently in force or not, exist that would render the subject matter of the proposed application neither new nor original.

The records are grouped into various classifications for ease of searching. The Intellectual Property Office of New Zealand uses the International Classification for Industrial Designs ("IDC") which categorises the items to which registered designs are applied into 32 classes (many of which are divided into further subclasses). A searcher may use Part III of the IDC (which is an alphabetical listing of articles) in order to determine which classes should be searched for similar items.

6.19.3 Correction of errors

Under s 29 Designs Act 1953, the Commissioner may correct any mistake existing in the Register, or any document issued under the Act, by reason of an error or omission on the part of the Intellectual Property Office. Where the Commissioner proposes to make such a correction he is required to give notice of the proposal to any persons who appear to him to be concerned, and give them an opportunity to be heard before making the correction.

Under s 29(3) such a correction may also be made on application by any person interested. As with the correction of mistakes initiated by the Commissioner, if the Commissioner considers the correction would materially alter the meaning or scope of any document he is required to give notice of the request by advertisement in the Patent Office Journal. Any person interested may oppose the correction of the error or mistake and the Commissioner must hold a hearing before a decision is made.

In *Wade's Application* (Commissioner's Decision No P01/1981, 9/1/81, Asst Commr Burton), Assistant Commissioner Burton held that an "interested person" for the purposes of the Patents Act 1953 is one who has a genuine commercial interest in the items the subject of the patent. It is likely that this test would be used for determining whether a person qualifies as "interested" under the Designs Act 1953.

6.19.4   Change of name or address

If the applicant or proprietor changes his or her name or address, these new details should be recorded on the Register. It is important to keep the Register accurate as various notices (for example, renewal fee reminders and notices for cancellation or rectification) must be responded to within a certain time frame. If such notices are not responded to, the registered design may lapse or be deemed to have been abandoned.

6.20   References and resource sites

6.20.1   Websites

Thomson Brookers	www.thomsonbrookers.co.nz
Intellectual Property Office of New Zealand	www.iponz.govt.nz
Interim Website of New Zealand Legislation	www.legislation.govt.nz
James & Wells	www.jaws.co.nz
World Intellectual Property Organisation	www.s.int
UK Intellectual Property Office	www.ipo.gov.uk

6.20.2   Texts and periodicals

Brown, B, and Grant, A, *The Law of Intellectual Property in New Zealand*, Wellington, Butterworths, 1988

Frankel, S, and McLay, G, *Intellectual Property in New Zealand*, Wellington, LexisNexis, 2002

Puri, K K, *Industrial Design Law in Australia and New Zealand*, Wellington, Butterworths, 1986

Intellectual Property Forum: The Journal of the Intellectual Property Society of Australia and New Zealand Inc, Melbourne, Australia

Chapter 7

TRADE MARKS

7.1 Introduction

7.1.1 Scope of this chapter

The Trade Marks Act 2002 establishes a system for registration of trade marks. As an incentive to registration the Act confers on the owner of a registered trade mark the exclusive right to use the mark on or in relation to certain goods or services in New Zealand.

One of the main benefits of registration is that a certificate of registration is taken as proof of ownership of the registered mark. Therefore, it is not necessary to prove reputation in the registered trade mark in an action for infringement where the infringing sign is identical to the registered mark, and the infringing sign is used in relation to the same goods/services for which the mark is registered.

A further benefit is that a trade mark registration is a defined property right, which can be licensed, sold or used as security.

While the Act prohibits the owner of an unregistered mark from bringing proceedings for infringement, it does not affect their rights under the tort of passing off or under the Fair Trading Act 1986. The topics of passing off and the Fair Trading Act 1986 are dealt with in subsequent chapters of this text (chapters 9 and 10 respectively).

The Trade Marks Act 2002, which repealed the Trade Marks Act 1953, came into force on 20 August 2003. The 2002 Act is largely based on the Trade Marks Act 1998 (Singapore), which is itself based on the Trade Marks Act 1994 (UK).

Some of the main reforms brought about by the new Act were:

- The provision of multi-class applications;

- A reduction of the non-use period from 5 years to 3 years;

- Simplification of the removal procedure for non-use;

- Simplification of the procedure for recording assignments of trade marks;

- New restrictions on the amendments which are permitted to pending applications;

- Removal of the right to amend registered trade marks;

- The abolition of defensive trade mark registrations;

- The abolition of infringement by use of a registered trade mark in comparative advertising;

- New provisions for criminal liability in certain cases of trade mark infringement;

- New measures to prevent registration of marks which may offend Maori or other sections of the community;

- A 10-year term for renewal of trade mark registrations;

- Removal of the distinction between Part A and Part B of the Register;

- New provisions regarding the infringement of well-known marks; and

- New provisions for invalidating trade mark registrations.

310

These changes are discussed in more detail in the corresponding sections of this chapter.

7.2 Legislation, treaties, and conventions

7.2.1 Governing law

The law relating to registered trade marks in New Zealand is found in the:

- Trade Marks Act 2002 ("the Act");

- Trade Marks Amendment Act 2003;

- Trade Marks Amendment Act 2005;

- Trade Marks Regulations 2003;

- Trade Marks Amendment Regulations 2006;

- Intellectual Property Office practice notes;

- Decisions of the Commissioner of Trade Marks; and

- Decisions of the New Zealand Courts.

As the Act is based on the Trade Marks Act 1998 (Singapore), which is in turn based on the Trade Marks Act 1994 (UK), decisions of the Courts in those jurisdictions may also be relevant and regarded as persuasive.

7.2.2 International conventions

(1)   *Paris Convention*

New Zealand is a contracting party to the Paris Convention for the Protection of Industrial Property (1883). New Zealand became party to the Convention on 29 July 1931. On 14 July 1946, New Zealand became an adherent to the London revision of the Act, and on 20 June 1984 became a party to arts 13-30 of the Stockholm revision. The actual text of the Convention can be viewed at www.wipo.int.

One of the most important features of the Paris Convention is that it establishes a "right of priority" for its members. A trade mark application filed within a member State creates a convention priority right. As long as the applicant meets certain criteria, it can use its first filed application in respect of a particular mark ("parent application") as the basis of a convention application for the same mark in other member states. If the later application is filed within 6 months of the parent application, then the later application will receive as its "priority date" the filing date of the parent application. The applicant will usually have to provide evidence of the parent application (such as a certified copy) to the appropriate body.

In order to claim convention priority in New Zealand the trade mark applied for must be identical to the mark applied for in the parent application. While additional goods or services may be added to the New Zealand application they will not receive the benefit of the convention priority date.

Additional information on applications with multiple priority dates can be found in the IPONZ Practice Guideline, "Priority of Trade Mark Applications", which is available on the IPONZ website (www.iponz.govt.nz).

The ability to file a convention-based application overseas which claims priority from a New Zealand application can be invaluable, because for up to 6 months a trade mark applicant can consider trade mark filing strategies and defer the cost of applying for trade mark protection in foreign jurisdictions, while retaining the New Zealand priority date in those jurisdictions.

(2)   *Nice Agreement*

New Zealand is an adherent to the Nice Agreement on the International Classification of Goods and Services for the Purposes of Trade Mark Registration. For more information on the Nice Agreement, see 7.3 ("The Register of Trade Marks") later in this chapter.

(3)   *Vienna Agreement*

New Zealand is also an adherent to the Vienna Agreement on the International Classification of the Figurative Elements of Marks. This agreement establishes a numbering system for describing trade mark representations for the purposes of searching.

7.2.3   Related legislation / common law causes of action

(1)   *The Geographical Indications (Wine and Spirits) Registration Act 2006*

This Act, which repeals the Geographical Indications Act 1994, was passed in late 2006, but is not yet in force. The main purpose of the Act is to provide a suitable legal framework for the registration of geographical indications in the wine and spirits industries in New Zealand. A "geographical indication" is defined in s 6(1) as an indication that identifies a wine or spirit as originating in the territory of a country, or a region or locality in that territory, where a given quality, or reputation, or other characteristic of the wine or spirit, is essentially attributable to its geographical origin.

Applications to register a geographical indication are made to the Registrar of Registered Geographical Indications and, if accepted, take effect from the date of application. There are some restrictions on registration including:

- It is not possible to register a geographical indication identical to a geographical indication that has already been registered;

- The geographical indication cannot be a customary name of a grape variety or a common name for a wine or spirit;

- Foreign geographical indications can only be registered if protected in their country of origin; and

- A geographical indication cannot be registered if it is identical to a New Zealand trade mark that has been registered or used in good faith in respect of identical goods or services, or that is the subject of an application covering identical goods or services that predates the application for registration of the geographical indication. The same applies for geographical indications which are similar to a trade mark and/or for similar goods and services if the use of the geographical indication would be likely to deceive or confuse. However, in all cases the owner of the trade mark may consent and/or the Registrar can allow registration of the geographical indication if the Registrar deems it is capable of co-existing with the trade mark.

Once registered there are certain restrictions on use of a registered geographical indication:

- For a New Zealand registered geographical indication for wine, at least 85 percent of the wine must be obtained from grapes harvested in the geographical region to which the indication relates; and

- Foreign registered geographical indications for wine may only be used in trade in New Zealand if the wine originated from the geographical region to which the foreign registered geographical indication relates.

Similar rules apply in respect of registered geographical indications for spirits. The restrictions for both wines and spirits apply whether or not:

- The true origin of the wine or spirit is indicated on the product or in advertising;

- The registered geographical indication is used in translation, or

- The use of the registered geographical indication is accompanied by any of the words "kind", "type", "style", "imitation", or any similar word or expression.

The restrictions do not apply to product which has never been in New Zealand or is in New Zealand in transit only, and do not apply to product which was bottled before the geographical indication was registered under the Act. There is also a saving for vested rights similar to that recognised in respect of registered trade marks (see s 29 of the Act). In addition, where the geographical indication has been used otherwise than in bad faith in an unregistered trade mark, the restrictions on use of the registered geographical indication cease to apply five years after such use has become generally known in New Zealand.

A breach of a restriction on the use of a registered geographical indication is a breach of s 9 Fair Trading Act 1986 and the provisions of that Act apply accordingly (see s 33 of the Act).

The procedure for registration is a simplified version of the procedure for registering a trade mark under the Trade Marks Act 2002. Applications are submitted to the Registrar of Registered Geographical Indications. Applications from two or more parties for the same product having the same or a similar geographical indication are given priority based on the filing date. The Registrar may obtain advice and consult on any application under the Act and must not exercise any power under the Act adverse to any person interested without giving them an opportunity to be heard. Regulations will be enacted to prescribe the procedure for such hearings. The Registrar may also register a geographical indication with any conditions he or she thinks fit. Where issues relating to the boundaries and the use of a place name arise, the Registrar may establish a Geographical Indications Committee to investigate and resolve them (see ss 53-56 of the Act).

The Registrar must also maintain a Register of registered geographical indications and allow public access to that Register. Registered geographical indications can be removed from the Register if the Registrar is satisfied that:

- A foreign geographical indication is not, or has ceased to be, protected in its country of origin;

- The registered geographical indication (whether foreign or New Zealand) has fallen into disuse in its country of origin;

- The registered geographical indication should not have been registered because it did not meet the requirements of the definition in s 6(1) of the Act;

- The registered geographical indication should not have been registered because it fell under one or more of the restrictions in the Act; or

- The registered geographical indication has become a common name for a wine or spirit in New Zealand.

The Registrar also has powers to alter the Register, and to refuse an application for removal/alteration that is vexatious or frivolous. Regulations will be enacted to govern the procedures for the exercise of these powers by the Registrar.

Any person who is aggrieved by a decision of the Registrar may appeal to the High Court within 20 working days from the date on which the decision appealed against was given.

Finally, s 20 Trade Marks Act 2002 prohibits registration of a trade mark that contains a registered geographical indication, or a geographical indication in respect of which registration has been applied for under the Geographical Indications (Wine and Spirits) Registration Act 2006, where that trade mark relates to a wine or spirit that does not originate from the geographical region to which the registered geographical indication relates. The Act also inserts a new s 98A into the Trade Marks Act 2002 which provides a defence to trade mark infringement through use of a geographical indication registered under the Act.

(2)   *The Major Events Management Act 2007*

The Major Events Management Act 2007 implements the Government's decision to enact protection against ambush marketing for major events given New Zealand's intention to host a number of major sporting events in the next few years including, notably, the Rugby World Cup in 2011 and co-hosting the Cricket World Cup in 2015. These kinds of major events attract large audiences and are therefore attractive to sponsors. "Ambush marketing" describes the actions of companies or advertisers who seek to capture the benefits enjoyed by sponsors without the authorisation of the event organiser.

The Act specifically deals with ambush marketing by association — which involves an advertiser misleading the public into thinking that the ambush marketer is an authorised partner or somehow associated with the event. The association will often be subtle and may not involve actual use of the event name or associated logo. Under the Act, the test for ambush marketing by association is whether the representation is likely to suggest to a reasonable person that there is an association between the major event and any product, service, or brand. This association will be presumed where any protected major event word or emblem is used.

The second form of prohibited activity is ambush marketing by intrusion — which occurs when an event is used to draw attention to the ambush marketer's brand from an audience gathered solely for the major event. This will usually occur in close proximity to the physical location of the event and/or major transportation routes leading into and out of that

314

location. In order to give effect to these provisions the Act allows for the Minister of Economic Development to declare geographically limited clean zones consisting of the venue and areas directly proximate to the venue of the major event in which marketing activities cannot be carried out except by those authorised by the event manager and/or its sponsors. These clean zones cannot include private land except that to which the public usually has access. The Act also prohibits advertising that is clearly visible from the clean zones.

Ambush marketing involves commercial activity that "free rides" on the publicity surrounding a major event and therefore undermines the value of official sponsorship and the viability of obtaining sponsorship for future events. In particular, it is noted that some major sponsors will not commit to sponsorship contracts unless there is some form of protection against ambush marketing in place.

In order to avoid overuse, the Act will only apply to major events that are of international significance. Following an application by an event organiser, the Minister of Economic Development will make a recommendation to the Governor General whether the event should be declared a major event. In making that recommendation the Minister is required to consult with the Ministers of Commerce and Sports and must also take into account whether the event will:

- Attract a large number of international participants or spectators and therefore generate significant tourism opportunities for New Zealand;

- Significantly raise New Zealand's international profile;

- Require a high level of professional management and co-ordination;

- Attract significant sponsorship and international media coverage;

- Attract large numbers of New Zealanders as participants or spectators; and

- Offer substantial sporting, cultural, social, economic, or other benefits for New Zealand or New Zealanders.

A declaration that an event is a major event will specify the period of time during which the ambush marketing protections will apply.

In terms of overlap with the Trade Marks Act 2002, the Act provides for protection of words and emblems that could denote a connection with a major event whether or not they are eligible for registration under the Trade Marks Act 2002 and/or actually registered. However, the Minister of Economic Development must take into account whether this is necessary to obtain maximum benefits for New Zealanders and to prevent unauthorised commercial exploitation at the expense of the major event organiser or sponsors, and will be required to consult with parties who are substantially affected (which may include parties with existing common law/registered rights in the same or similar words and emblems). Border protection measures equivalent to those under the Trade Marks Act 2002 are provided in relation to materials bearing protected major event words or emblems.

Given the potentially broad nature of these prohibitions the Act also introduces a number of safeguards. So long as they are carried out in accordance with honest practices in industrial or commercial matters, the following sorts of activities will not amount to an infringement:

- The use by a person of his or her own real name or address;

- The use of the proper name of any town, road or other place in New Zealand;

- The use of a person's legal or trade name or an existing registered trade mark;

- Existing businesses and organisations continuing to carry out their current activities;

- The use of indications concerning the kind, quality, quantity, value, geographical origin, time of production of goods or of rendering of services, or other characteristics of goods or services;

- Where incorporated into a context where the major event is substantially irrelevant;

- The use of representations necessary to indicate the intended purpose of a product or service; and

- The editorial use of names and indicia, such as for current affairs, criticism or review.

As part of the prohibition on ambush marketing by association, the Act prohibits offering, giving away, or selling a ticket to a major event activity in connection with the promotion of goods or services. Perhaps more controversially the Act also renders the scalping of tickets to major events (that is, the sale for a value greater than the original sale price) illegal.

A combination of enforcement measures is provided for in the Act including: the civil remedies of an account of profits, damages and corrective advertising; criminal penalties applying to intentional or knowing breaches (similar to existing offences in the Trade Marks Act 2002); and administrative remedies entitling enforcement officers to issue formal warnings to ambush marketers, seize offending material (such as scalped tickets or counterfeit merchandise), cover offending material (for example, billboards or signs in a clean zone or visible from a clean zone) and enter a premise under limited circumstances.

(3) *The Fair Trading Act 1986*

This Act prohibits misleading and deceptive conduct in trade, and in particular certain acts in relation to trade marks, such as forgery. These are discussed in more detail in the Fair Trading Act 1986 chapter of this text (chapter 10).

(4) *Passing off*

Passing off is a common law cause of action which provides a remedy for unfair competition between traders. It prohibits one trader making a misrepresentation calculated to injure the business reputation or goodwill of another trader by passing off his or her goods or services as those of the other trader. This cause of action is discussed in more detail in the passing off chapter of this text (chapter 9).

7.3 The Register of Trade Marks

IPONZ keeps a Register of all trade mark applications and registrations. The Register records the:

- Mark;

- Status and type of mark;

- Filing date;

- Usage (ie, whether or not the mark was in use at the time of filing);

- Convention priority date (if any);

- Specification of goods and/or services;

- Name(s), address(es) and description(s) of the owner(s);

- Notifications of assignments and transmissions (if any);

- Name(s) and address(es) of any licensee(s); and

- Disclaimers, conditions or limitations to which registration of the mark is subject.

7.3.1 Searching

The Register is recorded electronically in the IPONZ database. It can be searched through the IPONZ website (www.iponz.govt.nz) or manually at IPONZ's Document and Information Services Centre. A search can be conducted in respect of any of the fields of information that are recorded on the Register.

7.3.2 Classification of goods and services

Under s 31 Trade Marks Act 2002, trade marks must be registered in relation to particular goods and/or services. For the purposes of the Register, these are divided into specific classes, and any question arising as to the class or classes within which any goods or services fall will be determined by the Commissioner (s 31(2)).

The practice of the Commissioner is to use the system of classifying goods and services established under the Nice Agreement on the International Classification of Goods and Services, as revised in Geneva in May 1977.

The 9th edition (which came into force on 1 January 2007) is the current edition of the Nice classification. There are now 45 classes in total, made up of 34 classes of goods and 11 classes of services. More information on the Nice classifications (including lists of goods and services within each class) can be found at www.wipo.int/classifications/en/index.html.

According to IPONZ Practice Guideline, "Classification and Specification", an examiner must consider four things when examining a specification of goods or services:

- Whether the nature of the goods and/or services is clear (s 31);

- Whether the goods and/or services are correctly classified in the class or classes applied for (s 31);

- Whether the applicant has applied for an unreasonably wide range of goods and/or services (s 32(2)); and

- Whether the specification contains a registered trade mark or the applicant's own mark.

If the examiner has any concerns regarding the content of the specification of goods and/or services, an objection will be raised. For example, if the examiner is unable to determine the correct classification of the goods and/or services based on the details available, he or she will write to the applicant requesting more information regarding the goods/services in question. If items in the specification of goods and/or services are incorrectly classified, the applicant will have the option of either deleting the items in question from the specification, or adding a class under reg 43 Trade Marks Regulations 2003 (provided the application to add a class is made within one month of the filing date of the application). This deadline cannot be extended. The addition of classes will only be allowed where the goods or services to which the additional class or classes relate are within the original specification, and such an addition will be subject to an additional application fee (reg 43(2)(b)).

Under s 32(1) of the Act, an applicant may apply to register a trade mark in more than one class in a "multi-class" application. In contrast, under the Trade Marks Act 1953, a trade mark registration could only cover one class of goods or services, so separate applications were required for each relevant class.

Where multiple applications have been made, or where the application is a multi-class application, the examiner may ask the applicant to transfer items from one application or class to another, to ensure that those items are correctly classified.

More information regarding the classification of goods and services can be found in the IPONZ Practice Guideline, "Classification and Specification".

7.3.3 The Journal

Matters relating to trade mark registrations and applications under the Trade Marks Act 2002 are published in the *Patent Office Journal* (pursuant to s 112 Patents Act 1953).

The Journal is currently published monthly and contains advertisements of:

- The material particulars of trade mark applications advertised for opposition purposes;

- The registration number of all applications that have proceeded to registration;

- The registration number of all registrations that have been renewed;

- The registration number of all registrations where the renewal fee has not been paid;

- The application numbers of all applications abandoned by the applicant;

- Subsequent owners under assignments of registrations that have been recorded on the Register;

- Registered users entered on the Register;

- Applications or registrations amended or altered;

- Registrations cancelled;

- Registrations rectified; and

- Registrations restored to the Register.

Publication in the Journal serves as public notice of any matter advertised. The primary purpose of the Journal is to advertise accepted trade mark applications so that interested parties have an opportunity to oppose them (discussed further at 7.7 ("Oppositions")).

7.4 Trade mark application process

7.4.1 Filing an application

The Trade Marks Act 2002 provides that any person may, on payment of the prescribed fee, apply for the registration of a trade mark or a series of trade marks in the prescribed manner (s 32). The Trade Marks Regulations 2003 set out the mandatory requirements to be included in any application, together with the information that must be supplied before an application can be accepted. Sections 32-45 of the Act set out the application process for the registration of a trade mark.

(1) *Commissioner's preliminary advice regarding distinctive character of trade mark*

Under s 13 Trade Marks Act 2002, the Commissioner may only register a trade mark if he or she is satisfied that there are no absolute or relative grounds that would prevent registration of a trade mark.

Under s 18(1)(b), the Commissioner must not register a trade mark that has no distinctive character. Under s 16, an applicant is entitled to seek the Commissioner's preliminary advice regarding the distinctive character of the proposed trade mark. Regulation 38 Trade Marks Regulations 2003 sets out the information which is required of an application for preliminary advice or a search of the Register. The applicant must provide the following:

- The applicant's name and communication address;

- A clear representation of the trade mark in question;

- A statement of the goods and/or services for which trade mark registration is sought;

- A transliteration of any foreign characters in the trade mark;

- A translation of any foreign words in the trade mark; and

- The prescribed fee.

Once this information is provided, the Commissioner will conduct a search of the Register and/or comment on whether the proposed mark has a distinctive character. If an application for the same trade mark is filed within 3 months of receiving the Commissioner's advice, and if, contrary to the Commissioner's preliminary advice, the application is rejected on the basis of lack of distinctiveness or due to an earlier conflicting mark, the application fee will be refunded.

(2) *Qualification as applicant/ownership*

Under regs 41 and 42 Trade Marks Regulations 2003, an application to register a trade mark must contain the applicant's name in order to obtain a filing date. For this purpose, the applicant must be a legal entity.

Under s 33 Trade Marks Act 2002, an application may be made by two or more persons, as joint applicants. If the application is successful, a joint applicant will only be entitled to use the trade mark on behalf of all joint applicants, or in relation to goods and services with which all joint applicants are connected in the course of trade.

Where an application is made in the name of a partnership, the application must contain the names of all of the partners.

Under s 183, no notice of any trust may be entered in the Register. If however the trust is incorporated, the application may be completed in the name of that incorporated body. Where the trust is unincorporated, the application may be made in the individual names of the trustees, as it is the trustees who legally own the property.

As to "ownership", s 26(1) of the 1953 Act used to require an application to be filed in the name of "any person claiming to be proprietor of a trade mark". This is the equivalent to s 25(1) of the 2002 Act (as amended by s 5 Trade Marks Amendment Act 2005) which refers to "a person claiming to be the owner of a trade mark". Despite use of the word "owner" it is generally accepted that the principles applicable to a valid claim to proprietorship under the 1953 Act continue to apply to ownership in respect of the 2002 Act. Those principles were summarised by the High Court in *Newnham v Table for Six (1996) Ltd* (1998) 44 IPR 269, at p 278 as follows:

(1)   There is no prior use or prior assertion of proprietorship;

(2)   The applicant is using or has a sufficiently definite intention to use the mark; and

(3)   There is no fraud or breach of duty involved.

As to the type and extent of use required to maintain a claim to proprietorship based on use, see *Moorgate Tobacco Co Ltd v Philip Morris Ltd (No 2)* (1984) 156 CLR 414 (HCA), at p 432:

> "The prior use of the trade mark which may suffice, at least if combined with local authorship, to establish that a person has acquired [in a particular country] the statutory status of 'proprietor' of the mark, is public use [in that country] of the mark as a trade mark, that is to say, a use of the mark in relation to the goods for the purpose of indicating or so as to indicate a connection in the course of trade between the goods with respect to which the mark is used and that person …"

These tests were applied by the Court of Appeal in *Aqua Technics Pool & Spa Centre NZ Ltd v Aqua-Tech Ltd* 22/3/07, CA257/05.

(3)   *Filing requirements*

Under s 32(1) Trade Marks Act 2002, an application to register a trade mark must be made in "the prescribed manner".

The application must contain all the mandatory requirements set out in regs 41 and 42 Trade Marks Regulations 2003.

Under reg 42, an application to register a trade mark must contain the following information, as a minimum:

•   The applicant's name or, in the case of a joint application, the name of each applicant;

•   An address for service in New Zealand;

•   A clear representation of the trade mark;

•   If the application is for registration of a series of trade marks, a clear representation of each trade mark in the series; and

- The goods and/or services for which registration is required.

Under reg 41(2), an application will only be processed and a filing date assigned once the minimum requirements in reg 42 have been satisfied. If they are not met, then the application will not be given a filing date, and examination of the application will be delayed until all of the filing requirements have been satisfied.

IPONZ will usually confirm the official number allocated to the application and the filing date within 2 days of manually filing an application for registration of a trade mark. It is also possible to file a trade mark application online (www.iponz.govt.nz), in which case confirmation of the filing date and application number is available almost immediately.

An application that meets the mandatory requirements set out in reg 42 "must" be given a filing date, and "may" be examined (reg 41(3)). The use of "may" might suggest that the Commissioner has a discretion to refuse to examine an application, but the wording of s 39 of the Act makes it clear that:

> "The Commissioner must examine an application in order to determine whether it complies with the requirements of this Act."

(4) *Clear representation*

Under reg 42 Trade Marks Regulations 2003, the representation of the mark filed must be sufficiently clear to allow examination of the application to commence. The representation of the mark must not bring the scope of the application into doubt. If there is any uncertainty regarding the scope of protection sought for the mark, a filing date may not be allocated (reg 42(b) and (c)).

In cases where an applicant seeks to register a colour or combination of colours as a trade mark, IPONZ Practice Guideline, "Filing Trade Mark Applications" states that the applicant should file with the application either:

- A representation of the colour(s); or

- A description of the colour(s), using a widely known and readily available colour standard (such as the colour indexing scheme of the Pantone® colour system).

The Guideline also states that the description of the trade mark should also include information on how the colour(s) is being used, or is to be used, in relation to the goods and/or services, such as in the following example: "The mark is the colour blue (Pantone xxx) as shown in the representation attached to the application, applied to the exterior surface of the goods".

If the requirements specified in reg 42(b), are not met, the application will not receive an application number and filing date.

In the case of three-dimensional shape marks, the application must clearly show all the features of the mark. Depending on the visual characteristics of the shape in question, a number of aspect views of the shape may be required. Applications describing three-dimensional shapes in words only will not be given a filing date until a pictorial representation of the shape is supplied.

Finally, in the case of sound marks, musical notation will be accepted as a means of graphically representing the mark. If the musical instrument used to produce the sound forms part of the mark, then this should be stated in the application.

For more information regarding the minimum filing requirements, see the IPONZ Practice Guideline, "Filing Trade Mark Applications".

(5) *Series marks*

Where an applicant applies to register more than one trade mark in a single application, this is called an application to register a series of trade marks. Like a normal application, an application for the registration of a series of trade marks may be made in respect of goods or services in one class, or goods and/or services in multiple classes.

All such applications must meet the requirements set out in the definition of "series of trade marks" in s 5 of the Act.

A "series of trade marks" is defined in s 5 of the Act as a number of trade marks for the same goods or description of goods or the same services or description of services (as the case may be) that:

"(a) resemble each other in their material particulars; and

"(b) differ only in respect of—

"(i) statements of the goods or services for which they are, or are proposed to be, used; or

"(ii) statements of number, price, quality, or names of places; or

"(iii) other matters of a non-distinctive character that do not substantially affect the identity of the trade mark; or

"(iv) colour."

While s 5 sets out specific criteria that must be met before two or more marks will be considered a valid series of trade marks, this list is not exhaustive. If the marks differ from one another in a way not mentioned in s 5, the applicant will still need to show that the extra material constitutes non-distinctive matter, which does not substantially affect the identity of the mark.

When making this determination, IPONZ Practice Guideline, "Series marks under the Trade Marks Act 2002" states that examiners will take into account:

- The appearance or "look" of the marks;

- The pronunciation or "sound" of the marks;

- The "idea" or meaning of the marks; and

- Any other factors that might change the "idea" of one mark when compared to the "idea" of the other mark(s).

According to the IPONZ Practice Guideline, IPONZ will also refer to the principles laid down in the Australian decision of *Re Lynson Australia Pty* (1987) 9 IPR 350.

In *Lynson*, the applicant applied to register a series of two trade marks; the plain word LYNSON and a stylised version of the word. The examiner objected on the basis that the stylisation of the second mark constituted distinctive matter that materially altered the identity of the trade mark. The applicant appealed.

In reaching the decision that the stylisation did not materially alter the identity of the second mark in the series, and that the application should therefore be allowed to proceed to acceptance, Chief Assistant Registrar Farquhar said:

> "the variation between members of a series must be such that no additional element or dimension is contributed thereby to the overall identity of the marks; the 'idea' of the marks must remain the same. If the marks consist of a word, then the word must be the only element in the identity of each member of the series. The typescript may be varied, but only between known, conventional scripts, not fanciful get-up. The spelling may be varied, but only if the pronunciation and meaning remain unaffected."

The relevant provisions of the 2002 Act are essentially the same as those series provisions under the Trade Marks Act 1953. However, recent IPONZ practice is to adhere more stringently to the terms of s 5 than it did to the terms of the corresponding provision under the 1953 Act. IPONZ has stated that it will not consider past registrations when determining the scope of what can be protected by a series application. There are a large number of current series registrations that would not be eligible for registration as a series if they were re-filed and examined under the current practice.

More information regarding series marks under the Trade Marks Act 2002 can be found in IPONZ Practice Guideline, "Series marks under the Trade Marks Act 2002".

7.4.2 Priority of applications

(1) *Priority of applications for identical or similar trade marks*

Under s 34(1) Trade Marks Act 2002, where the Commissioner receives separate applications from different persons for identical or similar trade marks, the application with the earliest filing date will have priority over all the other applications and will be allowed to proceed (s 34(1)). It is the filing date and not the time of application that is important. Therefore applications which are received on the same day will be treated as if they had been received at the same time.

Where different persons separately apply for the registration of identical or similar trade marks on the same date, but independent of each other, both applications will proceed with equal priority. In such cases, the Commissioner must notify each applicant of the other's application (s 34(2)(b)), and each will have the opportunity to approve registration of the other's mark.

In *Nortel Networks Corp v Telecom Corp of NZ* 24/6/04, Goddard J, HC Wellington CIV-2003-485-2631, the appellant, Nortel, had held a registered trade mark for goods since 1976 in relation to telecommunication equipment. On 1 May 1988, the Trade Marks Act 1953 was amended to permit registration of service marks. On 2 May 1988, Nortel applied to register a service mark for a stylised version of the words "NORTHERN TELECOM". On the same day, the respondent, Telecom, applied to register service marks for

"TELECOM" in word and stylised form. Telecom's application for registration of its service marks was eventually approved over a decade later.

Nortel did not oppose Telecom's applications, as it considered that there was no likelihood of deception or confusion between Telecom's service marks and its own. However, Telecom opposed Nortel's application under s 17(3) Trade Marks Act 1953, on the basis that Nortel's logo was confusingly similar to Telecom's registered service mark for the word "TELECOM". At the opposition hearing, Nortel submitted that because both parties' applications had been filed on the same day, Telecom's service mark was not "already on the Register" for the purposes of s 17(3) of the 1953 Act.

At first instance, the Assistant Commissioner of Trade Marks refused to register Nortel's service mark on the basis that, inter alia, once accepted, Telecom's service mark was deemed to be registered from the date of application by virtue of s 28(1) Trade Marks Act 1953. In the High Court, Goddard J upheld that decision, noting, at para 13, that:

> "The practical interpretation of the words 'already on the Register' must mean that the event of registration gives priority in a situation where two applicants applied for registration on the same date but one applicant achieved registration before the other. If that were not so, neither of two applicants who applied in respect of similar marks on the same date could ever achieve registration, if application alone met the definition of 'already on the Register'. That would be an 'absurd' result ... A pending application does not confer such rights: for example, infringement proceedings cannot be brought until a mark is registered, but once registered infringement and any resultant damages date back to the date of application."

This reasoning applies equally to the rights attaching to a registered trade mark, once accepted, from the date of application for registration of the trade mark under the Trade Marks Act 2002.

(2)   *Convention priority applications*

When filing an application in New Zealand, it is possible for the applicant to claim priority from an earlier application filed in a convention country. The priority claim must be made within 6 months of the first application for the trade mark in a convention country. Section 36 Trade Marks Act 2002 and regs 46-47 Trade Marks Regulations 2003 govern convention priority applications.

Regulation 46 states that a claim for convention priority must be made within 2 working days of the filing date of the New Zealand trade mark application. This time period cannot be extended.

Regulation 47 states that a claim for convention priority must contain:

- The date of the application from which priority is claimed;

- The country in which the application was made;

- The goods and services to which the claim relates; and

- If the application in New Zealand is an application for registration of a series of trade marks, a statement specifying to which of the marks in the series the claim for convention priority relates.

Regulation 47 also allows the Commissioner the option of requesting a certified copy of the relevant convention document. This differs from the Trade Marks Act 1953, which required a certified copy of the convention document to be filed for all convention based applications.

The "deemed date of registration", as defined in s 5 of the Act, differs in the case of an application which has successfully claimed convention priority. The deemed date of registration for a convention based application will be the date of application in the convention country, as opposed to the New Zealand filing date.

Under s 36, a person who has applied for the registration of a trade mark in a convention country is entitled to registration of his or her trade mark "in priority to other applicants". On a strict reading of s 36, applicants taking advantage of the priority date of an earlier convention country application will have priority over all conflicting applications, even if the priority date of an earlier conflicting mark is earlier. It is most unlikely that this consequence was intended by the legislative draftsmen.

7.4.3 Post-filing

Under reg 44 Trade Marks Regulations 2003, the following information need not be supplied at the time of filing, but must be submitted before an application can be accepted:

- The applicant's business or residential address (if different from the address for service);

- Whether the application is for a certification or a collective trade mark;

- The class or classes of the Nice Classification in which registration is sought;

- In the case of a certification trade mark, the regulations governing the use of the trade mark approved by the Commissioner;

- A transliteration of any foreign characters in the trade mark;

- If the trade mark is a colour or colours, a description acceptable to the Commissioner of the colour or colours;

- If the trade mark is limited as to colour, a description acceptable to the Commissioner of the colour or colours in the trade mark;

- If the applicant has made a claim for convention priority, the information required by reg 47; and

- A statement by the applicant that the trade mark is being used or is proposed to be used.

If a trade mark contains a word in a language other than English, IPONZ will request an English translation of the word if the examiner's research indicates that the word may raise a concern on absolute and/or relative grounds. If the foreign word is represented in a foreign alphabet (eg Japanese katakana), then a transliteration of the characters will be required in addition to a translation (reg 44). Refer also to IPONZ Practice Guideline, "Examination of Trade Mark Applications".

Under reg 45, the Commissioner has discretion to request further information from an applicant that will assist in the examination of the application.

As to what constitutes "proposed use", the intention to use must be a settled purpose, and the absence of a bona fide intention to use the mark will prevent it from being a trade mark and may result in its revocation: *Imperial Group Ltd v Philip Morris & Co Ltd* [1982] FSR 72 (CA). However, in *Aston v Harlee Manufacturing Co* (1960) 103 CLR 391 (HCA), at p 401, it was held that the application itself should be regarded as prima facie evidence of an intention to use the mark the subject of the application — it is not for the Registrar to institute an inquiry as to the intention of any applicant, and on an opposition the burden of proving the absence of intention rests on the Opponent. The decision was followed in New Zealand by White J in *Philip Morris (NZ) Ltd v Ligget & Myers Tobacco Co (NZ) Ltd (No 3)* (1978) 1 TCLR 1; 1 NZIPR 195.

These authorities were considered by the High Court in *Effem Foods Ltd v Cadbury Ltd* 21/3/07, Miller J, HC Wellington CIV-2005-485-1487. Cadbury had applied to register the trade mark EARTH which was opposed by Effem Foods. Evidence submitted by Cadbury in support of its application suggested that the mark was filed to protect its MOTHER EARTH mark which had been used in New Zealand since 1981. At the opposition stage, the Assistant Commissioner held that Effem had the onus of proving absence of intention and had failed to do so. That decision was overturned on appeal, Miller J finding, at para 35:

> "In this case, the inference of intention to use that arose from the application itself was displaced by Cadbury's own evidence, which established that the purpose of registration was purely defensive. That being so, Cadbury failed to establish intention to use. The application ought to have been rejected."

7.4.4 Examination

Under s 39 Trade Marks Act 2002, the Commissioner must examine an application to determine whether it complies with the requirements of the Act. He or she will issue a compliance report within one to two weeks.

An IPONZ trade mark examiner will conduct a trade mark search for the purpose of identifying any confusingly similar marks (refer to 7.6.4 ("Comparison of trade marks") for a more detailed discussion of identical and similar marks).

The examiner will also examine the application, as to:

* Registrability of the mark (refer to 7.5 ("Registrability") and 7.6 ("Grounds for not registering") later in this chapter); and

* The specification of goods/services, to ensure that all goods/services are correctly classified and that the specification is not unduly broad (s 32). This aspect of the examination process is discussed at 7.3.2 ("Classification of goods and services") earlier in this chapter.

Under s 13(2) of the Act, a trade mark is registrable where:

* An application to register the trade mark was made in accordance with the Act;

* All prescribed fees have been paid in respect of the application; and

* The Commissioner is satisfied that there are no absolute or relative grounds that would prevent the registration of the trade mark.

In *Re Build-A-Bear Workshop Inc* 21/6/07, Miller J, HC Wellington CIV-2007-485-196; CIV-2007-485-775, the High Court confirmed the importance of the examination process in ensuring compliance with the requirements of the Act. Build-A-Bear appealed a decision of the Assistant Commissioner of Trade Marks rejecting its applications on the ground that the subject mark (a three-dimensional heart shape in respect of toys and retail services related to toys) was ineligible for registration because it had no distinctive character. Build-A-Bear argued that the Assistant Commissioner acted prematurely as, had there been any risk of legitimate use of the same mark by its trade competitors, that would have been revealed when the application was advertised. That argument was rejected by the High Court, which held, at para 12:

> "The Commissioner has a duty to consider whether an application complies with the Act, whether or not anyone opposes it. That is understandable, since registration confers a monopoly on the owner of the mark. There is a public interest involved. The Commissioner must be satisfied that the mark is eligible for registration before it is allowed to proceed to advertising, and if no notice of opposition is filed the Commissioner must register the mark. It follows that the Commissioner's initial consideration of the application before it is advertised is in no sense a preliminary hearing. The test is the same as that which is applied after an opposed proceeding. That is, the Commissioner must be satisfied that the mark complies with the requirements of the Act. The onus is on the applicant throughout, and the applicant may insist on a hearing at which it is able to submit evidence."

(1) *Maori trade marks*

All trade mark applications received by IPONZ will be assessed to determine whether they contain, or are derived from, a Maori sign, including text or imagery.

According to IPONZ Practice Guideline, "Examination of Trade Mark Applications", where a Maori sign is identified, IPONZ will add the trade mark type descriptor "Maori" to the application details. If the sign contains Maori imagery, appropriate New Zealand specific descriptors will also be assigned.

Under ss 177 and 178 Trade Marks Act 2002, the Commissioner is required to appoint an advisory committee "to advise the Commissioner whether the proposed use or registration of a trade mark that is, or appears to be, derivative of a Maori sign, including text or imagery, is, or is likely to be, offensive to Maori" (s 178). All applications identified as relating to Maori signs will be forwarded to that Maori Trade Marks Advisory Committee.

For more information on the Maori Advisory Committee and Maori trade marks, see the IPONZ Practice Guideline, "Maori Trade Marks Advisory Committee and Maori Trade Marks".

(2) *Prosecution time limits*

IPONZ anticipates that trade marks will usually be registered within 12 months of an application being lodged (reg 61). Accordingly, if after 10 months IPONZ has not received a response to a compliance report, a warning of abandonment notice will be issued. If a response to the compliance report is not received within the time prescribed in the notice, the application will be marked off as abandoned.

It is important to note that any subsequent correspondence from IPONZ after the initial compliance report, which contains a warning that the application will be abandoned if not placed in order for acceptance within a given time, may be considered a non-completion notice: IPONZ, "Information for Clients", No 7, 17 August 1999. Accordingly, such deadlines should always be adhered to.

(3) *Division and merger*

(a) *Division*

The concept of division is new to New Zealand trade mark law and is governed by regs 49-53 Trade Marks Regulations 2003. Division applies only to trade mark applications and can take a number of forms. The following areas can form the basis of division:

- Part of a series of marks, in the case of a series application;
- Classes within an application; or
- Specific goods or services within an application.

Division may be a useful tool in a number of situations. For instance, if an examiner opposes or objects to a particular matter within a trade mark application, the applicant may divide out the compliant matter (for example, a certain class of goods) so that the compliant part of the application may proceed to acceptance and registration, under a new application number. The divided applications can also be merged later, once any objections or oppositions have been addressed.

It is not permissible to divide out all of the marks in a series application as this would amount to a re-filing of that application, which is not allowable under the Act. Also, current IPONZ practice is to refuse to allow the division of a series application where IPONZ is of the view the marks in question do not constitute a valid series of marks.

An application for division of a trade mark application may be made in respect of one or more of the classes of goods/services specified in the initial application (reg 49(b)). Such a request must be for the same mark or series of marks as in the initial application. A request for the division of an application cannot be made for all of the classes in the initial application, where those classes include all of the goods and services in the initial application.

An application for division of a trade mark application may also be made for some of the goods and services specified in the initial application (reg 49(c)). Such a request must be for the same mark or series of marks as in the initial application.

The information required for an application for division is specified in reg 51:

- The applicant's name and address;
- If the applicant has an agent, the agent's name;
- The initial application number of the application for registration;
- In the case of division of a series of marks, the marks in the series to be divided out;
- In the case of division of classes, a list of the classes to be divided out;
- In the case of division of goods and services, a list of the goods and services to be divided out; and

- If a notice of opposition to the application for registration has been filed with the Commissioner, a statement that the opponent has consented to the application for division.

It is also possible to file a divisional application based on more than one initial application, provided that the initial applications all have the same filing date and are for the same mark. In addition, the goods and services specified in each class must be narrower in scope than those covered by each initial application. A multi-class divisional application based on more than one initial application may also be made where the initial applications are valid series applications.

The effect of division is defined by reg 52. If the Commissioner allows an application for division, the part that is divided out:

- Is independent of the original application(s) for registration; and

- Retains the filing date of the original application(s) for registration.

For more information on the IPONZ policy with respect to the division of trade mark applications, see IPONZ Practice Guideline, "Division".

(b) *Merger*

Regulation 54 Trade Marks Regulations 2003 provides that an applicant for registration of a trade mark, or the owner of a trade mark, may apply for the merger of two or more applications or registrations.

Pursuant to reg 55, an application for merger must be made in writing and contain the information specified in reg 56, namely:

- The name of the applicant for merger;

- If the applicant has an agent, the agent's name; and

- The number of each application or registration to be merged.

Regulation 54(2) provides that the Commissioner may merge the applications or registrations if they:

- Are for the same trade mark;

- Have the same filing dates and, if applicable, same convention priority dates;

- Have the same status, for example, accepted for registration, or registered;

- Are in the name of the same applicant or owner; and

- Are classified according to the same edition of the Nice Classification.

For more information regarding mergers, see IPONZ Practice Guideline, "Merger".

(4) *Applications which do not comply with statutory requirements*

If after examining the application the examiner considers the application does not comply, he or she will issue a notice of non-compliance under s 41 Trade Marks Act 2002. The non-compliance notice will specify the areas of non-compliance and provide the applicant with an opportunity to respond to the objection or amend the application to comply. The non-compliance notice may also specify certain conditions which must be met before the application can proceed.

The examiner may specify a deadline of not less than 12 months from the filing date for the applicant to either respond to the non-compliance notice or amend the application to comply with statutory requirements. If the applicant does not respond to the non-compliance notice before the deadline expires, the Commissioner must treat the application as abandoned.

If the applicant responds to a non-compliance notice and the examiner considers that the application does not comply with statutory requirements, he or she may issue further non-compliance notices under reg 61(2) Trade Marks Regulations 2003.

The IPONZ Practice Guideline, "Examination of Trade Mark Applications" has outlined further internal procedures with regard to non-compliance notices. IPONZ will send a written communication to the applicant which warns of the impending abandonment of the application 2 months before the deadline set in the most recent non-compliance report. This notice will confirm the deadline and warn the applicant that, in order to avoid abandonment, the applicant must either:

- Send a response to the compliance report on or prior to the expiry of the deadline; or

- Request a further extension of time and have received notification that that extension has been granted.

In *Lloyd IP Ltd's Application* (Commissioner's Decision No T11/2006, 26/6/06, Asst Commr Walden), the applicant sought a hearing in respect of IPONZ's decision to treat its application as abandoned through failure to respond to a final non-compliance notice sent after the applicant had failed to put its application in order for acceptance (despite obtaining a number of extensions to enable it to do so). The applicant claimed that it never received the non-compliance notice and therefore IPONZ had fallen into error by abandoning the application. The Assistant Commissioner agreed. The method of service of notices set out in s 197 of the Act provides that a document sent to any person by post will be deemed to have been delivered to that person at the time when the letter would, in the ordinary course of post, be delivered, provided delivery can be proved. There was no proof before the Assistant Commissioner that the non-compliance notice was actually posted. As that was a pre-condition to the exercise of the Commissioner's powers under s 41, the Assistant Commissioner found that IPONZ had fallen into error in treating the application as abandoned. The application was reinstated.

(5)   *Extensions of time*

Under reg 62 Trade Marks Regulations 2003, the Commissioner may grant an extension of time to comply with a notice of non-compliance provided that the request:

- Is in writing;

- Is received by IPONZ on or prior to the date to be extended; and

- Includes reasons for the extension.

Where an applicant seeks an extension of time, the request must be sufficiently detailed to demonstrate the existence of genuine and exceptional reasons for the extension. Each extension of time request will be assessed based on the information provided by the applicant in support of the request. In the absence of genuine and exceptional reasons, the request will be declined.

The Commissioner has no discretion to, and must not, grant an extension of time to respond to a non-compliance notice retrospectively. Where the Commissioner denies a request for an extension of time, the applicant may request a hearing, provided the request is made within 10 working days of the notification of refusal.

There are currently no fees for extension requests.

For more information on IPONZ policy with respect to extensions of time, see IPONZ Practice Guideline, "Examination of Trade Mark Applications".

(6)   *Abeyance*

Under s 44(1) Trade Marks Act 2002, if an applicant fails to respond to a notice of non-compliance in the time specified, the Commissioner must treat the application as abandoned.

However, s 44(2) provides that:

> "The Commissioner must not treat an application as abandoned under subsection (1) if the application is awaiting the outcome of—
>
> "(a)   opposition proceedings in respect of a prior application; or
>
> "(b)   cancellation, revocation, or invalidity proceedings in respect of a prior registration."

The IPONZ Practice Guideline, "Examination of Trade Mark Applications" also states that, where the circumstances set out in s 44(2) do not apply, an applicant may nonetheless request that its application be placed in abeyance where:

- The application is waiting the outcome of some other proceeding before the Commissioner of Trade Marks in New Zealand; or

- The application is awaiting the outcome of some other legal challenge in New Zealand.

Therefore, an application may be placed in abeyance (or frozen), pending the resolution of matters relating to:

- A hearing;

- An opposition or other legal challenge; or

- The citation of a confusingly similar mark, which has been removed from the Register for non-renewal, but for the purposes of the Act remains on the Register for a further period of one year from the date when the renewal fell due.

Any request for an application to be placed in abeyance:

- Must be made in writing;

- Must be received by IPONZ on or before the expiry of the deadline set by the compliance report; and

- Must set out the reasons for the request.

Under reg 63(1), if an applicant has been issued with a notice of non-compliance, the applicant must advise IPONZ if the application is awaiting the outcome of an opposition proceeding in respect of a prior application, or cancellation, revocation, or invalidity proceedings in respect of a prior registration. As aforesaid, the applicant's advice must be in writing, and be received by IPONZ prior to the expiry of the deadline specified in the notice of non-compliance (reg 63(2)). Upon receipt of the applicant's advice, the Commissioner will, upon verification of the facts, place the application in abeyance pending the outcome of the proceedings in question (reg 64).

Under reg 64(1), the applicant must notify IPONZ of the outcome of the proceedings in question as soon as practicable. On notice of the outcome of the proceedings, the Commissioner must extend the deadline for compliance by "a period that the Commissioner considers reasonable" (reg 64(2)).

7.4.5 Acceptance/advertisement

In the event that an application is examined and is considered to comply with statutory requirements, s 40 Trade Marks Act 2002 states that the Commissioner must, subject to any conditions the Commissioner thinks appropriate, accept the application. Once the Commissioner considers that the trade mark application complies, a Notice of Acceptance will issue. The Notice of Acceptance specifies the date on which the application will be published in the IPONZ journal for opposition purposes. A Notice of Opposition must be filed within 3 months of the advertisement date, unless an extension of time for filing the Notice of Opposition has been secured.

The opposition procedure is discussed in more detail at 7.7 ("Oppositions") later in this chapter.

7.4.6 Revocation of acceptance

Section 42 and regs 71 and 72 Trade Marks Regulations 2003 govern the revocation of an application's acceptance status. Acceptance will be revoked if the Commissioner is satisfied that:

- The application was accepted because of an error or omission made by the Commissioner; or

- Another application, that relates to the trade mark, has priority under s 36.

The first criterion is self-explanatory. The second criterion relates to situations where an application (application A) is filed (and subsequently accepted) after an earlier application (application B) has been accepted, where application A claims a convention priority date prior to the filing date of application B. In this case, where application A is identical or confusingly similar to application B, the acceptance of application B will be revoked.

Where the acceptance of an application is revoked, the application will be treated as if it had never been accepted. It will be re-examined and a notice of non-compliance will issue.

Before revocation of acceptance can be effected, the Commissioner must notify the applicant and the notification must:

- Specify the ground or grounds for revocation;

- Advise the applicant that the applicant may request a hearing;

- Specify a period of not less than one month after the applicant has received the notification for the applicant to request a hearing; and

- Advise the applicant that the Commissioner will revoke acceptance at the end of that period, if the applicant has not requested a hearing.

For an example of a case in which acceptance of a mark has been revoked based on a subsequent application being filed claiming an earlier convention priority date, see *Unilever Plc's Application* (Commissioner's Decision No T09/2006, 15/5/06, Asst Commr Walden). Unilever unsuccessfully appealed the decision of Assistant Commissioner Walden to the High Court (*Unilever Plc v The Commissioner of Trade Marks* 20/7/07, Wild J, HC Wellington CIV-2006-485-1208). The judgment is notable for its rejection of Unilever's argument that the Assistant Commissioner was required to consider the registrability of the earlier mark claiming priority under the Paris Convention (Unilever argued it was incapable of registration) when exercising his or her discretion under s 42 of the Act.

7.4.7 Registration

Once an accepted application is more than 6 months old and the opposition period has expired, IPONZ will issue the Certificate of Registration.

The 6-month delay is to accommodate overseas originating trade mark applications filed under the Paris Convention. At the time an application is accepted for registration, a subsequent convention application for a confusingly similar mark, filed within the 6-month convention period, may still be entitled to a priority date earlier than the accepted application.

By imposing a 6-month waiting period before registering an accepted application, IPONZ avoids registration of a mark in contravention of s 25 Trade Marks Act 2002.

7.4.8 Amendments

(1) *Amendment pre-registration*

There are certain situations where an application can be amended prior to registration. Sections 37 and 38 prescribe the types of amendments that can occur:

- The application may be withdrawn or the specification may be limited;

- The application may be altered at the request of the applicant, by the correction of:

  – The name or address of the applicant; or

  – An error or omission, the correction of which does not materially alter the meaning or scope of the application.

(a) *Amendment of a trade mark specification*

The IPONZ Practice Guideline, "Amendments to Trade Mark Applications" advises that amendments to the specification of goods or services of a trade mark application will only be allowed:

- If the amendment constitutes a narrowing of the specification; or

• If the amendment does not add anything new to the specification.

The Practice Guideline goes on to say that once the specification has been limited, the applicant may not subsequently request a reversion to the original or a previous specification. Thus, amendments to the specification of goods or services are only allowed if the new specification constitutes a limitation of the specification in existence at the time of the amendment request.

(b) *Correcting errors or omissions that do not materially alter the meaning or scope of the application*

The IPONZ Practice Guideline, "Amendments to Trade Mark Applications" advises that a correction will be deemed to materially alter the meaning or scope of the application if:

• Implementation of the correction would substantially alter the nature and scope of the rights that would accrue to the applicant upon registration; and/or

• Implementation of the correction would necessitate a different type of examination in order to determine whether the application complies with the statutory requirements.

(c) *Amendments to the trade mark*

Under the Trade Marks Act 2002, it is possible to amend the actual trade mark during the application stage. However, such an amendment will only be allowed if it does not alter the mark to any material extent.

According to the IPONZ Practice Guideline, "Amendments to Trade Mark Applications", an amendment will be considered to alter the mark to a material extent if:

• The correction would materially alter the visual, phonetic, or conceptual identity of the trade mark;

• The correction would require re-indexing of the trade mark and/or a new search and/ or examination of the trade mark application, due to the fact that distinctive material has been added or removed from the trade mark.

Amendments to the actual mark are not common, and the 2002 Act has tightened the law in this area. It will no longer be possible for a trade mark application to be amended by the addition of a house mark or logo, something which was possible under the Trade Marks Act 1953.

(d) *Other types of amendment*

(i) *Convention priority amendments*

Previous IPONZ policy with regard to the amendment of convention priority claims prescribed that the following amendments would not be allowed:

• Corrections whereby convention priority is claimed more than 2 days after filing as per reg 46 Trade Marks Regulations 2003; or

• Corrections whereby the convention priority date is changed to a date that is earlier than that originally claimed.

Notwithstanding this, in *Lino Manfrotto & Co SPA's Application* (Commissioner's Decision No T01/2006, 16/1/06, Asst Commr Walden), the applicant sought a hearing in respect of the Office's refusal to allow it to correct the date of the convention document stated in its application from 30 August 2004 to 13 August 2004. After considering the matter, the Assistant Commissioner held that, as there was no dispute regarding whether the application was made within the 6-month convention period, the correction would not materially alter the scope of the application and therefore complied with s 37(2)(b) of the Act.

In light of this decision, IPONZ will now allow any of the following types of corrections within 2 days of filing:

- Correction to the country in which the convention application was made; or

- Correction to the date the convention application was made; or

- Correction to the application number pertaining to the convention country application.

Such requests will be considered on their merits.

Corrections to the goods or services pertaining to the convention priority claim(s) may be considered corrections that materially alter the meaning or scope of the application. Such requests will also be considered on their merits.

(ii) **Amendment of class**

The Trade Marks Act 2002 allows for the amendment of errors or omissions relating to the class number or numbers specified by the application. Depending on the circumstances, IPONZ will allow amendments to:

- Correct a reference to an incorrect class number; or

- Allow an extra class or classes to be added, as long as the scope of the specification allows it. See reg 43 in this regard.

It is very important to note that an application of this nature may only be made within one month of the filing date of the application, and extra fees will be required. Regulation 43(4) does not allow for an extension of time in this situation.

(2) *Cancellation of registration*

(a) *Voluntary cancellation*

The registration of a trade mark may, at any time, be cancelled by the owner in relation to all or any of the goods or services in respect of which it is registered.

(b) *Rectification or correction of the Register*

Sections 76, 77, and 78 Trade Marks Act 2002 govern the amendment of registered trade marks. The types of amendments fall into two classes, namely, rectification or correction of the Register, and alteration in relation to registered trade marks.

Any person, who has an interest, may apply for the rectification of an error or omission in the Register of Trade Marks. Such an application can be made either to the Commissioner or to the Court. However, an application of this nature can not be made in respect of a matter that affects the validity of the trade mark registration. If the Commissioner or the Court decides to rectify the Register, the error or omission will normally be treated as if it had never existed. However the Commissioner or the Court does have the authority to decide to the contrary.

Sections 77 and 78 govern alterations to a registered trade mark. Section 77 states that the owner of a registered trade mark may not alter the registered mark after the actual date of registration. This relates to the mark itself and not ancillary information such as owner details and the specification of goods or services. However, the Commissioner may alter a number of matters once the trade mark has proceeded to registration, including:

- The owner's or licensee's name or address on the Register;

- Goods or services, or classes of goods or services, covered by the trade mark registration (union may be struck off);

- A memorandum relating to the trade mark may be entered, as long as it does not in anyway extend the rights given by the existing registration.

7.5 Registrability

Under the Trade Marks Act 1953, the Register was divided into two parts, known as Part A and Part B.

Part A was reserved for distinctive signs which were "inherently adapted to distinguish" or "[b]y reason of the use of the trade mark or of any other circumstances … in fact adapted to distinguish". Signs which were "*capable of* distinguishing" either "inherently" or "[b]y reason of the use of the trade mark or of any other circumstances … in fact", were registered in Part B (emphasis added).

The Trade Marks Act 2002 removed the distinction between Part A and Part B of the Register and created "absolute" and "relative" grounds upon which the Commissioner must refuse registration. The absolute grounds preventing registration are set out in ss 17-21, and the relative grounds in ss 22-26 of the Act.

The new registrability provisions in Part 2 of the Act are similar to the registrability provisions of the Trade Marks Act 1994 (UK) ("the 1994 Act"). As such, English case law decided under the 1994 Act is of assistance when interpreting and applying the provisions of Part 2. In addition, despite the change in legislative wording, many of the principles relevant under the 1953 Act continue to apply under Part 2.

7.5.1 Summary of basic requirements

For a mark to be registrable under the Trade Marks Act 2002, it must satisfy the definition of a trade mark under s 5(1) of the Act. In addition, under s 13(2), the trade mark must not be prevented from registration by any absolute or relative grounds under ss 17-28 of the Act. The absolute and relative grounds for refusing registration are discussed in more detail at 7.6 ("Grounds for not registering") later in this chapter.

7.5.2 What is a "trade mark"?

Section 5(1) Trade Marks Act 2002 defines a "trade mark" as a sign that is capable of being represented graphically and that is capable of distinguishing the goods or services of one person from those of another.

One definition of what is meant by "trade mark" was given in *Re Powell's Trade Mark* [1893] 2 Ch 388 (CA), at pp 403-404:

> "The function of a trade mark is to give an indication to the purchaser or possible purchaser as to the manufacture or quality of the goods — to give an indication to his eye of the trade source from which the goods come, or the trade hands through which they pass on their way to the market. It tells the person who is about to buy, or considering whether he shall buy, that what is presented to him is either what he has known before under the similar name, as coming from a source with which he is acquainted, or that it is what he has heard of before as coming from that similar source."

The statutory definition incorporates all "signs" that are capable of functioning as a trade mark, that is, by distinguishing the goods or services of one person from those of another.

7.5.3 What is a "sign"?

Section 5 Trade Marks Act 2002 defines a "sign" as including:

"(a) a brand, colour, device, heading, label, letter, name, numeral, signature, shape, smell, sound, taste, ticket, or word; and

"(b) any combination of signs."

The use of the word "including" means that this is not an exhaustive definition of what may be a sign for the purposes of trade mark registration. Instead the definition provides examples of the forms that trade marks may take.

7.5.4 The meaning of "capable of being represented graphically"

Under s 5(1) Trade Marks Act 2002, a sign must be "capable of being represented graphically" to be registrable as a trade mark. Accordingly, all applications to register a trade mark must contain a clear graphic representation of the mark (see 7.4.1(4) ("Clear representation") earlier in this chapter). This requirement is designed to enable the trade mark to be recorded and published in the Journal and on the Register. It allows third parties to determine the scope of rights that have been granted to a trade mark owner by searching the Register, and to assess whether their activities are likely to infringe those rights.

The majority of trade marks should be capable of graphical representation without difficulty. For example, in the case of a word mark, a logo, or a picture, a facsimile of the trade mark will suffice. Word marks should be shown in upper case unless the typeface or presentation is of significance to the protection sought by registration. Logo or picture marks should be shown clearly enough so that all details of the protection sought are evident.

More care must be taken where the trade mark is not a word or a pictorial mark, as in the case of smell or sound marks. In order to represent such marks graphically, a verbal description of the mark is required. For example:

- "The mark consists of the sound of a dog barking."

- "The trade mark is a squeak produced by the friction of thumb and forefinger on dishware." (Registration No 247094, covering "hand dishwashing products".)

- "The mark consists of the words 'The Warehouse, The Warehouse, Where Everyone Gets A Bargain' in conjunction with the listed musical notes." (Registration No 252035, covering wholesaling, retailing, and other services.)

- "The mark consists of the smell of cinnamon." (Application No 248231, covering "pharmaceutical preparations and substances". This application was abandoned by the applicant and did not mature to registration.)

Accurate representations of the mark are important. The trade mark will be examined in the exact form shown on the application. If accepted and registered, the representation of the trade mark provided will be shown in the Register and on the Certificate of Registration. Errors in the trade mark application may not be corrected once the mark is registered (see 7.4 ("Trade mark application process") earlier in this chapter).

7.5.5 What is meant by "capable of distinguishing"?

Under s 5(1) Trade Marks Act 2002, a sign must be "capable of distinguishing" the goods or services of one trader from those of another in order to be registrable as a trade mark. The only way that a sign can fulfil this function is if it is distinctive.

There are two ways that a sign may be distinctive:

- The sign may possess "inherent distinctiveness", that is, the sign itself possesses an intrinsic capacity to distinguish. An example of such a sign is an invented word, such as ZESPRI.

- Alternatively, a sign may acquire "factual distinctiveness" through use. In this case, while the sign is not inherently adapted to distinguish, consumers have come to recognise the sign as identifying the goods or services of the applicant.

In *McCain Foods (Aust) Pty Ltd v Conagra Inc* [2002] 3 NZLR 40 (CA), the Court of Appeal considered the meaning of the phrase "capable of distinguishing" in the context of the 1953 Act. In that case, Conagra applied to register HEALTHY CHOICE as a trade mark under Part B of the Register. McCain opposed the registration on the ground, inter alia, that the mark lacked the necessary distinctiveness to qualify for registration as a trade mark.

At first instance, the Assistant Commissioner allowed the registration in Part B. On appeal to the High Court, Wild J accepted that to be registrable, the mark must be both inherently capable of distinguishing and, by reason of use or other circumstances, in fact capable of distinguishing. On the facts, Wild J found that these requirements had been satisfied and upheld the Assistant Commissioner's decision. McCain Foods appealed the decision.

In the Court of Appeal, Gault P held, at paras 14 and 15, in a judgment delivered for the Court, that:

> "Since the quality of being capable of distinguishing must be present before the date of registration (it must be a trade mark), the meaning to be given to the quality of capable of distinguishing must involve an existing capacity rather than merely a capability (in the sense of potential) for becoming distinctive in the future. That must be correct; otherwise it would be possible to obtain registration and sue for

infringement before a mark had realised the very quality essential to any trade mark — that of distinguishing the goods or services of the proprietor from those of competitors …

"Accordingly, to be capable of distinguishing, a mark must at the date of registration have that as an inherent quality or have it demonstrated in fact by prior use or 'other circumstances'. There seems no reason why subsequent events might not constitute 'other circumstances': where they assist in establishing the essential quality at the time of registration."

His Honour also cited Lord Parker in *Registrar of Trade Marks v W & G du Cros Ltd* [1913] AC 624 (HL), at pp 634-635:

"The applicant for registration in effect says, 'I intend to use this mark as a trade mark, i.e. for the purpose of distinguishing my goods from the goods of other persons' and the Registrar or the Court has to determine before the mark be admitted to registration whether it is of such a kind that the applicant, quite apart from the effects of registration, is likely or unlikely to attain the object he has in view. The applicant's chances of success in this respect must, I think, largely depend upon whether other traders are likely, in the ordinary course of their business and without any improper motive, to desire to use the same mark, or some mark nearly resembling it, upon or in connection with their own goods. It is apparent from the history of trade marks in this country that both the Legislature and the Courts have always shown a natural disinclination to allow any person to obtain registration under the Trade Marks Act a monopoly in what others may legitimately desire to use."

The same passage was cited by the Court of Appeal in *Cadbury Ltd v Effem Foods Ltd* 20/7/07, CA247/05; [2007] NZCA 303 when determining whether Cadbury's application for PURPLE was distinctive of confectionery products. The application was ultimately rejected due to a lack of distinctiveness, although the case is notable for the manner in which the Court of Appeal reached that conclusion, confirming:

- There is no requirement to limit the goods (which other traders might legitimately wish to use the mark on or in relation to) to the same goods covered by the application;

- The chilling effect of possible proceedings on the activities of other traders (should the mark be registered) might be relevant; and

- It is legitimate for the Court to have regard to the reaction of consumers — as consumer confusion will likely inhibit traders in their use of the mark.

Cadbury's application had earlier been rejected by the High Court (*Effem Foods Ltd v Cadbury Ltd* 12/12/05, MacKenzie J, HC Wellington CIV-2004-484-2127) on the basis that it did not meet the *W & G Du Cros* test. The High Court held that, in relation to that test, there is no requirement to limit the goods (that other traders might wish to use the mark on or in relation to) to goods identical with those covered by the subject mark. Thus, it was permissible for the High Court to consider use of the mark in relation to purple coloured goods, notwithstanding Cadbury's voluntary exclusion of "goods being coloured purple" from the registration.

Adopting that broader view, the High Court held that defining the goods which are to be distinguishable by reference to a characteristic which does not alter their inherent nature will not achieve distinctiveness. It considered that those in the trade seeking to distinguish the goods in question would not be expected to know that purple ice cream, for example, was to be regarded as a different category of goods from non-purple ice cream. Even if the person had knowledge of the details of the registration, a degree of mental agility would be needed to understand, after encountering the word PURPLE in relation to goods, that, if the goods were not coloured purple, they would be Cadbury's goods but, if they were coloured purple, they could belong to another trader.

Further, the High Court held, if an advertisement related to purple ice cream, it would be impossible to distinguish whether the word PURPLE was used to indicate that it was Cadbury's ice cream without seeing the goods or a coloured picture of the goods. Even then, if the packaging was not purple, it would be necessary to open the container to ascertain if the contents were purple. Thus, to allow the registration of the word PURPLE would in effect extend the protection of the mark to purple goods, notwithstanding the voluntary exclusion.

On appeal, Cadbury took issue with the approach of the High Court on a number of grounds, including that MacKenzie J was wrong to take into account goods which are expressly excluded from the specification (ie purple goods) in assessing distinctiveness, as such approach is contrary to the plain words of the legislation. The Court of Appeal disagreed, holding, at paras 28-29 and 32:

> "We do not accept Cadbury's criticisms of the Judge's decision. We, like the Judge, are unable to divorce the word PURPLE from the colour purple, despite Cadbury's submission as to other connotations of the word such as royal, imperial and regal. We also consider that the Judge was correct to examine the question of whether other traders would be inhibited in their use of the word PURPLE in relation to goods in the same market as those for which registration is sought. As Effem submits, the test of distinctiveness is wider than merely whether use of the mark would lead to successful infringement proceedings. This means that a narrow view restricting the inquiry to the actual goods in relation to which registration is sought would be inappropriate, despite the terms of s 14(2) of the TMA. Section 14(2) may define distinctiveness for the purposes of s 14(1)(e). It does not define it for the purpose of the extra-statutory requirement of distinctiveness under the other paragraphs of s 14(1).

> "Arguably, the s 14(2) definition may also be read in light of the extended reach of infringement proceedings under the Trade Marks Act 2002 (TMA 2002). While the test for distinctiveness is wider than that of whether infringement proceedings would be successful, it may include a consideration of whether infringement proceedings might be brought. The possibility of infringement proceedings would clearly inhibit other traders in their legitimate use of the word. Under s 89(1) of the TMA 2002, which applies to infringement proceedings after 20 August 2003, the use of the word PURPLE on similar goods to those specified in the registration would constitute infringement (subject to any defences, such as for honest practices under s 95 of the TMA 2002 which, as noted above at [26], are ignored for these purposes). It is uncertain the extent to which purple goods might be held to be

similar to non-purple goods and thus the extent to which the use of PURPLE even on purple goods might constitute infringement. This is particularly the case as there remains a question as to the extent of any exclusion — whether it covers goods coloured lilac for example — see at [10] above.

•   •   •   •   •

"We also consider that it was legitimate for the Judge to have had regard to the reaction of consumers. The *Du Cros* test is whether other traders would be inhibited in their legitimate use of the word PURPLE. However, if consumer confusion is likely, then this will, in all likelihood, inhibit traders in their use of the word. We refer to Kitchen and others *Kerly's Law of Trade Marks and Trade Names* (14ed 2005) at [8.121] - [8.123] where it is stated that the ultimate source of evidence as to whether distinctiveness has been acquired comes from the body of consumers for the goods or services in question. We also note the European test, as set out in [*Koninklijke KPN Nederland NV v Benelux-Merkenbureau (C-363/99) [2005] 3 WLR 649; [2004] ETMR 57 (ECJ)*, at para 34] ('POSTKANTOOR'). That case held that the test of distinctiveness is to be assessed first by reference to the goods and services and then by reference to the perception of them by the relevant public, which consists of average consumers of the goods or services in question who are reasonably well informed and reasonably observant and circumspect."

In *Fredco Trading Ltd v Miller* 16/12/02, Venning J, HC Auckland CIV-2004-404-895, Miller was the registered proprietor of a trade mark relating to the shape of a tie used to secure kiwifruit vines ("the Klipon vine tie"). Fredco had been accused of infringement and brought separate proceedings seeking a declaration of invalidity under s 73 of the 2002 Act. In support of its application, Fredco claimed, inter alia, that the shape of the vine tie was not a valid trade mark under s 18(1)(a) of the Act.

In order to determine whether the sign was a trade mark for the purposes of s 18(1)(a), Venning J had to determine whether the shape was capable of distinguishing the goods of one trader from those of another in accordance with the definition of trade mark under s 5(1) of the Act.

Venning J cited, at para 30, Lord Parker's speech from *W & G du Cros Ltd* (above) and, at para 32, Gault P's judgment for the Court of Appeal in *McCain* (above). His Honour noted, at para 33, that in *Philips v Remington* [1999] RPC 809, Aldous LJ found, at pp 817-818, that the phrase "capable of distinguishing" required consideration of the features of the trade mark itself, not the results of its use (ie, capability of distinguishing concerned inherent distinctiveness not factual distinctiveness).

Venning J applied *McCain*, asking, at para 34, whether the shape of the Klipon vine tie had an inherent quality about it, or by use or other circumstances had acquired the capability of distinguishing it from other vine ties. His Honour noted that consumers did in fact distinguish between the Klipon vine tie and its competitor products based on shape, and concluded, at para 35, that the Klipon vine tie was factually distinctive and therefore capable of distinguishing the Klipon vine tie from competing products as the phrase had been interpreted by the Court of Appeal in *McCain*.

The decision of Venning J was upheld on appeal (*Fredco Trading Ltd v Miller* (2006) 8 NZBLC 101,761 (CA)).

In *Colgate Palmolive Co's Applications* (Commissioner's Decision No T4/2004, 10/3/04, Asst Commr Frankel), the Applicant unsuccessfully attempted to register two trade marks depicting two-dimensional slug representations of tooth paste containing stripes in particular colour combinations. Evidence was provided that the Applicant was not the only trader using such slug representations. In addition, there was insufficient evidence that the slugs were actually used to identify the goods of the Applicant and therefore functioned as a badge of origin. The Assistant Commissioner relied expressly on *Yakult Honsha Kk's Trade Mark Application* [2001] RPC 39 in which Laddie J stated "The fact that a particular design is eye catching because it is unusual or decorative is not enough by itself. At all times the Registry has to ask whether the design is distinctive as a badge or origin … the relevant question is not whether it is of memorable appearance, but whether by itself its appearance would convey trade mark significance to the average consumer".

Note, however, that the European Court of Justice has confirmed that a trade mark which has only been used in combination with other marks can acquire distinctiveness in its own right, if it is shown that "the relevant consumer groups understand that the element in question, if used separately, designates a product as originating from a specific undertaking, thus distinguishing it from products of other undertakings": *Société des Produits Nestlé SA v Mars UK Ltd* Case No C-353/03 (ECJ). This decision is particularly relevant to applications to register shape or single colour marks which will rarely be the only trade mark applied to a product. Shape and colour marks are discussed in more detail at 7.6 ("Grounds for not registering"). The decision of the European Court of Justice was cited with approval by the Court of Appeal of New Zealand in *Fredco Trading Ltd v Miller* (2006) 8 NZBLC 101,761 (CA), at para 81, in response to a submission by the appellant in that case that the shape trade mark was a "limping" mark because it was used in conjunction with the distinctive word "Klipon". These cases are discussed in more detail at 7.6.1(3) ("Factual distinctiveness") later in this chapter.

Finally, it is not necessary that the mark exhibits a "capacity to distinguish" particular goods or services in respect of everyone who may be exposed to the trade mark. Thus, in *Aqua Technics Pool & Spa Centre NZ Ltd v Aqua-Tech Ltd* 22/3/07, CA257/05, the appellant challenged a decision of the High Court permitting the respondent, Aqua-Tech Ltd, to register the trade mark AQUA TECH in relation to certain goods including pools and spa pools. One of the grounds upon which the High Court's decision was challenged was that the evidence of the respondent showed use of AQUA TECH as a masthead on a trade brochure only and evidence of use of the mark on physical goods was equivocal at best. The appellant therefore argued that the evidence showed use of the AQUA TECH mark as a service mark to indicate the retail source of goods only, and the respondent's application to register the mark in relation to goods should be refused. This argument was rejected by the Court of Appeal which, at para 40, confirmed the finding in the High Court that it is sufficient for those in the trade to see a connection between the respondent and the relevant goods by means of the catalogue. The Court of Appeal continued, at para 50:

> "In this case, even if the ultimate buyer did not know that Aqua Tech was the source of the pools, Cascade [a related trade supplier of pools manufactured by the respondent] would certainly know that. Because of this connection with the quality of the goods, Venning J was correct to conclude that the respondent was not using the mark simply as a provider of services."

Leave to appeal to the Supreme Court was refused: *Aqua Technics Pool & Spa Centre NZ Ltd v Aqua-Tech Ltd* 9/7/07, SC24/07; [2007] NZSC 52.

7.5.6 Registrability — specific examples

(1) *Signatures*

Due to their inherent distinctiveness, the signature of an applicant or his or her predecessor in title is prima facie registrable, although the protection afforded by the registration of such a mark is very narrow.

(2) *Invented words*

A trade mark which comprises an invented word or words will be prima facie registrable. However, there is considerable debate in case law on what actually constitutes an "invented word".

Despite its age, the leading case on the subject is *SOLIO (Eastman Photographic Materials Co Ltd's Application* (1898) 15 RPC 476 (HL)), in which Lord Shand made the following comments:

> "It is not possible to define the extent of invention required, but the words, I think, should be clearly and substantially different from any word in ordinary and common use. The employment of a word in such use, with a diminutive or a short and meaningless syllable added to it, or a mere combination of two known words, would not be an invented word; and a word would not be 'invented' which, with some trifling addition or very trifling variation, still leaves the word one which is well known or in ordinary use, and which would be quite understood as intended to convey the meaning of such a word."

(a) *Allusion to goods or services permitted*

According to the *SOLIO* case, an invented word does not have to be totally meaningless, but can instead contain a "skilful and covert allusion" to the nature of the goods or services.

However, an invented word cannot contain an obvious allusion to the character or quality of the goods — for example ARSENOID in relation to arsenide: *Yalding Mfg Co Ltd Trade Mark* (1916) 33 RPC 285.

(b) *Obviousness of meaning relevant consideration*

The degree of inventiveness is immaterial. What is relevant is obviousness of meaning, as opposed to obviousness of derivation.

In *Hallgarten's (S F & O's) Application* (1949) 66 RPC 105, a p 107, the word WHISQUEUR was held to be registrable in Part A as an invented word in respect of liqueurs containing whisky:

> "Although its derivation from the words 'whisky liqueur' is somewhat obvious, nevertheless the word whisqueur is not in my opinion merely a misspelling, nor a trifling variation of these words compounded, particularly when one considers that it is a word of two syllables, whereas the words 'whisky liqueur' contain four syllables."

(c) *Other examples*

Other cases have held that:

- Invented words cannot be misspellings of known words. For example, the trade mark ORLWOOLA was rejected as a misspelling of "all wool": *ORLWOOLA Trade Mark* (1909) 26 RPC 683.

- An invented word may comprise two foreign words joined together, provided the languages in question were not commonly known — for example PARLOGRAPH in relation to sound-recording and reproducing machines and parts and accessories: *In re Carl Lindstroem Aktiengesellschaft's Trade Mark* [1914] 2 Ch 103.

- A registration for DIABOLO for tops (for use in a rehashed version of the once popular game, "Devil on Two Sticks") was cancelled on the basis that the word was not an invented word, despite the word not being a word in the English language at the date of registration. It was held that as a variant of the Italian word meaning "the devil", the meaning of the mark would be known to "the ordinary Englishman": *Philippart v William Whiteley Ltd* (1908) 25 RPC 565.

(3) *Surnames*

Like any other sign, surnames that have no distinctive character are not registrable pursuant to s 18(1)(b) of the Act. Uncommon surnames or surnames with a better known meaning are therefore more likely to be prima facie registrable.

Previously IPONZ practice was to assess the registrability of a mark that had surname significance based on the following factors:

- How common the surname is in New Zealand;

- The size of the market (in terms of the number of traders in it) in the goods or services specified in the application; and

- How the mark is likely to be understood in light of the nature of the goods or services.

To assess how common a surname is in New Zealand, previous IPONZ practice was to check the number of occurrences of that surname on the New Zealand Electoral Roll. Based on the number of times the name appeared on the Roll, IPONZ would then make a decision as to the eligibility of the mark for registration.

However, following the European Court of Justice decision in *Nichols Plc v Registrar of Trade Marks* [2005] All ER (EC) 1; [2005] 1 WLR 1418; [2004] ECR 8499; [2005] RPC 12 (ECJ), IPONZ now considers that it is not appropriate to apply a strict criteria to determine whether a surname may or may not be distinctive of the goods or services in question. In light of the ECJ's decision, IPONZ no longer raises concerns as to the eligibility of a mark that consists of a surname solely on the basis that the surname appears a certain number of times on the New Zealand Electoral Roll. Instead, IPONZ will consider whether the mark is capable of distinguishing the goods or services of one trader from the same or similar goods or services supplied by other traders.

Therefore, according to IPONZ Practice Guideline, "Absolute Grounds: Distinctiveness", when assessing the registrability of a mark that has surname significance, IPONZ will now consider the following factors:

- Whether the mark is capable of distinguishing the goods or services of one trader from the same or similar goods or services supplied by other traders; and

- Whether the surname has another meaning which may give rise to an objection to registration under s 18(1)(c) of the Act.

(4) *Foreign words*

Marks that comprise foreign words may be prohibited from registration under s 18(1)(b), (c), or (d) (as applicable).

When assessing the registrability of a mark comprising a foreign word or words, IPONZ will consider whether the foreign language concerned is generally known to the relevant class of persons (being a class of persons in New Zealand). If the foreign word is unlikely to be understood by the relevant New Zealand trade or consumer, it is unlikely registration will be refused.

IPONZ Practice Guideline, "Absolute Grounds: Distinctiveness" gives the following example of how this practice may be applied. KIKU, the Japanese word for chrysanthemum, was found to be registrable in Ireland for perfumes and cosmetic preparations by the Irish Supreme Court, as the average consumer would need to have the word translated from the Japanese in order to know its meaning (*Kiku Trade Mark* [1978] FSR 246).

In *Tip Top Investments Ltd's Application* (Commissioner's Decision No T278, 13/4/04, Asst Commr Walden), the applicant was permitted to register DULCE DE LUCHE in class 30 for "ice creams, ice cream products; frozen and chilled confectionary; ices; desserts in this class" despite their being evidence that the trade mark was "sweet milk" in a Spanish language. Upon reviewing the authorities the Commissioner concluded that the fact the mark consisted of descriptive words in a foreign language did not automatically make it ineligible for registration. It was necessary to determine how obscure the foreign words in the mark were to the ordinary New Zealander in order to determine the weight which should be given to the English translation. The Assistant Commissioner considered that even if the connection between DULCE DE LUCHE and the English translation "sweet milk" could be made by the average consumer, the term was meaningless in relation to the applicant's goods and therefore not descriptive.

Similarly, in *Automobile Club de l'Ouest, ACO's Application* (Commissioner's Decision No T02/2005, 18/1/05, Asst Commr Walden), the Assistant Commissioner permitted registration of LE MANS despite its geographical significance on the basis that the ordinary New Zealander would associate the trade mark with the applicant's well known car race rather than a geographical location. This decision was unsuccessfully appealed: *Automobile Club de L'Ouest ACO v South Pacific Tyres NZ Ltd* 29/3/06, Wild J, HC Wellington CIV-2005-485-248.

See also Trade Mark Practice Guideline Amendment 2006/13 — Translation.

(5) *Shapes*

Despite the definition of "sign" being inclusive, before the introduction of the 2002 Act the question of whether it was possible to register three-dimensional shapes as trade marks, where the trade mark in question was simply the shape of goods themselves, or a bottle or container remained vexed.

The leading authority on this topic was the House of Lords' decision in *Coca-Cola Trade Marks* (1986) 103 RPC 421. The case concerned Coca-Cola's unsuccessful attempt to register its "waisted" bottle as a three-dimensional trade mark (although, a picture of the bottle was successfully registered).

In rejecting the application, Lord Templeman made the following observations, at pp 457-458:

> "The respondent registrar of trade marks has always taken the view that the function of trade mark legislation is to protect the mark but not the article which is marked … The word 'mark' both in its normal meaning and in its statutory definition is apt only to describe something which distinguishes goods rather than the goods themselves. A bottle is a container not a mark."

Lord Templeman also referred to Lindley LJ's observations in *Re James's Trade Mark* (1886) 33 Ch D 392 (CA), at p 395:

> "A mark must be something distinct from the thing marked. The thing itself cannot be a mark of itself."

However in 1994 the definition of "trade mark" was amended so that it specifically referred to a new, inclusive, definition of "sign". As this amendment was to give effect to the obligations under the TRIPS agreement, it was interpreted by IPONZ as acknowledging the potential registrability of a broader range of "signs" as trade marks (including smells, sounds, colours, and shapes) notwithstanding that "shape" was not mentioned in the definition of "sign". Accordingly IPONZ began accepting shape trade marks applications provided they met the other legislative requirements for registrability (ie, distinctiveness etc).

However, in an IPONZ decision involving applications filed by Société des Produits Nestlé SA to register the shapes of its two- and four-finger KIT KAT products as three-dimensional trade marks, in relation to confectionery products and associated goods: *Société des Produits Nestlé SA v Horizon Biscuit Co Ltd* (Commissioner's Decision No T45/2002, 30/8/02, Asst Commr Brown QC), the Assistant Commissioner declined to follow IPONZ practice, preferring instead the reasoning of the *Coca-Cola* case.

One of the grounds of opposition was that the alleged trade marks were nothing more than outline shapes of chocolate bars, and as such, were purely descriptive of the goods themselves. In his decision, Assistant Commissioner Brown QC made the following comments, at p 14:

> "The absence of reference to 'shape' [in the section 2(1) definition of 'sign'] cannot be attributed to legislative oversight. The addition of 'colour' to the list of items which had been included in the previous definition of 'mark' demonstrates that the legislature's attention was directed to the scope of the definition … Consequently, approaching the matter solely on the basis of the definition of 'sign', I consider that that definition does not include three-dimensional shapes of products."

and, at p 16:

> "Consequently, I consider that the ratio of the Coca Cola Trade Marks case continues to apply in New Zealand. Hence it is my view that three-dimensional

shapes of products are not 'signs' within the meaning of that term as introduced in the 1994 Amendment."

Notwithstanding this decision, in its IPONZ, "Information for Clients", No 22, 29 November 2002 IPONZ indicated that it would continue to treat shape marks as registrable under the Act on the basis that the definition of "sign" was an inclusive one.

The issue was put to rest with the enactment of the 2002 Act which specifically includes "shape" in the s 5 definition of "sign".

Current IPONZ practice with regard to the registrability of shape marks is set out in IPONZ Practice Guideline, "Absolute Grounds: Distinctiveness". According to the guidelines, shapes are registrable as trade marks unless:

- The sign is not a trade mark;

- The mark has no distinctive character;

- The mark consists only of signs or indications that serve in trade to designate characteristics of the goods or services; or

- The mark consists only of signs or indications that have become customary in the current language or in the bona fide and established practices of trade.

In addition to the above, the guideline states that IPONZ will consider the following matters when assessing whether a shape mark has distinctive character:

- Whether the mark is the shape of the goods themselves;

- Whether the shape is common to the specific trade, for example, as packaging;

- Whether the shape is in some way functional, for example, resulting from the nature of the goods themselves, or necessary to achieve a technical result.

A shape that falls within one or more of the above categories is unlikely to have distinctive character (IPONZ Practice Guideline, "Absolute Grounds: Distinctiveness").

Although the guidelines acknowledge the registrability of shape marks per se, in practice meeting the criteria has proven difficult, with many applicants being rejected on the basis that the shape of the goods is functional and therefore lacks distinctiveness as a trade mark.

For example in *Mag Instrument Inc's Application* (Commissioner's Decision No T55/2002, 4/11/02, Asst Commr Frankel) Mag Instrument had applied to register the shape of its MAG-LITE™ as a three-dimensional trade mark. While the Assistant Commissioner accepted that shapes are included in the definition of "sign" under the Act, she held that applications to register such marks must nonetheless meet the other registrability criteria set out in the Act, commenting, at p 3:

> "no doubt a truly distinctive shape might be one that has excellent design features, but the test for trade mark distinctiveness is not one of 'eye appeal' which is part of the test for design registrability."

and, at p 8:

> "A shape determined by function is unlikely to be distinctive because other traders may legitimately desire to use it."

After canvassing a number of earlier decisions, the Assistant Commissioner concluded that for the shape of a product to be inherently distinctive, it has to identify the origin of the goods before the public is educated about its use. The shape must be considered on its own (assuming no use), and it is not, of itself, sufficient that the shape is different to other goods of the same kind. Applying those criteria, the Assistant Commissioner concluded that the shape of the MAG-LITE™ torch was not inherently distinctive. Accepting that there was something aesthetically pleasing about the shape of the torches themselves, she nonetheless found no evidence to suggest that the shape and overall appearance were used as an indication of origin such that the shape would function as a trade mark. For similar reasons Mag Instrument was unable to show that the shape of its MAG-LITE™ torch had acquired trade mark significance through use.

Similarly, in *Philips Electronics NV's Application* (Commissioner's Decision No T23/2003, 4/8/03, Asst Commr Frankel), the Assistant Commissioner upheld the Intellectual Property Office's refusal to register as a trade mark the shape of a three-headed electric shaver. The Assistant Commissioner was primarily concerned that the shape of the goods was entirely functional, was a representation of part of the goods and was descriptive of the goods, and that other traders were likely to use the same or similar three-dimensional shape for their own electrical shaving apparatus. Hence registration was declined.

In *Société des Produits Nestlé SA's Application* (Commissioner's Decision No T14/2005, 9/5/05, Asst Commr Walden), an application to register the shape of the LIFESAVER sweet (without the LIFESAVER trade mark embossed on it) was successfully opposed by Effem Foods Ltd and Cadbury Ltd on the basis that it lacked both inherent and acquired distinctiveness.

In *Beaute Prestige International's Application* (Commissioner's Decision No T20/2006, 18/09/06, Asst Commr Walden), the applicant unsuccessfully applied to register two three-dimensional shapes of a container in class 3. The Assistant Commissioner deemed each mark to have no distinctive character, as the shapes did not appear to have any unusual features that a consumer could use as a reference point, were largely functional and were therefore likely to be something which other traders without improper motive might wish to use. The Assistant Commissioner also considered one of the marks too close to an earlier registration for a similar container held by the same applicant.

(a) *Can the goods themselves be the mark?*

In *Fredco Trading Ltd v Miller* 16/12/02, Venning J, HC Auckland CIV-2004-404-895, the Court considered an application for a declaration of invalidity of a registered trade mark for the shape of a plastic kiwifruit vine tie ("the Klipon vine tie"). The application was made, inter alia, on the grounds that the shape was incapable of distinguishing the goods or services of one person from those of another person and that it lacked distinctive character (under s 18(1)(a) and (b) respectively).

Venning J concluded that the shape was a sign and did meet the requirements of a trade mark in accordance with s 5 of the Act, ie, it was capable of distinguishing the goods or services of one person from those of another person (s 18(1)(a)).

His Honour went on to find that, though the mark was not inherently distinctive in terms of s 18(1)(b), it had, on the evidence, acquired a distinctive character through use sufficient to support its registration under s 18(2) Trade Marks Act 2002. Venning J relied upon the following evidence:

- Miller was the manufacturer/distributor of the Klipon vine tie in New Zealand for over 24 years;

- Miller sold over 1 billion units in 24 years;

- Consumers distinguished a competing product from the Klipon vine tie;

- The Klipon vine tie was marketed by its shape along with the brand name;

- Consumers used the shape to identify the product;

- Alternative shapes may have been used to achieve the same purpose; and

- The shape contained aesthetic components.

The application for a declaration of invalidity was declined and the decision of Venning J was upheld on appeal (*Fredco Trading Ltd v Miller* (2006) 8 NZBLC 101,761 (CA)).

One of the questions considered by the Court of Appeal in *Fredco Trading* was whether the goods themselves could be the mark. The appellant submitted that, where the sign is the goods, the mark cannot convey information about the origin of the goods because, if the shape is removed, there is nothing left to comprise a mark. The Court of Appeal rejected this submission, citing with approval the following passage from the judgment of French J in *Kenman Kandy Australia Pty Ltd v Registrar of Trade Marks* (2002) 122 FCR 494; 56 IPR 30 (FCA), at para 45:

> "The shape which distinguishes the goods may be their shape taken as a whole. The inclusion of 'shape' in the definition of 'sign' stands against the suggestion that it can never be an attribute separate from the goods to which it relates. It mandates consideration of shape as a distinctive attribute although not a necessary feature of the particular goods."

The Court of Appeal concluded, at para 42:

> "Any other approach would not give effect to the statutory recognition that a shape can be a mark."

(b) *Other factors*

Applicants for registration of shape marks may also find the European Court of First Instance's decision in *Nestlé Waters France v Office for Harmonisation in the Internal Market* [2003] ECR II-5207; [2004] ETMR 41 (CFI) helpful. In September 1998, Perrier Vittel France filed an application for a community trade mark for registration of a three-dimensional sign comprising the features of its Perrier water bottle. In May 2000, the examiner refused the application on the basis that it was devoid of distinctive character. That decision was upheld by the Fourth Board of Appeal in July 2002. Nestlé appealed, and the European Court of First Instance issued its decision in December 2003.

The Court of First Instance found that the Board of Appeal erred in finding that the mark was devoid of distinctive character and annulled its decision. In reaching its conclusion, the Court made four crucial findings:

- **Definition of trade origin**: the essential function of a trade mark is to define "trade origin". Trade marks enable consumers who have bought products bearing them to identify them at a later date and repeat the experience (if it is positive) or avoid it (if it is negative). If the trade mark does not do this, it cannot act as a badge of origin and is not capable of distinguishing. Distinctiveness must be assessed only in relation to the goods or services for which registration is sought and in relation to the public perception of those goods.

- **Public perception of trade marks**: the way in which the public perceives trade marks is influenced by its level of attention which varies according to the category of goods or services in question. In the case of mineral waters, the Court acknowledged that for many years operators within that sector sought to distinguish their products from those of others by the shape of their packaging. Thus, the purchasing public had been educated to distinguish products of different trade origin in the mineral water sector by means of the shape of packaging. The Court explicitly recognised that purchasers were able to perceive the shape of packaging of the goods concerned as an indication of commercial origin, insofar as that shape presents characteristics which were sufficient to hold the consumer's attention.

- **Classic shape**: in relation to the Board of Appeal's refusal of the application on the basis that it considered the general shape of the bottle to be "classic", the Court of First Instance, while acknowledging that some of the individual components may be non-distinctive, found that the combination was distinctive. Thus, the sum of the components was deemed to be greater than its individual parts.

- **Consistent approach**: finally, and perhaps most importantly, the Court of First Instance recognised that applications to register shape marks should be treated no more stringently than those for more "usual" trade marks, such as words, logos, or colours.

(6)   *Colours*

As "colour" is included in the definition of "sign" in s 5 Trade Marks Act 2002, colours are potentially registrable as trade marks, provided they have distinctive character (s 18(1)(b)). A colour will not be registrable as a trade mark if that colour is a sign or indication which has become customary in the current language or the bona fide and established practices of trade (s 18(1)(d)).

IPONZ Practice Guideline, "Absolute Grounds: Distinctiveness" states that when assessing the registrability of a mark that is a colour or a combination of colours, the following will be taken into account:

- An application for a single colour is considered prima facie to lack distinctive character. Evidence of use will always be required to demonstrate the mark has acquired a distinctive character. The evidence of use will need to show that the mark is exclusively associated with the applicant's goods or services.

- The greater the specificity of the mark's description, the more distinctive character the mark is likely to have.

- Some colours may be associated with certain trades and will therefore have no distinctive character within those trades.

In practice, the majority of applications to register single colour marks in New Zealand have been rejected or, if granted, successfully revoked.

Thus, in *Effem Foods Ltd's Application* (Commissioner's Decision No T43/2003, 26/11/03, Asst Commr Walden), a decision under the Trade Marks Act 1953, Effem Foods Ltd applied unsuccessfully to register the colour orange in relation to various food and confectionery goods in class 30, including rice. The application was opposed on the basis that, inter alia, the alleged trade mark was not able to distinguish Effem's goods from those of other traders. On considering whether the colour mark was capable of distinguishing the applicant's goods, Assistant Commissioner Walden stated, at p 17, that "single colour marks tend to have a very low amount of inherent distinctiveness because of the many uses of colour other than as a badge of origin". The Assistant Commissioner also stressed at p 16 the importance of ensuring that an application for a colour mark includes a description of how the colour mark is to be applied to the goods in question, so that it is possible to determine whether the colour mark is capable of being represented graphically, and the scope of the monopoly sought.

While the Assistant Commissioner did not consider that orange was a colour inherently generic to the goods claimed, she concluded that the colour mark had a very low amount of inherent distinctiveness, and that "other traders, without improper motives, may wish to use the colour orange in relation to their own rice products". As such, Effem needed to establish "a very substantial amount of factual distinctiveness by reason of the prior use of the mark or of any other circumstances". On the evidence Effem had not established that its colour mark would be perceived as a badge of origin by consumers. Therefore the opposition was successful.

Similarly, in *Telecom Directories Ltd's Application* (Commissioner's Decision No T19/2003, 21/5/03, Asst Commr Frankel) the colour yellow was deemed insufficiently distinctive of "electronic telephone and business directories and reference works including related computer software" and the application for registration refused. The Assistant Commissioner noted that there was a heavy onus on the applicant to show factual distinctiveness which it had failed to meet.

In *Frucor Beverages Ltd's Application* (Commissioner's Decision No T30/2003, 23/7/03, Asst Commr Brown QC), the applicant also unsuccessfully applied to register the colour green in classes 5 and 32.

In *The NZ Automobile Assoc Inc's Application* (Commissioner's Decision No T05/2006, 20/2/06, Asst Commr Walden) and *AMI Insurance Ltd's Application* (Commissioner's Decision No sT04/2006, 20/2/06, Asst Commr Walden), the NZAA and AMI Insurance successfully cross-opposed each other's application to register a combination of the colours yellow and black. The decisions turned primarily on the evidence that each party had been using the colour combination in respect of its business making it unlikely that the mark was distinctive in fact of either one of them. However, trade mark practitioners should also note the Assistant Commissioner's comment that the AA's description of the mark in its application (the colours yellow and black "as applied to signage, including vehicle signage, premises, printed matter and promotional and advertising matter in any media") was vague and uncertain because of its wide description and wide application without spatial delineation of the colour combination and no indication of the form that the colour combination might take.

(7) Other examples

Examples of marks which have been deemed insufficiently distinctive include:

- A device consisting of the side view of a pregnant woman with a prohibitory sign consisting of a circle with a diagonal bar across it in class 5 for "pharmaceutical preparations, including preparations for the treatment of acne, but not including pharmaceutical preparations for the purposes of prohibiting or preventing pregnancy" (*F Hoffman — La Roche AG's Application* (Commissioner's Decision No T11/2002, 5/4/02, Asst Commr Gallagher));

- The device of a solid three-dimensional shape coloured yellow with seven sides in class 5 for "pharmaceuticals in the nature of anti-inflammatory analgesics" (*GD Searle & Co's Application* (Commissioner's Decision No T12/2002, 2/5/02, Asst Commr Hastie));

- CONTINENTAL ROAST in class 30 for "coffee, coffee essences, mixtures of coffee and chicory" (*Fresh Food Holdings Pty Ltd's Application* (Commissioner's Decision No T17/2002, 28/5/02, Asst Commr Hastie));

- THE MUSIC WE GREW UP WITH in class 41 for entertainment and recreational services (*Steam Radio Co Ltd's Application* (Commissioner's Decision No T18/2002, 31/5/02, Asst Commr Duffy));

- THE ONE CLICK SHOP in class 35 (*The NZ Automobile Assoc Inc's Application* (Commissioner's Decision No T22/2002, 12/6/02, Asst Commr Gallagher)).

- The colours green and yellow applied to the visible surface of gloves (*Showa Inc's Application* (Commissioner's Decision No T20/2005, 27/6/05, Asst Commr Walden)).

- A three dimensional shape comprising a black rugby jersey (or casual shirt made in the style of a rugby jersey) bearing a fern with a white collar (*The NZ Rugby Football Union Inc's Application* (Commissioner's Decision No T31/2005, 12/12/05, Asst Commr Walden)). The Assistant Commissioner found that the mark was unlikely to function as a badge of origin. In particular, the general definition of the mark, and the fact that goods could be made from any fabric and worn by a variety of people in different contexts, were deemed to increase the likelihood of other traders wanting to use the mark without improper motive (per the *W & G du Cros* test for capacity to distinguish). Evidence of use of the mark tendered by the New Zealand Rugby Football Union was deemed insufficient to establish acquired distinctiveness — possibly due to contrary evidence from the opponents that other traders had made extensive sales of similar goods before the date of application.

- AIR SAFARIS in relation to "tourist offices, air transport, passenger transport, sightseeing (tourism), arranging of tours, transport of travellers" (*Air Safaris & Services (NZ) Ltd's Application* (Commissioner's Decision No T26/2006, 9/11/06, Asst Commr Walden)). The Assistant Commissioner acknowledged that, although the word combination "AIR SAFARIS" must be considered as a whole, in accordance with the

Court of Appeal's decision in *McCain Foods (Aust) Pty Ltd v Conagra Inc* [2002] 3 NZLR 40 (CA), she must first understand the meaning of each word in the mark to determine whether the words in combination convey a different meaning from that conveyed separately. However, as the combination of words added nothing to their separate meaning, and that combination was so descriptive as to essentially be a description of the services covered by the application, the mark was held to be incapable of distinguishing the applicant's services from those of other traders.

- EASE in block capital and stylised form for "medicines, natural and synthetic dietary supplements, medicinal plant compounds for use as dietary supplements and therapeutic preparations for human use" (*Stargate International Ltd's Application* (Commissioner's Decision No T27/2006, 13/11/06, Asst Commr Walden)). The Assistant Commissioner found that the EASE trade marks had no distinctive character as other traders were likely to want to use the term to indicate that the relevant goods may be taken or administered with ease, to indicate that the relevant goods ease symptoms such as pain or discomfort, or to indicate that the relevant goods will put the person at their ease in the sense of making the person feel comfortable or relaxed. As there was no evidence that the marks had acquired distinctiveness through use, the applications were rejected.

- A three dimensional heart shape for retail services and toys (*Build-a-Bear Workshop Inc's Application* (Commissioner's Decision No T01/2007, 15/1/07, Asst Commr Walden)). As no evidence of use was filed, the Applicant had to establish that the trade mark had inherent distinctiveness at the date of filing. The Assistant Commissioner found that it didn't, primarily because other traders were likely in the course of their business, and without improper motive, to want to use the same shape as a trade mark in connection with their own goods or services. The decision was unsuccessfully appealed to the High Court (*Re Build-A-Bear Workshop Inc* 21/6/07, Miller J, HC Wellington CIV-2007-485-196; CIV-2007-485-775).

- FASTGEL in relation to pharmaceutical and medicinal substances and preparations (*Wyeth's Application* (Commissioner's Decision No T08/2007, 20/2/07, Asst Commr Walden)).

Examples of marks which have been permitted to proceed to registration include:

- COIN FOR A CURE — COINS FOR A CURE in class 36 for "charitable fundraising services including funding of research for leukaemia and blood disorders; funding of medical equipment services and facilities for use in relation to leukaemia and blood disorders" (*The Leukaemia and Blood Foundation of NZ's Application* (Commissioner's Decision No T13/2002, 3/5/02, Asst Commr Duckworth));

- STEP BY STEP in class 41 for education and training services (*Christine Partridge's Application* (Commissioner's Decision No T15/2002, 12/5/02, Asst Commr Duffy));

- LAWLINE (in stylised form and in combination with a device in class 42 for legal telephone services with separate disclaimers of the words "law" and "line" or any combination of those words (*Lawline Telephone Consultations Ltd's Application* (Commissioner's Decision No T16/2002, 27/5/02, Asst Commr Duffy));

- CLINICALLY PROVEN MILDNESS (in stylised form and in combination with a device) in classes 3 and 5 with disclaimers of the words "clinically", "proven" and "mildness" individually or in combination (*Johnson & Johnson's Application* (Commissioner's Decision No T19/2002, 7/6/02, Asst Commr Duffy)).

- ULTRA in relation to lighting apparatus and related parts and fittings (*Marexim Export-Import Ltd's Application* (Commissioner's Decision No T10/2007, 19/3/07, Asst Commr Walden)). The Assistant Commissioner considered that "ultra" meant "going beyond what is usual or ordinary; excessive, extreme" and that the word, which is commonly used as a prefix or in a compound word, is not usually used by itself because the concepts of excessive or extreme need to be linked to something in order to understand what is being described as excessive or extreme. On that basis she considered it unlikely that other traders in New Zealand would wish to use ULTRA as a trade mark without any improper motive. The mark was also deemed insufficiently similar to a cited ULTRALAMP trade mark on the same basis.

- KiwiClams in relation to New Zealand greenshell mussels (*Te Huia's Application* (Commissioner's Decision No T11/2007, 19/3/07, Asst Commr Walden)). The Assistant Commissioner considered it unlikely that an ordinary New Zealander would see KiwiClams to be descriptive of New Zealand greenshell mussels because "clam" is not an apt term for mussels in New Zealand. One of the meanings of "clam" in the New Zealand Oxford Dictionary described it as a type of edible North American shellfish, which indicated to the Assistant Commissioner that it was a term used in North America rather than in New Zealand and/or understood by New Zealanders to relate to North American produce. For this reason, the Assistant Commissioner considered it unlikely that other traders in New Zealand would want to use KiwiClams, "Kiwi" or "Clams" as a description of New Zealand greenshell mussels.

7.5.7 Registrability under the Trade Marks Act 1953

Under the Trade Marks Act 1953, the Register was divided into two parts, known as Part A and Part B. Part A was reserved for distinctive signs which were "inherently adapted to distinguish" or "[b]y reason of the use of the trade mark or of any other circumstances … in fact adapted to distinguish". Signs which were "capable of distinguishing" either "inherently" or "[b]y reason of the use of the trade mark or of any other circumstances … in fact", were registered in Part B (emphasis added).

The registrability of trade marks in Part A was governed by s 14 of the 1953 Act. In order for a trade mark to be registered in Part A, the applicant for registration had to show that the mark contained or consisted of at least one of the following "essential particulars":

- The name of a company, individual, or firm represented in a special or particular manner;

- The signature of the applicant for registration or some predecessor in business;

- An invented word or invented words;

- A word or words having no direct reference to the character or quality of the goods or services, and not being according to its ordinary signification a geographical name or a surname; or

- Any other distinctive sign, being one other than those referred to above, on evidence of its distinctiveness as at the date of the application for registration.

These "essential particulars" were alternatives. Therefore, to be eligible for registration in Part A, the applicant needed only to show that the mark fell within one of the five categories and exhibited a capacity to distinguish. This separate requirement of distinctiveness (ie in addition to qualifying under s 14 of the 1953 Act) was confirmed by the Court of Appeal in *Cadbury Ltd v Effem Foods Ltd* 20/7/07, CA247/05; [2007] NZCA 303, at paras 13-16.

The eligibility for registration of a trade mark in Part B was governed by s 15 of the 1953 Act. The standard of distinctiveness for Part B was lower than that required for Part A.

In order for a trade mark to be registered in Part B, the applicant for registration had to show that the mark was "capable of distinguishing" the goods or services of the proprietor from those of other traders.

In determining whether a trade mark was capable of distinguishing, s 15(2) permitted the Commissioner or the Court to have regard to the extent to which:

- The trade mark was inherently capable of distinguishing; and

- The trade mark was in fact capable of distinguishing, due to use of the trade mark or "any other circumstances".

7.6 Grounds for not registering

7.6.1 Registration requirements — absolute grounds

The absolute grounds for refusing registration of a trade mark are found in ss 17-21 Trade Marks Act 2002.

(1) *Section 17 — absolute grounds: general*

Section 17 Trade Marks Act 2002 provides:

"(1) The Commissioner must not register as a trade mark or part of a trade mark any matter—

"(a) the use of which would be likely to deceive or cause confusion; or

"(b) the use of which is contrary to New Zealand law or would otherwise be disentitled to protection in any court; or

"(c) the use or registration of which would, in the opinion of the Commissioner, be likely to offend a significant section of the community, including Maori.

"(2) The Commissioner must not register a trade mark if the application is made in bad faith.

"(3) Despite subsection (1)(b), the Commissioner may register a trade mark even if use of the trade mark is restricted or prohibited under the Smoke-free Environments Act 1990."

IPONZ will take the above prohibitions into account when examining new trade mark applications (discussed at 7.4 ("Trade mark application process") earlier in this chapter).

The s 17 prohibitions on registration also apply as grounds for opposition to registration and for rectification of the Register (discussed at 7.7 ("Oppositions") and 7.14 ("Revocation") later in this chapter).

Under s 16 Trade Marks Act 1953, registration of a trade mark was unlawful if its use was likely to deceive or cause confusion or was contrary to law or morality. Case law decided under s 16 of the 1953 Act continues to apply in respect of s 17 Trade Marks Act 2002.

Although not specifically mentioned in s 17, it is generally accepted that a false claim to ownership of a mark will also be treated as an absolute ground for refusing registration. In practice such challenges are usually made at the opposition stage of an application (or following registration) under s 17(2) on the basis that by filing the application without being the rightful owner, the applicant has acted in bad faith. Ownership is discussed in more detail at 7.4 ("Trade mark application process") earlier in this chapter.

A challenge to a mark under s 17(1)(a) and (b) of the Act most often arises where a third party is using a confusingly similar mark and the Commissioner is concerned to avoid sanctioning conduct which might deceive or confuse the public by permitting a mark, the use of which is likely to deceive or confuse, to be registered. As the objection is usually based on third party rights it is often brought in tandem with an objection under s 25 of the Act (which prohibits the registration of a mark if it is identical or similar to a mark already on the Register and its use is likely to deceive or confuse). Accordingly the principles of comparison of trade marks, and of goods and services, discussed under that section will also be applicable to an enquiry under s 17(1)(a) and (b). See 7.6.4 ("Comparison of trade marks") and 7.6.5 ("Comparison of goods and services") later in this chapter.

It should be noted that under s 17 of the Act (as under the old s 16) the Court is required to consider notional use of the trade mark applied for. Thus, in the context of an opposition based on a third party's use and/or registration of a similar mark, the Court should have regard to the actual use of the opponent's mark as at the date of application, and ask whether it is satisfied that the applicant's mark, if used in a normal and fair manner in connection with all of the goods/services covered by the application, is reasonably likely to deceive or cause confusion amongst a substantial number of persons: *Smith Hayden & Co Ltd's Application* (1946) 63 RPC 97, at p 101. In *Telecom IP Ltd v Beta Telecom Ltd* 27/9/06, Ronald Young J, HC Wellington CIV-2004-485-2789, the High Court found, at para 26, that the Assistant Commissioner had fallen into error by focusing on what Beta Telecom currently did rather than the identified services for which registration of the mark had been sought, and accordingly overturned the decision of the Assistant Commissioner permitting registration of the trade mark BETA TELECOM.

In *Platinum Homes (NZ) Ltd v Golden Homes (1998) Ltd* 11/8/06, Miller J, HC Wellington CIV-2005-485-1870, Miller J confirmed, on appeal, that, where an opponent is alleging that the mark sought to be registered is confusingly similar to another trade mark which is either registered or in use by another party, it is not necessary for the opponent to be the owner of the marks it says will be confused with the opposed trade mark.

(a)   Section 17(1)(a) — likely to deceive or cause confusion

In *AMI Insurance Ltd v NZ Automobile Assn Inc* 15/7/04, Miller J, HC Wellington CIV-2003-485-836, AMI Insurance opposed registration of a mark under s 16 Trade Marks

Act 1953 on the grounds that it was likely to deceive or cause confusion. Miller J noted, at para 34, that the leading decision on s 16 was *Pioneer Hi-Bred Corn Co v Hy-Line Chicks Pty Ltd* [1978] 2 NZLR 50. In that case, Richardson J cited *Southern Cross Refrigerating Co v Toowoomba Foundry Pty Ltd* (1953) 91 CLR 592 (HCA), where Kitto J set out, at pp 594-596, a number of principles to assist the Court in determining whether use of a mark would be likely to deceive or cause confusion, as follows:

- The onus is on the person applying to register the mark to show that the mark is not likely to deceive or cause confusion;

- The likelihood of deception or confusion should be determined as at the date of application for registration of the mark;

- The relevant use is the possible future use of the mark in relation to goods which come within the specification for which registration is sought;

- The relevant use is of the mark in a manner that may be regarded as a fair and proper use, not of the particular mode or presentation of the product adopted or proposed to be adopted;

- When considering the likelihood of deception or confusion, all the surrounding circumstances must be taken into account, including the circumstances of use of the mark, the market in which the specified goods may be bought and sold, and the character of those involved in that market;

- The relevant use is the use of the mark in New Zealand, not its association with a similar mark used by another trader overseas unless that use bears on the likelihood of deception or confusion in the New Zealand market;

- The likelihood of deception or confusion must be determined from the perspective of the prospective potential purchasers of the specified goods and others involved in the purchase transaction;

- It is not necessary to prove that there is a commercial probability of deception leading to passing off or infringement. Detriment or financial loss to an opponent need not be established. It is sufficient if registration of the mark will be likely to cause persons to whom the mark is addressed to be deceived or confused. "Deceived" implies the creation of an incorrect belief or mental impression and causing "confusion" may go no further than perplexing or mixing up the minds of the purchasing public. Where the deception or confusion alleged is as to the source of the goods, deceived is equivalent to being misled into thinking that the goods bearing the mark come from another source, and confused is equivalent to being caused to wonder whether that might not be the case;

- The test is not that all persons in the relevant market are likely to be deceived or confused but it is not sufficient that someone in the relevant market is likely to be deceived or confused. A balance has to be struck. A number of persons, a substantial number of persons, a considerable section of the market, or a significant number of persons in the market must be likely to be deceived or confused;

- Where goods are sold in a specialist market consisting of persons engaged in a particular trade, evidence of persons accustomed to dealing in that market as to the likelihood of deception or confusion is essential.

These principles continue to apply in relation to s 17(1)(a) Trade Marks Act 2002 and will arguably be relevant in consideration of whether use of the mark constitutes a breach of the Fair Trading Act 1986 for the purposes of s 17(1)(b) of the 2002 Act as well: *Platinum Homes (NZ) Ltd's Application* (Commissioner's Decision No T22/2005, 22/8/05, Asst Commr Hastie).

The decision of the Assistant Commissioner in *Platinum Homes (NZ) Ltd's Application* was overturned on appeal (*Platinum Homes (NZ) Ltd v Golden Homes (1998) Ltd* 11/8/06, Miller J, HC Wellington CIV-2005-485-1870) on the basis that the marks were not confusingly similar. However, Miller J did not take any issue with the applicability of the *Pioneer* principles to s 17(1)(a) Trade Marks Act 2002. The *Pioneer* principles were also applied by the Court in *Telecom IP Ltd v Beta Telecom Ltd* 27/9/06, Ronald Young J, HC Wellington CIV-2004-485-2789.

(b) Section 17(1)(b) — contrary to law

Use of a mark will be contrary to law, and therefore the mark will be incapable of registration, if that use constitutes:

- Passing off;

- A breach of the Fair Trading Act 1986;

- Copyright infringement; or

- A breach of any other statutory provision.

(i) **Passing off or breach of the Fair Trading Act 1986**

If use of a trade mark would constitute passing off or a breach of the Fair Trading Act 1986, an application to register the mark may be successfully opposed on the grounds that it offends against s 17 Trade Marks Act 2002.

Refer to 7.6.1(1)(a) ("Section 17(1)(a) — likely to deceive or cause confusion") for a discussion of the principles applicable to determine whether use of a mark is likely to deceive or cause confusion. Also see the chapters entitled Passing Off (chapter 9) and The Fair Trading Act 1986 (chapter 10) for a discussion of what constitutes passing off or a breach of the Fair Trading Act 1986.

(ii) **Copyright infringement**

If use of a mark, for example a device or logo mark, will infringe copyright owned by a person other than the applicant, and the applicant's use is unauthorised, then the mark will be prohibited from registration. Refer to the Copyright chapter of this text (chapter 4).

(iii) **Other statutory provisions**

Marks for which registration is commonly prohibited include certain flags, emblems, representations of royalty and famous people, and words such as "registered", "patented" and the like. Their use is prohibited under the Flags, Emblems, and

Names Protection Act 1981. The Geographical Indications (Wines and Spirits) Registration Act 2006 also prohibits registration of a trade mark that contains a registered geographical indication where the mark relates to a wine or spirit that does not originate from the applicable geographical region. This is reflected in s 20 Trade Marks Act 2002.

(c)   *Section 17(1)(c) — likely to offend a significant section of the community, including Maori*

Under s 16 Trade Marks Act 1953, the Commissioner had to determine whether a trade mark contained matter that was scandalous or contrary to morality having regard to the widely held values of society at the time of consideration. Similarly, under s 17(1)(c) Trade Marks Act 2002, the Commissioner should determine whether use or registration of the mark would be likely to offend a significant section of the community, including Maori, by reference to the widely held values of society at the date of application.

In *Trade Mark Applications by Red Bull GmbH* (Commissioner's Decision No T33/2001, 19/7/01, Asst Commr Gallagher), the mark BULLSHIT was held by the Assistant Commissioner to be both "scandalous" and "contrary to morality". In that case, the Assistant Commissioner stated, at p 4:

> "it is sufficient to refuse registration if a significant number of New Zealanders would find the word offensive, improper or shocking."

The BULLSHIT case also refers to *HALLELUJAH Trade Mark* (1976) 93 RPC 605 in which an application to register HALLELUJAH was refused because a minority in the community, who were nevertheless substantial in number, were likely to be offended by use of HALLELUJAH as a trade mark on the basis that it is an exhortation to praise God.

Section 177 of the 2002 Act requires the Commissioner to appoint an advisory committee to advise the Commissioner whether the registration of a trade mark that is, or appears to be, derivative of a Maori sign, including text or imagery, is likely to be offensive to Maori.

According to IPONZ Practice Guideline, "Maori Trade Marks Advisory Committee and Maori Trade Marks", all applications containing Maori text or imagery will be forwarded to the advisory committee, and the applicant advised accordingly. The advisory committee will meet to consider the application and determine whether the trade mark is:

- Not offensive to Maori;
- Not likely to be offensive to Maori;
- Likely to be offensive to Maori; or
- Offensive to Maori.

The advice of the advisory committee is not binding on the Commissioner. The Commissioner must consider the advice, taking into account all relevant factors affecting registrability, and may determine the eligibility of a trade mark for registration contrary to the advice received from the advisory committee.

(d) *Section 17(2) — application made in bad faith*

Section 17(2) Trade Marks Act 2002 obliges the Commissioner to refuse an application for the registration of a mark which has been made in "bad faith". The scope of what is meant by bad faith is unspecified. However, it will include situations where:

- The applicant is not the true owner of the mark in question, that is, where the applicant knows that the mark belongs to someone else (see 7.4.1 ("Filing an application") earlier in this chapter); or

- An application is made without any genuine intention to use the mark in relation to the relevant goods and/or services (see 7.4.3 ("Past filing") earlier in this chapter).

Gromax Plasticulture Ltd v Don & Lowe Nonwovens Ltd [1999] RPC 367 provides the leading test as to what constitutes bad faith. In relation to the corresponding UK provision, Lyndsay J stated, at p 379:

> "Plainly it [bad faith] includes dishonesty and, as I would hold, includes also some dealings which fall short of the standards of acceptable commercial behaviour observed by reasonable and experienced men in the particular area being examined. Parliament have wisely not attempted to explain in detail what is or is not bad faith in this context; how far a dealing must so fall short in order to amount to bad faith is a matter best left to be adjudged not by some paraphrase by the Courts (which leads to the danger of the Courts then construing not the Act but the paraphrase) but by reference to the words of the Act and upon a regard to all material surrounding circumstances."

Subsequently, in *Harrison v Teton Valley Trading Co Ltd* [2004] 1 WLR 2577 (CA), the English Court of Appeal held that the test for bad faith involves a combination of an objective and a subjective standard. In reaching its decision, the Court of Appeal approved of Lord Hutton's combined test for dishonesty in *Twinsectra Ltd v Yardley* [2002] 2 AC 164; [2002] 2 WLR 802 (HL), at para 36. Delivering the judgment of the majority of the UK Court of Appeal, Sir William Aldous discussed the *Twinsectra* case and the "combined test" derived from it, at paras 24-26:

> "Clearly the court, when considering bad faith, cannot apply a purely subjective test, called by Lord Hutton 'the Robin Hood test'. The dishonest person or one with low standards cannot be permitted to obtain trade mark registrations in circumstances where a person abiding by a reasonable standard would not. The registration of a trade mark is designed to enable bona fide proprietors to protect their proprietary rights without having to prove unfair trading. Registration is not provided to help those with low moral standards.

> "Lord Hutton went on to conclude that the true test for dishonesty was the combined test. He said:

>> '36. Therefore I consider that your Lordships should state that dishonesty requires knowledge by the defendant that what he was doing would be regarded as dishonest by honest people, although he should not escape a finding of dishonesty because he sets his own standards of honesty and does not regard as dishonest what he knows would offend the normally accepted standards of honest conduct.'

"For my part, I would accept the reasoning of Lord Hutton as applying to considerations of bad faith. The words 'bad faith' suggest a mental state. Clearly when considering the question of whether an application to register is made in bad faith all the circumstances will be relevant. However the court must decide whether the knowledge of the applicant was such that his decision to apply for registration would be regarded as in bad faith by persons adopting proper standards."

Bad faith does not necessarily equate with a breach of legal obligation: *Demon Ale Trade Mark* [2000] RPC 345, at p 356.

In the first Court decision to consider the application of the equivalent section under the Trade Marks Act 1998 (Singapore), *Rothmans of Pall Mall Ltd v Maycolson International Ltd* [2006] SGHC 51, the Singaporean High Court confirmed that breach of a legal obligation was not necessary for bad faith to arise. It also commented, at para 19, that a trade mark applicant should bear a positive duty to investigate into the bona fides of a mark before seeking registration, as to not require the applicant to do so would have the result that:

"In borderline cases, such as those where suspicious circumstances exist as to the bona fides of the mark, registration would be allowed since an applicant's failure to investigate would not lead to a finding of bad faith. Viewed in this light, the omission of a duty to investigate is fundamentally flawed, as it gives scant protection to registered trade marks and encourages an applicant to turn a blind eye to any impropriety in relation to the proposed mark for registration."

Interestingly, the Court also considered that it was entitled to make a finding of bad faith despite the fact that the marks in question might not be so similar as to cause confusion.

As to the standard and/or type of proof required for a finding of bad faith to arise, the Court adopted *Kundry SA's Application: Opposition by the President and Fellows of Harvard College* [1998] ETMR 178 as authority for the view that an application would be tainted with bad faith if an applicant knew of the opponent and its concern about the possibility of confusion and did not respond to the allegations.

(2)   *Section 18 — absolute grounds: non-distinctive trade marks*

Section 18 Trade Marks Act 2002 provides as follows:

"(1)   The Commissioner must not register—

"(a)   a sign that is not a trade mark:

"(b)   a trade mark that has no distinctive character:

"(c)   a trade mark that consists only of signs or indications that may serve, in trade, to designate the kind, quality, quantity, intended purpose, value, geographical origin, time of production of goods or of rendering of services, or other characteristics of goods or services:

"(d)   a trade mark that consists only of signs or indications that have become customary in the current language or in the bona fide and established practices of trade.

"(2)   The Commissioner must not refuse to register a trade mark under subsection (1)(b), (c), or (d) if, before the date of application for registration, as a result

361

of either the use made of it or of any other circumstances, the trade mark has acquired a distinctive character."

Subsection (1)(a), (b), (c) and (d) are independent. Therefore, a particular trade mark may be rejected on any one or more of these grounds.

In instances where the Commissioner considers a mark is not registrable, the applicant must satisfy the Commissioner that registration should be allowed (s 13(2)(c)).

(a)   Section 18(1)(a) — not a trade mark

Under s 18(1)(a) Trade Marks Act 2002, a sign that is not a "trade mark" cannot be registered. Under s 5(1), a trade mark means a sign that is capable of being represented graphically and capable of distinguishing the goods or services of the applicant from those of another person. A sign includes a brand, colour, device, heading, label, letter, name, numeral, shape, signature, smell, sound, taste, ticket, or word or any combination of signs.

In theory, if the graphic representation of the mark applied for is not clear, or inadequately defines the scope of protection sought, an objection will be raised under s 18(1)(a). However, as prior to substantive examination of the application the applicant would have dealt with any irregularities regarding the graphic representation of the mark in order to secure a filing date, objections on this ground are likely to be rare.

Essentially, to be capable of distinguishing the goods or services of one trader from those of another, a mark must have an inherent quality of distinctiveness, or have demonstrated distinctiveness in fact by prior use or other circumstances, including subsequent events where they assist in establishing the essential quality at the time of registration: *McCain Foods (Aust) Pty Ltd v Conagra Inc* [2002] 3 NZLR 40, at p 43-44, per Gault P (delivering judgment for the Court of Appeal).

In *Fredco Trading Ltd v Miller* 16/12/02, Venning J, HC Auckland CIV-2004-404-895, the High Court had to consider an application under s 73 for a declaration that the registration for the shape of vine tie ("the Klipon vine tie") was invalid. Fredco's application was made on the grounds, inter alia, that the shape of the Klipon vine tie was not a sign capable of distinguishing the goods of one trader from those of another under s 18(1)(a).

Venning J noted, at para 33, that in *Philips v Remington* [1999] RPC 809, Aldous LJ found, at 817-818, that the phrase "capable of distinguishing" required consideration of the features of the trade mark itself, not the results of its use (ie, capability of distinguishing concerned inherent distinctiveness not distinctiveness in fact).

Venning J noted that consumers did in fact distinguish between the Klipon vine tie and its competitor based on shape, and concluded at para 35 that the Klipon vine tie was factually distinctive and therefore capable of distinguishing the Klipon vine tie from the competing vine tie, as the phrase had been interpreted by the Court of Appeal in *McCain*.

The decision of Venning J was upheld on appeal (*Fredco Trading Ltd v Miller* (2006) 8 NZBLC 101,761 (CA)).

The phrase "capable of distinguishing" is discussed further at 7.5 ("Registrability") and below in relation to the phrase "distinctive character".

(b)   *Section 18(1)(b) — no distinctive character*

Marks that have no distinctive character are prohibited from registration under s 18(1)(b).

The corresponding provision of the Trade Marks Act 1994 (UK) uses the wording "devoid of any distinctive character", however, the meaning of "no distinctive character" is probably the same.

The meaning of the phrase "devoid of distinctive character" was discussed in *British Sugar Plc v James Robertson & Sons Ltd* (1996) 113 RPC 281. Jacob J said, at pp 305-306:

> "If a mark on its face is non-distinctive (and ordinary descriptive and laudatory words fall into this class) but is shown to have a distinctive character in fact then it must be capable of distinguishing …

> "What does devoid of distinctive character mean? I think the phrase requires consideration of the mark on its own, assuming no use. Is it the sort of word (or other sign) which cannot do the job of distinguishing without first educating the public that it is a trade mark? A meaningless word or a word inappropriate for the goods concerned (North Pole for bananas) can clearly do so. But a common laudatory word such as 'Treat' is, absent use and recognition as a trade mark, in itself (I hesitate to use the word from the old Act but the idea is much the same) devoid of any inherently distinctive character."

In *AD2000 Trade Mark* [1997] RPC 168, Appointed Person Geoffrey Hobbs QC stated, at p 175, that a trade mark possesses a distinctive character "if and when it is endowed by nature and/or nurture with the capacity to communicate that the goods or services with reference to which it is used recurrently are those of one and the same undertaking".

Under s 5 of the Act a sign must be "capable of distinguishing the goods and services of one person from those of another person" in order to be considered a trade mark for the purposes of registration. The question arises as to whether there is any real difference between this requirement under s 18(1)(b) that a mark has "distinctive character". These two requirements were compared by Venning J in *Fredco Trading Ltd v Miller* 16/12/02, Venning J, HC Auckland CIV-2004-404-895. The case concerned a challenge to Miller's registration for the shape of a tie used to secure kiwifruit vines on the basis, inter alia, that it had no distinctive character.

Venning J noted, at para 36, that there is some debate about whether "capable of distinguishing" and "distinctive character" mean the same or different things. He referred to the doubts expressed by Jacob J in *British Sugar Plc v James Robertson & Sons Ltd* (1996) 113 RPC 281 as to the different meanings of the two phrases, but concluded that their meanings were different. He noted, at para 38, that the draftsperson had used different words in s 18(1)(b) even though the phrase "capable of distinguishing" was employed a number of times elsewhere within the Act. Furthermore, if the phrases were intended to mean the same thing s 18(1)(b) may be considered superfluous as it would not add anything to the definition of a trade mark under s 5 of the Act. His Honour stated, at para 41, that:

> "s 18(1)(b) is particularly applicable where the trade mark inherently lacks distinctive character. In other words, while the sign (in this case shape) may be capable of distinguishing, it does not have inherent qualities that mark it out as of a distinctive

character. In such a case it could only acquire such a distinctive character through use, or, in the words of the statute, other circumstances."

Venning J noted, at para 47, that s 3(2) Trade Marks Act 1994 (UK) imposes a prohibition on registering signs that consist exclusively of the shape of the goods which is necessary to obtain a technical result. He held that the reasoning applied in English cases concerning s 3(2) Trade Marks Act 1994 (UK) was applicable in determining whether a shape mark has distinctive character for the purpose of s 18(1)(b).

His Honour reviewed the functional parameters that constrain the design of kiwifruit vine ties and noted, at para s 44-45, that although there were certain aspects of the vine tie shape that were not solely determined by those functional considerations, the essential features of the shape of the Klipon vine tie were necessary to achieve the practical end of a working vine tie. He concluded, at para 48, that the Klipon vine tie did not have an inherently distinctive character and was prima facie caught by s 18(1)(b) of the Act.

On the facts however, the shape of the vine tie was deemed to have acquired distinctiveness for the purposes of s 18(2) and thus his Honour declined the application for a declaration of invalidity of the shape mark. Section 18(2) is an exception to s 18(1)(b), (c) and (d).

The decision of Venning J was upheld on appeal (*Fredco Trading Ltd v Miller* (2006) 8 NZBLC 101,761 (CA)). The Court of Appeal, at paras 60 and 61, endorsed the view of Venning J that, as the legislature had used different phrases, on the face of the Act, a staged approach is envisaged. The Court of Appeal did however acknowledge that there was authority to support the respondent's view that there is no difference between the test for determining whether a sign is "capable of distinguishing" under s 5 and the tests under s 18(1)(b)-(d) noting, at para 61, that: "[t]here may well be overlapping considerations between s 18(1)(a) and (b) and in some cases very little, if any, difference in the inquiry taken".

IPONZ has issued the following guidelines regarding the assessment of whether a trade mark possesses a distinctive character (IPONZ Practice Guideline, "Absolute Grounds: Distinctiveness"):

- The question whether a particular sign possesses a distinctive character cannot be considered in the abstract. It must be considered in relation to the goods or services for which registration is sought.

- The mark must possess enough of a distinctive character to be regarded as an indication of trade origin by the relevant class of persons or at least a significant proportion thereof.

- The relevant class of persons consists of the trade and average consumers of the specified goods and services in the territory covered by the application for registration.

- The average consumer of the goods or services concerned is to be regarded as reasonably well-informed and reasonably observant and circumspect.

- It is to be remembered that the average consumer normally perceives a mark as a whole and does not proceed to analyse its various details.

- The average consumer's level of attention is likely to vary according to the category of goods or services in question.

- The perceptions of the average consumer must be assessed in context, with due regard for the realities of the market place. It will be relevant to have regard to the various methods and practices of marketing that the average consumer of the relevant goods or services is likely to encounter under normal and fair trading conditions.

The fact that a trade mark may only have been used in combination with other trade marks does not preclude it from having acquired distinctive character in its own right: *Société des Produits Nestlé SA v Mars UK Ltd* Case No C-353/03 (ECJ). This cases is discussed in more detail at 7.6.1(3) ("Factual distinctiveness") later in this chapter.

(c) *Section 18(1)(c) — designate the character of the goods or services*

Under s 18(1)(c) Trade Marks Act 2002, the Commissioner must not register

> "a trade mark that consists only of signs or indications that may serve, in trade, to designate the kind, quality, quantity, intended purpose, value, geographical origin, time of production of goods or of rendering of services, or other characteristics of goods or services"

Subsection (1)(c) prevents the registration of marks that are descriptive or laudatory of goods or services or some characteristic of them.

The European Court of Justice addressed the purpose of the English equivalent of s 18(1)(c) in *Procter & Gamble v OHIM (BABY DRY Trade Mark)* [2001] CEC 325 (ECJ). The Court said, at para 37 that:

> "the purpose of the prohibition of registration of purely descriptive signs or indications as trade marks is ... to prevent registration as trade marks of signs or indications which, because they are no different from the usual way of designating the relevant goods or services or their characteristics, could not fulfil the function of identifying the undertaking that markets them and are thus devoid of the distinctive character needed for that function."

(i) *"... that consists only ..."*

The use of the word "only" in s 18(1)(c) refers to the content of the mark. It does not mean that the subsection only applies when the sole meaning that can be given to the mark is the descriptive meaning. For example, PROMPT would not be registrable in respect of courier services on the basis that it is descriptive of the speed of the service under s 18(1)(c), even though it has further meanings such as "something said to incite to action" or "to help the memory" that are not descriptive of courier services.

(ii) *"... that may serve, in trade ..."*

Section 18(1)(c) does not just prohibit the registration of signs which are already in use by other traders to designate a characteristic or characteristics of the goods or services in question; it also prohibits the registration of descriptive signs as trade marks where those signs are likely to be used by other traders in the future as designations of a characteristic or characteristics of the goods or services. For the subsection to apply, there must be a reasonable likelihood that the mark will be associated, in the mind of the relevant class of persons, with a characteristic or characteristics of the goods or services.

365

(iii) **Characteristics of the goods or services**

In IPONZ Practice Guideline, "Absolute Grounds: Distinctiveness", the following are given as examples of characteristics of goods or services:

- "Kind" includes the name of the goods or services, as well as any other words that indicate kind or type. Examples include JUMBO, MINI, LIGHT (for low tar cigarettes), PERSONAL (for computers), and VERTICAL (for blinds).

- Laudatory words such as SUPERIOR, BEST, PREMIUM, and NUMBER ONE serve to designate the quality of the goods or services and should remain free for all traders to use.

- Indications of quantity are frequently used by traders and are therefore unlikely to function as trade marks. For example, 12 would not be registrable for wine, and 200 would not be registrable for cigarettes.

- Words that refer directly to the use to which the goods are put, or that describe the consequences of using the goods or providing the services, are not registrable. For example, ROACH FREE would not be registrable for pest eradication services, and BATHROOM would not be registrable for cleaning products.

- Words or symbols that merely serve to indicate the value, merit, or importance of the goods or services are not registrable. For example, TWO FOR ONE and BARGAIN.

- Marks consisting only of signs designating the time the goods were produced, or the time the services are rendered, are not registrable. For example, FRESH EACH DAY for fruit and vegetables, and 24 HOUR BANKING for banking services.

- A mark will not be registrable if it consists only of a sign that designates the geographical origin of the goods or services. However, trade marks which include geographical names may still be registered if they have another more commonly understood meaning and/or if the geographic location indicated has no special relevance to the goods or services in the application. For example, WELLINGTON might be registered as a trade mark for bananas, given that the region of Wellington has no reputation for producing such goods. The trade mark MARLBOROUGH, on the other hand, could not be registered in respect of wine.

- There must be a reasonable likelihood of the sign being used in trade to indicate the geographical origin of the goods or services. If the geographical significance of a sign is obscure or remote, and suggests no connection with the goods or services, then there may not be a reasonable likelihood that the sign will be used in trade to designate geographical origin.

(iv) **Normal usage**

It is only the normal usage of a sign or indication that will be considered when determining whether a mark consists only of signs or indications that serve to designate characteristics of the goods or services in question: *Procter & Gamble v OHIM (BABY DRY Trade Mark)* [2001] CEC 325 (ECJ), at para 39.

The *BABY DRY* case is also authority for the proposition that, when assessing whether a trade mark is capable of distinguishing, the determination to be made depends on whether the mark in question "may be viewed as a normal way" of designating a characteristic or characteristics of the goods or services (para 42). The fact that there may be other normal ways to designate the goods or services does not make the mark registrable.

Where a reference can only be found by searching for a meaning or by "academic exercise", the mark is unlikely to be refused registration under s 18(1)(c).

(v)   ***Examples***

In *Nortel Networks Corp v Telecom Corp of NZ* 24/6/04, Goddard J, HC Wellington CIV-2003-485-2631, the Appellant, Nortel, unsuccessfully appealed against refusal of the Assistant Commissioner of Trade Marks to register its service mark for a stylised version of "NORTHERN TELECOM". On appeal, the High Court upheld Telecom's opposition on the grounds inter alia that Nortel's logo was confusingly similar to Telecom's registered service mark for the word "TELECOM".

Nortel's submission in defence of Telecom's opposition was that Telecom's registered service mark lacked distinctiveness and should not have been registered because "TELECOM" was a generic term, an ordinary word or an abbreviation.

Goddard J accepted, at para 28, that the words "telecommunications" and "telecom" are descriptive terms and might be described as generic. However, her Honour (perhaps in reference to the saving for factually distinctiveness marks under s 18(2)) stated that generic trade marks are not a special category precluded from use in trade. She noted, at para 31, that Telecom had developed an almost instant and extreme reputation in New Zealand in connection with the word "TELECOM" and, at para 36, that the word had become factually distinctive in New Zealand because of Telecom's use of the word in connection with telecommunication services. Her Honour therefore rejected Nortel's submission that Telecom's service mark lacked distinctiveness and concluded that Nortel had failed to discharge the onus of showing that the use of its logo was not likely to deceive or confuse the public.

Although the distinctiveness requirement was discussed in relation to the validity of Telecom's service mark, rather than in relation to the registrability of Nortel's logo, the High Court's recognition that a generic term can become factually distinctive through use is notable. This aspect of the case is also discussed at 7.6.1(3) ("Factual distinctiveness") below.

In *Cadbury Ltd v Effem Foods Ltd* 20/7/07, CA247/05; [2007] NZCA 303, the Court of Appeal upheld a finding of the High Court (*Effem Foods Ltd v Cadbury Ltd* 12/12/05, MacKenzie J, HC Wellington CIV-2004-484-2127) refusing registration of the trade mark PURPLE in relation to chocolates, confectionary and ice cream etc, none of the foregoing goods being coloured purple. The Court of Appeal held, at para 10, that Cadbury's submission that the word PURPLE had no direct reference to the character or quality of the goods could only be correct if the exclusion was taken as excluding all goods which might be seen as being purple. However, the Court of Appeal considered that there was an issue as to how much purple there had to be in goods, or on the packaging, before the goods could be described as being purple and thus come within the exclusion. Thus, the word PURPLE was deemed to be descriptive of at least some of the goods coming within the registration.

The Court of Appeal also held, at paras 36-40, that a negative restriction relating to a characteristic of goods, as opposed to an exclusion of certain categories of goods, was contrary to relevant overseas authority (*Koninklijke KPN Nederland NV v Benelux-Merkenbureau (C-363/99)* [2005] 3 WLR 649; [2004] ETMR 57 (ECJ), at para 34 ("POSTKANTOOR"); *Croom's Trade Mark Application* [2005] RPC 2, per Geoffrey Hobbs QC) and IPONZ's own guidelines and therefore impermissible.

(d) Section 18(1)(d) — signs or indications that have become customary in the current language or in the bona fide and established practices of trade

Section 18(1)(d) Trade Marks Act 2002 prevents the registration of trade marks that consist only of signs or indications that other traders customarily use, either in the current language of trade or in the "bona fide and established practices of trade". Section 18(1)(d) therefore prevents the registration of marks that are generic.

There is a significant degree of overlap between s 18(1)(d) and (c). The former has a role in excluding from registration signs or indications where the descriptive element is not readily apparent, yet a number of traders actually use the signs or indications in question.

(3) Factual distinctiveness

Section 18(2) provides as follows:

"The Commissioner must not refuse to register a trade mark under subsection (1)(b), (c) or (d) if, before the date of application for registration, as a result of either the use made of it or of any other circumstances, the trade mark has acquired a distinctive character"

If an objection has been raised to the registrability of a trade mark under s 18(1)(b), (c), or (d), the applicant may be able to overcome the objection by showing that, *prior to the date of the application for registration*, the mark had acquired a distinctive character, either as a result of use of the mark, or "any other circumstances".

There are a number of factors which must be considered when assessing whether a mark has acquired a distinctive character through use. Some of these factors were considered in *Windsurfing Chiemsee Produktions-und Vertriebs GmbH v Boots-und Segelzubehör Walter Huber and Franz Attenberger* [1999] ETMR 585 (ECJ). These include:

- The market share held by the mark;

- How intensive, geographically widespread, and long-standing the use of the mark has been;

- The amount invested by the applicant in promoting the mark;

- The proportion of the relevant class of persons who, because of the mark, identify the goods or services as originating from a particular undertaking; and

- Statements from chambers of commerce and industry or other trade and professional associations.

These factors were cited with approval by the Court of Appeal in *Fredco Trading Ltd v Miller* (2006) 8 NZBLC 101,761 (CA), at paras 67-68.

For a trade mark to be accepted for registration on the basis of distinctiveness in fact, evidence of use, in the form of a statutory declaration, must be filed. The evidence should comprise details of the nature, extent, period, and area of use of the trade mark in question.

(a) *Extent of use may vary depending on nature of mark*

If it can be shown that through use a sign functions as a trade mark, then, in theory, there will be no reason to refuse registration. However, the sign may itself be of a type that does not immediately suggest that it functions as a trade mark. Put another way, although the trade mark may have been used by the applicant and, although the applicant may claim that the sign has the necessary distinctiveness as a result of such use, an objective assessment of the trade mark may not support this.

This situation was considered in *British Sugar Plc v James Robertson & Sons Ltd* (1996) 113 RPC 281. British Sugar Plc had registered the trade mark TREAT in relation to dessert sauces and syrups. It argued that the registration was infringed by James Robertson & Sons' sale of a toffee flavoured spread known as either ROBERTSON'S TOFFEE TREAT or TOFFEE TREAT. British Sugar had secured the registration by arguing that the mark was distinctive for dessert sauces and syrups. This argument was supported by substantial evidence of use. James Robertson and Sons challenged the validity of the mark.

The Court held that British Sugar's trade mark registration for TREAT was invalid. Whilst British Sugar had shown that it had a reputation in TREAT for the goods in question, the facts did not show that TREAT was recognised as a trade mark by the consuming public. The Judge did not consider it fair to grant monopoly rights in what he perceived to be a description of the goods, ie, a "treat".

Conversely, in *Nortel Networks Corp v Telecom Corp of NZ* 24/6/04, Goddard J, HC Wellington CIV-2003-485-2631, the New Zealand High Court upheld a registration for the word "TELECOM" based on the extent of use of that word having established an "almost instant and extreme reputation".

At first instance the Assistant Commissioner of Trade Marks had declined to register Nortel's service mark for a stylised version of the words "NORTHERN TELECOM" on the grounds that Nortel's logo was confusingly similar to Telecom's registered service mark for the word "TELECOM" and Nortel's use of its logo was likely to deceive or confuse the public.

On appeal, Nortel submitted that Telecom's registered service mark should be revoked because the word "TELECOM" was a generic term, an ordinary word or an abbreviation, and thus lacked distinctiveness. Accepting that the words "telecommunications" and "telecom" are descriptive terms and might be described as generic, Goddard J proceeded to consider some of the factors outlined above.

369

Her Honour noted, at para 31, that by 31 March 1988, 1,370,000 access lines were connected to the Telecom network, Telecom was the sole provider of telecommunications in New Zealand, and by 2 May 1988 there was a complete connection between the provision of telecommunication services in New Zealand and Telecom (as the sole provider of such services). Her Honour concluded that Telecom had developed an almost instant and extreme reputation in New Zealand in relation to the word "TELECOM" and that its service mark featuring the generic word had nonetheless become distinctive.

Accordingly, her Honour rejected Nortel's submission that Telecom's service mark lacked distinctiveness and concluded that Nortel had failed to discharge the onus of showing that the use of its logo was not likely to deceive or confuse the public.

Whether the trade mark will be accepted for registration on the basis of distinctiveness in fact is usually determined by the extent of use. As the *Nortel* decision clearly illustrates, a trade mark may have acquired sufficient factual distinctiveness even though it has been used for a short period of time, particularly where public exposure to the mark has been intense.

In general, the lower the inherent capacity to distinguish, the more extensive the evidence of factual distinctiveness required for registration of the mark. In *Fredco Trading Ltd v Miller* 16/12/02, Venning J, HC Auckland CIV-2004-404-895, Fredco Trading Ltd claimed, inter alia, that a registered trade mark that consisted of the shape of a vine tie ("the Klipon vine tie") should be declared invalid under s 73 Trade Marks Act 2002 on the basis that it did not have distinctive character under s 18(1)(b) of the Act.

After applying the test laid down by Gault P in *McCain Foods (Aust) Pty Ltd v Conagra Inc* [2002] 3 NZLR 40 (CA) (ie, did the mark at the time of registration have an inherent distinguishing quality or was its distinguishing quality demonstrated in fact by prior use or other circumstances?), Venning J concluded that the Klipon vine tie did not have an inherently distinctive character and was prima facie caught by s 18(1)(b) of the Act.

His Honour then proceeded to consider whether there was evidence of use or other circumstances which established the distinctive character of the Klipon vine tie for the purposes of s 18(2). He held that evidence of the:

- Duration of the product on the market compared to its competitors;

- Quantity of sales since the product was released onto the market;

- Consumer appreciation of the differences between the Klipon vine tie and competing products;

- Consumer recognition of the shape of the Klipon vine tie and its use in marketing along with the Klipon brand;

- Range of alternative shapes that may fulfil the function of the product; and

- Existence of an aesthetic component to the product,

satisfied him the Klipon vine tie had acquired distinctive character through use sufficient to support its registration under s 18(2). The decision of Venning J was upheld on appeal (*Fredco Trading Ltd v Miller* (2006) 8 NZBLC 101,761 (CA)).

Finally, the "use" leading to the distinctiveness needs to be sales of the goods or services under the subject mark. For example, in *Kapiti Cheeses Ltd's Application* (Commissioner's Decision No T21/2003, 15/5/03, Asst Commr Walden), the applicant successfully registered KIKORANGI in class 29 for "milk products; cheese; edible oils and fats". While initially concluding that the mark was descriptive because "KIKORANGI" is Maori for "blue" the Assistant Commissioner was satisfied that the mark was factually distinctive on the basis of evidence regarding the annual New Zealand cheese awards where KIKORANGI cheese consistently won the prize for the best blue cheese. The Assistant Commissioner held that the fame attached to such a prestigious cheese award helped to cement the association of the word KIKIORANGI with the applicant's goods.

(b) *Use in a monopoly situation*

One of the questions addressed by the Court of Appeal in *Fredco Trading* was whether, in considering the scale of the applicant's use of the trade mark, it was necessary to discount links between the mark and the goods which exist solely because of a monopoly position enjoyed by the applicant. After considering the relevant authorities, including the decision of the European Court of Justice in *Philips Electronics NV v Remington Consumer Products Ltd* [2003] Ch 159; [2003] 2 WLR 294; [2003] RPC 2 (ECJ), in which the Court said, at para 65:

> "Where a trader has been the only supplier of particular goods to the market, extensive use of a sign which consists of the shape of those goods may be sufficient to give the sign a distinctive character for the purposes of Article 3(3) of the Directive [New Zealand s 18(2)] in circumstances where, as a result of that use, a substantial proportion of the relevant class of persons associates that shape with the trader and no other undertaking or believes that goods of that shape come from that trader. However, it is for the National Courts to verify that the circumstances in which the requirement under that provision is satisfied are shown to exist on the basis of specific and reliable data, that the presumed expectations of an average consumer of the category of goods or services in question, who is reasonably well-informed and reasonably observant and circumspect, are taken into account and that the identification, by the relevant class of persons, of the product as originating from a given undertaking is as a result of the use of the mark as a trade mark."

the Court of Appeal concluded, at para 73:

> "As the respondent submits, the focus is on the end result. If it [the applicant's mark] is distinctive that is enough and it does not matter whether that was acquired as a result of a monopoly situation."

(c) *Must the use be use "as a mark"?*

The Court of Appeal in *Fredco* also commented, at para 50, in reference to the question of whether the use considered had to be "use as a trade mark":

> "If the essence of the inquiry is to determine factually whether a functional shape has acquired secondary meaning in the marketplace which transmits trade source information, then the use of the product itself may be considered. Such an approach is not inconsistent with the legislation as it can be seen to be condoned by 'or any other circumstances'."

Accordingly, the decision of the Court of Appeal appears to confirm that, when considering acquired distinctiveness, the focus is on the end result and not so much how the applicant got there. Any use which results in a sign acquiring distinctiveness can be taken into account even if that use is not, in the strict sense, use as a trade mark and even if it results from a monopoly situation (for example conferred by another registered intellectual property right). That approach is consistent with the opinion of the Advocate General of the European Court of Justice in *Société des Produits Nestlé SA v Mars UK Ltd* Case No C-353/03 (ECJ), at paras 25-33, who had the following to say regarding the concept of "use":

> "The concept of the use of a mark is employed not only in Article 3(3) and Article 10 of Directive 89/104 but also in the context of Article 5 thereof which defines the rights conferred by the mark. The proprietor of a mark is entitled to prevent third parties from using his mark or other signs where there is a likelihood of confusion. In that connection the Court has restricted the concept of use to cases in which use of the sign by a third party affects or could affect the functions of the mark and in particular its chief function which is to guarantee to consumers the origin of the goods. This limitation results from the fact that the objectives of trade-mark protection do not justify the prohibition of uses and thus restrictions on the freedom of users where the use in question has no appreciable effect on the function of the mark.

> "However, the concept of use in the context of Article 3(3) of Directive 89/104 is wider than it is in Article 5(1) because it has a wholly different function. In Article 3(3) that concept is not intended to define the scope of trade-mark protection but only to describe the manner in which a sign which is not inherently distinctive may acquire distinctive character, namely by use. Therefore, in the case of parts of a mark the decisive factor is also whether a use leads to the acquisition of distinctive character.

> "According to Mars the Judgment in *Philips* is said to contradict that interpretation. In that case for acquisition of distinctive character the Court expressly required 'use of a mark as a trade mark'.

> "In *Philips* the Court examined inter alia whether a sign consisting of the shape of a product could acquire distinctive character. That case involved the graphic representation of the upper surface of a 3-headed rotary electric shaver, comprising three circular heads with rotating blades in the shape of an equilateral triangle. For a long time Philips had sold electric shavers in this form on an exclusive basis and took the view that the representation notified as a trade mark had acquired distinctive character by virtue of such exclusive marketing over a long period.

> "The Court proceeded on the basis that the distinctive character of a sign consisting in the shape of a product, and even the distinctive character acquired by the use made of it, must be assessed in the light of the presumed expectations of an average consumer of the category of goods or services in question, who is reasonably well informed and reasonably observant and circumspect.

> "However, it went on to qualify that statement in the following terms:

'[T]he identification, by the relevant class of persons, of the product as originating from a given undertaking must be as a result of the *use of the mark as a trade mark* and thus as a result of the nature and effect of it, which make it capable of distinguishing the product concerned from those of other undertakings.'

"Mars infers therefrom that the use of a sign as an element of a mark cannot be relied on in order to prove the acquisition of distinctive character. However, that conclusion does not carry conviction because the judgement in *Philips* makes no indication that the use of a sign as part of a mark does not constitute the use of a mark as a trade mark.

"In addition, the passage cited above can be categorised in the overall context of the case-law on trade mark law only if use of a mark as a trade mark includes all use leading to acquisition of distinctive character. If it were otherwise signs could not be protected as marks although they have acquired distinctive character only because the use of the sign which led to that distinctiveness did not constitute 'use as a trade mark'. For, as a matter of principle, the Court has regard solely to distinctive character and rejects specific criteria for certain types of marks. Distinctive signs can only not be recognised as trade marks if one of the obstacles to registration under Article 3(1) and (3) of Directive 89/104, referred to as insuperable and in the language of the *Linde* case as preliminary, occurs.

"The concept of use in Article 3(3) of Directive 89/104 is therefore to be construed from the perspective of the result. Any use which confers on a sign the distinctive character necessary for registration as a mark must be deemed to be use of a mark as a trade mark and meets the requirements of Article 3(3). This interpretation is confirmed by the passage of the Judgment in *Philips*, inasmuch as the Court also concentrates on the 'nature and effect' of a mark. However, the nature and effect of a mark precisely constitutes the distinguishing function. A use leading to acquisition of distinctiveness must therefore be considered in the context of Article 3(3)."

(d) *Composite marks*

Providing evidence of distinctiveness may prove problematic if the mark is normally used in combination with other distinctive elements such as word marks or logos. Shape and single colour marks can be particularly problematic. The question of whether a trade mark can acquire distinctiveness when only used as part of a combination has, until recently, remained vexed.

Fortunately, the position has been clarified to some degree by the decision of the European Court of Justice in *Société des Produits Nestlé SA v Mars UK Ltd* Case No C-353/03 (ECJ).

In 1995, Société des Produits Nestlé SA applied for registration in the UK of the mark "HAVE A BREAK" in class 30 in respect of "chocolate; chocolate products; confectionery; candy; biscuits". An opposition to registration was lodged by Mars UK Ltd on the basis that the mark was inherently non-distinctive and that the mark had not acquired the requisite distinctive character as a result of use. The Hearings Officer confirmed that slogans are not inherently distinctive, and therefore evidence was required that showed:

"a concrete expectation among consumers that the goods originate from one undertaking, not just that consumers may be caused to wonder whether or not this might be the case or simply be 'reminded' of the undertaking concerned."

Nestlé provided evidence that the slogan had been used since 1957, and that in the year prior to filing the application, £5 million was spent on advertising, with sales amounting to £139 million. However, the majority of the evidence was concerned with the use of the registered trademark HAVE A BREAK, HAVE A KIT KAT and use of HAVE A BREAK in combination with other distinctive elements. The opposition therefore succeeded on the basis that the slogan HAVE A BREAK had not acquired independent distinctiveness.

In December 2002, Nestlé appealed to the UK High Court of Justice. The appeal was dismissed by Rimer J, who confirmed that independent use of the mark HAVE A BREAK was needed in order to acquire distinctiveness.

In 2003, Nestlé filed an appeal to the UK Court of Appeal. The Court confirmed that the Hearings Officer and Rimer J had correctly applied the law to the question of inherent distinctiveness, but was uncertain in relation to the question of acquired distinctiveness. The Court of Appeal therefore asked the ECJ for guidance on whether distinctive character of a mark may be acquired following, or in consequence of, the use of that mark as part of, or in conjunction with, another mark.

In January 2005, Advocate General Kokott of the ECJ issued an opinion on the question, which was persuasive but not binding on the ECJ. The Advocate General affirmed the ECJ's earlier dicta (in *Windsurfing Chiemsee Produktions-und Vertriebs GmbH v Boots-und Segelzubehör Walter Huber and Franz Attenberger* [1999] ETMR 585 (ECJ)) that part of a composite mark can acquire distinctiveness if it is shown that:

"the relevant consumer groups understand that the element in question, if used separately, designates a product as originating from a specific undertaking, thus distinguishing it from products of other undertakings."

The ECJ followed the Advocate General's opinion and issued its decision confirming that a mark may acquire distinctive character "in consequence of the use of that mark as part of or in conjunction with a registered trade mark" and reverted the case back to the UK to reconsider the particular evidence filed in relation to the HAVE A BREAK slogan.

As the distinctiveness requirements of the New Zealand's Trade Marks Act mirror those clarified by the ECJ, it is likely that Nestlé's success in Europe will shape the assessment of similar trade mark applications in New Zealand.

(4)   *Restraint of registration of registered geographical indication*

Section 20 Trade Marks Act 2002 prohibits the registration of a trade mark that:

- Contains a registered geographical indication for a wine or spirit, or a geographical indication in respect of which an application for registration has been made in good faith under the Geographical Indications (Wine and Spirits) Registration Act 2006; and

- Which relates to a wine/spirit that does not originate from the geographical origin to which the registered geographical indication relates.

The Geographical Indications (Wine and Spirits) Registration Act 2006 is discussed in more detail at 7.2 ("Legislation, treaties, and conventions") earlier in this chapter.

(5)   *Commonly used chemical names*

Section 21 Trade Marks Act 2002 prohibits registration of trade marks that contain commonly used and accepted names for single chemical elements or compounds if the application relates to chemical substances or preparations. The rationale is that such names should be free for all traders to use.

7.6.2 Registration requirements — relative grounds

In addition to the absolute grounds in the Act for refusing to register a trade mark (ss 17-21), an application will be examined under the relative grounds set out in ss 22-30.

Section 25 of the Act is concerned with a comparison between two rival marks, relating to the same or similar goods or services, where one of those marks is already on the Register (either as an application or a registration) and there is a likelihood of confusion or deception.

Section 25 provides that:

> "(1)   The Commissioner must not register a trade mark (trade mark A) in respect of any goods or services if—
>
> > "(a)   it is identical to a trade mark (trade mark B) belonging to a different owner and that is registered, or has priority under section 34 or section 36,—
> >
> > > "(i)   in respect of the same goods or services; or
> > >
> > > "(ii)   in respect of goods or services that are similar to those goods and services, and its use is likely to deceive or confuse; or
> >
> > "(b)   it is similar to a trade mark (trade mark C) that belongs to a different owner and that is registered, or has priority under section 34 or section 36, in respect of the same goods or services or goods or services that are similar to those goods or services, and its use is likely to deceive or confuse; or
> >
> > "(c)   it is, or an essential element of it is, identical or similar to, or a translation of, a trade mark that is well known in New Zealand (trade mark D), whether through advertising or otherwise, in respect of those goods or services or similar goods or services or any other goods or services if the use of trade mark A would be taken as indicating a connection in the course of trade between those other goods or services and the owner of trade mark D, and would be likely to prejudice the interests of the owner.
>
> "(2)   Section 26 overrides subsection (1)."

Section 25 therefore provides that a trade mark shall not be registered if there is a trade mark belonging to a different owner that falls into one (or more) of the following four categories:

- An identical mark for the same goods or services that is registered, or in respect of which an application has been made that has earlier priority;

- An identical mark for similar goods or services that is registered, or in respect of which an application has been made that has an earlier priority, where there is likelihood of deception or confusion;

- A similar mark, for the same or similar goods or services, that is registered, or in respect of which an application has been made that has earlier priority, where there is a likelihood of deception or confusion.

- An identical or similar mark:

  - That is well known in New Zealand in respect of the same or similar goods or services; or

  - That is well known in New Zealand in respect of any other goods or services, if the use of the applicant's mark would be taken as indicating a trade connection with the owner of the well known trade mark and would be likely to prejudice the interests of that owner.

In considering s 25, the scope of future use is assessed on the basis of the marks as they appear on the Register. In the context of a trade mark opposition, the full range of goods covered by the opponent's mark must be considered, not just the goods in relation to which the opponent actually uses its mark. Section 25 can be distinguished from s 17 in this regard.

Under s 60(1), expired registrations will be taken into account for the purposes of s 25 for a period of one year from the date of their expiry. This is to take into account the fact that expired registrations may be restored to the Register up to 12 months from expiry. For further information on restoration of lapsed registrations, refer to 7.9 ("Term, renewal, and restoration").

7.6.3 Onus and time of assessment

The onus is on the applicant to show that its mark does not so nearly resemble the trade mark already on the Register as to be likely to cause deception or confusion under s 25 Trade Marks Act 2002: *NZ Breweries Ltd v Heineken's Bier Browerij Maatschappij NV* [1964] NZLR 115. Although the likelihood of confusion must be assessed as the date of application for the mark in issue, subsequent experience may be relevant as providing an indication of a tendency to confuse. The longer the use continues without confusion, the less likely a finding of confusion is. See, for example, *Helena Rubinstein Ltd's Application* [1960] RPC 229 in which Jacob J held, at p 231, (in respect of an opposition by the proprietor of the trade mark "SKIN DEEP" to the registration of "SKIN DEW"):

> "In the present case, the time interval between the date of application for this trade mark and the date of hearing of the opposition has allowed a period of upwards of two years wherein the goods of both parties have been sold side by side in the same shops under their respective marks, and a number of declarants have stated their experience of such trading. They all declare that their assistants and their customers have found no difficulty arising from this conjoint use. Such practical experience is a far more reliable guide than the anticipatory fear of the Opponents' declarants."

7.6.4 Comparison of trade marks

The most commonly applied test for comparing trade marks under s 25 Trade Marks Act 2002 is that set out in *Pianotist Co's Application* (1906) 23 RPC 774, at p 777:

> "You must take the two words. You must judge them, both by their look and by their sound. You must consider the nature and kind of customer who would be likely to buy those goods in fact, you must consider all the surrounding circumstances; and you must further consider what is likely to happen if each of those trade marks is used in a normal way as a trade mark for the goods of the respective owners of the marks."

Accordingly, when comparing trade marks consideration must be given to:

- The look and sound of each mark;
- The nature and kind of customer likely to buy or use the related goods or services; and
- The surrounding circumstances in which the marks will be used.

Other relevant factors to consider include:

- The whole of each mark (ie, not just the constituent parts);
- The idea of each mark; and
- The effect of an imperfect recollection of the essential features of each mark.

(1) *The look and sound of the marks*

For the purposes of comparison under s 25 Trade Marks Act 2002, the look and sound of similar marks is an important consideration. The more visually and phonetically similar two marks are, the more likely it is that they will be considered confusingly similar.

The primary significance of the look and sound of the respective marks in determining confusing similarity was emphasised in *Stichting Lodestar v Austin, Nicholls & Co Inc* 12/3/07, CA94/05. The Court of Appeal upheld the decision of the Assistant Commissioner that there was no likelihood of deception or confusion between the marks WILD GEESE and WILD TURKEY. The Assistant Commissioner found that, whilst there was a degree of similarity between the marks, the marks were visually and orally significantly different and thus were not confusingly similar. This case is discussed in more detail at 7.6.4(4) ("The idea of the mark") later in this chapter.

In *Nortel Networks Corp v Telecom Corp of NZ* 24/6/04, Goddard J, HC Wellington CIV-2003-485-2631, the appellant, Nortel, sought to register a service mark featuring a stylised version of the words "NORTHERN TELECOM" in relation to telecommunication services. Telecom opposed the application on the basis that Nortel's logo would be likely to deceive or confuse the public having regard to its similarity to Telecom's registered service mark.

In response, Nortel submitted that the use of its logo was not likely to deceive or confuse the public because it did not look or sound like Telecom's service mark. Goddard J disposed of this ground of appeal, at para 41, on the basis of an "essential feature" test (which her Honour found to be an established part of the common law in New Zealand (paras 14-18)).

Applying that test, her Honour, at para 47, found that the word "TELECOM" was an essential feature of Telecom's service mark as well as Nortel's logo, and, as such, the look and sound of the marks was sufficiently similar to deceive or confuse the public.

Although Goddard J's decision was based upon the provisions of the Trade Marks Act 1953, her Honour's reasoning appears to apply equally to the Trade Marks Act 2002.

However care needs to be taken in applying the "essential feature" test, as the assessment under s 25 calls for a comparison of the marks in their entirety. The fact that two marks share a common element, or even an essential feature, should not automatically lead to a finding of confusing similarity, and such cases may be limited to those (such as *Nortel Network*) in which the complainant has an unquestionable monopoly in the common element or essential feature. Where it does not, there may well be room for both parties to use the essential element without confusion.

Thus, for example, in *Champion Products Inc v Champions of the World Ltd* 29/8/03, Gendall J, HC Wellington CIV-2003-485-45; AP49/03, which concerned an appeal from a decision of Assistant Commissioner Walden (*Champion Products Inc's Application* (Commissioner's Decision No T07/2003, 14/2/03, Asst Commr Walden)) to allow the registration of the mark CHAMPIONS OF TOMORROW under the Trade Marks Act 1953 in the face of an earlier registration for CHAMPION, Gendall J held, at para 41:

> "Given the nature, size, visual and aural impact of the mark [CHAMPIONS OF TOMORROW], which in sight, sound, idea and impression is very different to the appellant's marks, I do not consider it likely or probable that a purchaser would be deceived or confused, applying the imperfect recollection test. He or she would not suppose the product containing the appellant's [sic] mark to be a product of the appellant. The only similarity is the use of the plural of the word used singularly by the appellant. But the use of the word in the overall mark, complete a phrase uniquely stylised, is not such as to infringe against s 17(1)."

Similarly in *Canstar Sports Group Inc's Application* (Commissioner's Decision No T05/2004, 29/3/04, Asst Commr Walden), the applicant was permitted to register BAUER in class 25 for clothing, footwear and headgear notwithstanding the Opponent's prior use of EDDIE BAUER. The Assistant Commissioner found that BAUER and EDDIE BAUER were not substantially identical (for the purposes of an enquiry into ownership) and were different in terms of their appearance, sound and ideas.

The essential features test is closely related to the tests applicable to composite marks, which are discussed in more detail at 7.6.4(7) ("Composite marks") below.

The first part of each mark is generally the most important for the purpose of comparison. Thus, in *Hannaford & Burton Ltd v Polaroid Corp* [1976] 2 NZLR 14 (PC), at p 19, Lord Fraser stated in relation to the marks POLAROID and SOLAVOID that:

> "an important matter is that the initial letters 'p' and 's' are not likely to be confused and their Lordships agree with Beattie J that the first syllables 'pol' and 'sol' look and sound dissimilar."

In *London Lubricants (1920) Ltd's Application (TRIPCASTROID)* (1925) 42 RPC 264 (CA), at p 279, Sargent LJ observed that:

"the tendency of persons using the English language to slur the termination of words also has the effect necessarily that the beginning of words is accentuated in comparison and, in my judgement, the first syllable of a word is, as a rule, far more important for the purpose of distinction."

However, note the comments of Ronald Young J in *Telecom IP Ltd v Beta Telecom Ltd* 27/9/06, Ronald Young J, HC Wellington CIV-2004-485-2789 where, at para 36, his Honour qualified the above authorities in the following terms:

"I have no difficulty in accepting as a general rule the first syllable of the first word or the first word in a phrase may be the more important. However, this proposition is not as the respondent has expressed it, some form of principle of law. It is no more than an observation about speech patterns and emphasis. However, in each case the actual phrase or words, as well as their place, will be significant."

That case involved a comparison between a logo mark containing the words BETA TELECOM and the word TELECOM. Ronald Young J concluded that the marks would be confused by a significant section of the public, the word TELECOM being such a strong trade name in New Zealand that its use in another mark would require substantial distinguishing features to set it apart from the TELECOM mark and avoid the similarity of marks causing confusion or deceit.

Consistent with the approach taken by Ronald Young J, where the first part of the mark is relatively non-distinctive, more importance will be attached to the remaining parts of each mark. Thus in *Lever Bros Ltd v J W McGill* [1917] NZLR 595, at p 597, Stout CJ held that:

"no intelligent person could … be led by the respondent's trade mark [HEALO] to believe that he was buying HEALATT balm."

Similarly, in *Effem Foods Ltd v Commissioner of Trade Marks* (1996) 7 TCLR 246; 5 NZBLC 104,209, Salmon J said, at pp 254-255; p 104,216:

"The opponent's mark [BISCATS] is in my judgement an abbreviation of the words 'biscuits for cats'. Biscrok on the other hand is clearly a made up word. It has no reference to any particular animal. All that it has in common with the word 'biscat' is the prefix which is a shortened form of the word 'biscuit'. Looking at the two words as a whole and bearing in mind the way they are likely to be used, I do not believe that purchasers of animal foods or other products will be confused either as to the product or as to origin. If the word 'Biscrok' is confined to the sale of dog biscuits in bulk, confusion is highly unlikely. If, on the other hand, the word 'Biscrok' is used for a line of products, such as for example, 'Biscrok dog food', 'Biscrok cat food' and so on, then once again I do not believe that there will be confusion with Biscats. For the above reasons I conclude that the Hearing Commissioner was wrong in determining that a purchaser might well suppose a common identity of origin."

In *Warner-Lambert Co v SmithKline Beecham Plc* 3/10/03, Hammond J, HC Wellington CIV-2003-485-959, Warner-Lambert Co appealed a decision of Assistant Commissioner Walden (Commissioner's Decision No T13/2003, 18/3/03, Asst Commr Walden) to allow SmithKline Beecham Plc's application for ACTIFAST to proceed to registration, despite Warner-Lambert Co having an earlier registration for ACTIFED. Hammond J concluded that the Assistant Commissioner was correct in allowing the application for ACTIFAST to proceed, and stated, at paras 41-42:

> "However this case is approached, at the end of the day this was a relatively straight forward trade mark application in which the determiner of this issue is driven back to basic elements: whether the look, sound, and idea of the marks is 'so close' that registration ought to be refused.

> "In my view, the Assistant Commissioner was correct. Nothing turns on the prefix 'Acti' which is widely used in the pharmaceutical trade and in respect of which SmithKline (as was appropriately conceded) can entertain no monopoly. ACTIFAST and ACTIFED are visually and aurally distinct and one has a distinct idea behind it, the other does not."

(2) *Type of customer and type of goods or services*

Further relevant considerations under s 25 Trade Marks Act 2002 include the type of customers likely to purchase the goods or services, and the type and price of the goods or services themselves.

If the goods or services are expensive, then consumers are less likely to buy or use them casually and without reflection. They are more likely to spend time considering whether to spend their money on those goods or services. Consequently, there is less likelihood of confusion or deception. Conversely, when the goods are lower priced, they are more likely to be purchased casually or on impulse and therefore there is an increased likelihood of confusion or deception. In such circumstances, consumers are considered likely to take less care in their purchases: *Dr Martens v Figgins* (1999) 44 IPR 281, at p 361.

By way of illustration, *Andrew John Van Lier's Application* (Commissioner's Decision No T24/2002, 27/6/02, Asst Commr Frankel) concerned Van Lier's applications for registration of ARMOURSHIELD, ARMOUR SHIELD ROOF COATINGS (and device) and ARMOURSEAL in class 2 and Ameron's application for removal from the Register of Van Lier's class 37 registrations for ARMOURSHIELD and ARMOURSEAL. The marks in question related to goods and services for the repair of roofs including paints and varnishes. The evidence showed that some of the likely purchasers of goods under these marks would be architects or engineers. The Assistant Commissioner considered that confusion or deception among that specialist type of customer was unlikely. In addition, the Assistant Commissioner considered that protecting roofs and choosing products to do so is an activity consumers will take care in doing. Given that it was not an impulse purchase, the Assistant Commissioner considered that confusion or deception would be unlikely.

Similarly, *Pfizer Laboratories Ltd's Application (AQUABABY)* (Commissioner's Decision No T48/2001, 15/11/01, Asst Commr Frankel) concerned an opposition to registration of AQUABABY by the registered proprietor of WATERBABIES, both in relation to suntan lotion. The Assistant Commissioner considered that suncare products for children are a type of goods that consumers would purchase reasonably carefully and that publicity about the ozone hole and concern about young children would mean that a purchase would not be a "casual or impulse one". The Assistant Commissioner continued:

> "The care consumers exercise when purchasing goods comprises a spectrum. With impulse, casual purchases, such as sweets, consumers will not take much care. At

the other end of the spectrum with products such as televisions and cars, consumers will purchase carefully. I believe suncare products fall between these two extremes. They are more towards the impulse end than the careful considered end, at least for repeat purchases."

In *Canstar Sports Group Inc's Application* (Commissioner's Decision No T05/2004, 29/3/04, Asst Commr Walden), the applicant was permitted to register BAUER in relation to clothing, footwear and headgear notwithstanding the Opponent's prior use of EDDIE BAUER in relation to similar goods. The Assistant Commissioner placed weight on the differences in trade channels through which the goods were sold by each party; the Opponent used catalogues whereas the applicant's goods were available through specialist and general sports stores.

In *Novartis AG's Application* (Commissioner's Decision No T31/2003, 30/7/03, Asst Commr Walden), ZANLAN, in class 5 for "pharmaceutical preparations for human use", was deemed insufficiently similar to ZANTAC in the same class. However, the Assistant Commissioner did not accept the applicant's argument that because the market and trade channels involved would include doctors, pharmacists and other health professionals the likelihood of confusion and deception would be less because the goods would be prescribed and administered by those highly trained professionals. She did however accept that pharmaceuticals were unlikely to be impulse purchases.

(3) *The whole of the mark*

While the marks being compared under s 25 Trade Marks Act 2002 may differ in part, they should not be divided up and compared in portions. It is the overall appearance of each mark that is important.

Thus, in *Bailey (William) Ltd's Application* (1935) 52 RPC 136, at p 151, Farwell J held:

> "I do not think it is right to take a part of the word and compare it with a part of the other word; one word must be considered as a whole and compared with the other word as a whole. In my judgment, it is quite wrong to take a portion of the word and say that, because that portion of the word differs from the corresponding portion of the word in the other case, there is no sufficient similarity to cause confusion. There may be two words which in their component parts are widely different but which, when read or spoken together, do represent something which is so similar as to lead inevitably to confusion."

The justification for this approach is that the commercial impression of a composite mark on an ordinary consumer is created by the mark as a whole, and not by its component parts: *Pfizer Laboratories Ltd's Application (AQUABABY)* (Commissioner's Decision No T48/2001, 15/11/01, Asst Commr Frankel).

As an example, in *The Meow Mix Co's Application* (Commissioner's Decision No T17/2004, 31/8/04, Asst Commr Hastie), the applicant was permitted to register MEOW MIX in class 31 for "cat food" despite the Opponent's prior use of CAT MEOW in relation to cat food since 1993. The Assistant Commissioner considered that the marks did not look alike or sound alike notwithstanding that they both included the word "MEOW". She considered that the position of the word "MEOW" in each mark, combined with the different second word ("mix" as opposed to "cat") sufficiently distinguished the two marks, that the idea of each mark was quite distinct and that they were unlikely to be visually or orally confused.

(4) *The idea of the mark*

In *CPC (UK) Ltd v Keenan* (1986) FSR 527, at p 531, the Court held that:

> "It is relevant to have regard to what is known as the idea of the mark, that is to say the idea which is given by the mark to a person who sees it, and if the mark gives rise to a particular association, that association may be important in relation to the question of deception or confusion."

The "idea of the mark" is the idea that each mark will naturally suggest to the mind of the consumer: *Jafferjee v Scarlett* (1937) 57 CLR 115 (HCA).

The classic example of the idea of the mark leading to confusion is *Hancock v American Steel & Wire Co* 203 F 2d 737 (CCPA, 1953). There the Court held that TORNADO on wire fencing was confusingly similar to CYCLONE on wire fencing. The Court held that CYCLONE was a well known mark, and that the ordinary purchaser would likely confuse TORNADO with CYCLONE because the two words meant the same thing to the ordinary purchaser. The case is notable because the idea was the only similarity between the two words (TORNADO and CYCLONE being visually and phonetically distinct).

However, the cases in which two marks are deemed confusingly similar based solely on a shared idea will be comparatively rare. Thus, in *Cooper Engineering Co Pty Ltd v Sigmund Pumps Ltd* (1952) 86 CLR 536 (HCA), the High Court of Australia emphasised that just because two marks convey the same idea, there may not necessarily be a deceptive resemblance between them. It is merely a factor to be taken into account when comparing marks. The case involved the marks RAIN KING and RAINMASTER applied to water spraying installations for horticultural or agricultural purposes. The High Court observed, at p 538:

> "In the present case, the prefix of the two words is the same word 'Rain', but the suffix 'master' differs from the suffix 'King' in appearance and in sound. This makes the two marks as a whole quite distinct and the marks must be judged as a whole. 'Rainmaster' does not look like 'Rain King' and it does not sound like it. There is not a single common letter in 'master' and in 'king'. The two words are so unalike to the eye and to the ear that counsel for the appellant was forced to rely on the likelihood of deception arising from the words conveying the same idea of the superiority or supremacy of the article as a mechanism for making a spray similar to falling rain or artificial rain as it was called during the argument. But it is obvious that trade marks, especially word marks, could be quite unlike and yet convey the same idea of the superiority of some particular suitability of an article for the work it was intended to do. To refuse an application for registration on this ground would be to give the proprietor of a registered trade mark a complete monopoly of all words conveying the same idea as his trade mark. The fact that two marks convey the same idea is not sufficient in itself to create a deceptive resemblance between them, although this fact could be taken into account in deciding whether two marks which really looked alike or sounded alike were likely to deceive."

The approach advocated in *Cooper Engineering* calls for a balanced assessment which takes into consideration all factors which might cause (or dispel) confusion. In particular it warns against awarding one party a de facto monopoly in word which conveys the same idea as the party's mark if too much emphasis is placed on the idea aspect of the comparison. The same rationale was adopted by the New Zealand High Court in *Platinum Homes (NZ) Ltd v Golden Homes (1998) Ltd* 11/8/06, Miller J, HC Wellington CIV-2005-485-1870, where the Court accepted the appellant's submission that the Assistant Commissioner had paid too much attention to the idea of the mark, and too little to the distinct differences in look and sound, in holding that PLATINUM HOMES was confusingly similar to GOLDEN HOMES. Miller J adopted the aforementioned reasoning of the High Court of Australia in *Cooper Engineering* as well as a similar decision of the Federal Court of Australia in *Sports Café Ltd v Registrar of Trade Marks* (1998) 42 IPR 552 (FCA) which concerned competing marks THE SPORTS CAFÉ and THE CIRCUIT SPORTS CAFÉ. Each was a device mark and a word mark. In relation to the device marks, the Federal Court held that the fact that the two marks conveyed a common idea becomes relevant only if the marks themselves look or sound alike; commonality of idea might then tip the balance in favour of a finding of deception. The Court accepted, at p 559, that the device marks both convey an idea of a café with a sporting ambience, but to hold that the appellant's device mark would thereby become deceptively similar to the cited mark would have the practical effect of giving the proprietor of the latter a monopoly over any mark that conveyed such an idea. The Federal Court concluded, however, that different considerations applied to the word marks. On the facts, confusion was likely because the THE SPORTS CAFÉ mark consisted of three words that were identical to three of the four words used in the cited mark THE CIRCUIT SPORTS CAFE.

Similarly, in *Stichting Lodestar v Austin, Nicholls & Co Inc* 12/3/07, CA94/05, the appellant successfully appealed against the High Court's decision to refuse registration of the mark WILD GEESE in respect of alcoholic and non-alcoholic beverages (*Austin, Nichols & Co Inc v Stichting Lodestar* (2005) 11 TCLR 265) where registration was refused on the basis of similarity of idea between WILD GEESE and the appellant's mark WILD TURKEY.

The respondent had unsuccessfully argued at a hearing before the Assistant Commissioner of Trade Marks that the use and registration of WILD GEESE would deceive or confuse given the reputation attached to the WILD TURKEY trade mark.

On appeal to the High Court Gendall J overturned the decision of the Assistant Commissioner, commenting (correctly), at paras 22-25, that the test to be applied should be as follows:

> "I must look at the sound and appearance of the two competing marks. But I must bear in mind that consumers rarely have the opportunity to view them side by side. Obviously the first word 'WILD' is identical. The words 'TURKEY' and 'GEESE' are not visually the same nor do they sound the same. Yet the whole mark must be considered. This includes the emphasis on the first word 'WILD', as it is associated with a largish bird, and the concept or idea behind the mark may be important. In this case I think that may be decisive. Both marks have as their concept the idea of a wild large bird, that is the subject of a hunt. That is clearly the idea or concept behind each mark. The issue is whether the use of the word 'GEESE' in conjunction with 'WILD' as associated with alcohol products produces such a similarity as is likely to confuse or deceive …

"Of course it is not the literal linguistic assessment that determines the test but whether as a part of an overall assessment of a mark it conveys the same 'idea', and despite the differences, it may deceive. If there is some literal similarity, but a different idea is conveyed, this may be taken into account, although it is not decisive on its own, in assessing whether by reason of the imperfect recollection confusion may arise.

"It is not so much the differences that matter, although of course they are relevant, but rather the similarities, whatever their form may be, that might lead to deception or confusion. Deception or confusion may arise in marks that appear to be related so that it could be thought that they denoted related products from the same source. It is not necessary that all persons in the market are likely to be deceived or confused but there must be a considerable section or significant number of the public who would be likely to be deceived or confused."

However, Gendall J went on to hold, at paras 30 and 31:

"I think in considering the respective marks as a whole in a case such as this, the idea or concept of the mark is critical. It is well known that marks are remembered rather by general impression or by significant detail or idea than by any photographic recollection of the whole. Certainly consumers of alcoholic products, or for that matter other consumers, do not have dictionaries with them when choosing the goods in question or ordering drinks on social or leisure occasions.

"In the present case the leading characteristic of each mark is the first word 'WILD' which is then juxtaposed with the word describing a large game bird that is the subject of a hunt … This is not a case of the Appellant having any monopoly over the use of the word 'WILD' but rather a case where the goods are similar, namely alcoholic beverages, and I am persuaded by the argument of the Appellant that the contextual or idea similarity through the combination of words, conveying the idea of a wild hunted game bird, is likely to lead to confusion."

The Court of Appeal rejected Gendall J's assessment of the mark on the basis that he had given insufficient weight to the views of the Assistant Commissioner, commenting, at para 11:

"She [the Assistant Commissioner of Trade Marks] noted that both marks contained the word 'WILD' as the first word and then the name of a bird. She noted that it was arguable that conceptually the two marks were the same, but said they neither looked the same, nor sounded the same as each other. Ultimately, she rejected the contention that confusion was likely because as a whole the two marks were conceptually similar. She noted the words 'Turkey' and 'Geese' were essential to each mark, and that these were distinctive and dominant components of the mark. She found that the fact that both marks used the name of a bird did not lead to a conclusion that consumers will assume an association between them. She said the general overall impression was a degree of similarity but visually and orally the marks were significantly different and thus not confusing."

The Court of Appeal agreed with the Assistant Commissioner that the concept of the word "WILD" with a large game bird was not the controlling consideration in the case and said, at para 31:

"We give much greater weight to the stark difference between the words 'Turkey' and 'Geese', both in spelling and phonetically. The latter is plural, which also differentiates it from the former. The use of these words with the word 'Wild' does not detract from those differences. The 'concept' is not a strong one – and the class of 'hunted birds' is both broad and ill-defined. The ideas associated with the two marks are quite different. 'Wild Turkey' is evocative of the region of the United States from which bourbon originated whereas 'Wild Geese' has distinct Irish connotations and thus is appropriately linked with a brand of Irish whiskey. Our assessment is that the two marks are unlikely to be confused for one another if used for liquor products sold in New Zealand in both bottled form in liquor outlets and as single drinks in bars."

Leave to appeal the decision of the Court of Appeal to the Supreme Court has been granted: *Austin Nichols & Co Inc v Stichting Lodestar* [2007] NZSC 41 (SC).

The Court of Appeal's decision in *Stichting Lodestar* can be contrasted with the decision of the High Court in *Carabao Tawandang Co Ltd v Red Bull GmbH* 31/8/06, Clifford J, HC Wellington CIV-2005-485-1975, in which a logo comprising a steer's skull and the word "carabao" on a red background was deemed to convey the same idea as the respondent's RED BULL trade mark and logo. The Court considered that confusion would result if the respective marks were used on energy drinks, as the central concept of the two marks was that of a horned cattle beast or bull in association with the colour red.

If two marks convey different meanings, or one mark has a meaning and the other is meaningless, there will be a lower likelihood of confusion or deception. For example, in *Hannaford & Burton Ltd v Polaroid Corp* [1976] 2 NZLR 14 (PC) the Privy Council held that POLAROID and SOLAVOID were not confusingly similar because the marks conveyed different ideas:

"it does not appear to their Lordships that the two words convey the same idea … The ideas are clearly different although their Lordships feel some doubt whether the idea of avoiding the sun would readily occur to members of the public as being associated with the Appellant's [POLAROID] mark if its derivation had not been explained to them. But even if they did not associate that idea with the Appellant's mark there would be no reason why they should associate it with the idea of polarisation. Accordingly, comparison of the marks does not in their Lordship's opinions suggest that confusion between the marks would be likely."

Other examples include:

* *Southern Producers Agriculture NZ Ltd's Application* (Commissioner's Decision No T14/2003, 1/4/03, Asst Commr Hastie), in which the trade mark SPANZ in class 29 for "meat, fish, poultry, game, meat extracts and other meat products in this class; dried and cooked fruits and vegetables; jellies, jams and fruit sources" was deemed insufficiently similar to the Opponent's trade mark SPAM partially on the basis that the inclusion of the letters "NZ" would identify the applicant's mark with New Zealand whereas the Opponent's mark had no apparent meaning.

* *Etam/Tommy Hilfiger Licensing, Inc's Applications* (Commissioner's Decision No T04/2005, 31/1/05, Asst Commr Walden), in which TOMMY and TAMMY were deemed capable of co-existing. The Assistant Commissioner's overall impression was

that the marks looked similar but sounded different and that there were sufficient conceptual differences between them (TOMMY was the name of a male and TAMMY the name of a female).

- *Telecom Corp of NZ Ltd v Chinese Yellow Pages Ltd* 18/11/02, Williams J, HC Auckland CL23/02, in which the plaintiff successfully argued that the defendant's use of "Chinese Yellow Pages" in Chinese ideographs infringed its registration for "Yellow Pages". The Court accepted that although the defendant's ideographs were only legible by readers of Chinese, there was still a reasonable likelihood of deception or confusion arising in those readers to whom the Chinese Yellow Pages was targeted.

- *Nortel Networks Corp v Telecom Corp of NZ* 24/6/04, Goddard J, HC Wellington CIV-2003-485-2631, in which the appellant, Nortel, sought to register a service mark featuring a stylised version of the words "NORTHERN TELECOM" in relation to telecommunication services. The respondent, Telecom, opposed the application on the basis that Nortel's use of its logo would be likely to deceive or confuse the public having regard to its similarity to Telecom's registered service mark for the word "TELECOM".

  In response, Nortel submitted that the use of its logo was not likely to deceive or confuse the public because the idea of Telecom's service mark for the word "TELECOM" was too commonplace and descriptive to indicate origin. Goddard J held, at para 42, that the likely deception and confusion must be gauged in the New Zealand telecommunications market, not the worldwide market. Her Honour noted that Telecom had a reputation in the word "TELECOM" and there was a complete connection between it and that word in the minds of the public in the New Zealand telecommunications market. The generic nature of the name did not detract from this. Accordingly, Goddard J rejected the appellant's submission.

- *Dualstar Entertainment Group, LLC's Application* (Commissioner's Decision No T16/2004, 23/8/04, Asst Commr Walden), in which the applicant was permitted to register MARY-KATEANDASHLEY despite the Opponent's prior use of the trade mark LAURA ASHLEY. The Assistant Commissioner considered that the marks looked and sounded different and were conceptually different in that LAURA ASHLEY gave the impression of one person compared to the applicant's mark which gave the impression of two people, neither of which were the person known as LAURA ASHLEY.

(5) *Imperfect recollection*

An important factor to be taken into account under s 25 Trade Marks Act 2002 is the imperfect recollection of consumers. At issue is whether ordinary consumers with imperfect recall using ordinary care and diligence are likely to confuse the marks.

The Privy Council, in *De Cordova v Vick Chemical Co* (1951) 68 RPC 103, at p 106, held that:

> "In most persons, the eye is not an accurate recorder of visual details and marks are remembered rather by general impression or by some significant detail than by photographic recollection of the whole."

Likewise, in *Rysta Ltd's Application* (1943) 60 RPC 87 (CA), at p 108, Luxmore LJ stated:

"It is the person who only knows one word, and who has perhaps imperfect recollection of it, who is likely to be deceived or confused. Little assistance therefore is to be obtained from a meticulous comparison of the two words, letter by letter and syllable by syllable pronounced with the clarity to be expected from a teacher of elocution. The court must be careful to make allowances for imperfect recollection and the effect of careless pronunciation in speech on the part not only of the person seeking to buy under the trade description but also of the shop assistant ministering to that person's wants."

In *ACCUTRON Trade Mark* (1966) 83 RPC 152, Buckley J summarised the approach to imperfect recollection as follows:

"I have got, first of all, to assume that the opponents are making fair and normal use of their registered marks in respect of the classes of goods to which the registrations relate. I have then to consider whether, in the ordinary course of commercial life, members of the public with imperfect recollection of those marks or of the proposed marks that the applicant seeks to register, would be likely to be confused as to the origin of the goods which they seek to register [and], as to whether they are products of the applicants or the opponents. Having regard to the fact that anyone seeking to buy any of those products in the ordinary way might well have an imperfect recollection of one mark and no knowledge of the others, I have to consider whether such person would be likely to be confused."

(6) *Not side-by-side comparison*

In *Sandow Ltd's Application* (1914) 31 RPC 196, at p 205, the English High Court of Justice observed that, because of the doctrine of imperfect recollection, it is not appropriate to undertake a side-by-side comparison.

"The question is not whether if a person is looking at two trade marks side by side there would be a possibility of confusion; the question is whether the person who sees the proposed trade mark in the absence of the other trade mark, and in view of his general recollection on what the nature of the other trade mark was, would be liable to be deceived and think that the trade mark before him is the same as the other, of which he has a general recollection."

The High Court of Australia made similar comments in *Australian Woollen Mills Ltd v F S Walton & Co Ltd* (1937) 58 CLR 641, at p 658:

"In deciding this question, the marks ought not, of course, to be compared side by side."

The reasoning behind the avoidance of a side-by-side comparison is that the consumer's state of mind must be determined when confronted by allegedly similar trade marks presented individually to the consumer. Differences which are obvious when marks are compared next to each other may be less apparent in recollection.

Notwithstanding the above authorities, in *Nortel Networks Corp v Telecom Corp of NZ* 24/6/04, Goddard J, HC Wellington CIV-2003-485-2631, the High Court relied upon a side-by-side comparison when considering the registrability of Nortel's logo as a service mark.

387

At first instance, the Assistant Commissioner of Trade Marks compared the two marks ("NORTHERN TELECOM" and "TELECOM") and found, despite visual and aural differences between the two, it was extremely likely that the general public in New Zealand would be deceived or confused by Nortel's service mark if registered. On appeal, Nortel submitted that this finding was inappropriate in the absence of any evidence of actual confusion. However, Goddard J, at para 46, rejected that submission on the basis that absence of confusion does no more than prove a negative. His Honour affirmed the Assistant Commissioner's "careful side-by-side comparison of the two marks" to conclude, at para 47, that the look, sound, and idea of the marks was sufficiently similar to deceive or confuse the public, and upheld the decision.

(7)   *Composite marks*

The question of whether the incorporation of a registered trade mark into another mark which contains additional detail is sufficient to give rise to a likelihood of confusion was considered by the European Court of Justice in *Medion AG v Thompson Multi Media Sales Germany and Austria GmbH* [2006] ETMR 13 (ECJ).

Medion was the owner of a German trade mark registration for LIFE and sought to prevent the use of THOMPSON LIFE for identical electronic leisure products. Under German practice on subsequent marks that incorporate earlier ones, a likelihood of confusion was deemed to exist where the shared element characterised the later composite mark to such an extent that the remaining components were secondary to the overall impression of the later mark. Where the shared element merely contributed to the overall impression of the later mark there would be no likelihood of confusion, even if the shared element had an "independent distinctive role" in the later mark. This was known as Pragetheorie.

The German Courts hesitated over Pragetheorie's compatibility with European Union law and asked the ECJ to advise whether the mere "dominance" of an element identical to an earlier mark in a later composite mark is enough, on its own, to give rise to a likelihood of confusion.

The ECJ ruled that the assessment of similarity in cases of composite marks was not simply a case of extracting one element from a composite mark and comparing it with another mark. Trade marks must, it affirmed, be considered as a whole. The ECJ acknowledged that in some cases the overall impression of a composite mark may be dominated by one element but that, in other cases, an element may not dominate but may still have an "independent distinctive role". Accordingly, declining to find a likelihood of confusion simply because a shared element was not dominant was inappropriate in such circumstances.

The ECJ held that the owner of an earlier mark would be deprived of its exclusive trade mark rights if there was a requirement that the earlier mark in the composite mark needs to dominate the overall impression of the later composite mark. Thus, a finding that there is a likelihood of confusion should not be subject to the condition that the overall impression produced by the composite mark should be dominated by the part of it that is represented in the earlier mark.

The ECJ's dismissal of "dominance" as the key issue where a later mark incorporates the whole of an earlier one is sensible. However, it remains to be determined when an element will play "an independent distinctive role" in the later mark. Obvious examples might include cases where the earlier mark is perceived (when used in a composite mark) as a main brand preceding a sub brand, or vice versa, and thus suggests a trade connection.

The decision does however strengthen the position of trade mark owners against owners of well known marks and company names that try to assert their rights by simply adding their company name or famous mark to the existing trade mark.

Composite marks were considered in New Zealand example in *Telecom IP Ltd v Beta Telecom Ltd* 27/9/06, Ronald Young J, HC Wellington CIV-2004-485-2789. In that case, the High Court overturned on appeal a decision of the Assistant Commissioner of Trade Marks allowing registration of a logo containing the words BETA TELECOM in the face of the opponent's prior registrations for TELECOM in block capital and stylised form. The High Court found, at para 31, that "the deceit or confusion [likely to be caused by the BETA TELECOM mark] is that potential customers of BETA will believe BETA is part of or closely connected to TELECOM". The High Court cited with approval the following passage from *Kodak (A'asia) Pty Ltd's Application* (1936) 6 AOJP 1724 (Reg) that this type of confusion or deceit arises from:

> "The well known trade practice of traders adopting a certain word as a trade mark in constructing other trade marks for distinguishing characteristics of their goods by using such word as a basis and adding thereto prefixes of a qualifying nature."

the High Court adding, at para 33:

> "Some of the words added are meaningless in themselves but may be seen to indicate a division or part of the primary word used in the trade mark. This of course is the very deceit and confusion alleged here with regard to the BETA mark."

7.6.5 Comparison of goods and services

The prohibition on registration contained in s 25 Trade Marks Act 2002 applies where the goods or services are the same or are similar.

In determining whether goods are the same or similar, the following factors, as set out in *Jellinek's Application* (1946) 63 RPC 59, are relevant:

- The nature and composition of the goods;

- The respective uses of the goods; and

- The trade channels through which the goods are bought and sold.

Those factors will require appropriate modification in relation to services.

In *British Sugar Plc v James Robertson & Sons Ltd* (1996) 113 RPC 281, at p 296, Jacob J elaborated on those principles to include:

- The respective use of the goods or services;

- The respective users of the goods or services;

- The physical nature of the goods or acts of service;

- The respective trade channels through which the goods or services reach the market;

- Where goods are found or likely to be found in trade channels; and

- The extent to which the respective goods or services are competitive.

In *QS by S Oliver Trade Mark* (1999) 116 RPC 520, at p 527, the British Trade Marks Registry held that "leather goods" and "leather bags" are similar to clothing because they would be regarded as clothing accessories, they are complementary to clothing, the users are the same, the trade channels are the same and they are found adjacent to each other in retail outlets.

In contrast, in *Colorado Group Ltd v Strandbags Group Pty Ltd (No 2)* (2006) 69 IPR 281 (FCA), backpacks were not considered to be goods "of the same description" as handbags, wallets and purses. The Court commented, at para 24, that goods are not of the same description simply because they can be used for the same purpose, for example for personal adornment. Furthermore, at para 26, the fact that goods may be found in the same shop or in the same department within a department store is more a symptom of modern marketing methods, which "tend to unify widely different types of products in the same retail outlet or distribution networks", than any great similarity of goods. Thus, the Court suggested that correspondence in channels of trade was no longer a very helpful line of enquiry in relation to many goods. The Court also considered it relevant that a person wishing to buy a backpack would not find a handbag, wallet or purse to be an acceptable substitute or alternative. The Court rejected a further submission that the bringing together of handbags, wallets and purses in a retail environment was a service "closely related" to backpacks themselves.

NZ Wines & Spirits Ltd's Application (SOLA) (Commissioner's Decision No T30/2002, 12/7/02, Asst Commr Hastie) involved an opposition to registration of SOLA in relation to alcoholic beverages by the proprietor of SOLA in relation to non-alcoholic beverages. The Assistant Commissioner considered that "alcoholic beverages including all general alcoholic beverages except beer" were not the same as "non-alcoholic beverages". The Assistant Commissioner noted that non-alcoholic products are never mixed with other non-alcoholic products but are consumed as is and that:

> "The mere fact that the opponent's product is also used as a mixer with alcohol does not in my view make it any more an RTD [ready to drink]."

Accordingly, the Assistant Commissioner held that the users, uses and trade channels of the two products under consideration were neither the same nor similar.

In *BALMORAL Trade Mark* (1999) 116 RPC 297, at p 302, Jeffrey Hobbs QC determined that "wines" are similar to "whiskey" and "bar services" because it is common to find whiskey and wine sold by merchants (in some cases under their own brands) whose customers expect them to stock both products.

Spa pools and spa baths were deemed to be similar goods in *Watkins Manufacturing Corp's Application (SOVEREIGN)* (Commissioner's Decision No 10/9, 23/12/97).

In contrast, in *Aqua-Tech Ltd's Application* (Commissioner's Decision No T09/2005, 22/3/05, Asst Commr Hastie), the applicant was permitted to register AQUA-TECH for pool and spa ladders, diving boards, pool covers and pool liners and related parts and accessories despite the opponent's prior use of AQUA-TECHNICS on swimming pools and spa pools since April 2001. The decision was overturned on appeal, although on different grounds: *Aqua-Tech Ltd v Aqua Technics Pool and Spa Centre NZ Ltd* 3/10/05,

Venning J, HC Auckland CIV-2005-404-2037; *Aqua Technics Pool & Spa Centre NZ Ltd v Aqua-Tech Ltd* 22/3/07, CA257/05.

Coffee, coffee beverages and coffee substitutes were found to be the same or similar to beverages that are chocolate or cocoa based and non-coffee based flavourings for beverages in *PT Indofood Sukes Makmur's Application* (Commissioner's Decision No T51/2001, 6/11/01, Asst Commr Popplewell).

Soft drinks and fruit juices were held not to be the same as or similar to mandarins in *Aenid 17 Ltd's Application* (Commissioner's Decision No T22/2001, 22/5/01, Asst Commr Howie).

7.6.6 Confusion or deception

A commonly applied test for the comparison of marks was set out by Evershed J in *Smith Hayden & Co Ltd's Application* (1946) 63 RPC 97, at p 101:

> "Assuming use by [the opponent] of its trade mark in a normal and fair manner for [the relevant goods or services], is the [court or Commissioner] satisfied that there will be no reasonable likelihood of deception or confusion among a substantial number of persons if [the applicant] used its mark in a normal and fair manner also for [the relevant goods or services]?"

The approach to confusion or deception set out in *Pioneer Hi-Bred Corn Co v Hy-Line Chicks Pty Ltd* [1978] 2 NZLR 50 (CA) in relation to s 17 (of the Trade Marks Act 1953) is applicable in this context to considerations under s 25 Trade Marks Act 2002 (refer to 7.6.1 ("Registration requirements — absolute grounds")).

7.6.7 Well-known marks

Section 25(1)(c) Trade Marks Act 2002 prohibits the registration of a trade mark where the trade mark, or an essential element of it, is identical or similar to, or a translation of, a trade mark that is well-known in New Zealand, provided certain other criteria apply.

In *John Goddard McCarthy's Application (AULD MUG)* (Commissioner's Decision No T47/2000, 13/10/00, Asst Commr Popplewell), the Assistant Commissioner noted, at p 17, that the "internationalisation of trade and the special position recognised for famous or well known trade marks or service marks laid the foundation for Article 16 and the amendments made to the New Zealand Act".

The corresponding section of the Trade Marks Act 1953 which dealt with well-known marks was s 17(2) and (4). Section 17(2) provided as follows:

> "(2)   Subject to subsection (5) of this section, no trade mark shall be registered in respect of any goods if the trade mark (or an essential element) is identical or similar to or a translation of a trade mark which is well-known in New Zealand (whether through advertising or otherwise)—
>
> "(a)   As respects those goods or any similar goods; or
>
> "(b)   As respects any other goods if use of the first-mentioned trade mark would be taken as indicating a connection in the course of trade between those other goods and the proprietor of the well-known

> trade mark, and would be likely to prejudice the interests of such proprietor,—
>
> where the use of the first-mentioned trade mark would be likely to deceive or cause confusion."

Section 17(4) provided the same in relation to services.

Section 25(1)(c) Trade Marks Act 2002 is similar to s 17(2) and (4) of the 1953 Act, with two major differences. These are set out in IPONZ Practice Guideline, "Relative Grounds: Identical or Similar Trade Marks" as follows:

- Section 17(2) of the 1953 Act prohibited registration of a trade mark in respect of goods if there was a trade mark belonging to a different owner that was well-known in New Zealand in respect of the same, similar or (in certain circumstances) other goods.

  Section 17(4) of the 1953 Act prohibited registration of a trade mark in respect of services if there was a trade mark belonging to a different owner that was well-known in New Zealand in respect of the same, similar or (in certain circumstances) other services.

  In contrast, s 25(1)(c) of the 2002 Act prohibits registration of a trade mark in respect of goods or services if there is a trade mark belonging to a different owner that was well-known in New Zealand in respect of the same, similar or (in certain situations) other goods or services.

- Under s 17(2) and (4) of the 1953 Act, the Commissioner could only refuse to register a trade mark if, in light of the existence of the well-known trade mark, its use would be likely to deceive or cause confusion.

  There is no such requirement under s 25(1)(c).

It follows that s 25(1)(c) of the 2002 Act gives greater protection to well-known trade marks than previously conferred in s 17(2) and (4) of the 1953 Act.

Section 25(1)(c) covers all well-known marks, that is, registered or unregistered. Thus, a common law trade mark may be considered a "trade mark that is well known in New Zealand" under s 25(1)(c).

Proving that a mark is "well known" is more difficult than establishing an awareness under s 17. It follows that an opponent or applicant for revocation will rarely succeed where a claim under s 17 has failed. In *Anheuser-Busch Inc v Budweiser Budvar National Corp* [2001] 3 NZLR 666, which was argued under the 1953 Act, the plaintiff, in attempting to revoke the defendant's registrations for "Budejovicky Budvar", submitted that "Budweiser" was "unarguably one of the world's best known brands" and that "Budejovicky" was simply a Czech translation of that word. The plaintiff further argued that there was a likelihood of confusion arising from use of the translated word.

Doogue J held that the plaintiff's case was "fundamentally flawed" in respect of s 17(2). Having already ruled out the possibility of confusion under ss 16 and 17(1), his Honour considered that "there can be no more likelihood of confusion under this section as a result of 'Budejovicky' and 'Budweiser' being comparable in the Czech and German languages than there can be under s 16 or s 17(1)."

The case was appealed to the Court of Appeal (*Anheuser-Busch Inc v Budweiser Budvar National Corp* [2003] 1 NZLR 472; (2002) 7 NZBLC 103,812 (CA)), although the Court of Appeal did not discuss in further detail, nor overturn, the findings in respect of s 17(2) and (4).

Well known marks are discussed in more detail at 7.11.3 ("Infringement of a well known trade mark") later in this chapter.

(1) *Examination procedure*

A party relying on s 25(1)(c) Trade Marks Act 2002 is required to show that the trade mark relied upon is well known in New Zealand. Alternatively, they need to show that the mark is a translation of a trade mark that is well known in New Zealand.

Where IPONZ, during examination, is of the view that the criteria in s 25(1)(c) apply, a citation will be raised. Reasons are to be provided as to why the cited mark is considered to be "well known in New Zealand" as at the date of application of the mark under examination (IPONZ Practice Guideline, "Relative Grounds: Identical or Similar Trade Marks").

(2) *Essential elements*

In *Nortel Networks Corp v Telecom Corp of NZ* 24/6/04, Goddard J, HC Wellington CIV-2003-485-2631, the High Court considered an appeal from a decision of the Assistant Commissioner of Trade Marks who declined to register Nortel's service mark for a stylised version of the words "NORTHERN TELECOM" because Nortel's logo contained an essential feature of Telecom's registered trade mark (the word "TELECOM"), and thus would be likely to deceive or confuse the public.

Nortel submitted that the use of its logo was not likely to deceive or confuse the public because it did not look or sound like Telecom's service mark. Goddard J disposed of this ground of appeal, at para 41, on the basis of an "essential feature" test (which her Honour found to be an established part of the common law in New Zealand (paras 14-18). Applying that test, her Honour, at para 47, found that the word "TELECOM" was an essential feature of Telecom's service mark as well as Nortel's logo, and, as such, the look and sound of the marks was sufficiently similar to deceive or confuse the public.

The essential feature test is expressly incorporated into s 25(1)(c) Trade Marks Act 2002.

Thus, in *Viva Time Corp's Application* (Commissioner's Decision No T14/2002, 14/5/02, Asst Commr Hastie), the applicant's trade mark PAUL PEUGEOT in class 14 for "watches" was deemed confusingly similar to the Opponent's PEUGEOT mark which had been used extensively in New Zealand for automobiles. In determining the question of whether confusion or deception was likely, the Assistant Commissioner noted that the applicant's mark incorporated the Opponent's PEUGEOT mark and PEUGEOT was not only an essential feature of the Opponent's mark, it was the entire mark.

7.6.8 Consent and honest concurrent use

Section 26 Trade Marks Act 2002 allows two marks that are identical or very similar to be entered on the Register if the owner of the earlier mark consents to the registration of the later mark, or where a case for "honest concurrent use" is made out by the applicant.

Section 26 provides:

"The Commissioner must register trade mark A if—

"(a)   the owner of trade mark B, trade mark C, or trade mark D (as the case may require) consents to the registration of trade mark A; or

"(b)   the Commissioner or the Court, as the case may be, considers that a case of honest concurrent use exists, or other special circumstances exist, that, in the opinion of the Court or the Commissioner, makes it proper for the trade mark to be registered subject to any conditions that the Court or the Commissioner may impose."

Pursuant to s 26(a), s 25 will not prevent the registration of a trade mark if consent to the registration has been provided by the owner(s) of the cited mark(s). Where an applicant has obtained consent, the applicant must forward the consent document to IPONZ. Specific guidelines regarding consent are set out in IPONZ Practice Guideline, "Methods of Overcoming a Citation". The rest of this section will focus on the requirements for proving honest concurrent use.

A case for honest concurrent use may be made out during examination if a prior mark is cited under s 25, by filing evidence in the form of a statutory declaration/affidavit. The other circumstance in which honest concurrent use may be proven is in opposition or infringement proceedings. For further information on opposition and infringement proceedings refer to 7.7 ("Oppositions") and 7.11 ("Enforcement of rights") later in this chapter.

While case law considering the issue of honest concurrent use under s 26 Trade Marks Act 2002 will take some time to emerge, there have been a number of decisions dealing with the issue of honest concurrent use under the equivalent provision of the 1953 Act, s 17(5). These decisions are discussed below with reference to s 26(b).

(1)   *Onus*

The onus of satisfying the requirements of s 17(5) rests with the applicant: *Dunn's Trade Mark* (1890) 7 RPC 311 (HL).

(2)   *Commissioner/Court has unfettered discretion*

The Commissioner/Court has an unfettered discretion under s 17(5) and each case has to be determined on its own particular circumstances: *VB Distributors Ltd v Matsushita Electric Industrial Co Ltd* (1999) 9 TCLR 349. Although the rights of the competing parties are generally determined as at the date of application, that does not prevent the Court from looking at conduct and events after that date in dealing with issues before it: *Matsushita*, at p 363.

(3)   *Factors to consider*

The relevant considerations for determining whether honest concurrent use exists are based on the decision of the House of Lords in *Pirie (Alex) and Sons Ltd's Application* (1933) 50 RPC 147 (HL). Those considerations were cited and used in *Re Trade Mark SOLPRENE* (1980) 1 NZIPR 310 and can be summarised as follows:

•   The extent of use of the mark in geographic area, time and quantity;

- The degree of confusion likely to ensue from the resemblance of the marks, which is to a large extent indicative of the measure of public inconvenience;

- The honesty of the concurrent use;

- Whether any instances of confusion have in fact been proved; and

- The relative inconvenience that would be caused if the mark were registered, subject if necessary to any conditions and limitations.

Each of these factors is discussed below.

(a)   *The extent of use in time and quantity, and the area of trade*

There is no minimum period of concurrent use. Generally, a substantial period of use must be shown, although each case is considered on its own merits.

In *The Goodyear Tire & Rubber Co's Application* (Commissioner's Decision No T20/2002, 12/6/02, Asst Commr Duckworth) the Assistant Commissioner considered a period of 6 months use of the mark before the date of application to be insufficient to establish that there had been honest concurrent use of the mark.

However, in other circumstances, such as where the applicant's use of his or her mark is much greater than that of the cited mark, or is on an extremely large scale, a short period may be acceptable: *Peddie's Application* (1944) 61 RPC 31.

In *Kiwi Polish Co v Kempthorne Prosser & Co* [1925] NZLR 26, the New Zealand Court of Appeal held that the concurrent trade mark use must be in New Zealand. Following that decision the Court in *VB Distributors Ltd v Matsushita Electric Industrial Co Ltd* (1999) 9 TCLR 349 refused to take into account use of the subject mark in Australia when determining whether there had been honest concurrent use in New Zealand.

This notwithstanding, the coexistence of marks on the Register of another country may be a relevant factor to take into account when determining whether a mark can also coexist on the Register in New Zealand. However, it will only be of persuasive value when the goods or services listed in the specification for the respective marks in New Zealand are the same or essentially similar to those covered by the corresponding overseas registrations: *Goodyear*.

It should be readily apparent that the use relied upon to support a claim of honest concurrent use must be in the same field as the conflicting mark. In *Telecom IP Ltd v Beta Telecom Ltd* 27/9/06, Ronald Young J, HC Wellington CIV-2004-485-2789, the High Court considered an appeal from a decision of the Assistant Commissioner of Trade Marks permitting registration of the BETA TELECOM logo in the face of registrations for the trade mark TELECOM and evidence that the opponent had an extensive and widespread reputation in the word TELECOM in relation to telecommunication services in New Zealand. The applicant relied, in part, on a claim to honest concurrent use of its mark. This claim was rejected by the High Court on the basis that there was limited evidence of use of the BETA TELECOM mark as applied for, and that the mark had not actually been used in relation to telecommunication services. The High Court commented, at para 58:

> "The statutory requirement in s 17(5) is that there must be concurrent use. This involves primarily a comparison between what services/retail sales in fact BETA

have been in the business of providing, compared with the services/retail sales by TELECOM to see if there has indeed been concurrent use of the marks. It is quite clear from the description of BETA's business and the use of the mark up until 2001 that it does not come within the description of concurrent use. Their work has been in the provision of what is essentially retail sales and installation and repair of goods. While some of the goods sold by BETA have a telecommunications aspect it is in my view stretching the ordinary use of telecommunication services to include them within this category. This is especially so when other categories [of goods/services] more naturally apply to BETA's use."

(b) *Degree of confusion likely to ensue*

The more likely it is that the public will be confused by the registration of two identical or similar marks, the weaker the case is for concurrent registration: *Indtex Trading Ltd's Application* (Commissioner's Decision No T21/2000, 9/6/00, Asst Commr Robinson).

In *Nortel Networks Corp v Telecom Corp of NZ* 24/6/04, Goddard J, HC Wellington CIV-2003-485-2631, the High Court considered an appeal from a decision of the Assistant Commissioner of Trade Marks who declined to register Nortel's service mark for a stylised version of the words "NORTHERN TELECOM" on the basis of honest concurrent use because confusion between Nortel's logo and Telecom's registered service mark for the word "TELECOM" was likely to adversely affect the public interest.

On appeal, Nortel submitted that the marks were not likely to deceive or confuse the public because Nortel's logo did not sound or look like Telecom's registered service mark, the idea of Nortel's logo differed to Telecom's service mark, the word "TELECOM" was not distinctive, Nortel held the same registered trade mark in relation to goods since 1976, and there was no evidence of actual confusion or deception proven.

Nortel also submitted that the use of its logo was not likely to deceive or confuse the public because the idea of Telecom's service mark for the word "TELECOM" was too commonplace and descriptive to indicate origin. Goddard J held, at para 42, that the likely deception and confusion must be gauged in the New Zealand telecommunications market, not the worldwide market. Her Honour noted that Telecom had a reputation in the word "TELECOM" and that, in the minds of the public in the New Zealand telecommunications market, there was a complete connection between Telecom and that word. The generic nature of the name did not detract from this.

Accordingly Goddard J upheld the decision of the Assistant Commissioner, concluding, at para 47, that the look, sound, and idea of the marks was sufficiently similar to deceive or confuse the public.

(c) *Actual instances of confusion*

The fact that there are no known instances of confusion is not of itself conclusive that the marks will not be confused, but it is a factor to be taken into account: *Re Trade Mark SOLPRENE* (1980) 1 NZIPR 310. However, the applicant's case for honest concurrent use will be stronger if no examples of actual confusion are provided. Thus, in *Pirie (Alex) and Sons Ltd's Application* (1933) 50 RPC 147 (HL), at p 160, it was stated that a lack of proof of confusion "cannot be regarded as unimportant even though allowance be made for difficulty of proof".

(d) *Honesty of the concurrent use*

It is essential that the concurrent use be honest. The standard of honesty has been described as "commercial honesty, which differs not from common honesty": *Parkington & Co Ltd's Application* (1946) 63 RPC 171, at p 182.

Accordingly, registration will not be granted to an applicant who adopted its mark with the knowledge that the mark was identical or very similar to an earlier mark: *Cohen v Fidler & Co* (1916) 33 RPC 129.

(e) *Relative inconvenience*

The relative inconvenience that would be caused if the later mark were registered is another relevant factor. The effect of registration on each owner must be considered.

(4) *"Other circumstances"*

Section 26(b) Trade Marks Act 2002 provides for registration of identical or nearly resembling marks in the case of honest concurrent use or in the case of "other special circumstances which in the opinion of the Court or Commissioner make it proper" to register the mark.

In *Kerly's Law of Trade Marks and Trade Names* (12th ed), London, Sweet and Maxwell, 1986, paras 10-21, it is suggested that:

> "The words 'other special circumstances', include any circumstances peculiar to the applicant in relation to the subject matter of the application, and this includes use by an applicant of his mark before the conflicting mark was registered or used, or the fact that the mark is the ordinary mark of a foreign company so that it would cause hardship if it could not be used here."

The authorities cited for those propositions are *Holt & Coy (Leeds) Ltd's Application* (1957) 74 RPC 289, at p 294, and *ACEC Trade Mark* (1965) 82 RPC 369.

(5) *Examples*

- In *The Goodyear Tire & Rubber Co's Application* (Commissioner's Decision No T20/2002, 12/6/02, Asst Commr Duckworth), the applicant's trade mark GOODYEAR VENTURA in class 12 for "motor vehicle tyres, excluding tyres for motorcycles" was deemed confusingly similar to a prior registration for the trade mark VENTURA in class 12 for "vehicle accessories".

- In *Timtech Chemicals Ltd's Application* (Commissioner's Decision No T23/2002, 13/6/02, Asst Commr Gallagher), the trade mark TIMTECH CHEMICALS (in stylised form and in combination with a logo) was deemed confusingly similar to prior registrations for the trade mark TANTECH CHEMICALS LTD in relation to the same goods and services.

7.6.9 Restraint of registration of certain words or representations

Under the Trade Marks Act 1953, the Commissioner had a discretion to refuse to register any application for a sign that included:

- The words "patent" or "patented" or "registered" or "registered design" or "copyright" or any abbreviations thereof, or any words to the like effect. For example, IPONZ would not permit the symbol ™ or ® to appear in a representation attached to an application; and

- Any representation of the Sovereign or any member of the Royal Family, unless consent to registration was obtained beforehand.

The provisions regarding the registrability of trade marks which contain representations of a member of the Royal Family or the Sovereign have been carried across into the 2002 Act (s 24). However, the prohibition against registration of trade marks containing the words "copyright", "patent", "patented" etc have been removed by s 22.

7.6.10 Restraint of registration of Royal Arms, etc

Sections 27-30 Trade Marks Act 2002 govern the registrability of trade marks which contain flags, armorial bearings, insignia, orders of chivalry, or decorations of any entity.

Where an application for registration contains any of the above matter, under s 27(1) the Commissioner may require the applicant to obtain the written consent of the person who appears to the Commissioner to be entitled to consent to the registration and use of the sign as a trade mark. However, s 27(1) of the Act applies subject to ss 28 or 29 of the Act.

Under s 28, the Commissioner must not register a trade mark where the mark contains a representation of the flag, armorial bearing, or other state emblem, or an official sign or hallmark of a convention country.

Section 29 prohibits the registration of a trade mark that contains a representation of an armorial bearing, flag or other emblem of an international intergovernmental organisation of which one or more convention countries are members (for example, the United Nations).

Under s 29(2), the Commissioner may register a trade mark if the Commissioner considers that use of the armorial bearing, flag, or other emblem, or the abbreviation or name of the international organisation concerned in the manner proposed:

- Is not likely to suggest to the public that a connection exists between the organisation and the trade mark; or

- Is not likely to mislead the public as to the existence of a connection between the user and the organisation.

7.7 Oppositions

Anyone may oppose registration of a trade mark, by filing a Notice of Opposition at IPONZ within 3 months of acceptance of the application being advertised in the Journal.

Oppositions are most frequently initiated by companies/persons concerned that:

- Registration of the subject mark will prevent them from legitimately carrying on business;

- The subject mark will be confused with their own trade mark; or

- They have a competing claim to ownership of the subject mark.

7.7.1 Grounds

The Notice of Opposition must include a statement of grounds on which the opponent objects to registration of the trade mark. The usual grounds are that:

- The mark sought to be registered is confusingly similar to another trade mark which is either registered or in use by another party: refer to 7.6 ("Grounds for not registering") earlier in this chapter;

- The mark is descriptive or incapable of distinguishing the applicant's goods or services from those of others: refer to 7.5 ("Registrability") earlier in this chapter;

- The mark is deceptive: refer to 7.6.6 ("Confusion or deception") earlier in this chapter; or

- The mark has been misappropriated from another party: refer to 7.6 ("Grounds for not registering") earlier in this chapter.

It is important that the Notice includes all of the grounds on which the opponent intends to rely, and that these grounds are pleaded accurately and fully: *Rainbow Technologies Inc v Logical Networks Ltd* [2003] 3 NZLR 553.

In *Platinum Homes (NZ) Ltd v Golden Homes (1998) Ltd* 11/8/06, Miller J, HC Wellington CIV-2005-485-1870, Miller J confirmed on appeal that, where the opponent is alleging that the mark sought to be registered is confusingly similar to another trade mark which is either registered or in use by another party, it is not necessary for the opponent to be the owner of the marks it says will be confused with the opposed trade mark.

7.7.2 Procedure

Trade mark opposition proceedings are dealt with under ss 47-49 Trade Marks Act 2002 and regs 73-85 Trade Marks Regulations 2003. The usual procedure is as follows:

- A Notice of Opposition to the grant of a trade mark can be filed within 3 months of acceptance of the trade mark application being first advertised. IPONZ considers a mark to be "first advertised" when it is advertised in the Patent Office Journal (IPONZ Practice Guideline, "Acceptance and Registration"). The Notice of Opposition must set out the grounds on which the opposition is based, and contain the minimum information required by reg 74.

  A copy of the Notice must be sent by the Commissioner to the applicant (reg 47(3)).

  Under reg 76, it is possible to file proceedings in opposition to the registration of a trade mark outside of the 3-month advertisement window. Regulation 76 provides that a Notice of Opposition, that has been sent to the Commissioner within 6 months of the filing date of the application in question, will be deemed to have been sent within the time for filing the Notice, if the applicant and the opponent each consent to this.

- A Counterstatement must be filed within 2 months of the applicant receiving the Notice of Opposition. The Counterstatement should set out which facts, if any, in the Notice of Opposition the applicant admits, and contain the minimum information required by reg 80(1). If not filed, the applicant is deemed to have abandoned the application, unless the Commissioner otherwise directs.

Again, the Commissioner is required under reg 48(3) to send a copy of the Counterstatement to every person who gave notice of an opposition.

- The opponent must file evidence in support of the opposition within 2 months of receiving the Counterstatement. If the opponent fails to file evidence or notice of its intention not to file evidence before the deadline, the opposition will automatically be deemed abandoned. Evidence may be in the form of statutory declarations or affidavits.

- The applicant may file evidence in support of its trade mark application within 2 months of receiving the opponent's evidence.

- If the applicant files evidence in support of the application, the opponent may file evidence in reply within one month of receiving the applicant's evidence. This evidence must be strictly in reply to matters raised in the applicant's evidence.

- Under reg 33, a party who files evidence with the Commissioner must, as soon as practicable, send a copy of the evidence to the opposite party and any party intervening.

- On completion of the evidence, the Commissioner will set the matter down for a hearing. Submissions may be given in writing or presented orally by counsel (or both). Each party is currently required to pay a fee before the hearing if he or she wishes to be heard (either in writing or in person at the hearing).

In *The NZ Rugby Football Union Inc's Application* (Commissioner's Decision No T17/2005, 7/6/05, Asst Commr Hastie), an application to consolidate two separate proceedings opposing the same trade mark on substantially the same grounds was rejected on the basis that there was no express power conferred on the Commissioner by the Act or Regulations, and therefore no inherent jurisdiction, to do so.

7.7.3 Extensions of time

Under reg 75(1), the deadline for filing a Notice of Opposition to the registration of a mark is 3 months after the date when acceptance of the application was first advertised. However, under reg 75(2), the Commissioner may, if requested in writing, extend the deadline for filing a Notice of Opposition by up to 2 months, with the consent of the applicant, or up to one month, in the absence of consent. Any such request for an extension of the deadline in this regard must be made on or before the deadline has expired. Regulation 75(3) prohibits the Commissioner from extending the deadline for opposing after the deadline has expired.

Apart from reg 75(3), it is generally possible to obtain an extension of time for taking any action in opposition proceedings under reg 32. An application for an extension of time must be made in writing setting out any grounds that justify the extension sought.

In *Natural Health NZ 2002 Ltd's Applications* (Commissioner's Decision No T20/2004, 7/9/04, Asst Commr Walden) it was confirmed that the Commissioner had the power to grant an extension of time retrospectively unless there is express wording in the regulations stipulating that the time must not be extended. The statement in reg 82 that the opposition would be discontinued if the Opponent did not, within the "applicable deadline", file evidence or notify the Commissioner that the Opponent did not intend to file evidence was deemed not to be an express provision preventing the granting of an extension, and the extension requested by the applicant was granted.

In *Cadbury Ireland Ltd's Application* (Commissioner's Decision No T26/2005, 19/9/05, Asst Commr Brown QC), the owner of a number of VAPOUR ACTION registrations (which were the subject of a non-use action), sought leave to file evidence out of time. Assistant Commissioner Brown QC noted that although the Trade Marks Regulations 1954 conferred a broad discretion on the Commissioner to accept evidence "in the interests of justice", the Trade Marks Regulations 2003 showed a clear intention to confine the Commissioner's power evidenced by inclusion of the phrase "genuine and exceptional circumstances that justify" the exercise of that discretion. Accordingly, the Assistant Commissioner rejected the filing of one affidavit which could have been prepared earlier, but allowed three further affidavits which could not have been filed earlier, one of which was intended to clarify earlier evidence to avoid ambiguity.

It is not uncommon to seek and obtain the other party's consent to an extension of time, particularly if it is within the guidelines set out in the practice note on extensions: IPONZ, Information for Clients, No 7, 17 August 1999. If consent is forthcoming, it would be unusual for the extension not to be granted by the Commissioner.

If a party does not give consent to an extension of time request, the Commissioner will exercise his or her discretion as to whether to grant the extension based on the reasons advanced by the applicant party.

The decision of *Amadeus Global Travel Distribution SA v Sabre Inc* 14/3/03, Ronald Young J, HC Wellington AP126/02 has had a significant impact on current IPONZ practice with regard to the granting of extensions of time. Although the facts concerned a patent opposition, the issues discussed have equal application to trade mark opposition proceedings.

Amadeus opposed Sabre's patent application in proceedings before the Commissioner. Both parties were slow in filing their Statement of Case and Counterstatement respectively. Amadeus sought an initial extension of time in which to file evidence in support of the opposition, and this was granted. A subsequent extension requested by Amadeus was refused. Amadeus sought a hearing before the Commissioner in relation to the refusal, but was unsuccessful, and appealed to the High Court.

IPONZ's guidelines for granting extensions of time in patent oppositions identified typical periods of extension. The guidelines also specifically stated that outside those standard extension periods exceptional circumstances would need to exist to justify an extension. The Court expressed doubt whether the guidelines were appropriate, as neither the Act nor the Regulations referred to "exceptional circumstances" or contained pre-ordained extension periods. The Court went on to note that the time-frames laid out in the Patents Act and Regulations were created 50 years ago and, with the complexity of modern litigation, were woefully inadequate.

Disregarding the guidelines, the Court took the view that the decision to grant an extension must depend on the circumstances of each individual case, and that it is vital that justice is done between the parties. This includes ensuring an expeditious hearing, and the proper exchange of information. However, most importantly, the parties should be afforded every opportunity to put their best case forward. The Court also commented that if there was any delay on the part of one or both of the parties, this could be taken into account when the issue of costs is addressed at the conclusion of proceedings.

Taking all the factors into account, the Court determined that the hearings officer was wrong to have refused Amadeus an extension of time in which to complete its evidence in relation to the proceedings.

This case (and *Royal NZ Yacht Squadron v Daks Simpson Group Plc* [2002] NZAR 187, which confirmed that the standard of evidence in proceedings before the Commissioner is the same as that required in the High Court) suggest that IPONZ practice is likely to be much more closely aligned with that of the District and/or High Courts in the future.

7.7.4 Halt in proceedings

If the Commissioner thinks it appropriate, or on the application of a party to the opposition proceedings, the Commissioner may halt the proceedings under reg 28 Trade Marks Regulations 2003. A halt in proceedings is effectively a stay of proceeding, and often this is requested where meaningful settlement negotiations are underway between the parties, with a realistic expectation of settlement. According to reg 28(2), the Commissioner may halt the proceedings for a period and on the terms and conditions that the Commissioner thinks appropriate. However, the proceedings must not be halted for more than 6 months at a time. Regulation 28(3) allows the Commissioner to halt the proceedings for further periods, but again for no more than 6 months at a time.

Under the Trade Marks Act 1953, a similar procedure was referred to as abeyance. Abeyance could only be achieved with the consent of all of the parties, which was required to be obtained and filed before any impending deadline. Although reg 28 does not specifically require the consent of the parties for a halt in proceedings to take place, it is assumed that a halt will only be granted with the consent of all parties. It is also expected that should any party's consent be withdrawn at any time, the proceedings will resume from the point at which they were halted. This would appear to be consistent with reg 28(4), which allows the Commissioner to recommence the proceedings at any stage.

The application of reg 28 in circumstances where a halt is requested by one party without the consent of the other was considered in *Tamsin Cooper's Application* (Commissioner's Decision No T23/2006, 2/10/06, Asst Commr Walden). The opponent had opposed three trade mark applications which were subsequently consolidated under a single notice. The opponent then filed its evidence and the applicant sought a halt in proceedings primarily on the basis that the opponent had filed High Court proceedings against the applicant subsequent to the opposition proceeding, and the applicant believed there was substantial similarity between the High Court proceedings and the opposition. Following the UK Registrar's decision in *GENIUS Trade Mark* [1999] RPC 741, the Assistant Commissioner agreed that multiple actions should be avoided if the issues between them were substantially the same. However, she was not convinced that the issues raised by the opposition and by the High Court proceedings were the same, as the legal tests would be different and, while the opposition would address the fair and notional use of the marks applied for, the High Court proceedings would address a range of matters relating to the actual conduct of the applicant. The Assistant Commissioner also noted that a halt would provide the applicant with an advantage over the opponent in terms of the time available to the applicant to prepare its evidence. Accordingly, the applicant's request for a halt in the proceedings was declined.

7.7.5 Cause of action estoppel

The fact that a party may have unsuccessfully opposed registration of a mark should not give rise to an issue estoppel in respect of subsequent application to revoke the registered mark by the same party, even if the revocation action is on substantially the same grounds as were alleged in the opposition. In *Special Effects Ltd v L'Oreal SA* [2006] RPC 33 (Ch), the English High Court found that the doctrine of cause of action estoppel did extend to a situation where the previous action was an opposition, however this finding was subsequently overturned on appeal.

Special Effects were the assignees of a UK trade mark registration for SPECIAL EFFECTS in class 3. When the predecessors in title of SPECIAL EFFECTS applied to register the mark L'Oreal filed an opposition based, in part, on alleged passing off of L'Oreal's own mark SPECIAL FX. The opposition failed on all counts and the mark proceeded to registration. Following its acquisition, Special Effects brought an infringement action against L'Oreal in respect of its use of the SPECIAL FX trade mark. In response, L'Oreal challenged the validity of the registration and issued its own counterclaim for passing off.

The High Court was required to consider whether L'Oreal was precluded by cause of action estoppel, issue estoppel, or an abuse of process, in challenging the validity of the SPECIAL EFFECTS registration on some or all of the grounds previously relied in the opposition proceedings, and whether the same estoppels would prevent L'Oreal from claiming passing off based on an unregistered trade mark right which had already been considered and dismissed in the opposition proceedings.

The High Court found that L'Oreal was indeed precluded from running these arguments by cause of action estoppel and issue estoppel. The finding seems to have been based primarily on the fact that the unsuccessful opposition proceedings before the Registry, and the invalidity proceedings before the High Court, contained almost identical issues, practice, and procedure. Thus, cause of action estoppel and issue estoppel applied because the cause of action and issues in the two actions were ostensibly identical.

However, the decision was overturned on appeal (*Special Effects Ltd v L'Oreal SA* [2007] RPC 15 (CA)). Lloyd LJ, delivering the judgment of the Court, said that to describe the application for registration as "a cause of action for registration" would be an inappropriate and artificial use of language. The same was true of an opponent, who did not have a cause of action at that stage for preventing the registration applied for. The decision of the Registry on opposition proceedings, or more generally a decision to register despite opposition, was not a final decision so as to be capable of being the basis of an issue estoppel. Even though the statute had created a specific jurisdiction for the determination of the issue of registrability, which established the existence of a legal right, in the sense of leading to the registration of the trade mark which was itself an item of property, the principle of res judicata did not apply to give finality to that determination because the provisions in the Act relating to a declaration of invalidity showed an intention to exclude that principle. Thus, it was not an abuse of process for L'Oreal to raise by way of defence or counterclaim matters which it raised in the opposition proceedings and which were found against it. In so doing, it simply wished to take advantage of opportunities expressly afforded by the Act, and it did not seek to do so in a manner which amounted to an abuse of process.

The decision of the Court of Appeal comes as a relief to many practitioners as the High Court decision threatened to undermine the current practice of using oppositions as a cheaper alternative (and possible dry run) for legal proceedings.

The decision in *Special Effects* is based on the difference between an opposition (in which the subject mark is not yet registered / and an invalidity/revocation action (in which it is) and may not be applicable where the nature of the challenge is the same in both forums. Thus, in *Hormel Foods Corp v Antilles Landscape Investments NV* [2005] RPC 28, the High Court of England and Wales barred in a second attempt to invalidate a trade mark on the basis of analogous law in the field of patent and registered design which obliges a party attacking the validity to put its full case in support of that attack at trial. Richard Arnold QC (sitting as a Deputy Judge) noted that, if unsuccessful, the party will be barred by cause of action estoppel from attacking the validity of that right in subsequent proceedings whether the attack is launched on the same or different grounds.

The decision in *Hormel Foods* seems to have been based on the fact that the two actions in the Trade Mark Registry and the High Court were both invalidity actions even though the grounds for the new attack were different.

7.7.6 Examples of successful oppositions

- In *Automobile Club de l'Ouest, ACO's Application* (Commissioner's Decision No T02/2005, 18/1/05, Asst Commr Walden), LE MANS for "Vehicles and their engines, tyres, parts, fittings and the aforesaid goods" was deemed confusingly similar to the Opponent's common law trade marks LE MANS and DUNLOP LE MANS for tyres. The application was allowed to proceed following removal of "tyres and parts, fittings and accessories relating to tyres" from the specification of goods. This was the subject of an unsuccessful appeal — *Automobile Club de L'Ouest ACO v South Pacific Tyres NZ Ltd* 29/3/06, Wild J, HC Wellington CIV-2005-485-248.

- In *Contact Energy Ltd's Application* (Commissioner's Decision No T40/2003, 15/9/03, Asst Commr Walden), the application to register DUAL ENERGY in class 4 in relation to "electricity and gas" was successfully opposed on the basis that the term was incapable of distinguishing the applicant's goods in terms of s 15 of the Act. The Assistant Commissioner found that the term DUAL ENERGY was in ordinary usage well before the relevant date and that other traders in the same industry were likely, in the ordinary course of their business and without improper motive, to desire to use the same term.

- In *Viva Time Corp's Application* (Commissioner's Decision No T14/2002, 14/5/02, Asst Commr Hastie), the applicant's trade mark PAUL PEUGEOT in class 14 for "watches" was deemed confusingly similar to the Opponent's PEUGEOT mark which had been used extensively in New Zealand for automobiles. In determining the question of whether confusion or deception was likely, the Assistant Commissioner noted that the applicant's mark incorporated the Opponent's PEUGEOT mark and PEUGEOT was not only an essential feature of the Opponent's mark, it was the entire mark.

- In *Boy London Ltd's Application: Doyles Trading Co Ltd's Application* (Commissioner's Decision No T20/2003, 19/5/03, Asst Commr Hastie), competing claims to proprietorship of the trade mark BOY LONDON were resolved in favour of Doyles which had used the mark in New Zealand between August 1992 and 1997/1998. Boy London Ltd and its successor's business had never used the mark here. Boy London's claim to spill over reputation was unsuccessful.

- In *Valley Girl Co Ltd v Hanama Collection Pty Ltd* (2005) 66 IPR 214, the High Court upheld on appeal a decision of the Assistant Commissioner of Trade Marks preventing registration of VALLEYGIRL in New Zealand in class 35 for "clothing retail". The respondent had used the same trade mark in Australia but not in New Zealand. The Court was not prepared to overturn the Assistant Commissioner's finding that the Respondent had established an awareness of the mark in New Zealand based on use in Australia together with travel statistics showing visitor arrivals from Australia of more than 600,000 and New Zealand resident departures to Australia of 600,000. The Assistant Commissioner also relied on evidence that the Respondent's VALLEYGIRL stores were advertised in catalogues and magazines and that the target market was highly brand aware.

- In *Primal Surf Ltd's Application* (Commissioner's Decision No T11/2005, 11/11/05, Asst Commr Hastie), the opponent successfully prevented registration of the trade mark PRIMAL in stylised form for clothing, headwear and footwear on the basis that he had developed the logo prior to entering into partnership with the applicant, had never assigned his rights in the logo to the partnership, and therefore remained the owner after the partnership was dissolved.

- In *Platinum Homes (NZ) Ltd's Application* (Commissioner's Decision No T22/2005, 22/8/05, Asst Commr Hastie), the opponent, which owned the trade mark GOLDEN HOMES, successfully opposed an application to register PLATINUM HOMES in relation to building materials and construction services. Golden Homes was found to have substantial reputation in the GOLDEN HOMES mark in New Zealand. The conceptual similarities of the marks persuaded the Assistant Commissioner that use of PLATINUM HOMES would be likely to cause confusion with GOLDEN HOMES. The decision was successfully appealed to the High Court (*Platinum Homes (NZ) Ltd v Golden Homes (1998) Ltd* 11/8/06, Miller J, HC Wellington CIV-2005-485-1870).

- In *Carabao Tawandang Co Ltd's Applications* (Commissioner's Decision Nos T24/2005 and T25/2005, 29/8/05, Asst Commr Walden), the opponent, Red Bull GmbH, successfully opposed registration of two logos comprising a steer's skull and the words "red carabao" or "carabao" in relation to energy drinks. The Assistant Commissioner found that the opponent had extensive reputation in the trade mark RED BULL in relation to energy drinks such that, although the marks sounded completely different and had significant visual differences, they might still be confused because they shared the common concept of "red" and a male bovine or bull. As energy drinks were a low involvement product, the Assistant Commissioner felt that the significant visual differences were not enough to neutralise the shared concepts and that use of the applicant's marks would be likely to deceive or cause confusion. The decision of the Assistant Commissioner was unsuccessfully appealed to the Wellington High Court (*Carabao Tawandang Co Ltd v Red Bull GmbH* 31/8/06, Clifford J, HC Wellington CIV-2005-485-1975).

- In *National Autoglass Supplies (Australia) Pty Ltd's Application* (Commissioner's Decision No T23/2005, 29/8/05, Asst Commr Duffy QC), the opponent, which had applied to register NAGS, successfully opposed an application to register a stylised logo comprising the letters NAGS and the words "National Auto Glass and Supplies". It was found that the opponent's mark was an abbreviation for "National Autoglass Specifications", and that the applicant had sufficient reputation in the wholesale market for automotive glass products for there to be a reasonable likelihood of deception and confusion occurring. The Assistant Commissioner seems to have been helped by evidence of actual confusion between the two marks.

- In *Dene Andre's Application* (Commissioner's Decision No T29/2005, 31/10/05, Asst Commr Walden), the opponent, Cadbury Confectionery Ltd, which owned the well known trade mark JAFFAS, successfully opposed registration of OJAFFS in relation to confectionery on the basis that it was confusingly similar. The decision seems to have been based in large part on the applicant's acknowledgment that OJAFFS was a blend of the trade marks JAFFAS and OJAYS (the trade mark of a bulk bin confectionery item available from supermarkets and confectionery shops).

- In *The NZ Automobile Assoc Inc's Application* (Commissioner's Decision No T05/2006, 20/2/06, Asst Commr Walden) and *AMI Insurance Ltd's Application* (Commissioner's Decision No T04/2006, 20/2/06, Asst Commr Walden), the NZAA and AMI Insurance successfully cross-opposed each other's application to register a combination of the colours yellow and black. The decisions turned primarily on the evidence that each party had been using the colour combination in respect of its business making it unlikely that the mark was distinctive in fact of either one of them. However, trade mark practitioners should also note the Assistant Commissioner's comment that the AA's description of the mark in its application (the colours yellow and black "as applied to signage, including vehicle signage, premises, printed matter and promotional and advertising matter in any media") was vague and uncertain because of its wide description and wide application without spatial delineation of the colour combination and no indication of the form that the colour combination might take.

- In *Peter Simpson's Application* (Commissioner's Decision No T06/2006, 1/5/06, Asst Commr Walden), the applicant was permitted to register the trade mark ONEBILLINFO in classes 35 and 36 for billing services, financial services etc. The opponent, Contact Energy Ltd, claimed the mark had no distinctive character, was not a trade mark and had become customary in the current language or in the bona fide and established practices of the trade, based on its own use of ONEBILL in respect of combined gas and electricity bills issued to its customers. However, the Assistant Commissioner, considering the trade mark as a whole, deemed that the addition of .INFO was not a natural extension of ONE and BILL and that the mark was eligible for registration.

- In *Paulo Saulualofaiga Ieriko's Application* (Commissioner's Decision No T07/2006, 1/5/06, Asst Commr Walden), the opponent successfully prevented the applicant from registering a logo for the "Evangelical Samoan Wesleyan Methodist Church of New Zealand". The opponent's evidence was that it established the Church in New Zealand and Australia in December 1999, during which time the applicant was a trustee.

The opponent developed and used an almost identical logo in 2000, 2001, and 2003 which had been supplied to the applicant as trustee. The applicant left the opponent's Church in December 2004 and was not authorised by the opponent to use its logo. The Assistant Commissioner deemed it almost inevitable that a substantial number of persons would be deceived or confused by the use of the trade mark, and also that its use would be contrary to law as the opponent was the legitimate owner of the trade mark. The opposition succeeded.

- In *Telecom IP Ltd v Beta Telecom Ltd* 27/9/06, Ronald Young J, HC Wellington CIV-2004-485-2789, the High Court overturned on appeal a decision of the Assistant Commissioner of Trade Marks allowing registration of a logo containing the words BETA TELECOM in the face of the opponent's prior registrations for TELECOM in block capital and stylised form. The High Court concluded that the marks would be confused by a significant section of the public, the word TELECOM being such a strong trade name in New Zealand that its use in another mark would require substantial distinguishing features to set it apart from the TELECOM mark and avoid the similarity of marks causing confusion or deceit.

- In *Liquid Development Ltd's Application* (Commissioner's Decision No T14/2006, 21/7/06, Asst Commr Frankel), the opponent successfully argued that a logo containing the words ORIGINAL HEMP HIGH ENERGY MORE POWER was likely to be confused with its HEMP trade mark. Both were used in relation to energy drinks and non-alcoholic beverages, and the parties had discussed going into business together which did not proceed, leading to an acrimonious relationship. Although the stylisation of each mark was entirely different, the Assistant Commissioner considered HEMP to be a distinctive word in relation to energy drinks such that the idea and imagery evoked by each mark would be the same and hence likely to lead to an association.

- In *Stefanel Next Pty Ltd's Application* (Commissioner's Decision No T15/2006, 10/7/06, Asst Commr Walden), the opponent Next Retail Limited successfully opposed registration of NEXT in relation to clothing, footwear and headgear on the basis of its spill over reputation in the NEXT trade mark from use in the UK. The opponent relied in particular on evidence from people travelling between the UK and New Zealand to show an awareness of the UK NEXT trade mark amongst a significant section of the New Zealand public.

- In *Wistbray Ltd's Application* (Commissioner's Decision No T05/2007, 12/1/07, Asst Commr B F Jones), an application to register TICK TOCK in relation to tea was successfully opposed by Ferrero SpA, in light of its use and registration of TIC TAC. The Assistant Commissioner found that the opponent had an established reputation in, and awareness of, its TIC TAC mark in New Zealand and that use of TICK TOCK would be likely to deceive or cause confusion.

7.7.7 Examples of unsuccessful oppositions

- In *The NZ Automobile Assoc Inc's Application* (Commissioner's Decision No T22/2002, 12/6/02, Asst Commr Gallagher), the trade mark LIFE ASSIST was deemed insufficiently similar to the Opponent's AMI ASSIST trade mark. Interestingly, the Opponent's strong reputation in "AMI" was a factor which militated against confusion.

- In *Nutripharm NZ Ltd's Application* (Commissioner's Decision No T03/2005, 25/1/05, Asst Commr Hastie), NUTRIBETIC for "pharmaceuticals, nutraceuticals, nutritional supplements, food for babies, infants and milk products" was deemed capable of co-existing with the Opponent's NUTRI-METICS trade mark which was used on skin care products and cosmetics.

- In *Laboratorios Phergal, S.A.'s Application* (Commissioner's Decision No T07/2005, 23/2/05, Asst Commr Walden), the Opponent's mark MATIS was found insufficiently similar to the applicant's mark NATURSTYLE HAIR MATISSE.

- In *The Meow Mix Co's Application* (Commissioner's Decision No T17/2004, 31/8/04, Asst Commr Hastie), the applicant was permitted to register MEOW MIX in class 31 for "cat food" despite the Opponent's prior use of CAT MEOW in relation to cat food since 1993. The Assistant Commissioner considered that the marks did not look alike or sound alike notwithstanding that they both included the word "MEOW". She considered that the position of the word "MEOW" in each mark, combined with the different second word ("mix" as opposed to "cat") sufficiently distinguished the two marks, that the idea of each mark was quite distinct and that they were unlikely to be visually or orally confused.

- In *Sediver Societe Europeenne D'Isolateurs en Verre et Composite's Application* (Commissioner's Decision No T22/2004, 13 September 2004, Asst Commr Walden), the applicant was permitted to register FLEXARREST FLEXIBLE LINE SURGE ARRESTER in stylised form in relation to "a device for protecting high voltage lines against voltage servers, the device being constituted by a lightening arrester and a discharge gap in air mounted on electrical insulators" despite the Opponent's prior use of the trade mark SURGEARREST. The Assistant Commissioner did not agree with the Opponent's suggestion that SURGE ARRESTER was a significant feature of the applicant's mark and also considered that there was a difference between markets for the respective parties' goods: people seeking to protect high voltage lines as compared to people seeking to protect home electronics and small business applications.

- In *Canstar Sports Group Inc's Application* (Commissioner's Decision No T05/2004, 29/3/04, Asst Commr Walden), the applicant was permitted to register BAUER in class 25 for clothing, footwear and headgear notwithstanding the Opponent's prior use of EDDIE BAUER. The Assistant Commissioner found that BAUER and EDDIE BAUER were not substantially identical (for the purposes of an enquiry into proprietorship) and were different in terms of their appearance, sound and ideas. The Assistant Commissioner also noted differences in the trade channels through which respective parties' goods would be sold — the Opponent used catalogues and the applicant's goods were sold through specialist and general sports stores.

- In *Newmans Chocolate Ltd's Application* (Commissioner's Decision No T27/2003, 2/7/03, Asst Commr Hastie), the applicant was permitted to register MILKBEARS in class 30 for "candy, chocolate, chocolate candies and pastries" despite the Opponent's prior use of MILKYBAR since the 1930s primarily on the basis of evidence that other traders had used the word "milk", it was a common descriptor word for chocolate, and the idea conveyed by the word BEARS was quite distinct from that of the word BAR.

- In *Tower Corp's Application* (Commissioner's Decision No T33/2003, 15/8/03, Asst Commr Hastie), the Assistant Commissioner considered that the trade mark TOWER and a lighthouse device was insufficiently similar to the Opponent's INSURANCE TOWERS trade mark.

- In *Bayer AG's Application* (Commissioner's Decision No T17/2003, 23/4/03, Asst Commr Walden), the trade mark ADVANEM was deemed insufficiently similar to the trade mark ADVEXIN both in class 5.

- In *Les Mills World of Fitness Ltd's Application* (Commissioner's Decision No T18/2003, 30/4/03, Asst Commr Hastie), the trade mark BODY PUMP in class 28 for "gymnastic and sporting articles not included in other classes" was deemed insufficiently similar to the Opponent's (Reebok International Ltd's), registrations for the trade mark THE PUMP and INSTA-PUMP.

- In *Ferring BV's Application* (Commissioner's Decision No T10/2005, 4/4/05, Asst Commr Walden), the trade mark ESELEN for "pharmaceutical products and substances" was deemed insufficiently similar to the opponent's trade mark EMSELEX used on similar goods. The Assistant Commissioner noted that when considering pharmaceuticals, purchases were not on impulse and tended to be considered carefully, militating against confusion amongst members of the public and/ or the medical profession.

- In *Village Roadshow Corporation Ltd's Application* (Commissioner's Decision No T15/2005, 23/5/05, Asst Commr Hastie), the applicant was permitted to register a logo containing a stylised V device and the word MAX in relation to entertainment services, despite the opponent's prior use of the trade mark IMAX for the same services. The Assistant Commissioner noted that while the word "MAX" was common to both marks, it was widely used in a descriptive sense in other trade marks and, when considering the two marks as a whole, was unlikely to lead to confusion. IMAX unsuccessfully appealed the decision to the High Court: *IMAX Corp v Village Roadshow Corp Ltd* 29/3/06, Williams J, HC Wellington CIV-2005-404-3248.

- In *Tracey Tillick's Application* (Commissioner's Decision No T18/2005, 27/6/05, Asst Commr Hastie), the applicant was entitled to register TRACE ELEMENT for clothing despite the opponent's prior use of the trade mark ELEMENT for the same goods on the basis that the respective marks were able to be distinguished visually and orally and that the idea of the marks differed considerably.

- In *Cadbury Confectionary Ltd's Application* (Commissioner's Decision No T19/2005, 27/6/05, Asst Commr Walden), the applicant was permitted to register "EARTH" in relation to chocolates, confectionary, snack foods, ice cream etc despite opposition from Effem Foods Ltd which claimed to have used the trade marks EARTH and MARS in a promotion surrounding its "MARS BAR" confectionary. The decision turned mainly on a finding that Effem had not actually used the EARTH mark in relation to goods in New Zealand as, while a product described as an "EARTH BAR" was shown in its television advertisement, there was no EARTH BAR product available to purchase in the New Zealand market and the use of the EARTH BAR in the advertisements was a clever way of advertising the MARS BAR product. While there was unquestionably evidence of use of the MARS trade mark, this was found to be insufficiently similar to the applicant's EARTH trade mark and the opposition was dismissed.

- In *Pacific Blue Airlines Pty Ltd's Application* (Commissioner's Decision No T27/2005, 26/9/05, Asst Commr Hastie), the opponent, which was the registered owner of BLUE PACIFIC TOURS, unsuccessfully opposed an application to register PACIFIC BLUE in relation to airline services and related goods. Although both marks contained the word PACIFIC and BLUE, the Assistant Commissioner noted that the first syllable of the mark was generally the most important, that the words were in reverse order, and that the opponent's mark also contained the word "tours" which made the idea of that mark sufficiently different to PACIFIC BLUE.

- In *United Airlines Inc's Application* (Commissioner's Decision No T28/2005, 1/11/05, Asst Commr Jones), United Parcel Service of America Inc unsuccessfully opposed registration of UNITED SERVICES on the basis of perceived similarity with its UNITED PARCEL SERVICE mark. The common word UNITED was deemed insufficient to establish similarity between the marks, and consumers were deemed able to distinguish between the marks on the basis of the additional word PARCEL. There was also evidence that users of the respective parties' services were likely to be different.

- In *Nu Vision Consultancy Ltd's Application* (Commissioner's Decision No T30/2005, 21/11/05, Asst Commr Jones), the opponent, Kraft Foods, which was the owner of the trade mark MILKA in relation to confectionery, unsuccessfully opposed an application to register MILKA SHAKE in relation to nutraceuticals, dietary supplements, and dietic foods. The Assistant Commissioner deemed the additional word SHAKE to change the look of the opposed mark. In addition, the marks were to be applied to different goods, appealed to different consumers and would be sold in different trade channels.

- In *Goodman Fielder NZ Ltd's Application* (Commissioner's Decision No T10/2006, 22/5/06, Asst Commr Walden), the opponent, George Weston Foods Ltd, unsuccessfully opposed applications by Goodman Fielder to register a series of trade marks comprising a sun device and the words SUNNY CRUST. George Weston relied upon its own use of a different sun device in conjunction with the words "Family Fresh Super Soft". The Assistant Commissioner found that the words contained in each trade mark immediately conveyed a different meaning. Also, comparing the devices, the overall impression was that they were visually and conceptually different. Although they both depicted suns with smiling faces, the applicant's device, being partially obscured, suggested a rising sun whereas the opponent's full sun logo conveyed the idea of a hot midday sun. The Assistant Commissioner also thought it relevant that the opponent's trade mark was used in conjunction with the well known TIP TOP brand which consumers were likely to look for.

- In *Carl Robert Bird's Application* (Commissioner's Decision No T13/2006, 3/7/06, Asst Commr Walden), the opponent, Rotary International, unsuccessfully opposed registration of the trade mark ROTARY ENGINE in stylised form for clothing. The Assistant Commissioner found that the overall impression of each trade mark was different, and the goods were also significantly different, the applicant being involved in clothing and the opponent being involved primarily in charitable and community services.

- In *Anthony Tesselaar Plants Pty Ltd's Application* (Commissioner's Decision No T17/2006, 31/7/06, Asst Commr Walden) the opponent, which was the owner of the well known CORUBA rum trade mark, unsuccessfully opposed registration of CARUBA for "plants, seeds and bulbs, flowers, shrubs and trees". While the Assistant Commissioner found that there was an awareness of the CORUBA mark in New Zealand through its extensive use in relation to Jamaican rum since 1967, and that the marks looked and sounded similar, there was a vast difference between the goods covered by each trade mark and the trade channels were also very different such that confusion was unlikely. The Assistant Commissioner also relied on evidence from the applicant as to a lack of precedent for any alcohol trade mark being used on or in relation to plants.

- In *Merck KGaA's Application* (Commissioner's Decision No T21/2006, 25/9/06, Asst Commr Walden), the opponent, which was the owner of the trade mark TYSABRI for pharmaceutical preparations, unsuccessfully opposed registration of GIABRI for pharmaceutical preparations. Comparing the two pharmaceutical names, the Assistant Commissioner found that the suffixes BRI and ABRI were not common and that the whole of the marks should be considered allowing for imperfect recollection. However, even on those terms, the Assistant Commissioner considered the marks insufficiently similar to cause confusion.

- In *Hui Lin's Application* (Commissioner's Decision No T24/2006, 9/10/06, Asst Commr Walden), the applicant was permitted to register KOSMO for food products and café/catering/accommodation services notwithstanding a finding that the opponent's COSMOPOLITAN/COSMO trade marks were well known in New Zealand in relation to magazines. The decision turns primarily on the different goods and services for which each mark will be used and the finding of the Assistant Commissioner that, while the general public could be reminded of the opponent's magazine when they see the applicant's mark, they would not be likely to think that there was a connection in the course of trade or that the applicant's goods and services were an extension of those of the opponent. The decision is also notable for the finding that the overall impression of the respective trade marks is quite different due to the applicant's mark beginning with the letter "K" and the opponent's mark having definite meanings.

- In *Valeant Pharmaceuticals International's Application* (Commissioner's Decision No T25/2006, 24/10/06, Asst Commr Walden), the applicant was permitted to register VALEANT in classes 5 (pharmaceutical preparations and dermatological products) and 42 (research and development services in the field of pharmaceuticals, except clinical research services) notwithstanding the opponent's use and registration of VALENT and VALENT BIOSCIENCES in respect of chemicals used in agriculture, horticulture and forestry, pesticides, herbicides, insecticides, fungicides etc for agricultural use. Once again, the decision turns in large part on the differences in the respective goods/services of the applicant and opponent as well as differences in the way in which the respective marks were likely to be pronounced (the applicant's mark being a three syllable word and the opponent's VALENT mark two syllable).

411

- In *Sons of the Desert, SL's Application* (Commissioner's Decision No T02/2007, 15/1/07, Asst Commr Walden), the owner of the applicant company (Mr Galdeano) and the opponent were directors and shareholders in a Spanish company which owned rights to the EL NINO trade mark. The opponent alleged that the application (which was for a stylised version of the EL NINO mark) had been filed in New Zealand in bad faith. The question to be determined was whether the trade mark application was dishonest or fell short of reasonable standards of commercial behaviour. The opponent's case turned on an alleged agreement or understanding between the opponent and Mr Galdeano. As the applicant was a company, there had to be a link between Mr Galdeano and the applicant, such that Mr Galdeano's knowledge could be imputed to the applicant. The Assistant Commissioner found such link on the basis that Mr Galdeano solely controlled the applicant company. However, the opposition failed because the opponent was unable to establish that there was an understanding or agreement regarding joint ownership of the trade mark which had been contravened by the filing of the New Zealand application.

7.7.8 Unsuccessful opposition may give rise to cause of action estoppel

Based on recent UK authority, in certain circumstances an unsuccessful opposition may give rise to an estoppel in subsequent invalidity proceedings launched by the same party and covering the same issues. This is discussed in more detail at 7.13 ("Defences") later in this chapter.

7.8 Rights given by registration

Section 10 Trade Marks Act 2002 gives the registered owner of a trade mark registration the exclusive right in New Zealand to use the registered trade mark in relation to the goods/ services for which the mark is registered.

7.8.1 Exclusive right

Under s 10(1)(b), the rights given by the registration of a trade mark are exclusive to the registered owner, although the registered owner may grant a licence to use the trade mark. The right is infringed by any person who uses the registered trade mark on the same (or in some circumstances, similar) goods or services without the consent of the registered owner. Infringement is discussed in more detail at 7.11 ("Enforcement of rights") later in this chapter.

7.8.2 Territory

Prior to the 2002 Act, registration of a trade mark in New Zealand had effect throughout New Zealand and in the Pacific Islands of Tokelau (s 86 of the 1953 Act), Niue (s 702 Niue Act 1966), and the Cook Islands (s 635 Cook Islands Act 1915). However, in view of the fact that these are independent island states trade mark registrations under the Trade Marks Act 2002 will not have effect until relevant legislation in those countries is enacted.

7.8.3 Unregistered trade marks

The Trade Marks Act 2002 cannot be used by the owner of an unregistered trade mark to enforce its rights. Where an unregistered trade mark is misused, the trade mark owner must rely on its rights under the tort of passing off and/or under the Fair Trading Act 1986 to restrain such use and to recover damages or an account of profits. These causes of action are discussed in more detail in the passing off and Fair Trading Act 1986 chapters of this text (chapters 9 and 10 respectively).

7.8.4 Jurisdiction

Although trade mark rights are territorial, and a New Zealand registered trade mark will have no effect in other countries, in certain limited circumstances it may be possible for the owner of the same trade mark granted in a number of jurisdictions to sue a New Zealand-based defendant for breaches of its foreign trade mark rights committed in those foreign jurisdictions. The question of whether and in what circumstances such actions are permissible was considered in *Kabushiki Kaisha Sony Computer Entertainment v van Veen* 14/12/06, MacKenzie J, HC Wellington CIV-2004-485-1520. The plaintiffs (collectively "Sony") were the owners of the PlayStation 2 computer games system, and owned intellectual property rights in some of the games played on that system. Those games were distributed on CDs and DVDs and, to assist in their protection, Sony embedded codes which prevented copying of the games from the CD or DVD to another medium. The defendants developed and distributed a software programme called HD Loader which enabled a user to circumvent the embedded copy protection code and copy Sony's games. The HD Loader programme was developed by the first defendant who sold or licensed the use of that programme in, amongst other countries, the UK and Hong Kong through the second defendant.

Sony commenced proceedings and obtained a number of interim orders. Following completion of the pleadings the first defendant admitted the material allegations in the Statement of Claim (breach of the New Zealand Copyright and Trade Marks Acts, breach of the UK Copyright, Designs and Patents Act 1988, breach of the Hong Kong Copyright Ordinance, and wrongful possession and use of confidential information) and Sony applied for judgment against the first defendant.

On each of the causes of action relating to breaches of the New Zealand legislation and wrongful use and possession of confidential information, the admitted facts clearly gave rise to liability which could be enforced in New Zealand. Those causes of action were based on New Zealand law and on actions admitted to have taken place in New Zealand. The more difficult question was whether the Court could determine causes of action relating to alleged breaches of UK and Hong Kong copyright legislation.

The starting point for the Court was the rule laid down by the House of Lords in *British South Africa Co v Companhia de Mocambique* [1893] AC 602 (HL), which stated that the Court has no jurisdiction to entertain an action for (1) the determination of the title to, or the right to possession of, any immoveable situate out of England (foreign land); or (2) the recovery of damages for trespass to such immoveable. MacKenzie J noted, at paras 9 and 10, that the rule had been applied in Australia and England in several cases involving intellectual property rights, and had been applied by Tipping J in New Zealand in *Atkinson*

413

Footwear Ltd v Hodgskin International Services Ltd (1994) 31 IPR 186 in respect of an application for an interim injunction to restrain the distribution of footwear allegedly infringing the plaintiff's copyright in New Zealand and Australia. Tipping J granted the application with respect to New Zealand but declined to extend it to Australia. However, MacKenzie J noted that since the decision of Tipping J in *Atkinson Footwear* the UK Court of Appeal had carefully reconsidered the position in *Pearce v Ove Arup Partnership Ltd* [1999] 1 All ER 769 (CA), a case involving the construction of a public building in Rotterdam which was a copy of a plan produced by an architectural student in London. The UK Court of Appeal held in *Pearce* that the English Courts did have jurisdiction to entertain a claim in respect of the alleged infringement of Dutch copyright by virtue of actions occurring in Holland on the basis that the *Mocambique* rule involves two limbs, the second of which makes a distinction between proceedings where issue of title, or the extent of rights available under a foreign law arise, on the one hand, and claims where the matter in issue is not the existence or nature of the title or rights, but whether some action has the effect of infringing the unquestioned rights of the plaintiff. MacKenzie J concluded, at para 19:

> "I find the reasoning [in *Pearce*] persuasive in favour of the proposition that, in the case of intellectual property rights governed by the law of a foreign country, the second limb of the *Mocambique* rule should not exclude justiciability in respect of actions for breach of intellectual property rights established under the law of another jurisdiction, when no question of the existence or validity of those rights arises."

adding, at para 22:

> "Nothing which I have said should be taken as questioning the applicability of the first limb of the rule in the *Mocambique* case to questions of title to intellectual property … nor should anything I have said be taken as questioning the applicability of the second limb in the *Mocambique* case to true immoveables such as land … The issue before me is whether the second limb should be extended to items of intellectual property such as those in issue here. The various forms of protection given under intellectual property statutes are territorial in nature, because the statutes conferring them are necessarily territorial in their application. To that extent, they have the characteristics of immoveable property. But the significant difference between such forms of intellectual property and true immoveables such as land is that the same item of intellectual property may be protected by statutory rights in many jurisdictions. A strict application of the second limb of the *Mocambique* case to such rights would mean that, where, as here, a defendant commits infringing acts against a single plaintiff in several jurisdictions, separate proceedings in each jurisdiction will be necessary to deal with those infringements. The inconvenience of such a requirement would outweigh the benefit of certainty that the application of the second limb to such claims would provide. I decline to apply the second limb to this case."

Having concluded that the justiciability of Sony's claim was not excluded by the *Mocambique* rule, MacKenzie J went on to consider whether, on the ordinary principles of the conflict of laws dealing with wrongs committed in another jurisdiction, the New Zealand Court had jurisdiction. In that regard, the common law double actionability rule applies. The double actionability rule states that, as a general rule, an act done in a foreign country is a tort and actionable as such in New Zealand, only if it is both (a) actionable as a tort according to New Zealand law or, in other words, is an act which, if done in New Zealand, would be a tort; and (b) actionable according to the law of the foreign country where it was done. However, a particular issue between the parties may be governed by the law of the country which, with respect to that issue, has the most significant relationship with the occurrence and the parties.

Having considered the double actionability rule, MacKenzie J went on to address (and resolve) a potential problem in applying that rule to the present case as follows, at paras 24 and 25:

> "In applying that Rule, it may be argued that, since the acts complained of must constitute a wrong actionable under New Zealand law, the acts complained of, being infringements in the United Kingdom and Hong Kong, do not constitute a wrong against New Zealand copyright, since New Zealand copyright is territorial in effect. Therefore, a strict application of the first limb of the double actionability rule would lead to the result that the infringement would not be actionable in New Zealand. That Rule was the subject of consideration in *Pearce*. Roch LJ discussed the difficulty which arises in a case such as this, if the first limb of [the Double Actionability] Rule … requires the [New Zealand] court to determine actionability by [New Zealand] domestic law. He dealt with the proposition that, if, despite the rule in the *Mocambique* case, the claim was justiciable, it was bound to fail the requirements in the first limb of the double actionability rule in these terms at page 803:

>> 'If that were a correct analysis, the effect would be that the first limb of r 203(1) imposed a requirement as to jurisdiction; and not simply a rule for the choice of law.'

> "He went on to note that the view that the first limb of the rule does impose a requirement as to jurisdiction had found expression in the dissenting judgment of Diplock LJ in [*Chaplin v Boys* [1969] 2 All ER 1085 (HL)], but had been plainly rejected by the House of Lords on the appeal. Roch LJ referred to [*Red Sea Insurance Ltd v Bouygues SA* [1994] 3 All ER 749 (PC)], where the Privy Council had accepted that the choice of the lex fori as the applicable law was not an invariable rule; rather that it was 'the general rule' or 'a starting point'. Roch LJ then went on to say, at page 803-804:

>> 'In the present case, the plaintiff's claim would be defeated if the court were to refuse to apply the exception. But the claim (if established on the facts) is one where the English court would have given a remedy, under United Kingdom copyright law, if the facts alleged had occurred in England. This is not a case in which the claim is in respect of some wrong which is conceptually unknown in English law. In our view this is a case where, if the claim is justiciable at all, the exception to the double actionability rule enables English court to apply Dutch law; and the English court ought to do so.'

> "I respectfully concur with that reasoning. It seems to me that, in applying the first limb of the double actionability rule, in an intellectual property infringement case, it is necessary to effect a notional transfer to New Zealand, for consideration under New Zealand law, of both the infringing act, and the intellectual property infringed. The infringing act and the intellectual property infringed cannot sensibly be

separated in applying the first limb of [the Double Actionability] Rule … The purpose of the rule is to consider how New Zealand law would regard an act, if that act were committed in New Zealand and subject to New Zealand domestic law. Where the act complained of is an infringement of an intellectual property right, a relevant inquiry, in considering the application of New Zealand domestic law, should be whether that particular form of intellectual property is one which is capable of protection under New Zealand law. The focus should be on the nature of the underlying intellectual property, not on the form in which that property is protected by the laws of the foreign jurisdiction. The laws of the foreign jurisdiction are relevant to the second limb, not the first limb, of the double actionability rule."

Accordingly, MacKenzie J entered judgment against the first defendant in respect of all causes of action. Finally, his Honour clarified, at para 27, that in reaching the conclusions which he had as to the applicability of the *Mocambique*, and double actionability, rules his findings should be limited to the case of a defendant who is resident in New Zealand and thereby subject to the jurisdiction of the New Zealand Courts.

Although this judgment relates specifically to allegations of breach of copyright and registered trade mark there is no reason in principal why it should not equally apply to other intellectual property rights, particularly those for which a process of registration is required (therefore providing certainty in terms of the scope of monopoly of the intellectual property right in various jurisdictions) such as patents and registered designs.

7.9 Term, renewal, and restoration

7.9.1 Term

Under s 57 Trade Marks Act 2002, a trade mark registration must be renewed every 10 years from the deemed date of registration. The "deemed date of registration" is defined in s 5 as the actual date of application, or the priority date of the application, whichever is the earlier.

A registration may be renewed for further periods of 10 years at a time (s 58). Provided the mark is being used, there is no limit on the number of times a registration may be renewed. Each expiry date of the registration will be the 10-year anniversary of the original deemed date of registration, for as long as the mark is renewed.

Under the Trade Marks Act 1953, the initial term of a trade mark registration was 7 years from the date of application, or the priority date of the application, whichever was earlier. Thereafter, a trade mark registration was renewable (again, indefinitely, provided it was being used) for additional periods of 14 years at a time.

Under s 208(3)(c) of the 2002 Act , if a trade mark was registered under the Trade Marks Act 1953 and was valid immediately before the Trade Marks Act 2002 came into force, it will retain its existing registration period of either 7 or 14 years, as applicable. When the registration next falls due for renewal, s 58 of the 2002 Act will apply, in which case the registration will be renewable for further periods of 10 years at a time (s 208(3)(c)).

If a renewal application was received before the commencement of the 2002 Act, the 1953 Act will apply in respect of the renewal application (s 203(1)(b)). This means that the registration will be renewed for a period of 14 years from the date of application/priority date, or of the last renewal of registration, as applicable (s 29(2)).

7.9.2 Renewal

Under reg 133(1)(b) Trade Marks Regulations 2003, an application for renewal of a trade mark must be made before the date of expiry of the registration. However, an application for renewal cannot be filed any earlier than 1 year before that date.

Regulation 133 sets out the minimum information which must be included in the application for renewal as follows:

- The trade mark registration number;

- A representation or description of the trade mark;

- The owner's name and address for service;

- If the owner has an agent, the agent's name;

- The name and communication address of the person paying the renewal fee; and

- If the trade mark is registered in more than one class, details of the class or classes for which the registration is to be renewed.

Under s 59(3) Trade Marks Act 2002, the Commissioner must remove a trade mark from the Register if notification of the date of expiry was sent to the owner, and the renewal fee was not paid.

Hence, if a trade mark registration is not renewed at expiry, it will cease to have effect after the date of expiry. IPONZ will advise the owner of the registration that it has expired, and the mark will be removed from the Register.

7.9.3 Restoration

Once a trade mark has been removed from the Register for non-payment of the renewal fee, under reg 134 Trade Marks Regulations 2003 the owner of the mark may apply to restore the mark within 12 months of the expiry of the trade mark. The 12-month period cannot be extended (reg 134(2)). If an application for restoration is filed outside the 12-month period, it will be refused.

An application to restore an expired trade mark may be made by submitting an application for restoration and renewal of the trade mark registration and paying the prescribed renewal fee. According to IPONZ Practice Guideline, "Renewal and Restoration", an application for the restoration of a trade mark registration must contain the same information as is required in an application for renewal under reg 133.

The Commissioner may impose any conditions on restoration that he or she thinks appropriate (reg 134). These will usually relate to preserving the position of third parties who may have inadvertently used the mark while the registration was lapsed.

Under s 60(1) Trade Marks Act 2002, the status of a lapsed registration is upheld for one year from the date of removal. During this period, a lapsed registration will be considered to be a trade mark on the Register for the purposes of trade mark examination and s 25(1)(a) and (b).

417

Under the Trade Marks Act 1953, restoration of a lapsed registration could be effected months, and sometimes years, after the original registration had been removed from the Register, provided the registration was not intentionally abandoned by the trade mark owner, and the Commissioner considered that it was just to restore the registration in light of all the circumstances of the particular case. Where the application for restoration was filed more than 12 months after the expiry of the registration, the details were to be provided in the form of a Statutory Declaration.

More information regarding the renewal and restoration of trade marks can be found in IPONZ Practice Guideline, "Renewal and Restoration".

7.10   Limitations on registration

7.10.1 Disclaimers

Before 1 June 1998 it was necessary to disclaim exclusive rights to any part of a trade mark that was purely descriptive or which others should be free to use. For example, WONDER WOOL might be registered for textiles subject to a disclaimer of the exclusive rights to the separate use of the words WONDER and WOOL. The effect of these disclaimers is that others who trade in textiles may use the words WONDER or WOOL separately without there being trade mark infringement, but trade mark infringement will occur if the two words are used in combination.

However, since 1 June 1998 IPONZ's practice has been not to require disclaimers. The rationale for this is that the rights conferred by registration apply to the sign as a whole regardless of whether any disclaimers have been entered. To ensure applicants understand the extent of their rights conferred by registration, IPONZ publishes a statement to this effect in each edition of the Journal.

Under the provisions of the Trade Marks Act 2002;

*   A trade mark owner may still disclaim voluntarily any right to the exclusive use of any part of a trade mark; or

*   The Commissioner or Court may still require the entering of a disclaimer in order to avert the revocation of a trade mark registration or where there are public interest reasons for the entering of a disclaimer.

7.10.2 Conditions and limitations

An application to register a trade mark that is likely to deceive or cause confusion is prohibited from registration under s 17 Trade Marks Act 2002. However, where conditions or limitations are entered which will remove the potential for deception or confusion, the examiner must accept the application if it complies with the requirements of the Act in all aspects (s 40).

For example, an examiner may require, as a condition of registration, that the applicant for the mark MAGIC WOOL in respect of clothing will use the mark only in relation to clothing made substantially from wool (in order to stop the mark from being used deceptively).

In the past, IPONZ has required a condition of registration to be entered in respect of marks covering live horticultural products (for example, plants and seeds) that the mark would not be used as a varietal name. The practice of requiring such conditions has now ceased.

Other instances where a mark can be registered subject to conditions and limitations are:

- Marks containing blank spaces;

- Marks filed in colour;

- Marks where particular goods or services must be excluded to avoid them being descriptive; and

- Marks with territorial limitations as to use.

(1) *Blank space conditions*

Blank space marks are device marks that include an area of blank space that is obviously intended for the insertion of other matter when used by the owner. IPONZ practice regarding blank space marks is to impose, as a condition of registration, a proviso that the blank space in the mark:

- Will remain blank;

- Will only be filled with matter of a non-trade mark character; or

- Will only be filled with another associated trade mark of the same owner.

The rationale behind this practice is to ensure that the proprietor does not (intentionally or unintentionally) represent that the owner has a monopoly in matter that is not capable of registration.

(2) *Colour limitations*

When a mark is filed in colour, the colour forms a distinctive aspect of the mark.

A colour limitation may sometimes be voluntarily entered, as doing so adds a distinctive element to the mark, making it easier to register. However, the limitation likewise restricts the scope of registration. For this reason, it has been common for a black and white and a colour version of a logo mark to be filed in one series application. However, since IPONZ began treating device marks which are not limited as to colour as covering all colours, series marks in black and white and colour are less common. For more information on series applications, refer to 7.20 ("Non-standard registrations") below and 7.4.1(5) ("Series marks") earlier in this chapter.

Section 19(2) Trade Marks Act 2002 states that trade marks filed in black and white or in colour, where no colour limitation is stated, are not limited as to colour. Therefore, where an application for a series mark is filed, no colour limitation will be required by the Commissioner.

Where an applicant chooses to limit the trade mark as to colour(s), the applicant must supply a description of the colour(s) acceptable to the Commissioner (reg 44(h)). In the situation where the Commissioner considers the mark is sufficiently distinctive on its own, the wording of such a colour limitation will be standardised as in the following example:

> "The mark is limited to the colours red, blue, and white as shown in the representation attached to the application."

419

On the other hand, where colour adds to the distinctiveness of the mark, allowing a mark to be eligible for registration which would otherwise not be eligible under s 18, or to overcome a citation raised under s 25, the Commissioner will request that a colour limitation be entered using a widely known and readily available colour standard (for example, the colour indexing scheme of the Pantone® colour system). The wording of such a colour limitation will be standardised as in the following example:

> "The mark is limited to the colours red (Pantone® 1234), blue (Pantone® 5678), and black and white, as shown in the representation attached to the application."

(3) *Limitations on the specification of goods/services*

In certain circumstances it may be possible to secure registration of a trade mark which might otherwise be descriptive of a characteristic of goods or services by excluding those goods and services from the statement of goods/services covered by the application/ registration. However, the Court of Appeal of New Zealand has confirmed in *Cadbury Ltd v Effem Foods Ltd* 20/7/07, CA247/05; [2007] NZCA 303 that such exclusions must relate to a particular type of product or service rather than a characteristic of those goods or services. The distinction is best illustrated by the facts of the case.

Cadbury had applied to register the word PURPLE in relation to chocolates, confectionery, ice cream etc but with a further exclusion of "goods being coloured purple". The High Court (*Effem Foods Ltd v Cadbury Ltd* 12/12/05, MacKenzie J, HC Wellington CIV-2004-484-2127) held that defining the goods which are to be distinguishable by reference to a characteristic which does not alter their inherent nature will not achieve distinctiveness. It considered that those in the trade seeking to distinguish the goods in question would not be expected to know that purple ice cream, for example, was to be regarded as a different category of goods from non-purple ice cream. Even if the person had knowledge of the details of the registration, a degree of mental agility would be needed to understand, after encountering the word PURPLE in relation to goods, that, if the goods were not coloured purple, they would be Cadbury's goods but, if they were coloured purple, they could belong to another trader.

Further, held the High Court, if an advertisement was for purple ice cream, it would be impossible to distinguish whether the word PURPLE was used to indicate that it was Cadbury's ice cream without seeing the goods or a coloured picture of the goods. Even then, if the packaging was not purple, it would be necessary to open the container to ascertain if the contents were purple. Thus, to allow the registration of the word PURPLE would in effect extend the protection of the mark to purple goods, notwithstanding the voluntary exclusion.

Those findings were upheld on appeal to the Court of Appeal. There is a more detailed discussion of this aspect of the case at 7.5.5 ("What is meant by 'capable of distinguishing'?") earlier in this chapter.

7.11　Infringement and enforcement of rights

Legal action for infringement can only be taken once the Certificate of Registration has issued. There is no provision for compensation under the Trade Marks Act 2002 for misuse of a trade mark before the issue of the Certificate of Registration, although remedies may be available under the Fair Trading Act 1986 or the tort of passing off.

Damages for trade mark infringement can run from the date of filing the application, so while legal proceedings cannot be instigated until a mark has been registered, damages for the period the application was pending may be recovered.

Infringement proceedings are heard and decided by a Judge alone without jury involvement.

7.11.1 Proceedings for infringement of registered trade mark initiated in High Court

In *Mitchell v Gulf Star Products Ltd* (1999) 9 TCLR 300, a case involving trade mark infringement brought before the High Court under the 1953 Act, the defendant denied infringement and sought an order transferring the proceedings to the District Court. The defendant's application for transfer was dismissed on the basis that, while the 1953 Act does not explicitly state that the High Court has exclusive jurisdiction in such matters, exclusive jurisdiction is implied. The 1953 Act defines "Court" as meaning "High Court" and this defined term is used in numerous places throughout the Act.

Under the Trade Marks Act 2002, s 101 specifically provides that the owner of a registered trade mark or, in the case of a collective trade mark, one or more members of a collective association acting on its behalf, may apply to the Court for relief if the trade mark is infringed. In s 5(1), Court is also defined as being the High Court.

7.11.2 Infringement where identical or similar sign used in course of trade

Section 89 Trade Marks Act 2002 sets out the acts which amount to infringement of a registered trade mark. Infringement occurs where there is unauthorised use of:

- A sign *identical* to that mark in relation to any goods or services in respect of which the trade mark is registered;

- A sign *identical* to the registered mark in relation to any goods or services that are *similar* to any goods or services covered by the registration, if such use would be likely to deceive or cause confusion; or

- A sign that is *similar* to the registered trade mark in relation to any goods or services that are *identical* or *similar* to any goods or services covered by the registration, if such use would be likely to deceive or cause confusion.

In addition, the use of the sign must be likely to be taken as being use in a trade mark sense.

(1) *Onus of proof*

The onus of proving the elements establishing infringement lies with the plaintiff.

(2) *Meaning of "identical" and "similar"*

In *Leafscreen NZ Ltd v Leafbusters Group Ltd* (2004) 10 TCLR 967, the plaintiff sought an interim injunction to prevent the defendant's use of the signs LEAFSCREEN and LEAFSCREENER in relation to the business of preventing the blockage of gutters by leaves, bird nests, and the like. The first defendant counterclaimed seeking revocation of the plaintiff's LEAFSCREEN trade mark, on the basis of prior use.

In considering whether or not to grant interim relief, Heath J noted, at para 22, that the plaintiff only had the ability to restrain use of the sign LEAFSCREENER if it was *identical* to the plaintiff's existing registered trade mark for LEAFSCREEN (pursuant to s 89(1)(a) of the Act) or *similar* and the use would be likely to deceive or confuse (pursuant to s 89(1)(c) of the Act).

His Honour held, at para 23, that there was no seriously arguable case that the term LEAFSCREENER was identical to the term LEAFSCREEN for the purposes of s 89(1)(a) and stated:

> "The distinction drawn in s 89(1) between an 'identical' registered trade mark and a sign 'similar to the registered trade mark' is, in my view, conclusive of the need to treat the term 'identical' as requiring a complete identity with the registered trade mark. That conclusion is reinforced by the need, when dealing with the use of a sign similar to the registered trade mark, to prove, in addition, that the use would be likely to deceive or confuse. While absolute protection is granted to a sign 'identical' with a registered trade mark, a qualified protection is granted for a sign 'similar' to the registered trade mark, and then only if its use would be likely to deceive or confuse."

Heath J concluded, at para 27, that, although the plaintiff succeeded in proving there was a serious question to be tried in relation to the use of the term LEAFSCREEN by the first defendant (which was *identical* to the plaintiff's registered trade mark), it had failed to prove there was a serious question to be tried in relation to the use of the term LEAFSCREENER as, although it was *similar* to the plaintiff's registered trade mark, the evidence did not indicate that such use was likely to cause deception or confusion of the public.

In a further decision of Heath J (*ABN Amro Holdings NV v ABN Union Treasury Management Ltd* 9/2/05, Heath J, HC Auckland CIV-2004-404-7200), his Honour maintained an interim injunction restraining the defendants, which traded as "ABN Union Treasury Management Ltd" and "ABN Union Building Society" from breaching the plaintiff's registered trade marks for ABN AMRO and ABN. The defendants argued that they were not using an identical sign because their trading names were different from the registered trade mark ABN. They relied on two UK decisions, *Reed Executive Plc v Reed Business Information Ltd* [2004] RPC 767 (CA), in which the English Court of Appeal held that "Reed Business Information" was not identical to the registered trade mark REED, and *Compass Publishing BV v Compass Logistics Ltd* [2004] RPC 809 in which "Compass Logistics" was held not to be identical to COMPASS. Heath J contrasted these decisions with the approach taken by the New Zealand Court of Appeal in *Anheuser-Busch Inc v Budweiser Budvar National Corp* [2003] 1 NZLR 472; (2002) 7 NZBLC 103,812 (CA), in which "Budweiser Budvar" was deemed identical to BUDWEISER. Heath J held that, to the extent the English Court of Appeal and the New Zealand Court of Appeal approaches were different, he was bound to follow the New Zealand Court of Appeal and was satisfied that the initials "ABN" in the defendants' respective trading names would be linked to the registered trade mark such that there was a seriously arguable case as to infringement. The decision is also notable for his Honour's decision to give no weight to the defendants' counterclaim to remove the registered trade marks — on the basis that the defendants had entered the market with knowledge that the marks were on the Register.

Notably, the Court of Appeal in *Anheuser-Busch* followed the approach taken by the English High Court at that time in *Decon Laboratories Ltd v Fred Baker Scientific Ltd* [2001] RPC 293. That approach no longer represents the law in the UK following the decision in *Reed*, in which Jacob LJ stressed the need to identify what the defendant's trade mark is, particularly in cases where descriptive or semi-descriptive words are added to a word mark.

As one commentator has noted (A Kingsbury, "IP Round-Up: Recent Decisions from the Courts" (2005) 4(5) NZIPJ 101) the tests in *Reed* and *Compass* (and indeed *Leafscreen*) more closely reflect the statutory test. Thus, where trade marks are identical the registered owner need not show confusion or a likelihood of confusion. However, where the marks are similar the likelihood of confusion must be proven. Accordingly, a strict approach to identity is appropriate to avoid situations where marks which may not infringe in practice are deemed to infringe solely because they are said to have identity with the registered trade mark.

(3) *Meaning of "use of sign"*

The word "use" is defined in s 6 Trade Marks Act 2002 as "use on, or in physical or other relation to" the goods or services. The definition therefore encompasses both use on the goods themselves, and use in advertising or promotional materials.

See, for example, *Aqua-Tech Ltd v Aqua Technics Pool and Spa Centre NZ Ltd* 3/10/05, Venning J, HC Auckland CIV-2005-404-2037 in which use by the appellant of its AQUA-TECH trade mark on brochures advertising goods manufactured by the appellant (often sold under various sub brands) was deemed to be use in relation to those goods by the appellant. The respondent argued that such use amounted to use in relation to retail services rather than in relation to the goods themselves and referred to two cases in support, *Pumps 'n' Pipes Pty Ltd* (1990) 18 IPR 378 and *The Hoyts Corp Pty Ltd v Hoyt Food Manufacturing Industries Pty Ltd* (2003) 61 IPR 344. However, that submission was rejected and the two authorities distinguished on the basis that in both cases the applicant was not the manufacturer of the goods in relation to which it had applied to register its mark, whereas the appellant in this case was. The decision of Venning J was upheld on appeal (*Aqua Technics Pool & Spa Centre NZ Ltd v Aqua-Tech Ltd* 22/3/07, CA257/05), the Court of Appeal reaching substantially the same conclusion. Leave to appeal the decision of the Court of Appeal to the Supreme Court was refused: *Aqua Technics Pool & Spa Centre NZ Ltd v Aqua-Tech Ltd* 9/7/07, SC24/07; [2007] NZSC 52.

In contrast, in *Colorado Group Ltd v Strandbags Group Pty Ltd (No 2)* (2006) 69 IPR 281 (FCA), the Federal Court of Australia rejected a submission that the use of the word "Colorado" on a shop front amounted to trade mark use in relation to goods. The Court held, at para 12:

> "I do not except that this use of the word, even if it were a fancy word, is use as a trade mark. In one way or other, the use of a word or device as a mark must involve its use in connection with particular goods. Unless there be some connection between the two the mark would not identify the source of the goods. A store front name does not serve that purpose particularly where a variety of goods and 'brands' are sold in the store. The average consumer would not think that a shop name is a badge of origin: rather he or she is likely to think that it is the name, or the business name, of the proprietor of the establishment."

423

Finally, although "use" includes use in other relation to goods or services (for example, in advertising), for such use to be relevant it remains necessary that the use is as a trade mark (ie sufficient to indicate the trade source of those goods or services). Although not an infringement action, the decision in *Effem Foods Ltd v Cadbury Ltd* 21/3/07, Miller J, HC Wellington CIV-2005-485-1487 illustrates the point. Effem appealed a decision of the Assistant Commissioner of Trade Marks permitting Cadbury to register the trade mark EARTH to protect its trade mark MOTHER EARTH which had been used by Cadbury since 1981. Cadbury's application had been filed on the basis of proposed use. Effem asserted that it had used EARTH as a trade mark before Cadbury's application had been filed. It also challenged Cadbury's intention to use the mark.

It was common ground that the only possible use before the relevant date was a TV advertisement for Effem's MARS bar depicting young men playing hackey sack with considerable skill and "casual disregard for the laws of gravity". Towards the end, a billboard appears behind the men depicting a chocolate bar in Mars getup but carrying the stylised word EARTH instead of MARS. A voiceover then intones "Earth. What you would eat if you lived on Mars" bringing the advertisement to a close.

At the opposition stage, the Assistant Commissioner rejected the advertisement as evidence of use of the trade mark EARTH on the basis that there was no actual trade or offered trade in the goods bearing the mark, or an existing intention to offer or supply goods bearing the mark in trade: *Moorgate Tobacco Co Ltd v Philip Morris Ltd (No 2)* (1984) 156 CLR 414 (HCA), at pp 433-434, and *Malibu Boats West Inc v Catanese* (2000) 51 IPR 134, at p 143. After considering those authorities in detail, the High Court concluded, at para 23, that the 1953 Act did not require that there be goods physically bearing the mark, or an intention to offer such goods. The s 2(2) definition envisaged that a sign might be used upon or in physical or other relation to goods. Thus the legislation contemplated that the mark might not be used upon the goods themselves and nothing in *Moorgate Tobacco* invited a different construction.

However, on consideration of the nature of use, Effem's claim to earlier ownership was rejected on the basis that, while the advertisement was a clever way of advertising Effem's MARS bar, it did so, not because the consumer drew a connection between "Earth" and Effem's product, but rather because "Earth" is used in juxtaposition with the word "Mars". Thus, the High Court concluded, at para 27, that there was no evidence that "Earth", used alone, was capable of indicating to consumers that Effem was the trade source of the MARS bars advertised.

(4)   *Meaning of "in the course of trade"*

"In the course of trade" means selling, hire purchase, leasing, exporting and any other commercial transaction: *Aristoc Ltd v Rysta Ltd* (1945) 62 RPC 65 (HL).

(5)   *Comparison of marks*

The general principles for comparison of marks under s 25 Trade Marks Act 2002 apply equally to comparison for the purposes of assessing infringement.

However, it is important to remember that one must consider the mark as it has been registered (rather than as used) by the plaintiff, bearing in mind any disclaimers or other limitations on the registration.

Also, in *Lever Bros v Newton & Sons* (1907) 26 NZLR 856 (CA) and *I & R Morely v Macky Logan Caldwell Ltd* [1921] NZLR 1001, it was held that a greater degree of similarity is required for a finding of infringement than for a finding of confusing similarity in respect of the relative grounds of refusal.

(6)   Meaning of "use as a trade mark"

The alleged infringing sign must be used in such a way that it refers to the owner of the registered mark or its goods or services. Use in a descriptive or non-trade mark sense will not constitute infringement.

The traditional idea of what constitutes trade mark use has been broadened by the UK decision of *Arsenal Football Club Plc v Reed (No 2)* [2003] 3 All ER 865; [2003] RPC 39 (CA). For many years a trader, Mr Reed, had been selling souvenirs and articles of clothing bearing Arsenal Football Club's registered insignia. The use of these insignia was not authorised by Arsenal, but Mr Reed displayed a sign on his wall indicating his goods were not official Arsenal merchandise. The club brought an action for passing off and trade mark infringement in the UK High Court. The passing off action failed, but the High Court referred the matter to the European Court of Justice ("ECJ") to decide whether Mr Reed was using Arsenal's trade marks to indicate a connection in the course of business with Arsenal, or simply as a badge of allegiance.

The ECJ ruled that Mr Reed's use of Arsenal's trade marks interfered with Arsenal's ability to guarantee the origin of goods bearing those marks, and referred the matter back to the UK High Court. However, instead of following the ECJ's ruling, the High Court found that Reed's use of the marks did not indicate trade origin, and therefore there was no trade mark infringement. Arsenal appealed.

The UK Court of Appeal took the view that the question to be answered was not whether the use in question was trade mark use, but rather whether that use interfered with Arsenal's ability to guarantee that products bearing its insignia came from a particular source. The Court of Appeal held that Reed's use did jeopardise this ability, and in any event also found that Reed's use of the insignia was use in a trade mark sense. Consequently, there was trade mark infringement.

Use of a mark by an innocent third party acting on instructions from another will not usually infringe. Thus in *Leafscreen NZ Ltd v Leafbusters Group Ltd* (2004) 10 TCLR 967, the claim against the first defendant was that it had used the mark LEAFSCREEN in relation to conducting the business of preventing gutter blockages. The claim against the second defendant, Telecom Directories Ltd, under ss 89(1) and 6 of the Act, was that it had used, or would use in trade, the plaintiff's registered trade mark, without permission, by agreeing to advertise the first defendant's business in a telephone directory that the second defendant published and provided to New Zealand businesses and consumers. The second defendant submitted that it was not liable for infringement of the registered trade mark on the basis that it was acting as a mere conduit for the first defendant.

Heath J, at para 34, noted with approval the Court of Appeal's decision in *Goldsbro v Walker* [1993] 1 NZLR 394; (1992) 5 TCLR 46; (1993) 4 NZBLC 102,946 (CA), at p 398; p 49; p 102,949 (per Cooke P), pp 402-403; p 53; p 102,952-102,953 (per Richardson J), and p 405; p 57; p 102,955-102,956 (per Hardie Boys J), who accepted that an innocent agent acting merely as a conduit and purporting to do no more than pass on instructions from a principal does not become responsible for anything misleading in the information he, she, or it conveys. Heath J observed, without deciding, that the second defendant, in the incarnation in which it was sued in this case, ought to be treated in a similar fashion and declined to grant interim relief against it.

Use of a mark for the purposes of comparison with one's own goods or services will be use in a trade mark sense: *Villa Maria Wines Ltd v Montana Wines Ltd* [1984] 2 NZLR 422 (CA). However, the Trade Marks Act 2002 now expressly permits comparative advertising, subject to certain requirements. Comparative advertising is discussed in more detail at 7.13 ("Defences") later in this chapter.

7.11.3   Infringement of a well known trade mark

Under the Trade Marks Act 2002, where a trade mark is well known in New Zealand, the owner of the mark is able to take action against use of a sign that takes unfair advantage of, or is detrimental to, the distinctive character or the reputation of the well-known mark, even though the mark is not registered. This is tantamount to the doctrine of trade mark dilution recognised in many overseas jurisdictions.

Generally speaking dilution encompasses two concepts: tarnishment and blurring. Tarnishment occurs when a well known trade mark is portrayed in a manner or context likely to invoke unflattering thoughts about the owner or its product/service associated with the mark. Blurring involves the erosion of the identity of a mark through its use on non-competing products.

Whether a mark is well known in New Zealand is a question of fact, to be decided based on the evidence available. It is worthy of note that the corresponding UK provision requires only that a mark must have "a reputation in the United Kingdom". Therefore, the test set out under the Trade Marks Act 2002 in relation to "well known" marks is, on the face of it, set at a higher level than the requirements in the UK. However, the distinction may be more perceived than actual. Article 16(2) of TRIPS (which the 2002 Act was in part drafted to give effect to) specifies that:

> "In determining whether a brand is well-known, Members shall take account of the knowledge of the trade mark in the relevant sector of the public, including knowledge in the Member concerned which has been obtained as result of the promotion of the trade mark."

In 1999, the Assembly of the Paris Union for the Protection of Industrial Property and the General Assembly of the World Intellectual Property Organisation adopted a joint recommendation which gives further detail to that definition. The recommendation provides that in determining whether a mark is "well-known" a competent authority should take into account any circumstances from which it may be inferred that the mark is well-known including, but not limited to:

- The degree of knowledge or recognition of the mark in the relevant sector of the public;

- The duration, extent and geographical area of any use of the mark;

- The duration, extent and geographical area of any promotion of the mark, including advertising or publicity and the presentation at fairs or exhibitions of the goods and/or services to which the mark applies;

- The duration and geographical area of any registrations, and/or applications for registration, of the mark to the extent that they reflect use or recognition of the mark;

- The record of successful enforcement of rights in the mark, in particular, the extent to which the mark was recognised as well known by competent authorities; and

- The value associated with the mark.

The recommendation emphasises that the determination in each case will depend upon the particular circumstances of that case and that the list is not a set of preconditions for reaching a determination that a mark is "well known".

In practice, this criteria is closely aligned with the criteria applied by the UK Courts in assessing whether a mark has "a reputation in the United Kingdom": *General Motors Corp v Yplon SA* [1999] 1 All ER 865. In *General Motors* it was held, at para 41, that the Court should look at "the degree of knowledge or recognition of the mark in relevant sectors of the public; the duration, extent and geographical area of use of the mark; and the scale and scope of investment in promoting the mark". Furthermore, the Court confirmed, at para 42, that the term "reputation" must be construed in the context of the section. Thus, if a reputation is to be material it must be sufficiently well known amongst a relevant section of the public before the use of the sign will cause unfair advantage or detriment.

Thus, while the wording of the UK section might suggest a lower threshold, the authorities show that proof of something much more than prima facie reputation is required (arguably akin to the level of proof required to establish that a mark is "well known").

The enquiry under s 89(1)(d) is whether the use of the mark takes unfair advantage of, or is detrimental to, the distinctive character or the reputation of the well known mark. The focus is on the impact of the alleged infringing use on the trade mark itself (or indirectly the trade mark owner) rather than the consumer. Accordingly, s 89(1)(d) does not require that there be any confusion or deception resulting from the use of the sign and the registered trade mark. However, the use must result in actual detriment or unfair advantage (or in the case of an application for interim injunction, a very real possibility of these events occurring).

In *DaimlerChrysler AG v Javid Alavi (t/a Merc)* [2001] RPC 813, DaimlerChrysler's claim that the defendant's use of "Merc" on clothing aimed at the skinhead market was detrimental to its "MERCEDES / MERC" trade mark was rejected by the Court, at para 98, on the basis that it failed to show:

> "there is established in the mind of the relevant public a connection between the mark with which they are familiar and the disparaging use. Thus, it is not sufficient to see the word MERC, note that this is the word which one uses to refer to Mercedes cars, see the disagreeable web-site and register it as disagreeable, if nothing actually rubs off on the sign MERC itself or on MERCEDES, or on DaimlerChrysler."

The Court posited, at para 92, the following test:

(1) Does the proprietor's mark have a reputation?

(2)   If so, is the defendant's sign sufficiently similar to it that the public are either deceived into the belief that the goods are associated with the proprietor so that the use of the sign takes unfair advantage of the mark, or alternatively causes detriment in their minds to either (a) the repute or (b) the distinctive character of the mark, or

(3)   Even if they are not confused, does the use of the sign nonetheless have this effect, and

(4)   Is the use complained of nonetheless with due cause.

Note that there is no provision in s 89(1)(d) for a "due cause" exception although the same sort of considerations may be taken into account when considering whether the exceptions to infringement provided in ss 92-98 of the Act apply.

As s 89(1)(d) is a new provision to New Zealand trade mark law, there is no New Zealand case law to shed any light as to what is meant by the wording "takes unfair advantage of, or is detrimental to, the distinctive character or the repute of the mark". However, the case of *Premier Brands UK Ltd v Typhoon Europe Ltd* [2000] FSR 767, at pp 789-791, provides some guidance as to what is meant by this wording in relation to the corresponding UK provision, as does the *DaimlerChrysler* decision discussed above.

7.11.4   Infringement by breach of restrictions

Infringement will occur where a person does, or authorises any other person to do, any of the acts specified in s 90(2) Trade Marks Act 2002 in relation to the goods covered by the registration if that person agreed in writing with the owner or licensee of the mark not to do those acts.

The specified acts are:

*   Applying the mark to the goods after their state or condition, get-up or packaging has been altered;

*   Alteration, part removal, or part obliteration of the mark affixed to the goods;

*   Removal or obliteration of all or part of the mark affixed to the goods without removing or obliterating all other matter indicating a connection in the course of trade between the owner or licensee of the mark and the goods;

*   Applying any other trade mark to the goods to which the registered mark is still affixed; or

*   Adding to the goods to which the mark is affixed, any other matter in writing that is likely to injure the reputation of the trade mark (or by implication the trade mark owner).

7.11.5   Joint infringement

In theory, it is possible for a person who becomes involved in counterfeiting or other infringement to be liable for directing, procuring or combining with others to infringe. For a discussion of the relevant principles see *CBS v Amstrad Consumer Electronics* [1988] 1 AC 1013.

In *Louis Vuitton Malletier SA v Toea Pty Ltd* (2006) 70 IPR 307 (FCA), Louis Vuitton unsuccessfully issued proceedings against Toea for breach of its registered trade marks as a joint torfeasor. Toea was the landlord of, and the party responsible for, operating, supervising and controlling a market at which counterfeit Louis Vuitton product was sold. Louis Vuitton argued that where Toea became aware over a period of years that some stall holders were selling counterfeit goods, and therefore infringing its registered trade marks, and took no action to stop that conduct, it tacitly accepted the conduct and became independently liable for the infringement as a joint torfeasor. That submission was rejected by the Court on a number of grounds including:

- A lack of evidence that Toea was actually aware, in advance of any sale, that the subject stall holders had counterfeit product or intended to sell such product. This evidence was crucial to Louis Vuitton's case given its central contention that Toea was a joint torfeasor in conjunction with the individual stall holders selling the counterfeit product, and

- Relying on *Thompson v Australian Capital Television Pty Ltd* (1996) 186 CLR 574; 141 ALR 1 (HCA), there was a distinction between joint torfeasors (being responsible for the same tort) and several torfeasors (being responsible only for the same damage). Thus, for joint torfeasors there must be a concurrence in the act or acts causing damage, not merely a co-incidence of separate acts which, by their co-joined effect, cause damage. Therefore, in order to find Toea liable for the stall holders' infringements there would need to be evidence of a concurrence in the act or acts causing damage, not merely a coincidence of separate acts which, by their conjoined effect, caused damage. There was no such evidence that the infringing conduct by the stall holders was committed towards some common purpose shared with Toea. Toea's purpose was to conduct an efficient and profitable market. The purpose of each stall holder was the successful conduct of his or her stall. The case was further hampered by the fact that the only revenue Toea received was rent on the space in the market. It did not receive a percentage of sales made by individual stall holders.

For an analogous case in the field of passing off see *White Horse Distillers Ltd v Gregson Associates Ltd* [1984] RPC 61. In this case, the plaintiffs were scotch whiskey distillers who took action in passing off against the defendants, who were whiskey exporters, for supplying scotch whiskey in bulk to Uruguay for admixture with local spirits. It was common ground that the plaintiffs were entitled to a share of the reputation of scotch whiskey in Uruguay and that, unless properly supervised by the exporter, the admixture trade was likely to result in products being passed off locally as scotch whiskey. The defendants had not printed the labels appearing on the whiskey sold in Uruguay but had supplied samples of the labels to their distributor and had also provided feedback in relation to revisions made to those labels to address concerns raised by the plaintiffs. The Court held, at pp 75-76, that, for the defendants to be liable as joint torfeasors to their Uruguayan distributor's passing off, it was essential that they should participate in the passing off. Thus, if the defendants not only supplied the goods, but also played a part in the deceptive marketing, they would be deemed to have committed a tort in England and held liable. The evidence showed that the defendants' predominant motive throughout was to interfere as little as possible with the wishes of the Uruguayan distributor by imposing on it a regime which it might find unduly restrictive, and since the labels had been supplied by the defendants, and had played a significant part in the marketing of the product, it was clear that the defendants had participated in the passing off and were liable.

Accordingly, to be jointly liable it is necessary to show that the alleged infringer must have participated in the very acts complained of. See also *Tot Toys Ltd v Mitchell* [1993] 1 NZLR 325, at p 354:

> "Passing off defendants are responsible for foreseeable deception of those ultimate customers who purchase from intermediaries as well as for deception of their own immediate customers … However, a manufacturer is not responsible for the misconduct of a retailer unless it is clearly shown that the manufacturer ought to have contemplated that such misconduct would be likely."

Care also needs to be taken to ensure that the alleged joint torfeasor is not a "mere conduit" acting on instructions from a principal. For example, refer to *Leafscreen NZ Ltd v Leafbusters Group Ltd* (2004) 10 TCLR 967 which is discussed at 7.11.2(6) ("Meaning of 'use as a trade mark'") earlier in this chapter. There is a more detailed discussion of the "mere conduit" defence in the Fair Trading Act 1986 chapter of this text (chapter 10).

7.11.6 Unjustified proceedings

Under s 105 Trade Marks Act 2002, a defendant, in infringement proceedings, may apply to the Court for a declaration that the infringement proceedings are unjustified, and also for an order for the payment of damages for any loss suffered by the defendant. Section 105 provides:

> "(1) If a person brings proceedings alleging an infringement of a registered trade mark, the Court may, on the application of any person against whom the proceedings are brought,—
>
> "(a) make a declaration that the bringing of proceedings is unjustified:
>
> "(b) make an order for the payment of damages for any loss suffered by the person against whom the proceedings are brought.
>
> "(2) The Court must not grant relief under this section if the person who brings the proceedings proves that the acts in respect of which proceedings are brought constituted, or would have constituted if they had been done, an infringement of the trade mark concerned.
>
> "(3) Nothing in this section makes a barrister or solicitor of the High Court of New Zealand liable to any proceedings under this section in respect of any act done in his or her professional capacity on behalf of a client."

7.12 Remedies

Unlike the Trade Marks Act 1953, the Trade Marks Act 2002 specifically sets out various remedies for infringement. These are governed by ss 106-116.

The usual relief available to a trade mark owner in an infringement action includes:

- Interim or permanent injunctions;

- An inquiry as to damages suffered by the owner or an account of profits earned by the infringer; and

- An order requiring erasure, removal or obliteration of the offending sign, or delivery up of infringing articles where the offending sign cannot be removed.

7.12.1 Interim injunctions

Several recent decisions of the High Court and the Court of Appeal would seem to suggest that the Courts will give increasing primacy to registered intellectual property rights when determining an application for interim relief. In many cases this seems to be at the expense of seemingly conclusive arguments going to the balance of convenience and the overall justice.

In *Aktiebolaget Hassle v Novartis NZ Ltd* 1/5/03, Potter J, HC Auckland CP51-SW/03, the plaintiffs sought an injunction to restrain Novartis from manufacturing an omeprazole product, PROBITOR, which they believed infringed their Patent No 220096 relating to their own similar product sold in New Zealand under the brand name LOSEC. Novartis resisted the application on a number of grounds including:

(1) That it was strongly arguable that the patent was invalid, the equivalent UK patent having already been overturned on the grounds of obviousness; and

(2) That it had contracted to supply Pharmac with PROBITOR, and was obliged to pay Pharmac \$350,000 per calendar month it was unable to supply same (presumably to compensate Pharmac for being obliged to subsidise the more expensive LOSEC during that period).

While recognising the significant losses likely to be suffered by Novartis if injuncted, the Court nonetheless found that the balance of convenience and the overall justice favoured the granting of an injunction, commenting, at para 43:

> "There is a reality to be recognised in the case of the patent, that the patent confers a monopoly during its currency, the benefit of which runs over to the post-patent period because of the strong market position usually developed during the monopoly period. This was expressed by Eichelbaum J in [*Monsanto Chemical Co v Stauffer Chemical Co (No 2)* (1984) 1 TCLR 129; 1 NZIPR 540]."

and later, at para 56:

> "Premature interference with the monopoly position which the patent confers during its currency will also impact on the ability of the proprietor to create or confirm its own market after the expiry of the patent (the 'bridgehead' opportunity)."

The decision of Potter J was upheld by the Court of Appeal in a decision of Blanchard J delivered on 4 July 2003 (*Novartis NZ Ltd v Aktiebolaget Hassle* [2004] 2 NZLR 721 (CA)).

Similar comments have also arisen in the context of applications for interim injunctions to restrain the infringement of registered design rights. See, for example:

- *Handitags Ltd v Warburton* 12/12/01, Glazebrook J, HC Auckland M1586-SW01, at paras 17 and 18:

"However, the main reason put forward by Handitags as to inadequacy of damages is the loss of the ability to manage their practical monopoly situation. This is because, at any stage during such a monopoly, an entry of a competitor can cause permanent damage and permanent inability to manage the monopoly and, in particular, the ending of the monopoly which will obviously occur at the end of the design and copyright period. This diminished advantage can mean a permanent effect which Handitags submits is exceedingly hard to quantify. It is noted that there is only some four years left in respect of the design and five years in respect of the copyright so the loss of a portion of the period at the end of the registration for the design and the copyright period is even more significant. These submissions are accepted. It is accepted that damages would not be an adequate remedy for Handitags."

- *BEP Marine Ltd v Aquatech Marine Ltd* 20/12/02, O'Regan J, HC Auckland M1568-SW02 (which applied *Handitags*).

- *Permanent Promotions Pty Ltd v Independent Liquor (NZ) Ltd* 10/6/04, Heath J, HC Auckland CIV-2004-404-2419, at paras 38 and 39:

"In my judgment, the scheme of the Act is clear. A Commissioner is appointed to examine designs submitted to him or her. In the course of that examination the Commissioner determines questions of novelty and compliance with statutory definitions. The underlying assumption is that the Commissioner is someone experienced in applying the Act and in making judgments of that sort. The scheme of the Act would be undermined significantly if the Courts failed to recognise the nature of the monopoly that flows from the registration process. In this case the design has been registered. I reject Mr Brown's submission that the Register is prima facie evidence only of what is contained in it rather than the fact that the Commissioner has found the design to comply with the definition contained in s 2(1) of the Act and has found the requisite degree of novelty. No item can be registered unless those conclusions have been drawn. That registration confers a monopoly. On an interim injunction application the Court must be slow to second guess the findings of the Commissioner."

and, at para 43:

"In my view the fact of registration confers a prima facie right sufficient to overcome the hurdle of establishing that a serious question exists to be tried."

If the view expressed by Heath J prevails, then there is considerable advantage to a litigant in having a registered (as opposed to common law) intellectual property right as the basis of the legal proceeding. In particular, it may dispense with the issue as to whether there is a serious question to be tried, and greatly increase the prospects of obtaining interim relief, which in intellectual property cases is more often than not determinative of the proceeding.

However as to balance of convenience and overall justice, some caution needs to be exercised, as the "bridgehead" argument may be limited to forms of intellectual property in which the rights expire after a finite period. Thus, for example, the bridgehead argument may not be appropriate in a case involving infringement of a registered trade mark. Similarly, if the ownership of the intellectual property is in dispute this may result in refusal of the application: *Golden Homes (1998) Ltd v Blue Chip Construction Ltd* 21/6/05, Allan J, HC Auckland CIV-2003-404-7090. See also *Lesa Systems Ltd v Canzac Ltd* 16/5/06, John Hansen J, HC Christchurch CIV-2006-409-624, at para 34.

(1) *The presumption of validity in interim injunction applications*

In *Gold Real Estate Group Ltd v GoldLeaf Real Estate Ltd* (2006) 11 TCLR 530, the Court considered the effect of the presumption of validity in s 162 Trade Marks Act 2002 in the context of an application for interim injunction. The plaintiff argued that s 162 meant that there was automatically a serious question to be tried as the registration was prima facie evidence of the validity and ownership of the trade mark. That argument was rejected by Fogarty J, his Honour noting that whether or not the plaintiff has a serious question to be tried is a forward looking assessment of the plaintiff's likely position at trial.

The defendant had called into question the validity of the plaintiff's registration on the basis that it comprised the laudatory word "Gold" and the descriptive words "Real Estate Group Limited". His Honour noted that at the trial it would be likely, if not inevitable, that one or both defendants would apply for a declaration of invalidity, and that for the plaintiff to sustain its cause of action for infringement of the trade mark registration and a final injunction, it would have to survive this likely challenge to the mark. Accordingly, his Honour felt that it would be wrong to assume, at the interlocutory stage, that the mark will be found to be validly registered at trial. His Honour also noted, at para 21, that s 162 was unlikely to have any practical advantage for the plaintiff at trial as the trial would not be a prima facie environment as:

> "The effect of s 162 is that a registered trade mark will be treated as valid in all legal proceedings in the absence of a challenge to the validity. But where there is a challenge the practical consequence will be that the Court will re-examine the merit of the original registration."

Fogarty J also noted, at para 41, that while s 162 applies to all legal proceedings and is a factor in the plaintiff's favour on the balance of convenience, it does not carry much weight as the principal consideration of the Court is to assess the justice of intervening now against the prospects at trial.

(2) *Injunction may be refused if determinative*

In *Gold Real Estate Group Ltd v GoldLeaf Real Estate Ltd* (2006) 11 TCLR 530, the plaintiff was the registered proprietor of the trade mark GOLD REAL ESTATE GROUP LIMITED and which claimed reputation in the word GOLD in relation to real estate services. It sought to injunct the defendant from using GOLD in relation to real estate services.

In respect of the overall justice, the defendants submitted that the granting of the interim injunction would effectively grant the plaintiff a monopoly in a common laudatory term and also one that was important to the Chinese community. Moreover, the defendants' evidence indicated that the order was likely to be determinative as, having changed their brand to comply with the order, they would be unlikely to carry on defending the proceedings and/or change back if successful at full trial.

Accordingly, the defendants submitted that the interim injunction should only be granted if there was very clear evidence to support such an exclusive right.

In response, counsel for the plaintiff relied upon the following passage of Davison CJ in *Klissers Farmhouse Bakeries Ltd v Harvest Bakeries Ltd* [1985] 2 NZLR 129, at pp 138-139:

> "Mr Brown submitted that to grant an interim injunction in the present case would have the effect of giving the plaintiff judgment in the action before trial because it is not commercially realistic for the defendants to cease using the present packaging, replace it with some other form of packaging, advertise and promote that new form of packaging and then if the defendants are successful in the action return to the present form of packaging and promote it in the marketplace. There may be some weight in that submission but the situation is one which must be faced by many defendants who suffer an interim injunction in passing off actions. If the defendants succeed in the action they can recover from the plaintiff the costs and expenses to which they have been put and such losses as they can establish in sales of their products. On the other hand, to deprive the plaintiff of the interim injunction because the defendants may not feel it commercially worthwhile to continue is to deprive the plaintiff of the most effective remedy for passing off and enable the defendants to further establish their products in the marketplace to the detriment of the plaintiff."

However, Fogarty J distinguished that case, at para 50, as follows:

> "I have considerable reservation as to the intrinsic merit of Davison CJ's proposition that to deprive the plaintiff of an interim injunction is to deprive the plaintiff of 'the most effective remedy for passing off'. This is particularly so if the interim injunction provides effectively the plaintiff with a final injunction and a monopoly on GOLD, against what is otherwise likely to be a strongly contested case …"

His Honour's decision may have been strongly influenced by the plaintiff's adoption of, and claim to exclusivity in, the laudatory word GOLD as his Honour went on to state, at para 53, that:

> "It is important that the remedy of interim injunction should not thwart the policy of common law and of statute, which is designed to protect distinctive names or marks and is cautious of allowing anyone to monopolise ordinary words in common use unless they have acquired a secondary meaning. Mr Arthur appeared to submit that there is no monetary value preserving for Mr Yap a choice of name. Financial value does not have to be put on a freedom of choice. Mr Marriott submitted that the plaintiff had taken a risk in developing a brand name using laudatory and then descriptive terms. I think that is right. The plaintiff may, in the long run, be able to sustain the argument that the word 'gold' has become distinctive of its business. But in the meantime, I cannot see any policy in the common law or statute to assist the plaintiff in this regard."

7.12.2 Costs

Costs in legal proceedings are entirely at the Court's discretion. Usually they will be awarded in favour of the successful party.

In *Disney Enterprises Inc v Guan t/a Balmoral Celestial Gifts* 19/6/02, Master Lang, HC Auckland M123-SD02, the plaintiff issued proceedings under s 141(3) Copyright Act. The defendant agreed to have judgment entered by consent once it had made its own determination that the goods the subject of the proceedings had been manufactured and distributed without the plaintiff's authority. The plaintiff sought costs and the defendant opposed.

In ruling that the plaintiff was entitled to its costs, Master Lang acknowledged that enforcement of the plaintiff's copyright interests was of vital importance to it, and that it was entitled to exercise its rights. He went on to say, at paras 45 and 47:

> "I accept also that the proceedings had to be issued as a matter of relative urgency because of the time limits imposed by the Act. The issuing of the proceedings was also a catalyst for the speedy resolution of the dispute, and it is impossible to say that that would necessarily have occurred if the proceedings had not been issued.

> •   •   •   •   •

> "I accept that the Defendant should receive some credit for the fact that it consented to orders being made against it at the earliest opportunity. In my view, however, that credit should be reflected in the fact that costs overall have been minimised through the resolution of the proceedings at an early stage and without resort to further interlocutory processes or unnecessary appearances."

The decision affirms a right holder's entitlement to protect its interests by issuing proceedings against an infringer, and further that right holders should not be financially impaired as a result.

7.13 Defences

Statutory defences to trade mark infringement include:

- Use in relation to genuine goods (eg, parallel imports);

- Reference to parts or accessories;

- Use of a registered trade mark beyond the rights conferred by registration;

- Vested rights;

- Use for comparative advertising;

- Use of a name, place of business or bona fide description of goods or services; or

- Use of a registered geographical indication.

In addition, a number of common law defences may be available including:

- Honest concurrent use; and

- Estoppel and acquiescence.

Infringement actions are most commonly defended on the basis that:

- The trade mark is invalid;

- There is insufficient similarity between the registered mark and the alleged infringing mark (and therefore no likelihood of deception or confusion; or

- The use complained of is not "as a trade mark".

7.13.1   Use in relation to genuine goods / parallel imports

Under s 97(a) Trade Marks Act 2002, it is a defence to trade mark infringement if the mark was applied to goods by, or with the express or implied authorisation of, the owner or licensee.

The primary intention of the section is to allow people to advertise and sell second-hand products. However, s 97(a) also raises interesting questions concerning parallel importation of trade-marked products. If the owner of the registered trade mark in New Zealand also owns the trade mark in the country in which the parallel imported goods were manufactured, the New Zealand trade mark owner cannot take action to stop the importation of those goods. That is because the marks have been applied to the goods by or with the consent of the New Zealand owner. This can be problematic for the New Zealand trade mark owner, particularly if it is an overseas company that owns the trade mark in New Zealand but which has granted exclusive distribution rights in New Zealand to another company.

In order to overcome this, foreign owners of New Zealand trade marks might assign the trade mark to their New Zealand agent. In *Transport Tyre Sales Pty Ltd v Montana Tyres, Rims & Tubes Pty Ltd* (1999) 43 IPR 481; [1999] FCA 329 the local distributor of a tyre manufacturer obtained an assignment of the manufacturer's registered trade mark in order to take action against parallel importers. The assignment was on terms that the mark would revert to the tyre manufacturer when the distributorship terminated. The Federal Court of Australia held that the trade mark assignment was lawful even though the assignor retained options to have the trade mark re-assigned to it.

However, the legitimacy of this practice in New Zealand may be questionable having regard to the implementation of s 97A Trade Marks Act 2002, pursuant to the Copyright (Parallel Importation of Films and Onus of Proof) Amendment Act 2003. Section 97A states:

> **"97A. Exhaustion of rights conferred by registered trade mark**
> "A registered trade mark is not infringed by the use of the trade mark (including use for the purpose of advertising) in relation to goods that have been put on the market anywhere in the world under that trade mark by the owner or with his or her express or implied consent."

The assignment in *Transport Tyre Sales* was effective because the party to whom the marks was assigned had only a contractual relationship with the manufacturer. Assigning the mark to a New Zealand subsidiary may be insufficient to avoid the operation of s 97A. The Courts in other Commonwealth jurisdictions (notably the line of authority commencing with *Revlon Inc v Cripps & Lee Ltd* [1980] FSR 85) have held that, as a parent company effectively controls the decisions of its wholly owned subsidiaries, the subsidiary impliedly consents to the application of the mark to the goods by the parent company (or any other subsidiary or licensee of the parent company) in a foreign country. Thus, in the case of a subsidiary company, the New Zealand courts would in all likelihood imply consent.

There are however some exceptions to this general rule of implied consent. They include:

- Where the goods being imported from a foreign country are of a much inferior quality to those sold or manufactured locally: *Colgate-Palmolive Ltd v Markwell Finance Ltd* (1989) 106 RPC 497;

- Where the foreign parent company includes an explicit term of sale of its goods in other territories (and possibly marks the goods themselves) to the effect that the goods are not to be resold outside the country in which they were purchased: *Castrol Ltd v Automotive Oil Supplies Ltd* (1983) 100 RPC 315; and

- Where there is only a contractual relationship between the foreign trade mark owner and the New Zealand registered owner (for example, a distribution agreement): *Fender Australia Pty Ltd v Bevk (t/a Guitar Crazy)* (1989) 15 IPR 257; *Transport Tyre Sales Pty Ltd v Montana Tyres, Rims & Tubes Pty Ltd* (1999) 43 IPR 481; [1999] FCA 329.

The only New Zealand decision to consider the application of s 97A to date is the decision of Heath J in *Leisureworld Ltd v Elite Fitness Equipment Ltd* 21/7/06, Heath J, HC Auckland CIV-2006-404-3499, an interlocutory decision dealing with Leisure World's application for an interim injunction. The decision also considers the inter-relationship between the removal of the prohibition on parallel importation under the Copyright Act 1994 and the Trade Marks Act 2002.

Leisureworld and Elite Fitness competed in the New Zealand market for the sale of fitness equipment. In early 2005, Leisureworld acquired the business of a further competitor (Progym NZ) which included a bundle of intellectual property rights for "Infiniti" branded equipment manufactured by an associated Taiwanese company Progym Taiwan. Among the assets transferred to Leisureworld on settlement were copyright in the products, and two registrations for the "Infiniti" trade mark in New Zealand. Elite subsequently imported "Infiniti" branded fitness equipment made by Progym Taiwan and Leisureworld sought an interim injunction restraining Elite from continuing to do so on the basis that its actions breached Leisureworld's copyright and registered trade mark rights in New Zealand. Elite's response was that its actions fell within the ambit of the parallel import exceptions under the Copyright Act 1994 and the Trade Marks Act 2002.

For reasons discussed in more detail in the copyright chapter of this text (chapter 4), Heath J had reservations about granting an interim injunction in respect of the alleged infringement of copyright. However, his Honour then went on to consider the allegation that Elite's actions might breach Leisureworld's registered trade marks, concluding that Leisureworld's case was much stronger and that an interim injunction should be granted to acknowledge the public interest in enforcing the monopoly rights created by the Trade Marks Act, pending resolution of substantive proceedings. It is useful to set out his Honour's reasoning, at paras 93-103, in full:

> "The critical issue, on the trade marks argument, is whether, for the purposes of s 97A of the Trade Marks Act, Leisureworld 'put on the market anywhere in the world' with its 'express or implied consent' equipment under the 'Infiniti' trade mark. If it did, s 97A provides that use of the trade mark by another person does not infringe the registered trade mark in New Zealand. I prefer to approach the question as one of statutory interpretation rather than on the basis of the cases to which reference is made is made in para [89](c) above.

"The focus of the s 97A inquiry is on the intentions of the New Zealand registered trade mark holder. The reference, in s 97A to 'anywhere in the world' emphasises the policy choice of the exhaustion model over the territorial model of trade mark law. It also envisages a worldwide, as opposed to a regional, model.

"I am attracted to the analysis undertaken by the European Court of Justice in *Zino Davidoff*. While Mr Sumpter, in his valuable text, suggests that the European Court's view may have been dominated by considerations relating to the peculiarities of the European Economic Area, with respect I find it difficult to draw a distinction in applying those principles based solely on the global approach taken in s 97A, compared with the regional approach taken in art 7 of the (European) Directive.

"Indeed, I see much merit in approaching questions of interpretation in a manner consistent with that used in the jurisdictions of major trading partners unless there are good reasons to suggest a contrary approach should be taken. The interpretation favoured by the European Court is consistent with the underlying principle that parallel importing occurs when 'goods are manufactured and put into circulation in another country either by, or with the consent of, the owner of the applicable intellectual property right': see the extract from policy paper set out in para [60] above.

"The starting point must be the rights conferred on the owner of the registered New Zealand trade mark by s 10(1) of the Trade Marks Act. Section 10(1) provides:

> **"10. Rights that attach to registered trade marks**
> '(1)   The owner of a registered trade mark has, in relation to all or any of the goods or services in respect of which the trade mark is registered, the rights and remedies provided by this Act and, in particular, has the exclusive right to—
>
> '(a)   use the registered trade mark; and
>
> '(b)   authorise other persons to use the registered trade mark; and
>
> '(c)   assign or transmit the registered trade mark (either in connection with the goodwill of a business or not); and
>
> '(d)   give valid receipts for any consideration for any such assignment or transmission.'

"Those acts which do not amount to infringement are set out in ss 92-98 (inclusive). Since 2003, that has included s 97A. There is no evidence that Leisureworld gave express consent to placement on the market, anywhere in the world, of the goods Progym Taiwan was contracted to manufacture for it. Indeed, the terms on which it acquired the intellectual property rights from Progym NZ and agreed to Progym Taiwan manufacturing the goods on its behalf seem to suggest that it intended the opposite: see the terms summarised in paras [16], [17] and [21] above.

"Can implied consent be inferred? For the purpose of this inquiry, I apply the principles set out in the European Court's decision in *Zino Davidoff*.

"On the evidence before me, there is no basis to infer, from established facts, implied consent on the part of Leisureworld to the gymnasium equipment in issue being placed on the market anywhere in the world. If, as Mr McGill contended, a company holding a registered trade mark in New Zealand became vulnerable to exploitation of its mark through the parallel importing regime by entering into a contract with a company overseas to manufacture the equipment, that would undermine the protections intended to be given to registered trade mark owners.

"'Put on the market', for the purposes of s 97A, connotes an intention that the goods be traded in markets outside New Zealand. The existence of a manufacturing agreement with a company in another jurisdiction is simply evidence of an agreement to manufacture: it is not evidence of consent for that manufacturer to make those goods available for sale elsewhere in the world. The need for a trade mark owner to give consent under s 97A would be undermined if a contrary view were taken. 'Implied' consent must still be actual consent.

"Those conclusions are reinforced by the ability of a party in the position of Elite to search the register of trade marks to ascertain whether anyone has exclusive rights in New Zealand in respect of the goods it intends to import. If unaware whether consent has or has not been granted, it would be open to the importer to make inquiry of that registered trade mark holder in the first instance. If those steps were not taken the importer must bear the risk that consent may not have been given, with the consequence that the registered mark has been infringed.

"I note that the register of trade marks is prima facie evidence of any matters required or authorised to be entered in it by the Act: s 181(3). Search may be undertaken under s 184 of the Act. Assignments of trade marks must be entered on the register: see s 182(c)."

In terms of an implied consent, his Honour adopted the following principles set out in the European Court of Justice's decision in *Zino Davidoff SA v A & G Imports Ltd* [2002] Ch 109 (ECJ), at p 146:

"(a)   While consent could be expressed or implied, it must be expressed positively. Evidence from which implied consent might be inferred must demonstrate unequivocally that the trade mark proprietor has renounced any intention to enforce its exclusive rights.

"(b)   Implied consent cannot be inferred from:

"(i)   Silence of the trade mark proprietor;

"(ii)   The fact that a trade mark proprietor has not communicated opposition to marketing goods in another market;

"(iii) The fact that the relevant goods do not carry any warning that it is prohibited to place them on the market elsewhere;

"(iv)   The fact that the trade mark owner transferred ownership of the goods bearing the mark without imposing contractual reservations or from the fact that, according to the law governing the contract, the property right transferred includes, in the absence of reservations, an unlimited right of re-sale or, at the very least, a right to market the goods subsequently in another jurisdiction;

"(c) It is not relevant to an assessment of consent that the importer of the goods bearing the trade mark is not aware that the proprietor objects to their being placed on the market elsewhere or should by traders other than authorised retailers. Nor is it relevant that authorised retailers and wholesalers have not imposed on their own purchasers contractual reservations setting out such opposition, even though they have been informed of it by the trade mark proprietor."

His Honour concluded, at para 86:

"In my view, the European Court's judgment goes no further than holding that consent might be implied by inference from proved facts. The inference drawn must, necessarily, be demonstrably stronger than other available inferences. That is the sense in which I understand the European Court to be saying that implied consent must be demonstrated unequivocally."

There is a fundamental conflict between the exhaustion of rights principle which underlies the removal of the prohibition on parallel imports carrying registered trade marks, and the territorial nature of these trade mark registrations. The decision of Heath J confirms that the focus of the enquiry under s 97A Trade Marks Act 2002 is on the intentions of the New Zealand registered trade mark holder, and that the starting point must be that the rights conferred on the owner of the registered New Zealand trade mark are territorial in nature. For s 97A to apply, there must be a demonstrably strong inference from proved facts that the owner of the New Zealand trade mark intended its goods to be traded in markets outside New Zealand. In the absence of this s 97A will not apply and these imports will be in breach of the New Zealand owner's rights.

7.13.2 Reference to parts or accessories

Under s 97(b) Trade Marks Act 2002, it is a defence to trade mark infringement if it is reasonably necessary to use the mark in relation to goods adapted to form part of, or which are accessory to, any genuine goods on which the mark has been applied. This covers the situation where, for example, spare parts for a car are made by someone other than the car manufacturer and it is necessary to use the car manufacturer's trade mark to indicate which make or model the spare parts fit.

7.13.3 Vested rights

Under s 96 Trade Marks Act 2002, a registered trade mark cannot be infringed by the use of an identical or similar mark in relation to goods or services, where that identical or similar mark has been used continuously in relation to those goods or services from a date before both:

- The filing date of the registered mark; and

- The date of first use of the registered mark in New Zealand.

7.13.4 Use for comparative advertising

Section 94 Trade Marks Act 2002 expressly permits the use of a registered trade mark for comparative advertising purposes subject to certain requirements. Section 94 provides as follows:

"A registered trade mark is not infringed by the use of the registered trade mark for the purposes of comparative advertising, but any such use otherwise than in accordance with honest practices in industrial or commercial matters must be treated as infringing the registered trade mark if the use, without due cause, takes unfair advantage of, or is detrimental to, the distinctive character or the repute of the trade mark."

The application of s 94 was considered in *Benchmark Building Supplies Ltd v Mitre 10 (NZ) Ltd* [2004] 1 NZLR 26; (2003) 10 TCLR 767; 7 NZBLC 104,002. Mitre 10 successfully obtained an interim injunction in the High Court restraining Benchmark from placing bright orange stickers, showing Benchmark's cheaper prices, on brochures produced by Mitre 10 and then displaying these brochures outside its shops. Benchmark appealed, relying on both s 94 Trade Marks Act 2002 (which excludes comparative advertising from infringement) and a concession on behalf of Mitre 10 that, if the section applied, no injunction could be sustained following the 2002 Act coming into force.

Being satisfied that Benchmark's use of the Mitre 10 trade marks constituted comparative advertising, the Court of Appeal found it necessary to consider Mitre 10's contention that the use was "otherwise than in accordance with honest practice in industrial or commercial matters in that, without due cause, it took unfair advantage of or was detrimental to, the distinctive character or repute of the trade marks".

That contention was rejected by the Court of Appeal, on the basis that the MITRE 10 trade marks, as used by Benchmark, continued to serve the purpose of identifying or distinguishing the retail source of the products advertised. Delivering the judgment of the Court, Gault P stated, at para 54:

"When Benchmark displays the brochures it does so with the intention that the trade marks of Mitre 10 perform precisely the same function as they performed upon Mitre 10's original distribution of the brochures. The very effectiveness of the comparisons Benchmark draws depends upon the public perceiving the marks are indicating Mitre 10's retail services and (in the case of BUTLERS) its goods. It cannot therefore be said that the distinctiveness of the marks is in any way damaged. Nor is it possible to say that the use by Benchmark takes unfair advantage of the distinctiveness or repute of the trade marks to any greater extent than more conventional forms of comparative advertising. Subject to the Fair Trading Act points with which we are not concerned, there is no issue of people being deceived or misled by the use of the trade marks."

The s 94 proviso mirrors s 10(6) Trade Marks Act 1994 (UK) and case law under that section will also assist the New Zealand judiciary in interpreting and applying the section.

In *Cable & Wireless v BT* [1998] FSR 383, at p 389-390, Jacob J adopted the following summary of the operation of s 10(6):

"(1)   The primary objective of section 10(6) of the 1996 Act is to permit comparative advertising;

"(2)   As long as the use of the competitor's mark is honest, there is nothing wrong in telling the public of the relative merits of competing goods or services and using registered trade marks to identify them;

"(3)   The onus is on the registered proprietor to show that the factors indicated in the proviso to section 10(6) exists;

"(4)   There will be no trade mark infringement unless the use of the registered trade mark is not in accordance with honest practices;

"(5)   The test is objective: would a reasonable reader be likely to say, upon being given the full facts, that the advertisement is not honest?;

"(6)   Statutory or industry agreed codes of conduct are not a helpful guide as to whether an advertisement is honest for the purposes of section 10(6). Honesty has to be gauged against what is reasonably to be expected by the relevant public of advertisements for the goods or services in issue;

"(7)   It should be borne in mind that the general public are used to the ways of advertisers and expect hyperbole;

"(8)   The 1994 Act does not impose on courts an obligation to try and enforce through the back door of trade mark legislation a more puritanical standard than the general public would expect from advertising copy;

"(9)   An advertisement which is significantly misleading is not honest for the purposes of section 10(6);

"I venture with diffidence to make a number of additional observations.

"(10)   The advertisement must be considered as a whole;

"(11)   As a purpose of the 1994 Act is positively to permit comparative advertising, the court should not hold words in the advertisement to be seriously misleading for interlocutory purposes unless on a fair reading of them in their context and against the background of the advertisement as a whole they can really be said to justify that description;

"(12)   A minute textual examination is not something upon which the reasonable reader of an advertisement would embark;

"(13)   The court should therefore not encourage a microscopic approach to the construction of a comparative advertisement on a motion for interlocutory relief." (citations omitted)

The test of "honest practice" in s 10(6) is an objective one: see *Vodafone Group Plc v Orange Personal Communications Services Ltd* [1997] FSR 34, at p 39, per Jacob J:

"In this case it is common ground that there is no infringement unless the use of Vodafone in the comparison falls within the qualification of section 10(6). This qualification was considered by Laddie J in *Barclays Bank Plc v RBS Advanta* [1996] RPC 307. He held that it is for the plaintiff to show that the use falls within the qualification and there the test of honesty is objective (ie, would a reasonable reader be likely to say, upon being given the full facts, that the advertisement is not honest?). Laddie J gave as an example the case where the advertisement is 'significantly misleading'. In trade marks, as Mr Mellor [counsel] rightly submitted, there is no 'one meaning rule'. If a comparison is significantly misleading on an objective basis to a substantial proportion of the reasonable audience, it is not an 'honest practice' within the section."

In *British Airways Plc v Ryan Air Ltd* [2001] FSR 541, the Court took a robust approach to the question of whether the advertisement in that case was "otherwise than in accordance with honest practices in industrial or commercial matters", Jacob J commented, at p 552:

> "It is of course the case that the average consumer has been exposed from birth to advertising. People get case hardened by it. They expect hyperbole and puff. One can almost say no advertisement is complete without them. The courts have long recognised this."

As Andrew Brown QC notes in his paper entitled "Trade Marks Act 2002: Big Changes to Some Key Provisions" Auckland District Law Society, 17 March 2003, the robust approach of the UK Courts accords with New Zealand authorities under the Fair Trading Act 1986: see, for example, *Telecom Directories Ltd v Ad.Viser (NZ) Ltd* (1992) 5 TCLR 60; 26 IPR 37.

The second part of the s 94 proviso requires that, as well as being "otherwise than in accordance with honest practices in industrial or commercial matters", the use of the mark must, without due cause, take unfair advantage of, or be detrimental to, the distinctive character or repute of the trade mark. In *Vodafone*, Jacob J took the view that this second requirement adds very little to the section, saying, at pp 39-40:

> "The provision contains a further qualification — 'that the use without due cause takes unfair advantage of, or is detrimental to, the distinctive character or repute of the mark'. Here Orange say that even if the slogan is misleading it does nothing to the distinctive character of the mark Vodafone. I think this is false. The slogan clearly takes advantage of the distinctive character or repute of the mark: it would be meaningless if no-one had heard of Vodafone. And, on the hypotheses that the mark is misleading, that would be an unfair advantage. I agree with Laddie J that these words 'in most cases add nothing of significance to the first part of the proviso'. If the slogan is misleading there will be infringement."

(1) Comparative advertising may breach other rights

While a comparative advertisement may not infringe a registered trade mark pursuant to s 94 Trade Marks Act 2002, it may still give rise to an action for copyright infringement. This prospect was considered by the UK Courts in *IPC Media Ltd v News Group Newspapers Ltd* [2005] EWHC 317 (Ch). IPC was the publisher of a weekly magazine entitled *What's on TV*. News Group, which published *The Sun* newspaper, included within it a free weekly television listing magazine entitled *TV Mag*. News Group published an advertisement in its newspaper promoting *TV Mag* which included a reproduction of the logo and a recent cover of IPC's *What's on TV* magazine. The logo and magazine cover also appeared in a letter sent to readers of *The Sun* newspaper which claimed *TV Mag* was bigger and had better content than *What's on TV* and also highlighted that *TV Mag* was free.

IPC complained of copyright infringement and News Group responded in part by relying on the defence of comparative advertising under the UK legislation. That defence was rejected by the trial Judge who noted that, even if the defence could apply to a copyright case, if the defendant did not need to infringe copyright to identify the product being compared, then the defence would not apply.

7.13.5 Use of name, place of business or description of goods or services

Section 95 Trade Marks Act 2002 provides a defence to trade mark infringement for any person who uses in accordance with honest practices in industrial or commercial matters:

- Their own name;

- The name of any of their predecessors in business;

- The name of their place of business;

- The name of their predecessor's place of business; or

- Any sign to describe the character or quality of that person's goods or services.

(1) *Meaning of "honest practices in industrial or commercial matters"*

The same phrase appears in s 94 which permits comparative advertising and is discussed in more detail at 7.13.4 ("Use for comparative advertising").

(2) *Use of own name*

A company does not automatically have a defence just because it used the name under which it is registered: s 91 Trade Marks Act 2002. What is important is whether the use is genuine.

In the case of companies, it is not necessary that a company uses its full name before it can avail itself of the s 95 defence. However, undue abbreviation may make the defence unavailable: *Parker-Knoll Ltd v Knoll International Ltd* (1962) 79 RPC 265 (HL).

The defence may be available to a distributor dealing in a manufacturer's goods, where the manufacturer has in good faith affixed its own name to the goods: *Smith & Nephew Plastics (Australia) Pty Ltd v Sweetheart Holding Corp* (1987) 8 IPR 285.

The decision of the Court of Appeal in *Advantage Group Ltd v Advantage Computers Ltd* [2002] 3 NZLR 741 (CA) has confirmed that the relevant time for assessing the own name defence is the date the application to register the mark alleged to have been infringed was filed (ie, the deemed date of registration).

Advantage Computers, which had been trading since 1986, applied to register the trade mark ADVANTAGE in 1992 for computer goods and services. Due to difficulties during the examination process the marks were not actually registered until March 1999. Advantage Group began using the same mark in early 1999, and applied to have Advantage Computers' trade mark registration cancelled. In response, Advantage Computers brought an action for trade mark infringement.

In the High Court (*Advantage Computers Ltd v Advantage Group Ltd* 28/6/02, Chambers J, HC Auckland CL41/99), Advantage Group Ltd unsuccessfully sought to rely on the corresponding provision in the 1953 Act relating to the own name defence, s 12. It was held that the s 12 defence did not apply, by virtue of s 13 (ie, if use of a company name will infringe another trade mark then s 12 will not be available by way of defence). However, even if the defence was available, the High Court found Advantage Group's use of the mark was not bona fide. These findings were upheld on appeal.

The fact that Advantage Group began using the ADVANTAGE mark in between the filing of Advantage Computers' applications to register the mark, and the date of registration, did not assist Advantage Group's case (the Court of Appeal noting that the alternative would be to encourage competitors to enter the market in the period between application and registration with every purpose of denying legitimate traders registration of their marks).

(3)   *Use of bona fide description*

The words must be an ordinary or natural description of the product or service, and in addition, must not be of a nature that will be taken as indicating a trade connection.

In *Mars GB Ltd v Cadbury Ltd* (1987) 104 RPC 387, Mars alleged that Cadbury's use of the words "Treat Size" on miniature confectionery infringed its registration for TREETS. The Court held that while the public would not take the words "Treat Size", as they appeared on Cadbury's packaging, as being used as a trade mark, "Treat Size" was not a bona fide description of Cadbury's product either.

The finding seems to have been largely based on the fact that Cadbury had applied to register "Treat Size" as a trade mark. Evidence of a Cadbury witness suggested that "Treat Size" would be a useful description of the product. The witness claimed that "Treat Size" was different from similar descriptions used by others in the confectionery trade (such as "Fun Size") and would distinguish the Cadbury product. The evidence showed that while Cadbury appreciated that "Treat Size" might not initially be registrable, it hoped that registration might be achieved in future through use.

"Ben Wear Thermal Sox" was held to infringe "Therm-O-Sox", as "thermal" was thought not to be descriptive of the character or quality of the goods, and in addition, imported a reference to a trade connection with the registered mark: *Rich VG v Bennetts & Co* (1978) 1 NZIPR 188.

In *Mainland Products Ltd v Bonlac Foods (NZ) Ltd* [1998] 3 NZLR 341 (CA), it was held that the word VINTAGE appearing on Bonlac's packaging for cheese was not a bona fide description of the cheese. In obiter Gault J stated, at p 351:

> "It is not difficult to envisage the use of the word 'Vintage' on a cheese wrapper in a purely descriptive sense. An obvious example is the incorporation of a statement such as 'The perfect complement to vintage wine'. That is the kind of usage contemplated by the statutory exclusion from infringement of the exclusive right to use a word trade mark. While care must be taken not to extend unduly the ambit of protection of registered marks which are known words with meanings suggestive of relevant goods or services, care also must be taken to prevent erosion of the distinctiveness of a good trade mark by competitors with strategic motives claiming descriptive use."

7.13.6   Use of registered geographical indication

In late 2006, the Act was amended by insertion of a new s 98A which provides that a registered trade mark is not infringed by the use of a geographical indication registered under the Geographical Indications (Wine and Spirits) Registration Act 2006. Similarly, s 20 of the Act prohibits the registration of a trade mark that contains a registered geographical indication unless it is limited to goods that originate from the place indicated in the registered geographical indication. The provisions of that Act are discussed in more detail at 7.2.3 ("Related legislation / common law causes of action") earlier in this chapter.

7.13.7 Honest concurrent use

Under s 26 Trade Marks Act 2002, a sign that is identical or similar to an existing registered trade mark may be registered where it can be shown that the applicant has made honest concurrent use of the sign. Accordingly, such honest concurrent use may also be a defence to infringement proceedings.

In *Leafscreen NZ Ltd v Leafbusters Group Ltd* (2004) 10 TCLR 967, the plaintiff claimed that the defendants infringed its registered trade mark for LEAFSCREEN by using the terms LEAFSCREEN and LEAFSCREENER in relation to the business of preventing gutter blockages. The first defendant counterclaimed seeking revocation of the plaintiff's registered trade mark on the basis of its prior use of the term.

The plaintiff was incorporated as a limited liability company in December 2001. It sought and obtained a registered trade mark for LEAFSCREEN in March 2002. The first defendant's claim of prior use was based upon the acquisition of the business of a company called Leafbusters 2001 Ltd. The first defendant acquired that company from an Australian company called Polymesh Australasia Group Pty Ltd. Polymesh allegedly used the marks LEAFSCREEN, LEAFSCREENER, and LEAFBUSTERS in Australia in connection with the business of preventing gutter blockages since 1993. It owned an Australian registered trade mark for LEAFSCREENER dating from 2000.

In interim injunction proceedings, Heath J considered whether the first defendant's alleged prior use of the sign LEAFSCREEN took precedence over the plaintiff's New Zealand registered trade mark for the same term. Heath J cited with approval, at para 25, the comments of the Privy Council in *Sprints Ltd v Comptroller of Customs (Mauritius)* [2000] FSR 814 (PC), a case concerning proceedings for infringement under a similarly worded statute. Their Lordships said, at p 819, that:

> "The rights of the legal owner of the mark cannot be ousted by the efforts of his rival to appropriate the mark. It has not been suggested that the appellant was an honest concurrent user of the mark."

Heath J observed, at para 25, that honest concurrent use of the LEAFSCREEN mark (as a defence to infringement proceedings) may well be an issue at full trial in this case, although, ultimately his Honour was not required to make a ruling on it at the interim injunction stage.

On the basis of the *Leafscreen* decision, it appears as though the defence will be available, provided the use can be shown to be honest. A company that acquires rights pre-dating the registered mark solely to legitimise use which would otherwise infringe runs the risk of a finding that such use lacks honesty — hence the defence will not be available.

7.14 Revocation

A trade mark registration may be removed from the Register or its scope reduced by a successful application for revocation of the trade mark.

The grounds upon which a trade mark may be revoked are set out in s 66 Trade Marks Act 2002. Broadly, a trade mark may be revoked if it has not been put to genuine use in the course of trade or its use has been suspended, it has become generic, it describes a product or service which is the subject of an expired patent, or it is likely to deceive or confuse the public.

An application for revocation of a registered trade mark may be filed by any person at any time provided they have the requisite standing (refer to 7.14.1 ("Standing") below).

For a discussion about the removal of a trade mark from the Register by means of an application for a declaration of invalidity, refer to 7.15 ("Invalidity") below.

7.14.1 Standing

A person has standing to file an application to revoke a registered trade mark under s 65(1) Trade Marks Act 2002 if that person is "aggrieved".

The term "aggrieved" should be given a wide interpretation: *Khalaf Stores v Phoenix Dairy Caribe NV* 3/9/03, Hammond J, HC Wellington CIV-2002-485-207.

An alleged infringer of a mark will always be an aggrieved person: *Baker v Rawson* (1891) 8 RPC 89.

A person who is in the same trade as the owner of the registered mark will usually be an aggrieved person. In *Powell v Birmingham Vinegar Brewery Co* (1894) 11 RPC 4 (HL), Lord Herschell stated, at p 7:

> "Wherever it can be shown, as here, that the applicant is in the same trade as the person who has registered the trade mark, and wherever the trade mark if remaining on the Register, would or might limit the legal rights of the applicant, so that by reason of the existence of the entry on the Register he could not lawfully do that which but for the existence of the mark upon the Register he could lawfully do, it appears to me he has a locus standi to be heard as a person aggrieved."

A person with a substantial or real interest in the removal of the registered trade mark will be an aggrieved person. The authors of *Kerly's Law of Trade Marks and Trade Names* (12th ed), London, Sweet and Maxwell, 1986 state, at para 11-07, that:

> "The persons who are aggrieved are, it is held, all persons who are in some way or other substantially interested in having the mark removed — where it is a question of removal — from the Register; including all persons who would be substantially damaged if the mark remained, and all trade rivals over whom an advantage was gained by a trader who was getting the benefit of a registered trade mark to which he was not entitled."

The authorities for this passage are said to be *Re Powell's Trade Mark* [1893] 2 Ch 388 (CA) and *DAIQUIRI Trade Mark* (1969) 86 RPC 600 (HL).

447

In *Nike International Ltd v United Pharmaceutical Industries (Aust) Pty Ltd* (1996) 35 IPR 385, a case concerning an application for revocation of a registered trade mark on the grounds of non-use under the relevant provisions of the Australian Act, the Court adopted the comments of McLelland J in *Ritz Hotel Ltd v Charles of the Ritz Ltd* (1988) 12 IPR 417, at p 454, as follows:

> "It is sufficient for present purposes to hold that the expression 'person aggrieved' would embrace any person having a real interest in having the Register rectified, or the trade mark removed in respect of any goods, as the case may be, in the manner claimed, and thus would include any person who would be, or in respect of whom there is a reasonable possibility of his being, appreciably disadvantaged in a legal or practical sense by the Register remaining unrectified, or by the trade mark remaining unremoved in respect of any goods, as the case may be, in the manner claimed. In my opinion, the concept does not admit of further refinement. In deference to a submission by the defendants based on, inter alia, [*Re Consort Trade Mark* (1980) RPC 160] at 166, I would merely add that in my view there is no legitimate basis for introducing into the concept of 'person aggrieved' for the purposes of s 22(1) or 23(1) any restriction based on the conditions required to be fulfilled by an applicant for registration of a trade mark. I reject the defendants' submission that 'the plaintiff must show a trade rivalry by demonstrating that it is either in trade or has a fixed and present intention to enter trade in Australia in goods sufficiently similar to those covered by classes 3 and 26 as to be likely to cause confusion.'"

Under the Trade Marks Act 2002, "an aggrieved person" may also include a person who is "culturally aggrieved".

An application to revoke a registered trade mark may not be based upon a trivial matter: *Wright, Crossley and Co* (1898) 15 RPC 131. Thus, under s 65(2), the Commissioner or Court may refuse any application to revoke a registered trade mark that is vexatious.

7.14.2 Forum

Under s 65(1) Trade Marks Act 2002, an aggrieved person may apply to the Intellectual Property Office of New Zealand ("IPONZ") or to the High Court to revoke a registered trade mark.

In most cases, an application is filed with IPONZ for determination by the Commissioner of Trade Marks. Under s 170, decisions of the Commissioner may be appealed to the High Court.

However, under s 158, where court action concerning the trade mark in question is pending, the application to revoke the trade mark must be filed in the High Court. The same section also permits the Commissioner to transfer a revocation action filed with IPONZ to the High Court at any stage.

Commonly, an application to revoke a registered trade mark will be filed as a defence or counterclaim to an action for trade mark infringement in the High Court.

For a discussion about the procedure to be followed where an application to revoke a registered trade mark is filed with IPONZ, refer to 7.14.3 ("Procedure") below.

7.14.3 Procedure

Where an application to revoke a registered trade mark is based on one of the grounds set out in s 66 Trade Marks Act 2002, other than non-use (under ss 66(1)(a) and (b)), and is filed with the Intellectual Property Office of New Zealand ("IPONZ") to be determined by the Commissioner, the following procedures must be followed:

- Under reg 96(1) Trade Marks Regulations 2003, within 2 months of receiving the application to revoke the registered trade mark, the owner or licensee may oppose the application by filing a counter-statement;

- Under reg 97(1), the counter-statement must contain the following information:

  - The name and address for service of the owner or licensee opposing the application;

  - If the owner or licensee has an agent, the agent's name;

  - A response to the applicant's grounds for revocation, by admitting, denying, or claiming lack of knowledge of each assertion made in the application for revocation;

  - A brief statement of the facts on which the owner or licensee relies in support of continued registration; and

  - If non-use is due to special circumstances of the kind referred to in s 66(2) Trade Marks Act 2002, a statement of the special circumstances;

- Under reg 96(2), if the owner or licensee fails to file a counter-statement within the relevant period, the Commissioner must (see discussion below) determine the application on the documents filed by the applicant;

- If a counter-statement is filed, then within 2 months of receiving a copy of the counter statement, the applicant must file evidence in support of the revocation application or notify the Commissioner that they do not intend to file evidence or that they withdraw their application;

- Within 2 months of receiving the applicant's evidence in support of the revocation application (or notification that no evidence will be filed), the trade mark owner or licensee may file evidence in support of registration or notify the Commissioner that they do not intend to file evidence; and

- If the trade mark owner or licensee files evidence then the applicant for revocation will be given one month to file evidence strictly in reply.

Where the application to revoke the registered trade mark is based on one of the grounds of non-use set out in s 66(1)(a) or (b), when filing a counter-statement the owner or licensee must also file evidence of use of the trade mark or of special circumstances restraining the use of the trade mark.

This extra procedural requirement in cases where the application for revocation is based on grounds of non-use differs from the previous legislation in which the applicant for revocation was required to "prove the negative" by making out a case of non-use before the trade mark owner or licensee was required to respond. It is generally accepted that this new procedure is now fairer to applicants for revocation. Onus is discussed in more detail below.

Where an application to revoke a registered trade mark is filed in the High Court, the ordinary rules of civil procedure which are governed by the High Court Rules will apply.

(1) *Procedure in undefended cases*

Where an application for a declaration of invalidity and/or revocation (other than for non-use) is undefended, IPONZ has adopted a practice similar to that used in the UK in *Firetrace Trade Mark* [2002] RPC 337: see for example *SportsGear NZ Ltd's Registration/White Holdings Ltd's Registration* (Commissioner's Decision No T13/2005, 9/5/05, Asst Commr Frankel). In *Firetrace*, the Hearing Officer considered the application of r 32(3) Trade Mark Rules 2000 (UK), which reads as follows:

> "Where a Notice and Counterstatement are not filed by the proprietor within the period prescribed by paragraph (2), the Registrar may treat his opposition to the application as having been withdrawn."

The Hearing Officer concluded that the absence of the word "shall" meant that it was not mandatory for the Registrar to exclude the owner from the proceedings on failure to file a Notice and Counterstatement and, because of the presumption of validity in s 72 Trade Marks Act 1994 (UK), the registration could not simply be revoked or declared invalid. It was therefore incumbent on the applicant for revocation to provide evidence which supported at least a prima facie case of invalidity.

The equivalent New Zealand provision to r 32(3) of the UK Rules is reg 101 Trade Marks Regulations 2003. Regulation 101 Trade Marks Regulations 2003 relates to the filing of a Counterstatement in revocation proceedings and states:

> "If the owner or licensee does not, within 2 months after the owner or licensee received the application, file the counterstatement the Commissioner must determine the application on the documents filed by the applicant."

The use of the word "must" in the New Zealand Regulations makes the decision in *Firetrace* distinguishable and requires the Commissioner to determine an undefended application on the basis of the papers filed at the point in time when the registered owner's Counterstatement fell due. Accordingly, notwithstanding IPONZ practice, there would seem to be no requirement on the applicant for revocation to file evidence supporting a prima facie case of revocation. On the contrary, if the registered owner declines to defend the proceedings then the undefended application for revocation creates a prima facie case that the mark is no longer valid.

7.14.4 Onus

In opposition proceedings, the onus to prove that a trade mark should be registered rests upon the person applying to register the trade mark.

In revocation proceedings, the onus to prove that a registered trade mark should be revoked rests upon different parties, depending on which of the grounds set out in s 66 Trade Marks Act 2002 are relied upon.

If the application is based on one of the grounds set out in s 66 other than non-use under s 66(1)(a) and (b), the onus is on the person applying to revoke the registered trade mark to prove that the relevant grounds exist.

If the application is based on one of the grounds of non-use set out in s 66(1)(a) or (b), the initial onus is on the trade mark owner or licensee to prove that the registered trade mark should not be revoked. Once use of the trade mark or special circumstances justifying non-use of the trade mark are established, the onus switches back to the person applying to revoke the registered trade mark to prove that the trade mark should be revoked on the relevant grounds of non-use.

7.14.5 Grounds

A registered trade mark may only be revoked on the grounds set out in s 66 Trade Marks Act 2002. The relevant grounds are that:

- The trade mark was not put to genuine use in the course of trade in New Zealand, by any owner for the time being, in relation to the goods or services in respect of which it was registered during the relevant period: s 66(1)(a);

- The use of the trade mark was suspended for an uninterrupted period of 3 years or more: s 66(1)(b);

- Due to the acts or inactivity of the owner, the trade mark has become a common name in general public use for a product or service in respect of which it is registered (ie, generic): s 66(1)(c);

- A product was formerly manufactured under a patent or a service was formerly a patented process and 2 or more years have elapsed since the expiry of the patent and the trade mark is the only practical name or description for the product or service: s 66(1)(d); and

- Due to the manner in which the trade mark is used, the trade mark is likely to deceive or confuse the public, for instance as to the nature, quality, or geographic origin of the goods or services: s 66(1)(e).

(1) *Non-use*

Under s 66(1)(a) Trade Marks Act 2002, a registered trade mark may be revoked if, up to one month before the application for revocation is filed, the trade mark has not been put to genuine use in the course of trade in New Zealand for an uninterrupted period of 3 or more years following the actual date of registration. Under s 66(1)(b), a registered trade mark may be revoked if use of the trade mark was suspended for an uninterrupted period of 3 or more years.

To avoid revocation of a trade mark on the grounds of non-use, the owner or licensee must prove that during the relevant uninterrupted period of 3 or more years:

- The trade mark was put to genuine use in the course of trade in New Zealand in relation to the goods and services in respect of which the trade mark is registered (s 66(1)(a)); or

- The use of the trade mark was not suspended (s 66(1)(b)).

Alternatively, if the trade mark was not put to genuine use during the relevant period, or use of the mark was suspended during the relevant period, the owner or licensee of the mark may avoid revocation by proving that:

- The non-use of the trade mark was due to special circumstances outside the control of the owner (s 66(2)); or

- The use of the trade mark resumed or commenced before the application for revocation was made (s 66(3)) and preparations to resume or commence such use began before the owner became aware that there may be an application for revocation of the mark on grounds of non-use (s 66(4)).

(a)   *Standard of evidence*

Where an application to revoke a registered trade mark is based on one of the grounds of non-use set out in s 66(1)(a) and (b) Trade Marks Act 2002, the trade mark owner or licensee bears the initial onus of establishing that the mark was put to genuine use on or in relation to some or all of the goods or services covered by the registration or that use of the mark was not suspended (s 67).

The standard of evidence required is the same whether the claim is filed at the Intellectual Property Office of New Zealand ("IPONZ") or at the High Court.

In *Royal NZ Yacht Squadron v Daks Simpson Group Plc* [2002] NZAR 187, the High Court considered an application to revoke a registered trade mark on the grounds of non-use under s 35 Trade Marks Act 1953 (under which the applicant for revocation bore the initial onus of establishing non-use). The Court held that the standard of evidence before the Commissioner in revocation proceedings should be the same as if the proceedings were taken in the High Court. Young J stated, at para 28, that:

> "It would be wrong for there to be different rules of evidence applying to a section 35 (non-use removal) application depending on whether the application was dealt with by the Court or by the Assistant Commissioner. The rules of evidence applicable to the High Court must therefore apply to both".

(b)   *Relevant period*

The interpretation of the relevant periods referred to in s 66(1)(a) and (b) Trade Marks Act 2002 have not been discussed in New Zealand case law to date.

The sections of the corresponding Singapore and English legislation relating to the revocation of a trade mark on the grounds of non-use are worded similarly to s 66. Both s 22 Trade Marks Act 1998 (Singapore) and s 46 Trade Marks Act 1994 (UK) state that:

> "The registration of a trade mark may be revoked on any of the following grounds:
>
> "(a)   That, within the period of [5/five] years following the date of completion of the registration procedure, [it/the registered trade mark] has not been put to genuine use in the course of trade in [Singapore/the United Kingdom], by the proprietor or with his consent, in relation to the goods or services for which it is registered, and there are no proper reasons for non-use;
>
> "(b)   That such use has been suspended for an uninterrupted period of [5/five] years, and there are no proper reasons for non-use;"

In *Kerly's Law of Trade Marks and Trade Names* (13th ed), London, Sweet & Maxwell, 2001, the learned authors state, at paras 9-38, that "the only difference between [ss 46(1)(a) and (b)] is in how the requisite five-year period is fixed."

In English revocation proceedings based on non-use, the Commissioner has stated that under s 46(1)(a) (ie, genuine use) the relevant period begins on the date that the trade mark was entered on the Register and ends 5 years later: see *Carte Bleue Trade Marks* [2002] RPC 599, at pp 605; 607; *BIG BLUE Trade Mark* (UKPO Decision O/118/04, 28/4/04, J MacGillivray), at paras 2-3; 22, and 23; *OMEGA Trade Mark* (UKPO Decision O/026/03, 30/1/03, D W Landau), at para 49; *OMEGA SCAN O VISION Trade Mark* (UKPO Decision O/029/03, 30/1/03, D W Landau), at para 51; *THE ORIGINAL EST 1954 EL TORITO RESTAURANT Trade Mark* (UKPO Decision O/119/02, 14/3/02, D W Landau), at para 31.

The English Commissioner has also stated that under s 46(1)(b) (ie, suspended use) the relevant period may begin and end at any time, provided it constitutes an uninterrupted 5-year period: *TRIDENT Trade Mark* (UKPO Decision O/111/04, 23/4/04, G W Salthouse), at paras 2-3; 28; *ASHWOOD GROVE Trade Mark* (UKPO Decision, 20/11/03, G W Salthouse), at paras 8-10; *RUBY BRAND Trade Mark* (UKPO Decision O/042/04, 12/2/04, M Foley), at para 18. This period may coincide with the period referred to under s 46(1)(a) but need not do so.

Where a party fails to specify the relevant period when making a claim under s 46(1)(a) and (b), the Commissioner or Court will determine both claims on the basis that the relevant period is that referred to in s 46(1)(a): *STRAIGHT EIGHT Trade Mark* (UKPO Decision O/094/04, 31/3/04, M Reynolds), at paras 1-3; 10-11.

Due to similar wording, the same conclusions would seem to apply in respect of our s 66(1)(b), that is, the relevant period may begin and end at any time provided it constitutes an uninterrupted period of 3 or more years during which use of the trade mark has been suspended. However, it is important to note that the wording of our s 66(1)(a) differs from that in the corresponding provisions of the UK and Singapore legislation. In particular, while the Singapore and UK legislation talk of there being non-use "within the period of five years following the date of completion of the registration procedure", and s 66(1)(a) similarly talks of a "continuous period of three years or more following the actual date of registration" it also refers to the non-use extending "up to the date one month before the date of the application for revocation of the registration of the trade mark". Arguably this might mean that the period in s 66(1)(a) works in reverse and is calculated backward from the date one month before the filing of the application for revocation rather than forward from the actual date of registration as in the UK/Singapore legislation.

While there have been no judgments to date, the position currently adopted by IPONZ seems to be the same as in the UK, namely, that under s 66(1)(a), the relevant period should begin on the date that the trade mark was actually entered on the Register and end 3 years or more later, and under s 66(1)(b), the relevant period may begin and end at any time provided it constitutes an uninterrupted period of 3 or more years, which may or may not coincide with the period referred to under s 66(1)(a). This interpretation might be reconciled with the difference in wording of s 66(1)(a) and the UK/Singapore legislation if s 66(1)(a) were treated as applying to the situation where the mark had never been used following its actual date of registration, and s 66(1)(b) to the situation where the mark had been used but then such use had been suspended for the requisite length of time.

Regardless of which interpretation is correct, when bringing an application to revoke a registered trade mark on the grounds set out in s 66(1)(b), the person applying to revoke the registered trade mark must specify the relevant 3-year period, otherwise it will be deemed to be the same as that under s 66(1)(a).

(c)   Use and non-use

The word "use" is defined in s 6 Trade Marks Act 2002 to mean "use on, or in physical or other relation to" goods or services. The definition of use therefore encompasses both use on the goods themselves and their packaging and use in materials advertising or promoting the goods or services.

Under s 7, applying a trade mark to goods in New Zealand where the goods will be exported from New Zealand will constitute use of the mark for any purpose for which use is relevant under the Act. Accordingly, manufacturing for export markets will still constitute use of the mark in New Zealand provided that the mark is applied in New Zealand.

"Use" also includes use in a form differing in elements that do not alter the distinctive character of the trade mark in the form in which it was registered (s 7(1)(a)).

References to "use" of a trade mark by the owner include use by a person other than the owner if that use is authorised by, and subject to the control of, the owner (s 7(2)).

(d)   Genuine use

In *Ansul BV v Ajax Brandbeveiliging BV* [2005] Ch 97 (ECJ), the European Court of Justice made the following comments in respect of genuine use:

*   "Genuine use" means "actual use of the mark"; the use should not be "token, serving solely to preserve the rights conferred by the mark";

*   Genuine use entails the use of the mark on the market for the goods or services protected by the mark. It does not include internal use by the undertaking concerned. Use of the mark must relate to goods or services which have already been, or are about to be, marketed and for which preparations to secure customers are underway (for example, in the form of advertising campaigns); and

*   In assessing the use of a mark, it is necessary to consider all facts and circumstances which establish whether the commercial exploitation of the mark is real, in particular whether the use is viewed in the sector as maintaining or creating a share in the market for the goods or services protected by the mark. Circumstances to be considered include the nature of the goods and services in question, the characteristics of the market and the frequency with which the mark is used.

Ansul was subsequently considered by the UK Court of Appeal in *Laboratoires Goemar SA v La Mer Technology Inc* [2005] EWCA CIV 978, which confirmed:

*   Internal use by the registered proprietor does not count as genuine use;

*   Token use of a mark does not count as genuine use, but equally it is illogical to assert that every case of non-token use qualifies as genuine use. Even if the use is not token,

it is still necessary to consider other factors in order to decide whether or not the use of the mark is genuine. For example, internal use by the registered proprietor may not be token or sham, but it will fail to qualify as genuine use because it is internal only;

- The act of importation of goods can constitute putting the goods bearing the mark on the market in the country into which they are imported, and therefore genuine use, even by a single importer. The crucial question is what type or kind of market use is in fact sufficient in the particular case; and

- When looking at market use, it is not always necessary to create a retail outlet for the consumer or end user. It may be sufficient if the use made of the mark has the purpose of doing so (for example the importation of goods with the intention of on-selling them to the pubic).

The Court in *La Mer* was concerned with a situation where products bearing the trade mark had been sold to a UK agent but there was no evidence of sales of those products under the mark to members of the UK public as consumers. The Court found, at para 34, that these circumstances amounted to genuine use, adding that what is important is the objective use of the mark, not the intention of the trade mark owner:

> "There was some discussion at the hearing about the extent to which Goemar was entitled to rely on its intention, purpose or motivation in the sales of the goods bearing the mark of Health Scope Direct. I do not find such factors of much assistance in deciding whether there has been genuine use. I do not understand the Court of Justice to hold that subjective factors of that kind are relevant to genuine use. What matters are the objective circumstances in which the goods bearing the mark came to be in the United Kingdom. The presence of the goods was explained, as Dr Trott found, by the UK importer buying and the French manufacturer selling quantities of the goods bearing the mark. The buying and selling of goods involving a foreign manufacturer and a UK importer is evidence of the existence of an economic market of some description for the goods delivered to the importer. The mark registered for the goods was used on that market. That was sufficient use for it to be genuine use on the market and in that market the mark was being used in accordance with its essential function. The use was real, though modest, and did not cease to be real and genuine because the extinction of the importer as the single customer in the United Kingdom prevented the onward sale of the goods into, and the use of the mark further down, the supply chain in the retail market, in which the mark would come to the attention of consumers and end users."

There is no New Zealand case law concerning the meaning of "genuine use". However, under s 35 Trade Marks Act 1953, a registered trade mark was revocable on the grounds that there was no "bona fide" use of the trade mark during the relevant period. It is suggested that the law relating to bona fide use of a registered trade mark should continue in relation to the requirement that the trade mark be put to genuine use within the relevant period under s 66(1)(a).

Under s 35, there was no set amount or frequency of use required to constitute bona fide use. The Court expressed bona fide use as being ordinary and genuine, substantial in amount, real commercial use on a substantial scale, not fictitious or colourable but a real or genuine use, and substantial and genuine judged by ordinary commercial standards.

The timing of the use was considered irrelevant in relation to whether or not the use was genuine in fact. In *Electrolux Ltd v Electrix* (1954) 71 RPC 23 (CA), the Court held that the fact that there may be a hurried motive for use of the registered mark to prevent it from being struck off for non-use is not relevant to the question of bona fides. However, under s 66(4) Trade Marks Act 2002, any commencement or resumption of use of the trade mark after the expiry of the 3-year period but within the period of one month before making the application for revocation must be disregarded unless preparation for the commencement or resumption began before the owner became aware that the application might be made.

The extent of the use was considered relevant under s 35 Trade Marks Act 1953. For example, it would be better to sell 100 items of clothing in each of 10 stores than 1,000 items of clothing in one store. Further, a course of continued use would be preferable to evidence of a one-off shipment or sporadic use.

The extent of use that was considered sufficient varied according to the context and the goods or services involved. For example, the threshold volume of sales required to constitute bona fide use would differ in relation to cigarettes as opposed to refrigerators or motor vehicles. Ultimately, the use needs to be genuine use judged by ordinary commercial standards.

If there are only limited examples of use, then compelling evidence of that use is likely to be required. The fewer the acts of use relied on, the more solidly proof of such acts of use must be established: *NODOZ Trade Mark* (1962) 79 RPC 1.

In *Royal NZ Yacht Squadron v Daks Simpson Group Plc* [2002] NZAR 187, the sale over a 3-year period of 11 jackets bearing the relevant trade mark was considered to be "not at all bona fide use of the trade mark" because the use was too infrequent and the evidence establishing that use was not strong.

Finally, it is at least arguable that "genuine" or "bona fide" use would exclude use of a mark in breach of another intellectual property right. Thus, for example, where the trade mark had been used, but in a form which breached copyright or which was otherwise likely to deceive or confuse the public. Such use might not be deemed "genuine" by the Courts.

(e) *Special circumstances*

Under s 66(2) Trade Marks Act 2002, an application to revoke a registered trade mark on the grounds of non-use under s 66(1)(a) and (b) will not succeed where the failure to put the trade mark to use resulted from special circumstances that were outside the control of the owner of the trade mark.

There is no New Zealand case law concerning the meaning of "special circumstances". However, under s 35(3)(a) and (b) Trade Marks Act 1953 it was a defence to a revocation claim based on lack of bona fide use for the trade mark owner or licensee to establish that they intended to use the trade mark but were prevented from doing so by reasons attributable to circumstances of trade or war.

It is suggested that the law relating to the defence of special circumstances under s 35(3) Trade Marks Act 1953 will continue to be applied under s 66(2) Trade Marks Act 2002.

Under the Trade Marks Act 1953, "special circumstances" also referred to a failure to use the mark due to circumstances beyond the owner's control. For example, an inability to obtain the necessary marketing approval from the Department of Health: *Pierre Fabre SA v Marion Laboratories Inc* (1986) 7 IPR 387. Such special circumstances do not include reasons peculiar to the owner itself (for example, lack of resources to exploit the trade mark).

Under s 46(1) Trade Marks Act 1994 (UK), an application to revoke a registered trade mark on the grounds that the trade mark was not put to genuine use, or the use was suspended, during the relevant periods will not succeed where there are "proper reasons" for the non-use. Section 66(1) Trade Marks Act 2002 contains no such proviso. However, in the absence of New Zealand case law, the English defence relating to proper reasons for the non-use of a registered trade mark may provide some guidance as to what constitutes "special circumstances" under s 66(2) Trade Marks Act 2002.

In *Invermont Trade Mark* (1997) 114 RPC 125, the hearing officer, M J Tuck, stated that the word "proper" in the context of s 46 Trade Marks Act 1994 (UK) means apt, acceptable, reasonable, or justifiable in all the circumstances, and was intended to cover abnormal situations in the industry or the market, or even temporary but serious disruption affecting the registered proprietor's business. It was not intended to cover normal situations or routine difficulties. Thus, abnormal delays caused by some unavoidable regulatory requirement (such as the approval of a medicine) might be acceptable but not the normal delays which are matters within the control of a business.

Where use of a trade mark commences prior to filing an application to register the trade mark, and the application is subject to an opposition proceeding whereby the owner of the trade mark ceases to use the trade mark for a period of 3 or more years pending resolution of the opposition proceedings, the period of non-use attributable to the resolution of the opposition proceedings may constitute proper reasons or special circumstances and the trade mark may not be revocable by reason of that period of non-use.

In *WORTH Trade Marks* [1998] RPC 875, negotiations to licence the use of a trade mark were not concluded because of the uncertainty caused by non-use attacks against the trade mark which was the subject of the negotiations for over 5 years. The Court held that these were proper reasons for non-use of the trade mark.

In *Magic Ball Trade Mark* [2000] RPC 439, Park J held that a delay of up to 9 years in the development of new manufacturing machinery for the satisfactory production of lollipops in relation to which the trade mark was to be used was a proper reason for non-use of the trade mark. Arguments that the delays were within the control of the business or a normal routine difficulty were rejected.

(f) *Commissioner's discretion*

Section 66 Trade Marks Act 2002 states that a trade mark "may be revoked" on the grounds specified in that section, which suggests that the Commissioner or Court has a discretion whether or not to revoke the registered trade mark even where the requisite grounds have been proved. However, the Commissioner or Court's discretion may be fettered in proceedings brought under s 66(1) Trade Marks Act 2002 on grounds of non-use, because of the shift in onus to the trade mark owner or licensee to prove use of the trade mark or special circumstances justifying non-use of the trade mark.

In *Premier Brands UK Ltd v Typhoon Europe Ltd* [2000] FSR 767, Neuberger J held that in revocation proceedings based on the grounds of non-use of a registered trade mark, there was no residual discretion to revoke or invalidate a trade mark despite the wording of s 46(1) Trade Marks Act 1994 (UK) which states that a trade mark "may be revoked" on grounds of non-use. He stated, at p 810, that "it would seem a little odd if there were a discretion, given the express exceptions at the end of section 46(1)(a) and (b) [Trade Marks Act 1994 (UK)], with their reference to 'no proper reasons for non-use'." After reviewing contradictory English authorities on the issue, Neuberger J stated the preferred view was that Parliament intended there to be no residual discretion in cases of non-use.

Similarly in *Reemtsma Cigarettenfabriken Gmbh v Hugo Boss AG* [2003] SGHC 205, it was held that in revocation proceedings based on non-use of a trade mark, the Court does not have discretion to maintain a mark on the Register where the grounds for revocation have been established. Section 22(1) Trade Marks Act 1998 (Singapore) also states that a trade mark "may be revoked" on grounds of non-use.

For further discussion of the Commissioner's discretion, see Ian Finch and Amanda Holling, "Discretion is the better part of …?" [2003] NZLJ 217 and Earl Gray and Karla Horstmans, "Does a residual discretion not to revoke a trade mark for non-use exist?" (2006) 4(8) NZIPJ 182.

(g)   *Transitional provisions*

Under s 66(1)(a) Trade Marks Act 2002, a registered trade mark may be revoked if the trade mark is not put to genuine use in the course of trade in New Zealand in relation to the goods and services in respect of which the trade mark is registered for an uninterrupted period of 3 years following its actual date of registration. By comparison, the non-use period of a trade mark registered under the Trade Marks Act 1953 was 5 years.

If a trade mark was registered under the 1953 Act more than 3 years but less than 5 years before the coming into effect of the Trade Marks Act 2002 and it had not been put to genuine use in the course of trade in New Zealand when the Trade Marks Act 2002 came into effect, then the trade mark would be susceptible to revocation under s 66(1)(a) Trade Marks Act 2002 prior to the expiration of the 5-year period of non-use required to revoke the trade mark under the Trade Marks Act 1953.

To remedy this inconsistency, s 208(4) Trade Marks Act 2002 provides that a trade mark that was registered under the Trade Marks Act 1953 within 5 years of the commencement of the Trade Marks Act 2002 cannot be revoked under s 66(1)(a) Trade Marks Act 2002 until 5 years have elapsed following the actual date of registration of the trade mark.

Similarly, under s 66(1)(b) Trade Marks Act 2002, a registered trade mark may be revoked on the ground that use of the mark was suspended for an uninterrupted period of 3 or more years. If a trade mark was registered under the 1953 Act and its use was suspended for a period of three or more years when the Trade Marks Act 2002 came into effect, the trade mark would be susceptible to revocation under s 66(1)(b) prior to the expiration of the 5-year period of non-use required to revoke the trade mark under the Trade Marks Act 1953.

Section 208(5) purported to remedy that situation. It read (pre-Trade Marks Amendment Act 2005):

> "A trade mark that was registered under the Trade Marks Act 1953, other than a defensive trade mark, before the period of 5 years before the coming into force of

this Act, cannot be revoked under section 66(1)(b) if use of the trade mark has been suspended for an uninterrupted period of 5 years and the use was suspended before the commencement of this Act."

However, on a strict interpretation of s 208(5), a trade mark cannot be revoked at all on grounds of suspended use under s 66(1)(b) if it was registered under the Trade Marks Act 1953 more than 5 years before the coming into force of the Trade Marks Act 2002 and its use was suspended for an uninterrupted period of 5 years commencing before the coming into force of the Trade Marks Act 2002.

Thus, s 208(5) failed to provide trade mark owners facing a revocation claim under s 66(1)(b) Trade Marks Act 2002 protection comparable to that offered by s 208(4) to trade mark owners facing a claim under s 66(1)(a). Indeed the protection appeared to be far greater.

It was also not clear why the indefinite period of protection provided in s 208(5) was extended only to those trade marks that were registered under the Trade Marks Act 1953 prior to 5 years before the commencement of the Trade Marks Act 2002, rather than to those trade marks that were registered under the Trade Marks Act 1953 within the period of 5 years before the commencement of the Trade Marks Act 2002 as in s 208(4).

The differences appeared to have been an oversight resulting from poor legislative drafting. The situation has been rectified by the Trade Marks Amendment Act 2005 which amended s 208(5) to read:

"(5)   For the purposes of section 66(1)(b), the uninterrupted period of suspension of use is 5 years (not 3) if all the following apply:

"(a)   the trade mark was registered under the Trade Marks Act 1953; and

"(b)   the trade mark is not a defensive trade mark; and

"(c)   the uninterrupted period of suspension of use began within the period of 5 years before this Act came into force."

Under s 208(6) Trade Marks Act 2002, a trade mark registered under the Trade Marks Act 1953 (other than a defensive trade mark) may be revoked under s 66(1)(a) and (b) Trade Marks Act 2002 after the periods specified in s 208(4) and (5) have elapsed.

(h)   *Examples*

- In *Sara Lee Corp's Registration* (Commissioner's Decision No T16/2003, 10/4/03, Asst Commr Frankel), the applicant for revocation successfully proved that there had been no use of the trade mark SILK REFLECTIONS by the registered proprietor in New Zealand for a continuous period of 5 years. The registered proprietor's claim that the mark had been promoted in New Zealand via the internet and advertisements contained in overseas publications was defeated by evidence that the proprietor's website stated it could only ship to addresses in the US.

- In *Cinq-Huitiemes SA's Registration* (Commissioner's Decision No T16/2005, 7/6/05, Asst Commr Walden), the applicant for revocation successfully proved that there had been no use of a logo featuring the words EDEN PARK by the registered owner in New Zealand for a continuous period of three years. Evidence of correspondence between the applicant for revocation and the owner of the mark exploring the possibility of the applicant for revocation selling EDEN PARK branded goods from Eden Park Stadium in Auckland was not considered to be use of the EDEN PARK marks in relation to the goods covered by the registration.

• In *Landmark NZ Ltd's Registration* (Commissioner's Decision No T18/2006, 31/7/06, Asst Commr Walden), Anchor Wall Systems Inc filed an application for partial revocation of the trade mark LANDMARK which was registered in class 19 for "buildings including houses; building materials and components" on the basis that the LANDMARK trade mark had not been used in respect of "building materials and components" for more than 5 years. The owner filed evidence to show that it had used LANDMARK in relation to the construction of houses which necessarily involved the supply of building materials. However, the Assistant Commissioner believed it necessary for customers to obtain building materials or components independent from a LANDMARK home and, in the absence of evidence to that effect, found a prima facie case of non-use. As there were no exceptional circumstances, partial revocation was successful and "building materials and components" were removed from the statement of goods.

(2) *Genericism*

If a mark has, since registration, lost its ability to distinguish the owner's goods/services from those of other traders, then the mark may have become generic, and be susceptible to removal from the Register (s 66(1)(c) Trade Marks Act 2002).

Under the Act, the test for genericism has been changed from a consideration of whether the *trade* uses the mark in a descriptive sense, to a consideration of whether the mark has become, as a consequence of acts or inactivity of the owner, a common name in "general public use" for a product or service in respect of which it is registered. The test for genericism, under the Trade Marks Act 1953, was based on whether the trade (not the public) used the registered trade mark descriptively.

Although decided under the 1953 Act, a similar approach was taken by the Court in *Waitomo Adventures Ltd v BWR Resources Ltd* 26/4/02, Randerson J, HC Hamilton CP72/00. There the Court was asked to determine whether the trade mark BLACK WATER RAFTING had become generic and should be removed from the Register. The phrase "black water rafting" was first coined by one of the directors of the defendant, BWR Resources Ltd, in 1984 to describe a commercial operation involving floating through caves on inner tubes or other flotation devices. The trade mark was registered in 1998.

In August 2000, the plaintiff, Waitomo Adventures Ltd, sought an order for the trade mark to be expunged from the Register. This was on the basis that the term "black water rafting" was descriptive of an activity (or was the generic term for the activity) and lacked the necessary distinction to justify continued registration.

BWR believed it had taken rigorous steps to police its trade mark by informing users that the correct term for the activity was "cave rafting/cave tubing" and argued that any remaining instances of descriptive public use were beyond its control. However, the Court agreed with the plaintiff and made an order for the mark to be removed from the Register.

Little weight was placed on the fact that four of the six companies providing similar services in New Zealand did not use the phrase in connection with their business. Instead, the Court focused on how the mark would be perceived by the New Zealand public.

(3)   *Use of name of patented article*

Section 66(1)(d) Trade Marks Act 2002 also provides that where the goods or services were formerly protected by a patent that expired 2 or more years earlier, and the trade mark used for those goods or services is the only practicable name or description for them, then the mark may be removed from the Register, so as to allow people exercising the expired patent the opportunity to accurately describe their goods or services without infringing the patentee's trade mark rights.

(4)   *Confusion or deception*

The concepts of confusion or deception are discussed in more detail at 7.6 ("Grounds for not registering") earlier in this chapter. This ground is most often relied upon where the revocation action is based on a claim that the owner is not the rightful owner of the mark (frequently because they are a distributor which has misappropriated the manufacturer's mark).

There is some debate as to whether a mark can be removed from the Register where that mark was not likely to deceive or confuse at the date of application, but subsequently became confusing or deceptive.

In the UK, it has been held that a mark that had become deceptive *after* registration could only be removed if the deception had arisen through some blameworthy act on the proprietor's part: *GE Trade Mark* (1973) 90 RPC 297 (CA).

The requirement of blameworthy conduct on the part of the proprietor is intended to prevent an infringer using the infringing mark so extensively that use by the proprietor of the registered mark would be likely to confuse or deceive the public, and then relying on that confusion or deception to remove the registered mark.

The reasoning in *GE* was followed in Australia in *NSW Dairy Corp v Murray Goulburn Co-operative Co Ltd* (1991) 108 RPC 144 (HCA). Section 28(a) Trade Marks Act 1955 (Aust), which prohibits registration of a mark the use of which is likely to confuse or deceive, was deemed to be read subject to s 28(d), prohibiting registration of a mark that was disentitled to protection in a Court of Justice. The Court held that for a mark to be removed as being "wrongly remaining on the Register", it must be both likely to deceive and confuse and disentitled to protection in a Court of Justice. Thus "blameworthy conduct" on the part of the proprietor was required.

The Court in *NSW Dairy Corp* did, however, note that the concept of blameworthy conduct had not been universally accepted, and in particular noted that the New Zealand Court of Appeal in *Pioneer Hi-Bred Corn Co v Hy-Line Chicks Pty Ltd* [1978] 2 NZLR 50 (CA) had stated that s 16 of the Trade Marks Act 1953 (which was the equivalent to s 22 Trade Marks Act 1955 (Aust)) did not require that the words "likely to deceive or confuse" be modified by "disentitled to protection in a Court of Justice".

However, the Court in the *Pioneer* case was not confronted with the issue of whether s 16 of the 1953 Act imposed a continuing obligation that a mark not be likely to deceive or

461

confuse. Accordingly, the issue remains at large as to whether a mark that was not likely to deceive or confuse at the date of application, but that has subsequently become deceptive or confusing, can be challenged as a mark "wrongly remaining" on the Register.

NSW Dairy Corp was also distinguished in *Campomar Sociedad Ltd v Nike International Ltd* (2000) 46 IPR 481 (HCA). In the *Nike* case, the High Court of Australia unanimously held that s 28 Trade Marks Act 1955 (Aust) did not have a continuing operation after the date of registration, that is, it was not possible to remove a mark where the likelihood of deception arose after the registration date. Accordingly, the question of blameworthy conduct does not arise.

(5)   *Contravention of condition of registration*

Contravention of, or failure to observe, a condition entered on the Register in relation to the registration may leave a registration susceptible to revocation: s 62 Trade Marks Act 2002.

For example, if it is a condition of registration of a certification mark that the mark must be used with an indication of its status as a certification mark (for example, "Cert ™"), and the mark is not used with such an indication, then it may be susceptible to rectification by any person aggrieved by the contravention of the limitation.

7.14.6   Cause of action estoppel

Finally, it is important to understand that a successful revocation action will not render earlier judgments for infringement of the mark nugatory.

Thus, a recent decision of the English High Court (Chancery Division, Patents Court), *Coflexip SA v Stolt Offshore MS Ltd* [2003] EWHC 1892 (Patent), has reaffirmed that cause of action estoppel may arise in patent infringement proceedings.

In that case, Stolt was found to have infringed Coflexip's patent, and its counterclaim for revocation was unsuccessful. An inquiry into damages was ordered. The patent was subsequently revoked in an unrelated action by another party and Stolt sought to stay the inquiry into damages. Relying upon *Poulton v Adjustable Cover & Boiler Block Co* (1908) 25 RPC 529 and *Poulton v Adjustable Cover & Boiler Block Co* (1908) 25 RPC 661 (CA), at p 663, Jacob J declined the stay and held:

> "The judgment obtained by the Plaintiff is a judgment which made the matter of infringement and the validity of the Patent *res judicata* between the parties and created a perfect estoppel.

> "An order for the revocation of a patent is conclusive *in rem*, as it extinguishes the patent, but it does not avoid prior estoppels from a prior decision *in personam* that the patent was valid and infringed.

> "There is a difference between a party saying 'there is no patent' and 'there was no patent'. Stolt cannot say there never was a patent, hence orders relating to the inquiry into damages are enforceable, yet an injunction preventing further infringement ceases to have effect, as there is no longer a patent to infringe."

There is no reason in principle why the same reasoning should not apply to damages in respect of a registered trade mark which is subsequently revoked/invalidated.

7.14.7 Examples

- In *Bio Cosmo (NZ) Ltd's Application* (Commissioner's Decision No T02/2004, 24/1/04, Asst Commr Walden), the applicant for rectification successfully obtained an order for removal from the Register of the owner's BIO-SURE trade mark on the basis that, at the date of application, the registered proprietor was the exclusive distributor in New Zealand of the applicant's goods under the BIO-SURE mark. A request for substitution of the applicant for rectification as the owner of the mark was declined.

- In *Speedy Parts (NZ) Ltd's Application* (Commissioner's Decision No T270, 22/8/02, Asst Commr Walden), the Assistant Commissioner upheld an application for rectification of a foreign owner's mark filed by a local distributor without its authority. The Assistant Commissioner confirmed that spending effort and money on the marketing of the goods under the mark in New Zealand did not give the distributor ownership of that mark.

- In *McPhail Sports Ltd's Registration* (Commissioner's Decision No T32/2005, 4/1/06, Asst Commr Jones), J & M Fashions Pty Ltd successfully applied to revoke the trade mark WET SEAL registered by McPhail Sports Ltd. McPhail Sports had applied to register the mark on 16 December 2002 but could only show use since March 2004. On the other hand, J & M Fashions was able to establish use on clothing since July 1993 which was sold in New Zealand since 1996. Accordingly, the Assistant Commissioner found that J & M Fashions was the true owner of the trade mark in New Zealand based on its prior use, and that, at the time McPhail Sports applied to register the mark, its use would have been likely to deceive or confuse a significant section of the relevant purchasing public and therefore the mark should not have been registered.

- In *Dick Smith (Wholesale) Pty Ltd's Registration* (Commissioner's Decision No T02/2006, 31/1/06, Asst Commr Walden), an application by Smiths City (Southern) Ltd to revoke a registration for a stylised version of the trade mark DICK SMITH POWERHOUSE was unsuccessful, primarily because Dick Smith had been able to show that the mark had been used in newspaper advertisements and a banner relating to the opening of a Hamilton store in March and April 2004. The decision is notable for the Assistant Commissioner's consideration of the existence of a residual discretion not to revoke the trade mark even had non-use been made out. The Assistant Commissioner considered that the residual discretion not to revoke remained but should only be exercised in exceptional circumstances. At least one commentator has questioned whether that is correct on legislative and policy grounds (Earl Gray and Karla Horstmans, "Does a residual discretion not to revoke a trade mark for non-use exist?" (2006) 4(8) NZIPJ 182).

- In *Astro Grass Allweather Surfaces Ltd's Registration* (Commissioner's Decision No T19/2006, 11/9/06, Asst Commr Walden), Australian Bowls Construction Pty Ltd successfully applied for revocation of the trade mark GREENGAUGE in classes 19 and 27, on the basis of prior use and a prior assertion of ownership of the mark in New Zealand. At the time of the application, the registered proprietor was the exclusive distributor of GREENGAUGE product in Australia and New Zealand and therefore an agent of the applicant for revocation. No counterstatement or evidence was filed by the registered proprietor to rebut this.

- In *The Derek Corp Ltd's Registration* (Commissioner's Decision No T22/2006, 25/9/06, Asst Commr Walden), the applicant for revocation sought to revoke the trade mark HAPPY HOUSE in class 24 for "textile products" on the basis of spill over reputation from Australia and the sale of HAPPY HOUSE goods in New Zealand. The applicant for revocation produced evidence of advertising of its goods in a magazine circulated in New Zealand, and actual use of the mark by a licensee in New Zealand, which the Assistant Commissioner deemed sufficient to make out a case of prior use. Again, no evidence was filed by the registered owner.

- In *Telecom Directories Ltd's Registration* (Commissioner's Decision No T3/2007, 29/1/07, Asst Commr B F Jones), Cabbage Tree Press Ltd applied to revoke Telecom's trade mark registration for the colour yellow covering "electronic telephone directory services enabling users to access business information". The Assistant Commissioner found that Cabbage Tree Press was an aggrieved person because it was using the colour yellow on its website for business services which were covered by Telecom's registration. Noting that single colour marks have a very low level of inherent distinctiveness, the Assistant Commissioner considered that the circumstances in which a single colour mark will be inherently adapted to distinguish services are probably limited to the following:

  - Where the colour does not serve a utilitarian function;

  - Where the colour does not serve an ornamental function;

  - Where the colour does not serve any economic functions; and/or

  - Where the colour mark is not sought to be registered in respect of goods or services in a market in which there is a proven competitive need for the use of the colour and in which other properly motivated traders might naturally think of the colour and use it in a similar manner in respect of the same goods or services.

  As the colour yellow was deemed by the Assistant Commissioner to have only a slight inherent capability of distinguishing, a substantial level of factual distinctiveness was required in order to obtain registration. Given that Telecom had failed to file any such evidence, the application for revocation was successful.

- In *Cadbury Ireland Ltd's Registrations* (Commissioner's Decision No T04/2007, 29/1/07, Asst Commr Walden), Nestlé successfully applied to revoke Cadbury's VAPOR ACTION registrations on the basis of non-use. Cadbury had filed evidence of use of similar marks and sought to rely on s 7(1)(a) which provides that use in relation to a trade mark includes use in a form differing in elements that do not alter the distinctive character of the trade mark in the form in which it was registered. The Assistant Commissioner found that the packaging in question featured the marks in a form which altered their distinctive character, and also questioned whether the use, which was by entities other than Cadbury Ireland Ltd, was authorised by, and subject to the control of, Cadbury Ireland Ltd such that Cadbury could avail itself of the provisions of s 7(2) of the Act.

- In *Fonterra Brands (Tip Top Investments) Ltd's Registration* (Commissioner's Decision No T06/2007, 12/1/07, Asst Commr B F Jones), Nestlé unsuccessfully applied to revoke Fonterra's FROSTY FRUITS registration on the grounds of non-use. In response to the application for revocation Fonterra was able to show that it had genuinely used the FROSTY FRUITS trade mark in relation to the goods covered by the registration during the relevant period. The Assistant Commissioner considered "genuine" (which is not defined in the Act) to encompass real and authentic use, and use which is not a sham.

- In *Unilever Plc's Registration* (Commissioner's Decision No T09/2007, 19/3/07, Asst Commr Walden), Goodman Fielder Consumer Foods Pty Ltd successfully applied to revoke Unilever's PRAISE registration for margarine. The Assistant Commissioner found that Goodman Fielder was an aggrieved person because it:

  - Had registrations for PRAISE in Australia, some of which included margarine;

  - Had used the mark in Australia since 1964; and

  - Wanted to launch its product in New Zealand.

  Goodman Fielder had filed an application to register PRAISE in New Zealand which was blocked by Unilever's registration. In support of its registration, Unilever filed a copy of scanned data relating to sales figures for its margarine products. However, the declarant did not compile the information, the person who did was not named, and the Declaration did not say why that person could not provide the Declaration him or herself. Accordingly, the Assistant Commissioner considered the evidence documentary hearsay and inadmissible.

- In *Goodman Fielder NZ Ltd's Registration* (Commissioner's Decision No T13/2007, 26/3/07, Asst Commr Walden), George Weston Foods (NZ) Ltd successfully applied to revoke Goodman Fielder's registration for GOLDENBAKE in logo form on the basis of non-use. Goodman Fielder had used the GOLDENBAKE trade mark but in a different manner of stylisation to that depicted in its registration and hence relied on s 7(1)(a) of the Act. In determining whether that use constituted use of the registration, the Assistant Commissioner applied *BUD and Budweiser Budbräu Trade Marks* [2003] RPC 25, at p 490, which held that the necessary enquiry required, firstly, identification of the points of difference between the trade mark as used and the trade mark as registered and, secondly, a consideration as to whether those differences altered the distinctive character of the mark as registered. As the Assistant Commissioner's view was that the overall impression of the whole of each mark was different, and that the differences altered the distinctive character of the GOLDENBAKE logo, the application for revocation was successful.

7.15 Invalidity

Under s 73 Trade Marks Act 2002, an aggrieved person (this includes a person who is "culturally aggrieved"), may apply to the Commissioner or the Court for a declaration that the registration of a trade mark is invalid, to the extent that the mark was not registrable under Part 2, as at the deemed date of its registration, ie, the date of application. Part 2 of the Act covers the registrability of trade marks, and in particular the absolute and relative grounds of refusal.

7.15.1 Standing

A person has standing to file an application for declaration of invalidity under s 73 Trade Marks Act 2002 if that person is "aggrieved". There is a detailed discussion of the meaning of "aggrieved" at 7.14.1 ("Standing") in the context of applications for revocation of a registered trade mark. The same principles apply to an application for a declaration of invalidity.

7.15.2 Forum

Under s 73(1) an aggrieved person may apply for a declaration of invalidity to the Commissioner or the Court. However, under s 158, where an action concerning the trade mark in question is pending, the application must be filed in the High Court. The same section also permits the Commissioner to transfer an application for a declaration of invalidity filed with IPONZ to the High Court at any stage.

Commonly, an application for a declaration of invalidity of a registered trade mark will be filed as a defence or counterclaim to an action for trade mark infringement.

Under s 73(3) the Commissioner or the Court has the power to refuse a vexatious application for a declaration of invalidity.

7.15.3 Procedure

Where an application for a declaration of invalidity is filed with the Intellectual Property Office of New Zealand to be determined by the Commissioner, the following procedures must be followed:

- Under regs 106(1) and 107 Trade Marks Regulations 2003 the application must be in writing and contain the following information:
  - The applicant's name and address for service;
  - The agent's name (if any);
  - A description or representation of the trade mark to which the application relates and the registration number;
  - The class or classes of goods or services to which the application relates; and
  - The grounds for a declaration of invalidity and a statement of the basis on which the applicant claims to be a person aggrieved.
- Under reg 108, within 2 months of receiving the application for a declaration of invalidity, the trade mark owner may oppose the application by filing a written counterstatement. Under reg 109, the counterstatement must contain the following information:
  - The name and address for service of the owner of the trade mark;
  - If the owner has an agent, the agent's name;

- A response to the applicant's grounds for a declaration of invalidity by admitting, denying or claiming a lack of knowledge of each assertion made in the application; and

- A brief statement of the facts which the owner relies upon in support of continued registration.

The counterstatement must be signed by the owner.

- Under reg 108(2), if the owner fails to file a counterstatement within the relevant period the Commissioner must (see discussion below) determine the application on the documents filed by the applicant.

- If a counterstatement is filed, then within 2 months of receiving a copy of the counterstatement, the applicant must file evidence in support of the application for a declaration of invalidity or notify the Commissioner that they do not intend to file evidence or that they withdraw their application.

- Within 2 months of receiving the applicant's evidence in support of the application for a declaration of invalidity (or notification that no evidence will be filed) the trade mark owner may file evidence in support of the registration or notify the Commissioner that they do not intend to file evidence.

- If the trade mark owner files evidence then the applicant for a declaration of invalidity will be given one month to file evidence strictly in reply; and

- The matter will then be determined by the Commissioner, usually at a hearing involving both parties at which they present written and/or oral submissions.

(1) *Procedure in undefended cases*

Where an application for a declaration of invalidity is undefended, IPONZ has adopted a practice similar to that used in the UK in *Firetrace Trade Mark* [2002] RPC 337: see, for example, *SportsGear NZ Ltd's Registration/White Holdings Ltd's Registration* (Commissioner's Decision No T13/2005, 9/5/05, Asst Commr Frankel). In *Firetrace*, the Hearing Officer considered the application of r 32(3) Trade Mark Rules 2000 (UK), which reads as follows:

> "Where a Notice and Counterstatement are not filed by the proprietor within the period prescribed by paragraph (2), the Registrar may treat his opposition to the application as having been withdrawn."

The Hearing Officer concluded that the absence of the word "shall" meant that it was not mandatory for the Registrar to exclude the proprietor from the proceedings on failure to file a notice and counterstatement and, because of the presumption of validity in s 72 Trade Marks Act 1994 (UK), the registration could not simply be revoked or declared invalid. It was therefore incumbent on the applicant for revocation to provide evidence which supported at least a prima facie case of invalidity.

The equivalent New Zealand provision to r 32(3) of the UK Rules is reg 108(2) Trade Marks Regulations 2003, which governs the filing of a counterstatement in opposition to an application for a Declaration of Invalidity. Regulation 108(2) states:

"If the owner does not, within the period specified, file the Counterstatement, the Commissioner must determine the application on the documents filed by the applicant."

The use of the word "must" in the New Zealand Regulations makes the decision in *Firetrace* distinguishable and requires the Commissioner to determine an undefended application on the basis of the papers filed at the point in time when the registered owner's Counterstatement fell due. Accordingly, notwithstanding IPONZ practice, there would seem to be no requirement on the applicant for a Declaration of Invalidity to file evidence supporting a prima facie case of invalidity. On the contrary, if the registered owner declines to defend the proceedings then the undefended application for a declaration of invalidity creates a prima facie case that the mark is no longer valid.

7.15.4   Onus

In *Fredco Trading Ltd v Miller* (2006) 8 NZBLC 101,761 (CA), the Court of Appeal cited with approval the following passage from *Kerly's Law of Trade Marks and Trade Names* (14th ed), London, Sweet & Maxwell, 2005 as to the onus of proof in an application for a declaration of invalidity:

"With one notable exception, if an application is made for a declaration of invalidity or for revocation, the onus lies on the person making the attack to prove the grounds of invalidity and/or revocation relied upon to the normal civil standard of the balance of probabilities. If one or more grounds are proved, this will automatically overcome the prima facie position provided for by s 72 of the 1994 Act. The rights and remedies, if any, which are then available in respect of the registered mark are subject to the temporal effect of the grounds relied upon."

The appellant in *Fredco Trading* had accepted that it had the onus of showing that it was more probable than not that the mark was not registrable. However, it argued that the effect of the evidence of its expert was to shift the evidential burden to the respondent. The respondent maintained that the evidential burden only shifted if there was evidence to overcome the prima facie validity of the registration. The appellant's expert was a branding expert giving theoretical evidence, and did not consider the actual market, nor did she speak to consumers of the goods. Accordingly, the respondent submitted that her evidence could not overcome the prima facie validity of the registration. The Court of Appeal agreed.

7.15.5   Grounds

The usual grounds of invalidity include:

- The original registration was invalid because:

  - The trade mark is not a "sign" or a "trade mark";

  - The applicant is not entitled to claim to be the owner of the mark;

  - The mark is not registrable in terms of s 18;

  - The mark is prohibited from registration by s 17;

  - The mark is prohibited from registration by s 25; and/or

- Use of the mark is contrary to law or otherwise disentitled to protection in any Court.

These grounds for obtaining a declaration of invalidity of a registered trade mark under s 73 Trade Marks Act 2002 are essentially the same as the corresponding grounds available for opposition to registration of a mark. Refer to 7.7 ("Oppositions") earlier in this chapter.

7.15.6 Presumption of validity

One proviso to the grounds listed above is that by virtue of s 75 Trade Marks Act 2002 the validity of a trade mark registration cannot be challenged after the expiration of 7 years from the deemed date of registration, unless the registration was obtained by fraud, the trade mark offends against s 17(1) or (2), or the registration may be revoked on any of the grounds set out in s 66.

7.15.7 Cause of action estoppel

It is important to note that a successful application for a declaration of invalidity may not render earlier judgments for infringement of the mark nugatory. There is a more detailed discussion of this at 7.14.6 ("Cause of action estoppel").

7.15.8 Examples

- In *Yeung Kwok Fung's Application* (Commissioner's Decision No T21/2005, Asst Commr Hastie), Nine Dots LLC successfully applied for a declaration of invalidity of a trade mark registration for DRUNKNMUNKY. Nine Dots established that it was the owner of registrations and applications for DRUNKNMUNKY in over 15 countries. It also produced evidence showing that Yeung Kwok Fung had 19 other registrations or abandoned applications demonstrating a clear pattern of adoption of well known overseas trade marks. The application was unopposed and was successful, the Assistant Commissioner finding that registration of the mark was in bad faith and without an intention to use it.

7.16 Rectification

Under s 76(1) Trade Marks Act 2002, a person who has an interest may apply for the rectification of an error or an omission in the Register. Such an application may be made either to the Commissioner or to the High Court (s 76(2)).

However, an application for rectification of the Register may not be made in respect of any matter that affects the validity of the registration of a mark (s 76(3)).

The effect of rectification of the Register is that the error or omission concerned is to be treated as if it had never existed, unless the Commissioner or the Court directs otherwise (s 76(4)).

7.17 Appeal against decision of Commissioner

Section 170 of the Act provides that a person who is aggrieved by a decision of the Commissioner may appeal to the Court. "Court" is defined in s 5 as the High Court. A Notice of Appeal must be filed within 20 working days after the date on which the Commissioner's decision was given. A copy of the Notice of Appeal must also be served on the Commissioner within the same timeframe (s 171). Both parties and the

Commissioner are entitled to be heard in relation to the appeal, although in practice the Commissioner normally agrees to abide by the decision of the Court. Without leave of the Court the only grounds of objection that may be advanced on appeal are those originally advanced by the opponent at IPONZ (s 172(3)(a)). If new grounds are permitted, the applicant will be given the opportunity to withdraw the application without payment of the opponent's costs.

In *AMI Insurance Ltd v NZ Automobile Assn Inc* 15/7/04, Miller J, HC Wellington CIV-2003-485-836 (an appeal against a decision of the Commissioner under the Trade Marks Act 1953) Miller J noted, at para 18, that the issues were to be determined by way of rehearing in accordance with s 66 Trade Marks Act 1953. His Honour considered the weight to be placed on the views of the Commissioner, referring to *VB Distributors Ltd v Matsushita Electric Industrial Co Ltd* (1999) 9 TCLR 349. In that case, Hammond J, at p 355, cited Salmon J in *Effem Foods Ltd v Commissioner of Trade Marks* (1996) 7 TCLR 246; 5 NZBLC 104,209 as providing the correct approach to appeals.

In *Effem Foods*, Salmon J stated, at p 248; p 104,211, that although it was appropriate to place great weight on the views of the Commissioner because of his position as an expert tribunal, the Court must come to its own decision as to whether the appellant had shown there was no reasonable possibility of confusion. His Honour also observed that the extent to which the Court should give weight to the Commissioner's views may depend upon the issue in dispute. He stated that the Commissioner's views regarding the practice in trade mark applications ought not to be lightly disregarded, however, there is benefit in subjecting tribunals to independent scrutiny. To the extent that the likelihood of confusion is determined by reason of a comparison of marks, the appellate Court may form its own view.

However, in *Stichting Lodestar v Austin, Nicholls & Co Inc* 12/3/07, CA94/05, it was noted that the approach outlined in *VB Distributors Ltd v Matsushita Electric Industrial Co Ltd* (above) (ie, deference should be paid to the Commissioner's views only in matters of trade mark practice) should not be so limited.

In *Stichting Lodestar*, the Court of Appeal upheld a decision of the Assistant Commissioner finding the appellant had discharged the onus of establishing there was no likelihood of deception or confusion arising out of the use of its mark WILD GEESE and ruling the mark could proceed to registration. On appeal to the High Court, Gendall J disagreed with the Assistant Commissioner's decision and refused registration of the mark (the reasoning is discussed in more detail at 7.6.4(4) ("The idea of the mark") earlier in this chapter).

The Court of Appeal held that this was a case where the High Court should have deferred to the expertise of the Assistant Commissioner commenting, at para 30:

> "She [the Assistant Commissioner] adopted an orthodox approach to the task and directed herself appropriately as to the legal tests she had to apply. Having done so, she reached a conclusion which involved a value judgment on the likelihood of confusion and deception, which appears to us to be soundly based. That being the case, the High Court Judge ought not to have embarked on a reconsideration of the issue without considering, and giving weight to, the Assistant Commissioner's conclusion. He was, of course, entitled to reach a conclusion contrary to that reached by the Assistant Commissioner, but not to do so without giving weight to her views."

Leave to appeal the decision of the Court of Appeal to the Supreme Court has been granted: *Austin Nichols & Co Inc v Stichting Lodestar* [2007] NZSC 41.

It will be appreciated that, where the Commissioner is exercising a discretion, this will be very difficult to overturn on appeal.

In *Aqua-Tech Ltd v Aqua Technics Pool and Spa Centre NZ Ltd* 3/10/05, Venning J, HC Auckland CIV-2005-404-2037, Venning J referred to the following passage of the Court of Appeal in *Ophthalmological Society of NZ Inc v Commerce Commission* [2003] 2 NZLR 145 (CA), at p 147, concerning the difficulty of defining when the process of applying the law to the facts turns into the exercise of a discretion:

> "It is by no means easy to define when the process of applying the law to the facts is the exercise of a discretion. The difficulty of this question of characterisation is brought out in the discussion of KJ Keith, 'Appeals from Administrative Tribunals' (1969) 5 VUWLR 123, pp134-153. The contrast is sometimes described as being between the exercise of a discretion and a finding based on evidence, as in *Merck & Co Inc v Pacific Pharmaceuticals Ltd* [1990] 2 NZLR 55 (CA) at p58, a case cited by Mr Brown. A key indication of a discretion is whether the area for personal appreciation by the first instance Court or decision maker is large (Keith at p135). In the context of the orders and decisions of Masters, whether the interests involved in a particular matter are purely procedural, or concern wider issues of principle in relation to the application of the law to the facts, will also be relevant to whether a decision is discretionary in nature. In the latter type of case it may more readily be seen that ultimately only one view is legally possible, even if there is scope for considerable argument as to what it is. If that is the case the decision maker does not have the margin of appreciation inherent in discretion."

While noting that the appeal was prima facie against an exercise of discretion having regard to the wording in s 26(2), his Honour found that the primary focus was essentially a question of fact (ie, whether the appellant had established use of its mark at the application date) and in that regard he was not bound to accept the Commissioner's findings: *G v NZ Medical Council* [1991] NZAR 1; *NZ Greyhound Racing Assoc (Inc) v Barron* (2002) 16 PRNZ 97.

The decision of Venning J was upheld on appeal (*Aqua Technics Pool & Spa Centre NZ Ltd v Aqua-Tech Ltd* 22/3/07, CA257/05. The decision of the Court of Appeal is also notable for its apparent criticism, at para 65, of the appellant's failure to cross-examine the chief witness for the respondent in respect of equivocal evidence as to the respondent's use of the subject mark, notwithstanding that the burden of proving ownership rested with the respondent at the trade mark opposition hearing stage. Note, however, the following comment of the Supreme Court in refusing leave to appeal to the Supreme Court, in *Aqua Technics Pool & Spa Centre NZ Ltd v Aqua-Tech Ltd* 9/7/07, SC24/07; [2007] NZSC 52, at para 5:

> "We do not consider that the Court of Appeal was doing anything more than stating the obvious, namely that it may be difficult to controvert assertions of fact by a witness without cross-examining the witness. The crucial point is that the Court of Appeal did examine the criticisms. But it rejected them. There is nothing in this point."

There is a further discussion regarding the tests in cases involving an appeal against a discretion in *Unilever Plc v The Commissioner of Trade Marks* 20/7/07, Wild J, HC Wellington CIV-2006-485-1208, at para 10.

Finally, *George Weston Foods Ltd v Goodman Fielder NZ Ltd* 27/3/07, Courtney J, HC Auckland CIV-2006-404-3347 confirms that s 173 Trade Marks Act 2002 empowers the High Court to reverse an IPONZ costs award. However, in that particular case, which dealt primarily with the question of costs on an appeal which was rendered nugatory by abandonment of the opposed trade mark applications before the appeal was heard, the Court was not prepared to enquire into the merits of the original opposition and found no basis on which it could interfere with the IPONZ decision on costs. The Court did confirm that the appellant would be entitled to its costs, the withdrawal of the subject applications rendering its appeal nugatory and making it, in effect, the successful party, and there being no evidence to support the respondent's assertion that it had a genuine commercial reason for abandoning the trade mark applications.

7.18   Assignments

A trade mark application or registration may be readily assigned by the owner of the trade mark to anyone entitled to own a trade mark registration. A trade mark may be assigned with or without the goodwill of the business associated with the trade mark. For a discussion on persons entitled to own a trade mark registration, refer to 7.4.1(2) ("Qualification as applicant/ownership") above.

Only the assignor need execute the deed of assignment for the purposes of recording the assignment on the Register.

The deed of assignment must be executed in a manner appropriate to bind the assignor. Therefore, an incorporated body should execute the document according to its rules. Individuals signing the document on their own behalf (as assignors) should have their signatures witnessed. No other legalisation is required.

7.18.1   Recording an assignment

Sections 81 and 82 Trade Marks Act 2002 allow for the assignment or transmission of a trade mark application or registration. Section 82(2) provides:

"A person to whom title to the trade mark is assigned or transmitted *must* apply to the Commissioner—

"(a)   for registration of the person's title if assignment or transmission is after the actual date of registration; or

"(b)   to change the name of the applicant on the application if assignment or transmission is before the actual date of registration." (emhasis added)

Therefore, pursuant to s 82(2), the assignee must apply to record his or her title in relation to the trade mark. However, there are no penalties for not recording an assignment, and there are also no timeframes as to when an application to record an assignment must be made.

Regulations 145 and 146 Trade Marks Regulations 2003 set out the requirements for recording an assignment of either a trade mark application or a trade mark registration.

While there are no specific forms with which to record a change in title of a trade mark application or registration, an application for the assignment or transmission of a trade mark application or registration must be in writing, and must contain the following information:

- The name of the assignor of the trade mark;

- If the assignor has an agent, the agent's name;

- The name, address for service in New Zealand and business or residential address of the assignee;

- If the assignee has an agent, the agent's name;

- The application/registration number of the trade mark;

- A description or representation of the trade mark;

- Whether the assignment or transmission was full or partial;

- The date on which the assignment or transmission became effective;

- The class or classes that were assigned or transmitted;

- In the case of the assignment or transmission of only some of the goods or services within a classification, a statement of the goods or services in respect of which the mark has been assigned or transmitted;

- A copy of the document of assignment or transmission or other documents acceptable to the Commissioner that are proof of the assignee's title to the trade mark; and

- If the assignment or transmission has resulted in the cancellation or amendment or registration of a licensee, a statement that the licensee has been notified of the assignment or transmission.

According to IPONZ Practice Guideline, "Assignments and Transmissions", the Commissioner will, on proof of the assignee's title, in the case of a trade mark application:

- Change the name of the applicant on the trade mark application;

- File the assignment, transmission or other document produced in evidence of title, or a copy of those documents, for the public record; and

- On completing the assignment, write to the applicant confirming the assignment or transmission has been completed.

In relation to a trade mark registration, the Commissioner will, on proof of the assignee's title:

- Register the assignee as the owner of the trade mark registration in relation to the goods or services in respect of which the assignment or transmission has effect;

- File the assignment, transmission or other document produced in evidence of title, or a copy of those documents, for the public record;

- On completing the assignment, write to the assignee confirming that the assignment or transmission has been completed; and

- Issue a replacement certificate, only where the old certificate is returned at the same time as the request for assignment or transmission is lodged.

With regard to the documentation required as proof of title, the document filed may be an original or a copy. The copy need not be certified. However, the assignment document should show the full name and address of both parties, the trade mark being transferred, and should be signed and dated by at least the assignor.

Where the assignment is requested and there is no change in the agent details, an authorisation of agent is not required. However, where the assignment will result in a change of agent, an authorisation of agent will be required from the assignee in favour of the new agent before the assignment can proceed (reg 22(1)).

The Commissioner has no discretion in respect of the recording of an assignment or transmission. If the application complies with the formal requirements and is supported by a document that establishes title to the trade mark, the Commissioner must record the change of ownership.

In general, there are no sanctions for failing to record an assignment. However, the transfer of ownership of a trade mark registration to a new owner must be recorded on the Register before the new owner can rely on the trade mark registration to enforce its rights. Unlike the 1953 Act, the 2002 Act does not distinguish between assignments with goodwill and assignments without goodwill. Nevertheless, it is important to mention in the assignment document whether the trade mark in question was assigned with or without goodwill. Failure to specifically mention whether the trade mark was assigned with or without goodwill may have adverse consequences for the assignee if, at a later date, the assignee wishes to rely on the common law rights accrued in the trade mark through use prior to the date of assignment: see *H & J Smith Ltd v The New Deal Skateboard Precincts Inc (ELEMENT)* (Commissioner's Decision No T02/2003, 10/1/03, Asst Commr Walden).

In proceedings for infringement, the Certificate of Registration will not be admitted in evidence as proof of the plaintiff's title to the trade mark, without leave of the Court, until the assignment is recorded.

7.18.2 Commissioner's certificate

Under s 81 Trade Marks Act 2002, the Commissioner may, if requested by either the applicant of a trade mark application or the owner of a registered mark, issue a certificate that states whether or not a proposed assignment or transmission is likely to deceive or confuse. This process is governed by regs 143 and 144 Trade Marks Regulations 2003. An application for a Commissioner's certificate must be in writing, signed by the person making the request, and must include the following minimum information (reg 144):

- The name and communication address of the person making the request;

- The name and communication address of the person to whom it is proposed to assign or transmit the application or trade mark;

- If the assignee has an agent, the agent's name;

- A description or representation of the trade mark to which the proposed assignment or transmission relates;

- Whether the proposed assignment or transmission is full or partial;

- The class or classes that are proposed to be assigned or transmitted;

- The application or registration number of the trade mark;

- Whether it is proposed that the registration of any licensees be cancelled or amended;

- A statement which, if the Commissioner requires it, must be verified by statutory declaration, setting out the circumstances of the proposed assignment or transmission; and

- In the case of the proposed assignment or transmission of only some of the goods or services within a classification, a statement of the goods or services in respect of which the mark has been assigned or transmitted.

The Commissioner may also require the person requesting the certificate to provide any additional information or documents that the Commissioner considers necessary (reg 144(2)).

The Commissioner will, once the requirements have been met, issue a certificate stating whether or not the request for an assignment or transmission is likely to deceive or confuse.

7.18.3 Association

Historically, IPONZ required "association" of trade mark registrations owned by the same owner, which were the same or similar in appearance, and which related to similar goods/ services.

The purpose of association was to avoid confusion which may occur if similar marks are owned and used by different parties. The effect of association was that one trade mark could not be assigned without also assigning the other trade mark(s) with which it was associated.

Just prior to the introduction of the 2002 Act, IPONZ altered its practice so as not to require associations. Pursuant to s 209(1) of the 2002 Act, any associations already entered on the Register ceased to have effect on the commencement of the Act.

Without the recording of associations as a warning of possible confusion if a registration is assigned, assignors and assignees should take care to consider this issue with any assignment.

7.19 Registered users and licensees

Historically, a trade mark owner was not entitled to sell the right to use his or her mark. A trade mark was considered to indicate a personal connection between the owner of the mark and the goods in respect of which it was used: *Pinto v Badman* (1891) 8 RPC 181. However, in *Pinto*, Lord Westbury LC upset the status quo by asserting that there might be property in a trade mark per se.

From *Pinto* the law developed so that a trade mark could be sold, but not separately from the business in which it was used. Nor could a trade mark be assigned where it connoted a personal connection between the original owner of the mark and the goods in respect of which it was used.

The introduction of the Trade Marks Act 1938 (UK) (on which New Zealand's 1953 Act was based) established what was described by Lord Nicholls of Birkenhead in *Scandecor Developments AB v Scandecor Marketing AV* [2001] UKHL 21; [2002] FSR 7 (HL), as a "somewhat complex system that cautiously opened the door to licensing". Although it "stopped short of any clear recognition of unrestricted licensing", the 1938 Act allowed proprietors to appoint "registered users" of a mark, so long as a "connection in the course of trade" was maintained between the trade mark proprietor and the registered user.

The enactment of the Trade Marks Act 1994 (UK) brought about substantial changes to English trade mark law, and in particular removed the remaining restrictions on assignment and licensing. Under that legislation, and the Trade Marks Act 2002, licences in the UK and New Zealand respectively are now registrable transactions.

7.19.1 Licensees

Section 83(1) Trade Marks Act 2002 allows somebody other than the owner (or, pre-registration, the applicant) to become a "licensee" of the trade mark in relation to any of the goods and services in respect of which the application has been made or the trade mark is registered.

Section 83(2) of the Act provides:

"If a person proposes to be registered as a licensee of a trade mark,—

"(a)   the owner and the proposed licensee must apply to the Commissioner in the prescribed manner; and

"(b)   the owner, or some person authorised to act on the owner's behalf and approved by the Commissioner, must make a statutory declaration that the person proposing to be registered as a licensee of a trade mark is entitled to be registered as a licensee; and

"(c)   the owner must give the Commissioner the statutory declaration."

Regulations 147 and 148 Trade Marks Regulations 2003 govern the requirements for filing an application for registration of a licensee in respect of a registered trade mark.

(1)   *Appointment of licensee may avoid finding of non-use*

Under the Trade Marks Act 1953, "permitted use" by a registered user was considered use by the registered proprietor for the purposes of s 35 of the Act (which related to non-use) and for any other purpose for which such use was material under the Act or at common law. Consequently, the registered user could never acquire independent goodwill and reputation in a trade mark.

However, amendments to the definition of "use" made by the Trade Marks Amendment Act 1994 meant that any use that was "authorised by and subject to the control of the proprietor" was to be considered "use" for the purposes of the Act. Accordingly, it was no longer necessary to appoint a party as a registered user in order to avoid a mark becoming vulnerable for non-use.

That amendment to the definition of "use" meant that the main benefit of appointing someone as a "registered user" was the ability of a registered user (subject to the user agreement) to commence infringement proceedings in his or her own name if the proprietor did not do so. Under the 1953 Act, an unregistered user was not able to do this.

The same position has been followed through into the Trade Marks Act 2002.

(2) *Licensee may file proceedings in own name*

Under s 102 Trade Marks Act 2002, and subject to any agreement between the parties, a licensee is entitled to commence infringement proceedings in his or her own name if the owner fails to take action within 2 months of the licensee's request. The owner must be joined as a defendant to the proceedings, although he or she will not be liable for any costs unless taking an active role in the proceedings (ss 103 and 104).

(3) *Owner must exercise sufficient degree of control*

An application for registration of a licensee must be accompanied by a statutory declaration by the owner attesting to the right of the proposed licensee to be registered as such (s 83(2)(b)), and the owner and the proposed licensee must apply to the Commissioner in the "prescribed manner" in order to register the licensee.

Pursuant to reg 148 Trade Marks Regulations 2003, an application for the registration of a licensee must contain the following information:

- The licensee's name, address for service, and business or residential address;
- If the licensee has an agent, the agent's name;
- The trade mark for which the licensee was to be registered;
- The registration number of the trade mark;
- The goods and services to which the licence relates; and
- Any conditions relating to the licence.

The Trade Marks Act 2002 and Regulations are silent as to what information the statutory declaration/affidavit should contain. Under the Trade Marks Act 1953, an application for registration of a registered user was to be accompanied by a Statement of Case, setting out a range of particulars, including:

- The relationship (existing or proposed) between the owner and the proposed user, including details of the degree of control that the owner would have over the use, and whether the user was a sole registered user;
- The goods or services in respect of which registration was proposed;
- Any conditions or restrictions proposed with respect to the characteristics of the goods or services and the mode or place of permitted use; and
- The term of the registered user agreement.

Although the 2002 Act and 2003 Regulations do not have any specific requirements in this regard, it is expected that similar information will be required in order to record a licensee.

Under s 84 of the 2002 Act, if the owner and the proposed licensee of a trade mark have complied with the requirements of the Act and Regulations, the Commissioner must register the proposed licensee as a licensee of the trade mark in respect of the goods and services set out in the application. Under the 1953 Act, the Commissioner had a discretion to register the proposed registered user as a registered user, provided the Commissioner was satisfied that the use of the trade mark by the proposed registered user would not be contrary to the public interest. The Commissioner was also entitled to place any conditions or restrictions on such use by the registered user as he or she thought proper.

(4) *Variation or cancellation of the licensee agreement*

Section 86 Trade Marks Act 2002 enables the Commissioner to alter the registration of a person as a licensee, on the application of the owner, in respect of the goods or services to which the licence relates, or the conditions or restrictions subject to which the registration has effect.

Under s 87(1)(a) and (b), the registration of a person as a licensee of a trade mark must be cancelled by the Commissioner if the trade mark is no longer registered or, in the case of an application for registration, if the application is withdrawn, abandoned, or rejected. In addition, under s 87(2), the registration of a person as a licensee of a trade mark may be cancelled by the Commissioner in the following circumstances:

- If, where the trade mark is no longer registered, the Commissioner received no advice within the time specified that the relationship between the owner and the licensee of the trade mark is current; or

- On written application in the prescribed manner by the owner or the licensee of the trade mark;

- On the application of "any person", showing that:

    - The licensee has used the trade mark otherwise than by way of the permitted use or in such a way as to cause, or to be likely to cause, deception or confusion;

    - The owner or the licensee misrepresented, or failed to disclose, some fact material to the application before registration, or that circumstances have materially changed since the date of the registration;

    - The registration of the licensee ought not to have been effected having regard to rights vested in the applicant by virtue of a contract the performance of which he or she is interested in. This provision is to allow a person who has been granted rights or an interest in the trade mark under an agreement, for example an unregistered licence, to apply to cancel the registration of a licensee, where that registration adversely affects his or her rights.

Under s 5, "permitted use" means use:

   "(a)   of a trade mark by a licensee of the trade mark in relation to any goods or services:

         "(i)   with which the licensee is connected in the course of trade; and

         "(ii)   in respect of which the trade mark is registered; and

   "(b)   that complies with any conditions to which the licensee's registration is subject."

7.19.2 Unregistered licences

The key character of a trade mark is that it must indicate a connection in the course of trade between goods and services and the manufacturer or provider of those goods/services. When the use of a trade mark is licensed to a person other than the owner, there is the potential for the connection in the course of trade with the owner of the mark to be severed.

The Trade Marks Act 2002 Act is silent on the status of licence agreements that are not registered under the Act. However, in *BOSTITCH Trade Mark* (1963) 80 RPC 183, Lloyd-Jacob J held that the failure to enter into a registered user agreement was immaterial to the validity of a registered trade mark.

The key concern in the *BOSTITCH* case was whether a connection in the course of trade had been maintained with the registered proprietor, regardless of whether the licence had actually been registered. His Honour commented, at p 195:

> "There is nothing anywhere in this section to justify the view that an arrangement between a registered proprietor of a trade mark and a party concerned to use such mark requires to be registered, still less that in the absence of registration, its affect upon the validity of the mark, if called into question, will be in any way different."

and, at p 197:

> "His mark only becomes vulnerable in this connection if he permits its use in a manner which is calculated to deceive or cause confusion.

> "The test of his actions is in consequence this: has he authorised such use of the mark as to deprive it of its very reason of existence, namely, as a mark which should distinguish his goods from the goods of other makers".

Amendments to the 1953 Act, which took effect on 1 January 1995, altered the definition of "use" such that any use that is authorised by and subject to the control of the trade mark owner will be deemed use by the owner. That amendment resolves many of the issues relating to validity of a licensed trade mark, as well as issues concerning non-use of the mark in question by the owner.

7.19.3 Control and connection in the course of trade

A trade mark licence must contain provisions that enable the owner to maintain control over the use of its mark. If not, then use of the mark may become deceptive or the mark may cease to function as a badge of origin. The mark will then become vulnerable to revocation.

In *GE Trade Mark* [1969] FSR 186; (1969) 86 RPC 418, the High Court of Justice held that a registered trade mark was valid if it indicated a connection in the course of trade between the registered proprietor and goods (or services). A registered trade mark could validly be licensed if the owner of the mark retained a sufficient degree of control over the nature and quality of the goods/services sold under the mark.

In *Pioneer Electronic Corp v Registrar of Trade Marks* (1978) 95 RPC 716 (HCA), Aickin J referred to the need for there to be a connection in the course of trade between the proprietor (or licensee) of the trade mark and the goods, to preserve the validity of a trade mark registration. Otherwise, the registration would become vulnerable to attack on the grounds of non-use. His Honour said:

> "the essential requirement for the maintenance of the validity of a trade mark is that it must indicate a connection in the course of trade with the registered proprietor, even though the connection may be slight, such as selection or quality control of the user in the sense in which a parent company controls the subsidiary. Use by either the registered proprietor or a licensee (whether registered or otherwise) will protect the mark from attack on the grounds of non-user, but it is essential both that the user maintains the connection of the registered proprietor with the goods and that the use of the mark does not become otherwise deceptive. Conversely, registration of a registered user will not save the mark if there ceases to be relevant connection in the course of trade with the proprietor or the mark otherwise becomes deceptive."

In *McGREGOR Trade Mark* (1979) 96 RPC 36, an agreement between the registered proprietor and registered user provided that the registered user was required to only use the trade mark so long as the goods were manufactured by him in accordance with directions as to the materials and methods to be used in the manufacture of the goods, as given from time to time by the registered proprietor. The High Court held that, because the registered proprietor never gave any such directions to the registered user of the McGREGOR trade mark, use of the mark by the registered user did not comply with the conditions and restrictions to which the registrations were subject and consequently was not "permitted use".

The common law requirement of controlling use to maintain a connection in the course of trade was incorporated into the Trade Marks Act 1953 by the Trade Marks Amendment Act 1994. The amendments, which took effect from 1 January 1995 altered the definition of "use" such that any use authorised by and subject to the control of the proprietor would be deemed use by the proprietor. This definition of "use" has been carried over into the Trade Marks Act 2002 (s 7). Hence the observation in *McGREGOR* remains applicable.

7.19.4 Effective control required

It is not sufficient to simply have quality control provisions in a licence agreement without monitoring or maintaining them. If quality control provisions are not monitored and maintained, there may cease to be any connection in the course of trade and the mark may become vulnerable to a rectification action.

In *Patience & Nicholson (NZ) Ltd v Cyclone Hardware Pty Ltd* [2001] 3 NZLR 490, one of the issues was who owned the goodwill in a New Zealand trade mark registration. In the 1960s, Patience & Nicholson Ltd ("Patience & Nicholson Australia") established a New Zealand subsidiary, registered the trade mark P&N in New Zealand, and entered into a registered user agreement with its New Zealand subsidiary. Both the Australian and New Zealand companies were later sold, with Patience & Nicholson Australia eventually being purchased by the Cyclone Group. The sale did not include the New Zealand P&N registration or other aspects of the New Zealand business.

The New Zealand company was sold to separate interests, who made little use of the P&N trade mark in New Zealand. In 1994, all of the business assets in the New Zealand business, including the goodwill, were sold to a company that was to rename itself Patience & Nicholson (NZ) Ltd.

In 1996, the P&N registration lapsed through non-payment of renewal fees and the next year Cyclone Hardware applied to register the P&N trade mark in New Zealand in its name. Patience & Nicholson (NZ) Ltd opposed such registration and sought an injunction alleging that use of P&N by Cyclone Hardware in New Zealand constituted passing off and a breach of the Fair Trading Act 1986.

To overcome s 37(2) Trade Marks Act 1953, which deemed use of the P&N mark by the New Zealand subsidiary (being a registered user) as use by Patience & Nicholson Australia (which was acquired by the defendant Cyclone), the plaintiff (Patience & Nicholson (NZ) Ltd) argued that use of the mark by the registered user had not been in compliance with the terms of the user agreement. Accordingly, the goodwill arising from the registered user's use of the mark did not accrue to Patience & Nicholson Australia (or to its successor Cyclone) because it was not "permitted use".

Although the plaintiff was ultimately successful in passing off (on the basis of its use of the name "P&N" as distinct from goodwill deriving from its use of "P&N" as a trade mark), Rodney Hansen J stated, at p 503, that he was satisfied that "at all stages specifications and standards of quality were approved by Patience & Nicholson Australia". His Honour distinguished the situation from that in *McGREGOR Trade Mark* (1979) 96 RPC 36, where the trade mark user was effectively given "carte blanche" to manufacture the goods as it saw fit. Hansen J was satisfied that Patience & Nicholson Australia had not abandoned its rights as registered proprietor of the mark in New Zealand and had maintained a connection in the course of trade at least up until the sale of the business in 1987. However, on an analysis of the rights of the parties following Cyclone's acquisition of the Australian business in 1987, his Honour concluded that neither party could rely on goodwill derived from use of the "P&N" trade mark in New Zealand, and based his decision solely on Patience & Nicholson (NZ) Ltd's reputation in "P&N" as a name at common law. The Court of Appeal (Keith, Blanchard and Tipping JJ) dismissed an appeal by Cyclone and upheld Hansen J's decision: see *Patience & Nicholson (NZ) Ltd v Cyclone Hardware Pty Ltd* [2001] 3 NZLR 490, at p 520.

7.19.5 Trafficking

Under the Trade Marks Act 1953, the Commissioner was entitled to refuse an application for registration of a registered user if it appeared that the grant of registration "would tend to facilitate trafficking in a trade mark".

Trafficking means treating the mark itself as a commodity in commercial dealings.

The leading decision in relation to trafficking is *HOLLY HOBBIE Trade Mark* (1984) 67 RPC 329 (HL). In that case, trafficking was referred to as "one of the cardinal sins of trade mark law". The trade mark applicants had used the HOLLY HOBBIE mark (which involved a drawing of a child dressed in a pinafore and bonnet) extensively on greeting cards and other stationery items. Following the success of the mark, they attempted to extend it to other ranges of goods, which they had not produced and would never produce. They filed 12 new trade mark applications covering a diverse range of goods. Each application was accompanied by a registered user application naming the relevant licensee who would trade in the goods in question.

Lord Brightman considered, at p 356, that:

> "trafficking in the trade mark context conveys the notion of dealing in a trade mark primarily as a commodity in its own right and not primarily for the purpose of identifying or promoting merchandise in which the proprietor of the mark is interested. If there is no real trade connection between the proprietor of the mark and the licensee or his goods, there is room for the conclusion that the grant of the licence is a trafficking in the mark. It is a question of fact and degree in every case whether a sufficient trade connection exists."

Although each agreement contained comprehensive quality control provisions, which were arguably sufficient under the *GE* ruling to constitute a "connection in the course of trade", the House of Lords rejected the applications on the grounds that the applicants were indulging in trafficking. On the basis of evidence showing "an open invitation to all and sundry to become licensees of the HOLLY HOBBIE mark" from the trade mark applicant, the House of Lords held that there was no connection in the course of trade between the proprietor of the mark and the licensee or his or her goods. After reviewing the relevant case law, Lord Brightman stated, at p 356, that he could not discern any "general rule that the mere ability to control quality is always to be sufficient to establish the required connection".

An allegation of trafficking was raised in *Reckitt & Colman (NZ) Ltd v Dominion and Overseas Agencies (NZ) Ltd (CANVAS)* (Commissioner's Decision No T05/1987, 24/12/87, Asst Commr Martin). In that case, the opponent claimed that an assignment of the CANVAS mark was ineffectual and invalid as the applicant had no intention to use the mark. The Assistant Commissioner agreed with the applicant's submissions that there was no suggestion of trafficking in the registered user application, because when the applicant applied to register the trade mark it had an intention that the mark would be used by a controlled subsidiary of the applicant.

Whether or not the control provisions in a license agreement suffice to maintain a connection between the owner of the mark and the licensee or his or her goods will always be a question of fact in every case.

The amendment to the definition of "use" in the Trade Marks Amendment Act 1994 (carried over into the 2002 Act) came into force subsequent to the *HOLLY HOBBIE* decision. However, the reasoning in the *HOLLY HOBBIE* case remains good law. The mere ability of the owner to control use of the mark may be insufficient to avoid a finding of trafficking or rectification of the mark on the basis of non-use, if such use is not in fact controlled.

Under the Trade Marks Act 2002, there is no obligation upon the Commissioner to refuse an application for the registration of a licensee where it appears that the grant of registration would tend to facilitate trafficking in a trade mark. In fact, s 84 obliges the Commissioner to register the proposed licensee if the requirements of s 83 are met.

7.20   Non-standard registrations

In addition to standard trade mark registrations, the Act provides for:

- Certification trade mark registrations; and
- Collective trade mark registrations.

7.20.1 Certification trade marks

The function of a certification trade mark is to indicate that goods or services provided under the mark comply with certain standards or possess a certain characteristic.

An example of a certification trade mark is the National Heart Foundation tick device, which distinguishes food products that have been certified as meeting Heart Foundation standards from food products that have not met those standards.

(1)   *Registrability*

Section 5 Trade Marks Act 2002 defines a "certification trade mark" as follows:

> "**certification trade mark** means a sign capable of—
>
> "(a)   being represented graphically; and
>
> "(b)   distinguishing, in the course of trade,—
>
>> "(i)   goods certified by any person in respect of origin, material, mode of manufacture, quality, accuracy, or other characteristic from goods not so certified; or
>>
>> "(ii)   services certified by any person in respect of quality, accuracy, performance or other characteristic from services not so certified."

A certification trade mark is a sign capable of distinguishing, in the course of trade, goods or services certified by a person as meeting certain standards or possessing a particular characteristic. As such, certification trade marks are used alongside "ordinary" trade marks, the former to guarantee some characteristic of the goods or services, the latter distinguishing the source of those goods or services.

As the words "capable of distinguishing" are also used in the definition under s 5 of "trade mark", the threshold for registration of certification marks is equivalent to that for normal trade marks. However, s 18 provides that the Commissioner must not register a trade mark that consists only of signs or indications that may serve, in trade, "to designate the kind, quality, quantity, intended purpose, value, geographical origin, time of production of goods or of rendering of services, or other characteristics of goods or services". Section 18(1)(c) specifically excludes certification trade marks from this requirement. This is indicative of the fact that, in practice, the threshold for certification marks tends to be lower as they must, by their nature, have an element of descriptiveness to serve their function.

(2)   *Application procedure*

Applications for registration of certification marks are dealt with in the same way as applications for ordinary marks. However, there are specific provisions under ss 54, 55, and 56 of the Act, and regs 57 and 58 Trade Marks Regulations 2003.

Registration of a certification trade mark involves filing a trade mark application, together with a Statement of Case in the form of a statutory declaration setting out grounds supporting the registration of the mark as a certification trade mark.

The certification mark must distinguish the goods or services to be certified in terms of their origin, quality or other distinctive characteristic that sets them apart from goods or services that are not certified.

Certification trade marks must be registered with regulations approved by the Commissioner governing the use of the mark. Section 54 provides as follows:

> "Before the Commissioner makes a decision on an application for the registration of a certification trade mark, the applicant must provide the Commissioner with draft regulations that govern the use of the certification trade mark for the Commissioner's approval."

The regulations should address such issues as:

- Who is authorised to use the mark;

- The characteristics to be certified by the mark; and

- How the certifying body is to test those characteristics and supervise the use of the mark.

After the application is filed, the Commissioner will examine the application and will also review the "suitability" of the draft regulations. Should any deficiencies be noted, the applicant will have an opportunity to correct these (reg 58). For example, the Commissioner must be satisfied that the applicant is competent to certify the goods or services for which the mark is to be registered. In some cases the applicant may be required to file a declaration of competency to verify this.

If there are no objections, or any objections are overcome, the application will be accepted by the Commissioner and advertised for opposition purposes. The Act does not contain separate provisions regarding the acceptance and advertisement of certification trade marks. Instead, s 50 states that relevant provisions of ss 46 and 47, regarding advertisement and opposition, will apply as if the certification trade mark was an "ordinary" trade mark. The opposition procedure and grounds of opposition are discussed in more detail at 7.7.2 and 7.7.1 respectively earlier in this chapter.

Upon registration of the certification trade mark, the regulations governing its use are deposited at IPONZ, where they remain open for public inspection.

(3)   *Ownership and use of certification trade marks*

The Act imposes restrictions on who is entitled to be the owner of a certification trade mark.

Any person, or organisation, who authorises or will authorise traders to use a certification mark in relation to certain goods or services, and who certifies or will certify that those goods or services possess certain characteristics, can apply to register a certification trade mark.

However, s 14 Trade Marks Act 2002 prohibits the registration of a certification trade mark in the name of any party who is using or will use the trade mark. For this reason, certification trade marks are usually owned by associations.

While there are restrictions as to who is entitled to be the owner of a certification trade mark, *any party* can use the certification trade mark provided they are able to meet the standards prescribed by the owner for the goods or services to which the registration relates. In practice the owners of certification marks get around this by making it a condition of use that the user be a member of the registered owner's organisation or association, or be approved by the registered owner.

(4)   *Infringement*

The owner of a certification trade mark registered in relation to goods or services has the exclusive right to use the trade mark in relation to those goods or services (s 10). Therefore only the owner of a certification trade mark may bring an action for infringement (s 101).

Unlike the Trade Marks Act 1953, the Trade Marks Act 2002 does not have specific provisions relating to the infringement of certification marks. Therefore the infringement of a certification mark is governed by the same provisions as the infringement of an ordinary trade mark under ss 88-116.

The defences to trade mark infringement and remedies available to an owner if the mark is found to have been infringed are discussed in more detail earlier in this chapter.

For more information regarding the filing and examination of applications for certification trade marks, see the IPONZ Practice Guideline, "Certification Marks".

7.20.2 Collective trade marks

Collective trade marks are fairly new to New Zealand trade mark law, having been introduced by the Trade Marks Amendment Act 1999, with effect from 1 April 2000.

A collective trade mark is a sign registered by a collective association in respect of goods or services provided by its members.

Therefore, the function of a collective trade mark is simply to indicate membership of an association.

(1)   *Collective trade marks v certification trade marks*

Collective trade marks, like "ordinary" trade marks, indicate the commercial origin of goods or services. However, instead of indicating origin in just one trader, a collective trade mark indicates origin in members of an association.

Although the association that owns a collective trade mark can set its own standards, which its members must meet when using the mark, it is not mandatory to set such standards in order to register a collective trade mark. In this way collective trade marks fall in between certification trade marks and "ordinary" trade marks.

(2)   *Registrability*

Section 5 Trade Marks Act 2002 defines a "collective trade mark" as follows:

> "**collective trade mark** means a sign capable of—

"(a)   being represented graphically; and

"(b)   distinguishing the goods or services of members of the collective association that is the owner of the sign from those of persons who are not members of the collective association."

As also provided by s 5, the owner of a collective trade mark is the collective association in whose name the trade mark is registered.

An application for the registration of a collective trade mark is governed by the same requirements as that for ordinary trade marks under the 2002 Act. This can be compared to the situation under the Trade Marks Amendment Act 1999, in which separate provisions governed the examination and registrability of collective trade marks.

(3)   *Application procedure*

Applications for registration of collective trade marks are dealt with in the same way as applications for ordinary marks. However, there are specific provisions under ss 10 and 15 Trade Marks Act 2002, and reg 59 Trade Marks Regulations 2003.

Registration of a collective trade mark involves filing a trade mark application, which is examined by the Commissioner and which, in the first instance, must meet the acceptance requirements for "ordinary" trade marks. Pursuant to reg 59, an application for registration of a collective trade mark must comply with the registrability requirements of ordinary trade marks, and also contain a declaration that the applicant is a collective association as defined in s 5(1) of the Act (reg 59(b)).

If there are no objections, or once any objections are overcome, the application will then be accepted and advertised for opposition purposes. As with certification trade marks, the Act does not contain separate provisions regarding the acceptance and advertisement of collective trade marks.

The opposition procedure and grounds of opposition are discussed in more detail earlier in this chapter.

(4)   *Ownership and use of collective trade marks*

Section 15 provides as follows:

"A collective trade mark may be registered in the name of a collective association, as owner, in respect of goods produced by its members, services provided by its members, or both."

Therefore, the applicant for registration of a collective trade mark must be a collective association.

A collective association is defined in s 5 Trade Marks Act 2002 as a body constituted for the joint benefit of its members such that its membership can be ascertained at any given time.

A collective trade mark confers on the members of the collective association the exclusive right to use the mark in relation to the goods or services for which it is registered. Consequently, non-members of the collective association do not have any rights in the mark.

As all members have equal rights to use a collective trade mark, collective associations will often register collective trade marks subject to limitations or conditions to control the circumstances in which the mark is used by members.

(5) *Infringement*

The registration by a collective association of a collective trade mark in respect of goods or services gives the association and its members the exclusive right to use the trade mark in relation to those goods or services.

A collective trade mark will be infringed by any person who, not being a member of the collective association, uses a similar or identical mark in relation to goods or services that are similar or identical, if such use is likely to deceive or cause confusion or create a wrongful impression that the person has the right to use the collective trade mark as a provider to, or member of, the collective association.

In the event that a collective trade mark is infringed either the collective association, or an individual member, may bring an action for infringement (s 101 Trade Marks Act 2002).

In accordance with s 107, in claiming damages for infringement of a collective trade mark, the party bringing the action, be it the collective association or a member, may take into account any damage or loss of profits sustained or incurred by any other member(s) as a result of the infringement.

The defence to trade mark infringement and remedies available to an owner if the mark is found to have been infringed, are discussed in more detail at 7.13 ("Defences") and 7.12 ("Remedies") earlier in this chapter.

For more information regarding the filing and examination of applications for collective trade marks, see IPONZ Practice Guideline, "Collective Marks".

7.21 Offences

An offence is committed under the Act in one of two ways, either by:

- Falsification of the Register; or

- Falsely representing a trade mark as being registered when it is not.

7.21.1 Falsification of the Register

Falsification of the Register occurs where a person:

- Knowingly causes a false entry to be made in the Register; or

- Holds out a document purporting to be copy of an entry in the Register knowing it to be false.

Under s 185 Trade Marks Act 2002, a person convicted of falsification of the Register is liable to imprisonment for up to 2 years.

7.21.2 Falsely representing a trade mark as registered

The second type of offence, falsely representing a trade mark as being registered, occurs where a person represents:

- A sign, or the whole or a part of a trade mark, as being registered;

- A trade mark as being registered in respect of goods or services outside the scope of the registration; or

- A trade mark as giving them exclusive rights to use the mark in circumstances where no such right exists due to a limitation or condition entered on the Register.

As the maximum fine for falsely representing a trade mark as being registered under s 186 is only $1,000, it is more common for people who are aggrieved to take an action under the Fair Trading Act 1986 for misleading and deceptive conduct, as it offers significantly harsher penalties.

7.21.3 Criminal offences

Under the Trade Marks Act 2002, there are new criminal offences for counterfeiting and the false application of trade marks, and for importing, selling, and possessing for the purpose of trade or manufacture, goods to which trade marks have been falsely applied.

These offences and penalties are governed by ss 120-125 of the Act. Under these sections, it is an offence to:

- Counterfeit a registered trade mark;

- Falsely apply a registered trade mark to goods or services;

- Make an object specifically designed or adapted for making copies of a registered trade mark or a sign that is likely to be mistaken for a trade mark with intent that the object be used for, or in the course of, committing the above offences;

- Possess an object specifically designed or adapted for making copies of a registered trade mark or a sign that is likely to be mistaken for that trade mark; and/or

- Import, sell, expose for sale, or possess for the purpose of trade or manufacture, goods to which that person knows a registered trade mark is falsely applied.

Every person who is convicted of an offence under ss 120-123 is liable, on conviction, for a fine not exceeding $10,000 for each of the goods or services to which the offence relates (not exceeding $150,000), or a term of imprisonment not exceeding 5 years. Every person who is convicted of an offence against s 124 is liable, on conviction, for a fine not exceeding $150,000 or imprisonment for a term not exceeding 5 years.

7.22   References and resources

7.22.1 Websites

Thomson Brookers	www.thomsonbrookers.co.nz
Interim Website of New Zealand Legislation	www.legislation.govt.nz
James & Wells	www.jaws.co.nz
Ministry of Economic Development	www.med.govt.nz

Intellectual Property Office of New Zealand	www.iponz.govt.nz
UK Intellectual Property Office	www.ipo.gov.uk
World Intellectual Property Organisation	www.wipo.int

7.22.2 Texts and periodicals

- Brown, A, and Grant, A, *The Law of Intellectual Property in New Zealand*, Wellington, Butterworths, 1988

- Blanco White, T A, and Jacob, the Hon Sir R, *Kerly's Law of Trade Marks and Trade Names*, London, Sweet and Maxwell, 1986

- Frankel, S, and McLay, G, *Intellectual Property in New Zealand*, Wellington, Butterworths, 2002

- Sumpter, P, *Trade Marks in Practice*, Wellington, LexisNexis, 2004

Chapter 8

Domain Names and Other Issues in Electronic Commerce

8.1   Introduction and scope of chapter

Intellectual property issues in electronic commerce are a complex and fast evolving area of the law. This chapter provides a brief overview of some of those issues, and the current state of the law in New Zealand and, where appropriate, other Commonwealth jurisdictions and the US.

The issues canvassed include:

- Registration of domain names;

- Trade marks and domain name disputes;

- Conflict resolution, the ICANN Uniform Dispute Resolution Policy, and New Zealand's Dispute Resolution Service Policy;

- Other intellectual property issues in e-commerce (meta tags, typo squatting, overstuffing, keyword buy agreements, hyperlinks, and framing);

- Liability;

- Jurisdictional issues;

- Website disclaimers; and

- Click wrap agreements.

There is significant overlap between the causes of action discussed in this chapter and other chapters in this text (specifically trade marks, passing off, and the Fair Trading Act 1986

493

(chapters 7, 9, and 10 respectively)). More information regarding those causes of action can be located in those chapters.

8.2 Domain names

8.2.1 What is a domain name?

A domain name acts as the address of a presence, or a website, on the internet. It is effectively an alphanumeric phone number. Generally the format of such an address is www.[identifier].[suffix].

8.2.2 Types of domain names

There are two main types of domain names. These are referred to as top level domains ("TLDs") and country-code top level domains ("ccTLDs").

(1) *Top level domains*

There were seven original TLDs:

Original TLD	Purpose	Website
.com	Unrestricted use	www.verisign-grs.com
.net	Unrestricted use	www.verisign-grs.com
.org	Unrestricted use	www.pir.org
.int	Reserved for inter-governmental organisations	www.iana.org/int-dom/int.htm
.mil	Reserved for US military use	www.nic.mil
.edu	Reserved for US or accredited educational institutions	www.educause.edu/edudomain
.gov	Reserved for US government sites	www.dotgov.gov

The *.com*, *.net*, and *.org* TLDs are available to anyone and are commonly called generic TLDs ("gTLDs").

From the introduction of the original gTLDs, the *.com* gTLD has stood out as the most desirable and well-recognised domain name suffix available. This has generated a large number of disputes between rival companies with the same, or a similar, name fighting for the associated .com domain name.

In an effort to cope with the demand and reduce the possibility of conflict, seven new TLDs were introduced by ICANN in 2001 and 2002:

TLD	Purpose	Website
.biz	Business use	www.neulevel.biz
.info	Unrestricted use	www.afilias.info
.pro	Accountants, lawyers, physicians, and other professionals	www.registry.pro

TLD	Purpose	Website
.name	Individuals	www.gnr.name
.museum	Museums	www.about.museum
.coop	Cooperatives	www.coop
.aero	Air-transport industry	www.nic.aero

A number of TLDs have been introduced since 2002:

TLD	Purpose	Website
.cat	Catalan linguistic and cultural community	www.domini.cat
.jobs	International community of human resource managers	www.goto.jobs
.mobi	Mobile content providers and users community	www.mtld.mobi
.travel	Travel and tourism community	www.tralliance.travel

The following TLDs are due to be launched in late-2007:

TLD	Purpose	Website
.tel	Designed to be a universal text naming system for contact information accessed from internet-enabled communications devices	www.telnic.org
.asia	From Asia / for Asia	www.registry.asia

Some of the new TLDs require that specific criteria be met before applicants will be eligible to use them. For more information on any of these TLDs please refer to the appropriate website.

(2) *Administration of TLDs*

The Internet Corporation for Assigned Names and Numbers ("ICANN") and the Internet Assigned Numbers Authority ("IANA") are responsible for the administration of the TLDs and ccTLDs.

ICANN has appointed Generic Names Supporting Organisation ("GNSO") to oversee the administration of gTLDs. GNSO maintains a list of the domain names within the gTLD name space and delegates responsibility for contracting with domain name purchasers to a number of Registrars located around the world. For more information, visit gnso.icann.org.

(3) *Country-code top level domain names*

ccTLDs, as the name suggests, are country-specific top level domains. New Zealand's ccTLD is *.nz*, Australia's is *.au* and the UK's is *.uk*. A registry within the respective country administers each ccTLD.

IANA/ICANN have made InternetNZ, the Internet Society of New Zealand Inc ("ISOCNZ") responsible for the administration of the *.nz* ccTLD. You can access the ISOCNZ website at www.isocnz.org.nz.

ISOCNZ has appointed a Domain Name Commissioner ("DNC") to be responsible for the administration of the *.nz* ccTLD. The Office of the DNC authorises Registrars, such as Domainz (www.domainz.co.nz), to register and manage .nz domain names. The Office of the DNC is an operational office of ISOCNZ. For more information, see www.dnc.org.nz.

The DNC provides a number of subsidiary domain names that may be selected in conjunction with the *.nz* ccTLD. The subsidiary domains or second level domains ("SLDs") provided by the DNC are:

SLD	Purpose
.co	Commercial organisations
.ac	Tertiary education organisations
.cri	Crown research institutes
.geek	Technical enthusiasts
.gen	Miscellaneous
.govt	Government organisations
.iwi	Traditional Maori tribes
.maori	Maori people, groups and organisations
.mil	Military organisations
.net	Internet related organisations
.org	Non-profit organisations
.parliament	Agencies and individuals who are a part of the parliamentary system, but not part of the executive government
.school	Primary, secondary, and pre-school education organisations

(4)   *Allocation of New Zealand's ccTLDs*

New Zealand ccTLDs are allocated on a "first come, first served basis". The system of domain name allocation is very similar to that provided by the New Zealand Companies Office for the allocation and registration of a company name. Applicants for a *.nz* ccTLD are not required to prove that they have the right to use a particular domain name. All that is required of applicants is that they declare they are entitled to their chosen domain name.

The Office of the DNC and its authorised Registrars are only concerned with ensuring that the domain name has the correct technical criteria and is unique, rather than whether the applicant is entitled to use the name, or will infringe some other party's rights by doing so. This may, and often does, lead to the types of conflict described later in this chapter.

For an example of the implementation of the "first come, first served" policy, see: *Pitman Training Ltd v Nominet UK* (1997) 38 IPR 341; [1997] FSR 797.

(5) *Contents of an application to obtain a New Zealand ccTLD*

An application to register a New Zealand domain name requires the following information:

- The preferred domain name, including the duration for which registration is sought (between 1-10 years);

- The name and contact details of the person or organisation in whose name the domain name will be registered; and

- The signature of the name holder / registrant or authorised officer of an organisation.

(6) *Anyone can register*

Applicants need not be a New Zealand citizen, or a New Zealand company, in order to register a *.nz* ccTLD. However, registrants do need to be identifiable individuals over the age of 18 years or properly constituted organisations.

8.2.3 Why register a domain name?

The internet explosion is over. The internet is no longer a radical new medium. It has become an integral part of everyday life. A large proportion of New Zealanders access the internet on a daily basis. It is present in our homes, workplaces and schools. We use it for everything from ordering groceries to checking our bank account balances.

The question is no longer "why register a domain name" but "can a modern business afford not to register a domain name and, in turn, establish a presence on the internet?".

8.2.4 Choosing a domain name

When selecting a domain name, it is essential to check that the domain name is not likely to lead to confusion with another person or business. This is particularly so where the domain name is an acronym, invented word or other distinctive name. Registration of a domain name may, in some circumstances, constitute trade mark infringement, a breach of the Fair Trading Act 1986, or passing off. If liable, it may be necessary to transfer ownership of the domain name to another party and, in some cases, to pay damages.

(1) *Perform basic checks*

The non-territorial nature of the internet makes it difficult (if not impossible) to unequivocally ascertain whether the use of a particular domain name will lead to conflict. However, there are a number of basic checks that can be carried out to minimise the possibility of conflict. These include:

- Checking the Trade Marks Register in New Zealand (and any other country into which goods/services might be promoted and sold via the website accessed by the domain name) to ascertain whether the proposed domain name (or something confusingly similar) has been registered as a trade mark in relation to the same, or similar, goods or services as those that may be offered on the website located by the domain name;

- Checking the Companies Register in New Zealand (and, if appropriate, any other country into which goods/services might be promoted and sold via the website accessed by the domain name) to ascertain whether any company is trading in goods/

services under a name which is the same as (or confusingly similar to) the proposed domain name;

- Reviewing the internet for similar domain names in the same field; and

- Reviewing brand guides, business directories, and telephone directories etc.

(2) *Domain name should be relevant and intuitive*

Businesses intent on marketing their goods and services on the internet will obviously want to take advantage of the goodwill in their name or trade mark by incorporating it into their domain name. For instance, the internet address for Thomson Brookers is www.thomsonbrookers.co.nz.

This address would be readily recognisable to most internet users as being associated with Thomson Brookers. It is also intuitive. Many internet users will locate a site by typing what they expect a company's domain name will be; www.thomsonbrookers.co.nz, for example, would be easily located by such users. The address may also be quickly and easily found by anybody wanting information on, or wanting access to the Thomson Brookers range of products via a search engine.

8.3 Domain name disputes

8.3.1 The nature of domain name disputes

As people have become more familiar with the internet as a forum for doing business it has become increasingly important for businesses to maintain an online presence. This has led to a number of problems. As domain names are often a user's entranceway onto the internet they have often become the focus of disputes. Such disputes can rise in a number of ways:

(1) *Unintentional misrepresentation*

Selection and use of a particular domain name may unintentionally lead the public to mistakenly assume that there is some association between the website and another party.

For example, two or more companies in different lines of business, or different geographical locations, may use the same name or trade mark. Because the internet does not distinguish between territories or fields of activity, only one business will be able to use its name as a domain name. When domain names are issued on a "first-come, first-served" basis, only one of the companies will be satisfied with the outcome.

In *Prince Plc v Prince Sports Group Inc* (1997) 39 IPR 225; [1998] FSR 21, two legitimate rights-holders entered into a dispute over the www.prince.com domain name.

Prince Plc, a UK company, had been providing services to the computer industry under the name Prince since 1985. In February 1995 the company registered the domain name www.prince.com.

Prince Sports Group Inc, a US sporting goods manufacturer with trade mark registrations in numerous countries, including the US and the UK, attempted to assert its rights under its trade mark registrations against Prince Plc. Prince Sports Group argued that Prince Plc's use of the domain name constituted trade mark infringement.

In response, Prince Plc took an action in the UK seeking a declaration of unjustified threats along with an injunction and damages. The Court held that Prince Sports Group's letter constituted a threat of proceedings for infringement of a registered trade mark under s 21(1) Trade Marks Act 1994 (UK). The Court went on to find that the threat was unjustified, and granted a declaration of non-infringement and an injunction against further threats in accordance with s 21(2).

The decision highlights the well recognised tenet of trade mark law that rights provided by registered trade marks are limited to defined fields of activity. The fact that Prince Sports Group had rights to the PRINCE mark in relation to sporting equipment was of little importance. Prince Plc was well within its rights to use the PRINCE trade mark and the domain name www.prince.com in relation to its own field of activity.

A number of disputes of this nature have occurred on the internet. Some of these disputes have been resolved by way of a mutual coexistence arrangement between the parties. The domain name in dispute will often be used to send the user to an intermediary page that includes links to the sites of the parties that have legitimate rights to the domain name. See www.scrabble.com for an example of such an arrangement.

(2) *Deliberate misrepresentation*

An unscrupulous party may deliberately secure a particular domain name (usually the name or trade mark of a successful business) to mislead or deceive the public for his or her own advantage. An example of this is typosquatting. Typosquatters register domain names that are nearly identical to domain names used by other businesses. The slight differences between the domain names are intended to catch internet users who make typographical or punctuation errors when entering a domain name into a web browser or search engine. Some examples of typo squatting are discussed at 8.4.2(4) ("Decisions of the *.nz* dispute resolution service") later in this chapter.

(3) *Cybersquatting*

A domain name may be registered by someone whose intention is not to mislead or deceive the public, but to sell the domain name. This is known as cybersquatting — the registration of domain names in bad faith with the intention of profiting from their sale to the owner of the goodwill in the name.

Many businesses have been successful in Court actions against cybersquatters, with the Courts finding cybersquatters liable for both passing off and trade mark infringement. For example, in *British Telecommunications Plc v One In A Million Ltd* (1998) 42 IPR 289; [1999] FSR 1 (CA), several trade mark owners succeeded in persuading the UK Court of Appeal to order One In A Million to transfer ownership of domain names that contained their trade marks on the grounds of passing off and trade mark infringement. This case is discussed in more detail at 8.5 ("Passing off, the Fair Trading Act 1986, and domain names") later in this chapter.

In *Saskatoon Star Phoenix Group Inc v Steven Noton* (2001) SKQB 153, the Canadian Court issued an injunction requiring the defendant, a cybersquatter, to transfer the domain name in dispute and also awarded "enhanced costs".

The plaintiff published the *StarPhoenix*, the largest daily newspaper in Saskatchewan, and maintained a website with the domain name and address www.thestarphoenix.com that contained the current day's lead stories and paid advertising.

The defendant created a website with the domain name and address "saskatoonstarphoenix.com". The main page of this site looked almost exactly the same as the plaintiff's. The bottom of the defendant's page also contained a notice that the site was "designed, hosted and marketed" by the defendant, and a message promoting the defendant's services.

The defendant inserted meta tags that contained repeated variations and combinations of the words "StarPhoenix" and "Saskatoon StarPhoenix". He also maintained a separate corporate website where he advertised for sale the "thestarphoenix.com" and "starphoenix.com" domain names.

The plaintiff attempted, through phone calls and letters, to persuade the defendant to cease his activities. After failing to obtain a satisfactory response, the plaintiff applied and was granted an interlocutory injunction.

The Court found that the plaintiff had established all three of the necessary components for passing off (reputation, a misrepresentation and damage), and issued an injunction restraining the defendant from using variations of the plaintiff's domain name, or directing public attention to his websites in such a way as to cause the public to think the defendant's website was, in fact, the plaintiff's. The defendant was also ordered to transfer registration of the three domain names to the plaintiff.

The plaintiff also sought punitive damages. The Court did not award these because it believed that there was very little precedent to guide would-be entrepreneurs of domain names before this and other recent decisions. However, it stated that punitive damages might be appropriate in the future if, after further decisions of this type, the defendant or others persisted in such activities.

However, the Court did disapprove of the defendant's unwillingness to investigate his legal position after being warned by the plaintiff that his activities were unlawful. It granted the plaintiff's request for "enhanced costs", finding that the defendant should be made aware that he could not, with impunity, cause other people to incur legal expenses to shut down his unlawful activity, as opposed to voluntarily ceasing such activity.

8.4 Dispute resolution

In cases where:

- A party considers it is entitled to a particular domain name; or

- A rights-holder considers the use of a domain name may lead to a breach of its rights,

it may be possible to prevent another party from using the subject domain name. It may also be possible to obtain an injunction requiring the domain name to be deregistered, or assigned to the entitled party.

The way in which the dispute is resolved will usually depend on the type of TLD at issue:

- Disputes arising in respect of most TLDs are administered under the ICANN Uniform Dispute Resolution Policy ("UDRP").

- Until recently, disputes in the .nz ccTLD domain space had to be resolved using more conventional forms of dispute resolution such as arbitration, mediation, and litigation. However, on 1 June 2006, the Office of the DNC, on behalf of ISOCNZ, issued its own Dispute Resolution Service Policy ("DRSP").

8.4.1 Uniform dispute resolution policy

Disputes arising in relation to the TLDs (listed at 8.2.2(1)) are administered under the ICANN Uniform Dispute Resolution Policy ("UDRP"). The UDRP is an international disputes body that was set up by ICANN to resolve disputes relating to TLDs.

The UDRP is a relatively cost-effective and quick way to resolve a dispute in the gTLD name space. In order to succeed under the UDRP the complainant must show that:

- The subject domain name is identical, or confusingly similar, to a registered trade mark or service mark in which the complainant has rights;

- The respondent has no rights or legitimate interest in respect of the domain name; and

- The domain name is both registered and actually used in bad faith.

(1)   *UDRP not available for disputes involving New Zealand ccTLDs*

A number of administrators of ccTLDs have adopted the UDRP on their own accord. ISOCNZ has not adopted the UDRP with regard to disputes over .nz ccTLDs, having instead created its own policy, the DRSP, which is very similar to the UK system administered by Nominet (UK).

(2)   *Other forms of dispute resolution not precluded*

The UDRP is a form of alternative dispute resolution ("ADR"). Complainants are not compelled to use the UDRP, and its existence does not preclude the complainant from initiating conventional legal proceedings and/or other forms of ADR.

(3)   *Complainants favoured*

The UDRP has been well received since its introduction in December 1999. Over 9,000 proceedings have been initiated under the policy, with more than 7,000 of them being resolved by way of a decision.

Since its inception there has been concern that the policy is flawed. Many believe that large companies could unjustifiably use the system to prevent small competitors from using certain domain names. In addition, UDRP panellists come from different countries with different legal systems, and this can lead to inconsistency. However, a recent study by the Max Plancke Institute for Foreign and International Patent, Copyright and Competition Law in Munich has concluded that, despite the odd inconsistent decision, the system is generally fair and free of major flaws.

The study found that in about three quarters of cases the decision resulted in the transfer of the domain name to the complainant. However, it should be noted that the complainant is required to pay a substantial fee to submit a complaint, and will usually only do so if it is reasonably certain of success.

A further study conducted by Dr Milton Mueller, a professor at the Syracuse University School of Information Studies, confirms this figure and also notes that in 50 percent of those cases the complainant prevailed because the respondent failed to reply to the complaint. Dr Mueller comments that, based on present rates, a complainant has a 50 percent chance of securing a domain name for no more than the initial outlay of lodging the complaint.

Both studies suggest clarification is required with respect to the following issues:

- The issue of "confusing similarity". At times the panel has held that there is confusing similarity between a domain name and a trade mark even when the domain name has clearly distanced itself from the trade mark;

- The issue of free speech. Some panels have found the use of a trade mark to be legitimate if the website contains critical comments on the product concerned, while others have held that the right of free speech on the internet should not extend to using someone else's trade mark;

- The use of precedents. Although the UDRP does not operate a formal precedent system, and previous cases are not binding, the top 20 precedent cases relied on by panellists all resulted in a win for the complainant, and in all but four the respondent defaulted; and

- The burden of proof. It is recommended that an investigation be carried out into the establishment of an appeals system. Currently, appeals are taken to the Courts.

(4)   *Delay may prejudice complainant*

In a 2002 decision before the World Intellectual Property Organisation ("WIPO") arbitration panel under the UDRP, Nike Inc was unsuccessful in trying to prevent another company, Circle Group Internet, from using the justdoit.net domain name, in part because it had stood by and knowingly allowed the domain name to be used without taking any action.

Nike was the registered proprietor of the JUST DO IT trade mark in the US, Canada, Australia, and the European Union, and argued that Circle's use of the domain name could be confused with its own domain names justdoit.com and justdoit.org. Nike argued that Circle must have been aware of its ownership of the trade mark when Circle registered the domain name in 1992.

Although the panel was troubled by Circle's argument that "using another's trademark as an automatic redirect to an unrelated website ... establishes legitimate interest", it found against Nike on the basis that it hadn't proven to the panel's satisfaction that Circle had registered the domain name in bad faith.

One of the factors affecting the panel's decision was that Nike had first become aware of Circle's registration of the domain name in 1997, but had taken no action. The panel noted that "proving bad faith registration has been made more difficult with the passage of time [for which Nike] has itself to blame".

(5) *Complainant must have rights in disputed domain name*

The importance of a complainant being able to demonstrate rights in the disputed domain name is highlighted in a 2002 case in which the New Zealand Government was unsuccessful in its claim to ownership of the newzealand.com domain name, and was instead found guilty of reverse domain name hijacking.

The case, heard by the WIPO Panel, was brought against US company Virtual Countries Inc. Virtual Countries had registered the domain name in 1996 and since that time had used it to like to an information website containing subject matter on New Zealand. It was also the proprietor of a US trade mark registration for NEW ZEALAND.COM.

The New Zealand Government claimed that it had acquired trade mark rights in NEW ZEALAND (it had filed five trade mark applications for NEW ZEALAND in 2001) and that the mark referred exclusively to the New Zealand Government. As a result, the New Zealand Government claimed that Virtual Countries had no rights or legitimate interest in respect of the domain name, and that the domain name had been registered, and was being used, in bad faith.

Virtual Countries denied these claims, and put into evidence the response of the New Zealand Government to a WIPO questionnaire, whereby the New Zealand Government had previously agreed that protection of country names was beyond the scope of WIPO policy, and should not extend to cover country names that are not registered trade marks.

The presiding panel concluded that the New Zealand Government had failed to provide sufficient evidence to show that it had acquired trade mark rights to NEW ZEALAND. It said that while a trade or service mark is able to indicate a precise trade origin or specific trader or the source of goods/services, indications of geographical origin cannot serve that purpose. The panel provided the example whereby a wine label that reads "New Zealand Wine" obviously indicates that the wine derives from New Zealand, but it does not specify from which of the many wine producers within New Zealand it derives.

After concluding that the New Zealand Government had failed in its claim, the panel also ruled that, because of its previous statement on the issue, the New Zealand Government had been aware that its claim against Virtual Companies was baseless. As a result, the New Zealand Government was found guilty of reverse hijacking the domain name, and abuse of the UDRP policy by putting Virtual Countries to unnecessary expense.

The New Zealand Government has since purchased the domain name from Virtual Countries for US$500,000.

(6) *More UDRP information*

For more information on the UDRP, visit ICANN's website at www.icann.org/udrp.

8.4.2 New Zealand's Dispute Resolution Service Policy

On 1 June 2006, the Office of the DNC issued its Dispute Resolution Service Policy ("DRSP"). The DRSP provides an alternative to other forms of dispute resolution. All *.nz* registrants agree to be bound by the DRSP when they register or renew a *.nz* domain name.

The DRSP was developed with the assistance of Nominet UK (www.nominet.org.uk). Nominet UK is the internet registry for *.uk* domain names and runs its own dispute resolution service.

The DRSP is not a modified version of the UDRP. Under the DRSP there is no requirement that the complainant show unfair registration and use. Furthermore, the complainant is not required to prove that the registrant is without rights or legitimate interest to the domain name.

The DRSP applies to a respondent when a complainant asserts to the DNC that:

- The complainant has rights in respect of a name or mark which is identical or similar to the domain name; and

- The domain name, in the hands of the respondent, is an unfair registration.

The DRSP has been reasonably successful since it came in to force in June 2006. As at 31 August 2007, 114 complaints had been received and of those complaints:

- 75 were valid; and

- 39 were deemed invalid (eg, involved non *.nz* domain names or no signed copy of the complaint was received)

Of the 75 valid complaints:

- 19 proceeded to an Expert determination, resulting in:

  - 14 orders that the domain name registration be transferred;

  - 1 order that the domain name registration be cancelled; and

  - 4 proceedings being dismissed.

- 31 complaints were resolved between the parties either at or prior to mediation;

- 17 complaints were withdrawn; and

- The remaining 8 complaints were continuing through the process.

(1) *Definition of rights*

The DRSP defines "rights" as including, but not being limited to, rights enforceable under New Zealand law. These rights can include:

- New Zealand registered trade marks;

- Foreign registered trade marks;

- Unregistered trade marks;

- Names of celebrities, sporting personalities etc; and

- Some geographical names.

A complainant will not be able to rely on rights in a name or term which is wholly descriptive of the complainant's business.

(2) Unfair registration

The DRSP defines "unfair registration" as a domain name which either:

- Was registered or otherwise acquired in a manner which, at the time when the registration or acquisition took place, took unfair advantage of or was unfairly detrimental to the complainant's rights; or

- Has been, or is likely to be, used in a manner which took unfair advantage of or was unfairly detrimental to the complainant's rights.

Unlike the UDRP, there is no requirement that the complainant show that the domain name was registered in "bad faith". In addition, the DRSP provides a non-exhaustive list of factors which may indicate that the domain name is an unfair registration. There will also be a presumption of unfair registration if the respondent is found to have made more than three unfair registrations in the 2 years before the complaint is filed.

The concepts of unfair advantage/detriment come from the Trade Marks Act 2002 and are discussed in more detail in the trade marks chapter of this text (chapter 7). They call for an evaluation of the domain name and the use made of it as a whole — and are not the same as passing off.

(3) Procedure and remedy

A complaint under the DRSP will proceed along the following lines:

- The complainant initiates the complaint by paying a fee and filing a submission setting out the nature of the complaint and supporting evidence. Informal evidence will be accepted, as will certain without prejudice correspondence (such as an offer to sell the domain name to the complainant);

- The respondent files a submission in reply;

- The matter will then be set down for an informal mediation;

- If the mediation does not result in a resolution an Expert is appointed from a panel to assess the complaint/response and issue a decision. All decisions are published on the DNC website; and

- Either party has the right to appeal the decision of the Expert to a panel of three Experts.

Experts have the power to cancel, transfer, suspend, or otherwise amend a domain name, but not to award costs.

In a recent article (Clive Trotman, "Disputed domain names — a moving target", Issue 73 (14/9/07) NZ Lawyer 14), Expert Clive Trotman gave the following advice for lodging a successful complaint:

- Set out clearly what your registered trade mark or common law rights are, and why the domain name is confusingly similar. If possible find a close precedent in which transfer or cancellation of the domain name was ordered;

- State clearly that you have not licensed the respondent to use the mark and that reasonable enquiries have not disclosed a legitimate interest in the word the subject of the respondent's domain name. This is important as it shifts the onus to the respondent (and many respondents do not respond);

- Choose the example of bad faith or unfair registration closest to your circumstances. One ground established well is better than a "scattergun" approach. However do give the others a paragraph in case the Expert needs to rely on them;

- Supporting documents should include a copy of the certificate of registration of the trade mark (if appropriate), or proof of use over time. You should also supply a screen shot of the offending web site highlighting aspects of bad faith (such as a copied logo, links to competitors or an offer to sell the domain name); and

- Above all, match the sequence of the complaint to the flow of the decision (ie, write the Expert's judgment for him or her).

(4)   *Decisions of the .nz dispute resolution service*

- In *InterCityGroup (NZ) Ltd v Traction Group Ltd* (DRS Decision No 101, 13/9/06, Hon Sir Ian Barker QC), the complainant challenged the respondent's rights to the disputed domain name www.intercity.co.nz on the basis of the complainant's trade mark rights in the word INTERCITY. However at the time of challenge the respondent was not technically in existence, having been struck off the Companies Register in December 2002. Nonetheless, the Expert found that disputes under the Dispute Resolution Service Policy ("DRSP") are proceedings in rem and considered that he was able to decide the dispute. The complainant satisfied the Expert that it had rights in respect of a name or mark identical or similar to the domain name. The Expert also found that the respondent had held the domain name passively for a number of years and was unable to demonstrate an apparent step to develop a website. The disputed domain name was found to be an unfair registration and the Expert ordered the domain to be transferred to the complainant.

- In *BOP Memorials v Jones & Co Funeral Services* (DRS Decision No 108, 8/9/06, Warwick Smith), the Expert considered the differences between descriptive trade names and fancy or "made-up" names. While the Expert considered the trade name "BOP Memorial Services" to be descriptive, the complainant was able to produce "(just) sufficient evidence to show that the name had become distinctive of the complainant's particular services". The domain name www.bopmemorials.co.nz was deemed to be an unfair registration in the hands of the respondent. The Expert ordered the domain to be transferred to the complainant.

- In *Harcourts Group Ltd v Sergei* (DRS Decision No 109, 18/8/06, Andrew Brown QC), the complainant was unable to establish any rights in the HARCOURTS name due to a licence agreement between the complainant and Harcourts International Ltd. The Expert dismissed the complaint.

- In *Barfoot & Thompson v Domain Admin* (DRS Decision No 113, 8/9/06, Clive Elliott), the respondent had registered the domain www.wwwbarfoot.co.nz. The Expert found that the complainant had rights in respect of the trade mark/name Barfoot & Thompson/Barfoot(s) and that the domain name was similar. The Expert considered the dispute to be a relatively clear case of "typosquatting" and found the respondent's conduct to be unfair and detrimental to the complainant's rights. The Expert ordered the domain to be transferred from the respondent to the complainant.

- In *Seek Ltd v Domain Admin* (DRS Decision No 137, 10/11/06, Hon Barry Paterson QC), the respondent had registered the domain name www.wwwseek.co.nz. The Expert found that the complainant had trade mark rights in respect of SEEK and seek.co.nz and that the domain name was similar. The respondent's use of www.wwwseek.co.nz in relation to an online employment and job related classified advertising service, and its featuring the complainant's domain name as a sponsored link, was an unfair registration on two grounds. First, the respondent was using the domain name in a way likely to confuse, mislead and deceive. The Export took particular note of the use of the additional "www" prefix to the domain name (a common typosquatting technique designed to capture people who mistakenly omit the full stop between the www and the domain name). Secondly, the respondent had engaged in a pattern of registrations in relation to well known names or trade marks to which it had no apparent rights (www.wwwbnz.co.nz, www.wwwbarfoots.co.nz, and www.wwwharcourts.co.nz). There was sufficient evidence before the Expert to make these findings without drawing any inference from the failure to file a response. This was, however, the second time the respondent had failed to answer a complaint and as a result the Expert would have been entitled to have drawn an adverse inference in that regard (see *Barfoot & Thompson v Domain Admin* (above)). The Expert ordered the domain name be transferred from the respondent to the complainant.

- In *Pacific Bereavement Solutions (NZ) Ltd v Cooper* (DRS Decision No 145, 5/12/06, Dr Clive Trotman), the administrative contact for the respondent was a former employee of the complainant. He registered the domain name www.geeandhickton.co.nz (whilst an employee of the complainant) without advising the complainant that he had done so. At the time of the complaint the domain name was being hosted by a service which offered free parking of domain names. The respondent filed no response and offered no explanation for his actions.

  The Expert found that the complainant's GEE & HICKTON mark was similar (noting it was technically identical — as the ampersand symbol could not be used in a domain name) and that the complainant had rights to the mark (in the form of a registered trade mark). The Expert considered that the respondent had paid money to register a unique and trade marked name as a domain name for which he had no legitimate use and had parked it out of use, at least for the time being. On that basis he concluded this was done with some ultimate objective in mind, which need not be monetary. As the ultimate effect of the registration was that the complainant was blocked from registering the domain name the Expert considered the registration was unfair. The Expert ordered the domain name be transferred to the complainant.

- In *Skype Technologies SA v Bellamy Price Mansfield Ltd* (DRS Decision No 150, 19/3/07, Andrew Brown QC), the domain names www.skypeshop.co.nz and www.skypestore.co.nz were found to be similar to the complainant's registered trade mark SKYPE. The complainant produced evidence that the respondent had offered to sell the domain name www.skypeshop.co.nz to the complainant for US$50,000 and had threatened the complainant with negative publicity if it did not purchase the domain name. The Expert considered this to be evidence that the respondent had

507

registered the domain name primarily for the purpose of on-selling it, blocking registration by the complainant or otherwise disrupting the complainant's business. There was also evidence that the respondent was using both domain names in a way which was likely to confuse, mislead or deceive people into assuming an association between the two businesses, such as through a licence agreement. As a result he found both domain names were unfair registrations and ordered both domain names be transferred from the respondent to the complainant.

- In *National Manager, Teach NZ, Ministry of Education v Powell* (DRS Decision No 156, 13/3/07, Mr Warwick Smith), the complainant had used and promoted the mark TeachNZ in a logo format since 1997, and had also used the domain name (www.teachnz.govt.nz). It did not, however, have a registered trade mark for TeachNZ. A third party had obtained a trade mark registration in respect of a TeachNZ device mark (which it was noted may be the subject of an application for a declaration of invalidity by the complainant in the future). Notwithstanding the third party's registration the Expert accepted the complainant had rights to the domain name, and that the domain name was similar to the complainant's TeachNZ logo.

The Expert found that the domain name (teachnz.co.nz) was an unfair registration, as it took unfair advantage of, and was unfairly detrimental to, the complainant's rights. In relation to the former, the respondent had used the domain name for commercial gain, as it was directed to another website which paid the respondent for the internet traffic he directed to it. In relation to the latter, the domain linked indirectly to "adult" websites, which the Expert considered to be at the very least embarrassing to the complainant and consequently constituted use which was unfairly detrimental to the complainant's rights.

The Expert ordered the domain name to be cancelled instead of transferring it to the complainant. This was because there was insufficient evidence to demonstrate the complainant had a greater right to the domain name than the third party who owned the trade mark registration.

- In *Financial Services v Insurance Agent* (DRS Decision No 168, 25/3/07, Clive Elliott), a dispute arose between the complainant and the respondent regarding ownership and use of the trading name Atlas Financial Services. As a result of the dispute the two ceased their business relationship. However, there remained a dispute over the use of the domain name www.atlasins.co.nz. The complainant originally registered the domain name in 1998 and had paid the renewal and hosting service fees until the domain name was transferred to the respondent in December 2006. The Expert found that the respondent had, as a means of resolving the dispute in his favour, procured transfer of the domain name into his name without the complainant's authority or consent, and as a result, it constituted an unfair registration. The Expert ordered the domain name be transferred from the respondent to the complainant.

- In *NZ Aerial Mapping Ltd v Terralink International Ltd* (DRS Decision No 172, 10/4/07, Hon Sir Ian Barker QC), the complainant had sought to put matters discussed in mediation before the Expert by seeking leave to file a non-standard submission. The Expert declined leave and commented:

"The Parties should 'get it right first time' and not file a half-strength application against the possibility of mediation failing and then follow up with a full-strength application."

The domain names in issue were www.nzaerialmapping.co.nz and www.aerialmapping.co.nz. It was accepted that the name NZ Aerial Mapping had been used by the complainant or its predecessor since 1936. By virtue of that use the complainant had rights to a domain which was similar to www.nzaerialmapping.co.nz and accordingly it was an unfair registration in the hands of the respondent. The respondent argued that confusion was unlikely as the domain name linked to its home page which in no way created an impression that it was connected with the complainant. Further it argued those seeking aerial mapping services were likely to be discerning in selecting the company providing the services. The Expert rejected this argument and commented "the fact of a discerning market is no excuse for using the trading name of a competitor as a domain name". However, the Expert was not satisfied that the complainant had rights in respect of www.aerialmapping.co.nz as this was a generic name and "could apply to any player in this specialised field". The Expert ordered the domain name www.nzaerialmapping.co.nz be transferred from the respondent to the complainant, but that www.aerialmapping.co.nz remain with the respondent.

- In *Mountain Buggy Trademarks Ltd v Gower* (DRS Decision No 186, 21/4/07, Dr Clive Trotman), the complainant challenged the respondent's right to the domain name www.mountainbuggy.co.nz and alleged it was an infringement of its registered trade mark MOUNTAIN BUGGY. The respondent (a director of Phil and Ted's Most Excellent Buggy Co Ltd) argued that the domain name and the complainant's trade mark were generic and that, as the domain name had been parked since registration in September 1999, it was not in use. It was accepted that the complainant had rights in the name and that it was similar to the disputed domain name. However the Expert found that the domain name was not "in use" as mere parking did not meet the criteria of use under the policy. Further given the descriptive nature of the domain name, and the respondent's bona fide reasons for registering the domain name, the complainant had not established that it was an unfair registration. The Expert noted there was a distinction "between a classic cyber squatter and the present respondent, who has registered a domain name containing two descriptive words, one of which is prominent in his genuine business name." However he also noted the respondent's apparent lack of purpose in registering the domain name but that the issue of how "he might make legitimate use of the domain name without infringing the complainant's trade mark need not be second-guessed." The complaint was dismissed.

- In *Kiwispy Ltd v Richard Gustin t/a Everlast* (DRS Decision No 188, 11/4/07, Hon Barry Paterson QC), the domain name www.kiwispy.co.nz was registered by the respondent under a trading name. This took place during his employment with Ozspy Pty Ltd (of which the complainant was a subsidiary) on the instructions of Ozspy's manager. There was evidence that Ozspy had paid for the registration (by a company credit card). The registration of the domain name in the respondent's name came to light after the termination of the respondent's employment for misconduct. The Expert found that this was an unfair registration, and that by virtue of either an equitable assignment of a chose in action from Ozspy to the complainant, or rights under the Contracts (Privity) Act 1982, the complainant was able to seek equitable relief against the respondent. The Expert ordered the domain name be transferred from the respondent to the complainant.

- In *Monarch Natural Health v DLE Investments* (DRS Decision No 198, 13/6/07, Mr Terence Stapleton), the complainant successfully challenged the respondent's rights to the domain name monarchnaturalhealth.co.nz. The respondent owned a business called Essential Remedies which employed the complainant until 28 February 2007 when she tendered her resignation to enable her to spend more time on setting up her new company. In tendering her resignation, the complainant requested the respondent allow her to continue using a consultation room at Essential Remedies' premises for her private practice as a natural health practitioner. A few days after tendering her resignation, the complainant received a call from the respondent telling her she was not required to work out her notice and asking her to collect her practitioner equipment from Essential Remedies' premises. The complainant further alleged that she was owed money by the respondent which debt had been registered with BayCorp and was now disputed by the respondent. On 23 April the complainant went to register a domain name for a website for her new business and found that name had been registered by the respondent on 18 April 2007. The complainant contended that the respondent had registered the domain name once privy to information about the complainant's proposed new business. The Expert agreed and ordered the domain name transferred to the complainant.

- In *TradeFree Ltd v AdNet.co.nz Ltd* (DRS Decision No 202, 31/7/07, Mr Andrew Brown QC), the complainant unsuccessfully challenged the respondent's rights to the domain name tradefree.co.nz. The complainant, TradeFree Ltd, was incorporated on 24 January 2007 to carry on the business of online advertising and auctions that are free to use. Having commenced business, the complainant discovered the respondent had already registered the tradefree.co.nz domain name. The complainant registered the .net.nz domain name and approached the respondent with an offer to purchase tradefree.co.nz. There was some negotiation between the parties but they were ultimately unable to agree on a price and negotiations broke down. The complainant asserted rights in the domain name dating back to 2005 on the basis that it "copyrighted" the TRADE FREE name in New Zealand on 10 February 2005. Thus, the sole issue was whether the complainant had any rights in the domain name sufficient to sustain its complaint. The 10 February 2005 date relied upon by the complainant as giving rise to its alleged rights in the TRADE FREE name related to an email of that date to an independent web developer enquiring as to the best way to go about promoting TRADE FREE. The Expert found that that email did not give rise to copyright or other rights in the TRADE FREE name, New Zealand and English copyright law being clear that copyright is not created in a single word or a combination of two words: *Exxon Corp v Exxon Insurance Consultants International* [1982] RPC 69. Rather, the email was simply evidence of an intention to use the TRADE FREE name at some point in the future. As that intention was never made public in such a way as to create rights in the TRADE FREE name prior to the respondent's registration of the .co.nz domain name, the complaint was dismissed.

- In *Thai Airways International Public Co Ltd v E-Promote* (DRS Decision No 203, 9/7/07, Mr Warwick Smith), the complainant successfully challenged the respondent's right to the domain name thaiairways.co.nz. Despite the fact that the complainant had not produced evidence of any registered trade mark in New Zealand, the Expert was satisfied on the basis of its use on the internet of THAI AIRWAYS, and a distinctive logo coupled with the word THAI, that it had established a reputation in those trade names in New Zealand. The Expert noted decisions of the appeal panels in the UK which held that the requirement under the policy to demonstrate "rights" is not a particularly high threshold test: *Seiko UK Ltd v Designer Time/Wanderweb* (Nominet Case No DRS00248). The Expert further found that the complainant's rights were identical or similar to the disputed domain name, and that the domain name was an unfair registration as the respondent's website was primarily travel-related and its use of the domain name to derive revenue on a pay-per-click basis demonstrated a lack of bona fides. Thus, in the absence of a response from the respondent, the Expert was prepared to draw an inference that the respondent registered the domain name with the intention of riding on the back of Thai Airways' goodwill in its rights, and attracting to its own website visitors who would be expecting to find Thai's official New Zealand website. This inference was supported by evidence from the complainant that that kind of confusion had in fact occurred.

- In *Telecom IP Ltd v E-Promote* (DRS Decision No 206, 16/7/07, Dr Clive Trotman), the Expert ordered the disputed domain names tellecom.co.nz and wwwferrit.co.nz to be transferred to the complainant in light of its rights in the trade marks and domain names TELECOM and FERRIT. The facts of the decision, and the findings of the Expert, are very similar to those in *YPG IP Ltd v E-Promote* (see below) as the same respondent was involved.

- In *YPG IP Ltd v E-Promote* (DRS Decision No 208, 23/7/07, Hon Sir Ian Barker QC), the complainant successfully challenged the respondent's rights to the domain names yelllowpages.co.nz, witepages.co.nz and whitpages.co.nz. The complainant was the assignee of the intellectual property rights of Yellow Pages Group Ltd which, until 30 April 2007, was a subsidiary of Telecom Corp of NZ Ltd and was authorised to use various New Zealand registered trade marks including YELLOW PAGES and WHITE PAGES. The complainant owned the domain names yellowpages.co.nz, yellowpages.net.nz, and whitepages.co.nz. It argued that the respondent's websites, accessed through the disputed domain names, were likely to cause confusion by directing users to sponsored websites under a number of business categories. The respondent was closely related to Domain Admin, which had been found to have made unfair registrations in *Barfoot & Thompson v Domain Admin* (DRS Decision No 113, 8/9/06, Clive Elliott) (barfoot.co.nz) and *Seek Ltd v Domain Admin* (DRS Decision No 137, 10/11/06, Hon Barry Paterson QC) (seek.co.nz). The respondent did not file a response to the complaint. After considering the evidence, the Expert found that the complainant was the legitimate successor to the original registrations for the trade marks WHITE PAGES and YELLOW PAGES and therefore had rights under the policy in respect of those registered trade marks and the related domain names. The Expert found that the complainant's domain names were classic examples of typo-squatting and were registered with slight misspellings of the complainant's trade marks and domain names in the hope that some people might be directed to the respondent's sites through mis-typing. Thus, the Expert deemed the registrations to be "unfair registrations" and ordered them transferred to the respondent.

(5) *More DRSP information*

For more information on the DRSP, visit the Office of the DNC's website at www.dnc.org.nz.

8.5 Passing off, the Fair Trading Act 1986, and domain names

8.5.1 Introduction

The operation of the DRSP is not intended to prevent either the complainant or the respondent from submitting the dispute to a New Zealand Court or decision making body of competent jurisdiction or an arbitral tribunal of competent jurisdiction. Businesses who believe that their intellectual property has been misappropriated by another party registering an identical, or confusingly similar, domain name may still rely on passing off and/or the Fair Trading Act 1986.

To prove passing off a plaintiff must establish:

- That he or she has a reputation in the word or words the subject of the domain name (or a similar word or words);

- That the defendant's registration or use of the domain name (and by implication the word or words in which the plaintiff has reputation) amounts to a misrepresentation. Usually the misrepresentation will be that the website associated with the domain name registered by the defendant is in some way connected with the plaintiff; and

- That the plaintiff is suffering, or is likely to suffer, damage as a consequence of the defendant's registration or use of the domain name.

The requirements in order to establish a breach of the Fair Trading Act 1986 are substantially the same although:

- The plaintiff may need to prove reputation amongst a substantial section of the relevant purchasing public; and

- It is not necessary to prove damage.

8.5.2 Misrepresentation essential

Assuming the requisite reputation can be proved, the important question is whether registration or use of the domain name constitutes a misrepresentation. Often this will come down to two essential inquiries:

- How the registration or use of the domain name is likely to be perceived by the public at large; and

- The legitimacy (or bona fides) of the defendant's registration or use.

8.5.3 Domain name more than just an address

Even though a domain name is technically only the electronic equivalent of a street address, it can also act as an indicator of origin. Selecting some other person's name or trade mark as one's web address will often cause consumers to believe:

- That they will locate that other person's website at the address; or

- That the website located at the address is in some way associated with the party with whom they associate the name or trade mark.

In *Panavision International LP v Toeppen* 141 F 3d 1316 (9th Cir, 1998), the defendant argued before the US Court of Appeal that its use of the plaintiff's registered trade mark "Panavision" as part of its domain name could not amount to unfair competition, because it was simply an address directing internet users to a site, that, once viewed, could be readily distinguished from the plaintiff's business. The US Court of Appeal rejected that argument stating, at p 1327, that:

> "A significant purpose of a domain name is to identify the entity that owns the web site. ...
>
> "Using a company's name or trademark as a domain name is also the easiest way to locate that company's web site. ...
>
> "Moreover, potential customers of Panavision will be discouraged if they cannot find its web page from typing in 'Panavision.com' ".

8.5.4 Use of an unrelated domain name a misrepresentation

In *Marks & Spencer Plc v One In A Million Ltd* [1998] FSR 265 (Ch D), the defendant had registered a large number of domain names that included a number of trade marks and names of well known commercial entities. The domain names were registered without the consent of the respective owners who took action against the defendant. At first instance, the Court considered registration of those confusingly similar domain names to be a misrepresentation, commenting, at p 271, that:

> "Any person who deliberately registers a domain name on account of its similarity to the name, brand name or trade mark of an unconnected commercial organisation must expect to find himself on the receiving end of an injunction to restrain the threat of passing off, and the injunction will be in terms which will make the name commercially useless to the dealer."

The UK Court of Appeal upheld this decision in *British Telecommunications Plc v One In A Million Ltd* (1998) 42 IPR 289; [1999] FSR 1 (CA). It has also been applied in New Zealand in a number of decisions discussed below.

8.5.5 Use of the domain name not essential

In *British Telecommunications Plc v One In A Million Ltd* (1998) 42 IPR 289; [1999] FSR 1 (CA), the UK Court of Appeal held that merely registering a domain name makes a representation to persons who consult the Register that the registrant is connected or associated with the name registered, and thus the owner of the goodwill in the name, and this amounts to passing off.

Similarly, in *Oggi Advertising Ltd v McKenzie* [1999] 1 NZLR 631, a case involving misappropriation of the www.oggi.co.nz domain name, it was not proved that the defendant had sold any goods or services via a website operated under the domain name. Indeed, after a certain date the site displayed only the contact details of the technical person responsible for the site. It appeared that the defendant had registered the domain name with the intent of selling it to the plaintiff, rather than trading on the plaintiff's reputation.

Nevertheless, after deciding that the plaintiff had the requisite reputation in the "Oggi" name, and relying on the decision in *British Telecommunications Plc v One In A Million Ltd* (1998) 42 IPR 289; [1999] FSR 1 (CA), Baragwanath J held that a misrepresentation had been made in the course of trade, and that it was likely to cause damage to the business of the plaintiff. He ordered the defendant to assign the domain name to the plaintiff (despite the fact that the matter was an interlocutory application for an interim injunction).

8.5.6 Misappropriated domain name as an "instrument of fraud"

In *British Telecommunications Plc v One In A Million Ltd* (1998) 42 IPR 289; [1999] FSR 1 (CA), the UK Court of Appeal held that if use of a domain name would result in passing off, the domain name is "an instrument of fraud". Furthermore, the Court would intervene by way of injunction in passing off cases, if by registration of a domain name:

- Passing off was established or threatened;

- The defendant was a joint tortfeasor with another in passing off (either actual or threatened); or

- The defendant equipped himself, or intended to equip another, with an instrument of fraud.

In *Qantas Airways Ltd v The Domain Name Co Ltd* 9/12/99, Anderson J, HC Auckland CP26-SD99, the defendant registered the domain name www.qantas.co.nz, effectively blocking the plaintiff from registering the same domain name. The defendant then offered to sell the domain name to the plaintiff, initially for a sum of $6,000. The evidence suggested that the defendant had taken similar steps in relation to a number of other well known trade marks in New Zealand.

The plaintiff relied on causes of action in passing off and for breach of s 9 Fair Trading Act 1986.

Anderson J followed the reasoning in *British Telecommunications*. He agreed that the registration of the domain name, and the fact that the registrant's details were recorded on the Domainz website, had the effect of representing a proprietary interest in that domain name to the public. His Honour went on to say, at p 3:

> "I do not doubt that the deliberate blocking of the lawful exploitation of goodwill by Qantas through registration if effectuated for that purpose or with that consequence is a fraudulent appropriation of part of the goodwill attaching to the

plaintiff's name … Such registration is, to use a term discussed in the *One In A Million* case, an instrument of fraud."

Anderson J found that the defendant was guilty of both passing off and of engaging in conduct, in trade, that was misleading or deceptive, or was likely to mislead or deceive, in breach of s 9 Fair Trading Act 1986. However, he was not willing to go so far as to grant the order sought by the plaintiff directing the defendant to assign ownership of the domain name to the plaintiff. His Honour thought it more appropriate for the defendant to deregister the domain name, and ordered accordingly.

In *NZ Post Ltd v Leng* [1999] 3 NZLR 219; (1998) 45 IPR 263, Mr Leng registered the domain name "nzpost.com". New Zealand Post had already registered the "nzpost.co.nz" domain name. Of prime concern to New Zealand Post was the material that could be viewed on the Leng site, some subsidiary pages of which were x-rated, and some of which sold phone cards. Leng had the ability to control the site from New Zealand. As New Zealand Post also sold phone cards, it argued that there was a considerable commercial overlap between the two sites, and took action against Leng.

As New Zealand Post had no registered trade mark at the time proceedings were commenced, the action was based on its reputation, with claims in respect of passing off and misleading and deceptive conduct under the Fair Trading Act 1986. An interim injunction was sought. The Court found that it was likely the two sites would be confused, and that there was a prima facie case under s 9 Fair Trading Act 1986 and granted an injunction accordingly.

In *Containerlift Services Ltd v Maxwell Rotors Ltd* (2003) 10 TCLR 807, the plaintiff, which had reputation in the UK and Europe in the name "Containerlift", successfully sought an injunction against a New Zealand based defendant for misrepresentations arising in those jurisdictions from the use of the domain name "containerlift.com". In deciding that the Court had jurisdiction, Salmon J relied upon the "double actionability" rule which forms part of traditional English common law in respect of torts committed overseas. There is a more detailed discussion of this aspect of the case at 8.10 ("Jurisdiction") later in this chapter.

8.6 Trade mark law and domain names

Can use of a domain name constitute trade mark infringement? The definition of "sign" under the Trade Marks Act 1953 and the Trade Marks Act 2002 is sufficiently broad to encompass domain names and their constituents. However, trade mark infringement requires:

- Use of the same sign on, or in relation to, the same goods or services (regardless of whether such use is likely to deceive or confuse);

- Use of the same sign in relation to similar goods/services if such use is likely to deceive or confuse; or

- Use of a similar sign in relation to the same or similar goods/services if such use is likely to deceive or confuse.

In addition, in all cases the sign must be used in a "trade mark sense".

8.6.1 Use in a "trade mark sense"

Use of a sign in a "trade mark sense" requires that the sign is used to distinguish the goods or services of one person from those of others. The immediate problem facing most litigants is that a domain name is essentially just an address that may be used to point internet users to a particular website. It is only when the domain name is actually associated with a site that trade mark infringement can be evaluated. Therefore:

- The mere registration of a domain name without use does not (technically) constitute trade mark infringement; and

- Using a domain name for a website that does not offer or promote goods or services is unlikely to be considered use of a sign "in a trade mark sense". Accordingly, it could be argued that there would be no trade mark infringement.

However, where the domain name is:

- The same as, or similar to, a registered trade mark; and

- Associated with a site that does promote or sell goods or services that are the same as, or similar to, those in relation to which that trade mark is registered,

the use of the domain name is likely to infringe the registered trade mark. In this situation, the domain name is being used as a mark (ie in a trade mark sense) to indicate the origin of the services provided, or the goods sold, on the website.

8.6.2 Class of goods/services important

The class of goods or services for which the mark has been registered is important, as are the specific goods or services nominated in that class.

For example, if the mark is registered in relation to "internet based advertising and retail services", use of the mark as a domain name will amount to trade mark infringement regardless of whether consumers are likely to be deceived or confused. That is because the same mark is being used in relation to the same services.

However, if the trade mark registration covers only the goods promoted on the site, then the registered proprietor may need to prove that use of the mark as a domain name is likely to deceive or confuse consumers. That is because it is arguable that the services in relation to which the mark has been used (retail and/or advertising of goods) are only similar to those for which the mark has been registered (the goods themselves).

In practice proprietors of valuable trade marks would be well advised to register them in relation to internet based services, so as to make proving infringement easier.

8.6.3 The DB case

In *DB Breweries Ltd v Domain Name Co Ltd* (2001) 52 IPR 280, the plaintiff issued proceedings in respect of the defendant's registration of the domain name www.db.co.nz. The plaintiff was a large New Zealand brewery with a substantial reputation in the "DB" trade mark. The plaintiff had registered the "DB" trade mark in New Zealand in relation to beer, and a range of related goods and services.

In an earlier decision the plaintiff successfully obtained an order in which the domain name was transferred to it on an undertaking it would transfer the domain name back to the defendant(s) in the event that its claim failed at full trial. A number of pre-trial proceedings followed with regard to the matter. The first and second defendants applied for an order striking out the claim against the second defendant. They also requested an order allowing the second defendant to deliver evidence in the trial by way of affidavit due to his residency in the UK. The plaintiff sought leave to issue interrogatories.

In considering the application to strike out the plaintiff's claim, the question arose as to whether the defendants were using the plaintiff's trade mark. Randerson J was satisfied that, although the mark had not actually been used by the defendants in relation to the goods and services covered by the plaintiff's registrations, the threat of such use in the future was sufficient to justify injunctive relief. However, he did recognise that, as the mark had not been used by the defendants in relation to the goods or services covered by the registrations, his interpretation "may be at the margins of the law of infringement of trade marks".

8.6.4 Other cases

In *Telecom Corp of NZ Ltd v Yellow Web Ltd* 14/4/99, Potter J, HC Auckland M316-SW99, the defendants maintained a website for "Yellow Web Pages" under the URLs www.yellowhomepages.co.nz and www.yellowweb.co.nz. The plaintiffs (who published the New Zealand Yellow Pages telephone directory) claimed that use by the defendants of these words, the URLs and/or the colour yellow for an internet directory constituted passing off, trade mark infringement and breaches of the Fair Trading Act 1986. In this respect the plaintiff had two registered trade marks, for "Yellow Pages" and for the colour yellow, in respect of business directories. An injunction issued.

In *NZ City Ltd v Baseline E-Com Ltd* 20/12/99, Heron J, HC Wellington CP300/99, passing off was alleged concerning a domain name for internet shopping malls. The respective sites were www.nzcity.co.nz and www.theCity.co.nz. Interim relief was granted.

In *YPG IP Ltd v Yellowbook.com.au Pty Ltd* 13/7/07, Allan J, HC Auckland CIV-2007-404-2839, the plaintiffs, which had rights in the YELLOW PAGES online directory, complained of the defendants' use of the domain names www.yellowbook.co.nz and www.yellowduck.co.nz in respect of a similar online directory. The plaintiffs alleged that the material accessible via those websites had been compiled in breach of their copyright rights, and that the use of the YELLOW BOOK trade mark on the website www.yellowbook.co.nz breached their YELLOW PAGES trade mark registrations, and sought injunctive relief. Allan J had no difficulty in holding, at para 103, that the defendants' use of the YELLOW BOOK trade mark on the website www.yellowbook.co.nz fell within the statutory definition of "use" under s 6 Trade Marks Act 2002 and was in relation to similar, if not identical, services. However, the decision is silent as to whether mere use of the domain name might have amounted to trade mark infringement. YPG had registered its mark in a number of classes and in relation to a broad range of services (including communication services, advertising and business services and information provided online from computer databases or from computer networks) so it is at least arguable that it would have.

8.7 Registration of domain names as trade marks

8.7.1 Domain names can be registered as trade marks

While it is possible to register a domain name as a trade mark, the Intellectual Property Office of New Zealand ("IPONZ") considers standard address code material such as *.com*, *.co.nz*, and *www.* is devoid of distinctive character and incapable of registration in its own right (IPONZ, "Information for Clients", No 6, 1999). As a result, the remainder of the domain name (or "identifier") must be distinctive for the domain name to be eligible for registration.

For example, the domain name www.zespri.com would be eligible for registration as a trade mark, as the identifier "Zespri" is distinctive in relation to fresh produce.

However, the domain name www.wine.com would not be eligible for registration in relation to a website that sold wines, as the identifier "wine" is directly descriptive of the products sold from the website.

8.7.2 Benefits not readily apparent

The benefits of registering a domain name as a trade mark are not readily apparent. The fact that the address code material is considered non-distinctive suggests that it is more important to protect the distinctive identifier as a trade mark. However, in situations where the domain name is consistently used as a trade mark, the registration of a complete domain name may provide better protection than registration of only the identifier.

8.8 Other intellectual property issues in e-commerce

8.8.1 Introduction

While domain name disputes have tended to be at the forefront of intellectual property-related internet issues, there are a number of other areas where intellectual property law has been brought into play.

For a business operating a website, the more visitors that are attracted to its site, and the more pages those visitors view, the better. Attracting and retaining visitors is important not only for promoting a business and generating direct sales, but also for generating brand awareness and secondary income streams (such as advertising revenue from the website). For those sites that rely on such secondary revenue streams, the number of visitors will often directly influence the sums that advertisers are willing to pay.

A website has the characteristics of a shop front window, a shop layout or the front cover and layout of a catalogue. Features of a website can be misappropriated by a competitor to pass off its website (and associated business) as that of the original. This is known as replicating the "look and feel" of a site.

In an attempt to attract visitors, some website owners and operators have employed practices that may be deemed objectionable. Being an electronic medium, a successful website, or elements of it, can be easily copied, or subtly varied and adapted, by an unscrupulous competitor who wants to trade on the success and reputation of the original. The name of the website and its address (ie the domain name) can also be made similar to the original. The result can be a rival website, with the look and feel of the original, which could easily deceive internet users as to the identity of the person or company they are dealing with.

The owner of the deceptive website can further perpetuate the deception by incorporating into the site keywords that will draw browsers using search engines to the site, or by linking or framing material from other websites so as to appear part of their own.

If customers are misled or deceived, a cause of action will lie under the Fair Trading Act 1986 or the tort of passing off.

These practices are discussed in more detail below.

8.8.2 Meta tags

Users of the internet may locate and access sites in a number of ways. Often they may already know the URL (uniform resource locator) of the site that they want to visit. However, where the URL is not known, the potential visitor may need to use a search engine.

Most search engines rank the sites disclosed by a search, with the highest ranked sites being the most relevant. There are a number of tricks that website designers and programmers can use to ensure that a site is ranked as high as possible in a search. Including keywords (known as "meta tags") behind the code of the website is a common method.

(1) *Meta tags defined*

Meta tags are keywords (usually relating to the subject content of the website) located in the programming language of a website, which are detected by internet search engines. Meta tags commonly include trade marks, business names and product descriptions. In certain circumstances, use of another person's trade mark or business name as a meta tag may amount to trade mark infringement, passing off and/or a breach of the Fair Trading Act 1986.

(2) *Infringing use*

Intellectual property rights in trade marks and business names can be infringed when they are incorporated into meta tags without the proprietor's consent. For instance, company A could include the trade marks of one of its competitors (company B) in the meta tags for its website. When an internet user looks for company B's products by reference to that company's trade marks, he or she may be directed to company A's website, and consequently to company A's rival products and services.

This conduct can be characterised as passing off, a breach of the Fair Trading Act 1986, and, arguably, if a registered trade mark is used as a meta tag, trade mark infringement.

Assuming company A has the requisite reputation in the mark used by company B as a meta tag, such use amounts to a misrepresentation, in the sense that the meta tag is likely to give consumers the impression that company B's site offers information on, or the ability to supply, certain products when in fact it does not. Naturally, damage will occur as custom is diverted from company A to company B and so passing off is also an available cause of action. In effect, this is the same as a shop advertising that it sells a certain brand of product when it does not, just to lure customers.

Where passing off is available as a cause of action, so is the Fair Trading Act 1986.

Whether use of a registered trade mark as a meta tag constitutes trade mark infringement turns on whether the mark is being used "in a trade mark sense" in relation to goods and/or services similar to those covered by the trade mark registration. However, as the reason for including the trade mark of another person as a meta tag can only be to attract browsers to the site, in almost all cases the mark will be deemed to have been used "in a trade mark sense". If the goods and/or services offered on the website are the same as, or similar to, the goods and/or services covered by the registration, then trade mark infringement is an available cause of action.

(3)   *Infringing use: examples*

In *Roadtech Computer Systems Ltd v Mandata (Management and Data Services) Ltd* [2000] ETMR 970 (Ch D), Mandata had been using two of Roadtech's registered marks as meta tags for a period of just over 2 months. Roadtech brought an action for summary judgment claiming royalties based on Mandata's unauthorised use of its property (the registered trade marks), the cost of corrective advertising, and damages for diversion of trade and loss of goodwill.

Finding that Mandata's actions were "a deliberate, albeit unsophisticated appropriation of the claimant's rights" Mandata was ordered to pay £15,000 as a royalty for unauthorised use of the marks.

The Court also indicated that, as a matter of principle, "a plaintiff is entitled to recover as damages a sum representing the costs of publishing advertisements to counter the effect of the infringement of its rights". However, as Roadtech had delayed too long in placing the corrective advertisements, no remedy was granted under this head.

In *Reed Executive Plc v Reed Business Information Ltd* [2003] RPC 207, the parties, despite sharing the same name "Reed", were unrelated. Reed Executive was a recruitment agency established in the 1960s. That company had registered the trade mark REED in relation to recruitment services, and maintained an online presence under the www.reed.co.uk domain name since the 1990s.

Reed Business Information Ltd ("RBI") was primarily a publishing company. In the mid 1990s it established the website www.totaljobs.com when its revenue from selling magazine advertising space began to fall in light of competition from the internet.

Along with words such as "jobs" and "recruitment" RBI included the name "Reed Business Information" in its meta tags. This meant that a search for "Reed jobs" would be likely to find RBI's website. RBI also arranged with a number of search engines for its advertising banner to appear when users typed in certain related terms such as "jobs" or "employment". RBI's arrangement with Yahoo! included the term "Reed" so that a search for "Reed jobs" would produce a banner advertisement for www.totaljobs.com.

At first instance, Reed Executive successfully sued RBI for trade mark infringement based on its use of the word "Reed" as part of its meta tags. The Court found that such use, and use of "Reed" as a keyword for the Yahoo! banner advertisements, constituted an invisible use of the registered mark. It was no defence that RBI's own name included the word "Reed", nor that there was no intention on the part of RBI to cause confusion, the Court noting, at p 249, that:

"the concept of use [in the course of trade] is wide enough to cover invisible use in metatags which is visible in the search results ... The short test, which must be applied with caution, is whether the sign tells the truth about the site."

On appeal (*Reed Executive Plc v Reed Business Information Ltd* [2004] RPC 767 (CA)), the UK Court of Appeal found that RBI's use did not amount to trade mark infringement, or passing off, based on a lack of confusion. The Court of Appeal held that this was a case of similar marks and services. Thus, in order to demonstrate infringement, Reed Executive would need to establish that the similarity of marks and services would result in a likelihood of public confusion. Reed Executive failed to do this, as the mere inclusion of a site in a search result does not necessarily suggest a connection with another trader. The Court did comment that, if the banner advertisement had led to a site bearing infringing material, the claim for trade mark infringement and passing off may have succeeded.

Given the earlier ruling in *Roadtech*, that the use of meta tags constitutes use of a trade mark, the *Reed* case has reignited the debate on this issue. The judgment seems to favour the view that users of internet search engines, who expect to see banner advertising and search results, are neither confused, nor deceived, into thinking there is trade connection between the term they enter and the results they receive.

(4)   *Source confusion not necessary*

In *Brookfield Communications Inc v West Coast Entertainment Corp* 174 F 3d 1036 (9th Cir, 1999), the US Court of Appeals for the Ninth Circuit was asked to consider whether it was permissible for the appellant to use the respondent's registered trade mark MOVIEBUFF and/or its domain name www.moviebuff.com as meta tags for its website. While the Court found that there would be no confusion as to the source of the products and services promoted on the appellant's site, it did find that there would be initial interest confusion. The Court considered there was a risk that the respondent's goodwill might be misappropriated because, even though visitors to the appellant's site would quickly realise it was not connected to the respondent, having arrived at that site they may not then necessarily choose to search further for the respondent's site.

Brookfield was applied with approval in *Playboy Enterprises Inc v Netscape Communications Corp* 354 F 3d 1020 (9th Cir, 2004). This case involved the internet practice of "keying", which allows advertisers to tie the placement of their ads on web pages to specific search terms. Netscape had made a number of search terms, including Playboy Enterprises' registered trade marks PLAYBOY and PLAYMATE, available to advertisers dealing with sex and adult oriented entertainment services for keying purposes. In some cases, the advertisements keyed to those terms were unlabelled, or were labelled in a confusing manner. For example, many of the advertisements required the user to "click here", which would then transport the user to the advertiser's own web page.

Playboy Enterprises sued for trade mark infringement, and successfully appealed to the Ninth Circuit where the lower Court had found in Netscape's favour. Citing *Brookfield*, the Appeal Court found that initial interest confusion could arise when a user, having searched for PLAYBOY or PLAYMATE and clicked on an advertising banner, found him or herself on the website of the advertiser keyed to those search terms. The Appeal Court found that, even if the internet user then realised he or she was not in an official Playboy Enterprises site, they may choose to stay at the site, thereby resulting in a possible diversion of trade from Playboy Enterprises to the advertiser.

(5) *Legitimate descriptive use of trade mark permitted*

In *Playboy Enterprises Inc v Terri Welles* 162 F 3d 1169 (9th Cir, 2002), Welles had been Playboy's 1981 Playmate of the Year and was using Playboy's registered trade marks "PLAYBOY" and "PLAYMATE" as meta tags for her website. Playboy sued for trade mark infringement. Rejecting the claim, the Court found that Welles needed to use the marks in order to refer to her past achievement and that, if she were not able to use them, it would be more difficult for people to find her website. The Court ruled that a finding of trade mark infringement in such circumstances could ultimately hinder "the free flow of information on the internet". Importantly Welles had made limited use of the marks and, as a result, her site did not appear above the Playboy site in search results.

8.8.3 Overstuffing / keyword stuffing

Trade marks are also often used by those engaged in a practice known as "overstuffing" or "keyword stuffing". Overstuffing involves using a trade mark (or indeed any word) dozens of times in the body of the site to increase the hit rate of that site. The words will often be typed in the same colour as the background so as to be invisible to the viewer. Given the decision in *Roadtech Computer Systems Ltd v Mandata (Management and Data Services) Ltd* [2000] ETMR 970 (Ch D), where such activities involve the unauthorised use of another person's trade mark they may also amount to trade mark infringement.

In *J K Harris and Co LLC v Steven H Kassel and Firse Tax Inc* 253 F Supp 2d 1120; 66 USPQ2d 1455 (ND Cal, 2003), the San Francisco District Court ordered the plaintiff to mention the defendant (which was one of its competitors) less often on its own website. This followed a complaint by the competitor, J K Harris, that the 75 references to its name on the defendant's www.taxes.com site were skewing search engine results, amounting to trade mark infringement.

The order against taxes.com is possibly the first decision of its kind concerning a website's primary content, rather than its hidden content (meta tags), in circumstances where internet users were clearly informed that the two sites were unconnected.

This practice is no longer as common as it once was, as many modern search engines no longer use meta tags as a major source of subject information.

8.8.4 Keyword buy agreements

Some internet search engine providers will sell the advertising rights attached to certain keywords. This arrangement is known as a "keyword buy agreement" or "keying".

Under a keyword buy agreement, every time a certain keyword is entered as a search parameter, the search engine displays the advertisement of the person to whom the keyword has been "sold". For instance, a browser might enter "intellectual property law" in the search category, and an advertisement for Thomson Brookers legal publications might appear. This is entirely legitimate.

However, if a keyword associated with one party is purchased by another party this may result in a breach of the first party's rights. For example, what would happen if the keyword

"Thomson Brookers" was purchased by a rival publisher so that the rival publisher's advertisement appeared whenever a user typed in "Thomson Brookers" on the search engine? Such actions would almost inevitably lead to confusion, and a possible diversion of trade, which would be actionable under the Fair Trading Act 1986 and/or the tort of passing off. However, a recent decision of the US Court of Appeals would suggest that such arrangements may not amount to a breach of registered trade mark. In *1-800 Contacts Inc v WhenU.com Inc* 414 F 3d (2nd Cir, 2005), the Second Circuit dismissed 1-800 Contacts' claim to infringement of its trade mark "1-800 CONTACTS" by WhenU on the basis that it had failed to establish use of the mark in commerce.

WhenU stored software on consumers' computers which monitored the words they typed into search engines and that appeared on the sites they visited. These words were checked against a directory of keywords purchased from WhenU by advertisers, and the software would cause a pop-up ad to appear on the consumers' screens if any such keyword was used. 1-800 Contacts complained that a competitor's advertisement appeared on the consumers' screens when they visited the website of 1-800 Contacts. The Court rejected that claim noting:

- WhenU did not display or use the trade mark at all. The pop-up advertisement that was triggered by the keywords did not display the trade mark;

- It was 1-800 Contacts' website address (rather than the "1-800 Contacts" trade mark) which WhenU placed in its directory. In that regard the Court viewed the website as functioning more like a "key" to 1-800 Contacts' website than a trade mark; and

- Consumers are accustomed to having multiple applications open at once and to windows opening spontaneously on their screens. The pop-up advertisements on 1-800 Contacts' site had no tangible effect on its appearance or functionality and WhenU's software did not alter the consumer's search results or the 1-800 Contacts' website and did not misdirect consumers to or from the site.

The judgment addressed only the question of trade mark use, and left open 1-800 Contacts' claims for unfair competition, cybersquatting, copyright infringement, and trade mark dilution.

For an example of a case in which a keyword buy agreement was deemed to amount trade mark infringement, see *Playboy Enterprises v Netscape* (discussed at 8.8.2(4) ("Source confusion not necessary") earlier in this chapter).

8.8.5 Hyperlinks

The linking of sites by means of hyperlinks raises questions as to whether or not a browser on a particular site ("the linking site") who is transferred to another site ("the linked site") might assume there is some connection or association between the owners of each site, or their respective goods and services.

While hyperlinks may be beneficial to the linked site because they increase traffic to that site, it can sometimes be objectionable, particularly where deep linking is involved. A deep link bypasses a site's homepage. As homepages often contain advertising, or give credit for their content, the owners of sites that are deep linked may object to this practice.

A website owner may not be aware that his or her site has been hyperlinked to another site. If the linking site is not user friendly, or offers inferior or competing goods/services, or if internet users assume a connection between the two sites, then the linked website owner may suffer damage to reputation and goodwill. In these circumstances, it is arguable that passing off and/or a breach of the Fair Trading Act 1986 have occurred.

A further form of deep linking known as "framing" is discussed at 8.8.6 below.

(1)   *Balance needs to be struck*

While it is possible to prevent deep linking, a balance needs to be struck between protecting the rights of those parties whose sites may be the subject of linking, and the general interest of the internet community to encourage freedom of use and dissemination of information.

If deep linking were prohibited entirely, internet users would always need to be sent to the homepage of the linked site, and would then need to find the information they required themselves. Therefore, there is some benefit to users in deep linking, provided it is done legitimately.

One way to legitimise deep linking might be to place advertisements for the linked site on an appropriate page of the linking site. This was the view taken by the Rotterdam District Court in *Algemeen Dagblad BV v Eureka Internetdiensten (Kranten.com)* [2002] ECDR 1, where the defendant was deep linking into PCM's site and bypassing the homepage.

(2)   *Hyperlinking will not normally amount to copyright infringement*

The US Courts considered hyperlinking in *Ticketmaster Corp v Tickets.com Inc* 2000 WL 1887522, 55 (CD Cal, 2000). In that case, the US District Court for the Central District of California found that hyperlinking does not amount to copyright infringement as no copying is involved. Rather, the viewer is automatically transferred to the genuine website of the original author. The decision would not preclude an action for a breach of the Fair Trading Act 1986 in similar circumstances in New Zealand.

The Scottish Courts have also addressed hyperlinks at the injunction stage. In *Shetland Times Ltd v Dr Jonathan Wills* [1997] FSR 604, the Court thought that newspaper headlines constituted a cable broadcast programme under s 7 Copyright, Designs and Patents Act 1988 (UK). The plaintiff argued that the headlines were literary works and that the defendant's activities constituted infringement under s 17. The case settled, so the Court did not make a final decision on the matter but found that it was at least arguable that copyright could subsist in short phrases.

It should be noted that the argument that copyright subsists in short words and phrases was unsuccessful in *No Fear Inc v Farmers Trading Co Ltd* 31/8/98, Morris J, HC Auckland M1616/95 and is contrary to English authority (*Exxon Corp v Exxon Insurance Consultants International* [1982] RPC 69).

8.8.6 Framing

Framing would seem to be a more obvious breach of a website owner's intellectual property rights.

Framing occurs when a browser travels by hyperlink from site A to site B. However, site B is framed so as to overlay the advertising of site B with site A's own advertising. In addition, the URL of site A is shown by the web browser instead of the URL of site B. This is similar to one law firm removing the cover of a client information text and replacing it with its own cover.

Framing is fundamentally hyperlinking to another site in a manner that enables the owner of the linking site to exploit the content of the linked site without any benefit or recognition accruing to the owner of the linked site. This practice may infringe the rights of the owner of the linked page where:

- The linked page contains the owner's trade marks; or

- The owner has a reputation in the style and get-up of the linked page.

Framing raises the same copyright infringement issues as hyper-linking in respect of implied licences and the debate over whether operating a website is operating a cable programme service. Technically, the practice of framing does not involve copying; the viewer is not actually downloading the material to his or her computer. However it could be argued that providing the link facilitates an unlicensed use of copyrighted material (by the user), which of itself amounts to infringement. This has been the approach of at least one German Court (see *Roche-Lexikon.de* 22/2/01, Hamburg Court of Appeal 3 U 247/00).

In relation to trade mark infringement, see *Washington Post Newsweek Interactive Co LLC v The Gator Corp* 16/7/02, CivA02-909-A (ED Va, 2002), where a US Federal Court issued a preliminary injunction against software company Gator, preventing it from causing its pop-up ads to appear on users' computer screens at the same time the user is viewing any of the plaintiffs' websites.

Gator developed software that provided free services to users, such as automatic entry of user passwords and addresses into web forms. It also monitored a user's internet usage and delivered ads specifically targeted to that user. For example, a user may see an advertisement for Pepsi, which is delivered by Gator, while visiting the coke.com website. The advertisements were delivered in a pop-up box that partially covered up the website when it appeared on screen.

With an estimated 25 million active users and 500 advertisers, Gator's advertisements, and the form in which they appeared, led the plaintiffs (a group of news organisations including the Washington Post, the New York Times and Dow Jones, all of which operated web versions of their publications) to brand Gator "a parasite" and to bring proceedings for, among other things, trade mark and copyright infringement and unfair competition.

The plaintiffs argued that Gator's conduct constituted an unauthorised use of their trade marks, and would cause confusion amongst users as to the sponsorship of the Gator ads. They also submitted that such activity involved the making of an unauthorised derivative copyright work, and violated their right to display and modify their own copyright works, thereby constituting copyright infringement.

Gator argued that the critical issue was a user's right to control what appeared on his or her computer screen. It contended that the practice of displaying pop-up ads on websites operated by a third party was a fundamental part of modern graphical user interfaces, and that its ads were used in the same way that Microsoft Windows, Outlook and other applications displayed pop-up alerts and reminders.

The Court disagreed with Gator and found (at an interim stage) that the plaintiffs were likely to prevail on their claims that the pop-up ads were an infringement of their registered trade marks. Accordingly, the Court issued a preliminary injunction barring Gator from delivering its pop-up ads on the plaintiffs' sites.

In New Zealand, framing is even more likely to result in a breach of the Fair Trading Act 1986 or passing off than deep linking. The act of framing may lead an internet user to incorrectly conclude that there is a relationship between the linked site and the linking site, thus constituting misleading and deceptive conduct.

8.9 ISP liability

The question of liability for infringement of intellectual property rights on the internet raises further interesting issues. Clearly anyone downloading or copying copyright material from the internet, without the authority of the copyright owner, infringes copyright. People who authorise the infringement of, or by their actions encourage others to infringe, copyright are also liable. This would include website owners who facilitate the copying of copyright materials by browsers. There is, however, another group who may be liable, namely internet service providers ("ISPs").

8.9.1 Copyright

Two landmark decisions in the US in the defamation field have led to the presumption that, where the ISP exercises editorial control, it will be treated as if it is a "publisher" and liable for any contraventions of law occurring within the ambit of its operation.

In *Cubby Inc v CompuServe* 776 F Supp 135 (SD NY, 1991), Cubby sued CompuServe over allegedly false and defamatory statements posted on a CompuServe bulletin board. CompuServe operated more than 150 bulletin boards, each on an individual topic. CompuServe contracted with a third party to screen messages before they were uploaded to its bulletin boards. This contracting out of the editorial process proved to be important, as the Court held that in so doing there was no opportunity for CompuServe to remove any messages before they were released to all subscribers. CompuServe would only be able to remove messages after they had been uploaded, and in that sense was more like a "news vendor" than a publisher. The decision seems to encourage a hands-off approach.

In *Stratten Oakmont Inc v Prodigy Services Co* 24/5/91, 31063/94 (NY Sup, 1994), the plaintiff commenced proceedings in relation to a statement posted on Prodigy's bulletin board that Stratten was involved in a major criminal fraud. Prodigy held itself out to be a family-oriented service and, as such, employed screening programs to filter unwanted postings.

The question that fell to be determined by the Court was whether Prodigy was in the nature of a distributor or publisher of information, or more akin to a "news vendor" as in the *Cubby* case. Relying on the fact that Prodigy employed a screening program to filter unwanted materials, and had employees whose job was to maintain control over individual bulletin boards, the Court found that Prodigy was a publisher and therefore liable for any materials appearing on its bulletin boards.

Applying the reasoning of the *Prodigy* and *Cubby* cases, it is reasonable to expect that an ISP will be liable for defamation in New Zealand where the ISP exercises some control over the material published by its subscribers. Similarly a bulletin board operator who exercises, or claims to exercise, editorial control over the content of a site, may be liable for material published on that site. That liability may extend to publications of which the bulletin board operator is unaware, given the purported exercise of editorial control.

Similar reasoning may apply in the copyright field. Thus in *Metro-Goldwyn-Mayer Studios Inc v Grokster Ltd* 545 US 913; 125 S Ct 2764; 75 USPQ 2d 1001 (US, 2005), the US Supreme Court unanimously held that the creators of the peer 2 peer ("P2P") file sharing systems Grokster and Morpheus could be sued for copyright infringement. This was contrary to an earlier decision in the Ninth Circuit, which ruled that the creators of the P2P systems were not able to exert sufficient control over users of the systems to prevent illegal file sharing. Souter J wrote in the decision:

> "We hold that one who distributes a device with the object of promoting its use to infringe copyright, as shown by clear expression or other affirmative steps taken to foster infringement, is liable for the resulting acts of infringement by third parties."

8.9.2 Lack of knowledge may provide defence

In *Religious Technology Centre v Netcom On-Line Communication Services Inc* 907 F Supp 1361 (ND Cal, 1995) and *Sega Enterprises v MAPHIA* 857 F Supp 679 (ND Cal, 1994), the ISP (*Netcom*) and the bulletin board operator (*Sega*) were found not to be liable for direct infringement of a copyright owner's distribution rights since they took no affirmative action that directly resulted in the copying, except for the creation and maintenance of the computer system which facilitated the copying.

In *Netcom*, an argument as to secondary infringement also failed. The Court held that, where an ISP could not reasonably verify a claim of infringement, they would not be liable for contributing to infringement by allowing the continued distribution of the alleged infringing work.

These cases would suggest that, in the absence of knowledge of an infringement, it is not the internet service provider who will be liable for an infringement of the copyright owner's rights, but rather the person who made the copyright work available on the server.

The case law in the area of secondary infringement (also known as contributory infringement) has been codified in the US by the Digital Millennium Copyright Act. This legislation came into effect in 1998.

US decisions subsequent to the enactment of this legislation have maintained the requirement that the contributory infringement include an element of knowledge. The most famous recent example is the decision in *A&M Records Inc v Napster Inc* (2000) 50 IPR 232.

8.9.3 The Australian and New Zealand situation

The Australian counterpart to the US Digital Millennium Copyright Act is the Copyright Amendment (Digital Agenda) Act 2000 (Aust). This amendment is, in part, a response to the High Court of Australia's decision in *Telstra Corp Ltd v Australasian Performing Right Assn Ltd* (1997) 38 IPR 294 (HCA), in which the Court recognised that the Australian law with regard to copyright infringement could have serious repercussions for ISPs. The amendment is not as specific as its US counterpart and is yet to be tested in the Courts. However, it does appear to provide more protection for ISPs than was previously available.

There are currently no decisions on this area of copyright law in New Zealand. Furthermore, the Copyright Act 1994 does not specifically address ISPs and the related liability issues. The Ministry of Economic Development released a discussion document on 10 July 2001 entitled "Digital Technology and the Copyright Act 1994: A Discussion Paper". The discussion paper was designed to enable the Ministry to explore the implications of digital technology on some key areas of copyright, one being the liability of ISPs for copyright infringement by their subscribers. The Ministry received submissions on the discussion paper, and published a position paper on 10 December 2002 and a Cabinet paper on 25 June 2003. The Cabinet paper contained the Government's proposals resulting from the legislative review. It recommended, at paras 24-25, that changes be made to the Copyright Act 1994 to limit the liability of ISPs where they:

- Merely provide the physical facilities that enable a communication to take place;

- Perform some form of caching in order to provide more efficient services; and

- Host material posted by third parties without knowledge that the material infringes copyright or take action to remove or disable access to the infringing material once they became aware of its infringing nature.

Following on from the Cabinet Paper, the Copyright (New Technologies and Performers' Rights) Amendment Bill was introduced into parliament in December 2006. The Bill proposes limiting the potential liability of internet service providers (ISPs) for both primary and secondary infringement in appropriate circumstances. In order to achieve this, the Bill introduces a definition of ISP and provides an exception to primary infringement where the ISP is merely providing the physical facilities to enable a communication to take place. The Bill also limits secondary liability in respect of the caching and storing of infringing material where the ISP does not know, or have reason to believe, that the material is infringing, and acts within a reasonable time to delete it or to prevent access to it upon obtaining such knowledge. These limitations on liability are not intended to preclude copyright owners from obtaining injunctive relief against ISPs.

On 27 July 2007, the Commerce Committee released a report recommending that the Bill be passed with minor amendments to the sections dealing with ISP liability.

The Bill is likely to be enacted in late-2007.

The legislative review of the Copyright Act 1994 is discussed in more detail at 4.2.2 ("Current developments / legislative amendments") in the copyright chapter of this text (chapter 4).

8.9.4 "Hands off" approach advocated

The effect of the US decisions, and corresponding legislation both in Australia and the US, is to encourage a "hands-off" approach from ISPs. In those jurisdictions, ISPs who do not exercise editorial control, and who make no inquiry as to whether their service is being used for infringing purposes, will be considered mere "distributors" or "innocent infringers" and thereby avoid liability.

In New Zealand, the Government's proposals resulting from the legislative review of the Copyright Act 1994 would encourage rights holders to inform ISPs of any infringing material posted on their site. The ISP would then be required to remove, or disable access to, the infringing material in order to avoid secondary liability for copyright infringement. It would be difficult to quantify the extent to which infringing material has been copied from a website, or to know how many people will have read or copied the infringing work on the site but it is likely that damages might be significant. This arrangement would place the onus upon rights holders to protect and enforce their copyright, which reflects the usual case with respect to the enforcement of other intellectual property rights.

8.9.5 Joint infringement of a registered trade mark

In theory, it is possible for a person or company to be liable for directing, procuring or combining with others to infringe a registered trade mark. For a discussion of the relevant principles see *CBS v Amstrad Consumer Electronics* [1988] 1 AC 1013.

An ISP is analogous to a market landlord in that it provides a forum by which infringing use of a trade mark may occur. However, unless it could be shown that the ISP stands to benefit in some way other than recovery of its usual fees (for example, by receiving from the trade mark infringement a percentage of sales made on sites which it hosted) it is difficult to see how a similar conclusion would not be reached by the New Zealand Courts in respect of ISP liability for third party trade mark infringement — even in circumstances where the ISP had been put on notice of the trade mark rights and failed to act.

In *Louis Vuitton Malletier SA v Toea Pty Ltd* (2006) 70 IPR 307 (FCA), Louis Vuitton unsuccessfully issued proceedings against Toea for breach of its registered trade marks as a joint tortfeasor. Toea was the landlord of, and the party responsible for, operating, supervising and controlling a market at which counterfeit Louis Vuitton product was sold. Louis Vuitton argued that where Toea became aware over a period of years that some stall holders were selling counterfeit goods, and therefore infringing its registered trade marks, and took no action to stop that conduct, it tacitly accepted the conduct and became independently liable for the infringement as a joint tortfeasor. That submission was rejected by the Court on a number of grounds including:

- A lack of evidence that Toea was actually aware, in advance of any sale, that the subject stall holders had counterfeit product or intended to sell such product. This evidence was crucial to Louis Vuitton's case given its central contention that Toea was a joint tortfeasor in conjunction with the individual stall holders selling the counterfeit product, and

- Relying on *Thompson v Australian Capital Television Pty Ltd* (1996) 186 CLR 574; 141 ALR 1 (HCA), there was a distinction between joint tortfeasors (being responsible for the same tort) and several tortfeasors (being responsible only for the same damage). Thus, for joint tortfeasors there must be a concurrence in the act or acts causing damage, not merely a co-incidence of separate acts which, by their co-joined effect, cause damage. Therefore, in order to find Toea liable for the stall holders' infringements there would need to be evidence of a concurrence in the act or acts causing damage, not merely a coincidence of separate acts which, by their conjoined effect, caused damage. There was no such evidence that the infringing conduct by the stall holders was committed towards some common purpose shared with Toea. The purpose of Toea was to conduct an efficient and profitable market. The purpose of each stall holder was the successful conduct of his or her stall. The case was further hampered by the fact that the only revenue Toea received was rent on the space in the market. It did not receive a percentage of sales made by individual stall holders.

A further difficulty would arise in proving that the ISP is not a mere conduit of information, acting on instructions from a principal. For example, in *Leafscreen NZ Ltd v Leafbusters Group Ltd* (2004) 10 TCLR 967 the claim against the first defendant was that it had used the mark "LEAFSCREEN" in relation to conducting the business of preventing gutter blockages. The claim against the second defendant, Telecom Directories Ltd, under ss 89(1) and 6 of the Act, was that it had used, or would use in trade, the plaintiff's registered trade mark, without permission, by agreeing to advertise the first defendant's business in a telephone directory that the second defendant published and provided to New Zealand businesses and consumers. The second defendant submitted that it was not liable for infringement of the registered trade mark on the basis that it was acting as a mere conduit for the first defendant.

Heath J, at para 34, noted with approval the Court of Appeal's decision in *Goldsbro v Walker* [1993] 1 NZLR 394; (1992) 5 TCLR 46; (1993) 4 NZBLC 102,946 (CA), at p 398; p 49; p 102,949 (per Cooke P), pp 402-403; p 53; p 102,952-102,953 (per Richardson J), and p 405; p 57; p 102,955-102,956 (per Hardie Boys J), who accepted that an innocent agent acting merely as a conduit and purporting to do no more than pass on instructions from a principal does not become responsible for anything misleading in the information he, she, or it conveys. Heath J observed, without deciding, that the second defendant, in the incarnation in which it was sued in this case, ought to be treated in a similar fashion and declined to grant interim relief against it. There is a more detailed discussion of the "mere conduit" defence in the Fair Trading Act 1986 chapter of this text (chapter 10).

Joint infringement of trade marks is discussed in more detail at 7.11.5 ("Joint infringement") in the trade marks chapter of this text.

8.9.6 Joint liability for passing off / breach of the Fair Trading Act 1986

For an ISP to be liable as a joint tortfeasor to passing off / for a breach of the Fair Trading Act 1986 it is essential that they should participate in the acts which amount to passing off / a breach. By analogy with the mere conduit defence articulated in *Goldsbro v Walker* (discussed at 10.4.5 ("Intention") in the context of the Fair Trading Act 1986), an innocent agent, who acts merely as a conduit and purports to do no more that pass on instructions or information does not become responsible for anything misleading passed on.

See also *Tot Toys Ltd v Mitchell* [1993] 1 NZLR 325, at p 354:

> "Passing off defendants are responsible for foreseeable deception of those ultimate customers who purchase from intermediaries as well as for deception of their own immediate customers … However, a manufacturer is not responsible for the misconduct of a retailer unless it is clearly shown that the manufacturer ought to have contemplated that such misconduct would be likely."

8.10   Jurisdiction

8.10.1   Introduction

Patent, design and trade mark rights are territorial, which creates an immediate conflict with the borderless nature of electronic commerce and the internet. Applying territorial concepts and laws to a medium in which there are no territorial constraints raises significant problems.

8.10.2   Trade marks

The monopoly granted to the proprietor of a New Zealand trade mark registration is restricted to New Zealand. The same is true of other jurisdictions. Under this territorial system, it is possible for two unrelated parties to own, and use, identical marks in relation to identical goods in their respective countries.

A business may market goods under its own trade mark in New Zealand, but be unable to do so in another country where someone else owns the same trade mark. Similarly, while it may be possible to manufacture and market a product in New Zealand, the sale or use of that product may constitute patent or design infringement elsewhere.

The reverse situation may pose problems for manufacturers and merchants in the New Zealand domestic market. Inevitably, domestic manufacturers will be faced with foreign businesses marketing goods on a website accessible by New Zealand consumers, which may infringe local intellectual property rights.

Customarily, a business will register its trade marks in the territories in which it trades, on a country-by-country or region-by-region basis. As its export business expands, a company will protect itself by registering its trade mark in the territories of interest. Problems of conflicting marks in these different regions are encountered gradually.

Incorporating a trade mark into a website may result in instantaneous use of that mark in almost every jurisdiction, and possibly infringement of the trade mark rights of others in some of those jurisdictions. For instance, while a New Zealand company may be the registered proprietor of a trade mark in New Zealand, another party may be the registered proprietor of that same mark in another country, such as the US. Use by the New Zealand company of its trade mark to sell its goods on the internet will constitute infringement of the US trade mark registration if the New Zealand company's internet site can be accessed from the US and/or if the New Zealand company supplies its branded goods to US customers.

8.10.3   Mere marketing may constitute infringement

The problem is compounded by the fact that in many countries, merely marketing a product under someone else's trade mark may constitute an infringement.

For example, under s 4(1)(b) Trade Marks Act 1994 (UK), a registered trade mark may be infringed where it is used in an advertisement issued to the public in a manner which imports a reference to the British proprietor of the mark.

A section equivalent to s 4(1)(b) was applied to find infringement in *R J Reuter Co Ltd v Mulhens* (1953) 70 RPC 235 (CA); a case involving the sending of an envelope by mail into the UK which featured a registered trade mark. Although the mark was applied to the envelope in another country, and posted from that country, it was deemed to be an advertisement received in the UK.

It is possible that the judgment in *R J Reuter Co Ltd* will be applied in New Zealand. Under s 8(1A)(e) and (f) Trade Marks Act 1953 a registration was infringed where the mark was used in an advertising circular or other advertisement "issued" to the public in circumstances where the mark imported a reference to the trade mark owner and/or its goods and services. Under s 89 Trade Marks Act 2002, the test is simply whether the sign has been used in a manner such that it will be viewed as a trade mark (rather than, for example, a description of the nature of the product or service).

Due to the passive nature of some web pages, there is some doubt as to whether the unauthorised use of a trade mark on, or in connection with, those web pages would constitute "issuing advertisements to the public". This is something that will undoubtedly receive judicial scrutiny once the use (and unauthorised use) of trade marks on the internet becomes more prevalent.

The New Zealand Court of Appeal's judgment in *Nationwide News Pty Ltd v The University of Newlands* 9/12/05, CA202/04, in which the Court considered jurisdiction in a defamation case, may also be of assistance. The issue before the Court of Appeal was whether the respondents were correct to serve proceedings on the appellant in Australia without leave. The respondents relied on r 219(a) High Court Rules which provided for them to do so in relation to "any act or omission for or in respect of which damages are claimed [which] was done or occurred in New Zealand". The respondents maintained that through downloading the defamatory material from the appellant's website, publication occurred in New Zealand and, on that basis, said that service without leave was justified. Without deciding the issue, the Court of Appeal took the High Court of Australia's decision in *Dow Jones & Co Inc v Gutnick* (2002) 210 CLR 575; 194 ALR 433 (HCA) as a correct statement of law in New Zealand. In *Gutnick*, Mr Gutnick, who was a resident of Victoria, alleged that an article published by the American company Dow Jones on its subscription news website defamed him in Australia. Unanimously, the High Court of Australia upheld the decision that the proceeding had been properly served out of Australia and that Victoria was the appropriate forum, noting that approximately 1,700 of the 500,000 subscribers to the Dow Jones website were in Australia and that Dow Jones had formally conceded that downloading had occurred in Victoria.

With reference to the occurrence of the tort of defamation, and identification of the real question for determination, the High Court of Australia said, at paras 26, 28, and 44, that:

> "Harm to reputation is done when a defamatory publication is comprehended by the reader, the listener, or the observer. Until then, no harm is done by it. This being so it would be wrong to treat publication as if it were a unilateral act on the part of the publisher alone. It is not. It is a bilateral act — in which the publisher makes it available and a third party has it available for his or her comprehension.

> •   •   •   •   •

> "If the place in which the publisher acts and the place in which the publication is presented in comprehensible form are in two different jurisdictions, where is the tort of defamation committed? That question is not to be answered by an uncritical application of some general rule that intentional torts are committed where the

tortfeasor acts or that they are committed in the place where the last event necessary to make the actor liable takes place.

•   •   •   •   •

"In defamation, the same considerations that require rejection of locating the tort by reference only to the publisher's conduct, lead to the conclusion that, ordinarily, defamation is to be located at the place where the damage to reputation occurs. Ordinarily that will be where the material which is alleged to be defamatory is available in comprehensible form assuming, of course, that the person defamed has in that place a reputation which is thereby damaged. It is only when the material is in comprehensible form that the damage to reputation is done and it is damage to reputation which is the principal focus of defamation, not any quality of the defendant's conduct. In the case of material on the World Wide Web, it is not available in comprehensible form until downloaded onto the computer of a person who has used a web browser to pull the material from the web server. It is where that person downloads the material that the damage to reputation may be done. Ordinarily then, that will be the place where the tort of defamation is committed."

By analogy, trade mark infringement requires that the sign is viewed as a trade mark. If the mark is used on the internet then it cannot be viewed until downloaded onto the computer of a person who has used a web browser to pull the material from the web server. Thus, it is where that person downloads the material that the actionable part of the infringement occurs.

The New Zealand Courts' approach to use of a registered New Zealand trade mark as a domain name for a website hosted within New Zealand is discussed at 8.6 ("Trade mark law and domain names") earlier in this chapter.

8.10.4 Infringement of New Zealand registered mark only if activity in New Zealand

What is certain is that infringement of a trade mark registered in New Zealand could only occur where there is infringing activity in New Zealand.

Apart from the obvious examples, infringing activity in New Zealand will include the unauthorised use of a trade mark on a website (based overseas or in New Zealand) in circumstances where it is possible for people within New Zealand to purchase goods or services from that website.

In the article Clive Elliott, "The internet: A new world without frontiers" [1998] 11 NZLJ 404, the author comments:

"If it could be established that a New Zealand resident accessed the web site in New Zealand and was misled or deceived, a relevant part of the cause of action arose in New Zealand. If, on the other hand, the only connection to New Zealand was the possible access to the web site in New Zealand, without any harm arising (to another New Zealand party), no jurisdiction would appear to arise."

The author goes on to suggest that the essential elements of establishing jurisdiction will be:

- A website;

- Conduct purposefully directed at the forum state (ie, New Zealand); and

- Knowledge that the plaintiff will be harmed in the forum state itself.

These comments were adopted by the Court in *NZ Post Ltd v Leng* [1999] 3 NZLR 219; (1998) 45 IPR 263. Substantially the same criteria have been adopted by the Federal Court of Australia in *Ward Group Pty Ltd v Brodie & Stone Plc* [2005] FCA 471 which confirmed that something more than an offer to the "world at large" on the internet is required for Australian trade mark owners to succeed in claims against foreign website owners for trade mark infringement.

8.10.5 Passing off and breach of the Fair Trading Act 1986

If the mark is not registered, but the common law owner of the mark in New Zealand can prove it has reputation in New Zealand, then passing off and a breach of the Fair Trading Act 1986 are available causes of action against the website owner. Although the action of creating the website with a deceptively similar mark may occur outside New Zealand, it is likely that the infringement will be held to have occurred inside New Zealand, provided that the offer to sell goods/services was received by internet users within New Zealand.

Passing off which occurs outside New Zealand may also be actionable within New Zealand, under the rule of "double actionability". This rule, which arises from traditional English common law with respect to torts committed overseas, states that an act done abroad may be actionable as a tort in England if:

(1)   It would have been actionable as a tort if it had been done in England; and

(2)   It was actionable, though not necessarily as a tort, under the law of the foreign country.

The application of this rule in New Zealand to torts committed outside New Zealand was affirmed by Salmon J in *Containerlift Services Ltd v Maxwell Rotors Ltd* (2003) 10 TCLR 807. The plaintiff, which had reputation in the UK and Europe in the name "Containerlift", successfully sought an injunction against a New Zealand based defendant for misrepresentations arising in those jurisdictions from the use of the domain name "containerlift.com", notwithstanding that the plaintiff did not operate in New Zealand and the domain name was registered in the US.

The double actionability rule was also considered in some detail in *Kabushiki Kaisha Sony Computer Entertainment v van Veen* 14/12/06, MacKenzie J, HC Wellington CIV-2004-485-1520 in the context of a claim for breach of copyright, breach of registered trade mark and wrongful possession and use of confidential information. The decision is discussed in more detail in the "Infringement and enforcement of rights" sections of the Patents (at 2.14), Copyright (at 4.10), Design (at 6.15), and Trade Marks (at 7.11) chapters of this text.

8.10.6 Must be use "in the course of trade"

If it is not possible for New Zealanders to purchase goods/services from the website then it is unlikely that the mark has been used in the course of trade in New Zealand. This would effectively rule out trade mark infringement, passing off and breach of the Fair Trading Act 1986.

This result can be observed from dicta in the US case of *Playboy Enterprises Inc v Chuckleberry Publishing Inc* 939 F Supp 1032; 39 USPQ 2d 1846 (SD NY, 1996). Playboy had been granted an injunction *Chuckleberry Publishing Inc v Playboy Enterprises Inc* 486 F Supp 414; 206 USPQ 70 (SD NY, 1980) to restrain the defendant from using the word "Playmen" anywhere in the world on the cover of a "male sophisticate magazine", which was published, distributed or sold in the US. Fifteen years later, the defendant created a website in Italy with the domain name www.playmen.it, which featured explicit images from its "Playmen" magazine. Playboy sued for contempt for violation of the 1981 injunction.

To succeed in the contempt proceedings, Playboy had to establish that:

- "Playmen" had been used as part of a trade mark, service mark, trade name or other business designation;

- The use was in relation to an English language publication; and

- The use was made in connection with a sale or distribution in the US.

The first two elements were easily established. The Court also found that the final element was established.

The defendant argued that it did not distribute the pictorial images in the US; rather it posted images on its server in Italy, which US citizens could only view by electronically "transporting" themselves to the Italian server. The Court rejected this argument, stating that the defendant had actively solicited US customers to its site. However, the Court allowed the defendant to continue its internet site, provided that it did not accept subscriptions from customers living in the US.

Applying the reasoning in *Playboy*, in the following situations, use of a foreign entity's mark on a website in one's own jurisdiction may be considered an infringement in the foreign entity's jurisdiction:

- Where the website displays content focused primarily on, or directed primarily toward, persons in the foreign jurisdiction; or

- Where the website displays content that is not focused on, or directed to, persons in the foreign jurisdiction, but it is possible for persons in that jurisdiction to purchase goods/services from the site, and such transactions have occurred.

The *Playboy* decision should be contrasted with that reached in *DB Breweries Ltd v Domain Name Co Ltd* (2001) 52 IPR 280, in which the defendant was injuncted from using the www.db.co.nz domain name, despite the fact that he had not actually used it to market any goods (discussed in further detail at 8.6 ("Trade mark law and domain names") earlier this chapter).

8.10.7 "Significant interest" test

In the Scottish Court of Session decision, *Bonnier Media Ltd v Smith* [2002] ETMR 86; [2002] SCLR 977 (CS), the plaintiff, a Scottish newspaper which traded under the name "Business a.m.", took action against Smith, the managing director of a Mauritius based company. The paper had previously published articles on Smith to which he objected. He took action against the paper in separate proceedings in the UK for defamation. During those proceedings it was disclosed that Smith had previously committed acts of domain name piracy regarding the "Business a.m." moniker. The Court issued an injunction preventing Smith from registering domain names featuring the "Business a.m." name.

Smith asked the Court to recall the injunction on the basis that a foreign website, which was visible in Scotland, would not necessarily give rise to an actionable wrong. The Court refused to recall the injunction stating, at para 19:

> "[T]he person who sets up the website can be regarded as potentially committing a delict [ie a tort] in any country where the website can be seen, in other words in any country in the world. It does not follow that he actually commits a delict in every country in the world, however. It is obvious that the overwhelming majority of websites will be of no interest whatsoever in more than a single country or a small group of countries. In my opinion a website should not be regarded as having delictual consequences in any country where it is unlikely to be of significant interest. That result can readily be achieved by a vigorous application of the maxim *de minimis non curat praetor*; if the impact of a website in a particular country is properly regarded as insignificant, no delict has been committed there. In determining whether the impact of a website is insignificant, it is appropriate in my opinion to look both at the content of the website itself and at the commercial or other context in which the website operates. In the *Crate & Barrel* case [*Euromarket Designs Inc v Peters and Crate & Barrel Ltd* [2001] FSR 288], for example, the commercial context of the defendants' website was a shop operating in Dublin, and obviously catering to a local clientele. The website itself dealt with goods that were available in that shop. In the circumstances, it was obvious that the defendants' trade with the United Kingdom was insignificant, and was accordingly insufficient to give rise to a case of trade mark infringement."

The Court held that any website accessible from outside its host country could potentially infringe foreign intellectual property rights, the only requirement being that the content of the site is of "significant interest" to users in the foreign jurisdiction.

The Federal Court of Australia applied a narrower form of the same test in *Ward Group Pty Ltd v Brodie & Stone Plc* [2005] FCA 471. Ward was the Australian manufacturer and owner of anti-greying hair creams and lotions marketed under the RESTORIA trade mark. In 1970, Ward sold the UK arm of its business and in the late 1990's Brodie & Stone acquired that business along with the UK trade mark registration for RESTORIA. Ward alleged that advertising and sale of Brodie & Stone's UK RESTORIA products on UK websites which were accessible in Australia amounted to infringement of Ward's Australian trade mark registration and passing off. The only evidence of actual sales in Australia via the website were a number of trap purchases carried out by Ward's solicitors.

Ward's action for trade mark infringement failed. The Federal Court did not consider the RESTORIA mark to have been "used" in Australia because the websites were not specifically targeted at consumers in Australia. In the Federal Court's view, the use of a trade mark on the internet, uploaded on a website outside of Australia, without more, is not a use by the website proprietor of the mark in each jurisdiction where the mark is downloaded. It is only once there is evidence that the use is specifically intended to be made in, or directed at, a particular jurisdiction that there is likely to be use in that jurisdiction when the mark is actually downloaded.

While the website operator's acceptance of the trap orders, and delivery of product to meet those orders, was deemed to be use of the mark, that use was found to be non-infringing because Ward's solicitors had procured the sales and therefore consented to the use.

The claim for passing off also failed because the UK RESTORIA product was more expensive than the local product (and hence it would not make economic sense for Australian consumers to actually purchase product from the UK via the internet) and, as the products were of common origin and were not materially different, any sale of the UK RESTORIA product in Australia was unlikely to damage the goodwill attaching to Ward's Australian product.

8.10.8 International developments

Internationally, the draft Hague Convention on Jurisdiction and Foreign Judgments in Civil and Commercial Matters outlines a system of rules relating to jurisdiction and cross-border litigation that provides similar enforcement rights for consumers and businesses around the world. The Hague Convention will apply to civil and commercial matters including intellectual property, contractual and tortious disputes. In the absence of express choice between the parties, an online vendor that provides trade or business services, or directs its activities at consumers, may be sued by a consumer in his or her home country. The definition of "directing an activity" may include a targeted national advertising campaign, or filtering access to certain services. The authors are not aware of any New Zealand cases in which the Hague Convention has been relied on to establish jurisdiction.

In the US, many Courts addressing jurisdictional issues and disputes involving the internet apply an "effects" test. The effects test derives from the US Supreme Court decision in *Calder v Jones* 465 US 783 (US, 1984), a pre-internet defamation case establishing jurisdiction based on a defendant's intentional conduct outside the forum that was calculated to cause injury in the forum. The effects test is often applied in the US cases involving defamation and other intentional torts, such as trade mark infringement. Under the effects test, the Court will look at both the interactivity of the website and other traditional connections such as:

- Conduct targeting the forum;

- The location of the contract of sale;

- The volume of online sales originating from the forum;

- Whether there are offices, property, personnel or agents located in the forum;

- Whether telephone calls have been made in the forum; and

- Whether income has been earned in the forum and, if so, how much.

In essence, the effects test involves focusing on the local impact that a website has in a particular jurisdiction. Where the online activity has a significant impact within a locality, the Court will usually assert jurisdiction.

A practical application of the effects test can be seen in two recent decisions of the California Court of Appeal.

In *Snowney v Harrah's Entertainment Inc* 11 Cal Rptr 3d 35 (Cal App 2D, 2004), hotel and casino operator, Harrah's Entertainment advertised in California, and provided an interactive website and toll-free telephone number to Californian residents for booking reservations. The Californian Court of Appeal found sufficient basis for jurisdiction, noting, at para 13, that:

> "The California Supreme Court in *Pavlovich* ... adopted a sliding scale analysis to determine whether internet use can justify the exercise of personal jurisdiction. The determination turns on the degree of interactivity of the Internet site and the commercial nature and extent of the exchange of information ... An interactive Internet site through which a non-resident defendant enters into contracts or conducts other business transactions with forum residents can be a means of purposefully directing activities at forum residents and, depending on the circumstances, may support the exercise of personal jurisdiction."

Similarly, in *West Corp v Superior Court of San Diego* 116 Cal App 4th 1167; 11 Cal Rptr 3d 145 (Cal App 4D, 2004), the California Court of Appeal found that West Corporation, a national telemarketing company based in Nebraska and operating call centres in Virginia, could be sued in California, noting, at p 16, that:

> "Companies such as [West Corporation] ... that deliberately engage in nationwide or multi-state commercial activities, whether by phone, via the Internet, by mail, or by sending agents into forum states should reasonably expect to be subject to suit in the states where they solicit business."

Although West Corporation's contact with Californian residents was primarily by telephone, it was significant that the Court felt it necessary to specify that it could find jurisdiction on the basis of such contacts regardless of whether they were made by phone or over the internet.

8.10.9 Enforcement difficult

The danger to businesses marketing their goods or services on the internet is clear. Once on the internet, they are marketing their goods and services internationally, and to regions with different laws, in which they could be infringing intellectual property rights. As a consequence, a New Zealand business promoting its brands and marketing its goods via the internet could face legal action, either from foreign intellectual property rights-holders overseas or from foreign purchasers. In addition, difficulties may be encountered when supplying goods into another territory due to border controls that prevent the entry of products likely to infringe intellectual property rights in those regions.

These jurisdictional problems also make it difficult to defend or enforce the right to market a particular product under a particular brand. The difficulties of being embroiled in foreign litigation, or of trying to enforce judgments against parties not resident in New Zealand, are obvious.

8.10.10 Safeguards

To absolutely safeguard against infringing intellectual property rights, it appears that one should now conduct international trade mark searches before marketing goods via the internet. If the domain name to be used is not fully searched, access to a website may be restricted to those within jurisdictions where trade marks have been cleared for use. For example, an initial entry page could require the browser to disclose his or her present location and, if that location is within a jurisdiction for which trade mark clearance has not been obtained, entry to the website should be refused. However, such entry pages are not particularly user friendly and may discourage potential customers from entering the site. An alternative is to screen persons from foreign jurisdictions at the contractual stage, and refuse orders received from persons in jurisdictions in which trade mark clearance has not been obtained.

8.11   Website disclaimers

Disclaimers, or exclusion clauses as they are also known, are an attempt by one party to exclude or limit their legal liability to another party.

A disclaimer is essentially a contractual term between the website owner and each browser concerning use of the website. Accordingly, a disclaimer relies on laws relating to contracts for its effect.

The principal rule of contract law is that there must be a clear act of acceptance of all relevant terms of an offer for there to be an enforceable contract. A clause that was not brought to the attention of the other party at the time the contract was made will not usually be enforceable. The more onerous the disclaimer, the greater the effort that must be made to draw it to the attention of the party whose rights will be restricted by it.

Unless it can be proven that sufficient efforts were made to draw the disclaimers to the browser's attention before using the relevant part of the website, the disclaimers are unlikely to be enforceable. Placing a hyperlink at the foot of a web page without any other reference is unlikely to be sufficient. Even including the disclaimers in terms and conditions that a browser must "click-accept" may not be enough without specific cross-reference to the disclaimers.

Disclaimers should be used carefully where the website purports to give advice of a professional nature, supplies high-value products, health-related products or high risk products, or offers to supply into litigious countries (for example, the US).

Other tips to avoid liability include:

- Have the relevant clauses reviewed by legal advisers from each major market that the website is likely to address;

- Include a specific reference to the disclaimers at any place on the website that is a potential source of risk;

- Hyperlink these references to the actual text of the disclaimers in the website terms and conditions;

- Prevent users from accessing the risk areas of the website, without first click-accepting the terms and conditions;

- Consider including a specific reference to the disclaimers in the area in which the "click-accept" box is located (eg "I have read and agree to these terms and conditions, including the disclaimers at clause X above"); and

- If the website has particularly high litigation risk, consider reverting to a traditional hand-signed agreement. If the arrangement will be ongoing, an initial hand-signed umbrella agreement could be used, with subsequent orders being made online under the terms of that agreement.

8.12 Click-wrap agreements

8.12.1 Introduction

Click-wrap agreements are standard form agreements entered into on the internet. Users are required to indicate their consent to the terms and conditions of an agreement by either typing "I agree", or by clicking on a box marked "I agree".

Click-wrap agreements developed out of the "shrink-wrap agreements" that became popular in the 1980s and 1990s when consumer interest in purchasing computer software was escalating. In a shrink-wrap agreement, the manufacturer places the terms and conditions of the software licence inside a box with the software disk or CD "shrink-wrapped" in plastic. The consumer is only able to read the terms and conditions once the software has been paid for. The customer is advised by a notice on the box to read the terms and conditions before unwrapping the disk. By unwrapping the disk the customer is taken to have accepted those terms and conditions.

In contrast, consumers entering into click-wrap agreements are usually given the opportunity to review the terms and conditions before indicating their acceptance. For that reason, click-wrap agreements are usually considered to be more readily enforceable than shrink-wrap agreements. So-called "browse-wrap" agreements, which do not require any act of affirmative assent, are generally not considered to be enforceable.

8.12.2 New Zealand

While, to the authors' knowledge, the New Zealand Courts have yet to examine the enforceability of either type of agreement, it is likely that they will adopt a similar approach to that taken overseas. The bulk of decisions in this area come from the US and refer back to traditional laws of contract, which provide that an agreement is unlikely to be effective unless both parties accept the terms and conditions before the contract is formed.

8.12.3 United States of America

One of the first click-wrap agreement cases in the US involved a law suit filed by Hotmail Corporation, a Silicone Valley company that provides free e-mail on the internet. Hotmail sued a number of its users (*Hotmail Corp v Van Money Pie Inc* 47 USPQ 2d (BNA) 1020 (ND CA, 1998), at p 1025) after it learnt that they were sending spam to thousands of e-mail users containing pornography, software and get-rich-quick schemes. Although the judgment in that case did not specifically address the enforceability of click-wrap agreements, the Court held that the defendants were bound by the terms of service posted on the website as a result of their act of clicking on a button marked "I agree".

Likewise, in *Register.Com v Verio Inc* 126 F Supp 2d 238 (SD NY, 2000), the Court held that Verio's actions were likely to constitute a breach of the plaintiffs' terms of use, which had been posted on the website with a statement that "by submitting this [database] query, you agree to abide by these terms". Even though Verio had not been required to click an "I agree" button indicating its agreement to be bound, the Court held that by submitting its query, Verio "manifested its assent to be bound" and therefore a contract was formed.

In *I.Lan Systems Inc v Netscout Service Level Corp* 183 F Supp 2d 328 (D Mass, 2002), the Court held that the plaintiff was bound by the terms of a licence agreement that appeared on its computer screen when it downloaded the defendant's software, because the plaintiff indicated its assent to be bound by clicking on an "I agree" icon at the foot of the licence agreement.

In *Specht v Netscape Communications Corp* 150F F Supp 2d 585 (SD NY, 2001), a Federal Judge ruled that the act of downloading Netscape Communication's SmartDownload software did not bind people to an online contract because the terms of that agreement were not specifically agreed to by consumers. When downloading the software, consumers saw a small box of text asking them to "please review the licensing agreement". However, they were not required to click on any link indicating that they had done so. The Court held that the agreement was not enforceable, despite language in the licence agreement whereby the user consented to be bound by the terms of the licence agreement by installing or using the software.

A similar decision was reached in *Williams v America Online Inc* 2001 WL135825 (Mass Superior Court, 8/2/01). There the Court ruled that America Online could not enforce the forum selection clause in its click-wrap agreement.

The *Netscape* and *Williams* cases serve as a warning to software publishers, and others seeking to attract customers to enter into online agreements, that click-wrap agreements will only be enforced if customers expressly agree to the terms of the contract.

8.12.4 Uniform Computer Information Transactions Act (US)

In the US, the Uniform Computer Information Transactions Act ("UCITA") was drafted as a model law to overcome many of the problems encountered by applying the technologically out-of-date provisions of the Uniform Commercial Code to commercial dealings on the internet.

UCITA creates rules for making and enforcing internet access contracts, and recognises non-negotiated standard form agreements like shrink-wrap and click-wrap licences as valid contracts. It provides that all shrink-wrap and click-wrap licences will be enforceable so long as the licence terms are revealed before the payment of the purchase price.

In cases where the disclosure of licence terms comes after the purchase price is paid, UCITA will give the customer an unqualified right to reject and return the goods, and obtain a refund, where there is dissatisfaction with any licence terms. Customers are, however, prevented from obtaining the benefits of the software or information and still obtaining a refund.

8.12.5 Canada

In *Rudder v Microsoft Corp* (1999) 2 CPR (4th) 474 (Ont SC), subscribers to a Microsoft network online service saw the Court reject the subscribers' excuse of ignorance of a clause that they claimed not to have seen.

MSN's sign-up procedure required potential members to view the membership agreement terms twice during the process, obliging potential members to signify their acceptance each time. The second time the terms were displayed, all users were advised "if you click 'I agree' without reading the membership agreement you are still agreeing to be bound by all of the terms of the membership agreement without limitation".

The Court noted that if it had upheld the subscribers' argument, rather than advancing the goal of "commercial certainty", such a decision would have led to "chaos in the marketplace". The Court considered that such a result would have made electronic commerce ineffectual, and undermined the integrity of any agreement entered into through the medium of the internet.

8.12.6 England

On 21 August 2002, e-commerce Regulations came into force in the UK, setting rules for UK businesses that advertise or sell goods via the internet, mobile phone or e-mail.

The Regulations are based on the European Union's E-Commerce Directive, which includes transparency requirements for internet advertising, new principles relating to online contracting and requirements regarding disclosure of any codes of conduct, such as for online dispute settlement.

The Regulations require companies providing e-commerce services to offer basic details about the supplier, its products and services, information about the ordering process, swift acknowledgement of orders and the chance for customers to amend their orders. If a company fails to meet the key criteria, the sale will not be considered valid and the customer cannot be forced to pay.

8.12.7 Electronic Transactions Act 2002 (NZ)

The primary difference between an ordinary contract and a click-wrap contract is the manifestation of acceptance of the terms of the offer. Traditionally, parties to a contract show their agreement by manually writing their signature on the document. The New Zealand Courts have not ruled on whether clicking an on-screen button is a sufficient act of acceptance of an agreement. However, if both parties are aware that clicking an on-screen icon is an acceptable mode of communicating acceptance, then it appears likely that a New Zealand Courts would enforce such an agreement.

The Electronic Transactions Act 2002 provides that transactions will not be invalidated merely because they are in electronic form, or in an electronic communication.

The Act does confirm that an electronic signature will be given legal effect as a signature, provided:

- The electronic signature identifies a person, and can indicate that person's approval of the information communicated;

- The electronic signature is as reliable as appropriate for the purposes of the communication; and

- There was consent by the person receiving the electronic signature to the use of such means.

However, the Act does not specifically address online contract formation. Accordingly, whether a click-wrap agreement will be considered a binding contract will be left to the common law as stated above.

Although "electronic signature" is defined to mean "a method used to identify a person and to indicate that person's approval of that information" no further attempts have been taken to define that term in the Act. Presumably, this is to avoid the definition becoming obsolete by changes in technology, and thereby to ensure that any application of electronic technology will be given legal effect under the Act if it is functionally equivalent to a corresponding application of traditional technology. Section 24 also includes some rebuttable presumptions about the reliability of electronic signatures.

A more detailed discussion of the Act is beyond the ambit of this text. More information can be found on the Ministry of Economic Development's website (www.med.govt.nz/irdev/elcom/transactions/index.html).

8.12.8 Tips for making online agreements enforceable

The key to ensuring that online agreements are enforceable is to make sure that customers entering into such agreements are made fully aware of the terms and conditions of the contract.

The following steps should be taken to ensure that a click-wrap agreement is enforceable:

- Make sure that the customer is aware as early as possible that any transaction between the parties is subject to the terms and conditions of a click-wrap agreement.

- Display the terms and conditions prominently, and in a clear and concise way. Make it mandatory for customers to physically scroll through the terms before getting to the "I agree" button.

- Require the customer to accept or reject the terms and conditions by typing "I agree" or "I do not agree", or by clicking on a button containing the same statement. Include a statement such as "if you click 'I agree' without reading the terms and conditions of this agreement, you are still agreeing to be bound by all of those terms and conditions, without limitation".

- Ensure that customers are required to indicate their consent to the terms and conditions of the agreement before they are physically able to proceed to the next stage of the transaction, for example, downloading the software (including free software).

- If the customer selects the "I agree" button, or types in those words, such conduct should either transmit the customer to a subsequent screen that allows him or her to reaffirm his or her consent to the agreement, or to a secondary procedure on the same screen that allows the customer to reaffirm his or her consent. A double consent procedure helps establish that the customer did agree to the terms and conditions of the contract, and will minimise arguments that the customer consented by mistake.

- Use commercially reasonable attribution procedures to ensure that the customer is who he or she claims to be. For example, following consent to the terms of a click-wrap agreement, require customers to fill out a user registration field requiring the disclosure of a previously agreed on user name and address.

- If the agreement involves the delivery of a product, provide a copy of the terms and conditions along with shipment of the product. Remind the customer that use of the product constitutes acceptance of those terms. Offer the option of a "cooling off" period, with a refund on return of the goods if the customer decides to reject the terms and conditions.

- For software that does not require physical delivery, consider requiring a further reaffirmation of the customer's consent to the terms and conditions a short period after the software has been downloaded. Consider installing a "self-help" style program in the software to allow remote disablement of the software in the event that the customer fails to reaffirm his or her consent.

  If you do elect to include the ability to remotely disable software, make sure that your ability to do so is made very clear in the terms and conditions of the agreement. Consider specifying your ability to do so in a separate agreement, providing details of the notice requirements and "cooling-off" period, with a refund on return of the goods if the customer decides to reject the terms and conditions.

- Encourage the consumer to print-off and retain a copy of the agreement for his or her own records and future reference.

- Keep electronic records of each transaction and the applicable terms. Details on websites can change, so readers should ensure that all variations of the terms and conditions of click-wrap agreements are retained.

8.13   Legislative developments

8.13.1   Code of Practice

InternetNZ has been working on a "Draft Internet Code of Practice" for some time. A copy of the draft is available at www.internetnz.net.nz/issues/current-issues/ICOP/ ("the Draft Code"). The Draft Code would, if adopted, require signatory service providers to abide by good standards of conduct and business practice on the internet. The Draft Code is intended to address the potential information imbalance between ISPs and consumers and the risks, security and privacy issues arising from the use of internet services.

Included in the Draft Code are provisions for:

- The publication by ISPs of minimum standards of service;

- An undertaking by ISPs to comply with the Privacy Act 1993 and any codes developed under that Act;

- The development of acceptable use policies upon which service is conditional;

- The development and implementation of security policies;

- The development and implementation of adult content, and offensive or illegal content policies;

- An undertaking by ISPs to engage in cooperative interactions with other ISPs;

- The development of an interim Executive Body to oversee the operation of the Draft Code in the first year;

- The creation of an Executive Body Constitution to govern the Executive Body; and

- The creation of a Complaints Panel, and Terms of Reference containing complaints procedures and information guiding the operation of the same.

It appears that progress is being made with this project, albeit slowly. In addition, ISOCNZ is talking with the Telecommunications Carriers' Forum ("TCF") with regard to this project. See the TCF website, at www.tcf.org.nz.

8.14 References and resource sites

8.14.1 Websites

Thomson Brookers	www.thomsonbrookers.co.nz
Office of the Domain Name Commissioner	www.dnc.org.nz
Intellectual Property Office of New Zealand	www.iponz.govt.nz
Interim Website of New Zealand Legislation	www.legislation.govt.nz
Internet Assigned Numbers Authority (IANA)	www.iana.org
Internet Corporation for Assigned Names and Numbers (ICANN)	www.icann.org
Internet Society of New Zealand	www.isocnz.org.nz
James & Wells	www.jaws.co.nz
Legal Information Institutes	www.worldlii.org
	www.bailii.org
	www.austlii.edu.au
	www.nzlii.org
Max Planck Institute for Foreign and International Patent, Copyright, and Competition Law	www.mpg.de/english/
Ministry of Economic Development	www.med.govt.nz
UK Intellectual Property Office	www.ipo.gov.uk
Uniform Dispute resolution Policy (UDRP)	www.icann.org/udrp

US Courts for the Ninth Circuit — source of online decisions from the US Federal Court	www.ce9.usCourts.gov
US Patent and Trade Mark Office	www.uspto.gov
WIPO Electronic Commerce and Intellectual Property	www.wipo.int/about-ip/en/studies/publications/ip_ecommerce.htm
World Copyright Law Report (incorporating World eBusiness Law Report)	www.worldcopyrightlawreport.com
World Intellectual Property Organisation	www.wipo.int

8.14.2 Texts and periodicals

- Cristal, L E, and Greenfield, N S, *Trademark Law and the Internet* (2nd ed), US, INTA, 2001

- Elliott, C, "The internet: A new world without frontiers" (1998) 11 NZLJ 404

- Gamboa, J, "Internet service provider liability in the US and Australia: Sentinels or landlords?" (2002) 50 *Intellectual Property Forum* 40

- Harvey, D J, *Internet.law.nz*, Wellington, LexisNexis, 2003

- Simpson Grierson X-Tech Group, *A Guide to E-Commerce Law in New Zealand*, Wellington, Brookers, 2002

Chapter 9

PASSING OFF

9.1   Introduction

"Passing off" is an action brought to redress, or protect against, unfair competition between traders. In particular it is concerned with misrepresentations made by one trader, which damage the goodwill of another.

The modern tort of passing off is a development of the principle enunciated by Lord Halsbury in *Reddaway v Banham* [1896] AC 199; [1895-9] ER REP 133 (HL):

> "The principle of law may be very plainly stated, and that is, that nobody has any right to represent his goods as the goods of somebody else."

Since that statement was made the Courts have come to recognise that what is really being protected, and what traders seek a quasi-property right in, is not the name, mark or get-up of their product, but the goodwill attached to the business of making or selling those goods. This was first expressly recognised in *Spalding & Bros v Gamage Ltd* (1915) 32 RPC 273 (HL), where the Court concluded that:

> "A passing off action is a remedy for the invasion of a right of property not in the mark, name or get up improperly used, but in the business or goodwill likely to be injured by the misrepresentation made by passing off one's goods as the goods of another."

More recently, in *Arsenal Football Club Plc v Reed (No 2)* [2003] 3 All ER 865; [2003] RPC 39 (CA), at para 70, Aldous LJ said:

> "The traditional form of passing off as enunciated in such cases as *Reddaway v Banham* [1896] AC 199, [1895 9] ER REP 133 is no longer definitive of the ambit of the cause of action."

His Lordship considered that the cause of action was now perhaps best referred to as "unfair competition".

9.1.1 Elements of passing off

In *Erven Warnink BV v J Townend & Sons (Hull) Ltd* [1979] 2 All ER 927 (HL), Lord Diplock established the following five criteria as the "minimum constituent elements" for passing off:

- A misrepresentation;

- Made by a trader in the course of trade;

- To a prospective customer of his, or ultimate consumers of goods or services supplied by him;

- Which is calculated to injure the business or goodwill of another trader (in the sense that this is a reasonably foreseeable consequence); and

- Which causes actual damage to the business or goodwill of the trader by whom the action is bought or (in a quia timet action) will probably do so.

His Lordship was careful to clarify, however, that not all fact situations satisfying the above criteria will necessarily give rise to passing off.

More recently the test has been simplified. The elements that a plaintiff must establish in order to succeed in an action for passing off are now generally accepted as being those described by Lord Oliver of Aylmerton in *Reckitt & Colman Products Ltd v Borden Inc* [1990] 1 WLR 499; [1990] 1 All ER 873 (HL):

- That the plaintiff's goods or services have acquired goodwill or reputation in the mind of the purchasing public and are known by some name, mark or a get-up distinctive of the plaintiff's goods or services;

- That there has been a misrepresentation by the defendant leading, or that is likely to lead, the public to believe that goods or services offered by the defendant are goods or services of the plaintiff; and

- That the plaintiff has suffered, or is likely to suffer, damage as a result of the defendant's misrepresentation.

Both of the above tests are commonly cited by the New Zealand Courts; however, recent cases have shown a preference for the simpler *Reckitt & Colman* test: see, for example, *Anheuser-Busch Inc v Budweiser Budvar National Corp* [2001] 3 NZLR 666 (HC), at p 690.

9.1.2 Comparison with s 9 Fair Trading Act 1986

The Fair Trading Act 1986 provides for statutory regulation of misleading and deceptive conduct, and false or misleading representations, with the general aim of achieving fair competition in trade. The common law action of passing off seeks to prevent unfair trading, the essence of the tort being an actionable misrepresentation. As a result the two causes of action are often pleaded in parallel.

However, there are significant differences between passing off and the various causes of action available under the Fair Trading Act 1986, largely stemming from the consumer protection aim of the Fair Trading Act. As a result, the emphasis in a Fair Trading Act claim is on the effect of the misrepresentation on consumers, and any interested person may bring such an action. Conversely, a passing off plaintiff must show actual or likely damage to his or her own goodwill or reputation.

There may also be differences between the remedies obtainable by plaintiffs under each head. A passing off plaintiff is entitled to damages for proven loss whereas under the Fair Trading Act all remedies are discretionary. Under the Fair Trading Act the quantum of damages is assessed according to the effect of the misleading conduct on consumers, whereas in passing off the assessment is of the amount of damage to the plaintiff's goodwill.

Misleading and deceptive conduct under the Fair Trading Act 1986 is discussed in more detail in the Fair Trading Act 1986 chapter of this text (chapter 10).

9.1.3 Types of passing off

Early passing off cases were confined to misrepresentations relating to the source of goods or services, such as, for example, where one trader misrepresented its goods or services as the goods or services of another. In *Erven Warnink BV v J Townend & Sons (Hull) Ltd* [1979] 2 All ER 927 (HL) however, the House of Lords expressly acknowledged that a misrepresentation that one trader's product has the same qualities as another may constitute passing off, notwithstanding that the source of each individual product was clear. These two forms of passing off have come to be known as "classic passing off" and "extended passing off" respectively.

(1) *Classic passing off*

Classic passing off occurs where a defendant misrepresents to the public that the defendant's goods or services are those of the plaintiff and in so doing causes damage to the plaintiff's goodwill. Commonly the plaintiff and the defendant will be trading within the same field of activity and the defendant will be misleading the plaintiff's customers through the use of a similar name, mark or get-up.

(2) *Extended passing off*

Extended passing off is based on a misrepresentation that the defendant's goods or services have characteristics belonging to the plaintiff. The action relies not so much on public confusion over the source of the goods or services, as on public deception about an association between them. Similarly, the goodwill misappropriated is not trading goodwill but promotional goodwill.

For example, in *Erven Warnink BV v J Townend & Sons (Hull) Ltd* [1979] 2 All ER 927 (HL) (the *Advocaat* case), the House of Lords held that the defendant's use of the name "Advocaat" would misrepresent to the public that the drink produced by the defendants had the same characteristics or qualities as that produced by the plaintiffs under the same name, notwithstanding that the defendants had clearly distinguished their product from that of the plaintiff.

With extended passing off the plaintiff and defendant may be engaged in differing but related enterprises. A common field of activity is not required.

The increased scope of extended passing off is particularly noticeable where a group of traders claim goodwill and/or reputation in a descriptive name derived from the geographical region in which their product originates. Examples include the *Advocaat* case (above) and the *Champagne* cases (such as the New Zealand Court of Appeal's decision in *Wineworths Group Ltd v Comité Interprofessionel du Vin-Champagne* [1992] 2 NZLR 327 (CA) and related cases overseas). In the *Champagne* cases the damage to goodwill alleged by the plaintiffs (makers of French sparkling wine in the Champagne region) was the damage to the ability of the name Champagne to indicate wine of a particular quality and geographical origin, rather than direct damage to the goodwill of their businesses.

(3) *Character merchandising cases*

It is possible that so-called "character merchandising" cases may have further extended the scope of passing off, or perhaps given rise to a further category of cases. The line of Australian cases commencing with *Radio Corp Pty Ltd v Henderson* [1960] NSWR 279; (1960) 60 SR (NSW) 576 (NSW SC) and culminating in *Hogan v Koala Dundee Pty Ltd* (1989) 20 FCR 314; 83 ALR 187; 12 IPR 508 (FCA), have gone so far as to recognise property rights in the identity of a celebrity or fictional character. In *Koala Dundee*, it was stated:

> "I think the law now is, at least in Australia, that the inventor of a sufficiently famous fictional character having certain visual or other traits may prevent others using his character ... Furthermore the inventor may do these things even where he has never carried on any business at all, other than the writing or making of the work in which the character appears."

This statement is tantamount to recognition that the essence of the wrong done in the character merchandising context is not a "misrepresentation" as to an association between the parties and/or their products or services, but rather a wrongful appropriation of reputation.

New Zealand Courts appear reluctant to further extend the scope of passing off in this way: *Tot Toys Ltd v Mitchell* [1993] 1 NZLR 325. However, they have been prepared to protect the reputation of celebrities against unwitting endorsements, particularly in the field with which the celebrity is customarily linked.

For example, in *NZ Rugby Football Union v Saint Publishing Ltd* 2/10/01, Williams J, HC Auckland M1458/01, Saint published a 2002 calendar entitled "Born to Lead — All Black test captains 1958-2001", which featured photographs of a number of All Black captains including the then captain, Anton Oliver. The Court held that consumers might think that Oliver had sponsored or endorsed the calendar and injuncted Saint (under the Fair Trading Act 1986 and the Trade Marks Act 1953) from continuing to print and sell it.

(4) *Reverse passing off*

Classic passing off involves the defendant claiming that his or her goods or services are the plaintiff's. However, a misrepresentation by the defendant that the plaintiff's goods or services are the defendant's may also be actionable. For example, in *Dominion Rent-A-Car Ltd v Budget Rent-A-Car Systems (1970) Ltd* [1987] 2 NZLR 395 (CA), the Court stated at p 412:

> "In principle a misrepresentation by the defendant that the plaintiff's business is a branch of the defendant's can support a passing off action, provided that damage to the plaintiff is shown — for instance, to take one obvious illustration, by way of damage to his reputation by associating him with inferior quality."

As a cautionary note however, in some instances what may at first appear to be reverse passing off, may in fact be a subtle form of ordinary passing off. For example if a defendant shows customers a catalogue of the plaintiff's goods, as if they were his or her own, the customer orders goods, and the defendant supplies his or her own goods, then passing off in the ordinary sense has occurred, as the defendant has sold his or her goods on the strength of those of the plaintiff.

(5) *Enabling passing off by others*

An indirect misrepresentation by a defendant may also be actionable. This was clarified in *Tot Toys Ltd v Mitchell* [1993] 1 NZLR 325, at p 354:

> "Passing off defendants are responsible for foreseeable deception of those ultimate customers who purchase from intermediaries as well as for deception of their own immediate customers … However, a manufacturer is not responsible for the misconduct of a retailer unless it is clearly shown that the manufacturer ought to have contemplated that such misconduct would be likely."

In a similar way, intermediaries such as retailers may also be liable for facilitating passing off.

9.2 Goodwill or reputation

Goodwill has been described as:

> "The benefit and advantage of the good name, reputation and connection of a business. It is the attractive force which brings in custom."

See *Inland Revenue Commissioner v Muller & Co's Margarine Ltd* [1901] AC 217 (HL), at p 223.

Care should be taken with the use of the term "reputation". In the ordinary sense reputation is used to mean "well known", and whether or not it exists is a question of fact. However, in a passing off sense reputation is often used in relation to trade marks to denote that they have become distinctive of a trader, or in some cases as a synonym for goodwill.

"Goodwill" is something more than a trading reputation, it is a property right, albeit intangible: *Dominion Rent-A-Car Ltd v Budget Rent-A-Car Systems (1970) Ltd* [1987] 2 NZLR 395 (CA), at p 420.

Arguably, reputation can become separated from goodwill — for example, where the public associates goods or services with a source other than the legal owner of the goodwill. In contrast goodwill cannot exist independently from the business to which it is attached.

9.2.1 Proving the existence of goodwill

In a passing off sense a plaintiff must be able to establish that its name, mark or get-up are sufficiently distinctive to be capable of conferring goodwill on the plaintiff in relation to the goods or services in question.

The goodwill in question must be concerned with trade or business, and with conduct in trade or commerce establishing or injuring that goodwill.

The parameters within which the elements of passing off must be established, including the requirement for goodwill and reputation, are succinctly described by Gault J in *Wineworths Group Ltd v Comité Interprofessionel du Vin-Champagne* [1992] 2 NZLR 327 (CA):

> "It is necessary to keep firmly in mind that it is in the market or trade setting that the issues arise for determination. It is the point at which goods or services are bought and sold, where business dealings are transacted that the elements of the tort are to be investigated. It is concerned with trade or business goodwill and with conduct in trade or commerce establishing or injuring that goodwill. The manner in which a name is presented in trade will dictate the goodwill that is generated. It is the understanding of those engaged in trade that will dictate whether or not they are, or will be, misled."

9.2.2 Relevant time for establishing goodwill

The relevant date for determining whether a plaintiff has established the necessary goodwill or reputation is the date of commencement of the conduct complained of, that is, when the defendant commenced marketing the goods or services objected to: *Cadbury Schweppes Pty Ltd v Pub Squash Co Pty Ltd* [1981] 1 All ER 213 (PC), at p 221.

In some cases a plaintiff may be able to establish goodwill and reputation before commencing trading such as, for example, through the use of advertising or media coverage. In *Fletcher Challenge Ltd v Fletcher Challenge Pty Ltd* [1982] FSR 1, the Court was prepared to find that the announcement of an intended merger between Challenge Corporation Ltd and Fletcher Holdings Ltd in New Zealand gave rise to sufficient reputation and goodwill in the name "Fletcher Challenge", within "hours" of the company's incorporation, to restrain the defendant from using the name in Australia.

9.2.3 Requirement for goodwill within the jurisdiction

To be protectable, a plaintiff's goodwill must be localised in the market within which the defendant's infringing conduct is alleged to take place. In *Dominion Rent-A-Car Ltd v Budget Rent-A-Car Systems (1970) Ltd* [1987] 2 NZLR 395 (CA), the Court of Appeal held:

- Some form of business connection with the jurisdiction is generally thought to be necessary to enable a successful suit;

- Mere reputation within the jurisdiction does not by itself constitute a property right which the law protects;

- Goodwill may in some cases transcend national boundaries; and

- Where a business has a large amount of international reputation very little activity within New Zealand might be required to establish goodwill.

The requirement that there be at least some business or market activity within New Zealand or the relevant market or jurisdiction was confirmed in *CardMember Wines Ltd v The Wine Society Ltd* (1992) 4 TCLR 556.

Note, however, that the jurisdiction need not necessarily be New Zealand. In *Containerlift Services Ltd v Maxwell Rotors Ltd* (2003) 10 TCLR 807, the plaintiff, which had reputation in the UK and Europe in the name "Containerlift", successfully obtained an injunction against a New Zealand based defendant for misrepresentations arising in those jurisdictions from the use of the domain name "containerlift.com". The Court applied the English common law rule of "double actionability"; an act done abroad is actionable as a tort in [New Zealand] only if it would have been actionable as a tort if it had been done in [New Zealand] and it was actionable (though not necessarily as a tort) under the law of the foreign country.

The double actionability rule was considered in some detail in *Kabushiki Kaisha Sony Computer Entertainment v van Veen* 14/12/06, MacKenzie J, HC Wellington CIV-2004-485-1520 in the context of a claim for breach of copyright, breach of registered trade mark and wrongful possession and use of confidential information. The decision is discussed in more detail in the "Infringement and enforcement of rights" sections of the patents (at 2.14), copyright (at 4.10), design registrations (at 6.15), and trade marks (at 7.11) chapters of this text.

Also, even where the goodwill relied upon is within New Zealand it is possible for it to be limited to particular geographic regions. Thus, in *Fresh Direct Ltd v Fresh Direct Wholesale Ltd* 18/12/03, Durie J, HC Blenheim CIV-2003-406-20, the High Court refused to grant the plaintiff, which had been selling fresh fruit, vegetables, flowers and pot plants under the name "Fresh Direct" since 1995, a permanent injunction to restrain the defendant from supplying a broader range of foodstuffs under the same name in the Nelson/Marlborough area. Although the Court accepted that the plaintiff had significant goodwill in the FRESH DIRECT name throughout most of New Zealand, the Court found that the plaintiff's reputation in the Nelson/Marlborough region was limited to the supply of fresh fruits and vegetables to only three supermarkets, each of which were serviced from the plaintiff's Christchurch branch. In counterpoint, fresh fruit and vegetables made up only 10 percent of the defendant's business and the defendant's supply was mainly to cafés and restaurants. The plaintiff's limited reputation in the Nelson/Marlborough region, combined with a "paucity of evidence of confusion amongst members of the public within the affected market area" resulted in the plaintiff's case falling "well short of providing the necessary confidence for judicial intervention".

9.2.4 Identity of source need not be known

It is not necessary that the public be able to associate the reputation or goodwill with any particular party. However, it is necessary that the public associate the goods or services as originating from a single source. In other words, the plaintiff must prove that the name, mark or get-up indicates its goods and no one else's.

For example, in *Wineworths*, French wine producers claimed to have established goodwill or reputation in the name "Champagne" for sparkling wine, wherever produced, including in New Zealand. The Court considered, at p 336, that:

> "It is not the name that indicates the characteristics but the name in conjunction with experience or repute. The name, therefore, will not have precisely the same significance to everyone who knows it but if it serves to distinguish the product or products they associate with the name from other competitive products it has an identifying function in the course of trade. To those who seek the characteristics they know, or have heard of, the name will serve as an attracting force. For suppliers the attracting force in the name constitutes a part of the goodwill of their business. That will be so whether the name is associated solely with one supplier or with a class of suppliers who stand in the same position as to the name. The goodwill may be enjoyed among the whole population or among a particular market segment."

9.2.5 Effect upon goodwill of cessation of business

Goodwill and reputation may continue notwithstanding that a plaintiff's business has ceased trading. Whether or not any residual reputation or goodwill subsists is a question of fact in each case. One significant factor is whether or not there was any intention on the part of the plaintiff to resume business at some later date.

For example, in *Pink v Sharwood & Co* (1913) 30 RPC 725, the Court found that the plaintiff's goodwill had come to an end when the receiver had discontinued the business and its assets were sold. In contrast, in *Poiret v Jules Poiret Ltd and AF Nash* (1920) 37 RPC 177, the plaintiff was successful even though his business had closed while he served in the First World War.

Proving an intention to resume the business at some later date will not assist the plaintiff, if the name, mark or get-up on which it relies has lost its distinctiveness in the intervening period.

9.2.6 Assignment of business or goodwill

As a property right, the goodwill of a business can be transferred voluntarily by assignment, by devolution upon death or by operation of law such as upon bankruptcy. Goodwill must be transferred with the business and an assignment of the business as a whole transfers the goodwill along with it.

An exception to the transferability of goodwill may occur where a name or mark has become so associated with a particular person that it cannot be assigned to anybody else. In most cases. however, the Courts will find that the association is with the business rather than the person, and will allow assignment provided the business is transferred at the same time.

See, for example, *Leather Cloth Co Ltd v American Leather Cloth Co Ltd* (1865) 11 HL Cas 523; 11 ER 1435. An assignment of a right to use a name or common law mark without assignment of the goodwill of the business will not be enforceable against members of the public: *Pinto v Badman* (1891) 8 RPC 181.

9.2.7 Licensing of goodwill

Generally speaking, goodwill itself is not licensed to others, but associated rights, such as the right to use names, marks or get-up are licensed. In this way the licensor is permitting another to do acts which would otherwise constitute passing off.

The wording of the licence is important, as the licensee will then be in a position to develop its own goodwill in the name, mark or get-up (in the eyes of the public at least). The licensor must be careful to maintain or retain a sufficient connection with the licensed business or he or she will no longer have the protectable right required to bring an action for passing off. Thus he or she will be unable to stop the licensee from continuing to use the name, mark or get-up upon the expiration of the licence, and may lose the right to use the distinctive feature himself or herself: *Thorneloe v Hill* [1894] 1 Ch 569.

9.2.8 Shared goodwill

In some cases more than one person or business may be legally entitled to use a particular name, mark or get-up, for example where a business has been split, divided or franchised. In such cases each co-owner may have an independent right to bring an action for passing off.

A further example arises in descriptive name cases, such as the *Advocaat* case (*Erven Warnink BV v J Townend & Sons (Hull) Ltd* [1979] 2 All ER 927 (HL)) where any trader whose goods possessed the qualities of *Advocaat* was said to enjoy goodwill and reputation in the name.

9.3 Distinctiveness

Unless the plaintiff can establish that its name, mark or get-up are distinctive, there will be nothing to attach that name, mark or get-up to the plaintiff's goodwill, and the plaintiff will have no action against the defendant for damage to that goodwill.

In the *Champagne* case (*Wineworths Group Ltd v Comité Interprofessionel du Vin-Champagne* [1992] 2 NZLR 327 (CA)), the Court of Appeal considered whether French sparkling wine manufacturers could protect the name "champagne" from use by New Zealand manufacturers. In considering the question of whether the name "champagne" was distinctive the Court stated, at p 336, that:

> "It is not the name that indicates the characteristics but the name in conjunction with experience or repute. The name, therefore, will not have precisely the same significance to everyone who knows it but if it serves to distinguish the product or products they associate with the name from other competitive products it has an identifying function in the course of trade. To those who seek the characteristics they know, or have heard of, the name will serve as an attracting force. To its suppliers the attracting force in the name constitutes a part of the goodwill of their business."

and later, at p 337:

"Of course, the situation may be reached where a name no longer does serve the purpose of distinguishing a particular product, service or business and comes to be used even in trade as applicable equally to products of other traders as to those of the trader whose goods it originally signified. Then it is no longer distinctive of that trader's goods and is generic. No longer can it constitute part of the trader's goodwill. It no longer serves to attract customers to his goods as distinct from others."

By analogy, the same applies to marks used on/in relation to, or the get-up of, goods or services.

9.3.1 Question of degree

Whether or not the plaintiff's name, mark, or get-up are distinctive of the plaintiff is a question of fact and degree. The key factors are the amount of use of the allegedly distinguishing feature and the inherent distinctiveness of the feature itself.

9.3.2 Use in a trade mark sense

Traditionally, only use of a name, mark or get-up in a trade mark sense can contribute to its distinctiveness. For example, where a word mark is used in a descriptive, rather than trade mark, sense (such as in conjunction with another more distinctive mark) the mark may not qualify as distinctive.

For example, in *Horlicks Malted Milk Co v Summerskill* (1917) 34 RPC 63 (HL), "malted milk" was found not to be distinctive despite 25 years of exclusive use by the plaintiff, on the grounds that "malted milk" had only been used descriptively in conjunction with the plaintiff's "Horlicks" mark.

However, recent trade mark authorities (notably *Philips Electronics NV v Remington Consumer Products Ltd* [2003] Ch 159; [2003] 2 WLR 294; [2003] RPC 2 (ECJ), *Fredco Trading Ltd v Miller* (2006) 8 NZBLC 101,761 (CA), and *Société des Produits Nestlé SA v Mars UK Ltd* Case No C-353/03 (ECJ)) have suggested that the focus of distinctiveness is on the end result. If an enquiry shows that the plaintiff's mark is distinctive to the public it doesn't matter how it became distinctive or whether it has been used with other distinctive marks.

"Use in a trade mark sense" and "distinctiveness" are discussed in more detail in the trade marks chapter of this text (chapter 7).

9.3.3 Distinctive get-up

In addition to names or marks, features of the appearance or "get-up" of a trader's goods may often be distinctive. Get-up was described in *Klissers Farmhouse Bakeries Ltd v Harvest Bakeries Ltd* [1985] 2 NZLR 129, at p 147, as:

> "the dress in which [goods] are presented to the buyer. It comprises in particular the size and shape of the packages, the material, the colour, and the decoration of their wrappers, and the lettering and arrangement of their labels."

If a plaintiff can establish that his or her get-up is distinctive, it may be protectable provided the necessary reputation and goodwill can be established.

The Courts have traditionally afforded protection only to non-functional features of get-up, on the basis that functional features ought to be available to all traders wishing to market goods that perform the same function. In *Tot Toys Ltd v Mitchell* [1993] 1 NZLR 325, the Court distinguished between aspects of get-up that were functional and those that were capricious, the capricious elements being eligible for protection. Capricious was defined, at p 335, as:

> "a design choice which is arbitrary, not uniquely desirable, and therefore not solely driven by considerations of logic or utility. If when presented with a range of possible choices a designer chooses one because it would be cheaper, easier to produce, or more useful to the consumer, the choice is not capricious. But it is capricious if it is a random selection from a range of equally acceptable solutions or is motivated by nothing more than aesthetics or a desire to be distinctive."

The Court identified the following principles in relation to the question of which aspects of the plaintiff's get-up might be protectable, at p 344:

"(a)   There is nothing in principle to preclude a plaintiff from relying upon the shapes, surface colours and markings of his or her product as get-up for passing off purposes.

"(b)   If the feature relied upon is a functional one it can qualify as part of the get-up only if the characteristic which distinguishes the product in the minds of the public is not the functional idea per se but the capricious way in which the idea has been expressed.

"(c)   For this purpose the design decision to adopt a particular characteristic can be regarded as capricious if it is arbitrarily chosen from a broad range of equally acceptable alternatives. It is not capricious if it is rationally dictated by the demands of function, efficiency, cost of production, available materials and like considerations.

"(d)   In marginal cases features of a product are more likely to be regarded as qualifying get-up if they are fanciful, original, unusual or selected from a vast range of available possibilities rather than simple, obvious, mundane or selected from a limited range; if they represent no more than the specific form or mode in which an idea has been expressed, rather than the idea itself; if there are obvious and equally effective alternatives readily available to erstwhile competitors; and if they do not embody ideas which would be uniquely useful to others.

"(e)   Get-up qualifying for passing off purposes is a combination of capricious features which satisfy the above test. It is the effective use by that combination which must distinguish the product in the minds of the public. Get-up is not disqualified if it serves to distinguish only when in association with the rest of the product but it must be a sine qua non to customer recognition. If recognition would occur with or without the qualifying get-up the action must fail."

9.3.4 Loss of distinctiveness

If the plaintiff's name, mark or get-up ceases to be distinctive of the plaintiff then he or she will have lost the goodwill in that name, mark or get-up.

For example, in *Kark (Norman) Publications Ltd v Odhams Press Ltd* (1962) 79 RPC 163, the Court upheld the right of the defendants to name their magazine *Today*, a name previously used by the plaintiffs, on the basis that the name had ceased to be distinctive of the plaintiffs some years after they discontinued using the name for their magazine.

9.4 Descriptive words, marks, or get-up

The distinctiveness of a mark is more difficult to establish when the words used are descriptive of the goods or services themselves, or some aspect of the goods or services (such as, for example, their name, appearance or geographical origin).

Dominion Rent-A-Car Ltd v Budget Rent-A-Car Systems (1970) Ltd [1987] 2 NZLR 395 (CA) summarises the proposition as follows:

> "There is a price to be paid for an eloquently descriptive trade name. Its very descriptiveness tends to make it not truly distinctive as to any particular business. The risk of confusion must be accepted, to do otherwise is to give one who appropriates to himself descriptive words an unfair monopoly in those words and might even deter others from pursuing the occupation which the words describe."

For example, in *Office Cleaning Services Ltd v Westminster Window & General Cleaners Ltd* (1946) 63 RPC 39 (HL), the Court refused to uphold a claim of passing off against the defendant who was trading as "Westminster Office Cleaning Association" on the basis that the words "Office Cleaning" were purely descriptive of the services performed or offered, and "Westminster" described only the geographical origin. In such circumstances the use by the defendant of "Association" rather than "Services" was sufficient to distinguish it from the plaintiff.

9.4.1 Secondary meaning

It is sometimes accepted that words with a primarily descriptive meaning may acquire a secondary meaning indicating that products or services originate from a particular source. The test is whether the words have in fact become distinctive of the plaintiff.

In *Dominion Rent-A-Car Ltd v Budget Rent-A-Car Systems (1970) Ltd* [1987] 2 NZLR 395 (CA), at p 408, the Court referred to the principle that allowing a trader an unfair monopoly in descriptive words might deter others from pursuing the occupation which the words describe, and said:

> "This principle does not altogether rule out the possibility that by usage the descriptive words may become distinctive of the business — but it means that true distinctiveness is especially hard to establish."

In *NZ Insurance Co Ltd v NZ Insurance Brokers Ltd* [1976] 2 NZLR 40, the Court held that the plaintiff had established that the words "New Zealand's Insurance" had acquired a secondary meaning, entitling the plaintiff to the exclusive right to their use, which could not be diminished by the defendant's addition of the word "Brokers".

9.4.2 Generic names

In some cases, words, whether descriptive from the outset or not, may be, or may have become, the name of the goods or services themselves, and as such incapable of denoting a particular trade source.

If a trader introduces novel goods or services that the English language does not currently have a name for, the trader faces the risk that his or her term for the goods or services may become descriptive of them unless he or she provides the public with a suitable generic term for identifying the new goods or services.

For example, in *Waitomo Adventures Ltd v BWR Resources Ltd* 26/4/02, Randerson J, HC Hamilton CP72/00, the defendant claimed to be the inventor of the term "black water rafting" used to describe an adventure tourism activity involving floating through underground caves in rubber tubes. The Court held that regardless of whether or not the defendant had invented the term, it was nonetheless descriptive of the activity and as such could never have been distinctive of the defendant or its service.

9.4.3 Geographical indications

Geographical names are another form of descriptive word that will rarely be protectable by a particular trader. However, in some cases where a defendant has no connection with the geographical name by which the plaintiff's goods (or a characteristic of those goods) are known or identified, the plaintiff may be able to bring an action for passing off. See, for example, *Wineworths Group Ltd v Comité Interprofessionel du Vin-Champagne* [1992] 2 NZLR 327 (CA) (discussed earlier in this chapter).

9.4.4 Small differences may suffice to distinguish

Where descriptive words or phrases are used, the Courts are more likely to accept small differences as distinguishing the defendant's goods or services from those of the plaintiff. In *Office Cleaning Services Ltd v Westminster Window & General Cleaners Ltd* (1946) 63 RPC 39 (HL), at p 42, the House of Lords held:

> "The courts will not readily assume that the use by a trader as part of his trade name of descriptive words if used by another trader as part of his trade name is likely to cause confusion and will easily accept small differences as adequate to avoid it."

In each case it is a question of fact as to whether confusion will be reduced by such a small difference.

9.5 Misrepresentation

An essential requirement of passing off is that there be an actionable misrepresentation by the defendant. The misrepresentation need not be an express statement made by the defendant, but may be implied from the use of names, marks or get-up that are sufficiently similar to cause confusion in the minds of the public.

The requirement for misrepresentation was described in *Reckitt & Colman Products Ltd v Borden Inc* [1990] 1 WLR 499; [1990] 1 All ER 873 (HL), at p 499; p 880, as:

"A misrepresentation by the defendant to the public (whether or not intentional) leading or likely to lead the public to believe that the goods or services offered by him are the goods or services of the plaintiff."

In *Klissers Farmhouse Bakeries Ltd v Harvest Bakeries Ltd (No 2)* [1985] 2 NZLR 143, at p 147, (subsequently upheld on appeal) the Court held:

"The misrepresentation is the foundation of a passing off action. Direct misrepresentation is comparatively rare. More commonly, passing off is alleged by way of indirect misrepresentation based on allegations that a mark or a get-up is distinctive of the plaintiffs goods exclusively and that the defendant has used the mark or get-up or an imitation so close as to be likely to deceive."

Proof of misrepresentation involves proof of two elements:

(1)   That the plaintiff's goods or services, by reason of their name, mark, or get-up, have become distinctive of the plaintiff, and that the name, mark, or get-up has given the plaintiff and the plaintiff alone the reputation as the marketer of such goods or services; and

(2)   Confusion of the defendant's goods or services with those of the plaintiff.

The *Klissers* case concerned get-up but the principles expressed are equally applicable to other forms of distinctive feature.

The misrepresentation must be material or relevant in the sense that confusion of the public must occur or be likely to occur as a result: *Erven Warnink BV v J Townend & Sons (Hull) Ltd* [1979] 2 All ER 927 (HL). However, even if confusion has resulted from the defendant's actions there will be no misrepresentation if, for example, the defendant has copied non-distinctive words or features, or the words or the statements were true. Similarly, mere copying of novel aspects of the plaintiff's goods, mark or name is not actionable as passing off if there has been no misrepresentation. See, for example, *Cadbury Schweppes Pty Ltd v Pub Squash Co Pty Ltd* [1981] 1 All ER 213 (PC).

See also *Universal College of Learning v ACP Computer Solutions Ltd* 22/10/03, Hammond J, HC Napier CP9/01, where the Court found no misrepresentation in the defendant's use of the brand "FutureCOL". To the extent that there was any "cause to wonder" in the minds of the public, the Court found that this was a risk that the plaintiff took when it used the element COL "a common abbreviation for College" in its own brand "Ucol".

Other examples where a defendant might use distinctive features of the plaintiff without misrepresentation include satire and comparative advertising.

However, the indication of future direction from the English Court of Appeal in *Arsenal Football Club Plc v Reed (No 2)* [2003] 3 All ER 865; [2003] RPC 39 (CA) might suggest otherwise. There Aldous LJ observed, in obiter, that he did not agree with the trial judge's finding that there could be no passing off without a representation that the allegedly infringing goods came from or were commercially connected with a particular source. His Lordship preferred the view of Cross J in *Vine Products Ltd v Mackenzie & Co Ltd* (1969) 86 RPC 1, that the use of another's mark in a way that diluted or destroyed their goodwill in the mark could be actionable as passing off in the sense that it was "unfair trading" or "unlawful competition", despite the fact that there was no misleading indication as to source. *Arsenal* does not appear to have been applied in New Zealand, as yet.

9.5.1 No fraudulent intention necessary

Proof of fraudulent intention on the part of the defendant is not a necessary element of the misrepresentation, nor indeed the action for passing off. However, if a fraudulent intention on the part of the defendant is proved, a Court is likely to be quicker to infer that the public has been, or is likely to be, deceived.

See *Klissers Farmhouse Bakeries Ltd v Harvest Bakeries Ltd (No 2)* [1985] 2 NZLR 143, at p 154:

> "[I]f it is shown that a defendant intended to deceive then the burden of proof on a plaintiff is much lighter: see *Rolls Razor Ltd v Rolls Lighters Ltd* (1949) 66 RPC 299, 303. If there is evidence of an intention to deceive, a court will not generally push its investigation further but will accept that if a party has intended to deceive then he is likely to be able to carry out his objective: see *Slazenger & Sons v Feltham & Co (No 2)* (1889) 6 RPC 531, 538. But if the court does not believe there is any probability of deception or confusion, the action must fail: see *Cadbury Schweppes Pty Ltd v Pub Squash Co Pty Ltd* [1981] 1 All ER 213 (PC)."

Similarly, although acknowledging that an honest or fraudulent intent is generally irrelevant to an action for passing off or breach of the Fair Trading Act, the Court in *Fresh Direct Ltd v Fresh Direct Wholesale Ltd* 18/12/03, Durie J, HC Blenheim CIV-2003-406-20 was prepared to look at the bona fides of the defendant's actions in adopting the trading name complained of, insofar as that enquiry assisted it in the exercise of its discretion whether or not to grant an injunction. The Court also commented, at para 13, that such an approach may assist in determining whether a particular result (ie confusion of the public) ought reasonably to have been foreseen and whether the defendant took all reasonable precautionary steps.

9.5.2 Likelihood of deception or confusion

As an element of the requirement for a misrepresentation, the plaintiff must establish that confusion or deception in the minds of the relevant public has resulted or is likely to result.

Confusion or deception is distinguishable from a mere "causing to wonder": *Universal College of Learning v ACP Computer Solutions Ltd* 22/10/03, Hammond J, HC Napier CP9/01.

The likelihood of confusion or deception is a question of fact. In *Office Cleaning Services Ltd v Westminster Window & General Cleaners Ltd* (1946) 63 RPC 39 (HL), Lord Simonds stated, at p 42, that:

> "The nature of the words which are used in the trade name, the circumstances and peculiarities of the trade, the motives, proved or presumed, of the trade who would use the words, all these and many other factors must be considered by the judge determining whether a plaintiff can succeed in his claim. It is a question upon which the judge who has to decide the case has to bring his own mind to bear and which he has to decide for himself."

Similarly, in *Klissers Farmhouse Bakeries Ltd v Harvest Bakeries Ltd (No 2)* [1985] 2 NZLR 143, at p 153:

"The test of confusion has been variously expressed. It has been said the courts must be satisfied that the defendant's conduct is calculated to pass off other goods as those of the plaintiff or, at least, to produce such confusion in the minds of probable customers or purchasers or other persons with whom the plaintiff has business relations as would be likely to lead to the other goods being bought and sold for his ... 'the likely impression on the casual and unwary customer'; and in the Privy Council case from New Zealand of *Hannaford & Burton Ltd v Polaroid Corp* [1976] 2 NZLR 14 at p 18 the test was accepted to be 'a reasonable likelihood of ... confusion among a substantial number of persons' ... The likelihood of confusion is a jury question for the Judge to be decided not only on the evidence before him but also on the basis of his own examination of the packaging involved."

The test for passing off calls for a comparison between the plaintiff's product presentation, as a whole, and the defendant's product presentation, as a whole, in the circumstances of actual use, including the respective trade marks used (if any) and the get-up of the products: *Anheuser-Busch Inc v Budweiser Budvar National Corp* [2003] 1 NZLR 472; (2002) 7 NZBLC 103,812 (CA), at p 501; p 103,836.

It follows that all of the circumstances of the case must be considered when determining whether or not confusion has resulted, or is likely to result, from the defendant's activities. These circumstances may include:

- Whether the product is of a type and cost likely to prompt inquiry over source. A Court may find that greater differences are required to distinguish products that are low cost or often used commodity items, as customers will take less care when making their selection. Similarly, regular or habitual purchasers of a product may be more likely to be deceived by something that appears similar, and is sold in similar circumstances to that which they normally purchase: *NZ Net Guide Ltd v IDG Communications Ltd* 24/1/01, Fisher J, HC Auckland M2039-SW00.

- Whether the product will be sold with packaging or labelling which would serve to distinguish.

- Whether the anticipated type of buyer is likely to be discerning.

- Whether retailers would be likely to present and represent the product in a way that would distinguish or confuse.

- Whether customers will have the opportunity of comparing the plaintiffs' and defendants' goods side by side, and if not, a customer's imperfect recollection is relevant: *Australian Woollen Mills Ltd v F S Walton & Co Ltd* (1937) 58 CLR 641.

9.5.3 Proof of actual deception not required

Evidence of actual confusion or deception is not essential, although as the Court of Appeal stated in *Wineworths Group Ltd v Comité Interprofessionel du Vin-Champagne* [1992] 2 NZLR 327 (CA), at p 342: "it is, of course, the best evidence of likely future deception".

9.5.4 Instruments of fraud or deception

In some instances a defendant's goods may have a name, mark or get-up that is so inherently deceptive, or so close to those distinctive of the plaintiff, that merely passing those goods to an intermediary will be viewed by the Courts as aiding that intermediary to pass those goods off as the plaintiff's. Such goods have been recognised as instruments of fraud or deception.

In such cases possessing or intending to equip another with an instrument of fraud will complete the requirements for passing off as the Court will be prepared to infer damage to the plaintiff's goodwill.

More recently names have also been held to be capable of being recognised as instruments of fraud. For example, the plaintiffs in *British Telecommunications Plc v One In A Million Ltd* (1998) 42 IPR 289; [1999] FSR 1 (CA) were successful in obtaining an injunction ordering the defendants to transfer internet domain names to the plaintiffs, on the basis that the internet domain names, which comprised or incorporated the names or trade marks of well known commercial enterprises (for example, marksandspencer.co.uk and britishtelecom.co.uk), were instruments of fraud. The Court found that the domain names were produced to enable passing off, adapted to be used for passing off, and if used, likely to be fraudulently used.

The Court also held that in considering whether a name was an instrument of fraud or deception it was appropriate to consider the similarity of the names, the intention of the defendants, the type of trade and all the surrounding circumstances.

9.5.5 Who must be confused

An important element in determining whether there has been or is likely to be confusion or deception is the identification of the relevant public, and the taking into account of the characteristics of that relevant public. The average customer will be different for different products or services. For example, customers will take more care with the selection of some types of products than with others, and such factors are relevant to the question of confusion and deception. The size of the relevant market may also have bearing on the number of persons who must be confused in order to satisfy the requirements of passing off. A useful summary was provided by the Court in *Tot Toys Ltd v Mitchell* [1993] 1 NZLR 325, at p 354.

It is not essential to show that all members of a relevant class of persons will be confused or deceived. The plaintiff needs to establish only that a substantial number of purchasers will be deceived: *Klissers Farmhouse Bakeries Ltd v Harvest Bakeries Ltd* [1988] 1 NZLR 16 (CA).

The question of substantiality was also considered by the Court in *Tot Toys Ltd v Mitchell* [1993] 1 NZLR 325, at p 355:

> "An injunction will not normally be granted unless the number or proportion of customers likely to be deceived is 'substantial' ... The numbers properly to be regarded as 'substantial' will no doubt vary according to the value of the product and the proportion of total transactions involved. In the context of selling ships even one deception might suffice, but not so for newspapers."

9.5.6 Common field of activity

In *Taylor Bros Ltd v Taylors Group Ltd* [1988] 2 NZLR 1; (1987) 2 TCLR 415 (HC), the High Court held that the question of whether, and to what extent, the plaintiff and defendant were engaged in a common field of activity was a factor to be taken into account in determining the likelihood of confusion. This was a clarification of earlier judicial disagreement as to whether a common field of activity was a factor, or a stand-alone requirement, of actionable passing off. The High Court held, at p 20, that:

> "The question to be determined is whether an activity on the part of the defendant may mislead potential customers into thinking the activity is that of the plaintiff. If the business of the plaintiff and the business of the defendant are in totally unrelated fields, the risk of such confusion is diminished. If, conversely, the fields of activity of the plaintiff and defendant are closely related, the risk is increased. And, of course, there are gradations in between. The important point is this: the existence or otherwise of a common field of activity is merely one pointer towards the probable presence or absence of confusion. It is no more."

In the *Taylors* case, there was a clear overlap between the respective businesses of the plaintiff and defendant, which pointed to a likelihood of confusion. In contrast, in *Lego Systems Aktieselskab v Lego M Lemalstrich Ltd* [1983] FSR 155, the Court found a likelihood of confusion despite the fact that there was no common field of activity at all.

9.6 Damage

Another essential element of actionable passing off is that the defendant's actions have caused or are likely to cause substantial damage to the plaintiff's business, goodwill or reputation. In *Dominion Rent-A-Car Ltd v Budget Rent-A-Car Systems (1970) Ltd* [1987] 2 NZLR 395 (CA), the Court held, at p 412, that:

> "One important limitation of the right of a trader to restrain another is that he must show an invasion of that intangible right of property compendiously described as goodwill."

There are many potential ways in which a plaintiff's goodwill can be damaged by actionable conduct on the part of the defendant, both direct and indirect.

At first instance in *Taylor Bros Ltd v Taylors Group Ltd* [1988] 2 NZLR 1; (1987) 2 TCLR 415 (HC), McGechan J identified three categories of actionable damage, at p 22; p 436:

> "Diversion is an appropriation of a part of the plaintiff's goodwill. Damage to reputation amounts to a poisoning of the plaintiff's goodwill. Damage by suggestion of association of the plaintiff's business amounts to a dilution of the plaintiff's goodwill."

Each of these is considered below in more detail, although it is important to note that in practice distinctions need not be drawn between different forms of damage. All forms of damage are actionable: *Taylor Bros Ltd v Taylors Group Ltd* [1988] 2 NZLR 1; (1987) 2 TCLR 415 (HC), at p 22; p 436:

> "At the end of the day there is nothing really arcane or specialised in these three categories of actionable damage. A common thread runs through all: damage to goodwill, differing only in type. … A plaintiff who is entitled in principle to the protection of his property right in goodwill is entitled to protection against all forms of attack without nice distinctions being drawn."

Indeed what may be suffered or claimed may well be a combination of forms of damage. For example, it is common to find damage by diversion and dilution pleaded together.

9.6.1 Diversion

The most common form of damage in a passing off action is the diversion of trade from the plaintiff to the defendant. In other words, customers may be confused as to the source of the product or service, and purchase the defendant's product or service believing it is that of the plaintiff.

In *Tot Toys Ltd v Mitchell* [1993] 1 NZLR 325, at p 351, the Court held that where damage by diversion is being claimed it is essential that the plaintiff establish that customers are motivated by the source of the product:

> "If in an alleged diversion of trade case the customer would have purchased the Defendant's product with or without any deception on the Defendant's part, that nexus is lacking. In that situation it will not be a passing off which has caused the damage to the Plaintiff; it will be conventional market forces."

9.6.2 Injury to the plaintiff's reputation

This form of damage occurs where the plaintiff's reputation, and hence goodwill, is damaged through association or confusion with the defendant's inferior goods or services, or where the nature or reputation of the defendant itself is such that the plaintiff's reputation is damaged by the inference that the plaintiff is in some way associated with the defendant. For example, in *Annabel's (Berkeley Square) Ltd v G Schock* (1972) 55 RPC 838, an escort agency was prohibited by injunction from trading under the same name as a well-known nightclub.

9.6.3 Dilution

Dilution of goodwill occurs where a plaintiff's distinctiveness is eroded or inundated by the defendant's use of similar distinctive features.

For example, in *Taylor Bros Ltd v Taylors Group Ltd* [1988] 2 NZLR 1 (CA), the Court found that there was a real risk that:

> "the point would come when the Plaintiff was no longer recognised by its own name but was seen by the public to be part of the Taylors Group; and that the goodwill attached to the name Taylors could be diluted to the point where the sale price of the name, at present no doubt very real, diminished and perhaps sharply."

Similarly, in *Wineworths Group Ltd v Comité Interprofessionel du Vin-Champagne* [1992] 2 NZLR 327 (CA), erosion of the distinctiveness of the name "champagne" as a result of use of the name by Australian manufacturers was viewed as an actionable form of damage to the goodwill of the French champagne producers.

9.7 Passing off and internet domain names

The misleading use of an internet domain name may be actionable as passing off in the same way as the use of any other mark that is, or may be, distinctive of a particular trader.

There is a more detailed discussion of passing off of internet domain names in the domain names chapter of this text (chapter 8).

9.7.1 Goodwill or reputation in a distinctive feature

The plaintiff must prove that he or she has goodwill and reputation in a distinctive word the subject of the domain name (or a similar word).

9.7.2 Misrepresentation

Usually the misrepresentation will involve the public being misled into thinking that the defendant's domain name relates to a website belonging to, or associated with, the plaintiff. Often whether or not there has been a misrepresentation will depend on:

- How the domain name is likely to be perceived by the public at large; and

- The legitimacy (or bona fides) of the defendant's proposed use.

Even though a domain name is technically only the electronic equivalent of a street address, it can also act as an indicator of origin. Selecting some other person's name or trade mark as one's web address will often cause consumers to believe:

- That they will locate that other person's web site at the address; or

- That the web site located at the address is in some way associated with the party with whom they associate the name or trade mark.

See *Panavision International LP v Toeppen* 141 F 3d 1316 (9th Cir, 1998).

(1)   *Use of the domain name by the defendant not essential*

Cybersquatting, or registering domain names similar to the well-known marks or names of other traders without the consent of the respective owners, and without any intention to use them, is also likely to constitute a misrepresentation.

In *Oggi Advertising Ltd v McKenzie* [1999] 1 NZLR 631, it was not proved that the defendant had used its www.oggi.co.nz domain name to offer any goods or services. It appeared that the defendant had registered the domain name with the intent of selling it to the plaintiff, rather than trading on the plaintiff's reputation. Nevertheless, after deciding that the plaintiff had the requisite reputation in the "Oggi" name, that a misrepresentation had been made in the course of trade, and that it was likely to cause damage to the business of the plaintiff, the Court ordered the defendant to assign the domain name to the plaintiff. The Court held that registering a domain name makes a representation to persons who consult the Register that the registrant is connected or associated with the name registered, and thus the owner of the goodwill in the name, and this amounts to passing off.

(2)   *Misappropriated domain name as an "instrument of fraud"*

In *British Telecommunications Plc v One In A Million Ltd* (1998) 42 IPR 289; [1999] FSR 1 (CA), the UK Court of Appeal held that if use of a domain name would result in passing off, the domain name is an "instrument of fraud". Furthermore, the Court would intervene by way of injunction in passing off cases if, by registration of a domain name:

- Passing off was established or threatened;

- The defendant was a joint tortfeasor with another in passing off (either actual or threatened); or

- The defendant equipped himself, or intended to equip another, with an instrument of fraud.

(3)   *Fraudulent intention*

Although the plaintiff does not need to show intention to deceive on the part of the defendant, the Court will more readily infer that a defendant who intended to deceive has succeeded in doing so: *Tot Toys Ltd v Mitchell* [1993] 1 NZLR 325, at p 354. In other words, a Court will be less sympathetic to a defendant who intended to deceive through its actions. However, proof of an intention to deceive will not of itself be conclusive. See, for example, *NZ Net Guide Ltd v IDG Communications Ltd* 24/1/01, Fisher J, HC Auckland M2039-SW00: "actual intent to deceive on the Defendant's part is neither necessary nor sufficient."

In a similar way, a finding that the defendant engaged in a course of conduct "with its eyes open" may be taken into account by the Court, particularly when weighing up whether to award an interim injunction. In the *NZ Net Guide Ltd* case the Court held:

> "The next factor is that IDG deliberately assumed the risk of proceeding. It cannot be suggested that IDG innocently entered the market only to discover NetGuide later. It has never been suggested that this was anything other than a deliberate attempt to produce something to compete with NetGuide ... Given that NetGuide was squarely within the eyes of IDG at the time that it chose its name and get-up, IDG must have known that with so many similarities it ran at least the risk of breach of the Fair Trading Act and/or passing off laws. Having gone into this venture with its eyes open it can scarcely be surprised if an interim injunction results."

9.8   Defences

9.8.1   Innocence not a defence

Intention to deceive is not a necessary element of the defendant's conduct in order to establish passing off. Hence, the absence of intent on the part of the defendant does not serve as a defence. Innocence may be a factor relevant in assessing the quantum of damages that ought to be awarded; however this is not always the case: *Gillette UK Ltd v EdenWest Ltd* (1994) 111 RPC 279.

9.8.2   Concurrent or antecedent rights

In some instances more than one person or entity may concurrently have independent rights to trade using the same name, mark or get-up, even though the use of that name, mark or get-up by a third party would constitute passing off.

There are a variety of ways in which such concurrent rights may have arisen, for example, through the division of a business or through acquiescence in respect of one potential defendant who subsequently accrues his or her own goodwill in the name, mark or get-up. See, for example, *Habib Bank Ltd v Habib Bank AG Zurich* [1981] 2 All ER 650 (CA).

"Antecedent rights" describes the situation where the defendant claims that it is the owner of pre-existing goodwill in the name, mark or get-up. If it can do so, then the defendant may be entitled to continue to use the name, mark or get-up notwithstanding that such use may constitute a misrepresentation, as the plaintiffs may have accrued substantial goodwill and reputation in the name, mark or get-up subsequently: for example, *Chelsea Man Menswear Ltd v Chelsea Girl Ltd* (1987) 104 RPC 189 (CA).

9.8.3 Bona fide use of the defendant's own name

A possible defence (or perhaps exception to liability) for misrepresentation exists where the defendant is using his or her own name. Early cases appear to reflect the fact that using one's own name was relatively important for traders. More recently, Courts have been more reluctant to recognise an exception or defence based on the use of one's own name, perhaps reflecting the decreased importance to traders of the use of their personal names.

This more restrictive approach is clearly illustrated in *Parker-Knoll Ltd v Knoll International Ltd* (1962) 79 RPC 265 (HL), which held that honest use of one's own name as a mark on goods could not be a defence although it left open the question of whether it might be a defence if used as a trading name.

This second aspect was clarified somewhat in *Taylor Bros Ltd v Taylors Group Ltd* [1988] 2 NZLR 1 (CA), which referred to the following limitations on "the own name exception":

- The name used, to come within the exception, must be the actual name of the defendant. Adaptations or the use of the name with additional words, even "and company", would not qualify;

- The exception does not extend to the use of the name if it will deceive as distinct from merely causing confusion, where deceiving is used in the sense of representing a thing falsely so as to cause another to believe that to be true which is not; and

- The exception extends to companies with an established business but not to new companies.

For further discussion, see Kevin Glover, "The own name defence to trade mark infringement in New Zealand" (2003) 3(8) NZIPJ 167.

9.8.4 The use of distinctive marks or disclaimers by the defendant

In theory a defendant can use features of name, mark or get-up distinctive of the plaintiff, in conjunction with an appropriate disclaimer, label or other marking indicating that there is no connection with the plaintiff, and thus avoid the possibility of confusion. In practice, it would seem the Courts are prepared to accept in principle that such indicia may serve to distinguish. For example, in *NZ Net Guide Ltd v IDG Communications Ltd* 24/1/01, Fisher J, HC Auckland M2039-SW00, the Court was prepared to accept that the publication of the defendant's magazine with an appropriate disclaimer on the cover would avoid passing off.

Whether labelling or disclaimers serve to distinguish notwithstanding the adoption of the plaintiff's distinguishing features is a question of fact in each case.

In *Clorox NZ Ltd v Elldex Packaging Ltd* 13/11/03, Williams J, HC Auckland CIV-2003-403-4292, the Court refused to grant an interim injunction restraining Elldex from marketing cling film in packaging having get-up similar to that of Clorox's "Glad

Wrap". Although it was common ground that Clorox had considerable reputation in the colours yellow, red, and blue (which were the prominent colours of Elldex's packaging), the Court said that the trade name "KiWi" was a strong feature of Elldex's packaging, and passing off causes of action based on get-up "are seldom successful if the brand name is prominent on packaging unless there is proof of actual deception or deliberate imitation".

In *Music Australia v Tansing* (1994) 27 IPR 649 (FCA), the Court refused an application to injunct the defendant from selling "unauthorised" recordings of Michael Jackson, which were clearly labelled as such, on the basis that the disclaimers were sufficient to ensure the public would not be misled as to the source of those recordings.

In contrast, the Courts have been slower to find a disclaimer or label effective where the features copied are particularly distinctive, or where the products are such that the purchaser is less likely to have regard to the label or any disclaimer: *Abundant Earth Pty Ltd v R & C Products Ltd* (1984) 59 ALR 211, at p 217:

> "There may well be cases where a disclaimer is effective to eliminate confusion … But, where the competing products are small, inexpensive items the efficacy of a disclaimer, however prominent, cannot be assumed."

For example, in *Cookie Time Ltd v Griffins Foods Ltd* 11/12/00, Glazebrook J, HC Auckland M1756-SW00, the Court held that, although it was likely that if compared side by side the respective labelling would distinguish the respective parties' buckets of biscuits, nonetheless "labelling and branding with the manufacturer's name are not always to be seen as definitive".

See also the comments of Aldous LJ in *Arsenal Football Club Plc v Reed (No 2)* [2003] 3 All ER 865; [2003] RPC 39 (CA), at paras 70-71, who indicated that (if the point had been appealed) he would have been prepared to find the defendant, who sold Arsenal Football Club memorabilia, liable for passing off, despite the fact that the memorabilia was clearly described as unauthorised. In his Lordship's view, such conduct could still lead to the dilution and/or destruction of Arsenal's goodwill in its marks, despite the fact that no one would be confused or deceived into thinking that the goods originated from or were authorised by Arsenal.

The use of disclaimers is also considered at 10.4.13 ("Disclaimers") in the Fair Trading Act 1986 chapter of this text (chapter 10).

9.8.5 Use of registered trade mark — no defence

It is no defence to an action for passing off that the defendant's mark was a registered trade mark. Section 6 Trade Marks Act 1953 provides:

> "nothing in this Act shall be deemed to affect the rights of action against any person for passing-off goods or services as the goods or services of another person or the remedies in respect thereof."

This saving is retained in s 88(a) Trade Marks Act 2002 (which came into force on 20 August 2003).

Section 88(a) does appear to contradict s 10(1) Trade Marks Act 2002, which grants the proprietor of a registered trade mark the "exclusive right" to the use of the trade mark in relation to the goods or services in respect of which it is registered. In *Sunshine Leisure Products*

(NZ) Ltd v The Great Outdoors Co Ltd (1985) 6 IPR 179, Gallen J, applying the English Court of Appeal decision in *Re Lyle and Kinahan's application* (1907) 24 RPC 249, held that the registered proprietor of the trade mark SUNLINE could not rely on the existence of its registered trade mark as a defence to a claim for passing off. Interestingly, the Court made no mention of s 6 Trade Marks Act 1953 (equivalent to s 88(a) Trade Marks Act 2002), although it is not clear whether s 6 was even brought to the attention of the Judge.

In contrast, the Ontario Court of Appeal in *Molson Canada v Oland Breweries Ltd* 159 OAC 396; 59 OR (3d) 607; 214 DLR (4th) 473 (Ont CA) distinguished *Lyle* and held that the holder of a registered trade mark had an exclusive right to use the mark over and above any common law rights. The case is unlikely to be followed in New Zealand as it turned on the fact that the Canadian trade marks legislation did not contain a corresponding provision to s 45 Trade Marks Act 1905 (UK) (a similar provision to s 88(a) Trade Marks Act 2002).

9.8.6 Custom or usage

In a passing off context, it might be pleaded that the defendant was entitled, either through custom or usage, to use the elements that the plaintiff sought to protect. In *Resene Paints Ltd v Orica NZ Ltd* [2003] 3 NZLR 709; (2003) 10 TCLR 795, the Court considered possible defences of custom or usage in the context of the defendant's unsuccessful claim that industry practice dictated that there could be no goodwill or reputation in the names of paint colours. The Court held that, for legal purposes, a "custom" is a particular rule which has long been recognised and which has attained the force of law. Usage, on the other hand, has no legal force, rather it is a question of fact involving an assessment of whether the usage is uniform and certain, fair, and proper, such that reasonable and right minded persons would adopt it, and that it does not offend against any existing law, in particular any Act of Parliament.

9.8.7 Estoppel

Estoppel, together with the related defences of acquiescence and delay, concerns circumstances where it would be unconscionable for the plaintiff to be allowed to enforce its rights against the defendant: *Wham-O MFG Co v Lincoln Industries Ltd* [1984] 1 NZLR 641 (CA).

9.8.8 Limitation

The limitation of actions in tort is governed by s 4(1) Limitation Act 1950. The limitation period for actions in tort is 6 years from the date on which the cause of action accrued.

In the passing off context the date on which the cause of action accrued would ordinarily be the date on which the misrepresentation by the defendant occurred, although if the defendant has concealed the existence of the cause of action by fraud then the limitation period may be said to run from the point at which the cause of action becomes discoverable.

9.9 Remedies

9.9.1 Injunctions

The primary remedy for a plaintiff in a passing off action will usually be some form of injunction to prevent further damage occurring.

(1)   *Interim injunctions*

In passing off actions obtaining interim relief will often be of vital importance to the plaintiff. This is primarily because of the perishable nature of the interest that the plaintiff seeks to protect, namely its goodwill. If the defendant's conduct is allowed to continue unabated pending a substantive hearing, the plaintiff's distinctiveness and hence its goodwill may have been eroded beyond redemption by the time substantive relief can be obtained.

Secondarily, the plaintiff will be seeking to prevent the name, mark or get-up in question from becoming distinctive of the defendant.

(a)   *Principles applicable to interim injunctions*

The principles to the grant of an interim injunction most often relied on by passing off litigants are those set out in *Klissers Farmhouse Bakeries Ltd v Harvest Bakeries Ltd* [1985] 2 NZLR 129, at p 142.

- Whether there is a serious question to be tried; and

- Where the balance of convenience lies?

The Court in *Klissers* emphasised the importance of viewing both of the above factors in light of the overriding requirement that the matter must be governed by the interests of justice.

(b)   *Interim injunction often determinative*

A key factor to be considered in passing off cases is that an interim injunction will often be determinative of the matter as the defendant will be forced to change its name, mark or get-up, and will henceforth begin to accrue independent reputation in that new name, mark or get-up. Further, provided the plaintiff has acted swiftly (note also that acquiescence on the part of the plaintiff may rule against the grant of an interim injunction) damages at this stage will only be minimal and it will rarely be cost effective for a plaintiff to pursue them substantively.

In formulating an interim injunction the Court will often be concerned to preserve the status quo. This will normally be the state of affairs immediately before the defendant's entry into the market.

In *Gold Real Estate Group Ltd v GoldLeaf Real Estate Ltd* (2006) 11 TCLR 530, the plaintiff was the registered proprietor of the trade mark GOLD REAL ESTATE GROUP LIMITED and which claimed reputation in the word GOLD in relation to real estate services. In this proceeding, the plaintiff sought to injunct the defendant from using GOLD in relation to real estate services.

In respect of the overall justice, the defendants submitted that the granting of the interim injunction would effectively grant the plaintiff a monopoly in a common laudatory term and also one that was important to the Chinese community. Moreover, the defendants' evidence indicated that the order was likely to be determinative as, having changed their brand to comply with the order, they would be unlikely to carry on defending the proceedings and/or change back if successful at full trial.

Accordingly, the defendants submitted that the interim injunction should only be granted if there was very clear evidence to support such an exclusive right.

In response, counsel for the plaintiff relied upon the following passage of Davison CJ in *Klissers Farmhouse Bakeries Ltd v Harvest Bakeries Ltd* [1985] 2 NZLR 129, at pp 138-139:

> "Mr Brown submitted that to grant an interim injunction in the present case would have the effect of giving the plaintiff judgment in the action before trial because it is not commercially realistic for the defendants to cease using the present packaging, replace it with some other form of packaging, advertise and promote that new form of packaging and then if the defendants are successful in the action return to the present form of packaging and promote it in the marketplace. There may be some weight in that submission but the situation is one which must be faced by many defendants who suffer an interim injunction in passing off actions. If the defendants succeed in the action they can recover from the plaintiff the costs and expenses to which they have been put and such losses as they can establish in sales of their products. On the other hand, to deprive the plaintiff of the interim injunction because the defendants may not feel it commercially worthwhile to continue is to deprive the plaintiff of the most effective remedy for passing off and enable the defendants to further establish their products in the marketplace to the detriment of the plaintiff."

However, Fogarty J distinguished that case, at para 50, as follows:

> "I have considerable reservation as to the intrinsic merit of Davison CJ's proposition that to deprive the plaintiff of an interim injunction is to deprive the plaintiff of 'the most effective remedy for passing off'. This is particularly so if the interim injunction provides effectively the plaintiff with a final injunction and a monopoly on GOLD, against what is otherwise likely to be a strongly contested case ..."

His Honour's decision may have been strongly influenced by the plaintiff's adoption of, and claim to exclusivity in, the laudatory word GOLD as his Honour went on to state, at para 53, that:

> "It is important that the remedy of interim injunction should not thwart the policy of common law and of statute, which is designed to protect distinctive names or marks and is cautious of allowing anyone to monopolise ordinary words in common use unless they have acquired a secondary meaning. Mr Arthur appeared to submit that there is no monetary value preserving for Mr Yap a choice of name. Financial value does not have to be put on a freedom of choice. Mr Marriott submitted that the plaintiff had taken a risk in developing a brand name using laudatory and then descriptive terms. I think that is right. The plaintiff may, in the long run, be able to sustain the argument that the word 'gold' has become distinctive of its business. But in the meantime, I cannot see any policy in the common law or statute to assist the plaintiff in this regard."

(c) *Registered intellectual property rights may confer advantage*

Several recent decisions of the High Court and the Court of Appeal would seem to suggest that the Courts will give increasing primacy to registered intellectual property rights when determining an application for interim relief. In many cases this seems to be at the expense of seemingly conclusive arguments going to the balance of convenience and the overall justice.

In the patent context, in *Aktiebolaget Hassle v Novartis NZ Ltd* 1/5/03, Potter J, HC Auckland CP51-SW/03, the plaintiffs sought an injunction to restrain Novartis from manufacturing an omeprazole product, PROBITOR, which they believed infringed their Patent No 220096 relating to their own similar product sold in New Zealand under the brand name LOSEC. Novartis resisted the application on a number of grounds including:

(1)   That it was strongly arguable that the patent was invalid, the equivalent UK patent having already been overturned on the grounds of obviousness; and

(2)   That it had contracted to supply Pharmac with PROBITOR, and was obliged to pay Pharmac $350,000 per calendar month it was unable to supply same (presumably to compensate Pharmac for being obliged to subsidise the more expensive LOSEC during that period).

While recognising the significant losses likely to be suffered by Novartis if injuncted, the Court nonetheless found that the balance of convenience and the overall justice favoured the granting of an injunction, commenting, at para 43:

> "There is a reality to be recognised in the case of the patent, that the patent confers a monopoly during its currency, the benefit of which runs over to the post-patent period because of the strong market position usually developed during the monopoly period. This was expressed by Eichelbaum J in [*Monsanto Chemical Co v Stauffer Chemical Co (No 2)* (1984) 1 TCLR 129; 1 NZIPR 540]."

and later, at para 56:

> "Premature interference with the monopoly position which the patent confers during its currency will also impact on the ability of the proprietor to create or confirm its own market after the expiry of the patent (the 'bridgehead' opportunity)."

The decision of Potter J was upheld by the Court of Appeal in a decision of Blanchard J delivered on 4 July 2003 (*Novartis NZ Ltd v Aktiebolaget Hassle* [2004] 2 NZLR 721 (CA)).

In the trade mark context in *Leisureworld Ltd v Elite Fitness Equipment Ltd* 21/7/06, Heath J, HC Auckland CIV-2006-404-3499, the Judge granted an interim injunction on the basis that it would acknowledge the public interest in enforcing the monopoly rights created by the Trade Marks Act.

However, f the ownership of the intellectual property is in dispute this may result in refusal of the application: *Golden Homes (1998) Ltd v Blue Chip Construction Ltd* 21/6/05, Allan J, HC Auckland CIV-2003-404-7090. See also *Lesa Systems Ltd v Canzac Ltd* 16/5/06, John Hansen J, HC Christchurch CIV-2006-409-624, at para 34.

Note also the approach of Fogarty J in *Gold Real Estate Group Ltd v GoldLeaf Real Estate Ltd* (2006) 11 TCLR 530. There the Court considered the effect of the presumption of validity in s 162 Trade Marks Act 2002 in the context of an application for interim injunction. The plaintiff argued that s 162 meant that there was automatically a serious question to be tried as the registration was prima facie evidence of the validity and ownership of the trade mark. That argument was rejected by Fogarty J, his Honour noting that whether or not the plaintiff has a serious question to be tried is a forward looking assessment of the plaintiff's likely position at trial.

The defendant had called into question the validity of the plaintiff's registration on the basis that it comprised the laudatory word "Gold" and the descriptive words "Real Estate Group Limited". His Honour noted that at the trial it would be likely, if not inevitable, that one or both defendants would apply for a declaration of invalidity, and that for the plaintiff to sustain its cause of action for infringement of the trade mark registration and a final injunction, it would have to survive this likely challenge to the mark. Accordingly, his Honour felt that it would be wrong to assume, at the interlocutory stage, that the mark will be found to be validly registered at trial. His Honour also noted, at para 21, that s 162 was unlikely to have any practical advantage for the plaintiff at trial as the trial would not be a prima facie environment as:

> "The effect of s 162 is that a registered trade mark will be treated as valid in all legal proceedings in the absence of a challenge to the validity. But where there is a challenge the practical consequence will be that the Court will re-examine the merit of the original registration."

Fogarty J also noted, at para 41, that while s 162 applies to all legal proceedings and is a factor in the plaintiff's favour on the balance of convenience, it does not carry much weight as the principal consideration of the Court is to assess the justice of intervening now against the prospects at trial.

(2) Permanent injunctions

The terms of a permanent injunction will commonly contain an unqualified prohibition against the defendant passing off its goods or business as those of the plaintiff, together with a specific prohibition against the conduct that gave rise to the complaint.

In some cases the Court may leave it open for the defendant to make use of the name, mark or get-up provided it clearly distinguishes its trade or business from the trade or business of the plaintiff: see, for example, *Noel Leeming Television Ltd v Noel's Appliance Centre Ltd* (1985) 5 IPR 249, at p 259.

(3) Mandatory injunctions

A variety of mandatory injunctions may be awarded in passing off cases including orders for delivery up and/or destruction of offending goods or promotional material. Other mandatory injunctions might include orders that names, marks or signage be removed.

9.9.2 Damages

If the plaintiff successfully establishes passing off then damages are a remedy that the Court has no discretion to refuse. The plaintiff is therefore entitled to at least nominal damages.

Because of the nature of harm to the plaintiff, damages for passing off are notoriously difficult to assess or quantify. Where the defendant has traded using a misappropriated name, mark or get-up, the plaintiff may make an election as to whether it seeks an inquiry into damages or an account of profits.

In many passing off cases the matter will be heard by way of a split trial, the first trial being to decide the issues of liability and whether the successful party is entitled to an inquiry as to damages or an account of profits, and a further hearing being conducted to determine quantum. See, however, the decision of Associate Judge Doogue in *Auravale Industries Ltd v Hallenstein Bros Ltd* 31/10/05, Associate Judge Doogue, High Court Auckland CIV-2004-404-4088, in which an application for split trial in a passing off case was refused. The Associate Judge noted, at paras 18 and 19, that cases which are particularly suitable for split trials are those where the issues of liability and quantum are sufficiently discrete as to involve separate enquiries. However, the law requires that in order to establish passing off, the plaintiff must show it suffered actual damage to its business or goodwill. That issue would therefore be common to both phases of a trial, that is, in establishing liability and quantum. For that reason, his Honour felt it would be difficult to compartmentalise the two phases of the case, and that granting the application for the split trial would not allow the Court to make orders restricting discovery in the first instance to matters that are relevant to liability only: *Island Records Ltd v Tring International Plc* [1995] FSR 560, at p 561.

The Associate Judge also noted the potential for multiple appeals consequent upon an order for split trial and thought that the same hazards identified by Fisher J in *Ashmont Holdings Ltd v Jurox Pty* (2000) 53 IPR 464, at para 4, might also apply:

- Unintended issues of estoppel;

- Organising the second fixture before the same Judge;

- Allegations of pre-determination against that Judge arising from comments made in resolving the earlier issues; and

- The potential for inconsistent findings.

(1) *Inquiry as to damages*

In determining the measure of any damages the onus is on the plaintiff to prove that the damages claimed have flowed from the defendant's misconduct. The Court is not entitled to make such an assumption in the absence of proof. Provided the plaintiff can discharge its onus then damage will ordinarily be claimable under the two heads of lost sales and/or damage to reputation and goodwill.

For example, in *Spalding & Bros v Gamage Ltd* (1915) 32 RPC 273 (HL), at first instance, the plaintiff was awarded £2,000 for general damage to reputation and £5,000 for loss of future profits. The Court of Appeal ultimately reset damages at £250 as representing proven damage to the plaintiff's goodwill but rejected the claim for damages in respect of future sales as unproven.

9.9.3 Account of profits

A successful plaintiff also has the option of electing an account of profits rather than an inquiry as to damages.

An account of profits is an equitable remedy and as such the Court has discretion whether to make such an order. In exercising its discretion the Court can take into account any inequitable conduct by the plaintiff such as delay or acquiescence.

When conducting an account of profits, damage suffered by the plaintiff is not relevant. The Court's inquiry is limited to profits made by the defendant that are attributable to the passing off. See, for example, *My Kind of Town Ltd v Soll* (1983) 100 RPC 15.

9.10 References and resource sites

9.10.1 Websites

Thomson Brookers	www.thomsonbrookers.co.nz
James & Wells	www.jaws.co.nz
Ministry of Economic Development	www.med.govt.nz
Intellectual Property Office of New Zealand	www.iponz.govt.nz
UK Intellectual Property Office	www.ipo.gov.uk
World Intellectual Property Organisation	www.wipo.int

9.10.2 Texts and periodicals

- Brown, A, and Grant, A, *The Law of Intellectual Property in New Zealand*, Wellington, Butterworths, 1988

- Frankel, S, and McLay, G, *Intellectual Property in New Zealand*, Wellington, LexisNexis Butterworths, 2002

- Todd, S, et al, *The Law of Torts in New Zealand* (4th ed), Wellington, Brookers, 2005

- Wadlow, C, *The Law of Passing Off* (2nd ed), London, Sweet & Maxwell, 1995

- *Halsbury's*, Wellington, LexisNexis Butterworths

- *Laws of New Zealand*, Wellington, LexisNexis Butterworths

Chapter 10

The Fair Trading Act 1986

10.1   Introduction

The Fair Trading Act 1986 ("the Act") came into force on 1 March 1987. The Long Title of the Act describes it as:

> "An Act to prohibit certain conduct and practices in trade, to provide for the disclosure of consumer information relating to the supply of goods and services and to promote product safety and also to repeal the Consumer Information Act 1969 and certain other enactments."

Like much of our legislation, the Act has been largely borrowed from an overseas statute, in this case Part 5 of the Trade Practices Act 1974 (Aust). While many sections have been taken straight from the Australian legislation, others have been amended specifically to suit the New Zealand market. Almost two decades of jurisprudence relating to the application and interpretation of the Act has also resulted in several departures from the Australian legislation and/or its interpretation.

The Act was implemented as part of The New Zealand-Australia Closer Economic Relations Trade Agreement ("CER"), with the express intention of harmonising trans-Tasman economic policies and practice, particularly as they relate to trade and competition.

10.1.1   Relationship with other causes of action

A breach of the Fair Trading Act may give rise to liability under other legislation and vice versa. Thus, in *Telecom Mobile Ltd v Commerce Commission* [2006] 3 NZLR 323; (2006) 11 TCLR 633; 8 NZBLC 101,708 (SC), Telecom's failure to advise consumers of their ability to cancel contracts under the Door to Door Sales Act 1967 was found to be a contravention of the Fair Trading Act 1986 as it also amounted to misleading and deceptive conduct. The High Court's conclusion that Telecom's actions were "misleading conduct/representations because the breach of the Door to Door Sales Act means in fact that the consumers had other rights of which they were not advised, in particular, the right to cancel at any time up to one month later without penalty" was not interfered with on appeal.

In general, however, the provisions of the Act will not provide relief where an action is barred under another specialist piece of legislation. Thus in *World TV Ltd v Best TV Ltd* (2005) 11 TCLR 247, the Court held that World did not have standing to obtain an injunction to restrain Best from broadcasting certain programmes under the Copyright Act and hence the Fair Trading Act. World held an exclusive licence with a third party, CCTV, to broadcast programmes from CCTV1, but not CCTV4. World sought to rely on a letter of authority from CCTV empowering it to enforce CCTV's rights in New Zealand to seek an injunction to prevent Best from broadcasting inter alia programmes from CCTV4. The action was unsuccessful as World was found to be neither an owner, nor an exclusive licensee. An action under the Fair Trading Act 1986 also failed as s 124 Copyright Act 1994 was deemed to act as a proviso to the more general provisions of the Fair Trading Act.

10.1.2   Comparison with passing off

In essence the Fair Trading Act 1986 provides for statutory regulation of misleading or deceptive conduct, and false or misleading representations, with the general aim of achieving fair competition in trade.

The Act is not simply a statutory version of the tort of passing off. The Act is first and foremost legislation for the protection of consumers through the eradication of unfair trade practices. Therefore, unlike passing off, an action under the Act can be advanced by any interested person. It is not necessary for a litigant to have an interest in the subject matter of the complaint.

Similarly, there is no requirement for the plaintiff to show that he or she has suffered damage as a consequence of the acts complained of, although actual damage can be redressed by suitable orders. These are discussed at 10.8 ("Legal remedies") later in this chapter.

Finally, as the action is governed by legislation, it is not restricted by the common law limitations that might apply to a passing off action. For this reason it has come to be perceived as something of a "catch all" cause of action by many practitioners and certain Judges. See, for example, the comments of Hammond J in *Crump v Wala* [1994] 2 NZLR 331; (1993) 6 TCLR 40; 4 NZBLC 103,383, who, when responding to a question from the appellant's counsel as to whether the respondent could "scramble home under the less refined provisions of the Fair Trading Act" complained of previous Courts having "allowed the Statute to float like oil across water" and further described the Act as "cancerous".

The differences between an action under the Act and the tort of passing off are discussed in more detail at 10.4.9 ("Act not to be read down") later in this chapter.

10.1.3   Role of the Commerce Commission

The Commerce Commission acts as a consumer watchdog. Its main purpose is to ensure that the public is aware of the provisions of the Fair Trading Act 1986, and that they are complied with, so that consumers and producers benefit from healthy competition.

The two main aims of the Commission are:

- Enforcement of the terms of the Act, and of consumer information and product safety standards made under the Act; and

- Education, mainly through the provision of free information about the requirements of the Act, and programmes for traders designed to help establish systems to ensure compliance.

The majority of summary prosecutions under s 40 are initiated by the Commission.

Part 6 of the Act provides the Commission with a limited range of powers to assist it in enforcement. They include the power to search premises and inspect documents and goods.

10.1.4   Scope of this chapter

As the subject matter of this text is intellectual property law, discussions in this chapter will be limited to the interface between the Fair Trading Act 1986 and more conventional intellectual property rights, such as trade marks, get-up, reputation and goodwill.

Aspects of the Act that deal with unfair practices (such as bait advertising and pyramid selling schemes), consumer information and product safety standards, and the powers conferred on the Commission, will not be discussed in detail. More comprehensive information can be obtained from the sources listed at 10.11 ("References and resource sites") later in this chapter.

10.2 Legislation

The law relating to fair trading in New Zealand is found in the following legislation:

- Fair Trading Act 1986 ("the Act");

- Fair Trading Amendment Act 1994;

- Fair Trading Amendment Act 1997;

- Fair Trading Amendment Act 1999;

- Fair Trading Amendment Act 2000;

- Fair Trading Amendment Act 2001;

- Fair Trading Amendment Act 2003;

- Fair Trading Amendment Act (No 2) 2003;

- Fair Trading Amendment Act 2006;

- A large number of Regulations and Orders relating to product safety and consumer information standards; and

- Consumer Guarantees Act 1993.

Discussions in this text will be limited to the Act (as amended).

10.2.1 Current developments / legislative amendments

The Ministry of Consumer Affairs has prepared a discussion document entitled "Review of the Redress and Enforcement Provisions of Consumer Protection Law: International Comparison Discussion Paper". It is available on the Ministry's website at www.consumeraffairs.govt.nz/policylawresearch/enforcement-review/paper-two/.

The paper reviews and compares the redress and enforcement provisions in the Fair Trading Act 1986 and the Consumer Guarantees Act 1993 with those found in consumer protection legislation in Australia, Canada, the US, and the UK.

It concludes that while there are no significantly different approaches in the overseas legislation, the analysis indicates that there may be some additional prohibitions, investigation, and enforcement tools and penalties that may strengthen the Fair Trading Act in terms of achieving the desired outcomes for consumers and businesses. The proposed amendments include:

- Prohibiting unfair terms in consumer contracts;

- Permitting the Minister of Consumer Affairs to authorise the seizure of unsafe products and to issue warnings to the public regarding potentially unsafe products that are the subject of an investigation;

- Empowering the Commerce Commission to make interim cease and desist orders to quickly restrain behaviour that contravenes the Act;

- Empowering the Commission to issue substantiation notices requiring businesses to substantiate claims or representations which might contravene the Act (effectively reversing the onus, which is currently on the Commission to demonstrate that a claim cannot be substantiated);

- Permitting the Commission to settle an investigation on receipt of a voluntary Court-enforceable undertaking which could be relied upon by the Commission for subsequent breach by the same offender;

- Empowering the Commission to require people to appear in person before the Commission to give evidence (with appropriate safeguards); and

- Empowering the Commission to issue orders banning recidivist offenders from supplying goods or services.

Submissions closed on 29 June 2006.

10.2.2 Related legislation

There may be considerable overlap between the causes of action available under the Fair Trading Act and those available under the tort of passing off and/or under the Trade Marks Act 2002 for infringement of a registered trade mark.

Readers are encouraged to familiarise themselves with the chapters in this text relating to the Trade Marks Act (chapter 7) (in particular, trade mark infringement) and passing off (chapter 9). However, caution needs to be exercised as the elements necessary to prove each cause of action differ in subtle and sometimes material respects. For example, what is likely to "deceive and confuse" under the Trade Marks Act may differ from that which is found "misleading and deceptive" under the Fair Trading Act, and it may be possible to succeed under the Fair Trading Act where a cause of action in passing off has failed or is likely to fail. In relation to the latter, see 10.4.9 ("Act not to be read down") later in this chapter on the overlap between passing off and the Fair Trading Act.

The Geographical Indications (Wine and Spirits) Registration Act 2006 is also relevant. Pursuant to s 33 of that Act, a breach of a restriction on the use of a registered geographical indication is deemed to contravene s 9 of the Fair Trading Act and the provisions of the Fair Trading Act are to apply accordingly.

10.3 Jurisdiction

10.3.1 Parties: plaintiffs

(1) *Plaintiffs not limited to consumers*

The right to issue proceedings under the Fair Trading Act 1986 is not limited to consumers, or even parties affected by the conduct complained of. The New Zealand Courts recognised at a very early stage that the statute is available to, and would be frequently utilised by, trade competitors. In *Taylor Bros Ltd v Taylors Group Ltd* [1988] 2 NZLR 1 (CA) the Court of Appeal noted, at p 30:

"It is clear that, although the Act is primarily consumer protection legislation, a rival trader may enforce s 9 and is indeed the usual applicant. In this way the Act operates for the benefit of the ethical trader."

In relation to the corresponding Australian statute, in *Janssen-Cilag Pty Ltd v Pfizer Pty Ltd* (1992) 37 FCR 526; 109 ALR 638 (FCA), Janssen had alleged that Pfizer had made false and misleading representations which induced members of the public and pharmacists to purchase Pfizer's drug rather than Janssen's competing drug thereby causing Janssen to lose sales. One of Pfizer's defences was that Janssen was not a person entitled to recover any loss or damage under the Trade Practices Act 1974 (Aust) because Pfizer was not a consumer within the meaning of the Act nor a person who relied on the allegedly false or misleading representations.

That proposition was rejected by Lockhart J who held, at p 530, that there was nothing in the language of the Act or its purpose to warrant the suggestion that the right of an applicant for damages was confined to a case where the applicant had relied upon, or personally been influenced by, the conduct of the respondent which contravened the relevant parts of the Act. His Honour emphasised however, at p 533, that there must be a significant causal link between the conduct and the recoverable loss or damage.

Janssen-Cilag was cited with approval in New Zealand in *Dorchester Finance Ltd v Conqueror Corporate Trustee Ltd* 3/3/04, Master Lang, HC Auckland CIV-2003-404-2847; CIV-2003-404-3780, *KA (Newmarket) Ltd v Hart* 4/7/02, Heath J, HC Auckland CP467-SD01, and *Darrell McGregor (Contractor) Ltd v Mountain Lake Holdings Ltd* (2006) 11 TCLR 643.

The majority of actions commenced by parties other than the Commerce Commission are by trade competitors.

(2) *Foreign plaintiffs*

Having regard to the extraterritorial application of the Fair Trading Act 1986 (discussed later in this section) plaintiffs could conceivably include persons overseas who have been misled or deceived by matter or goods originating from New Zealand.

10.3.2 Parties: defendants

(1) *Meaning of "person"*

The Fair Trading Act 1986 applies to any "person" engaging in conduct prohibited by the Act. "Person" includes a local authority and any association of persons whether incorporated or not (s 2(1)), as well as individuals, companies and partnerships.

(2) *Vicarious liability*

Under s 45 Fair Trading Act 1986, anyone to whom the Act applies will also generally be bound by:

• The acts of their servants or agents acting within their actual or apparent authority (s 45(2)(a) and (4)(a)); and

- The acts of any other person directed by, consented to, or otherwise agreed to by a servant or agent acting within their actual or apparent authority (s 45(2)(b) and (4)(b)).

(3)   *Act applies to Crown*

The Fair Trading Act 1986 applies to conduct in trade by the Crown (s 4) and Crown corporations (s 5). Although the Crown cannot be prosecuted for an offence, the Commerce Commission, or any person directly affected by any Crown conduct amounting to an offence, can apply to the Court for a declaration, and in the case of Crown corporations any other remedy under Part 5 of the Act (which may include injunctive relief and payment of damages).

(4)   *Liability of directors, servants, or agents*

Individuals who breach the Act are not exempt from liability simply because they have acted in the capacity of a director or employee of a company. This is clear from the decision in *Giltrap City Ltd v CC* [2004] 1 NZLR 608 (CA) in which the chief executive of the appellant company was found personally liable for entering into a price-fixing arrangement contrary to s 27 Commerce Act 1986. The Court considered that because of the language of the Act (which speaks of conduct engaged in "on behalf of" a company, and says that a company may "also" be liable), and the policy that "no person" should enter into such an arrangement, both the company and its CEO were vicariously liable. The Court noted that Tipping J had offered a similar interpretation of s 45 Fair Trading Act 1986 in *Megavitamin Laboratories (NZ) Ltd v CC* (1995) 6 TCLR 231, at p 236, and agreed with that approach.

See also *Kinsman v Cornfields Ltd* (2001) 10 TCLR 342 (CA), at para 27, a case dealing with representations concerning the turnover of a franchise made by a director:

> "It will be a rare case where a director who participates directly in negotiations as to his or her company's business will be able to avoid s 9 liability simply on the basis that he or she was acting only on the company's behalf. The Fair Trading Act is in our view intended to cast its net wider than that".

The Court of Appeal in *Newport v Coburn* (2006) 11 TCLR 831; 8 NZBLC 101,717 (CA) did question whether the line of authority in *Kinsman* remained good law, but was not prepared to overturn the decision without full argument as the point was not taken at trial and was raised on appeal only in response to questions from the bench. The Court commented, at para 56:

> "We note that at least one academic commentator, Professor Peter Watts, has suggested that the decisions of this Court in *Kinsman* and *Specialised Livestock* should be overruled: P Watts, 'Directors' and Employees' Liability Under the Fair Trading Act 1986 — The Scope of "Trading" ' (2002) 8 *Company and Securities Law Bulletin* 77. Our preliminary view is that the points made by Professor Watts may have some validity. But we consider that, if a change is to be made to the law in this regard, it should occur only after the point has been fully argued either in this Court or the Supreme Court. We will therefore proceed on the basis that an employee can be liable under s 43(1)(a) on the basis that he or she is 'in trade', subject to the 'mere conduit' defence to which we will refer below."

10.3.3   Territory

As well as covering conduct within New Zealand, the Fair Trading Act 1986 covers conduct outside of New Zealand by any person who is resident, or carries on business, in New Zealand provided that the conduct relates to the supply of goods or services from or within New Zealand.

(1)   *Meaning of "relates to"*

The term "relates to" is not defined in the Fair Trading Act 1986. In *Sterling Pharmaceuticals (NZ) Ltd v Boots Co (NZ) Ltd (No 2)* [1991] 2 NZLR 634, the Court held that the printing in the UK of a pamphlet containing allegedly misleading information, intended to accompany drugs to be sold in New Zealand (which were also manufactured in the UK), was conduct "relating to" New Zealand.

(2)   *Extraterritorial application*

Perhaps the most far-reaching judgment regarding extraterritorial application of the Fair Trading Act 1986 is *Douglas Pharmaceuticals Ltd v Nutripharm NZ Ltd* 23/12/97, Randerson J, HC Auckland CP515/97 which related to the defendant's manufacture in New Zealand, and marketing in Taiwan, of a goat's milk infant formula. The issue before the Court was whether there was a breach of s 9 and/or s 13 of the Act by means of the labelling of a product in New Zealand that was intended solely for export to another jurisdiction. Starting from the premise that the question was one essentially of statutory construction, and noting, at p 6, that:

> "Where the statute is clearly and unambiguously expressed, neither comity nor a rule of international law can be invoked to prevent a sovereign state from passing legislation which has extraterritorial effect."

Randerson J concluded, at p 9, that the Act could be applied to prevent the misleading and deception of consumers in a foreign jurisdiction:

> "The Fair Trading Act is primarily intended to control misleading or deceptive conduct which occurs wholly and partly within New Zealand even if the person or persons deceived are beyond New Zealand. If misleading or deceptive conduct or a material part thereof has occurred within New Zealand, then in my view the Fair Trading Act has application even if other parts of the conduct ultimately occur beyond our shores."

In *Containerlift Services Ltd v Maxwell Rotors Ltd* (2003) 10 TCLR 807, the plaintiff, which had reputation in the UK and Europe in the name "Containerlift", sought an injunction against a New Zealand based defendant for misrepresentations arising in those jurisdictions from the use of the domain name "containerlift.com". The Court referred to *Douglas Pharmaceuticals*, but found it unnecessary to determine the issue of jurisdiction under the Fair Trading Act, having already made a finding that the defendant's conduct amounted to passing off.

10.3.4   Courts

As a matter of practice, most contraventions of the Fair Trading Act 1986 will be heard in the High Court. That is because the majority of actions are brought under s 9 by rival traders seeking to restrain conduct which is alleged to contravene a proprietary right, often in tandem with an action for passing off.

The relief most commonly sought is an injunction restraining the conduct complained of, and damages. Neither the District Court, nor the Disputes Tribunal, has jurisdiction to grant an injunction (ss 38 and 39) and the Disputes Tribunal is statute-barred by s 39 from making orders in respect of contraventions of s 9 of the Act.

The Act also establishes certain limits on the value of the orders made by the District Court and Disputes Tribunals. Hence, the monetary value of the orders made may not exceed $200,000 for the District Court (s 43(3)) or $7,500 for the Disputes Tribunal. In the case of the Disputes Tribunal the limit may be extended to $12,000 by agreement between the parties (s 43(4) and (4A)). These limits may be prohibitive for many actions, especially those brought by rival traders to recover damages from a competitor.

(1) *High Court*

The High Court has jurisdiction to hear and determine:

- Appeals from criminal proceedings in a District Court for offences against s 40 of the Act (discussed at 10.9 ("Criminal liability") later in this chapter) and s 47J of the Act (which relates to powers exercised by the Commission and is beyond the scope of this text);

- Appeals from proceedings in a District Court for orders under s 40A of the Act (which relates to pyramid selling schemes and is also beyond the scope of this text);

- Applications for injunctions under s 41 of the Act (discussed at 10.8 ("Legal remedies") later in this chapter); and

- Applications for orders under s 42 and s 43 of the Act (discussed at 10.8 ("Legal remedies") later in this chapter).

There are no monetary limits on the exercise of the High Court's jurisdiction.

(2) *District Court*

The District Court can hear and determine:

- Proceedings for offences against s 40 of the Act (discussed at 10.9 ("Criminal liability") later in this chapter) and s 47J (which relates to powers exercised by the Commission and is outside the ambit of this text);

- Applications for orders under s 40A of the Act (which relates to pyramid selling schemes and is outside the ambit of this text); and

- Applications for orders under s 43 of the Act (discussed at 10.8 ("Legal remedies") later in this chapter),

provided that the money, value of property, consideration, damages and/or value of goods or services ordered to be provided does not exceed $200,000 (s 43(3)).

(3) *Disputes Tribunal*

The Disputes Tribunal has jurisdiction to hear and determine applications for orders under s 43(2)(c)-(f) provided that:

- The order is not sought in respect of a contravention of s 9 of the Act; and

- The money, value of property, consideration, damages and/or value of goods or services ordered to be provided does not exceed $7,500 (or $12,000 by agreement between the parties).

10.4   Misleading or deceptive conduct

Misleading or deceptive conduct is governed by ss 9-12 Fair Trading Act 1986.

The broadest and most commonly cited provision imposing civil liability is s 9, which reads:

> "No person shall, in trade, engage in conduct that is misleading or deceptive or is likely to mislead or deceive."

Sections 10 and 11 impose both civil and criminal liability on certain forms of misleading conduct in relation to goods and services respectively. Sections 10 and 11 read:

"10. Misleading conduct in relation to goods
"No person shall, in trade, engage in conduct that is liable to mislead the public as to the nature, manufacturing process, characteristics, suitability for a purpose, or quantity of goods."

"11. Misleading conduct in relation to services
"No person shall, in trade, engage in conduct that is liable to mislead the public as to the nature, characteristics, suitability for a purpose, or quantity of services."

The lower threshold of "liable" for these sections (which impose criminal liability), as opposed to "likely" for s 9 (which imposes only civil liability), can probably best be rationalised on the basis that, in the case of the types of conduct referred to in ss 10 and 11, the detriment or loss will be felt by members of the purchasing public in the sense that they will not be getting what they purchased or intended to purchase. In contrast, for other forms of conduct such as the more common passing off type complaint usually dealt with under s 9 of the Act, the detriment or loss will usually be felt primarily by some rival trader or other entity.

In practice, any breach of s 9 in respect of conduct that falls within the types covered by ss 10 or 11 will also constitute a breach of one of those sections.

Section 12 of the Act deals with misleading conduct in relation to employment. An analysis of that section is not included within this text.

10.4.1   The meaning of "in trade"

"Trade" is defined in s 2 Fair Trading Act 1986 as follows:

> "any trade, business, industry, profession, occupation, activity of commerce, or undertaking relating to the supply or acquisition of goods or services or to the disposition or acquisition of any interest in land."

The terms "business", "acquire", "supply", "goods", and "services" are each also defined in s 2. The inclusive nature of the majority of those definitions means that "trade" may be broadly interpreted.

"In trade" refers to the defendant's trade, not the plaintiff's trade. See, for example, *Solid Energy NZ Ltd v Mountier* 26/7/07, Chisholm J, HC Christchurch CIV-2007-409-441, in which the Court was satisfied that there was arguable case in relation to s 16 of the Act as Mountier (the first defendant), a representative of the Save Happy Valley Coalition, was not engaged in trade when she prepared a mock report regarding the activities of Solid Energy for the Coalition's website.

(1) *Multiple transactions not required*

In *Bevanere Pty Ltd v Lubidineuse* (1985) 59 ALR 334 (FCA), the full Federal Court of Australia considered whether the sale by a company of its only capital asset was in trade or commerce, even though the company was not engaged in the business of buying or selling capital assets. Rejecting the suggestion that a person or company must engage in multiple transactions of a similar kind in order to be engaged in trade, the Court found that the appellant had engaged in conduct that was in trade and had subsequently breached s 52 Trade Practices Act 1974 (Australia).

Bevanere has subsequently been applied in New Zealand in *Newell v Garland* (1989) 3 TCLR 598 regarding the purchase of a motel business.

In *Sunnylea Farms Ltd v Gray* (2004) 21 NZTC 18,667; (2005) 5 NZCPR 664, a case concerning a contract for sale and purchase of farm land, the High Court held that where farm land was owned by one entity, and a farming business conducted by another, the land owner was not "in trade" for the purposes of s 9 Fair Trading Act 1986 when it made a one-off sale of land.

(2) *Director or employee may be "in trade"*

In *Gloken Holdings Ltd v The CDE Co Ltd* (1997) 8 TCLR 278, the Court found that the manager and director of the defendant company, who made representations as to a hotel's turnover, had engaged "in trade". However, the decision seems to turn on the finding that the director was the alter ego of the company and the only person who could effectively act for it. This was affirmed in *Kinsman v Cornfields Ltd* (2001) 10 TCLR 342 (CA).

The correctness of the decisions in *Gloken* and *Kinsman* has been questioned by the Court of Appeal: *Newport v Coburn* (2006) 11 TCLR 831; 8 NZBLC 101,717 (CA). In dealing with the question of whether an employee who is not a director should properly be considered to be "in trade" for the purposes of concurrent liability, the Court commented, at para 56:

> "We note that at least one academic commentator, Professor Peter Watts, has suggested that the decisions of this Court in *Kinsman* and *Specialised Livestock* should be overruled: P Watts, 'Directors' and Employees' Liability Under the Fair Trading Act 1986 — The Scope of "Trading" ' (2002) 8 *Company and Securities Law Bulletin* 77. Our preliminary view is that the points made by Professor Watts may have some validity. But we consider that, if a change is to be made to the law in this regard, it should occur only after the point has been fully argued either in this Court or the Supreme Court. We will therefore proceed on the basis that an employee can be liable under s 43(1)(a) on the basis that he or she is 'in trade', subject to the 'mere conduit' defence to which we will refer below."

and subsequently, at paras 88-91:

"The question of the concurrent primary liability of the officers of the company and the company itself is a matter of some controversy. As we indicated earlier, we consider ourselves bound by the decisions of this Court in *Kinsman* and *Specialised Livestock*, both of which decided that a director of a company can be primarily liable along with the company itself on the basis that the director is independently engaged 'in trade'. That conclusion is based on a particular interpretation of s 45(2), which relevantly provides:

'(2)   Any conduct engaged in on behalf of a body corporate—

'(a)   By a director, servant, or agent of the body corporate, acting within the scope of that person's actual or apparent authority;

'[(b)]   …

shall be deemed, for the purposes of this Act, to have been engaged in also by the body corporate.'

"As this Court noted in *Kinsman* at [19], the use of the word 'also' suggests liability under the Fair Trading Act for both the director and company where the director is acting within his or her actual or apparent authority. Issue can be taken with that conclusion for the reasons given by Professor Watts, but we proceed on the basis that it correctly states the law.

"Both *Kinsman* and *Specialised Livestock* were cases involving directors who were intimately involved in the running of a company, as were a number of the High Court decisions relied on in those cases such as *Gloken Holdings Limited v The CDE Co Limited* (where the director was described as the 'alter ego' of the company), [*Megavitamin Laboratories (NZ) Ltd v Commerce Commission* (1995) 6 TCLR 231; 5 NZBLC 103,834] and [*T & P Developments Ltd v Yu* 11/4/01, Glazebrook J, HC Auckland CP18-SD99].

"Mr Newport is, of course, in a different position. While we have found he was an employee, and as sales manager he must be seen as a senior employee, he was not a director or shareholder of ISL and could certainly not be described as its 'alter ego'. But that raises the question as to whether we should impose a different rule for persons who are mere employees as opposed to directors. We can see no basis for doing so, given that the decisions in *Kinsman* and *Specialised Livestock* involved an application of s 45(2), which refers to 'a director, servant, or agent of the body corporate', without distinguishing between them in any way."

(3)   *Dealings with regulatory authorities may be in trade*

In *Norbrook Laboratories Ltd v Bomac Laboratories Ltd* 2/12/02, Heath J, HC Auckland CP241-SW02, the Court held that representations to the Agricultural, Chemical and Veterinary Medicines Authority for the purposes of securing approval to market an animal remedy were conduct "in trade" for the purposes of s 9 of the Act. The Court noted, at para 215, that:

"Although Mr Barker was unable to point me to any decisions under the Fair Trading Act which have imposed liability in a case involving representations to a regulatory authority in the course of obtaining regulatory approval to do something in trade,

> I am satisfied that the purpose underlying s 9 of the Act is sufficient to justify such a representation, if false, falling within the boundaries of s 9."

It is unclear whether the applicability of s 9 in such circumstances is to be limited to representations to a regulatory authority in order to obtain approval "to do something in trade" or whether it applies to any representation regardless of its underlying purpose.

Note however, the finding in *ABB Ltd v NZ Insulators Ltd* 20/9/06, Courtney J, HC Auckland CIV-2004-404-4829, a case concerning misrepresentations concerning the safety and suitability for purpose of goods made to the Energy Safety Service ("ESS"), a branch of the Ministry of Consumer Affairs. Courtney J found, at para 92, it difficult to see why a governmental agency undertaking a statutory investigation should be viewed as a section of the public capable of being misled or deceived for the purposes of ss 9 and 10 of the Act, despite the possibility that misrepresentations made to the ESS might indirectly affect consumers, as ESS was not the intended object of the consumer protection provided by the Act.

10.4.2 Section 9

Section 9 Fair Trading Act 1986 prohibits conduct in trade that is misleading or deceptive, or that is likely to mislead or deceive.

A comprehensive review of the provisions of s 9 Fair Trading Act by the Court of Appeal can be found in *Neumegen v Neumegen & Co* [1998] 3 NZLR 310; (1998) 8 TCLR 299 (CA). The appellant, an Auckland barrister and solicitor who had practised under his own name, Peter Neumegen, since 1984, was about to be joined in partnership by his cousin, Mark Neumegen. Together they proposed to adopt the firm name "Neumegen & Neumegen". The respondent, another Auckland firm, which had practised as "Neumegen & Neumegen" from 1931 until 1983, when it changed its name to "Neumegen & Co", objected on the basis that the proposed name of the new firm was likely to mislead or deceive, and would therefore be in breach of s 9 of the Act. In the alternative, Neumegen & Co argued that the adoption of the name would falsely represent that there was some connection between the respective businesses.

In the High Court, Paterson J found that "Neumegen & Co" still had some residual reputation in the name "Neumegen & Neumegen" such that present and past clients, and potential clients, would be misled or deceived by the new firm's adoption of the same name. Peter Neumegen appealed, primarily on the finding that a substantial number of consumers of legal services would be affected by the alleged misleading or deceptive conduct.

Blanchard J, giving the majority judgment, summarised the provisions of s 9, at pp 316-317; pp 305-306, as follows:

> "This is a provision to protect the consuming public from unfair trading practices, namely from being misled or deceived. In its particular application to the use of a trade name, which has the function of identifying the source of goods or services and has acquired a secondary signification, s 9 prohibits any use which will in a deceptive or misleading way affect the recognition or identification of the goods or services ...

"The question is whether that conduct is likely to deceive or mislead the consuming public or a significant section of that public, namely the clients or potential clients identified by Paterson J, including persons like real estate agents, who are assisting clients by making referrals. 'Members of the public have a right not to be misled about with whom they are dealing': per Cooke P in *Taylor Bros Ltd v Taylors Group Ltd* [1988] 2 NZLR 1, at p 40. In the same case Cooke P said that the degree of impact or likely impact on consumers is important and goes both to whether there is a real likelihood that persons will be misled or deceived and to whether the court in its discretion should grant an injunction or other remedy under the Act.

"Generally, indeed it may be thought in virtually all cases, a defendant's conduct will not be deceptive or misleading unless it amounts to a misrepresentation. The misrepresentation may be express or arise from silence or from conduct. It need not be intentional and often will not be. (*Bonz Group Pty Ltd v Cooke* (1996) 7 TCLR 206 (CA))

"However, there will be no misrepresentation by means of the adoption of a trading name unless the name has already acquired a reputation amongst a class of consumers as denoting the goods or services of another trader, so that members of that class will be likely mistakenly to infer that the goods or services are connected with the business of that other trader (*Chase Manhattan Overseas Corp v Chase Corp Ltd* (1986) 8 IPR 69, at p 78 and [*Taco Co of Australia Inc v Taco Bell Pty Ltd* (1982) 42 ALR 177 (FCA)]). The more unusual the name, the more likely it will be that its use by another trader has given rise to a secondary signification.

"It is not necessary to show that any consumer has suffered economic loss nor that a rival trader has lost custom because of the defendant's conduct.

"However, in our view, if the number of affected members of the public is or will be very small and the impact upon those persons is or will be minimal a court may be justified in taking the view that, looked at in the round, the conduct of the defendant is not properly to be characterised as deceptive or misleading or that, even if it has to be so characterised, what has occurred or is likely to occur is so lacking in real importance to any consumers who may be affected that the court's discretion may fairly be exercised against the granting of a remedy. In considering these questions the court will make a judgment about whether the conduct is of a kind which it is the object of the legislation to curb."

After considering the evidence, the Court concluded that, in at least three situations, there was a likelihood that a substantial section of the relevant public (consumers of legal services) might be misled or deceived by the adoption of the firm name "Neumegen & Neumegen" and dismissed the appeal.

10.4.3 Meaning of misleading or deceptive conduct

There is no statutory definition of "misleading or deceptive" in the Act. In the majority of decisions it is accepted that the words should be interpreted on the basis of their plain and ordinary meaning and in the context of the individual facts of each case. Thus, in *Taylor Bros Ltd v Taylors Group Ltd* [1988] 2 NZLR 1 (CA), Cooke P said, at p 39:

"As to when conduct is to be characterised as misleading or deceptive, judicial exegesis probably can do little at a general level to expand upon the ordinary words of the section; and obviously it cannot be allowed to supersede them. In the end one must always return to them and apply them to the particular facts."

See also the comments of Thomas J in *Paper Plus NZ Ltd v Robert Mitchell Ltd* 10/3/93, Thomas J, HC Auckland CL53/92:

"The section uses plain language and its meaning and intent are clear enough without refining or adding to its terms. It does not need a glossary."

and the comments of Lockhart J in *Henjo Investments Pty Ltd v Collins Marrickville Pty Ltd* (1988) 39 FCR 546; 79 ALR 83 (FCA), at pp 554-555; pp 92-93:

"The Compact Edition of the *Oxford English Dictionary* 1987 defines the word 'mislead' in its transitive sense as 'to lead astray in action or conduct; to lead into error; to cause to err'. 'Deceive' is defined as 'to ensnare; to take unawares by craft or guile; to overcome, overreach, get the better of by trickery; to beguile or betray into mischief or sins; to mislead' ...

"The two words, 'misleading' and 'deceptive', are plainly not synonymous. That is not to say that each word may not catch some of the same conduct and that there may not be some degree of overlap. 'Mislead' does not necessarily involve an element of intent and it is a word of wider reach than 'deceive'. However, it is difficult, in my opinion, to read the word 'deceive' in s 52 other than as involving some degree of moral turpitude as it does in ordinary English usage. Trickery, craft and guile, though not essential elements of liability, are typically at the heart of this second element of the statutory provision directed to the protection of the public from unfair trading practices.

"Misleading or deceptive conduct generally consists of representations, whether express or by silence; but it is erroneous to approach s 52 on the assumption that its application is confined exclusively to circumstances which constitute some form of representation. The section is expressed briefly, indeed tersely, in plain and simple words which, if I may be forgiven for repeating them, say simply: 'A corporation shall not, in trade or commerce, engage in conduct that is misleading or deceptive or is likely to mislead or deceive'. There is no need or warrant to search for other words to replace those used in the section itself. Dictionaries, one's own knowledge of the developing English language and ordinary experience are useful touchstones, but ultimately in each case it is necessary to examine the conduct, whether representational in character or not, and ask the question whether the impugned conduct of its nature constitutes misleading or deceptive conduct. This will often, but not always, be the same question, as whether the conduct is likely to mislead or deceive."

As to conduct, both acts and omissions are included in the definition, but whether silence is misleading or deceptive will turn on the facts of each case. Silence was considered misleading and deceptive in *Money World NZ 2000 Ltd v KVB Kunlin NZ Ltd* [2006] 1 NZLR 381. Money World sought to exchange $360,000 worth of commemorative $2 Fijian notes with KVB for New Zealand dollars. Money World failed to advise KVB of the existence of a dispute regarding the notes with the Reserve Bank of Fiji. KVB made independent enquiries with the Reserve Bank and was advised that the notes would not be redeemed by the Reserve Bank. The ability of KVB to redeem the notes was held to be a fundamental element of the transaction, hence Money World's silence constituted misleading and deceptive conduct.

See also *Stevens v Premium Real Estate Ltd* (2006) 11 TCLR 854, in which Premium's failure to disclose to Stevens that the purchaser of his property was a property speculator, with whom Premium was involved in other transactions, amounted to misleading and deceptive conduct as this information would have been regarded by Stevens as important and would have affected Stevens' view of the offer (which was below market value, the speculator having sold the property 5 months later for $980,000 more than the purchase price).

(1) *Level of misleading conduct required*

In relation to the level of misleading or deceptive conduct required, in *Taylor Bros Ltd v Taylors Group Ltd* [1988] 2 NZLR 1 (CA), at p 39, Cooke P delivering the judgment of the Court stated:

> "The essential requirement of s 9 is simply misleading or deceptive conduct. It is not enough that the conduct causes a state of wonder or doubt in the minds of people about, for example, the identity or otherwise of two businesses. The line in the latter respect can be a fine one, we think, for if the court is satisfied (on the balance of probabilities) that some consumers will wonder, it may at times not be difficult to take the further step of concluding that some are likely to be misled; but of course that is not necessarily so."

The distinction between misleading and deceptive conduct and a mere "causing to wonder" was relied upon by Hammond J in refusing the plaintiff's application for an interim injunction in *Universal College of Learning v ACP Computer Solutions Ltd* 22/10/03, Hammond J, HC Napier CP9/01.

(2) *The Taco Bell criteria*

In *Taco Co of Australia Inc v Taco Bell Pty Ltd* (1982) 42 ALR 177 (FCA), at p 202, the full Federal Court of Australia set out what were said to be "established propositions", which were "guidelines upon the path to decision" as to whether conduct was misleading or deceptive. These are the need to:

- Identify the relevant section (or sections) of the public (which may be the public at large) to whom the question of whether conduct is misleading or deceptive falls to be tested;

- Consider the matter with reference to all who come within the relevant section of the public, including "the astute and the gullible, the intelligent and the not so intelligent, the well educated as well as the poorly educated, men and women of various ages pursuing a variety of vocations";

- Determine, by objective test, whether the evidence that some person has in fact formed an erroneous conclusion is admissible. Such evidence, if admitted, may be persuasive but is not essential; and

- Inquire why the misconception has arisen. This is fundamentally important as it is only through investigating evidence of those who have been shown to have been led into error that it can be determined whether they were confused because of the misleading or deceptive conduct, or some other reason. In other words, there must be a causal link between the confusion and the conduct.

(3)   The AMP Finance test

In *AMP Finance NZ Ltd v Heaven* (1997) 8 TCLR 144, the New Zealand Court of Appeal applied a three-stage approach to the question of whether there was a breach of s 9:

- Ask whether the conduct was capable of being misleading;

- Decide whether the public were in fact misled by that conduct; and

- Decide whether it was reasonable for the public to have been misled by that conduct.

This test has been subsequently applied in a number of New Zealand cases.

10.4.4   Meaning of "likely" and "liable"

In *Bonz Group (Pty) Ltd v Cooke* [1994] 3 NZLR 216; (1994) 6 TCLR 23 (CA), the question arose as to the degree of likelihood required before it could be said that conduct is "likely" to mislead or deceive. Tipping J held that, although "likely" imported a lesser degree of likelihood than something that was more probable than not, the degree of likelihood must involve a real risk, and not a mere possibility. On appeal (*Bonz Group Pty Ltd v Cooke* (1996) 7 TCLR 206 (CA), at p 213), the Court of Appeal saw no error in this reasoning.

"Likely" has also been held to equate to a real or not remote chance or possibility, regardless of whether it is less or more than 50 percent: *Global Sportsman Pty Ltd v Mirror Newspapers Pty Ltd* (1984) 6 ATPR 45,339.

The most noticeable difference between ss 10 and 11 of the Act and the more commonly cited s 9 is the requirement for the offending conduct to be "liable to mislead" (as opposed to the "likely to mislead" found in s 9 of the Act). In *Sound Plus Ltd v Commerce Commission* [1991] 3 NZLR 329, Anderson J held, at p 332, that "it is plain to my mind that this legislature intended that different tests should be applied in respect of the differing statutory provisions". His Honour found, at p 332, that although "liable" was not defined in the Act, the word invoked "a concept importing a potential less than likelihood or probability" and could perhaps be rephrased as "looking at the issue sensibly, could the conduct mislead the public?" His Honour's analysis was applied in *ABB Ltd v NZ Insulators Ltd* 20/9/06, Courtney J, HC Auckland CIV-2004-404-4829. Thus "liable to mislead" represents a lower threshold than the "likely to mislead or deceive" found in s 9 and elsewhere within the Act. See also: *Commerce Commission v A & W Hamilton Ltd* (1989) 3 TCLR 398.

At first glance, it might seem inappropriate to impose a lower threshold for sections importing criminal liability. However, this is perhaps best rationalised by noting that particular types of conduct covered by ss 10 and 11 will have a direct effect upon the purchasing public as opposed to other persons such as rival traders. This view was supported by Anderson J in *Sound Plus* who held, at pp 332-333, "I am inclined to the view that the legislature intended that where the public is concerned a lesser tendency for misleading than likely shall be prescribed".

10.4.5   Intention

It is commonly held that an intention to mislead is not necessary to establish a breach of s 9 Fair Trading Act 1986. In *Bonz Group Pty Ltd v Cooke* (1996) 7 TCLR 206 (CA) the appellants argued that, by requiring proof of a misrepresentation, Tipping J had wrongly introduced intention as a necessary element of a breach of s 9. After discussing the meaning of "misrepresentation" the Court of Appeal commented, at pp 212-213:

> "It is of course clear that there is no element of intention necessary for contravention of s 9. There will be breach where the conduct results in a substantial section of the public being misled or deceived or a likelihood of that. Where misrepresentation is said to be required, that is to exclude from the ambit of the prohibition wholly accurate indications which, in particular circumstances, give rise to misunderstanding (as was the issue in *Unilever NZ Ltd v Cerebos Gregg's Ltd* (1994) 6 TCLR 187) not to introduce an element of intention."

However, the defendant's intention may be relevant to the exercise of the Court's discretion in granting an injunction under s 41(1) of the Act. Thus, although acknowledging that an honest or fraudulent intent is generally irrelevant to an action for passing off or breach of the Fair Trading Act, in *Fresh Direct Ltd v Fresh Direct Wholesale Ltd* 18/12/03, Durie J, HC Blenheim CIV-2003-406-20, the Court was prepared to look at the bona fides of the defendant's actions in adopting the trading name complained of, insofar as that enquiry assisted it in the exercise of its discretion. The Court also commented, at para 13, that such an approach may assist in determining whether a particular result (ie, confusion of the public) ought reasonably to have been foreseen, and whether the defendant took all reasonable precautionary steps.

In some circumstances, a lack of intention to mislead may avoid a finding of breach. In *Muollo v Creative Engineering Design Ltd* (2006) 8 NZBLC 101,675 (CA), the Court of Appeal allowed Muollo's appeal against a High Court decision that she was liable to Creative Engineering Design Ltd under s 9 Fair Trading Act 1986 for a promise that an invoice to a company would be paid. The Court of Appeal held that the promise Muollo made was in her capacity as a director of the company not personally, and, having given an undertaking and subsequently resiled from it, it did not automatically follow that she never intended to honour the promise — the decision to resile from the promise may have been made subsequently (and thus not have been misleading at the time it was made) and that was Muollo's unchallenged evidence.

See also *Commerce Commission v Vero Insurance NZ Ltd* (2006) 11 TCLR 779; [2007] DCR 115; (2006) 8 NZBLC 101,871, where the Court held that a representation must relate to an existing and verifiable state of affairs. In promotional material relating to an insurance policy underwritten by Vero, consumers were advised that, by taking up the policy, they would be in to win a year's free power, but no draw was held until more than 2 years after the first promotion. The District Court held that the delay in conducting the draw was explicable, and found against the Commission. The Commission's appeal was unsuccessful — the High Court holding that the promise of a future draw was not a "representation" for the purposes of the Act, there was no question of deceit or misrepresentation of the promoter's state of mind, nor was there any basis to imply into the promoter's statement a representation that arrangements were in hand for a draw or that the draw would be held within a reasonable time.

(1) *Breach more likely if intended*

Like passing off, where the Court finds that the defendant intended to mislead or deceive, it will more readily conclude that it was successful in doing so: *Tot Toys Ltd v Mitchell* [1993] 1 NZLR 325, at p 343.

See also, *Wineworths Group Ltd v Comité Interprofessionel du Vin-Champagne* [1992] 2 NZLR 327 (CA), at p 334:

> "Jeffries J was not prepared to hold the appellant in breach even though he found its conduct deceptive. He said the appellant should not be 'branded' as in breach suggesting that contravention of the section involves an element of culpability. That is not so. Even if it was required, however, the whole tenor of the judgment indicates that Jeffries J was of the view that Penfolds (if not the appellant) deliberately intended to ride on the reputation of Champagne in New Zealand which would, of course, involve deliberately misleading or deceiving members of the public."

The Court of Appeal overturned the decision of Jeffries J who had held that Wineworths' description of Australian wine as champagne did not breach the Act.

(2) *Not everyone who misleads will breach*

Although intention is not an element of a breach, it does not follow that everyone who misleads or deceives will contravene the Act. See *Yorke v Lucas* (1985) 158 CLR 661 (HCA), at p 666:

> "That does not, however, mean that a corporation which purports to do no more than pass on information supplied by another must nevertheless be engaging in misleading or deceptive conduct if the information turns out to be false. If the circumstances are such as to make it apparent that the corporation is not the source of the information and it expressly or impliedly disclaims any belief in its truth or falsity, merely passing it on for what it is worth, we very much doubt that the corporation can properly be said to be itself engaging in conduct that is misleading or deceptive."

This has become known as the "mere conduit" defence. The mere conduit defence was considered by the Court of Appeal in *Newport v Coburn* (2006) 11 TCLR 831; 8 NZBLC 101,717 (CA). Mr Newport was employed as the Sales Manager for a franchisor which was found to have misled and deceived its franchisees by providing false information concerning the success of the franchised business including, inter alia, fabricated sales figures. One of the questions on appeal was whether Mr Newport was a "mere conduit" of the misleading information. The Court began by examining the "mere conduit" defence as follows, at paras 93-97:

> "The 'mere conduit' defence was first articulated by this Court in [*Goldsbro v Walker* [1993] 1 NZLR 394; (1992) 5 TCLR 46; (1993) 4 NZBLC 102,946 (CA)]. Cooke P put it this way (at 398[; 49; 102,949]):
>
> > 'There is no difficulty in accepting that an innocent agent who acts merely as a conduit and *purports* to do no more than pass on instructions from his

principal does not thereby become responsible for anything misleading in the information so passed on.' (Emphasis in original.)

"Richardson J expressed it in these terms (at 402[; 53; 102,952-102,953]):

'It is not sufficient to attract liability that the communication simply purports to pass on information ostensibly provided by a third party. In such a case any misleading conduct is that of the third party not of the intermediary.

.   .   .   .   .

'The test under s 9 is objective and on which side of the line a particular case falls turns on an assessment of what was conveyed. Was it a representation by the person charged or was it the passing on of information for what it was worth to the receiver without any inference that the person charged was vouching for it?'

"Hardie Boys J suggested the following test (at 405[; 57; 102,955-102,956]):

'... [F]or the conduit to avoid liability it must be apparent that he is not the source of the information, that he expressly or implicitly disclaims any belief in its truth or falsity, and is merely passing it on for what it is worth.'

"All of the Judges referred to, and relied on, the dicta of the majority judgment in [*Yorke v Lucas* (1985) 158 CLR 661 (HCA)] at 666, where it was stated:

'That does not, however, mean that a corporation which purports to do no more than pass on information supplied by another must nevertheless be engaging in misleading or deceptive conduct if the information turns out to be false. If the circumstances are such as to make it apparent that the corporation is not the source of the information and that it expressly or impliedly disclaims any belief in its truth or falsity, merely passing it on for what it is worth, we very much doubt that the corporation can properly be said to be itself engaging in conduct that is misleading or deceptive.'

"Both *Goldsbro* and *Yorke* were cases involving independent agents: in *Goldsbro*, solicitors acting for a purchaser in a property transaction, and in *Yorke* a land agent acting for the vendor of a business."

Counsel for Mr Newport argued that the application of the "mere conduit" defence to an employee raises particular difficulties not faced in cases involving independent agents. Counsel submitted that it was quite reasonable to require that an independent agent make it clear that he or she is simply passing on information from a principal as those dealing with an independent agent might reasonably expect the agent to be making statements on his or her own behalf. Counsel argued that it was not appropriate to require employees to state, when repeating information provided by their employer, that the information was not verified by the employee because, unlike independent agents, employees have no independent status and would not reasonably be considered by a person with whom they are communicating as having any separate status from their employer.

While accepting the submission that there are difficulties in applying a test that was devised to deal with the situation involving an independent agent to employees, the Court was not prepared to pronounce a new test for "mere conduit" in the case of an employee. The Court commented, at para 104:

> "We think that the best approach is not to pronounce a new test for 'mere conduit' in the case of employees, but simply to apply the test to the facts of the case. The reality is that there are many situations, particularly where information has been conveyed by a relatively junior employee, in which will be obvious to the recipient that the representation is made by the body corporate which employees the employee, rather than independently by the employee himself or herself. We do not think that there is anything in the *Goldsbro* test which requires that an employee specifically distances himself or herself from the information in order to satisfy the mere conduit test. Rather, if, on the facts, it should be apparent to the recipient of the information that the employee is not personally the source of the information, then in the absence of any other factor indicating to the contrary, the mere conduit test should be satisfied."

In the end result the "mere conduit" defence was available to Mr Newport as, although he was a senior employee, he was subordinate to a director who was the "alter ego" of the company, and was found to have done no more than convey information prepared by that director.

This statement must be qualified by the duty of care that conduits of information owe to their recipients, and should also be read subject to the law in relation to disclaimers and contractual limitations discussed later in this chapter (see 10.4.13(2) ("Disclaimers to limit liability") and 10.4.14 ("Contractual limitations")).

10.4.6 Evidence

As with passing off, evidence of actual deception or confusion is not required. It is enough that on the balance of probabilities the conduct is likely to mislead or deceive the relevant section of the public: *Taylor Bros Ltd v Taylors Group Ltd* [1988] 2 NZLR 1 (CA), at p 39.

See also, the comments of the full Federal Court of Australia in *Taco Co of Australia Inc v Taco Bell Pty Ltd* (1982) 42 ALR 177 (FCA), at p 202:

> "Evidence that some person has in fact formed an erroneous conclusion is admissible and may be persuasive but is not essential. Such evidence does not itself conclusively establish that conduct is misleading or deceptive or likely to mislead or deceive. The court must determine that question for itself. The test is objective."

These comments were cited with approval by Fisher J in *Tot Toys Ltd v Mitchell* [1993] 1 NZLR 325, at p 367.

However, it is not unusual for actions to fail because the allegations of deception are not supported by the evidence.

See, for example:

- *Clorox NZ Ltd v Elldex Packaging Ltd* 13/11/03, Williams J, HC Auckland CIV-2003-403-4292, in which the Court refused to grant an interim injunction restraining Elldex from marketing cling film in packaging having get-up similar to that of Clorox. Although it was common ground that Clorox had considerable reputation in the colours yellow, red, and blue (which were the prominent colours of Elldex's packaging), the Court considered that the presence of Elldex's "KiWi" brand name was sufficient to avoid confusion in the absence of any proof of actual deception or deliberate imitation; and

- *Universal College of Learning v ACP Computer Solutions Ltd* 22/10/03, Hammond J, HC Napier CP9/01, in which the Court declined to grant the plaintiff an interim injunction restraining the defendant's use of a brand comprising the word "FutureCol" (which was alleged to be confusingly similar to the plaintiff's "Ucol" brand). One of the reasons for refusing the application was that the relevant purchasing public would be unlikely to subscribe to a course based simply on a name or the look of a brand.

10.4.7 Class of consumer

Whether conduct is misleading or deceptive is always to be decided by reference to the section of the public affected by the conduct.

If the conduct is directed towards the market as a whole, then the Court will be required to ascertain the effect of the conduct on a large variety of people.

Conversely, where the conduct is directed towards a specific section of the public, the Court will be required to identify that section, and then determine whether people falling within that group are likely to have been misled or deceived. For example, in *Neumegen v Neumegen & Co* [1998] 3 NZLR 310; (1998) 8 TCLR 299 (CA), the relevant section of the public was deemed to comprise potential clients of the respondent, including people like real estate agents who were assisting clients by making referrals.

(1)   *Consumer must be "reasonable"*

A number of decisions held that the effect of conduct should be assessed only by reference to "reasonable" consumers. See, for example, *Parkdale Custom Built Furniture Pty Ltd v Puxu Pty Ltd* (1982) 149 CLR 191 (HCA), at p 199, where the High Court of Australia said:

> "It seems clear enough that consideration must be given to the class of consumers likely to be affected by the conduct. Although it is true, as has often been said, that ordinarily a class of consumers may include the inexperienced as well as the experienced, and the gullible as well as the astute, the section must in my opinion be regarded as contemplating the affect of the conduct on reasonable members of the class. The heavy burdens which the section creates cannot have been intended to be imposed for the benefit of persons who fail to take reasonable care of their own interests."

See also the comments of Gault J in *Bonz Group Pty Ltd v Cooke* (1996) 7 TCLR 206 (CA), at p 212:

> "That which is misleading or deceptive (where there is no evidence of actual deception) will be that which is assessed as likely to mislead or deceive in postulated circumstances — that is when encountered by reasonable members of a significant section of the public."

In *Universal College of Learning v ACP Computer Solutions Ltd* 22/10/03, Hammond J, HC Napier CP9/01, the Court declined to grant the plaintiff an interim injunction restraining the defendant's use of a brand comprising the word "FutureCol" (which was alleged to be confusingly similar to the plaintiff's "Ucol" brand) in part on the basis that the relevant purchasing public would be unlikely to subscribe to a course based simply on a name or the look of a brand. The Court considered that the absence of evidence of actual confusion reinforced this finding.

In *Carter Holt Harvey Ltd v Cottonsoft Ltd* (2004) 8 NZBLC 101,541, Carter Holt Harvey complained that Cottonsoft's promotion as "made in New Zealand" of toilet tissue and paper towels manufactured from tissue imported from various Asian countries breached ss 9 and 13(j) Fair Trading Act 1986. In determining the claim, the Court resorted to an enquiry into the "mind of the average New Zealand shopper" commenting, at para 30, that:

> "a statement on packaging that a product is made in New Zealand is a representation not so much about the source and origin of its raw materials but about the place where it was produced or manufactured. The average shopper is alive to the modern economic reality that some New Zealand companies manufacture products here from imported raw materials. He or she would accept as true a statement that goods are made in New Zealand even if the raw materials originate elsewhere provided the manufacturing process occurred substantially here."

On the facts, the toilet tissue processed by Cottonsoft underwent four discrete stages of manufacture, of which only the last stage occurred within New Zealand. The Court found that the third stage, which involved transforming a bale of pulp into a sheet of tissue, was determinative in producing the base characteristics of the tissue sheet. These characteristics remained unchanged throughout the subsequent conversion stage. Hence, as this process occurred in Indonesia, the Court concluded, at paras 38 and 39, that Cottonsoft had misled consumers by representing that products formed from that tissue sheet originated in New Zealand:

> "I doubt that the average New Zealand shopper would be aware of each of the specific stages required to produce toilet and towel tissue. He or she would know only that it is produced by some process or processes which transform it from wood into the packaged goods stocked on a supermarket shelf. What the average shopper would assume from a representation that tissues are 'New Zealand Made' is that this entire conversion process occurs in New Zealand, not just the last or specific stage.

> "A promotional label which restricts the manufacturing nomination to New Zealand is therefore false and misleading. But it would not be misleading for Cottonsoft to describe the tissue as made both in Indonesia (or another Asian country) and New Zealand. They are the product's joint countries of origin and both should be listed on all packaging."

Ultimately, the Court did not need to grant an injunction under s 41(1) of the Act, as Cottonsoft had offered appropriate undertakings.

The decision is also notable for the finding that the use of a kiwi logo on some of Cottonsoft's products would be associated by the average New Zealand consumer with the local company behind the product rather than the product itself, and hence did not amount to a misrepresentation as to the origin of the product.

In *Gold Real Estate Group Ltd v GoldLeaf Real Estate Ltd* (2006) 11 TCLR 530, the plaintiff was the registered proprietor of the trade mark GOLD REAL ESTATE GROUP LIMITED and claimed to have reputation in the word GOLD in relation to real estate services. It sought an interim injunction restraining the defendant from using GOLD in relation to real estate services.

The injunction was sought on the basis of a potential for trade mark infringement and also passing off and breach of the Fair Trading Act 1986. In assessing the strength of the passing off cause of action, Fogarty J noted, at para 34, that there was likely to be evidence that vendors are relatively cautious when entering into real estate transactions and part of that caution will be requiring a measure of certainty that any company with GOLD in its name or branding is the same as another company with GOLD in its name or branding, given the general use of GOLD and GOLDEN in all sorts of markets by numerous firms. Similarly, his Honour felt that potential real estate agents would be careful about which company they joined and therefore there was at least some uncertainty as to whether purchasers would be materially deceived.

10.4.8 Correction of misrepresentation

Deception at any time constitutes a breach of the Act. If there is initial deception, immediate correction at the point of sale will be too late to retrospectively nullify the breach.

In this regard see *Trust Bank Auckland Ltd v ASB Bank Ltd* [1989] 3 NZLR 385 (CA). There the defendant alleged that initial customer confusion was irrelevant if rectified at the point of sale. Cooke P disagreed, at p 389:

> "There seems to us to be no reason why s 9 should not protect the public from being led into business premises by being misled as to the ownership of the business. Once a prospective customer has entered, he or she will often be more likely to buy."

10.4.9 Act not to be read down

Many of the considerations in relation to passing off are equally applicable to a breach of the Act. The essence of both causes of action is some misrepresentation by the defendant. That misrepresentation must arise from a reputation established by the plaintiff. However, the question of misleading conduct under s 9 is to be decided separately from the principles of passing off. The Act should not be read down so that the particular requirements of passing off must be made out before conduct will be deemed misleading or deceptive.

(1) *Differences between passing off and an action under the Act*

The differences between the Act and passing off, and the tendency of Courts to override the consumer protection aspects of the Act, were specifically addressed in the dissenting judgment of Thomas J in *Neumegen v Neumegen & Co* [1998] 3 NZLR 310; (1998) 8 TCLR 299 (CA), at p 325; p 314:

> "Certainly, the experience of the courts [in passing off cases] should not be abandoned nor the principles ignored. The case law is too well entrenched for that. The problem lies not so much with the principles which have evolved through experience as with the approach or mode of thinking when the courts' attention is

redirected from passing off to an action based on s 9. What is then required is not so much a shift in gear, as a change from a 'private' vehicle to a 'public' conveyance.

"Although the importation of the principles and terms of art used in formulating the tort of passing off may be understandable, it must be fully recognised that the cause of action in passing off and the cause of action based on s 9 are quite different beasts. Passing off is a tort of a private nature directed at the protection of the trader's intangible property right in his or her reputation and goodwill. An action under s 9 may be brought by a rival trader, but it remains an action of a public character directed at the protection of consumers. The danger is that the public interest elements which should dominate a proceeding under s 9 become subverted by the language and concepts of a private proprietary action. Formulae appropriate to the latter divert the courts from the consumer-oriented analysis of the case which is required in order to give effect to the object of the statute.

"It will do no injury to the doctrine of precedent if the courts strive to keep the two causes of action analytically separate and distinct so that the approach adopted in the one does not infect the approach adopted in the other. The public concerns which underlie the consumer legislation are not to be submerged by the case law which has developed around the proprietary tort, or more particularly the attitudes or mode of thinking it engenders. The courts must deliberately accommodate this difference as they move from a private cause of action to a cause of action having a public character and the public interest as its touchstone."

Similarly, in *ABB Ltd v NZ Insulators Ltd (No 2)* 28/8/07, Courtney J, HC Auckland CIV-2004-404-4829, the Court held, at para 44:

"I do not consider that I am constrained by the limitations imposed on a plaintiff in a passing-off action when assessing the loss caused by misleading and deceptive conduct under the FTA. Goodwill is not required to prove a breach of the FTA and it would be illogical if the absence of goodwill were to be a barrier to proving causation and loss."

(2) *Easier to establish cause of action under the Act*

In *Tot Toys Ltd v Mitchell* [1993] 1 NZLR 325, at p 367, Fisher J identified several aspects in which it would be easier to establish a cause of action under the Act as opposed to passing off. These were:

- The application of s 9 is not restricted by common law limitations that might apply to a passing off action. In *Tot Toys,* a case regarding "buzzy bee" look-alikes, much of the argument centred around whether the features of the defendant's toy were capricious features chosen by the plaintiff from a range of equally viable alternatives. The defendant could only be found to have passed off the plaintiff's product by adoption of those capricious elements. Commenting on the significance of the same inquiry under the Act, his Honour doubted whether the distinction would apply, noting that the words "conduct that is misleading or deceptive" are unqualified, and that strong reasons would be needed to introduce the gloss that if misleading or deceptive conduct amounts to no more than copying of non-capricious get-up it will escape the ambit of s 9;

- Damage to the plaintiff is not an essential element of a cause of action under the Act;

- Source motivation on the purchasers' part is also not an essential element of the cause of action even when a plaintiff's complaint is diversion of trade. As the test under s 9 is simply whether customers have been, or will be, misled or deceived, a plaintiff does not need to go on and demonstrate the adverse consequences of that deception. In other words, there need not be any adverse impact on the economic interests of consumers;

- There is no requirement that the plaintiff show that the reputation (necessary for there to be a misrepresentation) belongs to him or her. By way of explanation Fisher J gave the following example, at p 368:

  "To misrepresent that a painting was painted by Goldie would contravene the Act even though there is no current painter of Goldies. The principal object of the Act is to protect the public, not to vindicate the rights of a competitor."

- Deception at any time constitutes a breach of the Act. If there is initial deception, immediate correction at the point of sale will be too late to retrospectively nullify the breach. This must be contrasted with passing off in which damage to the plaintiff is an essential element. In the context of passing off, if the misleading or deceptive conduct has been corrected before any damage has occurred, the plaintiff may be deprived of a remedy.

A final significant difference noted by his Honour relates to the availability of remedies. Under passing off, if a plaintiff successfully establishes a reputation, misrepresentation and damage, it will, in most cases, be entitled to a remedy as of right. Under the Act, the remedies are discretionary. Therefore, even if all the technical ingredients of a cause of action are made out, the plaintiff must also satisfy the Court as to its entitlement to one of the statutory remedies. See also *Carter Holt Harvey Ltd v Cottonsoft Ltd* (2004) 8 NZBLC 101,541.

10.4.10 Significant section of the public

The statutory remedies available under the Act are discretionary. Therefore, even though a plaintiff may successfully establish the technical requirements of a breach of s 9 of the Act (conduct in trade which misleads or deceives and/or which is likely to mislead or deceive), the Court may decline to grant a remedy. One of the more important inquiries is whether a significant section of the public will be affected by the contravening conduct. As was noted in *Telecom Directories Ltd v Ad.Viser (NZ) Ltd* (1992) 5 TCLR 60; 26 IPR 37:

"Therefore, the court should, in exercising jurisdiction under the Fair Trading Act, be astute to avoid misuse of its injunctive powers under s 41 where the risk of deception to consumers is minimal or non-existent and the heavy-handed use of such powers may wrongfully hinder or lessen competition."

See also, *Magellan Corp Ltd v Magellan Group Ltd* (1995) 5 NZBLC 103,852, at p 103,860:

"an injunction is likely to be granted only if the number of consumers likely to be misled is significant in the context of that particular market and if the way in which they will be misled is likely to be of real consequence."

The consequence of the misleading or deceptive conduct (or likely impact) was a point also raised by Cooke P in *Taylor Bros Ltd v Taylors Group Ltd* [1988] 2 NZLR 1 (CA), at p 40:

> "Certainly the degree of impact or likely impact on consumers is important. It goes both to whether there is likelihood that persons will be misled or deceived and to whether the court in its discretion should grant an injunction (or other remedy) under the Act. The case has to be sufficiently serious to warrant a remedy."

The above quote was cited with approval in *Neumegen v Neumegen & Co* [1998] 3 NZLR 310; (1998) 8 TCLR 299 (CA), at p 317; p 306.

Note also, the relevant section of the purchasing public may be limited to those in a particular geographical region. Thus, in *Fresh Direct Ltd v Fresh Direct Wholesale Ltd* 18/12/03, Durie J, HC Blenheim CIV-2003-406-20, the Court refused to grant Fresh Direct, which had been selling fresh fruit, vegetables, flowers, and pot plants under the name "Fresh Direct" since 1995, a permanent injunction to restrain Fresh Direct Wholesale from supplying a broader range of foodstuffs under the same name in the Nelson/Marlborough area. Although the Court accepted that Fresh Direct had significant goodwill in the FRESH DIRECT name throughout most of New Zealand, it found that Fresh Direct's reputation in the Nelson/Marlborough region was limited to the supply of fresh fruits and vegetables to only three supermarkets, each of which were serviced from Fresh Direct's Christchurch branch. In counterpoint, fresh fruit and vegetables made up only 10 percent of Fresh Direct Wholesale's business and their supply was mainly to cafés and restaurants. Fresh Direct's limited reputation in the Nelson/Marlborough region, combined with a "paucity of evidence of confusion amongst members of the public within the affected market area", resulted in its case falling "well short of providing the necessary confidence for judicial intervention".

10.4.11 No criminal liability

As a breach of s 9 does not constitute a criminal offence, a breach will not give rise to any of the criminal sanctions available following conviction under s 40. A breach will, however, give rise to the civil remedies available under s 41 and s 43 of the Act. These are discussed in more detail at 10.8 ("Legal remedies") later in this chapter.

10.4.12 Erroneous assumptions

In *McWilliam's Wines Pty Ltd v McDonald's System of Australia Pty Ltd* (1980) 33 ALR 394 (FCA), the full Federal Court of Australia held that McWilliam's use of "Big Mac" in relation to wine did not constitute a breach of s 52 Trade Practices Act 1974 (Aust) notwithstanding McDonald's extensive use of the name for a type of hamburger. There was ample evidence that the public associated "Big Mac" with McDonald's and assumed that the use of the expression by McWilliam's indicated some arrangement between the two companies. However, the Court held that any confusion which had arisen did so on the basis of a mistaken assumption that the expression could not have been used by McWilliam's in the absence of a formal arrangement with McDonald's, rather than from the use of the phrase of itself.

The finding of the Court in that case had been interpreted by some as giving rise to a general proposition that anything that could be labelled "erroneous assumption" would break the causal link between the conduct and its misleading or deceptive effect, and deprive any complainant of a remedy.

The matter was subsequently clarified by the full Federal Court in *Taco Co of Australia Inc v Taco Bell Pty Ltd* (1982) 42 ALR 177 (FCA), as follows:

> "In truth, of course, no conduct can mislead or deceive unless the representee labours under some erroneous assumption. Such an assumption can range from the obvious, such as a simple assumption that an express representation is worthy of credence, through the predictable, such as the common assumption in a passing-off case that goods marketed under a trade name which corresponds to the well-known trade name of goods of the same type have their origins in the manufacturer of the well-known goods, to the fanciful, such as an assumption that the mere fact that a person sells goods means that he is the manufacturer of them. The nature of the erroneous assumption which must be made before conduct can mislead or deceive will be a relevant, and sometimes decisive, factor in determining the factual question where conduct should properly be categorised as misleading or deceptive or as likely to mislead or deceive. Beyond that, generalizations are themselves liable to be misleading or deceptive."

As Brown and Grant note in *The Law of Intellectual Property in New Zealand*, at para 7.13, the essential inquiry of every case will be whether the conduct said to contravene the Act gave rise to the erroneous assumption. If it did, then there will be a breach of s 9. If, however, the erroneous assumption is based on a pre-existing notion held by those who were misled or deceived then there will be no breach. In that regard every case is to be decided on its own facts, and evidence of people who have been misled or deceived as to why they were misled or deceived will assume increased importance.

10.4.13   Disclaimers

While the Courts have been prepared to accept in principle that disclaimers may operate to prevent misleading or deceptive conduct, in practice they have generally been found to be ineffective.

In essence there are two types of disclaimer:

- Those that seek to prevent misleading or deceptive conduct from arising, by informing or educating consumers as to the nature of the goods/services supplied (informative disclaimers); and

- Those that seek to limit liability in the event that the Act has been breached (disclaimers to limit liability).

(1)   *Informative disclaimers*

The first form of disclaimer was discussed extensively in *Hutchence v South Sea Bubble Co Pty Ltd* (1986) 64 ALR 330 (FCA), at pp 338-339. The respondent, which was selling t-shirts bearing the name and insignia of the rock group INXS, had placed signs and labels on them disclaiming that they were approved by the members of that group. The respondent also relied on a reference to "Bootleg" Industries on the t-shirt to say that consumers would realise they were not purchasing genuine merchandise. Wilcox J gave the following warning as to the efficacy of such disclaimers:

"There are occasions upon which the effect of otherwise misleading or deceptive conduct may be neutralized by an appropriate disclaimer: see *Abundant Earth Pty Ltd v R & C Products Ltd* (1984) 59 ALR 211, at p.217 and the authorities there cited. But such cases are likely to be comparatively rare and to be confined to situations in which the court is able to reach satisfaction — the onus resting on the party relying upon the disclaimer — that the disclaimer is likely to be seen and understood by all those — leaving aside isolated exceptions — who would otherwise be misled before they act in relation to the relevant transaction. In the present case, it seems to me that it is difficult to feel satisfied, both as to seeing and understanding, in respect of both the name of the stall and the labels and stickers.

"The assumptions underlining counsel's reliance upon the first matter are that all potential purchasers would notice the use of the trading name 'Bootleg Industries' and would understand from it that the items offered for sale were unapproved, or may be unapproved, by those with whom they were apparently associated ... But the word is not one in every day parlance. Not all potential purchasers will be persons of wide vocabulary. The word 'bootleg' was new to one of the three witnesses approached at Pier One at the time of that interview. Particularly in the absence of any evidence as to public acquaintance with the word, I am unable to feel satisfied that his is an isolated case.

"One problem about the stickers and labels is that they may not come to notice before purchase ... If a purchaser did see and read the sticker or label on a particular T-shirt, it is by no means clear that he or she would understand it as a statement that the garment had no association whatever with INXS. Indeed I suspect that many potential purchasers would not understand it at all. A number of studies have demonstrated that legalistic English is not widely understood in the Australian community; hence the movement for 'Plain English' drafting of legal documents and legislation ... In this situation it would be a brave assumption that the meaning of words such as 'warrant', 'depiction' and 'authorised' would be readily appreciated by all but an insignificant proportion of potential T-shirt buyers."

The disclaimer in *Hutchence* read:

"The manufacturer does not warrant the depiction hereon has been authorised."

Disclaimers will be particularly inappropriate in a case of low cost consumer items, which purchasers do not, as a habit, examine in detail before purchase: *Abundant Earth Pty Ltd v R & C Products Ltd* (1984) 59 ALR 211, at p 217:

"There may well be cases where a disclaimer is effective to eliminate confusion ... But, where the competing products are small, inexpensive items the efficacy of a disclaimer, however prominent, cannot be assumed."

(2) *Disclaimers to limit liability*

Disclaimers that limit liability after misleading or deceptive conduct has arisen will rarely be effective. See *Smythe v Bayleys Real Estate Ltd* (1993) 5 TCLR 454, in which Thomas J, discussing a series of exclusion clauses in documents associated with a real estate transaction that purported to exclude the operation of the Act, commented, at p 472:

"I do not consider, however, that these clauses have the effect of excluding the operation of the Fair Trading Act. The requirements of the Act are mandatory. In enacting the legislation, Parliament sought to protect the consumer from unfair trading and it would be inconsistent with that objective to permit a person engaged in trade to exempt him or herself from liability under the Act. In effect, this would be to allow such persons to opt out of the operation of the Act and the regime decreeing fair trading in the public interest".

10.4.14   Contractual limitations

The terms of a contract that purport to limit or exclude liability have generally been held to be ineffective. The reasons for this are explained by Lockhart J in *Henjo Investments Pty Ltd v Collins Marrickville Pty Ltd* (1988) 79 ALR 83, at pp 98-99:

"Section 52 is a section in the consumer protection provisions of an Act concerned to protect the public from misleading or deceptive conduct and unfair trade practices which may result in contravention of the Act. It has been held that exclusion clauses … cannot operate to defeat claims under s 52. It may be, as the judgment of Sweeney J in *P J Berry Estates Pty Ltd v Mangalone Homestead Pty. Ltd* (1984) 6 ATPR 45,626 at 45,638 suggests, that such exclusion clauses will generally be ineffective because they cannot break the nexus between the conduct and contravention of s 52 and the making of the agreement in issue. Where the conduct of the defendant is alleged to be fraudulent in character, [then] an exclusion clause will be no more effective to defeat the action than it would be effective if the action was brought in the tort of deceit in relation to conduct antecedent to the contract …

"There are wider objections to allowing effect to such clauses. Otherwise the operation of the Act, a public policy statute, could be ousted by private agreement. Parliament passed the Act to stamp out unfair or improper conduct in trade or in commerce; it would be contrary to public policy for special conditions such as those with which this contract was concerned to deny or prohibit a statutory remedy for offending conduct under the Act."

10.4.15   Sections 10 and 11

Section 10 of the Act prohibits conduct in trade that is liable to mislead the public as to the nature, manufacturing process, characteristics, suitability for a purpose, or quantity of goods. Section 11 contains an analogous prohibition in relation to services. Under s 40 of the Act, there are criminal sanctions available for a breach of ss 10 or 11 in addition to the civil remedies available under ss 41-43 of the Act.

There have been very few cases decided concerning the interpretation of ss 10 and 11 although the Commerce Commission commonly seeks criminal sanctions for breach of these sections.

(1)   *Price of goods or services may be a "characteristic"*

In some circumstances the price of goods or services may be a characteristic in terms of ss 10 or 11. In *Sound Plus Ltd v Commerce Commission* [1991] 3 NZLR 329, the Commerce Commission alleged that Sound Plus had, in describing goods as duty free, alleged that they were being sold at discount prices. In fact the goods were of a type for which no duty was payable. Anderson J commented, at p 335:

> "In this case, the impression having been given that the goods were duty-free, the concept conveyed is first that the goods on sale were of a type which would normally be subject to excise duty, and second that the appellant was able to offer them to the general public free of duty which would otherwise attach. The only benefit to the public of such facts, if they were true, would be a benefit in terms of price because it would allow the appellant to pass such goods on, free of an extraneous element of price. It is not only, of course, that the goods could clearly be considered duty-free in the context of such a description, but also that the price would be duty-free in a sense relevant to the understandings of ordinary New Zealanders. I therefore hold that the appellant was rightly convicted pursuant to s 10 of the Fair Trading Act and that the particular advertisement amounted to conduct liable to mislead the public as to a characteristic of the goods it displayed, namely the price."

It is implicit from the passage above that, if the representation concerning price did not convey a message that the goods were of a particular type, there would have been no breach of s 10.

10.5   Section 13: false representations

Section 13 Fair Trading Act 1986 sets out a range of false or misleading representations, which, if made in trade, and in connection with the promotion, supply or possible supply of goods or services, will contravene the Act.

The types of false or misleading representations prohibited by s 13 of the Act are as follows:

- That goods are of a particular kind, standard, quality, grade, quantity, composition, style, or model, or have had a particular history or particular previous use (s 13(a));

- That services are of a particular kind, standard, quality, or quantity, or that they are supplied by any particular person or by any person of a particular trade, qualification, or skill (s 13(b));

- That a particular person has agreed to acquire goods or services (s 13(c));

- That goods are new, or that they are reconditioned, or that they were manufactured, produced, processed, or reconditioned at a particular time (s 13(d));

- That goods or services have any sponsorship, approval, endorsement, performance characteristics, accessories, uses, or benefits (s 13(e));

- That a person has any sponsorship, approval, endorsement or affiliation (s 13(f));

- As to the price of any goods or services (s 13(g));

- Concerning the need for any goods or services (s 13(h));

- Concerning the existence, exclusion, or effect of any condition, warranty, guarantee, right, or remedy (s 13(i)); and

- Concerning the place of origin of goods (s 13(j)).

Given the ambit of this text it is not proposed to discuss these individual sections in further detail.

10.5.1 Meaning of "in trade"

"Trade" is defined in s 2 Fair Trading Act 1986 as:

> "any trade, business, industry, profession, occupation, activity of commerce, or undertaking relating to the supply or acquisition of goods or services or to the disposition or acquisition of any interest in land."

The terms "business", "acquire", "supply", "goods", and "services" are each also defined in s 2. The inclusive nature of the majority of those definitions means that "trade" may be broadly interpreted.

The meaning of "in trade" is discussed in more detail at 10.4 ("Misleading or deceptive conduct") earlier in this chapter.

10.5.2 Meaning of "supply"

"supply" is given an inclusive definition in s 2(1) Fair Trading Act 1986 as follows:

> "(a) In relation to goods, includes supply (or re-supply) by way of gift, sale, exchange, lease, hire, or hire purchase; and
>
> "(b) In relation to services, includes provide, grant, or confer;—
>
> "and 'supply' as a noun, 'supplied' and 'supplier' have corresponding meanings:"

10.5.3 Meaning of "goods" and "services"

The meanings of "goods" and "services" (in s 2(1) Fair Trading Act 1986) are also inclusive and cover, amongst other things:

- Ships, aircraft and vehicles;

- Animals including fish;

- Minerals, trees, and crops whether on, under or attached to land or not;

- Gas and electricity; and

- Any rights (including rights in relation to, and interests in, real or personal property), benefits, privileges, or facilities that are, or are to be, provided, granted or conferred whether or not under contract.

Rights or benefits in the form of the supply of goods, or the performance of work under a contract of service, are specifically excluded from the definition of "services".

Since 8 July 2003, the definition of "goods" has also included "personal property of every kind (whether tangible or intangible)" and "water and computer software", and "services" has included "the supply of electricity, gas, telecommunications, or water, or the removal of waste water". These additional definitions were inserted by virtue of the Fair Trading Amendment Act (No 2) 2003 in order to ensure that the definitions more accurately encompassed all the goods and services that are ordinarily acquired for personal, domestic or household use or consumption. The amendment appears to have been primarily motivated by the decision in *Electricity Supply Assn of NZ Inc v Commerce Commission* (1998) 6 NZBLC 102,555, in which the High Court held that electricity, and associated line function services, are not goods or services for the purposes of the Consumer Guarantees Act 1993.

The extension of the definition of "goods" to include personal property of any kind including intangible property at first glance appears far-reaching. Previously, the definition of "goods" was limited to true tangible goods. However, as is noted by Dr Noel Cox in his article "Proposed Consumer Protection Bill defines goods and services including software and utilities from their respective Acts" *Northern Law News*, No 33, 6 September 2002, there will be very few intangibles acquired by consumers that are not already acquired under a contract of service. Hence the amendment is unlikely to broaden the ambit of the Act to any significant extent.

Misleading and deceptive conduct in relation to "money" was considered in *Money World NZ 2000 Ltd v KVB Kunlin NZ Ltd* [2006] 1 NZLR 381. Money World sought to exchange $360,000 worth of commemorative $2 Fijian notes with KVB for New Zealand dollars. Money World failed to advise KVB of the existence of a dispute regarding the notes with the Reserve Bank of Fiji. KVB made independent enquiries with the Reserve Bank and was advised that the notes would not be redeemed by the Reserve Bank. The ability of KVB to redeem the notes was held to be a fundamental element of the transaction and Money World's silence misleading and deceptive conduct. Although decided under s 9 of the Act, it is likely that "money" would meet the definitions of "goods" and "services" and therefore a representation in respect of money would also be actionable under s 13 of the Act. "Goods" are defined in the Act as "personal property of every kind", and the definition of "personal property" under the Personal Property Securities Act 1999 includes "money".

10.5.4   False or misleading representation

The words "false or misleading representation" are common to all the subparagraphs of s 13.

(1)   *Meaning of "representation"*

The term "representation" is not defined in the Fair Trading Act 1986. However, many New Zealand Courts have adopted the comments of Franki J in *Given v Pryor* (1979) 24 ALR 442 that a representation encompasses not only oral or written statements, but may also extend to conduct.

Franki J also cited with approval the following passage from *Halsbury's Laws of England*:

> "A representation is a statement made by a representor to a representee and relating by way of affirmation, denial, description or otherwise to a matter of fact. This statement may be oral or in writing and may arise by implication from words or conduct."

Given v Pryor was cited with approval in *Commerce Commission v Kimberley's Fashions Ltd & Marcol Manufacturers Ltd* (1989) 3 TCLR 405.

It is also clear from the authorities that it is an offence under the Act to make a false or misleading representation regardless of whether that representation was actually communicated to any person. That is consistent with the aim of the Act to curtail misleading or deceptive conduct even in the absence of any damage being caused.

In *Commerce Commission v Telecom Mobile Ltd* [2006] 1 NZLR 190; (2005) 11 TCLR 436; 8 NZBLC 101,657 (CA), contractual terms were considered to be false or misleading representations. Telecom Mobile conducted a telephone marketing campaign which targeted Vodafone customers. Customers were telephoned by a third party telemarketing company and asked if they wanted to join Telecom Mobile's network. If they agreed, a credit check would be performed. If the outcome of the credit check was favourable a mobile phone would be sent to the customer. Telecom Mobile's contracts stated that once the seal on the box containing the phone was broken customers had no right to return the goods and that the contract would be enforceable on that basis. This was deemed to be misleading as it was contrary to the right of return provisions of the Door to Door Sales Act 1967, and consequently was unenforceable.

The decision of the Court of Appeal was appealed to the Supreme Court (*Telecom Mobile Ltd v Commerce Commission* [2006] 3 NZLR 323; (2006) 11 TCLR 633; 8 NZBLC 101,708 (SC)) on a narrow and unrelated point concerning the interpretation of certain provisions of the Door to Door Sales Act.

In *Commerce Commission v Vero Insurance NZ Ltd* (2006) 11 TCLR 779; [2007] DCR 115; (2006) 8 NZBLC 101,871, the Court held that a representation must relate to an existing and verifiable state of affairs. In promotional material relating to an insurance policy underwritten by Vero, consumers were advised that, by taking up the policy, they would be in to win a year's free power, but no draw was held until more than 2 years after the first promotion. The District Court held that the delay in conducting the draw was explicable, and found against the Commission. The Commission's appeal was unsuccessful — the High Court holding that the promise of a future draw was not a "representation" for the purposes of the Act, there was no question of deceit or misrepresentation of the promoter's state of mind, nor was there any basis to imply into the promoter's statement a representation that arrangements were in hand for a draw or that the draw would be held within a reasonable time.

(2) *Meaning of "misleading"*

There is no definition of "misleading" in the Fair Trading Act 1986.

Guidance as to its meaning can be found in the body of case law interpreting whether particular conduct is "misleading or deceptive" under s 9 of the Act. That case law is discussed in more detail at 10.4 ("Misleading or deceptive conduct") earlier in this chapter.

As with s 9, the inquiry as to whether a representation is misleading is an objective one to be determined on the facts of each case. Evidence that someone has, or has not, been misled will be helpful, but not conclusive.

The tests articulated in *Taco Co of Australia Inc v Taco Bell Pty Ltd* (1982) 42 ALR 177 (FCA) and *AMP Finance NZ Ltd v Heaven* (1997) 8 TCLR 144 (also discussed at 10.4 ("Misleading or deceptive conduct") earlier in this chapter) may be of assistance to the Courts.

(3) *Meaning of "false"*

Again, there is no definition of "false" in the Fair Trading Act 1986. In *Commerce Commission v A & W Hamilton Ltd* (1989) 3 TCLR 398, the Court adopted the *Concise Oxford Dictionary* definition of "wrong" or "incorrect".

10.5.5 No intention necessary

As with a breach of s 9 Fair Trading Act 1986, a party does not have to intend a representation to be false for it to contravene the section.

This was confirmed in *Given v C V Holland (Holdings) Pty Ltd* (1977) 15 ALR 439, at p 443:

> "I am satisfied that, if a representation is in fact not correct, it comes within the words of the section, even if it is not false to the knowledge of the person making the representation."

However, a finding that a party intended to make a false or misleading representation may make the Court more willing to conclude that the representation was false and/or misleading.

Intention is discussed in more detail at 10.4 ("Misleading or deceptive conduct") earlier this chapter.

10.5.6 Lack of knowledge may offer defence

Although intention is not an element of a breach of s 13, a lack of knowledge that a particular representation was false or misleading may give rise to the defences available under s 44 Fair Trading Act 1986 including, in particular:

- That the contravention was due to a reasonable mistake; or

- That the contravention was due to reasonable reliance on information supplied by another person.

These defences are discussed in more detail at 10.9.5 ("Criminal defences") later in this chapter.

10.5.7 Breach of section gives rise to criminal liability

Unlike s 9 Fair Trading Act 1986, a breach of s 13 may give rise to both criminal and civil sanctions. This means that a contravention of the section must be proven beyond a reasonable doubt.

10.6 Section 16: forgery and false application of trade marks

It is an offence under s 16(1) Fair Trading Act 1986 to:

- Forge a trade mark;

- Falsely apply a trade mark (or a sign closely resembling the trade mark) to goods, if that would be likely to mislead or deceive; or

- Falsely use a trade mark (or a sign closely resembling the trade mark) in respect of services, if that would be likely to mislead or deceive.

10.6.1 Meaning of forgery

Forgery is defined in s 16(2) Fair Trading Act 1986 as either:

- Making the trade mark (or a sign closely resembling the trade mark) without the consent of the proprietor so as to be likely to mislead or deceive; or

- Falsifying any genuine trade mark for example by alteration or effacement.

10.6.2 Meaning of "sign"

The definition of "sign" corresponds with the definition in the Trade Marks Act 1953 (but not the Trade Marks Act 2002, which includes the additional word "shape"). It includes a brand, colour, device, heading, label, letter, name, numeral, signature, smell, sound, taste, ticket, word, or any combination of those elements.

10.6.3 Meaning of "trade mark"

The definition of "trade mark" also corresponds with the definition in the Trade Marks Act 1953, which is as follows:

> "'Trade Mark',—
>
> "(a) Except when immediately preceded by the word 'certification' or the word 'collective' means a sign—
>
> > "(i) Capable of being represented graphically;
> >
> > "(ii) Capable of distinguishing the goods or services of one person from those of another; and
>
> "(b) Includes a certification trade mark and a collective trade mark."

There is a similar definition in the Trade Marks Act 2002.

(1) *Definition more expansive than under Trade Marks Act 2002*

However, unlike the definitions in the Trade Marks Act 1953 and Trade Marks Act 2002, the section goes on to provide a number of specific examples in which a "trade mark" would be applied to, or used in connection with, goods or services that fall within the definition of trade mark. These include:

- **In the case of goods**: any sign used on, or in connection with, the goods for the purpose of indicating that they are:

  - Goods of the proprietor of the sign by virtue of manufacture, selection, certification, dealing with or offering to supply;

  - Goods of a member of a body of persons (for example a club, unincorporated society or similar organisation) that is the proprietor of the sign; or

  - Goods certified by the proprietor of the sign in respect of origin, material, mode of manufacture, quality, accuracy or other characteristic.

- **In the case of services**: any sign used in connection with the provision of the services for the purposes of indicating that they are:

  - Services of the proprietor of the sign; or

  - Services of a member of a body of persons that is the proprietor of the sign.

(2) *Selection, certification, or dealing with*

The use of these words in the definition of "trade mark" recognises that not all trade marks are manufacturer's marks. On occasion, the purpose of a mark will be to indicate that goods have passed through a particular retailer's hands, or have been subjected to a selection process having regard to certain characteristics. The broad definition of "trade mark" under the Act encompasses this.

(3) *Collective and certification marks*

A "collective mark" is a mark that distinguishes the goods or services of members of an association that owns the mark on behalf of those members. Owners of collective trade marks are usually professional bodies or trade associations.

A "certification mark" is a mark that is used by its owner to certify the origin, quality, performance, accuracy, or some other recognisable characteristic, of goods or services.

The function of a collective mark is to indicate a trade connection between the goods or services of members of the association that owns the mark, and to distinguish those goods or services from goods and services provided by non-members. By contrast, a certification mark is more akin to a consumer protection measure, in the sense that it denotes some quality of the good or service itself, rather than of the person or company with whom it is connected in the course of trade.

On a rare occasion, a mark will function as both a collective and certification mark. "Champagne" is a good example of this.

(4) *Trade mark need not be registered*

It is clear that the definition of "trade mark" in s 16 Fair Trading Act 1986 is not limited to marks registered under the Trade Marks Act 1953 and/or Trade Marks Act 2002 . Similarly, a plaintiff relying on s 16 need not be the registered proprietor of the trade mark. Whether the plaintiff is, or is not, the "proprietor" of the mark for the purposes of this section will depend on his or her ability to establish reputation. This will usually fall to whether the mark exhibits a capacity to distinguish the goods or services of the plaintiff from those of other traders: *Joico Laboratories Inc v Beauty Products Co Ltd* (1990) 4 TCLR 48.

10.6.4 No definition of "falsely applied"

There is no definition of "falsely apply/use" in the Fair Trading Act 1986. In *Collector of Customs v Number Lock Ltd* 11/10/96, Salmon J, HC Auckland M783/94 the Court was required to consider whether imported shoes that bore invalid trade marks had had those marks falsely applied to the goods, and in turn whether the goods had been properly seized and forfeited under the Customs Act 1966. The Court held that the words "false" and "falsely" mean "erroneous; not according to rule, principle or law; wrong; incorrect".

Extending that definition to the application of trade marks, the Court concluded that a mark is falsely applied to goods in any case where those goods are sold without the permission of the owner of the mark.

At least one commentator (A Brown and A Grant, *The Law of Intellectual Property in New Zealand*, Wellington, Butterworths, 1988, at para 7.33) has suggested that the term "falsely applied" should be defined consistently with the corresponding definition of application of a false trade description in s 26(4) of the Act. However, the authors believe that the concept of "application" is much broader than that defined in s 26(4) and more likely to equate to the concept of use "upon, or in physical or other relation to" goods as defined in s 2(2) Trade Marks Act 1953 (cf s 6 Trade Marks Act 2002). Interpretation on this basis would also be consistent with the identical definitions of "trade mark" and "sign" in each Act.

The following passage from Lord Diplock in *Smith Kline & French Laboratories Ltd v Sterling-Winthrop Group Ltd* (1976) 93 RPC 511 (HL) also gives some guidance, at p 534, as to when a mark will be construed as having been "applied" to goods:

> "So, if it is to be a trade mark, a 'mark' must be something that can be represented visually and may be something that can be applied to the surface of the goods ('use upon') or incorporated in the structure of the goods ('use in physical relation to'). The inclusion of 'heading' (viz. coloured threads woven into the selvedge of textile goods) in the meaning of 'mark' also confirms that a mark, provided it can be seen upon visual examination of the goods, may be incorporated into their structure."

10.7   Section 26: Importation of goods bearing false trade description

Section 26(2) Fair Trading Act 1986 prohibits the importation of goods to which a "false trade description" has been applied.

Goods imported in contravention of s 26 will be treated as goods prohibited under s 54 Customs and Excise Act 1996. Through s 225 of that Act such goods are immediately forfeited to the Crown.

10.7.1 Meaning of "false trade description"

"False trade description" is defined in s 26(3) Fair Trading Act 1986 as being any representation that, if made in connection with the supply, possible supply or promotion of goods, contravenes s 13(a), (d) or (j) of the Act.

10.7.2 Meaning of "applied"

In accordance with s 26(4) Fair Trading Act 1986 a false trade description will be deemed to have been "applied" to goods if:

- It is woven in, impressed on, worked into, annexed or affixed to the goods; or

- It is applied to a covering, label, reel, or thing in which the goods are supplied.

Hence the definition is broad enough to encompass not only goods that carry the false trade description, but also the packaging and labelling.

In *Collector of Customs v Number Lock Ltd* 11/10/96, Salmon J, HC Auckland M783/94 one of the issues before the Court was whether counterfeit goods were goods to which a "false trade description" was applied. The defendant had imported a large number of shoes bearing L A GEAR and NIKE trade marks, which the proprietors of those marks considered to be counterfeit. The goods were consequently seized by NZ Customs and forfeited to the Crown for destruction. Both trade mark proprietors considered that the goods were counterfeit and that the trade marks were not validly applied, although under cross-examination each conceded the possibility that parts of the shoes were genuine.

Relying on the ordinary definition of "false" as set out in the *Shorter Oxford Dictionary*, the Court concluded that a trade mark is falsely applied to goods in any case where those goods are sold without the permission of the owner of the mark, and that the present goods, the sale of which was not authorised by the New Zealand proprietor of each mark, accordingly bore a false trade description.

The Court also noted that false application of a trade mark may also relate to the quality or selection of goods that the proprietor chooses to offer for sale in a particular market:

> "the sale of goods to which the mark is applied is a representation from the owner of the mark that the goods are theirs and meet their quality control standards. If the goods are not theirs and do not meet their standards the mark is falsely or wrongly applied."

10.8 Legal remedies

10.8.1 Section 41: injunctions

Under s 41(1) Fair Trading Act 1986, the High Court may grant an injunction restraining any person from:

- Contravening any of the provisions of Parts 1-4 of the Act;

- Attempting to contravene any such provision;

- Aiding, abetting, counselling, or procuring any other person to contravene such provision;

- Inducing, or attempting to induce, any other person whether by threats, promises or otherwise, to contravene such provision;

- Being in any way directly or indirectly knowingly concerned in, or party to, the contravention by any other person of such a provision; and

- Conspiring with any other person to contravene such provision.

10.8.2 Additional powers

Section 41 also contains supplementary provisions permitting the High Court to:

- Rescind or vary any injunction granted under the section (s 41(2));

- Grant an injunction against someone who has previously engaged in the conduct complained of (whether or not the person intends to continue that conduct or engage in similar conduct in the future) (s 41(3)(b)); or

- Grant a pre-emptive injunction to stop misleading or deceptive conduct from occurring (s 41(4)).

10.8.3 Mandatory injunctions

It is important to note that every subsection of s 41 Fair Trading Act 1986 uses the words "restraining a person from engaging in conduct". At first glance it would appear that the powers conferred by s 41 are limited to the granting of restrictive injunctions only. This view has been expressed in a number of cases including *E R Squibb & Sons (NZ) Ltd v ICI NZ Ltd* (1988) 3 TCLR 296 and *Alan H Reid Engineering Ltd v Ramset Fasteners (NZ) Ltd* (1990) 3 PRNZ 676.

In the latter case, the defendant had issued a circular alleging that pins produced by the plaintiff, that were designed to be fired from guns manufactured by the defendant, were unsafe. The plaintiff sought a number of orders including an interim injunction compelling the defendant to write to the addresses to which the circular was sent admitting the misleading nature of the circular. In declining the orders sought, the Court commented, at p 680, that remedial relief in the nature of a mandatory injunction is not available to a litigant (other than the Commerce Commission, which is entitled to seek mandatory orders and corrective advertising under s 42 of the Act). The Court went on to note that a mandatory order might be made in the equitable jurisdiction of the Court in appropriate circumstances, and affirmed the view expressed by McGechan J in *Squibb* that, in cases involving alleged breaches of the Act, there may be some merit in including claims for common law relief in passing off or malicious falsehood in order to avail oneself of the Court's equitable jurisdiction to make appropriate mandatory orders.

The ability to seek mandatory injunctive relief in tandem with an action under the Act was touched on again in *TV3 Network Ltd v Eveready NZ Ltd* [1993] 3 NZLR 435 (CA). The plaintiffs (the respondents, Eveready NZ Ltd and another distributor) pleaded malicious falsehood and defamation against the defendants (the appellants, TV3 Network Ltd and a subsidiary company) arising out of a documentary about ionisation smoke detectors broadcast by TV3 as part of the *60 Minutes* current affairs programme. The plaintiffs sought, amongst other things, a mandatory injunction directing the defendants to broadcast corrective advertising in a form similar to the broadcast complained of. The appeal raised the question as to whether the remedy of mandatory injunction was available to a litigant in an action for malicious falsehood or defamation.

The majority of the Court held that, in principle, there was no jurisdictional bar to the grant of a mandatory injunction, and that the remedy of injunction would be available whenever it was required by justice. Cooke P went on to observe, at p 438:

> "Especially since the mingling of law and equity, which is accepted in New Zealand, the remedy of injunction should be available whenever required by justice. To impose jurisdictional limits, as distinct from identifying factors which on practical grounds will tell against the discretionary grant of the remedy, would be a backward step."

Gault J, concurring, mentioned in passing both *Squibb* and *Reid* before specifically addressing, at p 445, the correlation between equity and the Act as follows:

"That there is no public policy imperative dictating non-intervention by orders to correct or retract is indicated by the enactment of powers conferred by the Broadcasting Act 1989 on the Broadcasting Standards Authority and on the courts under the Fair Trading Act 1986 (s 42)."

On the strength of those passages it would appear that the remedy of mandatory injunction might be available to a litigant under the Act by reference to the over-arching principle that equity will intervene when justice is required, notwithstanding the wording of s 41, and notwithstanding that no alternative action has been brought under the common law.

10.8.4   Interim injunctions

The power to grant injunctions under s 41 Fair Trading Act 1986 extends to interim injunctions (s 41(3)(b) and (4)(b)).

(1)   *Principles for the grant of interim injunctions*

The principles for the grant of an interim injunction most often relied on by litigants under the Fair Trading Act 1986 are those set out in *Klissers Farmhouse Bakeries Ltd v Harvest Bakeries Ltd* [1985] 2 NZLR 129, at p 142:

- Whether there is a serious question to be tried;

- Where the balance of convenience lies; and

- What is the overall justice of the case?

The Court in *Klissers* emphasised the need for flexibility in all circumstances, and the overriding requirement that the matter is governed by the interests of justice.

In *Blue Star Consumer Retailing Ltd v Book Find Ltd* (2001) 9 TCLR 691 Paterson J noted a "divergence of judicial opinion" as to whether the principles applicable to interim injunctions apply in an unmodified form to applications brought under s 41.

In *Alan H Reid Engineering Ltd v Ramset Fasteners (NZ) Ltd* (1990) 3 PRNZ 676, at pp 679-680, Gault J noted that the section permits the granting of interim relief if it is "desirable" in the opinion of the Court, although he expressed doubt whether that introduces any significantly different test from other cases, except perhaps closer scrutiny to the public interest given the consumer protection aims of the legislation.

In *Resene Paints Ltd v Orica NZ Ltd* [2003] 3 NZLR 709; (2003) 10 TCLR 795, the plaintiff successfully obtained an interim injunction to restrain the defendant from using two of its "iconic" paint names "Spanish White" and "Pearl Lusta". While confirming the *Klissers* principles, his Honour noted the inevitability that, in certain cases, the Court would be required to consider and determine the merits of a case at an interlocutory stage, commenting, at para 22:

"without in any way departing from the principles laid down by our Court of Appeal, it is useful to remember that increasingly in recent years, interlocutory injunctions have become to a respectable degree interfaced with the case management system. This remedy is essentially a 'holding' remedy to address a present position until the merits of the case can be fully adjudicated. Sometimes Judges prefer to go straight to the merits; and sometimes the Court may have no alternative (because of the exigencies of the litigation) to deliver what in functional effect is a judgment on the merits, doing as best the Court then can."

His Honour also expressed concern as to the lack of a Statement of Defence, and the late filing of the Notice of Opposition, commenting, at para 24, that "failure to file a statement of defence is not best practice, and indeed it can embarrass a Court in trying to identify and adjudicate (to the extent then appropriate) on just what is being run as a defence."

(2)   *Undertakings as to damages*

Ordinarily, all applicants for an interim injunction are required to file an undertaking as to damages with the Court (under rr 238(3) and 627B High Court Rules).

However, since 8 July 2003 the Commerce Commission has been exempted from providing such undertaking, and the Court is not permitted to take the lack of undertaking into account when determining whether an interim injunction should be granted (s 11(5) and (6)).

(3)   *Registered intellectual property rights may confer advantage*

Several recent decisions of the High Court and the Court of Appeal would seem to suggest that the Courts will give increasing primacy to registered intellectual property rights when determining an application for interim relief. In many cases this seems to be at the expense of seemingly conclusive arguments going to the balance of convenience and the overall justice.

In *Aktiebolaget Hassle v Novartis NZ Ltd* 1/5/03, Potter J, HC Auckland CP51-SW/03, the plaintiffs sought an injunction to restrain Novartis from manufacturing an omeprazole product, PROBITOR, which they believed infringed their Patent No 220096 relating to their own similar product sold in New Zealand under the brand name LOSEC. Novartis resisted the application on a number of grounds including:

(1)   That it was strongly arguable that the patent was invalid, the equivalent UK patent having already been overturned on the grounds of obviousness; and

(2)   That it had contracted to supply Pharmac with PROBITOR, and was obliged to pay Pharmac $350,000 per calendar month it was unable to supply same (presumably to compensate Pharmac for being obliged to subsidise the more expensive LOSEC during that period).

While recognising the significant losses likely to be suffered by Novartis if injuncted, the Court nonetheless found that the balance of convenience and the overall justice favoured the granting of an injunction, commenting, at para 43:

"There is a reality to be recognised in the case of the patent, that the patent confers a monopoly during its currency, the benefit of which runs over to the post-patent period because of the strong market position usually developed during the monopoly period. This was expressed by Eichelbaum J in [*Monsanto Chemical Co v Stauffer Chemical Co (No 2)* (1984) 1 TCLR 129; 1 NZIPR 540]."

and later, at para 56:

"Premature interference with the monopoly position which the patent confers during its currency will also impact on the ability of the proprietor to create or confirm its own market after the expiry of the patent (the 'bridgehead' opportunity)."

The decision of Potter J was upheld by the Court of Appeal in a decision of Blanchard J delivered on 4 July 2003 (*Novartis NZ Ltd v Aktiebolaget Hassle* [2004] 2 NZLR 721 (CA)).

Similar comments have also arisen in the context of applications for interim injunctions to restrain the infringement of registered design rights. See, for example:

- *Handitags Ltd v Warburton* 12/12/01, Glazebrook J, HC Auckland M1586-SW01, at paras 17 and 18:

  "However, the main reason put forward by Handitags as to inadequacy of damages is the loss of the ability to manage their practical monopoly situation. This is because, at any stage during such a monopoly, an entry of a competitor can cause permanent damage and permanent inability to manage the monopoly and, in particular, the ending of the monopoly which will obviously occur at the end of the design and copyright period. This diminished advantage can mean a permanent effect which Handitags submits is exceedingly hard to quantify. It is noted that there is only some four years left in respect of the design and five years in respect of the copyright so the loss of a portion of the period at the end of the registration for the design and the copyright period is even more significant. These submissions are accepted. It is accepted that damages would not be an adequate remedy for Handitags."

- *BEP Marine Ltd v Aquatech Marine Ltd* 20/12/02, O'Regan J, HC Auckland M1568-SW02 (which applied *Handitags*).

- *Permanent Promotions Pty Ltd v Independent Liquor (NZ) Ltd* 10/6/04, Heath J, HC Auckland CIV-2004-404-2419, at paras 38 and 39:

  "In my judgment, the scheme of the Act is clear. A Commissioner is appointed to examine designs submitted to him or her. In the course of that examination the Commissioner determines questions of novelty and compliance with statutory definitions. The underlying assumption is that the Commissioner is someone experienced in applying the Act and in making judgments of that sort. The scheme of the Act would be undermined significantly if the Courts failed to recognise the nature of the monopoly that flows from the registration process. In this case the design has been registered. I reject Mr Brown's submission that the Register is prima facie evidence only of what is contained in it rather than the fact that the Commissioner has found the design to comply with the definition contained in s 2(1) of the Act and has found the requisite degree of novelty. No item can be registered unless those conclusions have been drawn. That registration confers a monopoly. On an interim injunction application the Court must be slow to second guess the findings of the Commissioner."

and, at para 43:

  "In my view the fact of registration confers a prima facie right sufficient to overcome the hurdle of establishing that a serious question exists to be tried."

If the view expressed by Heath J prevails, then there is considerable advantage to a litigant in having a registered (as opposed to common law) intellectual property right as the basis of the legal proceeding. In particular, it may dispense with the issue as to whether there is a serious question to be tried, and greatly increase the prospects of obtaining interim relief, which in intellectual property cases is more often than not determinative of the proceeding.

Previous doubts regarding whether the "bridgehead" argument could be applied to forms of intellectual property in which the rights did not expire after a finite period, such as for example a registered trade mark, may have been extinguished by the decision in *Leisureworld Ltd v Elite Fitness Equipment Ltd* 21/7/06, Heath J, HC Auckland CIV-2006-404-3499. Heath J held that an interim injunction should be granted to acknowledge the public interest in enforcing the monopoly rights created by the Trade Marks Act, pending resolution of substantive proceedings.

If the ownership of the intellectual property is in dispute this may result in refusal of the application: *Golden Homes (1998) Ltd v Blue Chip Construction Ltd* 21/6/05, Allan J, HC Auckland CIV-2003-404-7090. See also *Lesa Systems Ltd v Canzac Ltd* 16/5/06, John Hansen J, HC Christchurch CIV-2006-409-624, at para 34.

10.8.5 Section 42 orders

(1) *Order to disclose information*

Under s 42, the Commerce Commission may apply to the District Court or High Court for orders that any person who has contravened the Act, or any other person involved in the contravention, disclose certain information that is in their possession, or to which they have access.

The disclosure is to be at the expense of the person so ordered, and both the type of information and class of person to whom the information must be disclosed is at the discretion of the Court.

The class of person can conceivably include the public as a whole and sections of the public, as well as the Commerce Commission for investigative purposes.

Although not specifically stipulated in the Act it is likely that the type of information ordered to be disclosed will be limited to that linked to the contravention giving rise to the order.

(2) *Order to publish advertisement*

Under s 42 of the Act, the Commerce Commission may apply to the Court for an order requiring any person who has contravened the Act, or any other person involved in the contravention, to publish corrective statements.

The nature of the statement, and the time and manner in which the statement is published, are entirely at the Court's discretion.

The person ordered to publish the statement is liable for the costs of publication.

(3) *Section 42 orders available to Commission only*

Applications for orders under s 42 may only be made by the Commerce Commission.

Thus, in *Carter Holt Harvey Ltd v Cottonsoft Ltd* (2004) 8 NZBLC 101,541, the Court, at para 53, expressed doubt as to whether it had jurisdiction to order publication of a corrective statement, as such power was restricted to applications by the Commerce Commission.

However, since 8 July 2003, the Court has had the power to hear and determine s 42 applications in conjunction with any other proceedings under any of ss 40, 40A, 41 or 43.

Litigants other than the Commission can also obtain similar orders to s 42 under the Court's equitable jurisdiction. This is discussed in more detail at 10.8.3 ("Mandatory injunctions") earlier in this chapter. The ability to do so does not appear to have been considered by the Court in the *Cottonsoft* case.

10.8.6 Section 43: Damages and other remedies (s 43)

Under s 43(1) Fair Trading Act 1986, if the Court finds that any person, whether or not a party to the proceedings, has suffered, or is likely to suffer, loss or damage by conduct that contravenes the Act, it may make any of the following orders:

- Voiding the whole or a part of a contract made between the person suffering, or likely to suffer, damage and the person contravening the Act (s 43(2)(a));

- Varying such contract at the Court's discretion, including the date on which the varied contract is deemed to commence (s 43(2)(b));

- Directing the person who contravened the Act to refund money, or return property, to the person who has suffered loss or damage (s 43(2)(c));

- Directing the person contravening the Act to pay the amount of loss or damage to the person who has suffered that loss or damage (s 43(2)(d));

- Directing any person who contravened the Act, and who has supplied goods to the person who suffered, or is likely to suffer, loss and damage, to repair, or provide parts for, those goods at their own expense (s 43(2)(e)); and

- Ordering the person who contravened the Act to supply specified services to the person who suffered, or is likely to suffer, loss and damage (s 43(2)(f)).

(1) *Orders against related parties*

The same orders are also available against any person who:

- Aided, abetted, counselled or procured the contravention (s 43(1)(b));

- Induced the contravention by threats, promises or otherwise (s 43(1)(c));

- Was in any way directly or indirectly knowingly concerned in, or a party to, the contravention (s 43(1)(d)); or

- Conspired with another person to contravene the Act (s 43(1)(e)).

In *Newport v Coburn* (2006) 11 TCLR 831; 8 NZBLC 101,717 (CA), the Court of Appeal confirmed that a lack of specific pleading under s 43(1)(d) would not be a bar to the imposition of liability although, for clarity, a separate pleading would be preferable. See also *T & P Developments Ltd v Yu* 11/4/01, Glazebrook J, HC Auckland CP18-SD99, at para 198.

(2)   *Orders available whether or not any other order made*

The orders identified in s 43 Fair Trading Act 1986 are available whether or not the Court grants an injunction or makes any other order under Part 5 of the Act.

(3)   *Damages generally*

In the majority of cases involving contravention of a proprietary intellectual property right, the "person" that has suffered loss or damage will be the plaintiff, and the measure of damage will be tortious (to restore the plaintiff to the position he or she would have been in had the contravention of the Act not occurred). Where the action is brought by a rival trader in tandem with an action for passing off, such damages will usually include diversion damages (ie, for sales of product which the plaintiff would have enjoyed were it not for the defendant's conduct). Damage to reputation, and inundation (dilution of exclusivity) are also actionable forms of damage: *Taylor Bros Ltd v Taylors Group Ltd* [1988] 2 NZLR 1 (CA), at pp 20-21:

> "At the end of the day there is nothing really arcane or specialised in these three categories of actionable damage. A common thread runs through all: damage to goodwill, differing only in type. Diversion is an appropriation of a part of the Plaintiff's goodwill. Damage to reputation amounts to a poisoning of the Plaintiff's goodwill. Damage by suggestion of association with the Plaintiff's business amounts to a dilution of the Plaintiff's goodwill. A plaintiff who is entitled in principle to the protection of his property right in goodwill is entitled to protection against all forms of attack without nice distinctions being drawn."

Although this passage relates to damage under the tort of passing off it is equally applicable to a claim for damages under the Act.

See also the comprehensive discussion regarding the calculation of damages in *ABB Ltd v NZ Insulators Ltd (No 2)* 28/8/07, Courtney J, HC Auckland CIV-2004-404-4829, at paras 13-63.

(4)   *No expectation damages*

The decision in *Cox & Coxon Ltd v Leipst* (1998) 8 TCLR 516 (CA) expressly precludes the recovery of expectation damages on the basis that they arise not from the conduct contravening the Act, but from the failure to implement a promise. Gault J said, at p 529:

> "More fundamentally however there is to be considered the basic rationale for the award of expectancy losses. As pointed out in the passage already quoted from *McGregor on Damages*, the loss of bargain or of expected future returns flows not from the conduct that is wrongful, but from the failure to implement a promise. Where no contract exists between the person who engaged in the conduct and the person who suffered the loss, there is no promise which failure to implement deprives the other party of expected benefits."

See also *ABB Ltd v NZ Insulators Ltd (No 2)* 28/8/07, Courtney J, HC Auckland CIV-2004-404-4829, where Courtney J, who had allowed substantial damages for breaches relating to ABB's S91 circuit breaker, held that ABB was not entitled to expectation damages for lost sales it expected to achieve on other products as a result of the success it would have enjoyed in relation to the S91 circuit breakers, but for NZI's conduct.

(5) Emotional harm/stress

In accordance with the Court's largely unfettered ability to award damages, under s 43(2) Fair Trading Act 1986 an award may be made to reflect:

- Mental anguish and emotional harm: *Crump v Wala* [1994] 2 NZLR 331; (1993) 6 TCLR 40; 4 NZBLC 103,383; and

- Stress: *AMP Finance NZ Ltd v Heaven* (1997) 8 TCLR 144, at p 158:

  "We can see no reason why stress damages should not be available in appropriate cases of this kind. The Act itself in s 43 authorises the court to order a person in breach of s 9 to pay to a person suffering 'loss or damage' by virtue of that breach 'the amount of the loss or damage'. The dual expression 'loss or damage' demonstrates that awards of damages under s 43 are not necessarily confined to financial loss. We can see no call to put a gloss on the words used in s 43 so as to prevent monetary compensation from being awarded for mental damage."

(6) Third party loss

An application to the Court under s 43 Fair Trading Act 1986 may be made by any person whether or not the person making the application was the one who suffered the loss or damage. The argument that s 43 does not apply in the case of loss or damage suffered by third parties was rejected in *Grain Processors Ltd v Bluebird Foods Ltd* (1999) 9 TCLR 383, at pp 392-393.

Indeed, the person who suffered the loss or damage need not be a party to the proceedings at all, although this might present practical difficulties to the plaintiff, and necessitate a further inquiry into damages, as occurred in *BMW NZ Ltd v Pepi Holdings Ltd* (1996) 7 TCLR 357.

The Court in *Grain Processors Ltd v Bluebird Foods Ltd* confirmed that damages recovered under s 43(2)(d) are to be paid to the party which has suffered the loss or damage. This means that actions to recover damages for third party losses are likely only to be initiated by the Commerce Commission (or similar organisations representing consumer interests), and plaintiffs representing multiple parties.

(7) Nexus between loss or damage and contravention

In order to avail oneself of the orders listed in s 43(2)(c) and (d) Fair Trading Act 1986 (refund of money, return of property and/or payment of loss or damage) there must be a finding that loss or damage has occurred. The remaining orders may be granted on the likelihood of loss or damage being suffered. It is also implicit from the choice of words "by conduct of any other person" in s 41(1) that it is the conduct of the person contravening the Act that has caused, or is likely to cause, the loss or damage.

However, there is nothing in the Fair Trading Act which limits claims for damages solely to those to whom the misleading or deceptive conduct is directed, provided there is a sufficient causal link between the conduct complained of and the recoverable loss or damage.

In *Janssen-Cilag Pty Ltd v Pfizer Pty Ltd* (1992) 37 FCR 526; 109 ALR 638 (FCA), Janssen had alleged that Pfizer had made false and misleading representations which induced members of the public and pharmacists to purchase Pfizer's drug rather than Janssen's competing drug thereby causing Janssen to lose sales. One of Pfizer's defences was that Janssen was not a person entitled to recover any loss or damage under the Trade Practices Act 1974 (Aust) because Pfizer was not a consumer within the meaning of the Act nor a person who relied on the allegedly false or misleading representations.

That proposition was rejected by Lockhart J who held, at p 530, that there was nothing in the language of the Act or its purpose to warrant the suggestion that the right of an applicant for damages was confined to a case where the applicant had relied upon, or personally been influenced by, the conduct of the respondent which contravened the relevant parts of the Act. His Honour emphasised however, at p 533, that there must be a significant causal link between the conduct and the recoverable loss or damage.

Janssen-Cilag was cited with approval in New Zealand in *Dorchester Finance Ltd v Conqueror Corporate Trustee Ltd* 3/3/04, Master Lang, HC Auckland CIV-2003-404-2047, CIV-2003-404-3780, *KA (Newmarket) Ltd v Hart* 4/7/02, Heath J, HC Auckland CP467-SD01, and *Darrell McGregor (Contractor) Ltd v Mountain Lake Holdings Ltd* (2006) 11 TCLR 643.

(8) *Measure of damages*

The leading case on the measure of damages under s 43 Fair Trading Act 1986 is *Cox & Coxon Ltd v Leipst* (1998) 8 TCLR 516 (CA), at p 520, which confirmed that the remedy under s 43(2) is statutory and discretionary, and is not to be restricted to the methods of assessing damage under contract or tort:

> "Although the distinction between the measure of damages available in tort and contract is well established, there is no need to classify a breach of the Act giving rise to a possible monetary claim under one or other of those categories. It is the statute which is the source of relief, and it is the statute which must be applied to the particular factual circumstances. Nevertheless, the rationale behind the two concepts may well be relevant when considering a particular set of circumstances."

and, at p 531:

> "The use of the words 'loss or damage' demonstrates that Parliament was intending to define the ambit of compensation available under the Act in a broad and general way. The Act does not expressly import any notions of contract or tort for the purpose of assessing compensation, nor indeed for any other purpose. Nothing in the language of the Act suggests that such notions were intended to be imported implicitly. In cases covered by the Act, Parliament was signalling a new approach untrammelled by historical causes of action and their criteria for the assessment of damages."

In certain circumstances it may be appropriate for damages to be apportioned between defendants according to the severity of their respective conduct. Thus, in *Newport v Coburn* (2006) 11 TCLR 831; 8 NZBLC 101,717 (CA) the High Court had awarded $25,000 compensation for a breach of the Fair Trading Act to be paid jointly and severally by the two directors of a franchisor company and its sales manager employee, Mr Newport. On appeal, the Court of Appeal accepted that Mr Newport's role was much less serious than that of the directors of the company and considered it appropriate that the liability of

Mr Newport be discounted to reflect this lesser wrong. Accordingly, the Court of Appeal discounted Mr Newport's liability to $5,000 with the remaining $20,000 being payable jointly and severally by the two directors.

The reduction in Mr Newport's liability also resulted in a reduction in the award of costs in the High Court. This was dealt with in a separate judgment of the Court of Appeal: *Newport v Coburn* 10/8/06, CA234/04.

10.9 Criminal liability

10.9.1 Criminal offences

Under s 40 Fair Trading Act 1986, every person who contravenes the provisions of Parts 1-4 of the Act commits an offence and is liable on summary conviction in the District Court. The exceptions to this are contravention of:

- Section 9 (misleading or deceptive conduct);

- Section 14(2) (the use of physical force, harassment or coercion in connection with the sale or possible sale of land);

- Section 23 (harassment and coercion generally); and

- Section 24 (pyramid selling schemes). It should, however, be noted that there appears to be an inconsistency in the Act as s 40(1A) provides that every person who contravenes s 24 commits an offence and *is* liable on summary conviction to a fine not exceeding $200,000.

10.9.2 Mainly sought by Commerce Commission

Although it is technically possible for any person to bring an action seeking orders under s 40 Fair Trading Act 1986, the Act seems to envisage that the majority of actions will be initiated by the Commerce Commission. Hence, Part 6 of the Act confers on the Commission broad powers, including the power of search and seizure, and to inspect and take copies of any documents obtained.

10.9.3 Monetary penalties only

The only penalties provided for are monetary penalties, which include a maximum fine for bodies corporate of $200,000, and a maximum fine for any other person of $60,000 ($200,000 if found to be in contravention of s 24 relating to pyramid selling schemes).

10.9.4 Sentencing principles

Commerce Commission v L D Nathan & Co Ltd [1990] 2 NZLR 160 contains some useful guidelines as to the principles the Court will apply when making an order under s 40 Fair Trading Act 1986. The appropriate level of penalty will vary according to the circumstances of each case. The class of relevant considerations is not closed. They include:

- The objectives of the Act;

- The importance of any untrue statement made;

- The degree of wilfulness, or carelessness, involved in making the statement;

- The extent to which the statements depart from the truth;

- The degree of the dissemination;

- The resulting prejudice to, or effect on, consumers;

- Whether any, and if so what, efforts have been made to correct the statements; and

- The need to impose deterrent penalties (which, it is noted, should not be so high as to be oppressive).

10.9.5 Criminal defences

A conviction under s 40 Fair Trading Act 1986 can be avoided if it can be shown that the contravention:

- Was due to a reasonable mistake (s 44(1)(a));

- Was due to reasonable reliance on information supplied by another person (s 44(1)(b)); or

- Was due to the act or default of another person (excluding a director, servant or agent of the defendant) and the defendant took reasonable precautions, and exercised due diligence, to avoid the contravention (s 44(1)(c)).

(1) *Person must be identified*

Where information supplied by another person, or the act or default of another person, are relied upon to establish a defence, the defendant must serve a notice in writing identifying that other person no less than 7 days before the hearing: s 44(3) Fair Trading Act 1986.

(2) *Onus of proof*

The onus of proof rests with the defendant, and although not specifically identified in the section, the standard of proof is the civil standard (balance of probabilities): *Foodtown Supermarkets Ltd v Commerce Commission* [1991] 1 NZLR 466.

(3) *Reasonableness*

All three of the defences to s 40 Fair Trading Act 1986 are based on the concept of reasonableness. The Court's inquiry is an objective one based on the individual circumstances of each case. The following factors will have a bearing on the Court's decision:

- Whether the defendant made reasonable inquiries to avoid a contravention of the Act;

- If the defendant did make inquiries, whether these were with a competent party. In particular, if the inquiry was as to a matter of law (rather than fact) did the defendant seek competent legal advice, and did the defendant follow that advice? and

- Whether the defendant had a compliance programme in place, and whether it took steps to ensure that that procedure was properly implemented and enforced.

(4) *Ignorance of law not a defence*

It is no defence that the defendant's ignorance of the law contributed to the offence under the Act. In *Fastlane Autos Ltd v Commerce Commission* [2004] 3 NZLR 513; (2004) 11 TCLR

173, the appellant, which had been convicted on six counts of misleading advertisements relating to motor vehicles, argued that its misrepresentations were due to a "reasonable mistake" (s 44(1)(a)) in ignorance of the law. Noting an absence of New Zealand authority, the Court took guidance from a decision of the full bench of the Supreme Court of South Australia (*Gilmore v Poole-Blunden* (1999) ATPR 46-197), concluding that if Parliament had intended to abrogate or qualify the general principle that ignorance of the law is not a defence, it would have done so in a clear and comprehensive way. Hence, the appeal was rejected.

10.9.6 Limitations

The limitation period for summary proceedings under s 40 Fair Trading Act 1986 is governed by s 40(3). That section was amended by s 16 Fair Trading Amendment Act 2003, which came into force on 8 July 2003. Hence:

- For summary proceedings commenced before 8 July 2003, the action must have been brought within 3 years of the matter that contravened the Act arising; and

- For proceedings commenced on or after 8 July 2003, the proceedings must have been commenced within 3 years of the date on which the contravention was, or ought reasonably to have been, discovered.

Section 16 Fair Trading Amendment Act 2003 specifically states that the amendment to the limitation period will have no effect on proceedings commenced before the change was enacted, and that the change will not enable any proceedings to be brought that were already barred under the pre-amended section.

The purpose of the amendment is to align the limitation period under s 40 with that under s 43 to ensure consistency in the application of the Act.

(1) *Limitation must be pleaded*

In order to rely on the limitation provision as a defence to a contravention of the Fair Trading Act 1986, it must be specifically pleaded by the defendant: *AMP Finance NZ Ltd v Heaven* (1997) 8 TCLR 144, at pp 154-155.

See the following section for more information on defences available under the Act.

10.10 Civil defences

10.10.1 Saving for publishers and advertisers

Section 44(4) Fair Trading Act 1986 provides a broad defence to all proceedings under Part 5 of the Act (including summary proceedings under s 40) in relation to the publication of a misleading or deceptive advertisement if the defendant can prove:

- That the defendant's business is publishing, or arranging the publication of, advertisements (for example an advertising agency); and

- That the advertisement (or information contained in the advertisement) was received by the defendant in the ordinary course of business, and that he or she did not know, and had no reason to suspect, that the publication of the advertisement containing the information would contravene the Act.

10.10.2   Saving for newspapers/broadcasters

Under s 15 Fair Trading Act 1986, ss 9-14 do not apply to the publication in a newspaper, or broadcast by a broadcasting body, of any information or matter other than:

- Advertisements; or

- Information or matter relating to the supply or use of goods/services, or the sale or grant of an interest in land by:

    (i)   The publisher/broadcasting body or a connected body corporate (being a subsidiary to, parent of, or company which shares the same parent as, the advertiser/broadcasting body); or

    (ii) Any person who is a party to any contract, arrangement or understanding relating to the content, nature or tenor of the information or matter.

The purpose of the exemption is to allow publishers and broadcasters to disseminate news items and similar material without fear of recrimination under the Act.

This section was applied by the Court of Appeal in *King v TV3 Network Services Ltd* (2003) 16 PRNZ 985 (CA). Mr King and his business were portrayed in a poor light in a partially covertly filmed excerpt featuring in a consumer affairs programme screened by TV3 Network Services. King sued TV3 and the producer, Top Shelf Productions Ltd, on a number of grounds including breach of the Fair Trading Act 1986. The Court of Appeal upheld the striking out of that cause of action on the basis that Mr King could not overcome the news media exclusion contained in s 15 of the Act, the Court commenting, at para 17:

> "The exclusion from the protection otherwise given to broadcasting bodies for what they broadcast does not apply when there is a contract, arrangement or understanding between the broadcaster and the other party relating to the content, nature or tenor of the information or matter to be broadcast. But here there was no relevant contract, arrangement or understanding between TV3 and Mr King because, as he has been at pains to point out, he had no idea there was to be any broadcast about him and his business. The contract between these parties related to the work to be done on a car. It did not, as is required, have anything to do with a proposed or anticipated broadcast. The Master and Wild J were therefore correct in their reading of s 15(2). On this basis the Fair Trading Act cause of action must be struck out as it is not exempted from the protection given by the introductory words of s 15(2)."

(1)   *Exemption applies only to publisher/broadcaster*

The exemption applies only to a publisher or broadcasting body that disseminates the information of another. It does not extend to the party orchestrating the misleading or deceptive information and matter, including the publisher or broadcasting body itself if the advertisement has been placed by the publisher/broadcasting body on its own behalf.

(2)   *Meaning of "advertisement"*

The exemption does not apply to advertisements. The definition of "advertisement" in s 2(1) Fair Trading Act 1986 is as follows:

"Any form of communication made to the public or a section of the public for the purpose of promoting the supply of goods or services or the sale or granting of an interest in land."

Consequently, the category of information that falls outside the exemption is very broad and may cover such things as billboards and sales pitches, as well as more conventional forms of television, radio and print media.

(3) *Newspaper*

"Newspaper" is defined by s 2 Film, Videos, and Publications Classification Act 1993 and means any periodical publication published (whether in New Zealand or elsewhere) at intervals not exceeding 40 days, or any copy of, or part of any copy of, any such publication; and includes every publication that accompanies and is distributed along with any newspaper.

(4) *Broadcasting body*

"Broadcasting body" is said to be defined in s 2 Broadcasting Act 1976. However, that Act was repealed as from 1 July 1989 by s 89(1) Broadcasting Act 1989. The new Act does not contain a definition of "broadcasting body". The closest definition is: "Broadcaster", which means a person who broadcasts programmes.

(5) *Duty of care*

The Fair Trading Act 1986 imposes a duty of care on publishers/broadcasters to ensure that advertisements they disseminate do not mislead or deceive. Consistent with this duty of care, publishers will have a defence under s 44(4) of the Act if they can show that the advertisement was published in the course of business and they had no reason to suspect it would breach the Act. The s 44(4) defence does not apply to broadcasters (although there appears to be no valid reason for this).

10.10.3 Limitations

Under s 43(5) Fair Trading Act 1986, applications for orders under s 43 Fair Trading Act 1986 must be brought within 3 years of the date on which the loss or damage, or likelihood of loss or damage, was discovered or ought reasonably to have been discovered.

Section 43(5) was substituted, as from 3 May 2001, by s 3 Fair Trading Amendment Act 2001. Prior to that the limitation period imposed on remedies available under s 43 of the Act was the same as under s 40 (ie, 3 years from when the matter giving rise to the contravention arose, as opposed to when damage was, or ought reasonably to have been, discovered). The amendment has clarified difficulties which have arisen in interpreting the precise nature of the "matter" giving rise to the application, and cases such as *Murray v Eliza Jane Holdings Ltd* (1993) 5 TCLR 272 (CA) (which contains a lengthy discussion of the pre-amended section) will only be of precedent value in respect of proceedings initiated before the section was amended (3 May 2001). In any event, the amendment may not be a significant one, as the majority of contravening conduct and loss is likely to be discovered or discoverable either at the time of the occurrence or shortly afterwards.

(1) *Limitation must be pleaded*

In order to rely on the limitation provision as a defence to a contravention of the Act, it must be specifically pleaded by the defendant: *AMP Finance NZ Ltd v Heaven* (1997) 8 TCLR 144, at pp 154-155.

(2) *No limitation on injunctive relief*

It would appear that there is no limitation on the bringing of an action for an injunction or other equitable relief under the Act (other than under s 4 Limitation Act 1950). Indeed, this is consistent with the consumer protection aims of the legislation. If someone is engaging in misleading or deceptive conduct then an interested party (including the Commission) ought to be able to obtain an injunction or similar remedy regardless of when that conduct came to that interested party's attention. Delay in bringing the action will go to whether the conduct remains misleading or deceptive and whether the injunction, or other equitable relief, is justified.

See also the comments of the Court in *TV3 Network Ltd v Eveready NZ Ltd* [1993] 3 NZLR 435 (CA) as to the availability of equitable remedies in tandem with an action under the Fair Trading Act 1986 (discussed at 10.8 ("Legal remedies") earlier in this chapter).

10.11 References and resource sites

10.11.1 Websites

Thomson Brookers	www.thomsonbrookers.co.nz
Australian Competition and Consumer Commission	www.accc.gov.au
Federal Trade Commission (US)	www.ftc.gov
Interim Website of New Zealand Legislation	www.legislation.govt.nz
James & Wells	www.jaws.co.nz
Ministry of Consumer Affairs	www.consumer-ministry.govt.nz
New Zealand Commerce Commission	www.comcom.govt.nz
Office of Fair Trading (UK)	www.oft.gov.uk
UK Intellectual Property Office	www.ipo.gov.uk

10.11.2 Texts and periodicals

- Brown, A, and Grant, A, *The Law of Intellectual Property in New Zealand*, Wellington, Butterworths, 1988

- *Fair's Fair*, Compliance and a number of pamphlets, guidelines and practice notices are available from the Commerce Commission website

- *Gault on Commercial Law* (Looseleaf), Wellington, Brookers, 1994

- *Fair Trading* (Looseleaf), Wellington, Brookers, 1991

Chapter 11

BORDER PROTECTION

638

11.1   Introduction

With the increasing prevalence of counterfeit or pirated goods in New Zealand, rights-holders must do all that they can to protect their markets. Given its comparatively small size (by international standards) the release of counterfeit goods onto the New Zealand market can result in a substantial loss of profit for rights-holders. Most counterfeit or pirated goods originate from overseas. Stopping their entry into New Zealand at the border is by far the most effective means for rights-holders to enforce their intellectual property rights, and to minimise any losses associated with the sale of counterfeit or pirated goods.

11.1.1   Border protection by way of customs notices

A customs notice ("notice") is one of most straightforward and effective forms of border protection available to a rights-holder.

Under the Trade Marks Act 2002 and the Copyright Act 1994, a proprietor of a registered trade mark or the owner of a copyright work (described collectively in this chapter as a "rights-holder") can lodge a notice ("trade mark notice" or "copyright notice" respectively) with the New Zealand Customs Service ("Customs"). A notice authorises Customs to detain any unauthorised goods that bear the rights-holder's registered trade mark or embody the rights-holder's copyright work.

(1)   *No detention without a notice*

Customs does not have the authority to detain counterfeit or pirated goods without a notice. Therefore, if no notice is lodged, unless the goods offend against any other legislation (for example the Customs and Excise Act 1996), items unlawfully featuring trade marks or embodying copyright works will be released to the importer.

(2)   *Most effective protection*

For obvious reasons it is impossible for Customs officers to physically check every item that is imported into New Zealand. However, notices have proven to be one of the most efficient and cost-effective means of preventing counterfeit or pirated goods from being sold in New Zealand.

11.1.2   Scope of this chapter and definitions

This chapter contains a description of the procedure for lodging and enforcing notices under both the Trade Marks Act 2002 and the Copyright Act 1994. Further details regarding registering trade marks and the rights conferred on registered proprietors of trade marks, and further details regarding the rights subsisting in copyright works, can be found in the trade marks and copyright chapters of this text (chapters 7 and 4 respectively).

The following definitions will be used for the purposes of this chapter:

- "Rights-holder" means the proprietor of a registered New Zealand trade mark, or the owner of copyright rights in a copyright work in New Zealand;

- "Claimant" means the party in whose name a trade mark notice or copyright notice has been lodged with Customs. Claimants may include a local agent, distributor or licensee of a rights-holder;

- "Counterfeit" means:

  - Any product that carries an "infringing sign", or

  - Any "pirated goods".

The meanings of "infringing sign" and "pirated goods" are set out in the following section of this chapter.

11.2   Legislation

Border protection measures are governed by:

- Section 135-157 Trade Marks Act 2002 ("the Trade Marks Act");

- Regulations 156-160 Trade Marks Regulations 2003;

- Sections 135-146 Copyright Act 1994 ("the Copyright Act");

- Copyright (Border Protection) Regulations 1994 ("the Copyright (Border Protection) Regulations"); and

- Copyright (Border Protection) Amendment Regulations 2003.

These provide the mechanism for notices to be filed and enforced in relation to both registered trade marks and copyright works.

11.2.1   History

The border protection measures were introduced into the:

- Trade Marks Act 1953, by virtue of s 21 Trade Marks Amendment Act 1994, and the

- Copyright Act 1994,

when those respective pieces of legislation took effect on 1 January 1995.

The Trade Marks Act 2002 has since repealed the Trade Marks Act 1953. Trade mark notices filed under the Trade Marks Act 1953 are to be treated as if they had been filed under the Trade Marks Act 2002 (s 204 Trade Marks Act 2002).

The border protection measures are in direct response to the Agreement on Trade-Related Aspects of Intellectual Property Rights ("TRIPS"). TRIPS arose out of the Uruguay Round of the General Agreement on Tariffs and Trade ("GATT") in 1994. New Zealand is a member of the World Trade Organisation, which heads GATT.

Article 51 of the TRIPS Agreement provides:

"Suspension of Release by Customs Authorities

"Members shall, in conformity with the provisions set out below, adopt procedures to enable a rights-holder, who has valid grounds for suspecting that the importation of counterfeit trademark or pirated copyright goods may take place, to lodge an application in writing with competent authorities, administrative or judicial, for the suspension by the customs authorities of the release into free circulation of such goods. Members may enable such an application to be made in respect of goods which involve other infringements of intellectual property rights, provided that the requirements of this Section are met. Members may also provide for corresponding procedures concerning the suspension by the customs authorities of the release of infringing goods destined for exportation from their territories."

11.2.2 Sections 135-157 Trade Marks Act 2002

Sections 135-157 Trade Marks Act 2002 govern the border protection measures available in relation to registered trade marks in New Zealand.

It is possible to lodge a notice in respect of any trade mark that has been registered with the Intellectual Property Office of New Zealand ("IPONZ"). Following acceptance of the notice, any goods:

- On which an infringing sign (ie a trade mark applied without the rights-holder's consent) has been used; and

- That are the same as, or similar to, those in respect of which the trade mark has been registered,

may be detained by Customs and the claimant notified.

Sections 135-157 fall into five broad areas as follows:

- Lodging a notice with Customs — ss 137-141;

- Investigation by Customs as to whether a sign is an infringing sign — ss 142-145;

- The issue of a determination by Customs — ss 146-148;

- The detention of goods bearing an infringing sign — ss 149-151; and

- Subsequent procedure for dealing with those infringing goods — ss 152-154.

Each of these sections is discussed in more detail later in this chapter.

(1) *Definition of "infringing sign"*

For the purposes of the border protection measures in the Trade Marks Act 2002, an "infringing sign" is defined in s 135 as a sign that is:

- *Identical* with the registered trade mark that is the subject of the trade mark notice and that has been used on, or in physical relation to, goods which are *identical* to the goods in respect of which the trade mark is registered;

- *Identical* with the registered trade mark that is the subject of a trade mark notice and that has been used on, or in physical relation to, goods that are *similar* to the goods in respect of which the trade mark is registered, if that use would be likely to deceive or confuse; or

- *Similar* to the registered trade mark that is the subject of a trade mark notice and that has been used on, or in physical relation to, goods that are *identical with*, or *similar to*, the goods in respect of which the trade mark is registered, if that use would be likely to deceive or confuse.

Whether a sign is infringing is for Customs to decide under ss 142-145 Trade Marks Act 2002.

(2)   *Trade Marks Regulations 2003*

The Trade Marks (Border Protection and Transitional Applications) Regulations 1994 were revoked by reg 166 Trade Marks Regulations 2003.

The Trade Marks Regulations 2003 came into force on 20 August 2003. Regulations 156-160 set out additional border protection legislation under ss 135-157 Trade Marks Act, and, in particular, contain the form that must be lodged with Customs. Reference to the Trade Marks Regulations will be made in this text, where applicable.

11.2.3   Sections 135-146 Copyright Act 1994

Sections 135-146 Copyright Act 1994 govern the border protection measures available in New Zealand in relation to copyright works. Where a copyright notice has been lodged and accepted by Customs, any pirated copy of the work the subject of the notice imported into New Zealand may be detained, and the claimant notified.

Sections 135-146 encompass six broad areas as follows:

*   The procedure for lodging a copyright notice with Customs — s 136;

*   Examination by Customs to determine whether an item is a pirated copy — s 137;

*   The issue of a determination by Customs — s 139;

*   Detention of pirated copies — s 140;

*   Proceedings in respect of pirated copies — s 141; and

*   Forfeiture of goods by consent — s 141A.

Section 141A was added to the Copyright Act 1994, pursuant to s 201 Trade Marks Act 2002.

(1)   *Definition of "pirated copy"*

A "pirated copy" is defined in s 135 Copyright Act 1994 as a copy of a literary, dramatic, musical, or artistic work, the typographical arrangement of a published edition, or a sound recording or film that has been made:

*   Directly or indirectly from the copyright work;

*   Without the licence of the person who owns copyright in the country where the copy is made; and

*   In circumstances where the making of the work, had it occurred in New Zealand, would have constituted an infringement of copyright under the Copyright Act 1994.

"Pirated copy" also includes an unlawful recording (as defined in s 169 Copyright Act which relates to performers' rights).

"Pirated copy" does not include copyright works sold in other countries by, or with the licence of, the owner of the copyright in the work in that country.

The definition of "pirated copy" used to exclude any copyright work in transit to another country. However, this part of the definition was repealed by s 201 Trade Marks Act 2002.

(2) *Copyright (Border Protection) Regulations 1994*

The Copyright (Border Protection) Regulations 1994 came into force on 1 January 1995. These regulations were further amended by the Copyright (Border Protection) Amendment Regulations 2003, which came into force on 23 September 2003. The regulations contain the forms that must be lodged with Customs. Where applicable, the regulations are cited in the Copyright Act 1994 (see, for example, s 136(3) and s 140(3)(b)). This approach differs from that adopted in the Trade Marks Act 2002, in which border protection regulations are made under a specific section (s 199(e)). Reference to the Copyright (Border Protection) Regulations 1994 (as amended) will be made in this chapter, where applicable.

11.3   Parallel importing

11.3.1   Copyright works

The exclusion of "any other copyright work sold in a country other than New Zealand by or with the licence of the owner of the copyright in the work in that country" from the definition of "pirated copy", means that it is not permissible for Customs to detain parallel imported copyright goods.

11.3.2   Trade marks

Under s 97A Trade Marks Act 2002 a registered trade mark is not infringed by its use (including use from the purposes of advertising) in relation to goods that have been put on the market anywhere in the world under the trade mark but the "owner" or with his or her implied consent. The issue of what constitutes "implied consent" is discussed in detail below.

This means that if the company who manufactured the goods overseas is a different company from that which has registered the mark in New Zealand, it may be possible for the New Zealand registered owner to have the foreign manufactured goods detained on the basis that they are goods that bear an "infringing sign" (in the sense that although they are genuine, the New Zealand owner was not the party that applied the trade marks to them).

One practice sometimes employed by overseas owners is to assign the New Zealand registration to a local distributor on terms that the mark reverts to the overseas owner when the distributorship terminates. In this way the local distributor will be the registered owner of the mark in New Zealand, and will be able to object to the importation of genuine product by third parties on the basis that it has not applied, nor consented to the application of, the registered trade mark on those goods. The legitimacy of this practice was discussed by the Federal Court of Australia (see *Transport Tyre Sales Pty Ltd v Montana Tyres, Rims & Tubes Pty Ltd* (1999) 43 IPR 481; [1999] FCA 329; (1999) 93 FCR 421) but has not been by the New Zealand Courts.

Accordingly, there remains some uncertainty as to how secure such an approach would be. A court looking at the arrangement could the view that the assignment was a legal fiction, or a sham transaction.

However, while untested, it remains a practical option for trade mark owners to consider when seeking to deter parallel importers.

The issue of "implied consent" to the use of the trade mark on parallel imported product may arise if there is some relationship between the registered owner of the New Zealand trade mark and the company which has applied the mark to those goods overseas. The most common circumstance would be where the two companies form part of the same corporate group.

The issue of implied consent was considered in some detail by Heath J in *Leisureworld Ltd v Elite Fitness Equipment Ltd* 21/7/06, Heath J, HC Auckland CIV-2006-404-3499, in which his Honour adopted the following principles set out in the European Court of Justice's decision in *Zino Davidoff SA v A & G Imports Ltd* [2002] Ch 109, at p 146:

> "(a)   While consent could be expressed or implied, it must be expressed positively. Evidence from which implied consent might be inferred must demonstrate unequivocally that the trade mark proprietor has renounced any intention to enforce its exclusive rights.

> "(b)   Implied consent cannot be inferred from:

>> "(i)   Silence of the trade mark proprietor;

>> "(ii)   The fact that a trade mark proprietor has not communicated opposition to marketing goods in another market;

>> "(iii)   The fact that the relevant goods do not carry any warning that it is prohibited to place them on the market elsewhere;

>> "(iv)   The fact that the trade mark owner transferred ownership of the goods bearing the mark without imposing contractual reservations or from the fact that, according to the law, governing the contract, the property right transferred includes, in the absence of reservations, an unlimited right of re-sale or, at the very least, a right to market the goods subsequently in another jurisdiction;

> "(c)   It is not relevant to an assessment of consent that the importer of the goods bearing the trade mark is not aware that the proprietor objects to their being placed on the market elsewhere or sold by traders other than authorised retailers. Nor it is relevant that authorised retailers and wholesalers have not imposed on their own purchasers contractual reservations setting out such opposition, even though they have been informed of it by the trade mark proprietor."

Heath J observed, at para 86:

> "In my view, the European Court's judgment goes no further than holding that consent might be implied by inference from proved facts. The inference drawn must, necessarily, be demonstrably stronger than other available inferences. That is

the sense in which I understand the European Court to be saying that implied consent must be demonstrated unequivocally."

There is a fundamental conflict between the exhaustion of rights principle which underlies the removal of the prohibition on parallel imports carrying registered trade marks, and the territorial nature of these trade mark registrations. The decision of Heath J confirms that the focus of the enquiry under s 97A Trade Marks Act 2002 is on the intentions of the New Zealand registered trade mark holder, and that the starting point must be that the rights conferred on the owner of the registered New Zealand trade mark are territorial in nature. For s 97A to apply, there must be a demonstrably strong inference from proved facts that the owner of the New Zealand trade mark intended its goods to be traded in markets outside New Zealand. In the absence of this s 97A will not apply and these imports will be in breach of the New Zealand proprietor's rights.

11.4 Customs notices

11.4.1 What is a customs notice?

A customs notice ("notice") is the official document posted with the New Zealand Customs Service ("Customs") instructing its officers to detain counterfeit or pirated goods imported into New Zealand. Notices may be filed in relation to either a registered trade mark ("trade mark notice") or copyright work ("copyright notice").

11.4.2 Who can file a notice?

The following people may file notices in New Zealand.

(1) *Rights-holders*

A rights-holder can file notices directly with Customs. When Customs detains counterfeit product relating to that notice, it will notify the rights-holder.

"Rights-holder" is defined in more detail at 11.1.2 ("Introduction") earlier in this chapter.

(2) *Local agent or licensee*

Customs will permit notices to be lodged by third parties on behalf of the rights-holder, as long as an appropriate authorisation is lodged with the notice. It is becoming increasingly common for overseas rights-holders to do this.

Provision for the lodgement of notices by parties other than the rights-holder is made under reg 7 Copyright (Border Protection) Regulations 1994. For trade mark notices, a trade mark licensee can call on the trade mark owner to lodge a notice on its behalf (subject to any agreement to the contrary) (s 141(1)). If the trade mark owner refuses or neglects to lodge a notice within 2 months of being asked, the licensee can lodge the notice itself: s 141(2).

The rights-holder can save valuable time and money by giving a local agent, licensee, or distributor day-to-day responsibility for the notice, particularly when it comes to enforcing a notice if a contravention occurs.

This arrangement is also particularly useful where a local distributor/licensee holds the rights to import and sell goods bearing the brand of more than one rights-holder. If the notices are lodged in the distributor's own name (on behalf of the overseas rights-holder (s)) the local distributor need not lodge a separate security bond in respect of each notice. This is discussed in more detail at 11.6 ("Documentation and other requirements for lodging notices") later in this chapter.

However, regardless of whether a rights-holder files a notice itself, or whether a local agent or distributor files the notice, the Trade Marks Regulations 2003 require that the address for service for trade mark notice is a New Zealand address.

11.4.3   Agents

The concept of agency arises either where a patent attorney or solicitor (or other third party) acts as agent for the rights-holder, or where an overseas rights-holder appoints a local New Zealand agent.

(1)   *Patent attorney / solicitor / third party as agent*

Although it is possible to file notices directly with Customs, the vast majority of rights-holders instruct an agent, usually a patent attorney or solicitor, to:

- Prepare and file the notice, and

- Receive and administer determinations under the notice,

on their behalf, or on behalf of a local licensee/distributor.

This is achieved by way of a "general authorisation to act" discussed in more detail at 11.6 ("Documentation and other requirements for lodging notices") later in this chapter.

(2)   *Appointment of local agent by overseas rights-holders*

The majority of notices lodged with Customs relate to registered trade marks and copyright works of foreign companies. In many cases the lodgement of the notice will have been prompted by that company's local distributor or licensee. Often the cost of preparing and lodging the notice, and the security bond, will be met by that local distributor/licensee, and the distributor/licensee will be the person providing instructions in respect of determinations under the notice.

In the interests of efficiency, most overseas rights-holders will appoint their local distributor/licensee as an agent in order to empower them to:

- File notices in their own name; or

- Post security on the rights-holder's behalf.

Depending on the nature of that relationship, a separate and distinct "authorisation of agent" will need to be filed. This is discussed in more detail at 11.6 ("Documentation and other requirements for lodging notices") earlier in this chapter.

11.4.4   Trade mark notices versus copyright notices

The bases upon which trade mark notices and copyright notices may be lodged are different.

(1)   *Trade mark must be registered*

Trade mark notices can only be lodged in respect of a registered trade mark. As trade marks are registered in relation to particular types of goods, any corresponding trade mark notice will be similarly limited to those goods.

However, it is possible to secure the exclusive right to the use of a word (or combination of words) as a trade mark regardless of the manner in which those words appear. Therefore, trade mark notices can provide a high level of protection for particular logos and words in relation to a specific class of goods.

The procedure for registering a trade mark and the level of protection afforded to proprietors of registered trade marks is discussed in more detail in the trade marks chapter of this text (chapter 7).

(2)   *Copyright notices have wider application*

A copyright notice can be lodged in relation to any work in which copyright subsists. There is no formal registration system for copyright works in New Zealand, and hence no cost. Notices are not limited to a specific class of goods.

A copyright notice is best utilised where a rights-holder wants to prevent the importation of goods that copy aspects of the shape and configuration of its products, or obtain protection for a broad range of products under a single notice (for example, by lodging a notice in respect of a catalogue featuring a range of products).

The rights conferred on the owner of a copyright work are discussed in more detail in the copyright chapter of this text (chapter 4).

(3)   *Differences between copyright and trade mark notices*

The following table sets out the primary differences between a trade mark notice and a copyright notice:

Trade mark notice	Copyright notice
Each trade mark must be formally registered before a trade mark notice can be lodged.	There is no formal system of registering copyright works in New Zealand and hence notices may be lodged at any time.
A trade mark notice can only apply to the class(es) of goods in which the trade mark has been registered. New notices must be lodged for each additional registered trade mark and/or new registration of the same trade mark in different classes.	As copyright rights are not limited to particular classes of goods, a copyright notice protects the work in relation to all types of goods.
A trade mark registered in plain block capital form (as opposed to stylised form) will provide the broadest protection against importation of counterfeits bearing the same trade mark.	The imported goods must be the same (or a substantially similar) as the copyright work to meet the definition of pirated copy.

Valid for 5-year periods. Can be continuously renewed, as long as the trade mark remains registered.	Valid for 5-year periods. Can continue to be renewed as long as copyright in the work still subsists (usually between 16 and 50 years).
In certain circumstances may be used to prevent parallel imported product.	Cannot be used to prevent parallel imported product.
Only applies to goods which carry an identical trade mark, or a similar trade mark where the use of that trade mark is likely to deceive or confuse.	Deception or confusion is not necessary.

11.5 Goods imported for private and domestic use exempted

Under s 137(4) Copyright Act 1994 and s 142 Trade Marks Act 2002, the border protection provisions do not apply to "goods that have been imported for private and domestic use".

Notwithstanding this exemption, Customs interprets the words "private and domestic" very narrowly. When making its determination Customs takes into account the nature of the goods themselves as well as all the known circumstances surrounding the importation of the goods and the importer. Thus, the importation of even a single item may be deemed otherwise that for "private and domestic" use given the right circumstances.

An obvious example might be a large shipment of one or two items of numerous brands of counterfeit product (ie, sample) by a known importer or distributor of counterfeits.

11.6 Documentation and other requirements for lodging notices

11.6.1 Requirements for filing a trade mark notice

Under ss 137 and 138 Trade Marks Act 2002, a trade mark notice must contain certain information before it will be accepted under s 139. The minimum information currently required by Customs is as follows:

- The New Zealand trade mark registration number, trade mark, and class(es) of goods to which the notice will relate;

- A statement that the claimant is the registered proprietor of that trade mark, or is authorised to lodge the notice on its own behalf as a registered licensee;

- A request that Customs detains any goods which come within its control on which any sign that would infringe the trade mark specified in the notice ("infringing sign") is used. (The definition of "infringing sign" is discussed in more detail at 11.2 ("Legislation") earlier in this chapter);

- The enforcement period of the notice;

- The name and contact details of the claimant or agent overseeing the notice; and

- Proof from IPONZ that the trade mark is registered and valid. A certified IP summary report can be obtained from IPONZ free of charge.

(1) *Form of trade mark notice*

Every notice lodged under s 137 Trade Marks Act 2002 must be in the prescribed form set out in Schedule 2 to the Trade Marks Regulations 2003.

(2) *Fee for lodging a trade mark notice*

There is currently no fee for lodging a trade mark notice with Customs.

11.6.2 Requirements for filing a copyright notice

The content of copyright notices is dictated by s 136 Copyright Act 1994. The minimum information currently required by Customs is as follows:

- A statement that the claimant owns the copyright in the work (s 136(1)(a));

- Particulars supporting such a claim, including the title of the copyright work, the name of the author (if known), and the country and year in which the work was first published (s 136(2)(a) and reiterated in reg 4 Copyright (Border Protection) Regulations 1994);

- A request that Customs detain any pirated copies that come into its control;

- The enforcement period of the notice; and

- The name and contact details of the claimant or agent overseeing the notice.

(1) *Form of copyright notice*

Every notice lodged under s 136(1) Copyright Act must be in the prescribed form set out in the Schedule to the Copyright (Border Protection) Amendment Regulations 2003.

(2) *Fee for lodging a copyright notice*

There is currently no fee for lodging a copyright notice with Customs.

11.6.3 Authorisations

There are three types of authorisations that may have to be filed in relation to a notice.

(1) *General authorisation to act*

When a rights-holder elects to have its patent attorney, solicitor, or other agent act on its behalf in relation to a notice, a general authorisation must be filed.

The authorisation must state in clear and unequivocal terms:

- The nominated agent's name and address; and

- That the patent attorney or solicitor etc is nominated by the rights-holder as its authorised agent to file, administer, renew, and receive correspondence relating to the notice on the rights-holder's behalf.

The authorisation will need to be signed by, or on behalf of, the rights-holder, and the original lodged with Customs.

(2) *Authorisation of local agent to file notices*

The Trade Marks Act 2002 and Copyright Act 1994 are both silent as to the lodging of notices by third parties (other than, in the case of trade marks, a registered licensee). In practice however, Customs will accept notices lodged by third parties with the appropriate authorisation.

A rights-holder (usually overseas) can authorise its local distributor or licensee ("local agent") to post a notice (and by implication to post security) on its behalf, by lodging an authorisation of local agent.

An authorisation of local agent must state that:

- The rights-holder authorises the local agent to prepare and file notices on its behalf under the Trade Marks Act 2002 and/or the Copyright Act 1994; and

- The local agent is authorised to take any action that may arise through enforcement of the notice.

Where the rights-holder is a company, the authorisation will usually be written on the company's letterhead, and in all cases must be signed by either the rights-holder or an authorised representative.

(3) *Authorisation of local agent to post security*

Under a more limited form of agency, the rights-holder may choose to file notices in its own name, but authorise a local agent to post security on its behalf. The authorisation will be of similar, although more limited, form to an authorisation of local agent.

Although Customs is obliged to refund the security bond to the party which actually posts it, local agents may run into difficulties if they voluntarily terminate their relationship with the rights-holder without reaching an agreement as to substitution of the security bond.

11.6.4 Security bond and indemnity

Any person lodging a notice with Customs must also:

- Pay a security bond, which is held in an interest bearing account and is refunded on termination of the notice; and/or

- Give an indemnity to Customs

(Regulation 159 Trade Marks Regulations 2003; and reg 6 Copyright (Border Protection) Regulations 1994).

The bond is currently set at $5,000 by the Chief Executive. It is held as an indemnity against any costs that Customs may incur in representing itself in legal proceedings in relation to the enforcement of the notice, or to recover costs Customs may have incurred as a result of disposing of any counterfeit goods forfeited to the Crown. Customs may further call on any indemnity given if its costs exceed the level of the security bond. In practice it is rare that the bond/indemnity will be called on.

(1) *Bond may be posted on rights-holder's behalf*

It is possible for a rights-holder to authorise a local agent or distributor to post the security bond on its behalf. This is discussed in more detail earlier in this section.

(2) *Single bond may cover several notices*

A single bond may cover several notices filed by the same party even if they relate to:

- Different trade mark registrations;

- Different copyright works; or

- Both trade mark registrations and copyright works.

For example, the distributor of clothing produced by several different companies may use a single bond to cover several registered trade marks provided the notices are lodged in the distributor's name (and not the respective rights-holders' names).

11.6.5 Customs to accept or decline notice

The Chief Executive of Customs has discretion to accept or decline notices submitted to him or her (s 139 Trade Marks Act 2002 and s 136(3) Copyright Act 1994). In practice, notices will normally only be declined if they do not comply with ss 137 and 138 Trade Marks Act 2002 and s 136(1) and (2) Copyright Act 1994 and the formalities set out in those sections.

11.7 Duration, renewal, and revocation of notices

11.7.1 Duration of trade mark notice

A trade mark notice will be valid for an initial period of either:

- 5 years from the date on which the notice is accepted; or

- The date on which the next renewal fee for the registered trade mark the subject of the notice falls due,

whichever occurs sooner (s 138(2) Trade Marks Act 2002).

11.7.2 Renewal of trade mark notice

The notice may be renewed for further 5-year periods on proof that the trade mark registration has been validated for the same period. There is no limit on the number of times a trade mark notice may be renewed in this way.

11.7.3 Revocation of trade mark notice

A notice may be revoked by the claimant at any stage during the term of the notice (s 140(a) Trade Marks Act 2002).

It may also be revoked by a Court order in s 153 proceedings (s 140(b)). These proceedings are discussed in more detail at 11.9 ("Post-acceptance procedure") later in this chapter.

11.7.4 Duration of copyright notice

In most cases a copyright notice will be valid for an initial period of 5 years from acceptance of the notice.

However, if copyright in the work the subject of the notice will expire within any 5-year period then the term of the notice will be the remaining term of the copyright.

651

The term of copyright works is discussed in more detail in the copyright chapter of this text (chapter 4).

(1)   *Term of industrially applied artistic works*

In the vast majority of cases the copyright work the subject of a copyright notice will be an artistic work (ie the original design drawing or prototype of the rights-holder's product), which will have been industrially applied.

"Industrial application" is defined in s 75(4) Copyright Act 1994 as the making of more than 50 copies in three dimensions of the work for the purposes of sale or hire.

Where an artistic work has been industrially applied its term will generally be 16 years from the date of first industrial application (s 75 Copyright Act 1994).

(2)   *Term of other copyright works*

Where the copyright work is a logo or artistic work (for example, applied to a t-shirt) then it is unlikely to have been industrially applied and the term of protection will generally be 50 years from the end of the calendar year in which the author of the work died (s 22 Copyright Act 1994).

11.7.5   Renewal of copyright notice

Copyright notices may be renewed for further 5-year periods as long as the copyright has not expired.

11.7.6   Revocation of copyright notice

A notice may be revoked by the claimant at any stage during the term of the notice (s 136(4)(a) Copyright Act 1994).

It may also be revoked by a Court order in s 141 proceedings (s 136(4)(b)). These proceedings are discussed in more detail at 11.9 ("Post-acceptance procedure") later in this chapter.

11.8   Assignment and changes to notices

If a registered trade mark or copyright right the subject of a notice is assigned to a new rights-holder, notice must be given to Customs (reg 158 Trade Marks Regulations 2003; reg 5 Copyright (Border Protection) Regulations 1994). Any corresponding notice may also be assigned by way of (the same) deed of assignment that assigned rights in the registered trade mark or copyright right the subject of the notice.

11.8.1   New documentation

Customs must be advised of an assignment of the relevant trade mark or copyright work or of any other changes in the particulars of the notice. Customs normally requires a revised notice to be lodged with the new rights-holder's information. New authorisations (if any) will also need to be filed and a new security bond posted. For this reason it is generally more cost-effective to lodge a new notice rather than assign an existing one.

11.8.2   Changes to notice particulars

Under reg 158(b) Trade Marks Regulations 2003 and reg 5(b) Copyright (Border Protection) Regulations 1994, Customs must be informed, in writing, of any changes to the particulars of a notice, or changes in evidence or information supplied in relation to the notice.

11.9   Post-acceptance procedure

Following acceptance of a notice, Customs will monitor goods imported into New Zealand to determine whether those goods are counterfeit.

Due to the vast volume of product imported into New Zealand on a daily basis, Customs cannot guarantee that it will be able to intercept, physically examine, and detain every item that contravenes a notice. Instead, a system of random checks and audits are carried out on inbound items.

11.9.1   Full information required

To enable Customs to carry out its job more effectively, claimants are encouraged to provide Customs with full information regarding:

- The names and addresses of known importers and merchants of counterfeit or pirated goods;
- The names and addresses of known manufacturers of counterfeit or pirated goods; and
- The likely countries of origin of counterfeit or pirated goods.

11.9.2   Authorised importers to be identified

Occasionally, genuine goods imported by an authorised licensee or distributor may be seized by Customs under a trade mark or copyright notice. To avoid any confusion, Customs generally requests, and holds on record, the names and addresses of any companies or individuals who are authorised to import goods bearing the registered trade mark/copyright work the subject of the notice. This will assist Customs to facilitate the quick release of genuine goods from its control and reduce the possibility that a determination is issued in respect of those genuine goods.

11.9.3   Determination procedure

The procedure for issuing determinations under trade mark and copyright notices is set out in ss 142-145 Trade Marks Act 2002 and s 137 Copyright Act 1994. Although the terminology between the two pieces of legislation differs, the procedure is substantially the same.

(1)   *Opinion and investigation*

Where a collector forms an opinion that any item imported contravenes an accepted trade mark or copyright notice he or she may conduct any investigation necessary to establish whether the notice is actually contravened.

Under s 137(2) Copyright Act 1994 and s 144 Trade Marks Act 2002, during the course of the investigation the collector may compel the importer, or any other person having an interest in the goods imported, to supply such information as the collector may specify within 10 working days.

Where the collector is left in any doubt as to whether the goods are genuine, he or she may request that the claimant inspect the goods (under s 155 Trade Marks Act 2002 and s 143 Copyright Act 1994) and provide a further opinion. Any person interested in the goods may also demand to inspect the goods (under the same sections) on 72 hours notice.

Whether or not the collector conducts an investigation he or she must make a determination as to whether the item contravenes the notice within a reasonable period of forming an opinion that it does.

(2) *Refusal to give information taken into account*

Under s 138(3) Copyright Act 1994 and s 145 Trade Marks Act 2002, the fact that a person has refused to give information to a collector during the course of his or her investigation may be taken into account when he or she is making a determination.

(3) *Limitations on requirement to supply information during investigation*

Section 138 Copyright Act 1994 and s 145 Trade Marks Act 2002 impose certain limitations on a collector's investigative powers.

In particular:

- A collector cannot request information unless he or she believes that information is reasonably necessary for the purposes of an investigation under the respective Act. By implication, the collector's inquiry must be limited to whether the goods carry an "infringing sign" and/or fall within the definition of "pirated copy". The collector could not, for example, request further information which might give rise to a contravention of any other Act; and

- People from whom the information is requested have the same rights and privileges in relation to the giving of information as witnesses in Court proceedings.

(4) *Notice of determination*

Where the collector determines that goods imported contravene any notice (because they are either pirated goods or contain an infringing sign) he or she is required, under s 147 Trade Marks Act and s 139 Copyright Act, to serve a written notice of that determination on:

- The claimant; and

- Any other person appearing to have an interest in the goods (which will include the importer).

Service is carried out by:

- Personal delivery;

- Facsimile; or

- Posting to the last known address of the claimant or person interested.

Section 148 Trade Marks Act 2002 and s 139(3) Copyright Act 1994 expressly state that detention of goods following the issue of a determination will not be rendered illegal through failure to correctly serve notice of the determination on the claimant or any other person interested.

In the event that a person interested does not receive a copy of the determination and s 153/s 141(3) proceedings issue, the failure can be rectified when the Court gives directions for service under s 153(3)/s 141(5) (discussed later in this section).

11.9.4 Detention of goods

Under s 149 Trade Marks Act 2002 and s 140 Copyright Act 1994, unless the importer voluntarily forfeits the goods to the Crown for destruction (discussed later in this section), goods the subject of a determination will be detained by Customs until any of the following events occurs:

- 10 working days have elapsed since the determination was served and Customs has not received notice of proceedings having been commenced under s 153 Trade Marks Act or s 141(3) Copyright Act;

- Proceedings under s 153(1) Trade Marks Act or s 141(3) Copyright Act result in a decision that the goods imported do not bear an infringing sign, are not pirated copies, or have been imported for private and domestic use;

- Proceedings under s 153 Trade Marks Act or s 141(3) Copyright Act are abandoned;

- Customs is served with an order made in proceedings under s 152 Trade Marks Act or s 141(1) Copyright Act that the notice be discharged;

- Customs is served with an order made in proceedings under s 152(b) Trade Marks Act or s 141(2) Copyright Act that the goods be released; or

- The Court makes an order as to the disposal of the goods.

Each of these is discussed in detail below.

(1)   *Goods may be detained for other reasons*

Section 150 Trade Marks Act 2002 and s 140(3) Copyright Act 1994 require Customs to release detained goods if every legal requirement as to their importation has been satisfied, or if their release of the goods is not contrary to law. The corollary is also true.

Counterfeit or pirated goods that initially come to Customs' attention under the border protection provisions of the Trade Marks Act 2002 and Copyright Act 1994 are sometimes also detained under the Customs and Excise Act 1996 on the basis that they contain a false statement as to their origin.

In such instances, Customs will seize the goods and notify both the importer and claimant.

Unlike the procedure for detention of goods under a customs notice, seized goods will not be released to the importer after 10 working days. Instead, the goods will be held for 3 months. If the importer fails to make the appropriate application under s 231 Customs and Excise Act 1996 for an order disallowing seizure, the goods will be disposed of in accordance with s 237(2) of that Act.

11.9.5 Voluntary forfeiture by importer

The importer of goods detained by Customs under a trade mark notice may consent to those goods being forfeited to the Crown by serving notice in writing to Customs (s 151 Trade Marks Act 2002; s 141A Copyright Act 1994).

Goods forfeited to the Crown under s 151 Trade Marks Act must be sold, destroyed, or otherwise disposed of, as directed by the Chief Executive (reg 160 Trade Marks Regulations). The usual consequence of voluntary forfeiture is that the goods are destroyed.

11.9.6 Proceedings by claimant

Goods are most frequently detained by Customs pending the outcome of proceedings initiated by the claimant under s 153 Trade Marks Act 2002 or s 141(3) Copyright Act 1994.

(1) *Time limit for issuing proceedings*

Under s 149(1)(e) Trade Marks Act 2002 and s 140(1)(e) Copyright Act 1994 the claimant has 10 working days in which to file the proceedings, and serve a copy on Customs, to avoid the goods being released to the importer.

Section 149(3) Trade Marks Act and s 140(2) Copyright Act empower Customs to extend the period to a maximum of 20 working days if it is considered appropriate in all the circumstances. Extensions are infrequently granted.

In *Disney Enterprises Inc v Guan t/a Balmoral Celestial Gifts* 19/6/02, Master Lang, HC Auckland M123-SD02, the claimant, which was based overseas but had legal representation in New Zealand, successfully obtained an extension of the period in which to take action to 20 working days with the consent of the importer.

(2) *Proceedings must be filed in High Court*

As:

- Both s 5(1) Trade Marks Act 2002 and s 135 Copyright Act 1994 define "Court" as "High Court"; and

- The High Court derives its powers to make orders in respect of notices from the Acts (s 154 Trade Marks Act and s 142(1) Copyright Act),

proceedings cannot be initiated in other forums (such as the District Court or Disputes Tribunal).

(3) *Purpose of proceedings*

The purpose of issuing proceedings under s 153 Trade Marks Act 2002 and s 141 Copyright Act 1994 is to have the Court make a decision whether the goods the subject of a determination are counterfeit or pirated, and accordingly whether they should be forfeited to the Crown or released to the importer.

(4) *Any interested party may apply*

Both the rights-holder, and any other person having an interest in the goods, can apply to the Court to make that assessment.

(5)   *Court to give directions*

Section 153(3)(a) Trade Marks Act 2002 and 141(5) Copyright Act 1994 require the High Court to give directions as to the service of the proceedings on any person who appears to have an interest in the goods (whether or not that person was also served with a copy of the determination). Any such person is permitted to appear in the proceedings, and to appeal the Court's decision. Each Act also requires a copy of the proceedings to be served on Customs, who may also elect to appear.

(6)   *Rights-holder may need to be joined*

Where the claimant is an agent, licensee, or distributor of the rights-holder he or she may need to join the rights-holder as a party to the proceedings, particularly if the proceedings contain additional causes of action (such as trade mark infringement, breach of copyright, passing off and/or breaches of the Fair Trading Act 1986).

In case of doubt, directions can be sought from the Court under s 153(3) Trade Marks Act 2002 and/or s 141(5) Copyright Act 1994.

(7)   *Proceedings should be under appropriate section*

In *G Sucess Co Ltd v CEO NZ Customs Service* [2001] 1 NZLR 506; (2001) 7 NZBLC 103,199, Fisher J suggested, at para 4, that parties wishing to avail themselves of the remedies under s 54I Trade Marks Act 1953 (the precursor to s 154 Trade Marks Act 2002) should expressly refer to those sections of the Act in their pleadings:

> "The proceedings [filed by Dragon Optical, the registered proprietor of the trade mark the subject of the notice] took the form of conventional civil proceedings alleging trade mark infringement and breach of the Fair Trading Act. The proceedings did not refer to s 54G(3) of the Trade Marks Act [s 153 Trade Marks Act 2002], nor did they seek relief in terms of s 54I [s 154]. I make no finding of my own that those proceedings should be treated as the legal equivalent of an application by Dragon Optical under s 54G(3) [s 153]. It is sufficient to say that in this hearing both parties to the application were content to proceed on that assumption. In a commercial dispute of this nature it is not for me to question that concession."

and at para 18:

> "Once the registered proprietor has given notice of proceedings under s 54G(3) [s 153 Trade Marks Act 2002] he or she may choose to include other causes of action in the claim. However the proceedings should expressly refer to s 54G(3) [s 153] and state that relief is sought under s 54I [s 154]."

(8)   *Abandonment of proceedings*

Where proceedings under s 153 Trade Marks Act 2002 and/or s 141(3) Copyright Act 1994 are abandoned, Customs is obliged to release the goods to the importer/owner.

(9)   *Powers of the Court*

If the Court determines that the goods the subject of a determination are counterfeit or pirated, and have been imported other than for private and domestic use, it is entitled (under s 154(1) Trade Marks Act 2002 and s 142(1) Copyright Act 1994) to make orders that the goods be:

- Forfeited to the Crown;

- Destroyed; or

- Otherwise dealt with as the Court thinks fit.

When considering which order to make, the Court is required by s 154(2) Trade Marks Act and s 142(2) Copyright Act to have regard to:

- Whether other remedies available in proceedings for infringement of a registered trade mark/copyright would be adequate to compensate the claimant and protect his or her interests; and

- The need to ensure that the goods are not disposed of in a manner that would adversely affect the claimant.

If there is more than one person with an interest in the goods, the Court may direct that the goods are sold and that the proceeds from the sale are divided between those people (s 154(3) Trade Marks Act and s 142(3) Copyright Act).

In practice the majority of goods are destroyed so as to avoid any possibility that they are resold in contravention of the claimant's interests.

(10) *Costs*

Costs in legal proceedings are entirely at the Court's discretion. Usually they will be awarded in favour of the successful party.

In *Disney Enterprises Inc v Guan t/a Balmoral Celestial Gifts* 19/6/02, Master Lang, HC Auckland M123-SD02, the plaintiff issued proceedings under s 141(3) Copyright Act. The defendant agreed to have judgment entered by consent once it had made its own determination that the goods the subject of the proceedings had been manufactured and distributed without the plaintiff's authority. The plaintiff sought costs and the defendant opposed.

In ruling that the plaintiff was entitled to its costs, Master Lang acknowledged that enforcement of the plaintiff's copyright interests was of vital importance to it, and that it was entitled to exercise its rights. He went on to say (at paras 45 and 47):

> "I accept also that the proceedings had to be issued as a matter of relative urgency because of the time limits imposed by the Act. The issuing of the proceedings was also a catalyst for the speedy resolution of the dispute, and it is impossible to say that that would necessarily have occurred if the proceedings had not been issued ...

> "I accept that the Defendant should receive some credit for the fact that it consented to orders being made against it at the earliest opportunity. In my view, however, that credit should be reflected in the fact that costs overall have been minimised through the resolution of the proceedings at an early stage and without resort to further interlocutory processes or unnecessary appearances."

The decision affirms a claimant's entitlement to protect its interests by issuing proceedings against an importer under a notice, and further that claimants should not be financially impaired as a result.

For a similar decision involving breach of a registered trade mark, see *Waikato Rugby Union Inc v Wellfit Ltd* 8/3/05, Cooper J, HC Auckland CIV-2004-404-4678.

(11) *Compensation*

In the event the Court finds that the goods the subject of a determination are not counterfeit or pirated they will ordinarily be released to the importer or owner of the goods.

The Court may order that any party to the proceedings pay compensation to the importer or owner of the goods (s 154(4) Trade Marks Act 2002 and s 142(4) Copyright Act 1994).

The importer/owner may also be entitled to recover a proportion of its legal costs.

Section 157 Trade Marks Act and s 146 Copyright Act preclude the recovery of compensation for loss or damage from Customs, unless Customs has acted in bad faith.

11.9.7 Application to discharge notice

Under s 152(a) Trade Marks Act 2002 and s 141(1) Copyright Act 1994, any person may apply to the Court for an order discharging a notice accepted under the respective Act.

In *G Sucess Co Ltd v CEO NZ Customs Service* [2001] 1 NZLR 506; (2001) 7 NZBLC 103,199, Fisher J made the following comments, at para 12, in respect of the application of s 54G(1) (the precursor to s 152(a) Trade Marks Act 2002):

> "Such an application would normally be made by the registered proprietor's competitor in order to negate the Customs protection in the future. It can also be sought by an importer retrospectively as a basis for release of goods that have already been detained …"

To date no decisions appear to have been made under s 152(a) or s 141(1).

11.9.8 Application for order that the goods be released

Under s 152(b) Trade Marks Act 2002 and s 141(2) Copyright Act 1994, any person may apply to the Court for an order that an item detained by Customs be released.

The ambit of s 152(b) (s 54G(2) Trade Marks Act 1953), and the overall procedure for determining and detaining goods under the border protection provisions of the Trade Marks Act, was examined in some detail by Fisher J in *G Sucess Co Ltd v CEO NZ Customs Service* [2001] 1 NZLR 506; (2001) 7 NZBLC 103,199.

In that case, Customs had detained 350 jackets under a trade mark notice lodged by the overseas proprietor of the registered trade mark the subject of the notice, Dragon Optical. Having unsuccessfully attempted to convince the importer to relinquish the goods to the Crown, Dragon Optical issued proceedings for trade mark infringement and a breach of the Fair Trading Act 1986.

At the same time, the importer applied to the Court for an order under s 54G(2) (s 152(b) Trade Marks Act 2002) for the release of the jackets, claiming insufficient similarity between the registered trade mark and the trade mark appearing on the detained jackets.

The Court had to decide whether a dispute as to whether the jackets carried an infringing sign could be resolved in the context of an application for release under s 54G(2) (s 152(b)).

Despite the fact that the section contains no express limitation on the grounds for releasing detained goods, Fisher J ruled that the primary purpose of the section was to provide an opportunity for vindication of the importer's rights where:

- The claimant has failed to bring proceedings, and give appropriate notice, within the requisite time limit; or

- The claimant has brought proceedings and since abandoned them,

and Customs continues to detain the goods.

Fisher J also considered the possibility that the section could be relied on in circumstances where there is a lack of seriously arguable case that there is a trade mark infringement, or where the importation was for private or domestic use.

His Honour concluded, at para 16, that in cases such as the present, where it was at least arguable that the goods detained featured an infringing sign, the appropriate remedy would be to seek a determination from the Court under s 54G(3) (s 153 Trade Marks Act 2002):

> "it seems to me that where goods have been detained, the primary provision for determining substantive rights between competing individuals was intended to be s 54G(3) [s 153 Trade Marks Act 2002], not s 54G(2) [s 152(b)]. I say that because the proceedings which must be commenced within a time limit (s 54F(1)(d) [s 149(1)]) and not abandoned (s 54F(1)(e) [s 149(1)(d)]) are proceedings under s 54G (3) [s 153]. It is in proceedings under s 54G(3) [s 153] that the directions as to service are mandatory (s 54G(5) [s 153(3)]). That ensures that in proceedings under s 54G (3) [s 153] all private individuals who have an interest in the detained goods will have an opportunity to be heard. Further, it is in proceedings under s 54G(3) [s 153] that there is the opportunity to make orders under s 54I [s 154] as to the ultimate fate of the detained goods. All of this suggests an intention that proceedings under s 54G (3) [s 153], or conventional civil proceedings, will be the occasion for determining the substantive trade mark rights of competing individuals, not proceedings under s 54G(2) [s 152(b)]."

Accordingly, Fisher J declined to order the release of the goods under s 54G(2) [s 152(b)] pending the result of the substantive proceedings commenced by Dragon Optical.

11.10   References and resource sites

11.10.1   Websites

Thomson Brookers	www.thomsonbrookers.co.nz
Intellectual Property Office of New Zealand	www.iponz.govt.nz
Intellectual Property Owners Association of Australia Ltd	www.ipo.org.au

Interim Website of New Zealand Legislation	www.legislation.govt.nz
International Anti-Counterfeiting Coalition	www.iacc.org
International Intellectual Property Investigators Association	www.iipia.com
James & Wells	www.jaws.co.nz
New Zealand Customs Service	www.customs.govt.nz
The Copyright Council of New Zealand	www.copyright.org.nz
World Trade Organisation	www.wto.org

TABLE OF STATUTES AND REGULATIONS

Abbreviations

M

N

P

U

TABLE OF CASES

Abbreviations

C

D

S

W

SUBJECT INDEX

A

D

G

H

M

N

O

R